D1384114

The PHOENIX Program

by Douglas Valentine:

The Hotel Tacloban
The Phoenix Program

THE PHOENIX PROGRAM

Douglas Valentine

William Morrow and Company, Inc.
New York

Recognizing the importance of preserving what has been written, it is the policy of William Morrow and Company, Inc., and its imprints and affiliates to have the books it publishes printed on acid-free paper, and we exert our best efforts to that end.

Library of Congress Cataloging-in-Publication Data

Valentine, Douglas.
The Phoenix program / Douglas Valentine.
p. cm.
Includes bibliographical references.
ISBN 0-688-09130-X
1. Vietnamese Conflict, 1961–1975—Underground movements.
2. Counter insurgency—Vietnam. I. Title.
DS558.92.V35 1990
959.704'3—dc20 90-34660
CIP

Printed in the United States of America

First Edition

1 2 3 4 5 6 7 8 9 10

BOOK DESIGN AND MAPS BY JEFFREY L. WARD

ACKNOWLEDGMENTS

This book is dedicated to my darling wife, Alice. Special thanks to my father for his editorial assistance; the Fitchburg Arts Council for its financial aid; Adria Henderson, Bill McCoy, Jack Madden, John Kelly, and Nick Proffitt for their comradeship; Sandy Kelson, Larry Hill, and Andy McKevitt for their generosity; Dave Coggeshall, Ian Fleming, the Fat Angel, and Robert Graves for inspiration; Lucy Nhiem Hong Nguyen, Lien Johnson, and Pham Thi Ngoc Chan for their efforts on my behalf; Larry Tunison for the night on the town; and all those who contributed to this book.

CONTENTS

Introduction 9

Chapter 1: Infrastructure 19
Chapter 2: Internal Security 31
Chapter 3: Covert Action 43
Chapter 4: Revolutionary Development 57
Chapter 5: PICs 73
Chapter 6: Field Police 89
Chapter 7: Special Branch 100
Chapter 8: Attack on the VCI 113
Chapter 9: ICEX 127
Chapter 10: Action Programs 142
Chapter 11: PRU 159
Chapter 12: Tet 174
Chapter 13: Parallax Views 193
Chapter 14: Phoenix in Flight 198
Chapter 15: Modus Vivendi 213
Chapter 16: Advisers 223
Chapter 17: Accelerated Pacification 253
Chapter 18: Transitions 266

Chapter 19: Psyops 280
Chapter 20: Reforms 291
Chapter 21: Decay 303
Chapter 22: Hearings 315
Chapter 23: Dissension 327
Chapter 24: Transgressions 340
Chapter 25: Da Nang 351
Chapter 26: Revisions 362
Chapter 27: Legalities 376
Chapter 28: Technicalities 389
Chapter 29: Phoenix in Flames 404

Epilogue 420
Appendix 431
Glossary 435
Notes 447
Index 463

INTRODUCTION

It was well after midnight. Elton Manzione, his wife, Lynn, and I sat at their kitchen table, drinking steaming cups of coffee. Rock 'n' roll music throbbed from the living room. A lean, dark man with large Mediterranean features, Elton was chain-smoking Pall Malls and telling me about his experiences as a twenty-year-old U.S. Navy SEAL in Vietnam in 1964. It was hot and humid that sultry Georgia night, and we were exhausted; but I pressed him for more specific information. "What was your most memorable experience?" I asked.

Elton looked down and with considerable effort, said quietly, "There's one experience I remember very well. It was my last assignment. I remember my last assignment very well.

"They," Elton began, referring to the Navy commander and Special Forces colonel who issued orders to the SEAL team, "called the three of us [Elton, Eddie Swetz, and John Laboon] into the briefing room and sat us down. They said they were having a problem at a tiny village about a quarter of a mile from North Vietnam in the DMZ. They said some choppers and recon planes were taking fire from there. They never really explained why, for example, they just didn't bomb it, which was their usual response, but I got the idea that the village chief was politically connected and that the thing had to be done quietly.

"We worked in what were called hunter-killer teams," Elton explained.

"The hunter team was a four-man unit, usually all Americans, sometimes one or two Vietnamese or Chinese mercenaries called counterterrorists—CTs for short. Most CTs were enemy soldiers who had deserted or South Vietnamese criminals. Our job was to find the enemy and nail him in place—spot his position, then go back to a prearranged place and call in the killer team. The killer team was usually twelve to twenty-five South Vietnamese Special Forces led by Green Berets. Then we'd join up with the killer team and take out the enemy."

But on this particular mission, Elton explained, the SEALs went in alone. "They said there was this fifty-one-caliber antiaircraft gun somewhere near the village that was taking potshots at us and that there was a specific person in the village operating the gun. They give us a picture of the guy and a map of the village. It's a small village, maybe twelve or fifteen hooches. 'This is the hooch,' they say. 'The guy sleeps on the mat on the left side. He has two daughters.' They don't know if he has a mama-san or where she is, but they say, 'You guys are going to go in and get this guy. You [meaning me] are going to snuff him.' Swetz is gonna find out where the gun is and blow it. Laboon is gonna hang back at the village gate covering us. He's the stoner; he's got the machine gun. And I'm gonna go into the hooch and snuff this guy.

"'What you need to do first,' they say, 'is sit alongside the trail [leading from the village to the gun] for a day or two and watch where this guy goes. And that will help us uncover the gun.' Which it did. We watched him go right to where the gun was. We were thirty yards away, and we watched for a while. When we weren't watching, we'd take a break and go another six hundred yards down the trail to relax. And we did that for maybe two days—watched him coming and going—and got an idea of his routine: when he went to bed; when he got up; where he went. Did he go behind the hooch to piss? Did he go into the jungle? That sort of thing.

"They told us, 'Do that. Then come back and tell us what you found out.' So we went back and said, 'We know where the gun is,' and we showed them where it was on the map. We were back in camp for about six hours, and they said, 'Okay, you're going out at o-four-hundred tomorrow. And it's like we say, you [meaning me] are going to snuff the guy, Swetz is going to take out the gun, and Laboon's going to cover the gate.'"

Elton explained that on special missions like this the usual procedure was to "snatch" the targeted VC cadre and bring him back to Dong Ha for interrogation. In that case Elton would have slipped into the hooch and rendered the cadre unconscious, while Swetz demolished the antiaircraft gun and Laboon signaled the killer team to descend upon the village in its black CIA-supplied helicopters. The SEALs and their prisoner would then climb on board and be extracted.

In this case, however, the cadre was targeted for assassination.

"We left out of Cam Lo," Elton continued. "We were taken by boat partway up the river and walked in by foot—maybe two and a half, three miles. At four in the morning we start moving across an area that was maybe a hundred yards wide; it's a clearing running up to the village. We're wearing black pajamas, and we've got black paint on our faces. We're doing this very carefully, moving on the ground a quarter of an inch at a time—move, stop, listen; move, stop, listen. To check for trip wires, you take a blade of grass and put it between your teeth, move your head up and down, from side to side, watching the end of the blade of grass. If it bends, you know you've hit something, but of course, the grass never sets off the trip wire, so it's safe.

"It takes us an hour and a half to cross this relatively short stretch of open grass because we're moving so slowly. And we're being so quiet we can hardly hear each other, let alone anybody else hearing us. I mean, I know they're out there—Laboon's five yards that way, Swetz is five yards to my right—but I can't hear them.

"And so we crawl up to the gate. There's no booby traps. I go in. Swetz has a satchel charge for the fifty-one-caliber gun and has split off to where it is, maybe sixty yards away. Laboon is sitting at the gate. The village is very quiet. There are some dogs. They're sleeping. They stir, but they don't even growl. I go into the hooch, and I spot my person. Well, somebody stirs in the next bed. I'm carrying my commando knife, and one of the things we learned is how to kill somebody instantly with it. So I put my hand over her mouth and come up under the second rib, go through the heart, give it a flick; it snaps the spinal cord. Not thinking! Because I think 'Hey!' Then I hear the explosion go off and I know the gun is out. Somebody else in the corner starts to stir, so I pull out the sidearm and put it against her head and shoot her. She's dead. Of course, by this time the whole village is awake. I go out, waiting for Swetz to come, because the gun's been blown. People are kind of wandering around, and I'm pretty dazed. And I look back into the hooch, and there were two young girls. I'd killed the wrong people."

Elton Manzione and his comrades returned to their base at Cam Lo. Strung out from Dexedrine and remorse, Elton went into the ammo dump and sat on top of a stack of ammunition crates with a grenade, its pin pulled, between his legs and an M-16 cradled in his arms. He sat there refusing to budge until he was given a ticket home.

In early 1984 Elton Manzione was the first person to answer a query I had placed in a Vietnam veterans' newsletter asking for interviews with people who had served in the Phoenix program. Elton wrote to me, saying, "While I was not a participant in Phoenix, I was closely involved in what I think was the forerunner. It was part of what was known as OPLAN 34. This was the old Leaping Lena infiltration program for LRRP [long-range reconnaissance patrol] operations into Laos. During the time I was involved it became the well-known Delta program. While all this happened before Phoenix, the operations were essentially the same. Our primary function was intelligence gathering, but we also carried out the 'undermining of the infrastructure' types of things such as kidnapping, assassination, sabotage, etc.

"The story needs to be told," Elton said, "because the whole aura of the Vietnam War was influenced by what went on in the 'hunter-killer' teams of Phoenix, Delta, etc. That was the point at which many of us realized we were no longer the good guys in the white hats defending freedom—that we were assassins, pure and simple. That disillusionment carried over to all other aspects of the war and was eventually responsible for it becoming America's most unpopular war."

The story of Phoenix is not easily told. Many of the participants, having signed nondisclosure statements, are legally prohibited from telling what they know. Others are silenced by their own consciences. Still others are professional soldiers whose careers would suffer if they were to reveal the secrets of their employers. Falsification of records makes the story even harder to prove. For example, there is no record of Elton Manzione's ever having been in Vietnam. Yet, for reasons which are explained in my first book, *The Hotel Tacloban,* I was predisposed to believe Manzione. I had confirmed that my father's military records were deliberately altered to show that he had not been imprisoned for two years in a Japanese prisoner of war camp in World War II. The effects of the cover-up were devastating and ultimately caused my father to have a heart attack at the age of forty-five. Thus, long before I met Elton Manzione, I knew the government was capable of concealing its misdeeds under a cloak of secrecy, threats, and fraud. And I knew how terrible the consequences could be.

Then I began to wonder if cover-ups like the one concerning my father had also occurred in the Vietnam War, and that led me in the fall of 1983 to visit David Houle, director of veteran services in New Hampshire. I asked Dave Houle if there was a part of the Vietnam War that had been concealed, and without hesitation he replied, "Phoenix." After explaining a little about it, he mentioned that one of his clients had been in the program, then added that his client's service records—like those of Elton Manzione's and my father's—had been altered. They showed that he had been a cook in Vietnam.

I asked to meet Houle's client, but the fellow refused. Formerly with Special Forces in Vietnam, he was disabled and afraid the Veterans Administration would cut off his benefits if he talked to me.

That fear of the government, so incongruous on the part of a war veteran, made me more determined than ever to uncover the truth about Phoenix, a goal which has taken four years to accomplish. That's a long time to spend researching and writing a book. But I believe it was worthwhile, for Phoenix symbolizes an aspect of the Vietnam War that changed forever the way Americans think about themselves and their government.

Developed in 1967 by the Central Intelligence Agency (CIA), Phoenix combined existing counterinsurgency programs in a concerted effort to "neutralize" the Vietcong infrastructure (VCI). The euphemism "neutralize" means to kill, capture, or make to defect. The word "infrastructure" refers to those civilians suspected of supporting North Vietnamese and Vietcong soldiers like the one targeted in Elton Manzione's final operation. Central to Phoenix is the fact that it targeted civilians, not soldiers. As a result, its detractors charge that Phoenix violated that part of the Geneva Conventions guaranteeing protection to civilians in time of war. "By analogy," said Ogden Reid, a member of a congressional committee investigating Phoenix in 1971, "if the Union had had a Phoenix program during the Civil War, its targets would have been civilians like Jefferson Davis or the mayor of Macon, Georgia."

Under Phoenix, or Phung Hoang, as it was called by the Vietnamese, due process was totally nonexistent. South Vietnamese civilians whose names appeared on blacklists could be kidnapped, tortured, detained for two years without trial, or even murdered, simply on the word of an anonymous informer. At its height Phoenix managers imposed quotas of eighteen hundred neutralizations per month on the people running the program in the field, opening up the program to abuses by corrupt security officers, policemen, politicians, and racketeers, all of whom extorted innocent civilians as well as VCI. Legendary CIA officer Lucien Conein described Phoenix as "A very good blackmail scheme for the central government. 'If you don't do what I want, you're VC.' "

Because Phoenix "neutralizations" were often conducted at midnight while its victims were home, sleeping in bed, Phoenix proponents describe the program as a "scalpel" designed to replace the "bludgeon" of search and destroy operations, air strikes, and artillery barrages that indiscriminately wiped out entire villages and did little to "win the hearts and minds" of the Vietnamese population. Yet, as Elton Manzione's story illustrates, the scalpel cut deeper than the U.S. government admits. Indeed, Phoenix was, among other things, an instrument of counterterror—the psychological warfare tactic in which VCI members were brutally murdered along with their families or neighbors as a means of terrorizing the neighboring population into a state of submission. Such horrendous acts were, for propaganda purposes, often made to look as if they had been committed by the enemy.

This book questions how Americans, who consider themselves a nation ruled by laws and an ethic of fair play, could create a program like Phoenix. By scrutinizing the program and the people who participated in it and by employing the program as a symbol of the dark side of the human psyche, the author hopes to articulate the subtle ways in which the Vietnam War changed how Americans think about themselves. This book is about terror and its role in political warfare. It will show how, as successive American governments sink deeper and deeper into the vortex of covert operations—ostensibly to combat terrorism and Communist insurgencies—the American people gradually lose touch with the democratic ideals that once defined their national self-concept. This book asks what happens when Phoenix comes home to roost.

SOUTHEAST ASIA
CHINA
NORTH VIETNAM
Hanoi
GULF OF TONKIN
BURMA
Loungphrabang
Plain of Jars
LAOS
Mekong River
DMZ
THAILAND
Da Nang
Bolovens Plateau
Bangkok
CAMBODIA
Tonle Sap
SOUTH VIETNAM
Phnom Penh
Saigon
GULF OF THAILAND
Mouths of the Mekong
SOUTH CHINA SEA

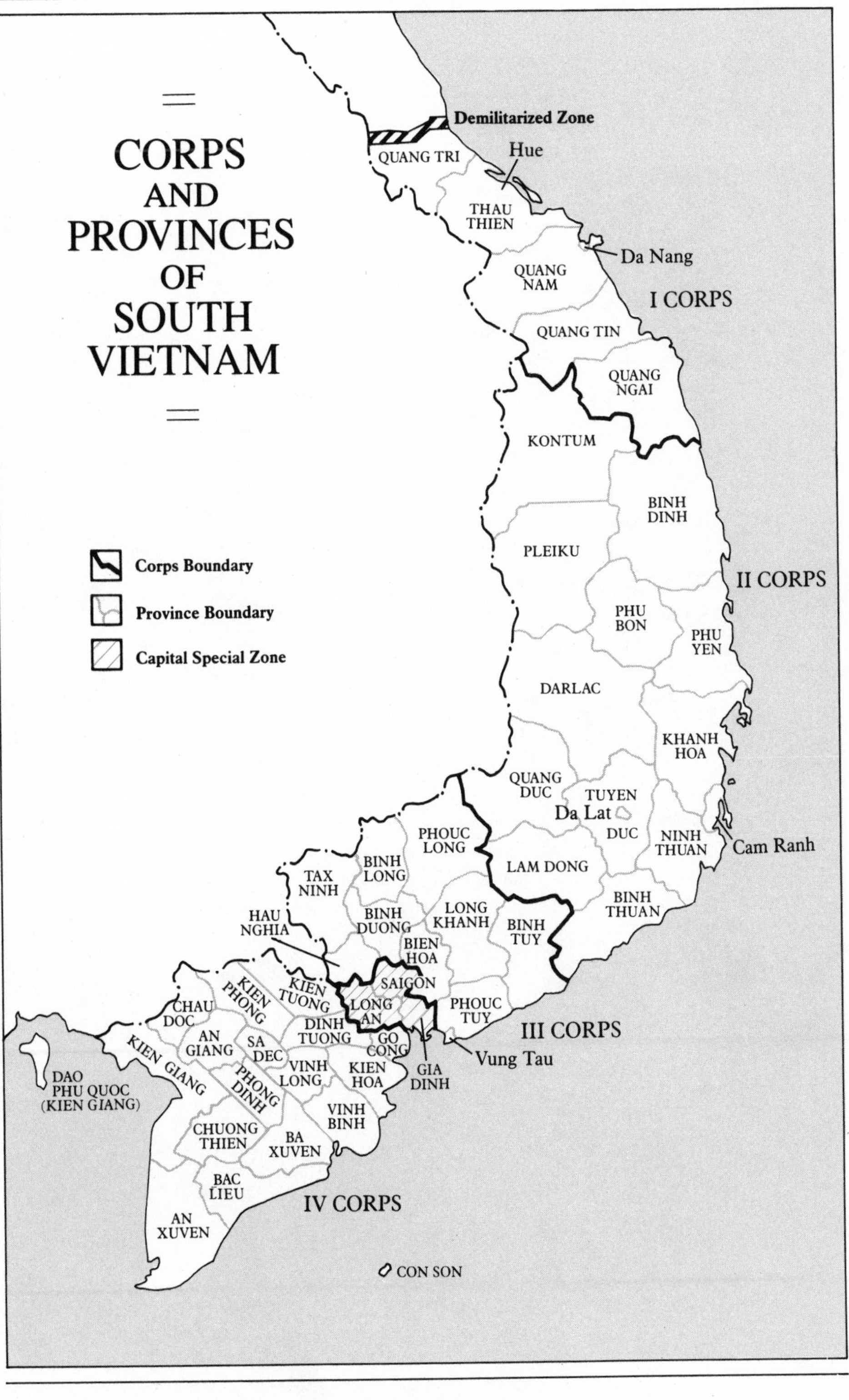
CORPS AND PROVINCES OF SOUTH VIETNAM
Demilitarized Zone
QUANG TRI
Hue
THAU THIEN
Da Nang
QUANG NAM
I CORPS
QUANG TIN
QUANG NGAI
KONTUM
BINH DINH
PLEIKU
Corps Boundary
Province Boundary
Capital Special Zone
II CORPS
PHU BON
PHU YEN
DARLAC
KHANH HOA
QUANG DUC
TUYEN
Da Lat
DUC
NINH THUAN
Cam Ranh
PHOUC LONG
BINH LONG
TAX NINH
LAM DONG
BINH THUAN
LONG KHANH
BINH DUONG
HAU NGHIA
BINH TUY
BIEN HOA
SAIGON
KIEN PHONG
KIEN TUONG
LONG AN
PHOUC TUY
CHAU DOC
DINH TUONG
III CORPS
AN GIANG
SA DEC
GO CONG
Vung Tau
KIEN GIANG
VINH LONG
KIEN HOA
GIA DINH
DAO PHU QUOC (KIEN GIANG)
PHONG DINH
VINH BINH
CHUONG THIEN
BA XUVEN
BAC LIEU
IV CORPS
AN XUVEN
CON SON

CHAPTER 1

Infrastructure

What is the VCI? Is it a farmer in a field with a hoe in his hand and a grenade in his pocket, a deranged subversive using women and children as a shield? Or is it a self-respecting patriot, a freedom fighter who was driven underground by corrupt collaborators and an oppressive foreign occupation army?

In his testimony regarding Phoenix before the Senate Foreign Relations Committee in February 1970, former Director of Central Intelligence William Colby defined the VCI as "about 75,000 native Southerners" whom in 1954 "the Communists took north for training in organizing, propaganda and subversion." According to Colby, these cadres returned to the South, "revived the networks they had left in 1954," and over several years formed the National Liberation Front (NLF), the People's Revolutionary party, liberation committees, which were "pretended local governments rather than simply political bodies," and the "pretended Provisional Revolutionary Government of South Vietnam. Together," testified Colby, "all of these organizations and their local manifestations make up the VC Infrastructure."[1]

A political warfare expert par excellence, Colby, of course, had no intentions of portraying the VCI in sympathetic terms. His abbreviated history of the VCI, with its frequent use of the word "pretended," deliberately oversimplifies and distorts the nature and origin of the revolutionary forces lumped under the generic term "VCI." To understand properly Phoenix and its prey, a more detailed and objective account is required. Such an account cannot begin in 1954—when the Soviet Union, China, and the United States split Vietnam along the sixteenth parallel, and the United States first intervened in Vietnamese affairs—but must acknowledge one hundred years of French colonial oppression. For it was colonialism which begat the VCI, its strategy of protracted political warfare, and its guerrilla and terror tactics.

The French conquest of Vietnam began in the seventeenth century with the arrival of Jesuit priests bent on saving pagan souls. As Vietnam historian Stanley Karnow notes in his book *Vietnam: A History,* "In 1664 . . . French religious leaders and their business backers formed the Society of French Missionaries to advance Christianity in Asia. In the same year, by no coincidence, French business leaders and their religious backers created the East India Company to increase trade. . . . Observing this cozy relationship in Vietnam, an English competitor reported home that the French had arrived, 'but we cannot make out whether they are here to seek trade or to conduct religious propaganda.'

"Their objective, of course," Karnow quips, "was to do both."[2]

For the next two centuries French priests embroiled themselves in Vietnamese politics, eventually providing a pretext for military intervention. Specifically, when a French priest was arrested for plotting against the emperor of Vietnam in 1845, the French Navy shelled Da Nang City, killing hundreds of people, even though the priest had escaped unharmed to Singapore. The Vietnamese responded by confiscating the property of French Catholics, drowning a few Jesuits, and cutting in half, lengthwise, a number of Vietnamese priests.

Soon the status quo was one of open warfare. By 1859 French Foreign Legionnaires had arrived en masse and had established fortified positions near major cities, which they defended against poorly armed nationalists staging hit-and-run attacks from bases in rural areas. Firepower prevailed, and in 1861 a French admiral claimed Saigon for France, "inflicting heavy casualties on the Vietnamese who resisted."[3] Fearing that the rampaging French might massacre the entire city, the emperor abdicated ownership of three provinces adjacent to Saigon, along with Con Son Island, where the French immediately built a prison for rebels. Soon thereafter Vietnamese ports were opened to European commerce, Catholic priests were permitted to preach wherever Buddhist or Taoist or Confucian souls were lurking in the darkness, and France was guaranteed "unconditional control over all of Cochinchina."[4]

By 1862 French colonialists were reaping sufficient economic benefits to hire Filipino and Chinese mercenary armies to help suppress the burgeoning insurgency. Resistance to French occupation was strongest in the north near Hanoi, where nationalists were aligned with anti-Western Chinese.

The rugged mountains of the Central Highlands formed a natural buffer for the French, who were entrenched in Cochin China, the southern third of Vietnam centered in Saigon.

The boundary lines having been drawn, the pacification of Vietnam began in earnest in 1883. The French strategy was simple and began with a reign of terror: As many nationalists as could be found were rounded up and guillotined. Next the imperial city of Hue was plundered in what Karnow calls "an orgy of killing and looting."[5] The French disbanded the emperor's Council of Mandarins and replaced it with French advisers and a bureaucracy staffed by *supplétifs*—self-serving Vietnamese, usually Catholics, who collaborated in exchange for power and position. The *supplétif crème de la crème* studied in, and became citizens of, France. The Vietnamese Army was commanded by French officers, and Vietnamese officers were *supplétifs* who had been graduated from the French military academy. By the twentieth century all of Vietnam's provinces were administered by *supplétifs,* and the emperor, too, was a lackey of the French.

In places where "security" for collaborators was achieved, Foreign Legionnaires were shifted to the outer perimeter of the pacified zones and internal security was turned over to collaborators commanding GAMOs—group administrative mobile organizations. The hope was that pacified areas would spread like oil spots. *Supplétifs* were also installed in the police and security forces, where they managed prostitution rings, opium dens, and gambling casinos on behalf of the French. From the 1880's onward no legal protections existed for nationalists, for whom a dungeon at Con Son Prison, torture, and death were the penalties for pride. So, outgunned and outlawed in their homeland, the nationalists turned to terrorism—to the bullet in the belly and the bomb in the café. For while brutal French pacification campaigns prevented the rural Vietnamese from tending their fields, terrorism did not.

The first nationalists—the founding fathers of the VCI—appeared as early as 1859 in areas like the Ca Mau Peninsula, the Plain of Reeds, and the Rung Sat—malaria-infested swamps which were inaccessible to French forces. Here the nationalists honed and perfected the guerrilla tactics that became the trademark of the Vietminh and later the Vietcong. Referred to as selective terrorism, this meant the planned assassination of low-ranking government officials who worked closely with the people; for example, policemen, mailmen, and teachers. As David Galula explains in *Counter-Insurgency Warfare: Theory and Practice,* "Killing high-ranking counterinsurgency officials serves no purpose since they are too far removed from the population for their deaths to serve as examples."[6]

The purpose of selective terror was psychologically to isolate the French and their *supplétifs,* while demonstrating to the rural population the ability of the insurgents to strike at their oppressors until such time as a general uprising was thought possible.

In the years following World War I, Vietnamese nationalists organized in one of three ways: through religious sects, like the Hoa Hao or Cao Dai, which secretly served as fronts for anti-French activity; through overt political parties like the Dai Viets and the Vietnam Quoc Dan Dang (VNQDD); or by becoming Communists. All formed secret cells in the areas where they operated, and all worked toward ousting the French. In return, the French intelligence service, the Deuxième Bureau, hired secret agents and informers to identify, capture, imprison, and murder core members of the underground resistance.

In instances of open rebellion, stronger steps were taken. When VNQDD sailors mutinied in 1932 in Yen Bai and killed their French officers, the French retaliated by bombing scores of VNQDD villages, killing more than thirty thousand people. Mass deportations followed, and many VNQDD cadres were driven into exile. Likewise, when the French caught wind of a general uprising called for by the Communists, they arrested and imprisoned 90 percent of its leadership. Indeed, the VCI leadership was molded in Con Son Prison, or Ho Chi Minh University, as it was also known. There determined nationalists transformed dark dungeons into classrooms and common criminals into hard-core cadres. With their lives depending on their ability to detect spies and agents provocateurs whom the French had planted in the prisons, these forefathers of the VCI became masters of espionage and intrigue and formidable opponents of the dreaded Deuxième Bureau.

In 1941 the Communist son of a mandarin, Ho Chi Minh, gathered the various nationalist groups under the banner of the Vietminh and called for all good revolutionaries "to stand up and unite with the people, and throw out the Japanese and the French."[7] Leading the charge were General Vo Nguyen Giap and his First Armed Propaganda Detachment—thirty-four lightly armed men and women who by early 1945 had overrun two French outposts and were preaching the gospel according to Ho to anyone interested in independence. By mid-1945 the Vietminh held six provinces near Hanoi and was working with the forerunner of the CIA, the Office of Strategic Services (OSS), recovering downed pilots of the U.S. Fourteenth Air Force. A student of American democracy, Ho declared Vietnam an independent country in September 1945.

Regrettably, at the same time that OSS officers were meeting with Ho and exploring the notion of supporting his revolution, other Americans were backing the French, and when a U.S. Army officer traded a pouch of opium for Ho's dossier and uncovered his links to Moscow, all chances of coexistence vanished in a puff of smoke. The Big Three powers in Potsdam divided Vietnam along the sixteenth parallel. Chinese forces aligned with General

Chiang Kai-shek and the Kuomintang were given control of the North. In September 1945 a division of Chinese forces advised by General Phillip Gallagher arrived in Hanoi, plundered the city, and disarmed the Japanese. The French returned to Hanoi, drove out the Vietminh, and displaced Chiang's forces, which obtained Shanghai in exchange.

Meanwhile, Lord Louis Mountbatten (who used the phoenix as an emblem for his command patch) and the British were put in charge in the South. Twenty thousand Gurkhas arrived in Saigon and proceeded to disarm the Japanese. The British then outlawed Ho's Committee of the South and arrested its members. In protest the Vietnamese held a general strike. On September 23 the Brits, buckling under the weight of the White Man's Burden, released from prison those French Legionnaires who had collaborated with the Nazis during the occupation and had administered Vietnam jointly with the Japanese. The Legionnaires rampaged through Saigon, murdering Vietnamese with impunity while the British kept stiff upper lips. As soon as they had regained control of the city, the French reorganized their quislings and secret police, donned surplus U.S. uniforms, and became the nucleus of three divisions which had reconquered South Vietnam by the end of the year. The British exited, and the *supplétif* Bao Dai was reinstalled as emperor.

By 1946 the Vietminh were at war with France once again, and in mid-1946 the French were up to their old tricks—with a vengeance. They shelled Haiphong, killing six thousand Vietnamese. Ho slipped underground, and American officials passively observed while the French conducted "punitive missions . . . against the rebellious Annamese."[8] During the early years of the First Indochina War, CIA officers served pretty much in that same limited capacity, urging the French to form counterguerrilla groups to go after the Vietminh and, when the French ignored them, slipping off to buy contacts and agents in the military, police, government, and private sectors.

The outgunned Vietminh, meanwhile, effected their strategy of protracted warfare. Secret cells were organized, and guerrilla units were formed to monitor and harass French units, attack outposts, set booby traps, and organize armed propaganda teams. Assassination of collaborators was part of their job. Company- and battalion-size units were also formed to engage the French in main force battles.

By 1948 the French could neither protect their convoys from ambushes nor locate Vietminh bases. Fearful French citizens organized private paramilitary self-defense forces and spy nets, and French officers organized, with CIA advice, commando battalions (Tien-Doan Kinh Quan) specifically to hunt down Vietminh propaganda teams and cadres. At the urging of the CIA, the French also formed composite airborne commando groups, which recruited and trained Montagnard hill tribes at the coastal resort city of Vung

Tau. Reporting directly to French Central Intelligence in Hanoi and supplied by night airdrops, French commandos were targeted against clandestine Vietminh combat and intelligence organizations. The GCMAs were formed concurrently with the U.S. Army's First Special Forces at Fort Bragg, North Carolina.

By the early 1950s American soldiers were fighting alongside the French, and the 350-member U.S. Military Assistance and Advisory Group (MAAG) was in Saigon, dispensing and accounting for U.S. largess. All in all, from 1950 through 1954, the United States gave over three billion dollars to the French for their counterinsurgency in Vietnam, including four million a year as a retainer for Emperor Bao Dai, who squirreled away the lion's share in Swiss bank accounts and foreign real estate.

In April 1952, American advisers began training Vietnamese units. In December 1953, an Army attaché unit arrived in Hanoi, and its officers and enlisted men began interrogating Vietminh prisoners. While MAAG postured to take over the Vietnamese Army from the French, the Special Technical and Economic Mission provided CIA officers, under station chief Emmett McCarthy, with the cover they needed to mount political operations and negotiate contracts with the government of Vietnam (GVN).

Finally, in July 1954, after the Vietminh had defeated the French at Dien Bien Phu, a truce was declared at the Geneva Conference. Vietnam was divided along the seventeenth parallel, pending a nationwide election to be held in 1956, with the Vietminh in control in the North and Bao Dai in control in the South. The French were to withdraw from the North and the Vietminh from the South, where the United States was set to displace the French and install its own candidate, Ngo Dinh Diem, a Catholic mandarin from Hue. The CIA did this by organizing a cross section of Vietnamese labor leaders and intellectuals into the Can Lao Nham Vi (Personalist Labor party). Diem and his brothers, Nhu, Can, and Thuc (the archbishop of Hue), thereafter controlled tens of thousands of Can Lao followers through an interlocking maze of clandestine cells present in the military, the police and security services, the government, and private enterprise.

In *Vietnamese History from 1939–1975*, law professor Nguyen Ngoc Huy, a Dai Viet politician who was exiled by Diem in 1954, says about the Diem regime: "They persecuted those who did not accept their orders without discussion, and tolerated or even encouraged their followers to take bribes, because a corrupt servant must be loyal to them out of fear of punishment. . . . To obtain an interesting position, one had to fulfill the three D conditions: Dang [the Can Lao party]; Dao [the Catholic religion]; and Dia phuong [the region—Central Vietnam]. Those who met these conditions and moreover had served Diem before his victory over his enemies in 1955 enjoyed unbelievable promotions."[9]

Only through a personality cult like the Can Lao could the CIA work its will in Vietnam, for Diem did not issue from or have the support of the Buddhist majority. He was, however, a nationalist whose anti-French reputation enabled the Americans to sell themselves to the world as advisers to a sovereign government, not as colonialists like the French. In exchange, Diem arranged for Can Lao businessmen and their American associates to obtain lucrative government contracts and commercial interests once owned exclusively by the French, with a percentage of every transaction going to the Can Lao. Opposed to Diem were the French and their *supplétifs* in the Sûreté and the Vietnamese Mafia, the Binh Xuyen. Together with the Hoa Hao and Cao Dai religious sects, these groups formed the United Sect Front and conspired against the United States and its candidate, Diem.

Into this web of intrigue, in January 1954, stepped U.S. Air Force Colonel Edward Lansdale. A confidential agent of Director of Central Intelligence Allen Dulles and his brother, Secretary of State John Dulles, Lansdale defeated the United Sect Front by either killing or buying off its leaders. He then hurriedly began to build, from the top down, a Vietnam infused with American values and dollars, while the Vietcong—as Lansdale christened the once heroic but now vilified Vietminh—built slowly from the ground up, on a foundation they had laid over forty years.

Lanky, laid-back Ed Lansdale arrived in Saigon fresh from having managed a successful anti-Communist counterinsurgency in the Philippines, where his black bag of dirty tricks included counterterrorism and the assassination of government officials who opposed his lackey, Ramón Magsaysay. In the Philippines his tactics earned him the nickname of the Ugly American. He brought those tactics to Saigon along with a team of dedicated Filipino anti-Communists who, in the words of one veteran CIA officer, "would slit their grandmother's throat for a dollar eighty-five."[10]

In his autobiography, *In the Midst of Wars,* Lansdale gives an example of the counterterror tactics he employed in the Philippines. He tells how one psychological warfare operation "played upon the popular dread of an asuang, or vampire, to solve a difficult problem." The problem was that Lansdale wanted government troops to move out of a village and hunt Communist guerrillas in the hills, but the local politicians were afraid that if they did, the guerrillas would "swoop down on the village and the bigwigs would be victims." So, writes Lansdale:

> A combat psywar [psychological warfare] team was brought in. It planted stories among town residents of a vampire living on the hill where the Huks were based. Two nights later, after giving the stories time to circulate among Huk sympathizers in the town and make

> their way up to the hill camp, the psywar squad set up an ambush along a trail used by the Huks. When a Huk patrol came along the trail, the ambushers silently *snatched* the last man of the patrol, their move unseen in the dark night. They punctured his neck with two holes, vampire fashion, held the body up by the heels, drained it of blood, and put the corpse back on the trail. When the Huks returned to look for the missing man and found their bloodless comrade, every member of the patrol believed that the vampire had got him and that one of them would be next if they remained on the hill. When daylight came, the whole Huk squadron moved out of the vicinity.[11]

Lansdale defines the incident as "low humor" and "an appropriate response . . . to the glum and deadly practices of communists and other authoritarians."[12] And by doing so, former advertising executive Lansdale—the merry prankster whom author Graham Greene dubbed the Quiet American—came to represent the hypocrisy of American policy in South Vietnam. For Lansdale used Madison Avenue language to construct a squeaky-clean, Boy Scout image, behind which he masked his own perverse delight in atrocity.

In Saigon, Lansdale managed several programs which were designed to ensure Diem's internal security and which later evolved and were incorporated into Phoenix. The process began in July 1954, when, posing as an assistant Air Force attaché to the U.S. Embassy, Lansdale got the job of resettling nearly one million Catholic refugees from North Vietnam. As chief of the CIA's Saigon Military Mission Lansdale used the exodus to mount operations against North Vietnam. To this end he hired the Filipino-staffed Freedom Company to train two paramilitary teams, which, posing as refugee relief organizations supplied by the CIA-owned airline, Civil Air Transport, activated stay-behind nets, sabotaged power plants, and spread false rumors of a Communist bloodbath. In this last regard, a missionary named Tom Dooley concocted lurid tales of Vietminh soldiers' disembowling pregnant Catholic women, castrating priests, and sticking bamboo slivers in the ears of children so they could not hear the Word of God. Dooley's tall tales of terror galvanized American support for Diem but were uncovered in 1979 during a Vatican sainthood investigation.

From Lansdale's clandestine infiltration and "black" propaganda program evolved the Vietnamese Special Forces, the Luc Luong Duc Biet (LLDB). Trained and organized by the CIA, the LLDB reported directly to the CIA-managed Presidential Survey Office. As a palace guard, says Kevin Generous in *Vietnam: The Secret War*, "they . . . were always available for special details dreamed up by President Diem and his brother Nhu."[13] Those "special" details sometimes involved "terrorism against political opponents."[14]

Another Lansdale program was aimed at several thousand Vietminh stay-behind agents organizing secret cells and conducting propaganda among the people. As a way of attacking these agents, Lansdale hired the Freedom Company to activate Operation Brotherhood, a paramedical team patterned on the typical Special Forces A team. Under CIA direction, Operation Brotherhood built dispensaries that were used as cover for covert counterterror operations. Operation Brotherhood spawned the Eastern Construction Company, which provided five hundred hard-core Filipino anti-Communists who, while building roads and dispensing medicines, assisted Diem's security forces by identifying and eliminating Vietminh agents.

In January 1955, using resettled Catholic refugees trained by the Freedom Company as cadre, Lansdale began his Civic Action program, the centerpiece of Diem's National Security program. Organized and funded by the CIA in conjunction with the Defense Ministry, but administered through the Ministry of Interior by the province chiefs, Civic Action aimed to do four things: to induce enemy soldiers to defect; to organize rural people into self-defense forces to insulate their villages from VC influence; to create political cadres who would sell the idea that Diem—not the Vietminh—represented national aspirations; and to provide cover for counterterror. In doing these things, Civil Action cadres dressed in black pajamas and went into villages to dig latrines, patch roofs, dispense medicines, and deliver propaganda composed by Lansdale. In return the people were expected to inform on Vietminh guerrillas and vote for Diem in the 1956 reunification elections stipulated by the Geneva Accords. However, the middle-class northern Catholics sent to the villages did not speak the same dialect as the people they were teaching and succeeded only in alienating them. Not only did Civic Action fail to win the hearts and minds of the rural Vietnamese, but as a unilateral CIA operation it received only lip service from Diem and his Can Lao cronies, who, in Lansdale's words, "were afraid that it was some scheme of mine to flood the country with secret agents."[15]

On May 10, 1955, Diem formed a new government and banished the French (who kept eighty thousand troops in the South until 1956) to outposts along the coast. Diem then appointed Nguyen Ngoc Le as his first director general of the National Police. A longtime CIA asset, Le worked with the Freedom Company to organize the Vietnamese Veterans Legion. As a way of extending Can Lao party influence, Vietnamese veteran legion posts were established throughout Vietnam and, with advice and assistance from the U.S. Information Service, took over the distribution of all existing newspapers and magazines. The legion also sponsored the first National Congress, held on May 29, 1955, at City Hall in Saigon. One month later the Can Lao introduced its political front, the National Revolution Movement.

On July 16, 1955, knowing the Buddhist population would vote overwhelmingly for the Vietminh, Diem renounced the reunification elections required by the Geneva Accords. Instead, he rigged a hastily called national referendum. Announced on October 6 and held on October 23, the elections, says Professor Huy, "were an absolute farce. Candidates chosen to be elected had to sign a letter of resignation in which the date was vacant. In case after the election the representative was considered undesirable, Nhu had only to put a date on the letter to have him expelled from the National Assembly."[16]

Elected president by a vast majority, Diem in 1956 issued Ordinance 57-A. Marketed by Lansdale as agrarian reform, it replaced the centuries-old custom of village self-government with councils appointed by district and province chiefs. Diem, of course, appointed the district chiefs, who appointed the village councils, which then employed local security forces to collect exorbitant rents for absentee landlords living the high life in Saigon. Universal displeasure was the response to Ordinance 57-A, the cancellation of the reunification elections, and the rigged election of 1955. Deprived of its chance to win legal representation, the Vietcong launched a campaign of its own, emphasizing social and economic awareness. Terror was not one of their tactics. Says Rand Corporation analyst J. J. Zasloff in "Origins of the Insurgency in South Vietnam 1954–1960": "There is no evidence in our interviews that violence and sabotage were part of their assignment." Rather, Communist cadres were told "to return to their home provinces and were instructed, it appears, to limit their activities to organizational and propaganda tasks."[17]

However, on the basis of CIA reports saying otherwise, Diem initiated the notorious Denunciation of the Communists campaign in 1956. The campaign was managed by security committees, which were chaired by CIA-advised security officers who had authority to arrest, confiscate land from, and summarily execute Communists. In determining who was a Communist, the security committees used a three-part classification system: A for dangerous party members, B for less dangerous party members, and C for loyal citizens. As happened later in Phoenix, security chiefs used the threat of an A or B classification to extort from innocent civilians, while category A and B offenders—fed by their families—were put to work without pay building houses and offices for government officials.

The military, too, had broad powers to arrest and jail suspects while on sweeps in rural areas. Non-Communists who could not afford to pay "taxes" were jailed until their families came up with the cash. Communists fared worse. Vietminh flags were burned in public ceremonies, and portable guillotines were dragged from village to village and used on active and inactive

Vietminh alike. In 1956 in the Central Highlands fourteen thousand people were arrested without evidence or trial—people were jailed simply for having visited a rebel district—and by year's end there were an estimated twenty thousand political prisoners nationwide.[18]

In seeking to ensure his internal security through the denunciation campaign, Diem persecuted the Vietminh and alienated much of the rural population in the process. But "the most tragic error," remarks Professor Huy, "was the liquidation of the Cao Dai, Hoa Hao and Binh Xuyen forces. By destroying them, Diem weakened the defense of South Vietnam against communism. In fact, the remnants . . . were obliged to join the Vietnamese stalinists who were already reinforced by Diem's anti-communist struggle campaign.

"Diem's family dealt with this problem," Huy goes on, "by a repressive policy applied through its secret service. This organ bore the very innocent name of the Political and Social Research Service. It was led by Dr. Tran Kim Tuyen, a devoted Catholic, honest and efficient, who at the beginning sought only to establish a network of intelligence agents to be used against the communists. It had in fact obtained some results in this field. But soon it became a repressive tool to liquidate any opponent."[19]

By then Ed Lansdale had served his purpose and was being unceremoniously rotated out of Vietnam, leaving behind the harried Civic Action program to his protégé, Rufus Phillips. Meanwhile, "Other Americans were working closely with the Vietnamese," Lansdale writes, noting: "Some of the relationships led to a development which I believed could bring only eventual disaster to South Vietnam.

"This development was political," Lansdale observes. "My first inkling came when several families appeared at my house one morning to tell me about the arrest at midnight of their men-folk, all of whom were political figures. The arrests had a strange aspect to them, having come when the city was asleep and being made by heavily armed men who were identified as 'special police.' "[20]

Sensing the stupidity of such a program, Lansdale appealed to Ambassador George Reinhardt, suggesting that "Americans under his direction who were in regular liaison with Nhu, and who were advising the special branch of the police, would have to work harder at influencing the Vietnamese toward a more open and free political concept." But, Lansdale was told, "a U.S. policy decision had been made. We Americans were to give what assistance we could to the building of a strong nationalistic party that would support Diem. Since Diem was now the elected president, he needed to have his own party."[21]

"Shocked" that he had been excluded from such a critical policy decision, Lansdale, to his credit, tried to persuade Diem to disband the Can Lao.

When that failed, he took his case to the Dulles brothers since they "had decisive voices in determining the US relationship with South Vietnam." But self-described "visionary and idealist" Lansdale's views were dismissed offhandedly by the pragmatic Dulleses in favor "of the one their political experts in Saigon had recommended." Lansdale was told he should "disengage myself from any guidance to political parties in Vietnam."[22]

The mask of democracy would be maintained. But the ideal was discarded in exchange for internal security.

CHAPTER 2

Internal Security

In 1954, in the professed belief that it ought to extend the "American way" abroad, Michigan State University (MSU) offered to provide the government of Vietnam with a huge technical assistance program in four areas: public information, public administration, finance and economics, and police and security services. The contract was approved in early 1955, shortly after the National Security Council (NSC) had endorsed Diem, and over the next seven years MSU's Police Administration Division spent fifteen million dollars of U.S. taxpayers' money building up the GVN's internal security programs. In exchange for the lucrative contract, the Michigan State University Group (MSUG) became the vehicle through which the CIA secretly managed the South Vietnamese "special police."

MSUG's Police Administration Division contributed to Diem's internal security primarily by reorganizing his police and security forces. First, Binh Xuyen gangsters in the Saigon police were replaced with "good cops" from the Sûreté. Next, recruits from the Sûreté were inducted into the Secret Service, Civil Guard, and Military Security Service (MSS), which was formed by Ed Lansdale in 1954 as "military coup insurance." On administrative matters the MSS reported to the Directorate of Political Warfare in liaison with the CIA, while its operations staff reported to the Republic of Vietnam Armed Forces (RVNAF)'s Joint General Staff in liaison with MAAG counterintelligence officers. All general directors of police and security services were military officers.

The Sûreté (plainclothesmen handling investigations, customs, immigration, and revenue) was renamed the Vietnamese Bureau of Investigations (VBI) and combined with the municipal police (uniformed police in twenty-two autonomous cities and Saigon) into a General Directorate of Police and Security Services within the Ministry of the Interior. This early attempt at bureaucratic streamlining was undermined by Diem, however, who kept the various police and security agencies spying on one another. Diem was especially wary of the VBI, which as the Sûreté had faithfully served the French and which, after 1954, under CIA management, was beyond his control. As a result, Diem judged the VBI by the extent to which it attacked his domestic foes, spied on the Military Security Service, and kept province chiefs in line.

Because it managed the central records depository, the VBI was the most powerful security force and received the lion's share of American "technical" aid. While other services got rusty weapons, the VBI got riot guns, bulletproof vests, gas masks, lie detectors, a high-command school, a modern crime lab and modern interrogation centers; and the most promising VBI officers were trained by the CIA and FBI at the International Police Academy at Georgetown University in agent handling, criminal investigations, interrogation, and counterinsurgency. The VBI (the Cong An to Vietnamese) is one of the two foundation stones of Phoenix.

Whereas the majority of Michigan State's police advisers were former state troopers or big-city detectives, the men who advised the VBI and trained Diem's Secret Service were CIA officers working under cover as professors in the Michigan State University Group. Each morning myopic MSUG employees watched from their quarters across the street as senior VBI adviser Raymond Babineau and his team went to work at the National Police Interrogation Center, which, Graham Greene writes in *The Quiet American*, "seemed to smell of urine and injustice."[1] Later in the day the MSUG contingent watched while truckloads of political prisoners—mostly old men, women, and children arrested the night before—were handcuffed and carted off to Con Son Prison. America's first colonialists in Saigon looked, then looked away. For four years they dared not denounce the mass arrests or the fact that room P-40 in the Saigon Zoo was used as a morgue and torture chamber. No one wanted to incriminate himself or get on the wrong side of Babineau and his protégés in the "special police."

The fear was palpable. In his book *War Comes to Long An*, Jeffrey Race quotes a province chief: "I hardly ever dared to look around in the office with all the Can Lao people there watching me, and in those days it was just impossible to resign—many others had tried—they were just led off in the middle of the night by Diem's men dressed as VC, taken to P-40 or Poulo

Condore [Con Son Prison] and never heard from again."[2]

While the VBI existed primarily to suppress Diem's domestic opponents, it also served the CIA by producing an annual *Ban Tran Liet Viet Cong* (Vietcong order of battle). Compiled for the most part from notes taken by secret agents infiltrated into VC meetings, then assembled by hand at the central records depository, the *Ban Tran Liet* was the CIA's biography of the VCI and the basis of its anti-infrastructure operations until 1964.

In 1959 Diem held another sham election. Said one Vietnamese official quoted by Race: "The 1959 election was very dishonest. Information and Civic Action Cadre went around at noon when everyone was home napping and stuffed ballot boxes. If the results didn't come out right they were adjusted at district headquarters." When asked if anyone complained, the official replied, "Everyone was terrified of the government. . . . The Cong An beat people and used 'the water treatment.' But there was nothing anyone could do. Everyone was terrified." Said another official: "During the Diem period the people here saw the government was no good at all. That is why 80% of them followed the VC. I was the village chief then, but I had to do what the government told me. If not, the secret police [VBI] would have me picked up and tortured me to death. Thus I was the very one who rigged the elections here."[3]

As is apparent, Diem's security forces terrorized the Vietnamese people more than the VCI. In fact, as Zasloff noted earlier, prior to 1959 the VCI carried out an official policy of nonviolence. "By adopting an almost entirely defensive role during this period," Race explains, "and by allowing the government to be the first to employ violence, the Party—at great cost—allowed the government to pursue the conflict in increasingly violent terms, through its relentless reprisal against any opposition, its use of torture, and, particularly after May 1959, through the psychological impact in the rural areas of the proclamation of Law 10/59."[4]

In *Phoenix/Phung Hoang: A Study of Wartime Intelligence Management,* CIA officer Ralph Johnson calls the 10/59 Law "the GVN's most serious mistake." Under its provisions, anyone convicted of "acts of sabotage" or "infringements on the national security" could be sentenced to death or life imprisonment with no appeal. Making matters worse, Johnson writes, was the fact that "The primary GVN targets were former Viet Minh guerrillas—many of whom were nationalists, not Communists—regardless of whether or not they were known to have been participating in subversive activities."[5]

The 10/59 Law resulted in the jailing of fifty thousand political prisoners by year's end. But rather than suppress the insurgency, Vietnamese from all walks of life joined the cause. Vietminh cadres moved into the villages from secluded base camps in the Central Highlands, the Rung Sat, the Ca Mau swamps, and the Plain of Reeds. And after four years of Diem style democracy, the rural population welcomed them with open arms.

The nonviolence policy practiced by Vietcong changed abruptly in 1959, when in response to the 10/59 Law and CIA intrusions into North Vietnam, the Lao Dong Central Committee organized the 559th Transportation and Support Group. Known as Doan 559, this combat-engineer corps carved out the Ho Chi Minh Trail through the rugged mountains and fever-ridden jungles of South Vietnam, Laos, and Cambodia. Doan 559 paved the way for those Vietminh veterans who had gone North in 1954 and returned in 1959 to organize self-defense groups and political cells in Communist-controlled villages. By the end of 1959 Doan 559 had infiltrated forty-five hundred regroupees back into South Vietnam.

Sent to stop Doan 559 from infiltrating troops into South Vietnam were U.S. Army Special Forces commandos trained in "behind-the-lines" anti-guerrilla and intelligence-gathering operations. Working in twelve-member A teams under cover of Civic Action, the Green Berets organized paramilitary units in remote rural regions and SWAT team-type security forces in cities. In return, they were allowed to occupy strategic locations and influence political events in their host countries.

Developed as a way of fighting cost effective counterinsurgencies, the rough-and-tumble Green Berets were an adjunct of the CIA—which made them a threat to the U.S. Army. But Special Forces troopers on temporary duty (TDY) could go places where the Geneva Accords restricted the number of regular soldiers. For example, in Laos, the "Sneaky Petes" wore civilian clothes and worked in groups of two or three, turning Pathet Lao deserters into double agents who returned to their former units with electronic tracking devices, enabling the CIA to launch air attacks against them. Other double agents returned to their units to lead them into ambushes. As Ed Lansdale explains, once inside enemy ranks, "they could not only collect information for passing secretly to the government but also could work to induce the rank and file to surrender." Volunteers for such "risky business," Lansdale adds, were trained singly or in groups as large as companies that were "able to get close enough in their disguise for surprise combat, often hand to hand."[6]

By the late 1950s, increasing numbers of American Special Forces were in South Vietnam, practicing the terrifying black art of psychological warfare.

Arriving in Saigon in the spring of 1959 as the CIA's deputy chief of station was William Colby. An OSS veteran, Princeton graduate, liberal lawyer, and devout Catholic, Colby managed the station's paramilitary operations against North Vietnam and the Vietcong. He also managed its political operations and oversaw deep-cover case officers like Air America executive Clyde Bauer, who brought to South Vietnam its Foreign Relations

Council, Chamber of Commerce, and Lions' Club, in Bauer's words, "to create a strong civil base."[7] CIA officers under Colby's direction funneled money to *all* political parties, including the Lao Dong, as a way of establishing long-range penetration agents who could monitor and manipulate political developments.

Under Colby's direction, the CIA increased its advice and assistance to the GVN's security forces, at the same time that MSUG ceased being a CIA cover. MSUG advisers ranging across South Vietnam, conducting studies and reporting on village life, had found themselves stumbling over secret policemen posing as village chiefs and CIA officers masquerading as anthropologists. And even though these ploys helped security forces catch those in the VCI, they also put the MSUG advisers squarely between Vietcong cross hairs.

So it was that while Raymond Babineau was on vacation, assistant MSUG project chief Robert Scigliano booted the VBI advisory unit out from under MSUG cover. The State Department quickly absorbed the CIA officers and placed them under the Agency for International Development's Public Safety Division (AID/PSD), itself created by CIA officer Byron Engel in 1954 to provide "technical assistance" and training to police and security officials in fifty-two countries. In Saigon in 1959, AID/PSD was managed by a former Los Angeles policeman, Frank Walton, and its field offices were directed by the CIA-managed Combined Studies Group, which funded cadres and hired advisers for the VBI, Civil Guard, and Municipal police. Through AID/PSD, technical assistance to police and security services increased exponentially. Introduced were a telecommunications center; a national police training center at Vung Tau; a rehabilitation system for defecting Communists which led to their voluntary service in CIA security programs; and an FBI-sponsored national identification registration program, which issued ID cards to all Vietnamese citizens over age fourteen as a means of identifying Communists, deserters, and fugitives.

Several other major changes occurred at this juncture. On the assumption that someday the Communists would be defeated, MSUG in 1957 had reduced the Civil Guard in strength and converted it into a national police constabulary, which served primarily as a security force for district and province chiefs (all of whom were military officers after 1959) and also guarded bridges, major roads, and power stations. CIA advisers assigned to the constabulary developed clandestine cells within its better units. Operating out of police barracks at night in civilian clothes, these ragtag Red Squads were targeted against the VCI, using intelligence provided by the VBI. However, in December 1960 the U.S. Military Assistance Advisory Group seized control of the constabulary and began organizing it into company, battalion, and regimental units armed with automatic rifles and machine guns. The constabulary was renamed the Regional Forces and placed under the Ministry of Defense. The remaining eighteen thousand rural policemen thereafter served to enforce curfews and maintain law and order in agrovilles—garrison communities consisting of forcefully relocated persons, developed by MSUG in 1959 in response to Ed Lansdale's failed Civic Action program.

With the demise of Civic Action teams, pacification efforts were by default dumped on the Vietnamese Army, whose heavy-handed tactics further alienated the rural Vietnamese and enabled the Vietcong to infiltrate the Self-Defense Corps and erode the program from within. In an attempt to stop the bleeding, Civic Action cadres were redirected toward organizing "community development" programs, in which class A and B Communist offenders were forced to build agrovilles, as well as roads leading to and from them. When construction had been completed, South Vietnamese army units leveled the surrounding villages, "resettled" the inhabitants in agrovilles, and manned outposts along the roads as a means of facilitating the movement of security forces in search of Communist offenders.

The idea behind agrovilles was to control the rural population by physically moving the *sea* of sympathetic people away from the guerrilla *fish*. By making relocated persons build agrovilles—tent cities protected by moats, mud walls, and bamboo stakes—internal security, it was imagined, could be established, laws enforced, and potential revolutionaries tacitly involved in the fight against the guerrillas and thus psychologically prone to act as informers to VBI case officers. Their information would then lead to the elimination of the insurgent political cells through their imprisonment, assassination, or defection. Agrovilles were defended by Regional Forces and the Popular Force—derived from Self-Defense Corps—trained and advised by U.S. Army, AID/PSD, and CIA personnel.

The secondary nation-building goal of the agroville program was physically to construct a social and economic infrastructure connected to the GVN. In reality, though, by uprooting the people from their ancestral homes, the program generated legions of Vietcong sympathizers. Moreover, the massive infusion of American aid amounted to a boondoggle for the corrupt government officials administering the program. Piled on top of a land reform program that stole from the poor and gave to the rich and of the 10/59 Law, agrovilles replaced Civic Action as the main target of the burgeoning insurgency and its North Vietnamese sponsors.

In response, when he became chief of the CIA's Saigon station in 1960, William Colby accelerated the pace of CIA operations into North Vietnam. He and Gilbert Lawton (a CIA officer disguised as a Special Forces colonel) also launched the Civilian Irregular Defense Group (CIDG) program as a means of preventing North Vietnamese Army (NVA) and roving Vietcong guerrilla units from moving through, drawing sustenance from, or maintaining agents in GVN-monitored villages. Extrapolated from the French commando program begun in 1951, the CIDG program used Vietnamese Special Forces to organize "favorable minorities" into static Self-Defense Corps through Civic Action, which were armed, trained, and targeted by the CIA against Communist political and military units.

Father Hoa's Sea Swallows exemplify the CIDG program in operation. Imprisoned in the 1940's by the Communist Chinese for conspiring with the Kuomintang, Father Nguyen Loc Hoa led two thousand Catholic converts into Laos in 1950, shortly after Chiang Kai-shek had fled to Taiwan with his Nationalist Army. Eight years later, after enduring religious persecution in Laos, Father Hoa was persuaded by Bernard Yoh—a Kuomintang intelligence officer on loan to the CIA—to resettle his flock in the village of Binh Hung on the Ca Mau Peninsula in southern South Vietnam. The deal was this: Father Hoa was appointed chief of a district where 90 percent of the people were Vietcong supporters. He was given quantities of military aid and advice from a series of CIA officers disguised as Special Forces colonels. In exchange, Father Hoa had merely to fight the Vietcong, as he did with vigor. As Don Schrande reported in the *Saturday Evening Post* of February 17, 1962, "Father Hoa personally led his pitifully small force into the swamps nightly to strike the enemy on his own ground."[8]

Stuck in the midst of a VC stronghold, Binh Hung village resembled a military outpost, replete with an obstacle course Father Hoa called "our own little Fort Bragg." As district chief Father Hoa used CIA funds to run "an intelligence network" consisting of "a volunteer apparatus of friendly farmers and a few full time agents." On the basis of this intelligence Father Hoa mounted raids against individual Vietcong cadres. By 1962 he had corralled 148 prisoners, whom he used as slave laborers in the village's rice paddies. In the evenings Sea Swallow cadres indoctrinated their captives with religious and political propaganda, prompting the weaklings to defect and join the ranks of Father Hoa's Popular Force battalion—five hundred Vietnamese dressed in ill-fitting U.S. Army-supplied khaki uniforms.

Because it was composed of Vietnamese, the Popular Force battalion was not trustworthy, however, and did not include the Sea Swallows' own cadre. Described by Schrande as former Boy Scouts who gave the three-fingered salute, this "group of black-clad commandos armed to the teeth" was "[c]lustered around the priest like a personal bodyguard."[9] Unlike their Vietnamese neighbors, Father Hoa's Chinese Catholic zealots held what Bernard Yoh calls "an ideology that there can be no compromise with Communism."[10]

The image of a defiant band of foreigners, transplanted by the CIA to Vietnam to suit its purposes and surrounded by captives, defectors, and enemies, symbolizes perfectly the state of the counterinsurgency in the early

1960's. Things were not going well inside the GVN either. The Military Security Service was infiltrated by Communist agents, and in June 1959 the VBI arrested the personal bodyguard to the ARVN chief of staff and charged him with spying. In January 1960 two officers in the Operations Division of the Vietnamese Joint General Staff (JGS) were arrested as Vietcong agents. Even the Can Lao was penetrated by Communist agents, as events proved.

The situation climaxed in November 1960, when a group of disgruntled Dai Viet paratroopers led a coup against Diem. Although a failure, the coup attempt drew attention to Diem's lack of popular support, a situation made worse when his brother Nhu sicced the secret police on the Dai Viets and their Buddhist allies. This purge sent the Buddhists underground and into alliances with the Communists, and what was called "the Buddhist crisis" ensued, eventually causing the demise of the Ngo regime.

Sensing that Diem was on the ropes and bolstered by the Buddhists' having joined their cause, the Communists on December 20, 1960, announced the formation of the National Front for the Liberation of South Vietnam and called for the expulsion of all Americans. Ho Chi Minh appointed Le Duan secretary-general of the southern branch of the party, and one year later the People's Revolutionary party (PRP) was activated in the South. The insurgency had begun in earnest.

How the insurgency was organized is essential to understanding Phoenix, which was targeted specifically against its leadership, the VCI. At the top of the VCI organizational chart was the Central Office of South Vietnam (COSVN), an executive committee answering to the Lao Dong Central Committee's Reunification Department in Hanoi. From its floating headquarters along the Cambodian border, COSVN in turn directed the activities of the People's Revolutionary party, the National Liberation Front, and the Liberation Army—aka the Vietcong. COSVN's marching orders were sent to six regional committees in South Vietnam, plus one more for the Saigon capital zone. Province committees in turn directed district committees, which were formed by groupings of at least three village committees. Likewise, each village committee was composed of at least three hamlet-level chapters, which constituted the fundamental link to the rural population. Hamlet chapters had three to five members, who were organized into cells with elected leaders. The cell was the smallest VCI organizational unit but could not exist unless integrated into a chapter.

The National Liberation Front sought to mobilize the "people" through associations encompassing all sectors of society. The NLF coordinated the Communist party with other South Vietnamese political parties through its Central Committee, which floated along the Cambodian border in the area referred to as the Parrot's Beak. When operations were mounted against it, the Central Committee slipped into the Iron Triangle area north of Saigon, or into the famous tunnels of Cu Chi, or into Tay Ninh City. Regardless of where it was headquartered, the NLF was most viable at the grass-roots level. There farmers' associations preached land reform; women's associations trained nurses; and liberation youth associations opposed the draft. Liberation associations existed for all classes of society, including writers and Buddhists.

Initially, only Communist party members headed NLF associations, and all ambitious revolutionaries sought admission to the People's Revolutionary party, which by 1962 boasted half a million members. Entrance to the PRP required a sponsor, a background check, and a trial membership. As the insurgency's managers, party members were *the* primary target of Phoenix and its predecessor organizations.

Topping the hit list were party secretaries—the people directing Vietcong operations at region, province, and district levels. Although usually known by name, they were nevertheless hard to find. VCI "duty expert" Robert Slater, a Marine captain on contract to the CIA from 1967 to 1969, writes: "In over three years in Vietnam, I knew of no Province Party Secretary ever being captured." Why so hard to kill? "Since he is the most important VC committee member in the province, access to him is limited to province and district committee members. This is to prevent any attempted assassination by Allied penetration agents or VC 'sell-outs.'"[11]

High on the list was the district party secretary, in Slater's words, "the indispensable link between COSVN, region, province and the villages." Armed and always on the move, the "DPS usually does not sleep in the same house or even hamlet where his family lives," Slater notes, "to preclude any injury to his family during assassination attempts or Allied raids." Such precautions did not always work. Writes Slater: "The Allies have frequently found out where District Party Secretaries live and raided their homes; in an ensuing fire fight the secretary's wife and children have been killed and injured."[12]

The village party secretary was another priority target. Traveling alone to hamlets to conduct person-to-person business in rice paddies, cafés, and barbershops, the village secretary was responsible for feeding, billeting, and guiding VC and NVA troops in the area. More visible than district or province cadre, village secretaries were considered easy pickings.

Managing revolutionary intelligence operations in South Vietnam was the Central Research Agency (Cuc Nghien Cuu), reporting to the National Defense Committee in Hanoi in conjunction with the Reunification Department of the Lao Dong Central Committee. The task of Cuc Nghien Cuu agents in South Vietnam, according to CIA officer Ralph Johnson, was the penetration of GVN offices, "to determine plans and capabilities, to recruit

GVN military members, and to provide intelligence for paramilitary activities, espionage, subversion, and other political operations."[13] Agents of the Cuc Nghien Cuu reported through an intricate radio and courier network directly to Hanoi, where intelligence data were analyzed and collated with information from elsewhere in South Vietnam and abroad. The Cuc Nghien Cuu maintained secret bases and courier networks in the South as a means of supplying its agents with direction and equipment.

Introduced into South Vietnam in 1960 as the insurgency's security service was the An Ninh. Composed mainly of North Vietnamese agents who reported to Hanoi's Ministry of Public Security, the An Ninh investigated VCI members suspected of being double agents or potential defectors. From its headquarters in COSVN, the An Ninh ran intelligence nets, propaganda campaigns, and counterespionage operations at the village level, drawing up blacklists of double agents and manning armed reconnaissance teams that kidnapped and assassinated GVN officials. More than any other branch of the Communist shadow government in South Vietnam, the An Ninh was responsible for destabilizing the GVN. Ralph Johnson calls it "the glue that held the VCI together."[14] The Cuc Nghien Cuu and the An Ninh were the CIA's archenemies and, ironically, the models for its Phoenix coordinators.

Indeed, as the CIA saw how the insurgency was organized, it structured its counterinsurgency accordingly. Unable to admit that nationalism was the cause of the insurrection and that the United States was viewed as an intruder like the French, the CIA instead argued that Communist organizational techniques, especially its use of selective terror, compelled the Vietnamese people to support the insurgency. As William Colby testified before Congress, "the implication or latent threat of force alone was sufficient to insure that the people would comply with Communist demands."[15]

In drumming up public support in America for military intervention, the CIA portrayed all armed anti-GVN sects as Communist puppets, and because the agency asserted that the "people" were not behind the insurgency but were mindless peasants who had been coerced by a clever mix of propaganda and terror, the legitimate grievances of the people—primarily their anger at Diem's dictatorship—could be ignored. This being the case, the GVN did not have to comply with the Geneva Accords, provide fair elections, or enact land reform. It did not have to end preferential treatment for Catholics, curb police corruption, or discipline ARVN soldiers. All grievances were dismissed as smoke and mirrors disguising the criminal ambitions of the Communists.

This revisionist view is what Stanley Karnow calls "the myth . . . that the Vietcong was essentially an indigenous and autonomous insurgent movement."[16] The revisionists argued that the wily Communists had recognized the legitimate grievances of people, then adapted their organization to exploit local conditions. Having gained toeholds in the villages, they used selective terror to eliminate GVN authority and frighten the people into joining NLF associations and armed VC units. Ipso facto the VCI and the "people" were in no real sense connected, and one had only to destroy the VCI—the apparatus—to stop the revolution.

Key to revisionist theory was the notion that selective terror was a more effective social control than the GVN's suppressive terror, which only fanned the revolutionary fires. As Jeffrey Race notes, "violence will work against the user, *unless* he has already preempted a large part of the population and then limits his acts of violence to a sharply defined minority."[17] Ironically, by using selective terror effectively, the VCI handed the CIA the rationale it needed to develop counterterror teams. And by announcing the formation of the NLF in a bid for political legitimacy—just as this notion of killing off the enemy's civilian leadership was being advanced—the VCI offered itself as a target.

Meanwhile, as the CIA became aware of what political warfare entailed, Diem and his brother Nhu began to be perceived as liabilities. Convinced that William Colby had organized the November 1960 coup attempt, Nhu prohibited his Can Lao followers from consorting with the CIA. This edict threw a wrench into CIA attempts to organize internal security in South Vietnam, and in May 1961 Ambassador Elbridge Durbow asked Diem to abolish the Can Lao, claiming it denied advancement to the majority of Vietnamese and nullified democratic reforms.

Unwilling to divest himself of his power base, Diem refused, and instead sought to appease the Americans by authorizing a statute legalizing the creation of the Central Intelligence Organization (CIO), a move Colby credits as the beginning of Phoenix. Station chief Colby then directed Raymond Babineau to provide the people and the equipment required to put the CIO in business.[18] Colonel Nguyen Van Y was named chief, a building in Saigon was selected as his headquarters, and he recruited his staff from a faction of the Can Lao that included General Tran Thien Khiem, the man who eventually managed Phoenix, and Nguyen Van Thieu, the army colonel who eventually became president of South Vietnam. Not limited to the coordination of police and military intelligence, the CIO also managed political and foreign intelligence operations. Smaller and more sophisticated than the Cong An, the CIO became the nerve center of the counterinsurgency.

Knowing that the single-minded Americans would carry the fight against the North, Diem, through his spymaster, Dr. Tuyen, and the Office of Political and Social Studies, redoubled his attack against his domestic opponents. However, Karnow writes, "Tuyen feared that Diem's failings would bring about a Communist takeover. Ironically, he filled his faction with dissenters he had blacklisted, and he also attracted disgruntled junior officers.

He teamed up as well with Colonel Pham Ngoc Thao, unaware of Thao's clandestine Communist ties. Thao's followers included a young air force pilot, Nguyen Cao Ky."[19]

Believing Thao to be trustworthy, Nhu appointed him to manage the strategic hamlet program, which replaced the agroville program in 1962. Thus, by forcing Diem and Nhu into greater dependence on reactionary programs and a Communist double agent, the formation of the CIO in 1961 further hastened the demise of the Ngo regime.

Meanwhile, in order to stem the tide of cheap little wars of liberation that Nikita Khrushchev promised would "bury" the West, President John Kennedy formed the National Security Council Special Group to manage U.S. counterinsurgency efforts in Vietnam and elsewhere. A special assistant for covert and special activities (SACSA) was assigned to the chairman of the Joint Chiefs of Staff, former Lansdale aide General William B. Rosson was made the special warfare assistant to the Army's chief of staff, and the CIA got a new headquarters in Langley, Virginia.

When, on September 18, 1961, an An Ninh terror squad decapitated the Catholic chief of Phuoc Long Province, President Kennedy, ignoring troop limits set at the Geneva Accords, rushed legions of Special Forces advisers to the South Vietnamese. The 704th Military Intelligence Group arrived and began advising the Military Security Service, and the Army sent its first province advisers to Vietnam, supplementing MAAG with the Military Assistance Command, Vietnam (MACV). CIA psywar and paramilitary officers, their brains bursting with big ideas and their Abercrombie and Fitch safari jacket pockets bulging with big bucks, converged on Vietnam from Cuba, Africa, Greece, Korea, the Philippines, Laos, and Indonesia. By the end of 1962 nearly twelve thousand American soldiers were in South Vietnam, flying helicopters, dropping napalm on Communist villages, spraying Agent Orange, advising ARVN battalions, patrolling rivers and the coast, conducting "behind-the-lines" missions, and mounting anti-infrastructure operations that included attacks on Diem's political opposition. The counterinsurgency, too, had begun in earnest.

CHAPTER 3

Covert Action

The dynamics of political warfare, as conceived by the Communists and copied by the CIA, revolved around armed propaganda teams. In South Vietnam a Vietcong armed propaganda team (APT) would enter a village at dusk, and the political cadres, being friendly and "upright," would go from person to person introducing themselves and getting everyone's attention. They would then gather everyone together for entertainment—old tunes with a revolutionary twist—followed by propaganda on GVN corruption and American war crimes, for example, a lecture on how American-made defoliants destroyed crops and caused disease or a skit depicting an American soldier raping a Vietnamese girl. Next came the obligatory self-criticism session, and last but not least, the recruitment of people into clandestine cells, liberation committees, guerrilla units, and informant nets.

As standard procedure, an armed propaganda team would return to the village to repeat the performance, and if the villagers resisted over a period of time, terror came into play. The APT would go through its routine, then announce that a spy had been discovered—usually a secret policeman or corrupt village chief, sometimes a wife and children, too. The unfortunate person was put on trial before a "people's court" and, after being summarily convicted, was brutally murdered in the center of the village. A death notice was pinned to the body, and the body put on display.

The message was clear. The CIA determined early the economic advantages of this village-level selective terror approach. Only when selective terror was used by the CIA, it was called counterterror. The origin of the CIA's counterterror doctrine in South Vietnam may be traced to political warfare pioneer Ralph Johnson. A Chicago native, veteran of the Flying Tigers, and notorious ladies' man, whose most famous liaison was with Nguyen Cao Ky's wife, Johnson was described by one colleague as "a good-looking, fast-talking snake-oil salesman."[1] Johnson dubbed his counterterror doctrine Contre Coup and, in *The Phoenix Program: Planned Assassination or Legitimate Conflict Management,* describes it as "Turning the Communist terrorist strategy, which had proven effective, into a US-Saigon pacification strategy."[2]

CIA officer Johnson formulated his theory in the Philippines in the mid-1950's and as a police adviser in Indonesia in 1957 and 1958, prior to the failed Sukarno coup. His cover having been blown in Jakarta, he was posted to Laos and assigned to the remote northern region bordering China and North Vietnam. There, working undercover for the Agency for International Development, Johnson began organizing Montagnard tribesmen and Pathet Lao defectors into Civic Action/commando teams on the Ed Lansdale "combat psywar" model.

In mid-1960, shortly before the Buddhist crisis, Johnson was transferred to Hue to serve as the CIA officer in charge of South Vietnam's northern provinces and to implement a program similar to the one he had created in Laos. In staffing the pilot programs they created, Johnson and his CIA colleagues spotted, vetted, and hired qualified military and police officers as agents. These Vietnamese nationals were detached from the military or the police and served at the pleasure of the local civilian authority. Such was the arrangement that enabled Johnson and Vietnamese Army Captain Le Xuan Mai to devise the Mountain Scouts, a political action program employing tactics and techniques Johnson had copied from the Communists and perfected in Laos.

According to Stu Methven, a veteran CIA officer who followed Johnson from Laos to Hue in early 1961, the Mountain Scouts were a unilateral CIA operation managed by CIA-funded province and district chiefs. The scouts were composed of Montagnard tribesmen recruited by Vietnamese agents in the CIA's employ. The "Yards" and their Vietnamese officers were then organized into fifteen-man teams that—like the VC's armed propaganda teams—had both paramilitary and political action capabilities. Their job, says Methven, was to "make the GVN presence felt outside the district capitals." Once inside a VC village, the Mountain Scout political officer would denounce the Communists and make a pro-GVN speech, cowritten by Mai and Johnson. Other team members would take a census and make a map of the village. If possible, the team returned with defectors, left informers behind, and stuck a VC head on a pole as they left. The latter was a counterterror function, distinct from any strictly paramilitary function, which involved combat with enemy units.

Now a special assistant to the vice-president of the Center for Naval Analysis, Methven co-managed the Mountain Scout program with Ralph Johnson in 1961 and 1962. To counter what he perceived as rampant VC terror, Methven began extracting the most aggressive individuals from Mountain Scout teams and hiring mercenaries—often Vietnamese convicts or Chinese Nungs—to act as counterterrorists, to do unto the Vietcong's armed propaganda teams what they were doing to GVN officials. With the creation of these counterterror teams, the second of Phoenix's foundation stones was set in place.

Ralph Johnson defines the CTs as "small teams . . . particularly well trained, aggressive, and consisting of a large percentage of former Viet Cong who had become disillusioned and were now violently anti-Viet Cong. Designed like SWAT units employed by the Police Departments of any major city, the Counter-Terror Teams were constituted of five to 20 men whose mission was to collect intelligence in Communist-controlled areas, as well as to apprehend key Viet Cong leaders. At maximum strength the Counter-Terror Teams never totaled more than 3,500 throughout all South Vietnam, but because of their CIA support, and the need to protect not only Team members but their families from Viet Cong reprisals, an aura of mystery and secrecy came to surround these units."[4]

With the appearance of CT teams in 1962, three separate and distinct programs began to emerge; political action, paramilitary, and counterterror. At this point Ralph Johnson was transferred to Saigon as an adviser to several important government officials, and the CIA station's chief of covert action, Cliff Strathern, assigned Methven the task of selling the Mountain Scout program to the province chiefs in I Corps and II Corps. Assisted by half a dozen CIA contract officers, Methven eventually installed the program in thirteen provinces with a force of fifteen thousand men.[5]

Selling the Mountain Scout program to province chiefs, what he called "fostering local initiatives," was easy, Methven recalled, "because we gave them money and supplies." Province chiefs also found the program attractive because as a unilateral CIA operation the Mountain Scouts were not under GVN control and because having the teams under their control strengthened the hand of province and district chiefs in their dealings with Saigon.

In expanding the Mountain Scout program, Methven noted, "MAAG was our biggest supporter." But in return for logistical support, MAAG ultimately assumed control. And being less concerned with political action than with fighting NVA and VC combat units, MAAG advisers began transforming the Mountain Scouts and other paramilitary CIDG teams from "static" defense groups into mobile strike (Mike) forces. The CIA, however, did not forsake its political action or counterterror missions, and while MAAG increased the size of the units under its control, the CIA purposely kept its CT and political action teams in small units—usually fewer than two hundred men in a province—and in this way maintained greater control over political developments at the local level.

With the militarization of the Mountain Scouts, hunter/killer teams first appeared on the scene. Composed of two or three Montagnards or mercenaries and one or two American advisers, the hunter team penetrated enemy areas, reconnoitered for intelligence, and conducted kidnapping and assassination (snatch and snuff) operations. When the hunter teams, which performed as counterterrorists, stumbled on large enemy troop concentrations, they called in killer teams in black, unmarked helicopters provided by the CIA. Although they worked in tandem, hunter teams were not under the operational control of killer teams.

Also at this time the CIA began using selective terror not just to do to the Vietcong what they were doing to GVN officials. Knowing that an act of selective terror against one Montagnard would send the whole village scurrying to a refugee center or a strategic hamlet, where they were then recruited into CIDG teams, the CTs began disguising themselves as Vietcong and committing acts of selective terror against ethnic rivals.

However, as became increasingly clear during the early 1960's, organizing favorable minorities through the CIDG program was not enough to stem the Communist tide. Through arrogance and repression, Diem had alienated the Buddhist majority, and even his generals were plotting against him. Meanwhile, the NLF was organizing more and more Buddhist villages, and the CIA was failing to do likewise on behalf of the GVN. As Jeffrey Race points out, "The [GVN] could not create a viable 'underground' apparatus like the Party's, because of the low level of motivation of the government's operatives and their lack of a sympathetic environment."[6]

For VC and CIA alike, the purpose of political action was threefold: to expand influence through propaganda and civic action, to organize villagers to fight enemy military units, and to destroy the enemy's infrastructure—meaning that if the counterinsurgency was to succeed, the CIA had to create cadres that were every bit as motivated as the Vietcong. So, in the spirit of Contre Coup, the CIA turned to defectors to spread its message in the rural villages of Vietnam, in effect, into enemy territory.

According to William Colby, "The Armed Propaganda Team has [a number of] former Vietcong who are recruited to work for you. . . . Their function is to go around in the countryside and indicate to the people that they used to be Vietcong and that the government has received them and taken them in and that the Chieu Hoi [amnesty] program does exist as a way of VC currently on the other side to rally. They contact people like the families of known VC" and provide transportation to defector and refugee centers.[7]

As Colby explained, communication is the essence of political warfare. Thus, to understand political warfare and how Phoenix fits within that context, it is essential first to understand the role of language.

In its broadest political warfare application, language is the means by which governments, through subtle suggestion and disinformation, shape public opinion on issues. Communists and capitalists alike recognize the power of slogans and packaging to sell political as well as commercial products. For example, the Vietcong used language to peddle a totalitarian state in the guise of social justice, while language allowed Ed Lansdale to wrap the Diem dictatorship in the robe of Jesus Christ and sell it as a democracy. The difference in Vietnam, of course, was that the Vietcong slung their slogans at the rural population, proclaiming, "Land for the Landless," while Lansdale (who prior to World War II handled accounts for an advertising agency in San Francisco) declared straight-faced that "Christ has moved South," a pitch obviously aimed at the American public.

Lansdale was not unaware of what he was doing. The first objective of a covert action program is to create plausible denial—specifically, in South Vietnam, to cloak the CIA's role in organizing GVN repression. The CIA did this by composing and planting distorted articles in foreign and domestic newspapers and by composing "official" communiqués which appeared to have originated within the GVN itself. This disinformation campaign led predisposed Americans to believe that the GVN was a legitimately elected representative government, a condition which was a necessary prerequisite for the massive aid programs that supported the CIA's covert action programs. Insofar as language—information management—perpetuated the myth that Americans were the GVN's advisers, not its manufacturer, public support was rallied for continued intervention.

Next, the CIA judges a covert action program on its intelligence potential—its ability to produce information on the enemy's political, military, and economic infrastructure. That is why the CIA's covert action branch operates as an intelligence arm under cover of civic action. What makes these intelligence operations covert is not any mistaken impression on the part of the enemy, but rather the CIA's ability to deny plausibly involvement in them to the American public. Here again, language is the key.

For example, during Senate hearings into CIA assassination plots against Fidel Castro and other foreign leaders, "plausible denial" was defined by the CIA's deputy director of operations Richard Bissell as the use of circumlocution and euphemism in discussions where precise definitions would expose covert actions and bring them to an end.[8]

The Church Committee report says, "In November 1962 the proposal for a new covert action program to overthrow Castro was developed. The President's Assistant, Richard Goodwin, and General Edward Lansdale, who was experienced in counter-insurgency operations, played major staff roles in creating this program, which was named Operation MONGOOSE." A special group was created to oversee Mongoose, and Lansdale was made its chief of operations. Those operations included "executive actions."[9]

A memo written by Lansdale and introduced during the hearings in part states that the "*Attack* on the cadre of the regime including key leaders . . . should be a 'Special Target' operation. CIA defector operations are vital here. Gangster elements might prove the best recruitment potential for *actions* against police G-2 officials." When questioned about his language, Lansdale testified that the words "actions" and "attack" actually meant killing. He also testified that "criminal elements" were contracted for use in the attack against Castro. He euphemistically called these gangsters the Caribbean Survey Group.[10]

Further to ensure plausible denial, the CIA conducts covert action under cover of proprietary companies like Air America and the Freedom Company, through veterans and business organizations, and various other fronts. As in the case of fake newspaper articles and official communiqués, the idea is to use disinformation to suggest initiatives fostering positive values—freedom, patriotism, brotherhood, democracy—while doing dirty deeds behind the scenes. In CIA jargon this is called black propaganda and is the job of political and psychological (PP) officers in the covert action branch. PP officers played a major role in packaging Phoenix for sale to the American public as a program designed "to protect the people from terrorism."[11]

Language, in its narrowest political-warfare application, is used to create defectors. Not only were defectors valued for their ability to sap the enemy's will to fight, but having worked on the inside, defectors were also the most accurate and timely source of intelligence on Vietcong and NVA unit strength and location. For that reason they made the best guides and trackers. After defecting, many returned immediately to their area of operations with a reaction force to locate hidden enemy arms or food caches. Others, upon turning themselves in, were screened and interrogated by security officers. Once turned, these defectors became penetration leads back into the VCI. Defectors who returned to their former positions inside enemy military units or political organizations were provided with a "secure" means of contacting their VBI case officer, whom they fed information leading to the arrest or ambush of enemy cadres, soldiers, and secret agents.

VBI case officers monitoring the defector program for potential recruits also conducted CIA-advised political reeducation programs for Communists and common criminals alike. Recycled wrongdoers were transformed by CIA advisers into counterterrorists and political action cadres who then co-opted former comrades, prepared leaflets, and conducted interrogations. Where hardened criminals were unavailable, counterterror elements were extracted from political action teams and hidden in sealed compounds inside Special Forces camps and CIA safe houses.

So it was that political and psychological warfare experts moved to the forefront of the counterinsurgency in the early 1960's, fighting, under cover of Civic Action, a plausibly deniable war against enemy agents and soldiers, using black propaganda, defectors, criminals (the entire Fifty-second Ranger Battalion was recruited from Saigon prisons), selective terror, forcible relocations, and racial hatred to achieve its goal of internal security.

The importance of information management in political warfare also meant a larger role in Vietnam for the U.S. Information Service (USIS). Ostensibly the overseas branch of the U.S. Information Agency—performing the same propaganda and censorship functions outside America as the USIA performs within—the USIS has as its raison d'être promotion of the "American way" in its narrowest big business sense. In its crusade to convert the world into one big Chamber of Commerce, the USIS employs all manner of media, from TVs, radios, and satellites to armed propaganda teams, wanted posters, and counterterror.

The USIS officer most deeply involved in Phoenix was Frank Scotton. A graduate of American University's College of International Relations, Scotton received a U.S. government graduate assistantship to the East-West Center at the University of Hawaii. About the CIA-sponsored East-West Center, Scotton said in an interview with the author, "It was a cover for a training program in which Southeast Asians were brought to Hawaii and trained to go back to Vietnam, Cambodia, and Laos to create agent nets." After passing the Foreign Service exam, Scotton was persuaded by a patron to join the USIS, which "dealt with people," unlike the State Department, which "observed from a distance."[12]

A fabulously charismatic personality, tall and swarthy, Scotton had recently returned from a trip to Thailand—which included taking his teenage son on a patrol into Cambodia, where they were shot at by Khmer Rouge guerrillas—when William Colby introduced us in 1986. According to Scotton, when he arrived in Saigon in November 1962, he was met by and fell under the influence of Everett Bumgartner, chief of USIS field operations in Vietnam. A Lansdale disciple, Bumgartner had launched wanted poster and defector programs in Laos in 1954 and implemented similar programs in Vietnam after he arrived there in 1959.

Bumgartner introduced Scotton to John Paul Vann, the senior adviser to the ARVN Seventh Division and a friend of Colonel Tran Ngoc Chau's, the controversial Kien Hoa Province chief. A graduate of Fort Bragg, where he roomed with Nguyen Van Thieu, Chau was a CIA asset who in 1962 had just finished a six-year tour as chief of the GVN's Psychological Warfare Service. Over the next ten years Chau's relationship with Scotton, Bumgartner and Vann came to symbolize Phoenix and the duplicitous nature of U.S.-Vietnamese relations.

Scotton, Bumgartner, and Vann are described by Ngo Vinh Long in *The CIA and the Vietnam Debacle:*

> Frank Scotton was the originator of the Provincial Reconnaissance Units program, the predecessor of the Phoenix program. For years he worked closely with John Paul Vann, the famous CIA operative who specialized, among other things, in black propaganda, which involved him in murder, forgery and the outright deception of the American press in order to discredit the NLF in particular and the opposition to American intervention in general. Everett Bumgartner was Colby's deputy and used to oversee pacification efforts in the central provinces of Vietnam. Any person who has the faintest knowledge of the pacification program would know what disasters have visited the Vietnamese people as a result of such programs. Bumgartner was also in charge of the Phoenix program in that area.[13]

When Scotton arrived in Vietnam, Bumgartner assigned him to the Central Highlands, the expansive area between Saigon and Qui Nhon City, the capital of Binh Dinh Province. Bumgartner thought there was "a vacuum of knowledge" in the highlands and directed Scotton "to energize the Vietnamese" in what Scotton calls "prerevolutionary development." As Scotton likes to say, "pacification wasn't even a term then."[14]

The emphasis at the time was on the strategic hamlet program—separating the guerrilla fish from the sea of people through forced relocations. Begun in March 1962 with Operations Sea Swallow in Ca Mau Province and Royal Phoenix in Binh Dinh Province, more than four million Vietnamese had been relocated into strategic hamlets in most of South Vietnam's forty-four provinces by the time Scotton arrived in-country. The program was administered by CIA-advised province security officers reporting to Ngo Dinh Nhu's confidential agent in Saigon, the notorious double agent Pham Ngoc Thao. However, because VC guerrillas had at least the tacit support of the rural population, police and security officials had difficulty conducting law enforcement and intelligence operations outside strategic hamlets or other secure, generally urban areas. In following Bumgartner's orders to fill the vacuum of knowledge in Central Vietnam, Scotton told me, "We would take a Vietnamese employee of the Vietnam Information Service (VIS) and put him in the provincial information system and have him provide resources—leaflets, school kits, films—that sort of thing. In return we expected reporting."

Having placed his agent net, Scotton turned his attention to the job of "energizing" the Vietnamese. However, as a result of CIA machinations against his regime, Diem had instructed his provincial appointees to resist American influence and to blunt U.S. efforts to escalate the war against the Communists. Indeed, Diem's brother Nhu was secretly negotiating with the North Vietnamese in hopes of reaching a settlement *before* the United States found a pretext to call in the Marines, as the Pentagon seemed intent on doing.

In looking for motivated individuals to mold into political cadres, Scotton turned to the CIA's defector program, which in April 1963 was placed under cover of the Agency for International Development and named the Chieu Hoi (Open Arms) amnesty program. There Scotton found the raw material he needed to prove the viability of political action programs. Together with Vietnamese Special Forces Captain Nguyen Tuy (a graduate of Fort Bragg's Special Warfare Center who commanded the Fourth Special Operations Detachment) and Tuy's case officer, U.S. Special Forces Captain Howard Walters (a Korean War veteran and psywar expert), Scotton worked through an extension of the Mountain Scout program Ralph Johnson had established in Pleiku Province.

As part of a pilot program designed to induce defectors, Scotton, Walters, and Tuy crossed the An Lao Valley, set up an ambush deep in Vietcong territory, and waited till dark. When they spotted a VC unit, Scotton yelled through a bullhorn, "You are being misled! You are being lied to! We promise you an education!" Then, full of purpose and allegory, he shot a flare into the night sky and hollered, "Walk toward the light!" To his surprise, two defectors did walk in, convincing him and his CIA sponsors that "a determined GVN unit could contest the VC in terms of combat and propaganda."

Back in camp, according to Scotton, "We told the VC defectors that they had to divest themselves of untruths. We said that certainly the U.S. perpetrated war crimes, but so did the VC. We acknowledged that theirs was the stronger force, but that didn't mean that everything they did was honorable and good and just." In this manner, Scotton indoctrinated cadres for his political action teams.[15]

But these were tumultuous times in South Vietnam, as wild as the 1955 battle for Saigon. In early 1963, two hundred lightly armed VC guerrillas routed an ARVN force of twenty-five hundred, advised by John Vann and supported by U.S. bombers and helicopters at Ap Bac, a mere forty miles from Saigon. The incident reaffirmed what everyone already suspected: that the top-heavy, bloated, corrupt ARVN was no match for the underequipped, starving, but determined Vietcong.

Next, Diem's brother Thuc, the archbishop of Hue, forbade the display of Buddhist flags at a ceremony in Hue commemorating the 2587th birthday of Buddha. A demonstration led by Buddhist priest Thich Tri Quang erupted on May 8, and Nhu sent the LLDB in to put it down. In doing so, they killed nine people, mostly women and children. Official communiqués blamed VC "terrorists," but the Buddhists knew better; they strengthened their alliance with the NLF and began organizing massive demonstrations. On June 11, 1963, a Buddhist monk doused himself with gasoline and set himself on fire in Saigon. Soon others were doing likewise across Vietnam. "Let them burn," Madame Nhu, the Dragon Lady, cooed, "and we shall clap our hands."[16]

Two months later, while Nhu negotiated with the North Vietnamese and the Joint General Staff pressured Diem to declare martial law, a South Vietnamese Special Forces unit disguised as ARVN troops attacked Saigon's Xa Loi Temple, the city's most sacred Buddhist shrine. Buddhists immediately took up arms and began fighting the LLDB in Hue. The spectacle was repeated across Vietnam, as thousands of Buddhists were arrested, jailed, and summarily executed. In response, on August 21, 1963, the Special Group in Washington ordered the CIA to pull the financial plug on the Vietnamese Special Forces. The search for a more dependable, unilaterally controlled army began, and the nascent counterterror teams emerged as the most promising candidates.

Meanwhile, in Saigon Diem's downfall was originating within his own palace guard. CIA asset Tran Van Don conspired with secret police chief Dr. Tran Kim Tuyen, NVA double agent Pham Ngoc Thao, and, among others, General Duong Van Minh (known as Big Minh), who had the backing of the Dai Viets in the ARVN. Colonel Nguyen Van Thieu and Tran Thien Khiem joined the plot. In October President Kennedy suspended economic aid, and the pope ordered Thuc to leave his post in Hue, a decision "that eased the conscience of the Catholic plotters."[17]

As plotters swirled around them, Nhu and Diem instructed the Vietnamese Special Forces chief Colonel Le Quang Tung to prepare a countercoup. But Tung was summoned to the senior officers' club at Joint General Staff headquarters and shot dead by Big Minh's personal bodyguard. That prompted III Corps Commander General Ton That Dinh to withdraw the Special Forces under his command from Saigon. The CIA-controlled palace guard vacated the premises, and the military began arresting Diem loyalists. Knowing the end was near, Nhu and Diem fled to a friend's house in Cholon, then sought sanctuary in a nearby church. Soon a military convoy arrived, arrested them, and took them for a ride. When the convoy reached Hong Thap Tu Alley, between Cao Thang and Le Van Duyet streets, the brothers were shot dead. "The military men in the vehicle, who hated Nhu, stabbed his corpse many times."[18]

America endured a similar bloodletting three weeks later, when President John Kennedy was caught in a crossfire of gunfire in Dallas, Texas. The assassination, curiously, came shortly after Kennedy had proposed withdrawing U.S. advisers from Vietnam. Three days after JFK's death, President Lyndon Johnson signed National Security Action Memorandum 273, authorizing planning for covert military operations against North Vietnam. Conceived in secrecy, the ensuing policy of "provoked response" paved the way for full-scale U.S. military intervention for which the CIA was laying the groundwork through its three-part covert action program in South Vietnam's provinces.

On December 19, 1963, the Pentagon's planning branch in the Pacific, CINCPAC (Commander in Chief, Pacific), presented its plans to the Special Group. Two weeks later LBJ approved OPLAN 34A, and Marine General Victor Krulak, SACSA, handed operational control to MACV. The Special Operations Group (SOG) was formed in Saigon to implement OPLAN 34A, and attacks against North Vietnam began in February from Phoenix Island off the coast of Da Nang.

On July 31, 1964, SOG achieved its goal of creating a provoked response. That night SEALs Elton Manzione and Kenny Van Lesser led twenty South Vietnamese marines in a raid against Hon Me Island. Dropped at the wrong end of the island, Manzione and Van Lesser failed to knock out their target—an NVA radar installation—but the raid did push the North Vietnamese into attacking the USS *Maddox*, which was monitoring NVA electronic defenses activated by the attack. The incident was sold to the American public as a North Vietnamese "first strike" and resulted in Congress's passing the Gulf of Tonkin Resolution. The resulting air strikes against North Vietnam are cited by many historians as the start of the Vietnam War. Tonkin Gulf also allowed LBJ to sell himself as tougher than Republican candidate Barry Goldwater and to win the 1964 presidential election.

In Saigon, South Vietnamese armed forces Commander Duong Van Minh, who was supported by the important generals, the Dai Viets, and the CIA, surfaced as the new chief of state. Big Minh appointed General Khiem III Corps commander, and, in league with Nguyen Van Thieu, had General Ton That Dinh, the Vietnamese Military Security Service chief Mai Huu Xuan, CIO chief Nguyen Van Y, and Tran Van Don arrested. Generals Thieu and Khiem then used the unpopular arrests to undercut Big Minh, their main adversary, whom they replaced with General Duong Van Khanh. General Khanh, in the spirit of the times, called for an invasion of North

Vietnam. But the plan was subverted three days later, when Air Marshal Nguyen Cao Ky—fired from Operation Haylift for smuggling opium on his "black" flights—revealed that the CIA had been sending teams into North Vietnam since July 1963. Diem's spy chief, Dr. Tuyen, was sent into honorable exile as ambassador to Egypt. NVA double agent Pham Ngoc Thao temporarily escaped detection and was appointed Ben Tre province chief; he served until 1965, when he was killed by Thieu, who suspected Thao of working against him on behalf of Ky. Thieu, Khiem, and Ky emerged as the big three power brokers and invited Dai Viet leaders Nguyen Ton Hoan and Professor Huy to return from ten years' exile in France to join a new but very loose coalition government.[19]

In the wake of the coup, according to Frank Scotton, "administrative paralysis set in. The VC exploited that and physically dismantled the strategic hamlets as despised symbols of the GVN." And as the grateful inmates returned to their villages, the country erupted in open revolt. Even the road leading from Saigon to John Vann's headquarters in My Tho was unsafe, so in December 1963 Ev Bumgartner sent Scotton to Long An Province, a few miles south of Saigon. Scotton brought along his political cadre from Quang Ngai Province, Civic Action recruits were provided by the Long An province chief, and Scotton set about "seeing what was wrong and getting a fix on the hamlets." He did this by using "small armed teams seeking information."[20]

Working with the American province adviser, Scotton organized three survey teams, which operated in three neighboring hamlets simultaneously. Each six-member team was equipped with black pajamas, pistols, a radio, and a submachine gun. Standard procedure was to regroup at the last moment before daybreak, then shift at dawn to a fourth hamlet, where the team would sleep during the day. At night they sat beside trails used by the VC cadres they had identified during visits to the hamlets. When Vietcong armed propaganda teams under their surveillance departed from a hamlet, Scotton's cadre would move in and speak to one person from each household, so the VC "would have to punish everyone after we left. But that never happened. A woman VC leader would bring in a unit after us," Scotton added, "but there were never any recriminations.

"The mission of these survey teams," according to Scotton, "was intelligence, not an attack on the VCI. But Long An proved the viability of small units. I felt confident that motivated small units could go in and displace the VC simply by their presence. Will and intent had to be primary, though; if they were, then the method generated useful reports."

With Diem dead, three quarters of South Vietnam's province chiefs fired from their jobs, and no more prohibitions on taking CIA money, the time was ripe for "local initiatives." Local officials, along with legions of Diem loyalists purged from government after the coup, were hired by the CIA and put in management positions in its covert action programs in the provinces and districts. But it was an American war now, with GVN stature at an all-time low, making it harder than ever to wage political war. And of course the situation was exploited by the North Vietnamese, who started infiltrating regular NVA troops, not just regroupees, into South Vietnam.

Other changes were also forthcoming as a result of the coup. With Operation Switchback and the transfer of the CIDG program to MACV, Ralph Johnson launched a new covert action program in Dam Pao outside Pleiku. Called Truong Son, it organized Montagnards into small units having civic action, counterterror, and intelligence functions. Meanwhile, Stu Methven was assigned to the Delta to stimulate "local initiatives" among the new generation of province chiefs.

Methven's plan was to create a three-part program with separate teams for civic action, counterterror, and intelligence. However, because the fighting was less intense in the Delta than in central Vietnam, Methven advocated easily monitored teams no larger than six men each—the type Scotton was toying with in Long An. Methven also incorporated ideas developed in Kien Hoa Province by Tran Ngoc Chau, whose innovative census grievance teams were proving quite successful. Using Chau's and Scotton's programs as his models, Methven sold "local initiatives" to province chiefs across South Vietnam.

Behind every province chief, of course, was a CIA paramilitary officer promoting and organizing the CIA's three-part covert action program. Walter Mackem, who arrived in Vietnam in early 1964, was one of the first. After spending two months observing the CIDG program in Ban Me Thuot, Mackem was transferred to the Delta to institute similar programs in An Giang, Chau Doc, Sa Dec, and Vinh Long provinces. Mackem also reported directly to Washington on the political activities of the various sects and favorable ethnic minorities in his area of operations, the most important of which were the Hoa Hao (Theraveda Buddhists) and the closely related ethnic Cambodians, the Khmer.

According to Mackem, there were no counterterror teams prior to his arrival on the scene. What did exist were private armies like the Sea Swallows, and those belonging to the sects. It was from these groups, as well as from province jails and defector programs, that Mackem got recruits for his CT teams. The composition of the teams differed from province to province depending "on what form opposition to the GVN took, and on the motives of the province chief"—as Mackem puts it, "if he wanted the CT program tidy or not." The biggest contributors to Mackem's CT teams were the Khmer, who "didn't get along with the Vietnamese," while the armed propaganda team served as "a Hoa Hao job corps."[21]

Mackem personally selected and trained his CT and political action cadres. He dressed in black pajamas and accompanied them on missions deep into enemy territory to snatch and snuff VCI cadres. "I wandered around the jungle with them," Mackem admitted. "I did it myself. We were freewheeling back then. It was a combination of *The Man Who Would Be King* and *Apocalypse Now*!"

To obtain information on individual VCI in GVN villages, according to Mackem, the CTs relied on advisers to the VBI, "the liaison types who set up an Embassy House." Information on VCI members in their own villages, or those in dispute, was provided by undercover agents in the villages, who, because of their vulnerability, "had a more benevolent approach [toward the VCI] than the police."

Such was the situation following the coup. The Vietcong controlled most of the countryside, and the Vietnamese Bureau of Investigations had little role to play outside Saigon and the major cities. In the countryside counterterror and armed propaganda teams, aided by secret agents in the villages, gathered intelligence on and attacked the Vietcong infrastructure. Meanwhile, U.S. airplanes, artillery, and combat units arrived and began driving the rural population into refugee camps or underground. However, the division of labor within the CIA station, which pitted police advisers against paramilitary advisers, had to be resolved before an effective attack on the VCI could be mounted, and first, the CIA would have to incorporate its covert action programs within a cohesive strategy for political warfare. Such is the subject of the next chapter.

CHAPTER 4

Revolutionary Development

In February 1964 Frank Scotton returned to Qui Nhon to work on what Ogden Williams, the senior American adviser in neighboring Quang Ngai Province, called "a Phoenix-type thing." In developing this Phoenix-type program, Scotton teamed up with Ian Tiege, an Australian paramilitary adviser on contract to the CIA, and Major Robert Kelly, the MACV district adviser. "Kelly was the American on the spot," Scotton recalled. "I advised on training and deployment."[1] Tiege was the professional soldier, deciding how to fight the enemy.

Formal relations between MACV and CIA officers at the district level had begun only one month earlier, when General William Westmoreland arrived in Saigon as MACV commander and, in an effort to strengthen the American hand, assigned MACV advisers to each of South Vietnam's 250 districts. Military intelligence advisers assigned to the Fifth Special Forces also entered the districts at this point. However, coordination among MACV advisers, CIA officers, and their Vietnamese counterparts depended primarily on personal relationships and varied from place to place.

Notably, the impetus for Scotton's Phoenix-type program on the Vietnamese side came from the Tu Nghia District police chief, Colonel Pham Tuong. A long-standing CIA asset, Tuong anted up a platoon of volunteers, all of whom had been victimized by the VC, in exchange for equipment, money, and advice. "They wanted to fight," Scotton said, "but they didn't want to lose." Money and supplies were provided by Ralph Johnson. A fifteen-day "accelerated" training cycle was set up using what Scotton called his motivational indoctrination program. Modeled on Communist techniques, the process began on "a confessional basis. On the first day," according to Scotton, "everyone would fill out a form and write an essay on why they had joined." The district's Vietnam Information Service representative "would study their answers and explain the next day why they were involved in a *special* unit. The instructors would lead them to stand up and talk about themselves." This motivational function was handled by the unit's morale officer, chosen by his peers through what Scotton referred to "as the only honest elections held in South Vietnam." The morale officer's job, he said, "was to keep people honest and have them admit mistakes."

Not only did Scotton co-opt Communist organizational and motivational techniques, but he also relied on Communist defectors as his cadre. "We felt ex-Vietminh had unique communication skills. They could communicate doctrine, and they were people who would shoot," he explained, adding, "It wasn't necessary for everyone in the unit to be ex-Vietminh, just the leadership."

In copying the Communists, Scotton was selective. "People from the other side knew the value of motivation, but they confessed too much. So we refined the technique based on what the Vietminh disliked the most: that the party set itself up as the sole authority. We didn't have the party as number one. We had the group as the major motivational factor."

Key to Scotton's motivational indoctrinational program was the notion of a "special" unit. To enhance this esprit de corps, Scotton's units were better equipped and better paid than regular ARVN units. Carbines were replaced with submachine guns, and instead of wearing uniforms, the cadres wore black pajamas—just like the average Vietnamese. Scotton's teams were also special insofar as they reported directly to the province security chief and, ipso facto, the CIA.

"Tuong's original group was thirty-four," Scotton said, noting that Quang Ngai was a more heavily contested province than Long An and that the teams required more men and greater firepower, "so we bumped it up to forty and started a second group in an adjacent district. That's three teams of twelve men each, strictly armed. The control element was four men: a commander and his deputy, a morale officer, and a radioman. These are commando teams," Scotton stressed, "displacement teams. The idea was to go into contested areas and spend a few nights. But it was a local responsibility so they had to do it on their own."

Scotton named his special unit the *Trung-doi biet kich Nham dou* (people's commando teams). "Two functions split out of this," Scotton said. "First was pacification under Nguyen Be. Second was the anti-VCI function taken out to form the Provincial Reconnaissance Units. The PRU thing directly evolves from this." Indeed, the phrase "Biet Kich," meaning "commando," is the name the Vietnamese applied to counterterrorists and later the PRU.

Concurrent with the creation of the people's action teams (PATs), as Scotton's teams were renamed by station chief Peer DeSilva, there began a synthesis of White House policies and police and paramilitary programs that culminated three years later in Phoenix. It was, in effect, a blueprint for political warfare, conceptualized by Ralph Johnson, adapted to Vietnamese sensibilities by Le Xuan Mai, and formalized by Frank Scotton, Bob Kelly, Ian Tiege, and Stu Methven. At its heart was the doctrine of Contre Coup, particularly the notion of counterterror, which more than any other factor seized the imagination of station chief DeSilva, under whose direction the synthesis began.

In his autobiography, *Sub Rosa,* DeSilva describes arriving in Vietnam in December 1963 and being introduced to VC terror by one of his CIA officers. Two VC cadres had impaled a young boy, a village chief, and his pregnant wife on sharp poles. "To make sure this horrible sight would remain with the villagers, one of the terror squad used his machete to disembowel the woman, spilling the fetus onto the ground." Having arrived on the scene moments after the atrocity had occurred, DeSilva writes, "I saw them, the three impaled bodies and the unborn child lying in the dirt. A Catholic member of the village was making the sign of the cross over each body, murmuring a prayer in Vietnamese."[2]

A white-collar intelligence officer who put agent work above political warfare, DeSilva was shocked by what he saw. "The Vietcong," he writes, "were monstrous in their application of torture and murder to achieve the *political and psychological* [author's emphasis] impact they wanted." But DeSilva also recognized that "This implacable use of terror in its own way served an intelligence purpose," that "A bloody act of terror in a populated area would immobilize the population nearby, make the local inhabitants responsive to the Vietcong and, in return, unresponsive to the government element requests for cooperation."[3]

So DeSilva authorized the extraction of counterterror teams from Scotton's Political Action Teams. He describes this "radically different form of activity" as "a counterterror program consisting of small teams," dressed in black pajamas, armed with folding stock carbines which could be hidden under their black tunics, and with grenades carried in the pockets of their loose-fitting shorts.[4]

The idea, DeSilva continues, was "to bring danger and death to the Vietcong functionaries themselves, especially in the areas where they felt secure. We had obtained descriptions and photographs of known cadres who were functioning as committee chiefs, recruiters, province representatives and heads of raiding parties. Based on these photographs and their known areas of operation, we had recruited really tough groups of individuals, organized in teams of three or four, who were willing and able by virtue of prior residence to go into the areas in which we knew the Vietcong senior cadres were active and to see what could be done to eliminate them."[5]

Here DeSilva is describing Phoenix, the attack on the VCI on its own turf, using intelligence provided by commandos and selective terror conducted by counterterrorists. One of the soldiers who participated in DeSilva's counterterror program was Elton Manzione. A self-described "supersoldier," Manzione received extensive training in hand-to-hand combat, combat swimming, sniping, parachuting, and demolition. When his schooling was completed, Manzione was dropped in the jungles of Panama with a knife and a compass and told to find his way out, and he did. "By then," he noted with no small degree of understatement, "I was fairly competent."

In December 1964 Manzione left California aboard an oil tanker and, ten days later, crossed over to a guided missile destroyer, the USS *Lawrence,* in the middle of the Pacific Ocean. To ensure plausible denial, Manzione's service records were "sheep-dipped" and indicate that he never got off the *Lawrence*.

Manzione stepped ashore in Cam Ranh Bay in January 1964 and was met by a Special Forces colonel who briefed him on his mission. Manzione was told he would be working for the Special Operations Group under a number of directives called OPLANS which had been drawn up to accomplish specific goals. Insofar as SOG had absorbed the Combined Studies Group, he would be working for U.S. Army and civilian personnel, as well as the U.S. Navy. He was sent to the Hoa Cam Training Center near Da Nang, where in 1961 Ralph Johnson had based the Mountain Scout training camp and where in 1964 the CIA trained its special operations personnel in long-range reconnaissance patrols.

At Hoa Cam Manzione completed an intensive orientation course. He was taught advanced tracking and camouflage techniques, made familiar with Soviet and Chinese weapons, put on a steady diet of Oriental food, told not to bathe and not to shave. And he was briefed on the various OPLAN directives and goals. "The actual goals were to stop the infiltration from the North of arms and supplies," he recalled. "How did they phrase it? 'Undermining the enemy's ability to fight in the South.' Another goal was to deal with enemy violations of the international accords—I'm assuming the 1962 Geneva Accords. It meant taking out command centers in Laos. And there was anti-infrastructure stuff, too."

Manzione was next assigned to Nam Dong in the Central Highlands, where he and two other SEALs were quartered inside a U.S. Special Forces camp. "Basically what they said was, 'Welcome to Nam Dong. This is the town you'll work out of. You're gonna get orders to do something, and the orders are going to be verbal.' The orders were always verbal and never said, 'Do this specifically.' It was always 'Go there and do what you think you ought to do.' It was so free-form it was hard to connect being in the military, let alone the Navy."

In March the SEALs started running "over-the-fence" missions as part of SOG's Leaping Lena program. Three quarters of the missions were in Laos, the demilitarized zone, and North Vietnam. At times the SEALs sat along the Ho Chi Minh Trail counting enemy troops and trucks. Other times they moved from one set of coordinates to another, reconnoitering. They also shot field-grade NVA officers, kidnapped prisoners, escorted defectors from the North to the South, demolished downed U.S. aircraft, and engaged in counterterror.

In regard to this last function, the SEALs worked with CTs, whom Manzione described as "a combination of ARVN deserters, VC turncoats, and bad motherfucker criminals the South Vietnamese couldn't deal with in prison, so they turned them over to us. Often they'd been pardoned to fight Communists. Some actually had an incentive plan: If they killed X number of Commies, they got X number of years off their prison terms." The CTs taught Manzione and his SEAL comrades the secrets of the psywar campaign, which in practice meant exploiting the superstitions, myths, and religious beliefs of the Vietnamese. One technique was based on the Buddhist belief that a person cannot enter heaven unless his liver is intact. So Manzione would snatch an NVA courier off the Ho Chi Minh Trail or sneak into a VCI's hooch at night, crush the man's larynx, then use his dagger to remove the man's liver. Some of the CTs would actually devour their enemies' vital organs.

In the summer of 1964 Manzione was assigned to SOG's northern headquarters in Dong Ha. "Back then," he said, "being as close to the DMZ as we were, it was hard to tell where any particular Vietnamese civilian came from." Here he referred to the fact that the demilitarized zone separated families and communities without regard for their political affiliations. In light of this ambiguity, counterterror was one way of co-opting uncommitted civilians. To facilitate their political awakening, according to Manzione, "We left our calling card nailed to the forehead of the corpses we left behind. They were playing card size with a light green skull with red eyes and red teeth dripping blood, set against a black background. We hammered them into the third eye, the pituitary gland, with our pistol butts. The third eye is the seat of consciousness for Buddhists, and this was a form of mutilation that had a powerful psychological effect."

Curiously, terror tactics often involve mutilating the third eye (the seat of insight and secret thoughts) and playing on fears of an "all-seeing" cosmic eye of God. Used by morale officers in World War I, the eye of God trick called for pilots in small aircraft to fly over enemy camps and call out the names of individual soldiers. Ed Lansdale applied the technique in the Philippines. "At night, when the town was asleep, a psywar team would creep into town and paint an eye (copied from the Egyptian eye that appears atop the pyramid in the Great Seal of the United States) on a wall facing the house of each suspect," Lansdale writes. "The mysterious presence of these malevolent eyes the next morning had a sharply sobering effect."[6]

To appreciate the "sobering effects" of the "malevolent" and "mysterious" eye of God, it helps to know something of the archetype's mythological origins. In ancient Egypt, the eye of God was plucked from Horus, an anthropomorphic sun-god with a falcon's head. Pictured as the morning sun cresting a pyramid, the eye of God represents the dawn of self-awareness, when the ego emerged from the id and no longer required human sacrifice to overcome its primeval anxiety. Awed by the falcon's superlative sight, talons, and flight, the Egyptians endowed Horus with the bird's predatory prowess, so he could avenge the murder his father, Osiris, whose name means "seat of the eye." Set on high, scanning the earth for the forces of darkness, the falcon as sun-god—as the manifestation of enlightenment—carries out the work of organization and pacification, imposing moral order on earth.

The eye of God assumes its mysterious "counterespionage" qualities through this myth of the eternal cycle—the battle between good and evil—in which, if the perfidious gods of darkness can guess the sun-god's secret name, they can rob him of his powers and trap him forever in the underworld. Thus a falcon emblem was placed above the gates of all Egyptian temples, scanning for the sun-god's enemies, while the sun-god relied on code names to conceal his identity.

Oddly enough, the eye of God was the symbol of the Cao Dai sect, whose gallery of saints include Confucius, Buddha, Joan of Arc, Jesus, and Victor Hugo. Inside the Cao Dai cathedral in Tay Ninh City, the Cao Dai pope divined upon his planchette the secrets of the Great Pyramid; over the temple door loomed a huge blue "all-seeing" eye surrounded by snakes and trees. For this reason, some people suggest that the Cao Dai eye of God endowed Phoenix, the all-seeing bird of prey that selectively snatched its prey, with its ubiquity.

In South Vietnam the eye of God trick took a ghastly twist. CIA officer Pat McGarvey recalled to Seymour Hersh that "some psychological warfare guy in Washington thought of a way to scare the hell out of villagers. When we killed a VC there, they wanted us to spread eagle the guy, put out his eye, cut a hole in the back [of his head] and put his eye in there. The idea was that fear was a good weapon."[7] Likewise, ears were cut off corpses and nailed to houses to let the people know that Big Brother was listening as well.

nailed to houses to let the people know that Big Brother was listening as well.

The subliminal purpose of terror tactics was to drive people into a state of infantile dependence. In this sense, CIA psywar experts were not exorcists come to heal Vietnam and free it from Communist demons; their spells were meant to break up the society and project its repressed homicidal impulses onto the Communists—cast as carrion and snakes.

"It was all part of the counterterror doctrine developed by the Ugly American to beat the enemy at his own game," Elton Manzione said. In beating the VC at their own game, the SEALs were told to ignore the rules of engagement. "Our camp was always separate," he explained. "Just CTs and us. Sometimes a Special Forces colonel would walk in, but rarely. Nam Dong was not populated by the spooky hunter-killer type folks you associate with the Green Berets. A lot of them were medical specialists, or agricultural specialists, or language specialists that worked with the villagers on different things. So the great majority of this particular Special Forces camp were not hit team types. We were, however, and our camp was separated by wire and a gate.

"Now everyone knows about the airborne interrogation—taking three people up in a chopper, taking one guy and saying, 'Talk,' then throwing him out before he even gets the chance to open his mouth. Well, we wrapped det [detonator] cord around their necks and wired them to the detonator box. And basically what it did was blow their heads off. The interrogator would tell the translator, usually a South Vietnamese intelligence officer, 'Ask him this.' He'd ask him, 'Who gave you the gun?' And the guy would start to answer, or maybe he wouldn't—maybe he'd resist—but the general idea was to waste the first two. They planned the snatches that way. Pick up this guy because we're pretty sure he's VC cadre—these other two guys just run errands for him. Or maybe they're nobody; Tran, the farmer, and his brother Nguyen. *But bring in two*. Put them in a row. By the time you get to your man, he's talking so fast you got to pop the weasel just to shut him up." After a moment's silence he added, "I guess you could say that we wrote the book on terror."

Having seen the intelligence potential in Scotton's PATs and CTs, DeSilva, according to Stu Methven, "decided he wanted a version in each province in South Vietnam." The job of standardizing the political action teams, along with the counterterrorists and Chau's Census Grievance program, was given to Methven, whose first step was to find them a permanent home on the Vung Tau Peninsula. Methven did this with the help of Tran Quoc Buu, a wealthy Vietnamese warlord and founding member of the Can Lao party who in 1954 had headed the CIA-funded Vietnamese Federation of Labor. Buu had been charged by Diem with laundering Can Lao rake-offs through the federation's foreign accounts. Buu, however, pocketed the money and used it to buy huge parcels of land, including a portion of Vung Tau.

After the coup the tables turned on Buu, whose association with Diem led to his imprisonment; in need of cash to buy his way out of jail, he sold Methven a choice piece of property on the Vung Tau Peninsula. Located at Cat Lo, Buu's estate had been used by the French as a transshipment point in their lucrative opium trade and as a training camp for their Montagnard maquis. Buu himself had used Cat Lo as a training camp for his private army of resettled Catholic refugees. Called the Shrimp and Cinnamon Soldiers, for their civilian jobs, Buu's troops were highly motivated and, according to Methven, were admired by Nguyen Van Thieu because "unlike the ARVN, they stayed at their posts at night." With Thieu's consent, Methven arranged for CIA contract employees to start training counterterror, census grievance, and political action cadres at Buu's Vung Tau facility. This was a unilateral CIA operation, extralegal, with no GVN oversight. Isolated and accessible only by Air America, Vung Tau was the perfect place for such a covert action undertaking.

Vung Tau became the seedbed of the CIA's political cadres, who were trained to enter VC villages, to convince the people that the GVN represented their interests and, having done that, to help the villagers form self-defense forces to fight the VC. However, the generals who dominated the GVN viewed the image of an armed citizenry with alarm and were reluctant to support the program. Even MACV commander Westmoreland argued that anyone with a gun should be in the army. Thus, before the GVN could join the synthesis, it first had to put its house in order—which, in the summer of 1964, was a remote possibility at best.

To begin with, the Montagnards had mutinied against their Special Forces officers in Ban Me Thuot and four other districts, temporarily diverting the CIA's attention. Meanwhile, the Dai Viets had assumed control of the government, created a Directorate of Political Warfare, and established their own pacification program managed by Professor Nguyen Van Huy. Called Rural Construction and centered in Thu Duc, the program used mobile cadre teams to organize villagers into pro-GVN associations. But the Dai Viets were split internally over the issue of allowing VNQDD cadres into the program, and when other, more powerful Dai Viets launched an unsuccessful coup against General Khanh in April, Huy and his associates were exiled once again.

With the CIDG program and the GVN in shambles, the CIA looked to its nascent Vung Tau program for stability. The CIA officer chosen to build the facility and create a national pacification program that could maintain operations independently of the GVN by fostering local initiatives was a garrulous, blustering Irish-American named Tom Donohue. A product and practitioner of Cook County politics, Donohue resembled W. C. Fields in looks and mannerisms and, you get the feeling, in ethics, too; to wit, he joined the CIA when he perceived the cold war as "a growth industry." When he spoke, his words came in melodramatic exclamations. As he pondered, he paced nervously, like a pool hustler circling the table, picking his next shot. In all these respects, Donohue was the prototypical CIA officer—a cagey position player using a glib exterior to mask a calculating mind.

When we met in 1986, Tom Donohue was working as the Mideast representative for a Filipino construction company. When he arrived in Saigon twenty-two years earlier to replace Cliff Strathern as chief of covert action, he worked under State Department cover in the embassy's political office. One of his jobs at the time, he said, was managing "a small training camp down in Vung Tau which had about a hundred students run by a very dynamic guy—Le Xuan Mai.

"I spent a lot of time with Mai," Donohue recalled, "and was mighty impressed. Mai was a wizard at appealing to a particular sensory element the Vietnamese seemed to have about the fatherland. He had the ability to interweave Vietnamese myth and modern-day nationalism that seemed somehow to make an impact on the tutored and the untutored alike. He was trilingual," Donohue said with admiration, "but he was controversial. What kind of army officer goes around talking about fairies and dragons?'"[8]

Donohue immediately picked up where Stu Methven had left off, hammering out a deal with the minister of the interior to rent an even larger chunk of the Vung Tau Peninsula. He then got Mai a promotion to major and arranged for "a guy who had been training agency people to come up with three or four others to run the camp. This is an early program called armed propaganda team," what he termed an armed social working element.

"Anyway," Donohue said, "I decided this was the route we should be following, and I began looking for a means of expanding the program. I got rid of most of the other stuff I had responsibility for, and from that point on programming evolved rapidly. We began to build up the program with more and more officers coming in from Washington on permanent change of station."

Donohue leased a Catholic seminary, whose owners had "decided it was time to cut and run," and used Seminary Camp, as it became known, as headquarters for his staff. "It was really just a stopgap," Donohue explained, "but it gave us the ability to have a good permanent base. "Then we started building our training facility—Ridge Camp. It was five miles beyond the airport, so we built roads. We built barracks, mess halls, classrooms, armories, and offices. We built a training camp for five thousand and opened it on the fifteenth of January, 1965."

Having put his management team and facilities in place, Donohue next had to demonstrate that the CIA could develop people's action teams for every province, which meant centralized training and using Scotton's forty-man model from Quang Ngai. Donohue also arranged for the training of CTs and Census Grievance cadre. To manage the CT training program, he imported "a couple of guys from headquarters. They were experts. They taught how to get in, how to abduct prisoners, and how to get the hell out with good sources for interrogation. I brought them out TDY and kept talking them into extending, and they both ended up doing a full tour." Both, Donohue said in 1986, "are still gainfully employed by the CIA."

Donohue's pet program was Census Grievance, "the most sophisticated program in the whole goddamned country—the most effective political tool, if you accept the fact that the government really didn't care what people thought or what their political needs were." Noting that the VC had made the problem worse by cutting the lines of communication, "through the skillful use of terror," Donohue said, "the population had been cut adrift, and Census Grievance was the ersatz system that allowed us to say, 'We accept the fact that there are no normal political lines of influence, so we'll put this on and hope to God we can jump-start this body politic.'"

Donohue explained Census Grievance like this: "Everybody knows the government takes a census, so you'd have a guy make a map of every house in the village—put everything into perspective. Then the edict was issued that once a month every head of household had to talk to the Census Grievance officer. We tried to get somebody from the village who was older—retired teachers, retired civil servants—older people who appeared harmless but were respected." To make it possible for a head of household to speak privately with the Census Grievance officer, "We would put together a little two-by-four shack (patterned on the Catholic confessional) so that there ain't nobody else around.

"Basically the census, scaled down, had three questions: (One) What would you like the GVN to do for you? All of the basic precinct-type needs. 'A bridge across this particular canal would save us a three-mile walk to get our produce to market.' Very legitimate needs. (Two) Is there anybody in the GVN giving you a hard time? Are the police at the checkpoint charging you a toll every time you take your rutabagas to market? (Three) Is there anything you want to tell me about the Vietcong? If the answer was no, the whole thing wasn't pursued, but once a month the head of household had to touch base. If the Census Grievance officer finds that X number of people say they need a bridge, you begin to get a consensus. Okay, money is allocated. If it went to the wrong things, you might as well keep it back here. So the point we would make with the province and district chiefs was 'This is a political need. If you are responsive to it, people will look at you in a different light.' "

"Census Grievance produced a good bit of intelligence," Donohue concluded. "So did the cadre program. But there were areas that were so tough and so inaccessible that there was just no intelligence coming out. Some of the Chieu Hois would bring it in, but we never really had what we thought was a good enough handle on *continuing intelligence*, which is a terrible blind spot if you're trying to win a war that's got all the built in problems that Vietnam had."

The next problem Donohue faced was "how to imprint a political system on a foreign country." That was no easy task, even for an irrepressible huckster like Tom Donohue. Donohue described the typical province chief as "a military officer who was a product of a mandarin system," a person with total discretion over how to spend funds, who "couldn't care less about what some grubby little old peasant lady in black pajamas had to say. He didn't have a political bone in his body." By way of comparison he added, "They're as bad as our military. They never understood either what we were doing." All that led Donohue to say, "We were running a coaching school for army officers."

Further complicating things was the fact that corruption in the provinces was a way of life. So Donohue spent a good deal of time "trying to keep the local parties from using it to their own advantage. The VNQDD element had to be goddamned careful that they weren't pushing the long-range interests of the party," he said, referring to Mai's habit of inserting four VNQDD cadres into every PAT team. "The same is true when you get into Hoa Hao country. If you had a province chief who looked upon it as a source of revenue or if a guy wanted to use it as a private army, then you had real trouble."

Donohue told each province chief, "If you use these people in the way they've been trained, we'll feed them, pay them, and equip them. If you decide at any time they're a hindrance rather than a help, you give me a call, and within thirty days we'll get them out of here. If I decide that you're not using them properly—that you're using them as a palace guard here in the province—I'll give you thirty days' notice and pull them out." And that was the agreement. It was that simple. Nothing in writing. Nothing went through the central government.

"Next, I'd take an agency officer—or officers in a big province—and stick him in the province and tell him, 'Find a place to live. Get some sandbags. We'll try to get you some Nung guards. Stay alive and do as you see fit.' And then he was responsible for the direction of the teams—payroll, logistics, the whole smear." The CIA officer then selected "a vigorous young lieutenant" whom the province security officer would appoint to his staff as the Rural Construction cadre liaison, "so we would have a guy we could work with day in and day out. Then we would work down to the district level, where we had a similar arrangement, and then into a village."

As soon as the district chief had vouched for his recruits, "We'd put them on an airplane and send them down to Vung Tau," Donohue said. "This is pretty heady stuff. These guys had never been out of the village before. The food was spectacular. Suddenly they had more protein in their systems than they've ever had before, and they're able to stay awake in class. Our training program was vigorous as hell, but they all put on weight. We treated them for worms as soon as they came in the door. Then Mai began telling them stories about the fairies and the dragons and the great cultural heritage of the Vietnamese people. He had all sorts of myths which were at least apparent to many of these people. Then he would work in the political applicability of today."

According to Donohue, this is "precisely" what political warfare is all about: Having been selected into a "special" program and given "special" treatment, CIA political cadres were taught the corporate sales pitch. In effect, rural youths were put on a political assembly line, pumped full of protein and propaganda, cross-trained as interchangeable parts for efficiency, then given one last motivational booster shot. "The graduation ceremonies at Vung Tau were something else." Donohue chortled. "At night. Total darkness. Then the one candle lit. Oh! This is the schmaltz! Remember, these are kids that have never seen anything like this. The pageantry!"

The New York Times reporter R. W. Apple described on February 21, 1965 the Ridge Camp graduation ceremony occurring in an amphitheater the size of a football field. Filipino trainers were present and, writes Apple, "The ceremony had a theatrical, almost religious quality. Vietnamese national symbols, including the old imperial flag, were arrayed before an altar. Multicolored pennants bearing the names of the nation's ancient heroes were mounted behind the speaker. Captain Mai stood at an illuminated lectern. The recruits were grouped on the three other sides of the arena. At a signal, all the lights except one focused on Captain Mai went out, and the recruits stripped off their white shirts and dark trousers. When the lights came on again, all were clad in black pajamas."

Whipped into an ideological fervor, the CIA's political cadres were then sent into villages to spread democratic values and undermine the infrastructure.

"It's a GVN presence that's really comprised of your own people that have, by God, gone off and been washed in the blood of the lamb. They've been trained and they've seen the light," Donohue palavered. "They spoke the local dialect, and they're there to defend and focus people on their own defense, to try to enlist the people into doing something positive. If the government can't protect you, it ain't no government."

Of course, the GVN was not a government but a military dictatorship which was opposed to independence in the countryside. The GVN at that time, writes Professor Huy, "could be curiously compared to that of the USSR with the Armed Forces Council as the Supreme Soviet, the Committee Leading the Nation as its Presidium, and the Central Executive Committee as the Soviet government before World War Two when its ministers were called commissars. General Nguyen Van Thieu was elected chairman of the Committee Leading the Nation and so became chief of state. General Nguyen Cao Ky was appointed chairman of the Central Executive Committee, i.e. the government."[9]

In June 1965 the National Council of Security was created and placed under Ky, who reported to Thieu but in fact exercised greater power than Thieu. As prime minister controlling the Interior Ministry, Ky appointed his people to the CIA's covert action program and appointed his confidential agent, General Nguyen Ngoc Loan, director of the Military Security Service in June 1965, director general of the National Police in October 1965, and head of the Central Intelligence Organization in April 1966.

Explains Huy:

> Nguyen Cao Ky was strongly backed by the Americans anxious to find a leader for the Vietnamese. A program called Rural Development, later called the Phoenix program, was set up. It aimed at detecting and destroying the communist cells in villages and reconstructing the countryside. This program was undertaken with means provided by the USA. It was smaller than what we had tried to apply when Nguyen Ton Hoan was deputy prime minister in charge of Pacification. The only difference was that now, the personnel in use were not politically motivated and trained cadres, but merely dispirited employees of the government.[10]

Frank Scotton was also critical of Vung Tau. "I shied away from Vung Tau," he said, "because the American hand became too big and because having a fixed complex was spiritually uncomfortable. Spiritually the thing to do was to go into the villages. At Vung Tau they were not dealing with unconventional warfare, but with warehousers. There was always the threat that 'We'll turn off the water' if you don't do it our way."[11]

He also criticized the "development of incantation and rote" and the resulting "doctrinaire" mind-set that led to the Rural Construction program's being compared with Hitler's Strength Through Joy camps. Its cadre studied the ninety-eight duties, the eleven-point criteria, and the twelve phases of action. They sang the "New Life Hamlet Construction" song, with its symbolic twelve stanzas and ninety-eight notes, and recited the ritual Five Oaths: "Standing before the altar of our Fatherland and the national Flag, we, in the capacity of rural construction cadres, take the oath . . . to remain faithful . . . to firmly believe . . . that cadres are created by the people . . . to mingle with the people . . . and to make constant efforts in study in order to progress in behavior, education and techniques."[12]

Scotton's biggest complaint, however, was the shift from intelligence and displacement to civic action. The change took place in early 1965, when Robert Kelly joined the CIA and took his team of instructors to duplicate the Quang Ngai program in other provinces. At that point Harry "The Hat" Monk took over in Binh Dinh Province and began working as case officer to Major Nguyen Be, the former insurgent who, before defecting, had been party secretary for the Ninth Vietcong Battalion. A visionary, Be wanted Rural Construction to be more than an attack on the VCI; he wanted to provide services to the people as well. Perceiving the PATs as "too American," he retrained his people as they returned to Binh Dinh from Vung Tau and, with the help of Monk, combined "mobile" Census Grievance cadres, PATs, and CTs, and came up with the fifty-nine-man Revolutionary Development (RD) team.

Be's fifty-nine-man RD teams had group leaders and psywar, intelligence, and medical specialists in staff positions. There were three eleven-man teams constituting an "action element" and having a counterterror mission, and there was a Rural Construction leader with a six-man Civic Action team; a six-man "mobile" Census Grievance team under the intelligence office; and a six-man economic unit. Be's teams were called Purple People Eaters by American soldiers, in reference to their clothes and terror tactics. To the rural Vietnamese they were simply "idiot birds."

Said Scotton: "Be was trying to create a climate to make the VC blunder into ambushes and fear the unpredictable." His goal was to neutralize the VC, but his style was "be nice to VC agents, give them gifts, smother them with affection, and then let them try to explain that to their superiors." It was a style Scotton did not approve of, although he loved Be himself. "Be was like an older brother to me and an uncle to my children," Scotton said. "He lived with us from 1976 until he died in summer of 1981."

Despite Scotton's compunctions, by mid-1965 the CIA was using Be's fifty-nine-man model as its standard team, at which point the Rural Construction Cadre program was renamed the Revolutionary Development Cadre program. With larger teams and standardization came the need for more advisers, so Donohue began recruiting military men like Joe Vacarro, a Special Forces sergeant working as a Public Safety adviser in Quang Nam Province. "I met Joe and chatted with him," Donohue said, "and he looked interesting, so I went to AID, and he was sort of seconded to me; although he still worked for AID, I wrote his fitness reports. Then I worked out a direct hire for him, and he came back here to D.C., did some formal Vietnamese training, then went back out for another tour." Vaccaro was to become heavily involved in the Provincial Reconnaissance Unit training program at Vung Tau. Donohue also hired Jean Sauvageot out of the Army. Sauvageot was to become the scion of Vung Tau and a close aide to Frank Scotton, his mentor, and William Colby.

"We get to the point," according to Donohue, "where the CIA was running a political program in a sovereign country where they didn't know what the hell we were teaching. So I had Thieu and Ky down to Vung Tau, and I did all the right things. But what kind of program could it be that had only one sponsor, the CIA, that says it was doing good? It had to be sinister. Any red-blooded American could understand that. What the hell is the CIA doing running a program on political action?

"So I went out to try to get some cosponsors for the record. They weren't easy to come by. I went to [USIS chief] Barry Zorthian. I said, 'Barry, how about giving us someone?' I talked to MACV about getting an officer assigned. I had AID give me a guy." But most of it, Donohue said, "was window dressing. We had the funds; we had the logistics; we had the transportation."

The CIA also had the approbation of Ky and Thieu. "Ky and Thieu saw the wisdom of it," Donohue said, "so they offered up (as their liaison to the program) General Nguyen Duc Thang. And he was indefatigable. He went everyplace." There was, however, one catch. As a way of monitoring the Saigon station, in August 1965 the Special Group assigned Ed Lansdale as senior liaison to General Thang, who instantly advocated transferring the entire Revolutionary Development program to the Defense Ministry.

"Ed Lansdale was an invention of Hubert Humphrey's," Donohue grumbled. "The idea was 'We did it before, we can do it again.' So Lansdale came out two years too late. He brought a lot of his old cohorts; some were agency guys that he'd suborned. He had some Army people and some retired folks, but there was really nothing," Donohue said wearily, "for them to do."

"My boss [Gordon Jorgenson, who replaced Peer DeSilva in February 1965] said, 'Tell them everything.' I said okay, and I spent two and a half hours briefing his full group about a week after they arrived. And they said, 'Let's have a joint office.' So we had our logistics people put in offices and all the right things. Then I had to get somebody to run the office. Thang said, 'Who do you want?' And I said, 'Chau.'"

Tran Ngoc Chau, according to Donohue, "was a farsighted, bright guy with an ability to keep meaningful statistics—which is not very Vietnamese. He'd been the apple of Diem's eye during the strategic hamlet program, and he had a special phone to the palace—Diem was on the horn to him constantly. Because he had that kind of sponsorship, he was able to do an awful lot of experimentation. So we used Kien Hoa as a proving ground. I spent a lot of time between Mai and Chau looking at programs," Donohue recalled, "trying to introduce refinements."

By having Chau transferred to Vung Tau, Donohue also got greater control over his pet project. "We took Census Grievance and expanded it," he said. "I got a villa in Gia Dinh and set up a training school for Census Grievance people. We would bring people in that had been spotted in various villages and run them through the training; then they would go back to their provinces. I had a French gent, Matisse, who ran the school. We trained in small groups, and it was a much faster process than the PATs; but these were literate people, so they were quick on the uptake. And it was very pleasant surroundings. It was a well-handled program." To it Donohue assigned John O'Reilly, John Woodsman, Dick Fortin, and Jean Sauvageot.

"But I had forced the transfer," Donohue confessed, "and Chau was so damn mad that he was in a permanent pout. So he decided to go down to Vung Tau and shape the place up. Which we really didn't need. 'Cause here you have two dynamic personalities [Mai and Chau] who couldn't stand each other."

The conflict was resolved in 1966, when Mai was reassigned to the Joint General Staff, while Chau took over the Vung Tau training program. Donohue minimized the effect. "I couldn't really do much business out there anyway," he noted, "because I needed our own system to talk to people. But at least for the record it looked pretty good. We had a MAVC guy, an AID guy, and a USIS guy down at Vung Tau, so all the bases had been touched. You see," he added, "at this point all we were trying to do was expand the thing and say that there's at least plausible denial that the agency is solely responsible."

Indeed, with the creation of Vung Tau and the synthetic Revolutionary Development Cadre program, South Vietnam began slouching toward democracy. But it was an empty gesture. The rule in South Vietnam was one step forward followed by two steps back.

CHAPTER 5

PICs

"A census, if properly made and exploited, is a basic source of intelligence. It would show, for instance, who is related to whom, an important piece of information in counterinsurgency warfare because insurgent recruiting at the village level is generally based initially on family ties."[1]

As counterinsurgency expert David Galula notes above, a census is an effective way of controlling large numbers of persons. Thus, while CIA paramilitary officers used Census Grievance to gather intelligence in VC-controlled villages, CIA police advisers were conducting a census program of their own. Its origins are traced to Robert Thompson, a British counterinsurgency expert hired in 1961 by Roger Hilsman, director of the State Department's Office of Research and Intelligence, to advise the United States and GVN on police operations in South Vietnam. Basing it on a system he had used in Malaya, Thompson proposed a three-pronged approach that coordinated military, civilian intelligence, and police agencies in a concerted attack on the VCI.

On Thompson's advice, the National Police in 1962 initiated the Family Census program, in which a name list was made and a group photo taken of every family in South Vietnam. The portrait was filed in a police dossier along with each person's political affiliations, fingerprints, income, savings, and other relevant information, such as who owned property or had relatives outside the village and thus had a legitimate reason to travel. This program was also instrumental in leading to the identification of former sect members and *supplétifs,* who were then blackmailed by VBI case officers into working in their villages as informers. By 1965 there were 7,453 registered families.

Through the Family Census, the CIA learned the names of Communist cell members in GVN-controlled villages. Apprehending the cadre that ran the cells was then a matter of arresting all minor suspects and working them over until they informed. This system weakened the insurgency insofar as it forced political cadres to flee to guerrilla units enduring the hardships of the jungle, depriving the VCI of its leadership in GVN areas. This was no small success, for, as Nguyen Van Thieu once observed, "Ho Chi Minh values his two cadres in every hamlet more highly than ten military divisions."[2]

Thompson's method was successful, but only up to a point. Because many VCI cadres were former Vietminh heroes, it was counterproductive for Political Action Teams and counterterrorists to hunt them down in their own villages. Many VCI were not terrorists but, as Galula writes, "men whose motivations, even if the counterinsurgent disapproves of them, may be perfectly honorable. They do not participate directly, as a rule, in direct terrorism or guerrilla action and, technically, have no blood on their hands."[3]

Thompson's dragnet technique engendered other problems. Mistakes were made, and innocent people were routinely tortured or subject to extortion by crooked cops. On other occasions VCI agents deliberately led Political Action Teams into arresting people hostile to the insurgency. Recognizing these facts, Thompson suggested that the CIA organize a police special branch of professional interrogators who would not be confused with PATs working to win hearts and minds. In 1964, at Thompson's suggestion, the Police Special Branch was formed from the Vietnam Bureau of Investigation and plans were made to center it in Province Intelligence Coordinating Committees (PICCs) in South Vietnam's provinces.

Creation of the police Special Branch coincided with the reorganization of the "Special Branch" of the Vietnamese Special Forces into the Special Exploitation Service (SES), the GVN's counterpart to the Special Operations Group. SOG and SES intelligence operations were coordinated with those of the Special Branch through the CIO, though only at the regional and national level, an inadequacy the PICCs were designed to overcome.

The birth of the police Special Branch also coincided with the Hop Tac (Pacification Intensive Capital Area) program, activated in July 1964 to bring security to the besieged capital. A variation on the oil spot technique, Hop Tac introduced twenty-five hundred national policemen into seven provinces surrounding Saigon. In October 1964 the National Identification and Family Census programs were combined in the Resources Control Bureau in the National Police Directorate, and a Public Safety adviser was placed in each region specifically to manage these programs. By December 1964 thirteen thousand policemen were participating in Hop Tac, seven thousand cops were manning seven hundred checkpoints, more than six thousand arrests had been made, and ABC-TV had done a documentary on the program. In the provinces, Public Safety advised policemen-enforced curfews and regulations on the movement of persons and goods under the Resources Control program.

Also in September 1964, as part of the effort to combine police and paramilitary programs, Frank Scotton was directed to apply his motivational indoctrination program to Hop Tac. Assisted by cadres from his Quang Ngai PAT team, Scotton formed paramilitary reaction forces in seven key districts surrounding Saigon. Scotton's cadres were trained at the Ho Ngoc Tau Special Forces camp where SOG based its C5 program for operations inside Cambodia. Equipment, supplies, and training for Scotton's teams were provided by the CIA, while MACV and Special Forces provided personnel. Lists of defectors, criminals, and other potential recruits, as well as targets, came from Special Branch files.

The aim of the motivational indoctrination program, according to Scotton, was to "develop improved combat skills—increased commitment to close combat—for South Vietnamese. This is not psywar against civilians or VC. This is taking the most highly motivated people, saying they deserted, typing up a contract, and using them in these units. Our problem," Scotton said, "was finding smart Vietnamese and Cambodians who were willing to die."[4]

The first district Scotton entered in search of recruits was Tan Binh, between Saigon and Tan Son Nhut airport, where he extracted cadres from a Popular Force platoon guarding Vinh Loc village. These cadres were trained to keep moving, to sleep in the jungle by day and attack VC patrols at night. Next, Scotton trained teams in Nha Be, Go Vap, and Thu Duc districts. He recalled going two weeks at a time without a shower, "subliminating the risk and danger," and participating in operations. "We had a cheap rucksack, a submachine gun, and good friends. We weren't interested in making history in the early days."

So successful was the motivational indoctrination program in support of Hop Tac that MACV decided to use it nationwide. In early 1965 Scotton was asked to introduce his program in SOG's regional camps, in support of Project Delta, the successor to Leaping Lena. Recruits for SOG projects were profit-motivated people whom Scotton persuaded to desert from U.S. Special Forces A camps, which were strung out along South Vietnam's borders. On a portable typewriter he typed a single-page contract, which each recruit signed, acknowledging that although listed as a deserter, he was actually employed by the CIA in "a sensitive project" for which he received substantially higher pay than before.

The most valuable quality possessed by defectors, deserters, and criminals serving in "sensitive" CIA projects was their expendability. Take, for example, Project 24, which employed NVA officers and senior enlisted men. Candidates for Project 24 were vetted and, if selected, taken out for dinner and drinks, to a brothel, where they were photographed, then blackmailed into joining special reconnaissance teams. Trained in Saigon, outfitted with captured NVA or VC equipment, then given a "one-way ticket to Cambodia," they were sent to locate enemy sanctuaries. When they radioed back their position and that of the sanctuary, the CIA would "arc-light" (bomb with B52's) them along with the target. No Project 24 special reconnaissance team ever returned to South Vietnam.

Notably, minds capable of creating Project 24 were not averse to exploiting deviants within their own community, and SOG occasionally recruited American soldiers who had committed war crimes. Rather than serve time in prison or as a way of getting released from stockades in Vietnam or elsewhere, people with defective personalities were likely to volunteer for dangerous and reprehensible jobs.

In June 1965 Colonel Don Blackburn commanded SOG. His staff numbered around twelve and included the commanders of the First and Fifth Special Forces groups, plus various special warfare Marine, Air Force, and Navy officers. SOG headquarters in Saigon planned operations for the four hundred-odd volunteers in its operational units. However, 1965 was rough going for border surveillance. The Montagnards were no longer effective after their revolt, and as compensation, Project Delta was organized to provide intelligence for newly arrived U.S. Army and Marine divisions. About the paramilitary police, SOG, and pacification programs he and his compatriots developed, Scotton said, "For us, these programs were all part of the same thing. We did not think of things in terms of little packages." That "thing," of course, was a grand scheme to win the war, at the bottom of which were the province interrogation centers.

John Patrick Muldoon, Picadoon to the people who knew him in Vietnam, was the first director of the PIC program in Vietnam. Six feet four inches tall, well over two hundred pounds, Muldoon has a scarlet face and a booming bass voice remarkably like Robert Mitchum's. He was friendly and not overly impressed with either himself or the CIA mystique. That makes Muldoon one of the few emancipated retired CIA officers who do not feel obligated to call headquarters every time a writer asks a question about Vietnam.

A Georgetown University dropout, Muldoon joined the agency in 1958, his entry greased by two sisters already in the CIA's employ. He did his first tour in Germany and in 1962 was sent to South Korea. "I worked interrogation in Seoul," Muldoon recalled. "I'd never been involved in interrogation before. Ray Valentine was my boss. Syngman Rhee had been replaced by Park Chung Hee, who was running the show. Park's cousin Colonel Kim Chong Pil was director of the ROK [Republic of Korea] CIA. There was a joint KCIA-CIA interrogation center in Yon Don Tho, outside Seoul."

Here it is worth pausing for a moment to explain that in recruiting cadres for the Korean CIA, the CIA used the same method it used to staff the Vietnamese CIO. As revealed by John Marks in *The Search for the Manchurian Candidate,* the CIA sent its top psychologist, John Winne, to Seoul to "select the initial cadre," using a CIA-developed psychological assessment test. "I set up an office with two translators," Winne told Marks, "and used a Korean version of the Wechsler." CIA psychologists "gave the tests to 25 to 30 police and military officers," Marks writes, "and wrote up a half-page report on each, listing their strengths and weaknesses. Winne wanted to know about each candidate's ability to follow orders, creativity, lack of personality disorders, motivation—why he wanted out of his current job. It was mostly for the money, especially with the civilians."[5]

In this way secret police are recruited as CIA assets in every country where the agency operates. In Latin America, Marks writes, "The CIA . . . found the assessment process most useful for showing how to train the anti-terrorist section. According to results, these men were shown to have very dependent psychologies and needed strong direction"—direction that came from the CIA. Marks quotes one assessor as saying, "Anytime the Company spent money for training a foreigner, the object was that he would ultimately serve our purposes." CIA officers "were not content simply to work closely with these foreign intelligence agencies; they insisted on penetrating them, and the Personality Assessment System provided a useful aid."[6]

Following his tour in Korea, Muldoon was assigned to Vietnam in November 1964. "I was brought down to the National Interrogation Center [NIC] and told, 'This is where you're going to work. . . . You're going to advise X number of interrogators. They'll bring you their initial debriefing of the guy they're working on; then you'll give them additional CIA requirements.' "

The CIA had different requirements, Muldoon explained, because "the South Vietnamese wanted information they could turn around and use in their battle against the Vietcong. They just wanted to know what was going on in the South. . . . But we were interested in information about things in the North that the South Vietnamese couldn't care less about. And that's where the American advisers would come in—to tell them, 'You gotta ask this, too.'

"We had standard requirements depending on where a guy was from. A lot of VC had been trained in North Vietnam and had come back down as volunteers. They weren't regular NVA. So if a guy came from the North, we wanted to know where he was from, what unit he was with, how they were organized, where they were trained.... If a guy had been North for any length of time, we wanted to know if he'd traveled on a train. What kind of identification papers did he need? Anything about foreign weapons or foreigners advising them. That sort of thing."

Built in 1964, the National Interrogation Center served as CIO headquarters and was where civilian, police, and military intelligence was coordinated by the CIA. "It was located down on the Saigon River," Muldoon recalled, "as part of a great big naval compound.... On the left was a wing of offices where the American military chief, an Air Force major, was located. In that same wing were the chief of the CIO... his deputy and the CIA advisers." Muldoon referred to the CIO chief by his nom de guerre, Colonel Sam. "There was only one CIO chief the whole time I was there," he added, "up until August 1966. His deputy was there the whole time, too, and the same interrogators."

Muldoon estimated there were several hundred prisoners in the NIC and four interrogator-advisers. Muldoon was the fifth. Three were Air Force enlisted men serving under an Army captain. Muldoon's boss, the CIA chief of the NIC, was Ian "Sammy" Sammers, who worked under the station's senior liaison officer, Sam Hopper, who had supervised construction of the NIC in early 1964.

One year later, according to Muldoon, "There was a conference in Nha Trang, in late April 1965. They were putting together an interrogation center in an existing building they had taken over, and they asked for help from the NIC. So I was sent up there with the Army captain to look at the place, figure out what kind of staff we needed, and how we were going to train them.... And while we were up there trying to break these guys in, the police liaison guy in Nha Trang, Tony Bartolomucci, asked Sammy if they could keep me there for this conference, at which all of our people were going to meet Jack 'Red' Stent, who was taking over from Paul Hodges as chief of foreign intelligence. Bartolomucci wanted to show off his new interrogation center to all these big shots.

"The military people from the NIC had done their job," Muldoon continued, "so they left. But I stayed around. Then Tucker Gougleman and Red showed up for this conference. Tucker was chief of Special Branch field operations, and things were just starting to get off the ground with the PICs. A couple were already under way—one in Phan Thiet and one in Phuoc Le—and Tucker told me, 'We're going to build, build, build, and I need someone to oversee the whole operation. I want you to do it.'

"So we had this big conference, and they packed the interrogation center full of prisoners. Bartolomucci wanted to show off with a bunch of prisoners, so he got his police buddies to bring in a bunch of prostitutes and what have you and put them in the cells. I don't think they had one VC in the place. After the conference they all went back to the regular jail, and I went to work for Tucker."

John Muldoon spoke affectionately about Tucker Gougleman. "Tucker was loud and foulmouthed, and he had a terrible temper; but it was all a big front. He was very easy to get to know . . . a likable guy. Always in a short-sleeved shirt and sneakers. He was married three times, divorced three times. He had adopted a girl in Korea, and in Vietnam he had what he called his family. He was back in Saigon trying to get them out when he was picked up. When the evacuation was over, he was still there, staying in the hotel. One day he came down, got off the elevator, walked into the lobby, and they were waiting for him. They took him out, threw him in a car, and took him to the National Police Interrogation Center. A French newspaper guy saw it happen. The North Vietnamese denied they had him, but they returned his body about a year later.

"It's funny, but me and Tucker used to talk about the PICs. He said something like 'John, if we lose this war one day, we could end up in these goddammed things if we get caught.'

"'Well,' I asked, 'what would you do if you were in there?'

"He said he thought he'd kill himself rather than go through interrogation. But he didn't. The report I heard was that when his body got to the graves registration people in Okinawa, the broken bones had yet to heal. So obviously they had tortured him right up until the time he died. And I'd be willing to bet he didn't say a damn thing to help them. I can see him spitting in their faces."

Muldoon laughed. "Tucker wanted to turn the PICs into whorehouses. The interrogation rooms had two-way mirrors.

"Tucker was a hero in the Marine Corps in World War Two," Muldoon added. "He joined the agency right after and worked with [station chief] John Hart in Korea, running operations behind the lines. He was in Afghanistan and worked in training, too. He got to Vietnam in 1962 and was base chief in Da Nang running everything* that had to do with intelligence and paramilitary operations. . . . He was no longer the Da Nang base chief when I arrived in Saigon," Muldoon continued, "but he hadn't taken over field operations yet either. He was in Saigon trying to set up the Province Intelligence Coordination Committees with Jack Barlow, a British guy from MI Six. Barlow had been in Africa and Malaya with Robert Thompson, and they were the experts. They'd succeeded in Malaya, and we wanted them to

*Karnow calls Gougleman "the principal adviser" to OPLAN 34A.

show us how to do it. Barlow and Tucker worked hand in hand. I shared an office with them at the embassy annex—which I had besides my office at the NIC—and that's where I first met Tucker."

Forerunner to the Province Interrogation Center program, the Province Intelligence Coordination Committee program, established in November 1964, was designed to extend CIO operations into the provinces. Each PICC was to serve as the senior intelligence agency within each province and to guide, supervise, and coordinate all military, police, and civilian operations.

"Barlow was the guy pushing the PICCs, and Tucker agreed it was a good idea," Muldoon recalled. "But they weren't able to convince the military to go along with them. It was bought by us and the embassy, but not by the military, and that's the one you needed—'cause they were the ones who initially had control of the prisoners. And the Vietnamese military wasn't going to go along unless the U.S. military approved it. So when the U.S. military said, 'Don't turn those prisoners over,' there was no way we were going to get them. So the PICC project never got off the ground. Then after the embassy bombing [February 1965] they had a reorganization, and Tucker became chief of field operations. We started building the Province Interrogation Centers, and it was thought that people would say, 'Hey, man, this is a great spot! We'll send all our prisoners here!' and that then they'd start moving in and set up the PICCs around the PICs. But that never happened either.

"So after the Nha Trang conference we went down to Phuoc Le to set up a training schedule for the PIC that had already been built down there. The paramilitary guy, Pat, wanted to cooperate, and he had great relations with the province chief and the military. The intelligence guy, Ben, was serious about making everything in his province work. He wasn't happy that he got stuck with building the interrogation center and being the adviser, but he wanted to be the best. And he had great relations with the Special Branch and the CIO. Now some paramilitary and liaison guys didn't even talk to each other, but together Pat and Ben were able to make the thing work. It cost a lot of loyal Vietnamese their lives, but Ben would get hamlet informants to tell us who the VC were; then Pat would send the CTs out to get the names."

What Muldoon described was the one-two punch of the counterinsurgency—the Province Interrogation Centers and the counterterrorists. Through the PICs, the CIA learned the identity and structure of the VCI in each province; through the CTs, the CIA eliminated individual VCI members and destroyed their organization.

The problem with the Phuoc Le PIC, according to Muldoon, was its design. "Ben had built his PIC with the guard posts outside each corner, so there was no way for the guards to get back into the inner compound during an attack. Once the shooting started and they ran out of ammunition, they were finished. So the first thing we did was change the design so they were still on each corner and could see in all directions but had a door leading inside the compound."

CIA architects settled on a standard design based on the modified Phuoc Le PIC. Strictly functional, it minimized cost while maximizing security. Under cover of Pacific Architects and Engineers (PA&E), the CIA's logistics staff hired local Vietnamese contractors to build interrogation centers in every province. Funds and staff salaries came from the Special Branch budget. After it was built, the CIA bought the interrogation center, then donated it to the National Police, at which point it became a National Police facility under the direction of the Special Branch. In practice, however—because they got their operating funds directly from the CIA—Special Branch employees wielded more power than their supervisors in the National Police, who received Aid-in-Kind funds indirectly from the Agency for International Development through the National Police Directorate in Saigon.

Each provincial capital would eventually have a PIC. However, regional interrogation centers were built first and were larger, holding two to three hundred prisoners each. In IV Corps's regional capital, Can Tho, where the French had built a jail capable of holding two thousand prisoners, existing facilities were renovated. In choosing where to build in the provinces, each CIA regional officer selected priority provinces. Then, according to Muldoon, it was up to the liaison officer in the province to talk to the province chief and his CIO counterpart to find a spot near the provincial capital. "'Cause that's where our guy lived. Some of the guys had a hell of a time getting PICs started," Muldoon noted, "because some province chiefs wanted money under the table."

Once the interrogation center was built, the liaison officer became its adviser, and Muldoon helped him recruit its staff. There were deadlines for each phase, and part of Muldoon's job was to travel around and monitor progress. "In one place construction would be half done," he recalled, "and in another they'd be trying to find a piece of land. It was a very big undertaking. We even had nit-PICs, which were smaller versions for smaller provinces." Most interrogation centers were built or under construction by the time Muldoon left Vietnam in August 1966, at which point he was transferred to Thailand to build the CIA's huge interrogation center in Udorn, "where the CIA ran the Laos war from the Air America base." Muldoon was replaced as PIC chief in Vietnam by Bob Hill, a vice cop from Washington, D.C. Hill replaced Muldoon in Thailand in 1968.

One story high, fashioned from concrete blocks, poured cement, and wood in the shape of a hollow square, an interrogation center was four buildings with tin roofs linked around a courtyard. In the center of the yard was a combination lookout-water tower with an electric generator under it. "You couldn't get the guards to stay out there at night if they didn't have lights," Muldoon explained. "So we had spotlights on the corners, along the walls, and on the tower shooting out all around. We also bulldozed around it so there were no trees or bushes. Anybody coming at it could be seen crossing the open area." People entered and exited through green, steel-plated gates, "Which were wide open every time I visited," said Muldoon, who visited only during the day. "You didn't want to visit at night," when attacks occurred. PICs were located on the outskirts of town, away from residential areas, so as not to endanger the people living nearby, as well as to discourage rubbernecking. "These were self-contained places," Muldoon emphasized. Telephone lines to the PICs were tapped by the CIA.

On the left side were interrogation rooms and the cellblock—depending on the size, twenty to sixty solitary confinement cells the size of closets. Men and women were not segregated. "You could walk right down the corridor," according to Muldoon. "It was an empty hallway with cells on both sides. Each cell had a steel door and a panel at the bottom where you could slip the food in and a slot at the top where you could look in and see what the guy was doing." There were no toilets, just holes to squat over. "They didn't have them in their homes." Muldoon laughed. "Why should we put them in their cells?"

Prisoners slept on concrete slabs. "Depending on how cooperative they were, you'd give them a straw mat or a blanket. It could get very cold at night in the highlands." A system of rewards and punishments was part of the treatment. "There were little things you could give them and take away from them, not a lot, but every little bit they got they were grateful for."

Depending on the amount of VCI activity in the province and the personality of the PIC chief, some interrogation centers were always full while others were always empty. In either case, "We didn't want them sitting there talking to each other," Muldoon said, so "we would build up the cells gradually, until we had to put them next to each other. They were completely isolated. They didn't get time to go out and walk around the yard. They sat in their cells when they weren't being interrogated. After that they were sent to the local jail or were turned back over to the military, where they were put in POW camps or taken out and shot. That part I never got involved in," he said, adding parenthetically, "They were treated better in the PICs than in the local jails already there for common criminals. Public Safety was advising them, working with the National Police. Sometimes they had sixty to seventy people in a cell that shouldn't have had more than ten. But they didn't care. If you're a criminal, you suffer. If you don't like it, too bad. Don't be a criminal."

The interrogation process worked like this. "As we brought prisoners in, the first thing we did was . . . run them through the shower. That's on the left as you come in. After that they were checked by the doctor or nurse. That was an absolute necessity because God knows what diseases they might be carrying with them. They might need medication. They wouldn't do you much good if they died the first day they were there and you never got a chance to interrogate them. That's why the medical office was right inside the main gate. In most PICs," Muldoon noted, "the medical staff was usually a local ARVN medic who would come out and check the prisoners coming in that day."

After the prisoner was cleaned, examined, repaired, weighed, photographed, and fingerprinted, his biography was taken by a Special Branch officer in the debriefing room. This initial interrogation extracted "hot" information that could be immediately exploited—the whereabouts of an ongoing party committee meeting, for example—as well as the basic information needed to come up with requirements for the series of interrogations that followed. Then the prisoner was given a uniform and stuck in a cell.

The interrogation rooms were at the back of the PIC. Some had two-way mirrors and polygraph machines, although sophisticated equipment was usually reserved for regional interrogation centers, where expert interrogators could put them to better use. Most province liaison officers were not trained interrogators. "They didn't have to be," according to Muldoon. "They were there to collect intelligence, and they had a list of what they needed in their own province. All they had to do was to make sure that whoever was running the PIC followed their orders. All they had to say was 'This is the requirement I want.' Then they read the initial reports and went back and gave the Special Branch interrogators additional requirements, just like we did at the NIC."

The guards—usually policemen, sometimes soldiers—lived in the PIC. As they returned from guard duty, they stacked their weapons in the first room on the right. The next room was the PIC chief's office, with a safe for classified documents, handguns, and the chief's bottle of scotch. The PIC chief's job was to *turn* those in the VCI—make them Special Branch agents—and maintain informant networks in the hamlets and villages. Farther down the corridor were offices for interrogators, collation and report writers, translator-interpreters, clerical and kitchen staff. There were file rooms with locked cabinets and map rooms for tracking the whereabouts of VCIs in the province. And there was a Chieu Hoi room where defectors were encouraged to become counterterrorists, political action cadre, or Kit Carson scouts—a play on the names Biet Kich and Kit Carson, the cavalry adviser who gave a reward for Navajo scalps. Kit Carson scouts worked exclusively for the Marines.

Once an interrogation center had been constructed and a staff assigned,

Muldoon summoned the training team from the NIC. Each member of the team was a specialist. The Army captain trained the guards. Air Force Sergeant Frank Rygalski taught report writers how to write proper reports—the tangible product of the PIC. There were standard reporting formats for tactical as opposed to strategic intelligence and for Chieu Hoi and agent reports. To compile a finished report, an interrogator's notes were reviewed by the chief interrogator, then collated, typed, copied and sent to the Special Branch, CIO, and CIA. Translations were never considered totally accurate unless read and confirmed in the original language by the same person, but that rarely happened. Likewise, interrogations conducted through interpreters were never considered totally reliable, for significant information was generally lost or misrepresented.

Another Air Force sergeant, Dick Falke, taught interrogators how to take notes and ask questions during an interrogation. "You don't just sit down with ten questions, get ten answers, then walk away," Muldoon commented. "Some of these guys, if you gave them ten questions, would get ten answers for you, and that's it. A lot of them had to learn that you don't drop a line of questioning just because you got the answer. The answer, if it's the right one, should lead you to sixty more questions. For example," he said, "Question one was 'Were you ever trained in North Vietnam?' Question two was 'Were you ever trained by people other than Vietnamese?' Well, lots of times the answer to question two is so interesting and gives you so much information you keep going for an hour and never get to question three, 'When did you come to South Vietnam?' "

For Special Branch officers in region interrogation centers, a special interrogation training program was conducted at the NIC by experts from the CIA's Support Services Branch, most of whom had worked on Russian defectors and were brought out from Washington to handle important cases. Training of Special Branch administrative personnel was conducted at region headquarters by professional secretaries, who taught their students how to type, file, and use phones. This side of the program was run by a former professional football player with the Green Bay Packers named Gene, who chain-smoked and eventually died of emphysema. "In between puffs, he'd put this box to his mouth, squeeze it, and take a breath of oxygen," Muldoon recalled.

On the forbidden subject of torture, according to Muldoon, the Special Branch had "the old French methods," interrogation that included torture. "All this had to be stopped by the agency," he said. "They had to be retaught with more sophisticated techniques."

In Ralph Johnson's opinion, "the Vietnamese, both Communist and GVN, looked upon torture as a normal and valid method of obtaining intelligence."[7] But of course, the Vietnamese did not conceive the PICs; they were the stepchildren of Robert Thompson, whose aristocratic English ancestors perfected torture in dingy castle dungeons, on the rack and in the iron lady, with thumbscrews and branding irons.

As for the American role, according to Muldoon, "you can't have an American there all the time watching these things." "These things" included: rape, gang rape, rape using eels, snakes, or hard objects, and rape followed by murder; electrical shock ("the Bell Telephone Hour") rendered by attaching wires to the genitals or other sensitive parts of the body, like the tongue; "the water treatment"; "the airplane," in which a prisoner's arms were tied behind the back and the rope looped over a hook on the ceiling, suspending the prisoner in midair, after which he or she was beaten; beatings with rubber hoses and whips; and the use of police dogs to maul prisoners. All this and more occurred in PICs.

One reason was inexperienced advisers. "A lot of guys in Vietnam were career trainees or junior officer trainees," Muldoon explained. "Some had been in the military; some had just graduated from college. They put them through a six-month course as either intelligence or paramilitary officers, then sent them over. They were just learning, and it was a hell of a place for their baptism of fire. They sent whole classes to Vietnam in 1963 and 1964, then later brought in older guys who had experience as region advisers. . . . They were supposed to hit every province once a week, but some would do it over the radio in one day.

"The adviser's job was to keep the region officer informed about *real* operations mounted in the capital city or against big shots in the field," Muldoon said, adding that advisers who wanted to do a good job ran the PICs themselves, while the others hired assistants—former cops or Green Berets—who were paid by the CIA but worked for themselves, doing a dirty job in exchange for a line on the inside track to the black market, where VC in need of cash and spies seeking names dealt in arms, drugs, prostitution, military scrip, and whatever other commodities were available.

PICs are also faulted for producing only information on low-level VCI. Whenever a VCI member with *strategic* information (for example, a cadre in Hue who knew what was happening in the Delta) was captured, he was immediately grabbed by the region interrogation center, or the NIC in Saigon, where experts could produce quality reports for Washington. The lack of feedback to the PIC for its own province operations resulted in a revolving door syndrome, wherein the PIC was reduced to picking up the same low-level VCI people month after month.

The value of a PIC, according to Muldoon, "depended on the number of people that were put in it, on the caliber of people who manned it—especially the chief—and how good they were at writing up this information. Some guys thought they were the biggest waste of time and money ever spent because they didn't produce anything. And a lot of them didn't produce anything because the guys in the provinces didn't push them. Other people say, 'It's not that we didn't try; it's just that it was a dumb idea in the first place, because we couldn't get the military—who were the ones capturing prisoners—to turn them over. The military weren't going to turn them over to us until they were finished with them, and by then they were washed out.'

"This," Muldoon conceded, "was part of the overall plan: Let the military get the tactical military intelligence first. Obviously that's the most important thing going on in a war. But then we felt that after the military got what they could use tomorrow or next week, maybe the CIA should talk to this guy. That was the whole idea of having the Province Intelligence Coordination Committees and why the PICs became part of them, so we could work this stuff back and forth. And in provinces where our guys went out of their way to work with the MACV sector adviser, they were able to get something done."

The military's side of the story is given by Major General Joseph McChristian, who arrived in Saigon in July 1965 as MACV's intelligence chief. McChristian recognized the threat posed by the VCI and, in order to destroy it, proposed "a large countrywide counterintelligence effort involved in countersabotage, countersubversion and counterespionage activities."[8] In structuring this attack against the VCI, McChristian assigned military intelligence detachments to each U.S. Army brigade, division, and field force, as well as to each South Vietnamese division and corps. He created combined centers for intelligence, document exploitation, interrogation, and matériel exploitation and directed them to support and coordinate allied units in the field. And he ordered the construction of military interrogation centers in each sector, division, and corps.

McChristian readily conceded the primacy of the CIA in anti-VCI operations. He acknowledged that the military did not have sophisticated agent nets and that military advisers at sector level focused on acquiring tactical intelligence needed to mount offensive operations. But he was very upset when the CIA, "without coordination with MACV, took over control of the files on the infrastructure located" in the PICs. He got an even bigger shock when he himself "was refused permission to see the infrastructure file by a member of the [CIA]." Indeed, because the CIA prevented the military from entering the PICs, the military retaliated by refusing to send them prisoners. As a result, anti-VCI operations were poorly coordinated at province level.[9]

Meanwhile, MACV assigned intelligence teams to the provinces, which formed agent nets mainly through Regional and Popular Forces under military control. These advisory teams sent reports to the political order of battle section in the Combined Intelligence Center, which "produced complete and timely intelligence on the boundaries, location, structure, strengths, personalities and activities of the Communist political organization, or infrastructure.[10]

Information filtering into the Combined Intelligence Center was placed in an automatic data base, which enabled analysts to compare known VCI offenders with known aliases. Agent reports and special intelligence collection programs like Project Corral provided the military with information on low-level VCI, while information on high-level VCI came from the Combined Military Interrogation Center, which, according to McChristian, was the "focal point of tactical and strategic exploitation of selected human sources."[11]

The South Vietnamese military branch responsible for attacking the VCI was the Military Security Service under the direction of General Loan. Liaison with the MSS was handled by MACV's Counter-Intelligence Division within the 525th Military Intelligence Group. The primary mission of counterintelligence was the defection in place of VCI agents who had penetrated ARVN channels, for use as double agents. By mid-1966 U.S. military intelligence employed about a thousand agents in South Vietnam, all of whom were paid through the 525th's Intelligence Contingency Fund.

The 525th had a headquarters unit near Long Binh, one battalion for each corps, and one working with SOG in third countries. Internally the 525th was divided into bilateral teams working with the Military Security Service and ARVN military intelligence, and unilateral teams working without the knowledge or approval of the GVN. Operational teams consisted of five enlisted men, each one an agent handler reporting to an officer who served as team chief. When assigned to the field, agent handlers in unilateral teams lived on their own, "on the economy." To avoid "flaps," they were given identification as Foreign Service officers or employees of private American companies, although they kept their military IDs for access to classified information, areas, and resources. Upon arriving in-country, each agent handler (aka case officer) was assigned a principal agent, who usually had a functioning agent network already in place. Some of these nets had been set up by the French, the British, or the Chinese. Each principal agent had several subagents working in cells. Like most spies, subagents were usually in it for the money; in many cases the war had destroyed their businesses and left them no alternative.

Case officers worked with principal agents through interpreters and couriers. In theory, a case officer never met subagents. Instead, each cell had a cell leader who secretly met with the principal agent to exchange information and receive instructions, which were passed along to the other subagents. Some subagents were political specialists; others attended to tactical military concerns. Posing as woodcutters or rice farmers or secretaries or auto mechanics, subagents infiltrated Vietcong villages or businesses and reported on NLF associations, VCI cadres, and the GVN's criminal undertakings as well as on the size and whereabouts of VC and NVA combat units.

Case officers handling political "accounts" were given requirements, originated at battalion headquarters, by their team leaders. The requirements were for specific information on individual VCIs. The cell leader would report on a particular VCI to the principal agent, who would pass the information back to the case officer using standard tradecraft methods—a cryptic mark on a wall or telephone pole that the case officer would periodically look for. The case officer would, upon seeing the signal, send a courier to retrieve the report from the principal agent's courier at a prearranged time and place. The case officer would then pass the information to his team leader as well as to other customers, including the CIA liaison officer at the embassy house, as CIA headquarters in a province was called.

The finished products of positive and counterintelligence operations were called army information reports. Reports and agents were rated on the basis of accuracy, but insofar as most agents were in it for money, accuracy was hard to judge. A spy might implicate a person who owed him money or a rival in love, business, or politics. Many sources were double agents, and all agents were periodically given lie detector tests. For protection they were also given code names. They were paid through the MACV Intelligence Contingency Fund, but not well enough to survive on their salaries alone, so many dabbled in the black market, too.

The final stage of the intelligence cycle was the termination of agents, for which there were three methods. First was termination by paying the agent off, swearing him to secrecy, and saying so long. Second was termination with prejudice, which meant ordering an agent out of an area and placing his or her name on a blacklist so he or she could never work for the United States again; third was termination with extreme prejudice, applied when the mere existence of an agent threatened the security of an operation or other agents. Case officers were taught, in off-the-record sessions, how to terminate their agents with extreme prejudice. CIA officers received similar instruction.

CHAPTER 6

Field Police

Four Opinions on Pacification

The corporate warrior: "Pacification was the ultimate goal of both the Americans and the South Vietnamese government. A complex task involving military, psychological, political, and economic factors, its aim was to achieve an economically and politically viable society in which the people could live without constant fear of death or other physical harm"—WILLIAM WESTMORELAND, *A Soldier Reports*

The poet: "Defenseless villages are bombarded from the air, the inhabitants driven into the countryside, the cattle machine gunned, the huts set afire with incendiary bullets: this is called pacification"—GEORGE ORWELL, *Politics and the English Language,* 1946

The reporter: "What we're really doing in Vietnam is killing the *cause* of 'wars of liberation.' It's a testing ground—like Germany in Spain. It's an example to Central America and other guerrilla prone areas"—BERNARD FALL, "This Isn't Munich, It's Spain," *Ramparts* (December 1965)

The warlord: "A popular political base for the Government of South Vietnam does not now exist. The existing government is oriented toward the exploitation of the rural and lower class urban populations. It is in fact a continuation of the French colonial system of government with upper class Vietnamese replacing the French. The dissatisfaction of the agrarian population . . . is expressed largely through alliance with the NLF"—John Paul Vann, 1965

In retaliation for selective terror attacks against Americans in South Vietnam, President Lyndon Johnson ordered in 1965 the bombing of cities in North Vietnam. The raids continued into 1968, the idea being to deal the Communists more punishment than they could absorb. Although comparisons were unforthcoming in the American press, North Vietnam got a taste of what England was like during the Nazi terror bombings of World War II, and like the Brits, the North Vietnamese evacuated their children to the countryside but refused to say uncle.

Enraged by infiltrating North Vietnamese troops, LBJ also ordered the bombing of Laos and Cambodia. To help the Air Force locate enemy troops and targets in those "neutral" countries, SOG launched a cross-border operation called Prairie Fire. Working on the problem in Laos was the CIA, through its top secret Project 404. Headquartered in Vientiane, Project 404 sent agents into the countryside to locate targets for B-52's stationed in Guam and on aircraft carriers in the South China Sea. The massive bombing campaign turned much of Laos and Cambodia into a wasteland.

The same was true in South Vietnam, where the strategy was to demoralize the Communists by blowing their villages to smithereens. Because of the devastation the bombing wrought, half a million Vietnamese refugees had fled their villages and were living in temporary shelters by the end of 1965, while another half million were wandering around in shock, homeless. At the same time nearly a quarter million American soldiers were mired in the muck of Vietnam, a small percentage of them engaged in pacification as variously defined above. The Pentagon thought it needed half a million more men to get the job done.

Reacting to the presence of another generation of foreign occupation troops, COSVN commander General Nguyen Chi Thanh called for a renewed insurgency. The head of the NLF, Nguyen Huu Tho, agreed. The battle was joined. And with the rejuvenated revolution came an increased demand by the CIA for VCI prisoners. However, the VCI fish were submerged in the sea of refugees that was rolling like a tidal wave over South Vietnam. Having been swamped by the human deluge, only three thousand of Saigon's eighteen thousand National Policemen were available to chase the VCI; the rest were busy directing traffic and manning checkpoints into Saigon.

Likewise, in the countryside, the hapless police were capturing few VCI for interrogation—far fewer, in fact, than U.S. combat units caught while conducting cordon and search operations, in which entire villages were herded together and every man, woman, and child subjected to search and seizure, and worse. As John Muldoon noted, the military rarely made its prisoners available to the police until they were "washed out."

Making matters worse was the fact that province chiefs eager to foster "local initiative" often made deals with the CIA officers who funded them. At the direction of their paramilitary advisers, province chiefs often pursued the VCI with counterterror teams, independently of the police, put the VCI in their own province jails and sent them to PICs only if the CIA's Special Branch adviser learned what was going on, and complained loud enough and long enough. Meanwhile, amid the din of saber-rattling coming from the Pentagon, the plaintive cries of police and pacification managers began to echo in the corridors of power in Washington. Something had to be done to put some punch in the National Police.

What was decided, in the summer of 1965, was to provide the National Police with a paramilitary field force that had the mission and skills of counterterror teams and could work jointly with the military in cordon and search operations. The man given the job was Colonel William "Pappy" Grieves, senior adviser to the National Police Field Forces from August 1965 till 1973.

"I was trying to create an A-One police force starting from scratch," Grieves told me when we met at his home in 1986.[1] A blend of rock-solid integrity and irreverence, Grieves was the son of a U.S. Army officer, born in the Philippines and reared in a series of army posts around the world. He attended West Point and in World War II saw action in Europe with the XV Corps Artillery. Then came the War College, jump school at Fort Benning (he made his last jump at age sixty) and an interest in unconventional warfare. As MAAG chief of staff in Greece in the mid-1950's, Grieves worked with the CIA, the Special Forces, and the Greek airborne raiding force in paramilitary operations behind enemy lines.

Grieves ended his career as deputy commander of the Special Warfare Center at Fort Bragg under General William Yarborough. "I've often thought that if he had gone to Vietnam instead of Westmoreland, the war would have taken a different course. More would have been put on the Vietnamese. Yarborough," said Grieves, "realized that you can't fight a war on the four-year political cycle of the United States—which is what we were trying to do. I'm convinced the war could have been won, but it would have taken a long time with a lot less U.S. troops." The notion that "you can't go in and win it for somebody, 'cause you'll have nothing in the end" was the philosophy Pappy Grieves brought to the National Police Field Forces.

Days before his retirement from the U.S. Army, Grieves was asked to join the Agency for International Development's Public Safety program in South Vietnam. "Byron Engel, the chief of the Public Safety Program in Washington, D.C., had a representative at the Special Warfare Center who approached me about taking the job," Grieves recalled. "He said they were looking for a guy to head up the paramilitary force within the National Police. They specifically selected me for the job with the Field Police, which were just being organized at the time, because they needed someone with an unconventional warfare background. So I went to Washington, D.C., was interviewed by Byron Engel, among other people, took a quick course at the USAID Police Academy, and as a result, when I retired in July 1965, by the end of the next month I was in Vietnam.

"Let me give you a little background on what the Field Police concept was," Grieves continued. "In a country like Vietnam you had a situation where a policeman couldn't walk a beat—like Blood Alley in Paris. In order to walk a beat and bring police services to the people, in most parts of Vietnam you had to use military tactics and techniques and formations just for the policeman to survive. So you walk a beat by squads and platoons. The military would call it a patrol, and, as a matter of fact, so did the police.

"That was the basic concept. Whether you had an outfit called Phoenix or not, there was a *police* need for a field force organization in a counterinsurgency role. The British found this necessary in Malaya, and they created Police Field Forces there. In fact, the original idea of the Vietnamese Police Field Forces came out of Malaya. Robert Thompson recommended it. And when I got to Vietnam, they had a contract Australian . . . who had taken over for himself the Police Field Forces: Ted Serong. If you looked at the paper, he was hired by AID as a consultant; but he was paid by the CIA, which was reimbursed by AID. This arrangement allowed the CIA to have input into how the Field Police were managed.

"When I got to Vietnam," Grieves continued, "I found myself responsible on the American side of this thing, and yet Serong was in there, not as an adviser, but directly operating. He had some money coming in from Australia, which he would dispense to get [Vietnamese] to come over to his side, and he had five or six Australian paramilitary advisers, paid by the Company [CIA], same as him."

The problem was that the CIA wanted to establish the Field Police under its control, not as a police force but as a unit against the infrastructure. The CIA tried to do that by having Serong suborn the Vietnamese officers who managed the program, so that he could run it like a private army, the way the agency ran the counterterror teams. "Under Serong and the CIA," Grieves explained, "the Field Police program was not for the benefit of the Vietnamese; when they were gone, there wasn't going to be anything left. Well, they could run it like the counterterror teams, or they could be advisers."

As a matter of principle, Grieves felt obligated to run his program legitimately. "Now Serong and I were both dealing with the same Vietnamese," he recalled, "with him on the ground trying to make it anti-VCI. Then I discovered that some very peculiar things were going on. There was no accountability. The CIA was furnishing piasters and weapons to get the Field Police going, but these things were dropped by the Company from accountability when they left Saigon. Serong would take a jeep, ship it by Air America up to the training center in Da Lat, ship it back on the next airplane out, and he'd have a vehicle of his own off the books! A lot of piasters were being used to pay personal servants, to buy liquor, things of that nature. And he had sources of information. He was going with the director of AID's administrative assistant, and she would take things Serong was interested in and let him see them before [USAID Director] Charlie Mann did. There were all sorts of things going on, and this just put me across the barrel.

"It took me a couple of months to figure it out"—Grieves sighed—"and it made it hard to put the Field Police back on the police track, which was my job. So the first thing we did was try to get rid of that crowd. But Bob Lowe, who was the head of Public Safety in South Vietnam and my boss through the chief of operations, wanted me to stay out of it. Serong had pulled the wool over his eyes, and he just wasn't interested. Then John Manopoli replaced Lowe, and John called me in and said he wanted to see me get into it; he had a directive to get rid of Serong, and I supplied the ammunition.

"It was just his personality," Grieves said in retrospect, "but his handling of funds, equipment, and everything else was completely immoral. And eventually it all came out. After about a year the services of Brigadier Serong were dispensed with; his and his people's contracts ran out or were turned over to the Company, and my relationship with the CIA station soured as a result."

The final parting of ways came when Grieves was asked to work for the CIA without the knowledge of his AID superiors. From his experience with the agency in Greece, Grieves knew that CIA staff officers were protected but that contract employees were expendable. He did not trust the CIA enough to put himself in the tenuous position of having to depend on it.

Grieves's refusal to bring the Field Police under CIA control had a significant effect. "In the eyes of Serong and that crew, the Field Police were to be an outlet of the Company," Grieves explained. "So when it became obvious they were a part of the National Police, the CIA developed the Provincial Reconnaissance Units (PRU)—units operating separately, hired and commanded by Company people." Unfortunately, he added, "The Field Police could never develop across the board as long as PRU existed." Indeed, the PRU and the Field Police worked at cross-purposes for years to come, reflecting parochial tensions between U.S. agencies and undermining the U.S. war effort in Vietnam.

The Field Police was formally established on January 27, 1965, at the same time as the Marine Police. Its mission, as written by Grieves, was "for the purpose of extending police services to the people of Vietnam in areas where more conventionally armed forces and trained National Police could not operate, and to provide a tool to assist in the extension of the National Police into the rural areas." Field Police units were to patrol rural areas, control civil disturbances, provide security for the National Police, act as a reserve, and conduct raids against the VCI based on information provided by the Special Branch.

Notably, Grieves placed the anti-VCI role last, a priority that was reversed two years later under Phoenix. In the meantime, he was intent on bringing order, discipline, and a public service purpose to the Field Police. "The headquarters was in Saigon, collocated with Public Safety," Grieves recalled. "As soon as we could, however, we constructed a separate headquarters and a warehouse on the outskirts of Saigon. We hired Nungs as security. There was a Nung platoon in Cholon at our central warehouse and forty to fifty Nungs at our training center in Da Lat. We got them through Chinese brokers in Cholon.

"Between 1965 and 1966," Grieves explained, "the Field Police were just getting organized. Under Serong the planned strength was eighteen thousand, but the actual force in July 1965 was two thousand." There were six companies in training at the original center in Nam Dong, which Serong moved to Tri Mot, about six miles outside Da Lat. "He was also dealing with piaster funds on the black market, using the profits to build a private villa for his vacations up there," Grieves revealed.

The Tri Mot facility accommodated twelve companies. The American in charge was retired Special Forces Sergeant Major Chuck Petry. Training of field policemen began with a two-month course at the National Police training center in Vung Tau, followed by a three-month course at Tri Mot. Field policemen were assigned to provinces initially as a unit, later as individuals. Offshore training in jungle operations and riot control was given to selected recruits at the Malayan Police Field Force training center (created by Serong) through the Colombo Plan, while other field policemen were trained at the International Police Academy in Washington. The first two Field Police companies, from Long An and Gia Dinh provinces, completed their training in December 1965.

Grieves then arranged for MACV to provide logistical support to the Field Police through U.S. Army channels on a reimbursable basis. In order to make sure that supplies were not sold on the black market, equipment was issued directly into the American warehouse and parceled out by Grieves and his staff. "We did not issue it to the Vietnamese," he said, "until they had the troops for it. We didn't give them twenty-seven companies' worth of equipment when they only had ten companies of people.

"We were the administrators," Grieves explained, "which forced us to account for funds and do a lot of things that were not in an advisory capacity. But it was the only way to get the job done. From the very beginning the idea was to turn it back to the Vietnamese when they could handle it, but at first we had to expand our advisory role to create this force.

"My first counterpart," Grieves recalled, "for about eight months was a Special Forces lieutenant colonel named Tran Van Thua. He was assigned to the National Police and was working with Ted Serong. Thua meant well but was not a strong officer. He was attempting to play us against each other by not allowing himself to become too aware of it. Then Nguyen Ngoc Loan became director general of the National Police, and he brought in Colonel Sanh, an army airborne officer." At that point Thua was reassigned as chief of the National Police training center at Vung Tau. "Colonel Sanh was an improvement over Thua, but he was also a little hard to get along with," according to Grieves. "He had no real interest in the police side of it. He came from one of the Combat Police* battalions and was interested primarily in the riot control aspect of the Field Police."

Reflecting General Loan's priorities, Colonel Sanh in early 1966 revised Field Police operating procedures to emphasize civil disturbance control, and he directed that Field Police units in emergencies would be available as a reserve for any police chief. Concurrently with this revised mission, the two existing Combat Police battalions—still advised by Ted Serong under CIA auspices—were incorporated into the Field Police. Available as a nationwide reaction force, the Combat Police was used by General Loan to suppress Buddhist demonstrations in the spring of 1966 in Da Nang, Hue, and Saigon. Likewise, Field Police units in provinces adjacent to Saigon were often called into the capital to reinforce ongoing riot control operations. In such cases platoons would generally be sent in from Long An, Gia Dinh, and Binh Duong provinces.

"The trained provisional Field Police companies were finally deployed to their provinces in July 1966," Grieves said, "after being held in Saigon for riot control during the Buddhist struggle movement, which dominated the first half of that year. By year's end there were forty-five Field Police companies, four platoons each, for a total of five thousand five hundred forty-

*The two Combat Police battalions (later called Order Police) were CIA-advised paramilitary police units used to break up demonstrations and provide security for government functions.

five men." By the end of 1967 the Field Police had twelve thousand men in fifty-nine companies.

"My counterpart for the longest time," said Grieves, "was Major Nguyen Van Dai, who started out as a ranger captain in the Delta. Dai was the best of the bunch—an old soldier and a real hard rock. He was the one who really built the Field Police."

From July 1968 until February 1971 Dai served as assistant director of the National Police Support Division and as commandant of the National Police Field Forces. "Over two years and a half," said Dai, "as commandant NPFF, my relationship with Colonel Grieves and his staff was very friendly. We had open discussions to find an appropriate and reasonable solution to any difficult problems. After twenty-two years in the army, most of that in combat units, I have only one concept: Quality is better than quantity. All soldiers in my command must be disciplined, and the leader must demonstrate a good example for others."[2]

"Dai," Grieves said with respect, "brought to the National Police Field Forces the attitude of 'service to the people.'

"My personnel," explained Grieves, "the Field Police advisers, were hired in this country and sent over to Vietnam. In addition, because they were coming over so slowly, we got a couple of local hires who were military and took their discharges in Vietnam. The Field Police advisers were all civilians. [Of 230 Public Safety advisers in Vietnam, 150 were on loan from the military.] We also had a bunch of peculiar deals. I needed advisers, and I needed them bad. The Fifth Special Forces at Nha Trang meanwhile had a requirement for men in civilian clothes in three particular provinces where I needed advisors, too. Theirs was an intelligence requirement, mine was a working function, but a guy could do both jobs. When this came out, I went and laid it on the table with my boss. I wasn't pulling anything underhanded, and I got their permission to do this. These guys came along and were documented as local hires by AID, but actually they were still in the military. They took over and did a damn fine job in the provinces.

"There were some officers, too," Grieves said, adding that "most of them were staff members. We also had an ex-military police major as an adviser to two Field Police companies working with the First Cavalry near Qui Nhon, rooting out VC. He was there two days and said he wanted a ticket home. He said, 'I'd have stayed in the Army if I wanted this.'

"So Ed Schlacter took over in Binh Dinh," Grieves continued. "Based on Special Branch intelligence that Vietcong guerrillas were in the village, around first light the First Cavalry would go in by chopper and circle the village, followed by a Field Police squad, platoon, or company. While the Cav provided security, the Field Police would search people and look in the rice pot. The Americans never knew what was going on, but the Vietnamese in the Field Police would know how many people were feeding by looking in the rice pot. If they saw enough rice for ten people but only saw six people in the hooch, they knew the rest were hiding underground."

About the Special Branch, Grieves commented, "They had a security and intelligence gathering function. Special Branch furnished the intelligence on which the Field Police would react. They could pick up two or three guys themselves and actually didn't need to call in the Field Police unless it was a big deal.

"What we did was put a company of Field Police in each province," Grieves explained. "Originally the plan was for a fixed company: four platoons and a headquarters. If you had a big province, put in two companies. Then it became obvious, if you're going to put platoons in the districts, that it would be better to have one company headquarters and a variable number of platoons. So the basic unit became the forty-man three-squad platoon. They had M-sixteens and were semimobile.

"In theory, each company had an adviser, but that was never the case. There were never enough. In fact, some of the places where we didn't have a Field Police adviser, the Public Safety adviser had to take it over. When I first went out there, some Public Safety people had to cover three provinces and were supposed to take the Field Police under their wing. In most cases, however, they didn't have any interest, and it didn't work too well. But when the thing got going, the Public Safety adviser had the Field Police adviser under him, and by the very end the companies were so well trained that they could run themselves."

Doug McCollum was one of the first Public Safety advisers to manage Field Police units in Vietnam. Born in New Jersey and reared in California, McCollum served three years in the U.S. Army before joining the Walnut Creek Police Department in 1961. Five years later one of McCollum's colleagues, who was working for Public Safety in Vietnam, wrote and suggested that he do likewise. On April 16, 1966, Doug McCollum arrived in Saigon; two weeks later he was sent to Pleiku Province as the Public Safety police adviser.

"There was no one there to meet me when I arrived," McCollum recalled, "so I went over to the province senior adviser . . . who didn't know I was coming and was surprised to see me. He didn't want me there either because of the previous Public Safety adviser, who was then living with his wife in Cambodia. Rogers didn't think Public Safety was any good."[3]

Not many people did. To give the devil his due, however, it was hard for a Public Safety adviser to distinguish between unlawful and customary behavior on the part of his Vietnamese counterpart. The province police chief bought his job from the province chief, and in turn the police chief expected a percentage of the profits his subordinates made selling licenses and paroles and whatever to the civilian population. Many police chiefs were also taking payoffs from black-marketeers, a fact they would naturally try to keep from their advisers—unless the advisors wanted a piece of the action, too.

The problem was compounded for a Field Police commander and his adviser. As Grieves noted, "the Vietnamese Field Police platoon leader could not operate on his own. He received his orders and his tasks from commanders outside the Field Police, and the National Police commanders he worked for were in turn subjected to the orders of province and district chiefs who had operational control of the National Police."

Another limitation on the Field Police was the fact that Vietnamese policemen were prohibited from arresting American soldiers. Consequently, Doug McCollum worked closely with the Military Police in Pleiku to reduce tensions between American soldiers and Vietnamese and Montagnard pedestrians who often found themselves under the wheels of U.S. Army vehicles. With the cooperation of his counterpart, McCollum and the MPs set up stop signs at intersections and put radar in place in an effort to slow traffic. To reduce tensions further, McCollum and the MPs restricted soldiers to bars in the military compound.

A dedicated professional who is now an intelligence analyst for the Labor Department, McCollum believed he "was doing something for our country by helping police help people." One of his accomplishments as a Public Safety adviser was to renovate the province jail, which before his arrival had male and female prisoners incarcerated together. He inspected the PIC once a week, did manpower studies which revealed "ghost" employees on the police payroll, and managed the national identification program, which presented a unique problem in the highlands because "it was hard to bend the fingers of a Montagnard." McCollum also led the Field Police in joint patrols with the MPs around Pleiku City's perimeter.

Soon McCollum was running the Public Safety program in three provinces—Pleiku, Kontum, and Phu Bon. As adviser to the police chief in each province McCollum was responsible for collecting intelligence "from the police side" on enemy troop movements, caches, and cadres and for sending intelligence reports to his regional headquarters in Nha Trang. Then, in February 1967, McCollum was reassigned to Ban Me Thuot, the capital city of Darlac Province. There he had the police set up "a maze of barbed wire, allowing only one way into the city. I put people on rooftops and had the Field Police on roving patrols." McCollum also began monitoring the Chieu Hoi program. "They'd come in; we'd hold them, feed them, clothe them, get them a mat. Then we'd release them, and they'd wander around the city for a while, then disappear. It was the biggest hole in the net."

McCollum's feelings reflect the growing tension between people involved in police programs and those involved in Revolutionary Development. At times the two approaches to pacification seemed to cancel each other out. But they also overlapped. Said Grieves about this paradoxical situation: "We used to send Field Police squads and platoons down to Vung Tau for RD training, which was political indoctrination, and for PRU training, which was raids and ambushes. Now the RD Cadre were patterned on the Communists' political cadre, and they paralleled the civilian government. But most were city boys who went out to the villages and just talked to the girls. On the other hand, the Vietcong had been training since they were twelve. So the CIA was trying to do in twelve weeks what the Communists did in six years."

Phoenix eventually arose as the ultimate synthesis of these conflicting police and paramilitary programs. And with the formation of the Field Police, its component parts were set in place. The CIA was managing Census Grievance, RD Cadre, counterterror teams, and the PICs. Military intelligence was working with the MSS, ARVN intelligence, and the Regional and Popular Forces. AID was managing Chieu Hoi and Public Safety, including the Field Police. All that remained was for someone to bring them together under the Special Branch.

CHAPTER 7

Special Branch

Nelson Brickham is fiercely independent, hungry for information, and highly skilled at organizing complex systems in simple terms. "I've been called an organizational genius," he said modestly, "but that's not true. I'm just well read."[1] He is also engaging, candid, and willful, with interests ranging from yachting and bird watching to religious studies. When we met in November 1986, he had just completed a master's thesis on the First Book of John.

His motive for speaking with me, however, had nothing to do with atonement; in his words, it was a matter of "vanity," the chance that "maybe I'll wind up as a footnote in history." Said Brickham: "I feel that I, as well as a number of other people, never got recognition for some of the things we did." Brickham also believed his analysis of the CIA's role in the Vietnam War might help reverse what he saw as a dangerous drift to the right in American politics. "The events we've seen in recent years," he told me, "are a reaction to the psychic trauma of the country following Vietnam, a reaction which, on a far more modest scale, is similar in character—and here's where it's dangerous—to the frustration and bitterness of the German nation after the First World War."

Coming from a CIA officer who did everything in his power to win the war, to the extent of creating Phoenix, such a warning carries double weight.

So, who is Nelson Brickham? Prior to joining the CIA in 1949, Brickham attended Yale University, from which he was graduated magna cum laude with a degree in international politics. His first CIA assignment was on the Czechoslovakian desk in the Office of Reports and Estimates. During the Korean War Brickham worked for the agency's Special Intelligence Branch, gathering intelligence on Soviet political and foreign officers. Next came a stint in the Office of Current Intelligence, where he got involved in "depth research" on the Soviet political process and produced with several colleagues the landmark Caesar Project on the selection process of Soviet leaders after Stalin's death. As a result of the Caesar Project, Brickham was invited to London as a guest of British intelligence—MI6. Overseas travel and liaison with foreign nationals appealed to him, and in 1955 he transferred from the sedate Directorate of Intelligence to the Soviet Russia (SR) Division in the freewheeling Directorate of Plans, where the CIA's clandestine operations were then being hatched.

In 1958 Brickham was appointed chief of the operations research branch of the SR Division, where he planned covert operations into Soviet territory. These operations included the emplacement of photographic and signet equipment near Soviet military bases and the preparation of false documents for "black" agents. Brickham also wrote research papers on specific geographic targets.

Then the Russians sent up *Sputnik,* which "scared everyone," Brickham recalled, "and so I was put in charge of a massive research project designed to develop collection targets against the Soviet missile program. Well, in 1954 I had read a report from British intelligence describing how they had developed a *target plot* approach to guiding espionage and other collection activities. In applying that target plot idea to the Soviet problem, it immediately occurred to me to magnify it as a systems analysis study so we could go after the whole Soviet missile program. It was the first time," he said, "that any government agency had taken a *systems approach* toward a Soviet target. We wanted to pull together all information from whatever source, of whatever degree of reliability, and collect that information in terms of its geographic location. And from that effort a series of natural targets sprang up."

A systems approach means assembling information on a weapons system from its theoretical inception, through its research and development stage, its serial production, its introduction to the armed forces, finally to its deployment. "For the first time," Brickham said, "there was a complete view of everything known about Russian military and missile development systems. The British called this the best thing achieved by American research since the war."

Insofar as Phoenix sought to combine all existing counterinsurgency programs in a coordinated attack on the VCI, Brickham's notion of a systems approach served as the conceptual basis for Phoenix, although in Phoenix the targets were people, not missile silos.

With yet another feather in his cap, Brickham was posted in 1960 to Teheran, where he managed intelligence and counterintelligence operations against the Soviets in Iran. As one of only three neutral countries bordering the USSR, Iran was a plum assignment. For Brickham, however, it devolved into a personality conflict with his desk officer in Washington. Frustrated, he requested a transfer and in 1964 was sent to the Sino-Soviet Relations Branch, where he managed black propaganda operations designed to cause friction between the USSR and China. At the heart of these black operations were false flag recruitments, in which CIA case officers posed as Soviet intelligence officers and, using legitimate Soviet cipher systems and methodology, recruited Chinese diplomats, who believed they were working for the Russians, although they were actually working for the CIA. The CIA case officers, on Brickham's instructions, then used the unsuspecting Chinese agents to create all manner of mischief. Although it was a job with "lots of room for imagination," Brickham was unhappy with it, and when the agency had its "call-up" for Vietnam in the summer of 1965, Brickham volunteered to go.

His preparation included briefings from experts on the Vietnamese desk, reading books and newspaper articles, and reviewing reports and cable traffic produced by every government agency. Upon arriving in Saigon in September 1965, he was assigned to the station's liaison branch as deputy chief of police Special Branch field operations. His boss was Tucker Gougleman.

The chief of station was Gordon Jorgenson, "a kindly, thoughtful person. He'd been through the bombing of the embassy the previous February. Peer DeSilva, who was hurt in the explosion, went home, and Jorgy, who had been his deputy, became station chief. But within a matter of months he went home, too, and John Hart came out as the new chief of station in January 1966." The subject of John Hart gave Brickham pause. "I have described the intelligence service as a socially acceptable way of expressing criminal tendencies," he said. "A guy who has strong criminal tendencies—but is too much of a coward to be one—would wind up in a place like the CIA if he had the education. I'd put John Hart in this category—a mercenary who found a socially acceptable way of doing these things and, I might add, getting very well paid for it.

"John Hart was an egomaniac," Brickham continued, "but a little bit more under control than some of the bad ones. He was a smart one. A big, imposing guy over six feet tall with a very regal bearing and almost a British accent. He claims to be Norman, and he spoke fluent French and was always trying on every occasion to press people to speak French. Red Stent used to say that you could tell somebody who parades his knowledge of French by the way he uses the subjunctive, and John Hart used it properly. But John Hart had both feet on the ground. He was a bright guy, very energetic, and very heavy into tennis—he played it every day.

"When John Hart came out as chief of station, I was one of his escort officers; our job was to take him on a tour of the whole country, to visit the facilities and explain what was going on. And my job was in question at that moment because Hart had another guy—his pet, John Sherwood—slated to replace Tucker as chief of field operations. . . . Anyway," Brickham said, "there's a great division in the Foreign Service world between people who get out on the local economy and try to eat native and find out what's going on versus the people that hole up in the American colony, the so-called golden ghetto people. So we're sitting around, talking about Vietnamese food and about the guys who go down to the MAAG compound for dinner every night, and Hart makes this sort of sneerlike remark to me at the restaurant where we're having dinner; he says, 'Well, really, I would have figured you for the kind of person who would eat dinner in the MAAG compound every night.' Well, he later found out that wasn't true, and he was persuaded to appoint me to the position of chief of field operations. And even though I started out with that base of insecurity, Hart respected me. And later on that became quite evident."

Perhaps as a result of his eating habits, Brickham got assigned as chief of Special Branch field operations in the spring of 1966, after Tucker Gougleman's tour had ended and he was transferred to New Delhi. And once installed in the job, he began to initiate the organizational reforms that paved the way for Phoenix. To trace that process, it is helpful to understand the context.

"We were within the liaison branch," Brickham explained, "because we worked with the Vietnamese nationals, dealing with the CIO and Special Branch on questions of intelligence and counterespionage. The chief of the liaison branch was Jack Stent." Brickham's office was in the embassy annex, while Special Branch headquarters was located in the National Police Interrogation Center. As chief of field operations Brickham had no liaison responsibilities at the national level. "I had field operations," Brickham explained, "which meant the province officers. I managed all these liaison operations in the provinces, but not in the Saigon-Gia Dinh military district. That was handled by a separate section under Red Stent within the liaison branch."

As for his duties, Brickham said, "In our particular case, field operations was working both positive intelligence programs and counterespionage, because police do not distinguish between the two. Within the CIA the two are separate divisions, but when you're working with the police, you have to cover all this." Brickham compares the Special Branch "with an intelligence division in a major city police force, bearing in mind that it is within a national police organization with national, regional, province, and district police officers. There is a vertical chain of command. But it is not comparable with FBI, not comparable with MI Five, not comparable with Sûreté. It's the British Special Branch of police. . . . And with the Special Branch being concerned specifically with intelligence, it was the natural civilian agency toward which we would gravitate when the CIA got interested. Under Colby, the Special Branch became significant."

If under Colby (who was then chief of the CIA's Far East Division) the Special Branch became significant, then under Brickham it became effective. Brickham's job, as he defined it, "was to bring sharpness and focus to CIA field operations." He divided those operations into three categories: the Hamlet Informant program (HIP), which concerned low-level informants in the villages and hamlets; the Province Interrogation Center program, including Chieu Hoi and captured documents; and agent penetrations. "I did not organize these programs," he acknowledged. "They were already in place. What I did do was to clean up the act . . . *bureaucratize*. . . . We had some province officers trying to build PICs, while some didn't care. We even had police liaison people putting whistles on kites at night to scare away the VC when that wasn't part of their job. We were not supposed to be propagandists; that's covert operations' job."

As Brickham saw it, a Special Branch adviser should limit himself to his primary duties: training Vietnamese Special Branch case officers how to mount penetrations of the VCI, giving them cash for informers and for building interrogation centers, and reporting on the results. Brickham did this by imposing his management style on the organization. As developed over the years, that style was based on three principles: "Operate lean and hungry, don't get bogged down in numbers, and figure some way to hold their feet to the fire.

"When I got there, we had about fourteen province officers who were not distributed evenly around the country but were concentrated in population centers, the major ports, and provinces of particular interest. A lot of provinces were empty, so we had to fill them up, and we eventually got our strength up to fifty."

Training of incoming officers was done in Washington, although Brickham and his staff (including John Muldoon and an officer who handled logistics) gave them briefings on personal security, aircraft security, emergency behavior, and procedure—"what to do if your plane is shot down in VC territory or if the VC overrun a village you're working in. . . . Some guys took it seriously; some did not," Brickham noted. "We also gave them reading material—a *Time* magazine article on the Chinese mind and several books, the most important of which was *Village in Vietnam*. But we had to cut back on this because the stuff was constantly disappearing. Then, as the police advisory program expanded, Washington set up another training program for ex-police officers being brought in on contract and for military officers and enlisted men assigned to the agency. . . . We had a bunch of guys on contract as province officers who were not CIA officers, but who were hired by the agency and given to us."

Not the sort of man to suffer fools, Brickham quickly began weeding out the chaff from the wheat, recommending home leave for province officers who had operational fund shortages or were not at their posts or otherwise could not cut the mustard. Brickham's method of evaluating officers was a monthly report. "I wanted a province officer to tell me once a month every place he'd been and how long he'd been there. Normally this kind of thing wouldn't show up in a report, but it was important to me and it was important to the Vietnamese that our people 'show the flag' and be there when the action was going on. Reporting makes for accountability.

"A Special Branch monthly report, as I designed it, would go up to four pages in length and would take province officers two or three days to complete. . . . The reports were then sent in from the province through the region officer [a position Brickham placed in the chain of command], who wrote his report on top of it. We studied them in Saigon, packaged them up, and sent them on to Washington, where they had never seen anything like it."

To streamline the rapidly expanding Special Branch advisory program further, Brickham set up six regional offices and appointed region officers; Gordon Rothwell in Da Nang, for I Corps; Dick Akins in Nha Trang, handling the coastal provinces in II Corps; Tom Burke in Ban Me Thuot, handling Montagnard provinces; Sam Drakulich in Bien Hoa in III Corps; Bob Collier in My Tho for the northern Delta; and Kinloch Bull in Can Tho for the southern provinces. Brickham's liaison branch was the first to have region officers; the rest of the station was not operating that way. In fact, while the liaison branch had one officer in each province, reporting to a region officer, the discombobulated covert action branch had five or six programs in each province, with an officer for each program, with more than two hundred officers coming in and out of headquarters, each operating under the direct supervision of Tom Donohue.

Donohue scoffed at Brickham's attention to reporting. "My point, of course, was quite the opposite of Brickham's," he said. "I felt it was better to keep those guys working and not tie them up with paper work (that can be handled elsewhere). What I did was take *raw* reporting and give it to an officer who was not really any good in the field, and he was responsible for doing nothing but producing finished reporting from raw reporting. That takes the problem off the guys in the field. It's the same problem that so many sales organizations have: Do they want their people on the street or doing reports?'"[2]

Donohue's budget ("about twenty-eight million dollars a year") was considerably larger than his archrival Brickham's, which was approximately one million dollars a year. Otherwise, according to Brickham, "The main difference between Foreign Intelligence and Paramilitary was the fact that we had region officers, but the PM people worked directly out of Saigon. . . . And it was this situation that Hart wanted to straighten out.

"Hart's first move was to adopt this regional officer concept from the liaison branch," Brickham explained. "Second was to establish province officers so all CIA operations in a particular province came under one coordinated command. The fact that it operated on the other basis for as long as it did is almost unbelievable, but there was just too much money and not enough planning.

"The covert action people are a breed apart"—Brickham sighed—"especially the paramilitary types. They've had a sort of checkered history within the agency, and in Vietnam most of them were refugees from the Cuban failure. More than one of them said they were damned if they were going to be on the losing end of the Vietnam operation, too." Backing away from the knuckle draggers, Brickham noted: "We had very little to do with one another. They were located across the hall from us in the embassy annex, and we knew each other, and we were friends, and we drank beer together. But we had our separate programs, theirs being the covert programs the station was conducting in the provinces. The PM shop was basically an intelligence arm under cover, getting its own intelligence through armed propaganda teams, Census Grievance, and the whole Montagnard program run out of Pleiku. . . . Then they had the so-called counterterror teams, which initially were exactly as leftist propaganda described them. They were teams that went into VC areas to do to them what they were doing to us. It gets sort of interesting. When the VC would come into villages, they'd leave a couple of heads sticking on fence posts as they left. That kind of thing. Up there in I Corps there was more than one occasion where U.S. advisers would be found dead with nails through their foreheads."

As for the Census Grievance program, managed by John Woodsman, Brickham said, "We wanted access to its intelligence because they could get intelligence we didn't have access to. But because we were more compartmented within ourselves than we should have been, the police could not necessarily absorb this stuff. . . . The basic contract with the Vietnamese peasant," Brickham explained, "was that anything that was learned through Census Grievance would not be turned over to the police authorities. This was to get the confidence of the rural population. So we had almost nothing to do with it. It was for the province chief's advice and guidance. They took

Census Grievance stuff and turned around and used it in the counterterror teams, although on occasion they might turn something over to the military."

Brickham cited Chieu Hoi as "one of the few areas where police and paramilitary advisers cooperated."

Regarding his own programs, Brickham said, "All counterinsurgency depends in the first instance on informants; without them you're dead, and with them you can do all sorts of things. This is something that can only be a local operation. It's a family affair. A few piasters change hands."

In "The Future Applicability of the Phoenix Program," written for the Air University in 1974, CIA Province Officer Warren Milberg calls the Hamlet Informant program the focus of the Special Branch's "bread-and-butter" activities, designed specifically "to gain information from and on the people who lived in rural hamlets. . . . The problem," he writes, "was in recruiting informants in as many hamlets as possible." This task was made difficult by the fact that informing is dangerous work, so "it became necessary to do detailed studies of various motivational factors." Consequently, at the top of Special Branch recruitment lists were "people who had been victims of Viet Cong atrocities and acts of terrorism."[3]

Recruiting victims of VC terror as informers was a condition that dovetailed neatly with counterterror and the doctrine of Contre Coup. For, as David Galula explains, "pseudo insurgents are another way to get intelligence and to sow suspicion at the same time between the real guerrillas and the population."[4]

By 1965 defectors who joined counterterror teams had the words *Sat Cong* (Kill Communist) tattooed on their chests as part of the initiation ceremony to keep them from returning to former VC and NVA units. Their unit insignia was a machete with wings, while their unofficial emblem was the Jolly Roger skull and crossbones. When working, CTs dispensed with the regalia, donned black pajamas, and plundered nationalist as well as Communist villages. This was not a fact reported only by the leftist press. In October 1965, upon returning from a fact-finding mission to Vietnam, Ohio Senator Stephen Young charged that the CIA hired mercenaries to disguise themselves as Vietcong and discredit Communists by committing atrocities. "It was alleged to me that several of them executed two village leaders and raped some women," the *Herald Tribune* reported Young as saying.[5]

Indeed, CT teams disguised as the enemy, killing and otherwise abusing nationalist Vietnamese, were the ultimate form of psywar. It reinforced negative stereotypes of the Vietcong, while at the same time supplying Special Branch with recruits for its informant program.

In his autobiography, *Soldier,* Anthony Herbert tells how he reported for duty with SOG in Saigon in November 1965 and was asked to join a top-secret psywar program. "What they wanted me to do was to take charge of execution teams that wiped out entire families and tried to make it look as though the VC themselves had done the killing. The rationale was that other Vietnamese would see that the VC had killed another VC and would be frightened away from becoming VC themselves. Of course, the villagers would then be inclined to some sort of allegiance to our side.[6]

"I was told," writes Herbert, "that there were Vietnamese people in the villages who were being paid to point the finger." Intrigued, he asked how they knew for certain that the informer might not have ulterior motives for leading the death squads to a particular family. "I suggested that some of their informers might be motivated, for instance, by revenge or personal monetary gain, and that some of their stool-pigeons could be double or triple agents."[7]

Milberg concedes the point, noting that the Special Branch recruited informants who "clearly fabricated information which they thought their Special Branch case officers wanted to hear" and that when "this information was compiled and produced in the form of blacklists, a distinct possibility existed that the names on such lists had little relation to actual persons or that the people so named were not, in fact, members of the VCI."[8]

Such concerns, unfortunately, were overlooked in the rush to obtain information on the VCI. "The Special Branch kept records of people who had been victims of Viet Cong atrocities and acts of terrorism, of people who had been unreasonably taxed by the Viet Cong, of families which had had sons and husbands impressed into Viet Cong guerrilla bands, and those people who, for differing reasons, disliked or distrusted the Viet Cong. Depending on the incentive, be it patriotism or monetary gain, many hamlet residents were desirous of providing information on the activities of the local VCI. The Special Branch then constructed sometimes elaborate, sometimes simple plans to either bring these potential informants into province or district towns or to send undercover agents to the hamlets to interview them on a regular basis."[9]

In recommending "safe, anonymous" ways for informers to convey information, counterinsurgency guru David Galula cites as examples "the census, the issuing of passes, and the remuneration of workers." Writes Galula: "Many systems can be devised for this purpose, but the simplest one is to multiply opportunities for individual contacts between the population and the counterinsurgent personnel, every one of whom must participate in intelligence collection."[10] The idea, of course, is that "intelligence collection" is the primary task of the counterinsurgent and that all his contacts with the population are geared toward this purpose, whatever ulterior motive they may appear to have.

Apart from the Hamlet Informant program, Special Branch advisers also managed the PIC program—what Brickham called "a foundation stone upon which it was later possible to construct the Phoenix program. The PICs were places where defectors and prisoners could be taken for questioning under controlled circumstances," he explained. "Responsibility was handled by a small group assembled by Tucker Gougleman. This group worked with province officers setting up training programs for translators, clerks doing filing and collation, and interrogators. John Muldoon was the chief of this little group. He was CIA staff, and he had a good program there. Everything led me to believe that he was top-notch."

The third major program run by the Special Branch was agent penetrations, what Brickham termed "recruitment *in place* of Vietcong," adding, "This is by far the most important program in terms of gathering intelligence on the enemy. My motto was to recruit them; if you can't recruit them, defect them (that's Chieu Hoi); if you can't defect them, capture them; if you can't capture them, kill them. That was my attitude toward high-level VCI."

The penetration process worked as follows, according to OSS veteran Jim Ward, the CIA officer in charge of IV Corps between 1967 and 1969. An athletic, good-looking man, Ward noted, when we met together at his home, that the Special Branch kept dossiers on all suspected VCI in a particular area of operations, and that evidence was gathered from PIC interrogations, captured documents, and "walk-ins"—people who would walk into a police station and inform on an alleged VCI. When the accumulated evidence indicated that a suspect was a high-ranking VCI agent, that person was targeted for recruitment in place. "You didn't send out the PRU right away," Ward told me. "First you had to figure out if you could get access to him and if you could communicate with him once you had a relationship. Everybody in the Far East operates primarily by family, so the only opportunity of getting something like that would be through relatives who were accessible people. Does he have a sister or wife in town that we can have access to? A brother? Somebody who can reach him? Somebody he can trust? If that could be arranged, then you looked for a weakness to exploit. Is there any reason to believe he's been in this position for five years and hasn't been promoted when everybody else around him has been moving up the ladder? Does he bear resentment? Anything you can find by way of vulnerability that would indicate this guy might be amenable to persuasion to work for us."[11] Bribes, sex, blackmail, and drugs all were legitimate means of recruitment.

Speaking of the quality of Special Branch penetration agents, Brickham remarked, "We had some that were fairly good. By which I mean their information checked out." That information, he added, concerned "the movements and activities of district and province and COSVN cadre. COSVN people might come around on an inspection tour or an indoctrination mission.

Sometimes they had major political conferences where you might have a number of province and COSVN cadre together in one place. Now this is the kind of thing we'd go right after however we could. It was usually militarily; artillery if you could reach it."

Because of the unparalleled "intelligence potential" of penetrations, one of the main jobs of liaison advisers was training Special Branch case officers to handle penetration agents. At the same time, according to Brickham, "if the opportunity came their way, our own people would have a unilateral penetration into the VCI without their Special Branch counterparts knowing. These things for the most part were low-grade, but occasionally we had some people on the payroll as penetration agents who worked at district level, and as I recall, we had three or four at province level, which is fairly high up."

In 1967, Brickham told me, the CIA had "several hundred penetration agents in South Vietnam, most of them low-level." They were not cultivated over a period of years either. "In a counterinsurgency," he explained, "it's either quickly or not at all. However, the unilateral operations branch in the station went after some very high-level, very sophisticated target penetration operations." Since this unit played a major role in Phoenix, it requires a brief accounting.

The CIA's special operations unit for unilateral penetrations was largely the work of Sam Drakulich, the senior Special Branch adviser in III Corps in 1965. "I've always had a notion ever since I was a kid," Brickham said, "that it's the crazy people that have the bright ideas. So I've always been willing to play along with people like that, even though they're ignored by the other kids in school. Same thing with Drakulich. He had a lot of good ideas, but he was a little flaky—and he got more so. He refused to live in Bien Hoa, and he was the region officer in charge. Now I wanted all the region officers to live in their capitals. Anyway, Drakulich had a place to live out there, and it hadn't been bombed in thirty years; but he was terrified, so he came to Saigon every night. The point came [March 1966] where he was not supervising the province operations, and therefore, I persuaded Tucker to relieve him of duty.

"Howard 'Rocky' Stone [Jack Stent's replacement as chief of Foreign Intelligence (FI)] had just come into country and was putting on pressure for VCI penetrations. So what Tucker and I did—to respond to Stone, on the one hand, and to solve the Drakulich problem, on the other—was to create a high-level VCI penetration unit and switch Drakulich to run it."

Drakulich claimed to me, in a 1986 interview, that he had written a proposal for the high-level penetration unit before he was given the job by Brickham. Big and powerfully built, Drakulich said he designed the unit specifically to identify a group of high-level VCI that had killed, in broad daylight, a CIA officer on the main street of Bien Hoa. Hence his angst about sleeping overnight in Bien Hoa. In any event, Drakulich devised a special unit for penetrating the high-level VCI who were targeting CIA officers for assassination, and it was his contention that this special unit, which supplied blacklists to a special CT unit in Saigon, was the prototype for Phoenix.[12]

The special unit organized by Drakulich consisted of several high-ranking CIA officers who traveled through the country reviewing all penetration cases. This team would visit each province officer, interview everyone on his staff, evaluate all the cases, in some instances meeting with the agent, then determine which of the cases were promising enough to set up special arrangements. The special unit would bring back to Saigon the cases that were promising, and in Saigon, Brickham said, "We would apply special care to their development. We would nurture them, generate requirements, and make sure they had communications and full exploitation.

"Regardless of the potential importance of this job," Brickham added, "Sam could never adjust to the fact that he had been relieved of his regional officer job, and so he left Vietnam in the summer of 1966. And that was the end of that. Then Rocky Stone set up his special unit [under Burke Dunn] to take over what Sam Drakulich was supposed to be doing, and suddenly these cases, if they were thought to be good, would disappear from our purview all together.

"Stone pressed very hard for unilateral operations. He was interested in high-level penetrations of the VCI; I was interested in fighting a counterinsurgency war. As a result, he set up this separate shop, which took away my best operations—which is always a source of resentment. Stone and I later became best of friends, but not in this period." Brickham took a deep breath, then said solemnly, "This competition for intelligence sources is one of the underlying, chronic conflicts that you can't avoid. There's a tension because there are two different purposes, but you're utilizing basically the same resources.

"Anyway, the penetrations Stone wanted to take away were our unilaterals. Out in the provinces we would provide advice and guidance to the Special Branch for their penetrations into the VCI. But on our side, maybe through Chieu Hoi or some other resource, we would develop independent unilateral penetrations unknown to the police. We had a number of these around the country, and it's that kind of thing that Stone's special unit was interested in reviewing. And if it was very good, they'd take it away from us."

Not only did Rocky Stone abscond with the special unit, but he also took steps to have Special Branch field operations expelled from the station. This issue is central to Phoenix. "There was always a big fight in the agency as to how covert it should be," Brickham explained. "In particular, there was a lot of opposition in the station to the extent of exposure we had in

Special Branch field operations. So Stone came in and tried to reduce that operation in favor of unilateral espionage into the VCI. Which I resisted."

A believer in David Galula's theories on political warfare, Brickham stated, "My feelings were simple. We're in a war, an intelligence war, meaning fought on the basis of intelligence. It will either succeed or fail on intelligence. Special Branch field operations are a crucial element of this whole thing with Special Branch operations—informants, defectors, PICs—critical against the enemy infrastructure. American boys are over here who are being killed. We don't have time to worry about bureaucratic niceties. We don't have time to worry about reputations. We got to win the goddamned thing!

"So I was all gung ho for continuation and improvement of field operations. But Stone said, 'Get rid of field operations. I don't want it as part of my responsibility.' So I was turned over to the new Revolutionary Development Cadre unit that was run by Lou Lapham, who was brought out from Washington especially for that purpose."

CHAPTER 8

Attack on the VCI

In the summer of 1966 steps were finally taken in Washington and Saigon to resolve the debate over who should manage the pacification of South Vietnam. At the heart of the problem was the fact that despite the U.S. Army's success against NVA main force units in the Central Highlands, the Vietnamese people were not supporting the GVN to the extent that President Lyndon Johnson could withdraw American forces and leave the Vietnamese to manage the war on their own.

On one side of the debate was the Pentagon, recommending a single chain of command under MACV commander Westmoreland. The reasons were simple enough: The military was providing 90 percent of pacification resources, a single chain of command was more efficient, and there was danger in having unsupervised civilians in a battle zone. On the other hand, the civilian agencies were afraid that if the military managed pacification, any political settlement calling for the withdrawal of troops would also require civilians under military management (in, for example, refugee programs) to depart from Vietnam along with U.S. soldiers.

In 1965 Ambassador Henry Cabot Lodge had handed the problem to Ed Lansdale, whom he appointed senior liaison to the Ministry of Revolutionary Development. But Lansdale (a "fifth wheel," according to Brickham) was unwanted and ignored and failed to overcome the bureaucratic rivalries in Saigon. By 1966 the problem was back in Washington, where it was determined that pacification was failing as the result of a combination of poor management and the VCI's ability to disrupt Revolutionary Development. As a way of resolving these interrelated problems, President Johnson summoned his war managers to a conference at Warrenton, Virginia, in January 1966, the result of which was an agreement that a single pacification manager was needed. Once again, this point of view was advanced by the military through its special assistant for counterinsurgency and special activities, General William Peers, who suggested that the MACV commander be put in charge of pacification, with a civilian deputy.

Although the civilians continued to object, Johnson wanted quick results, the kind only the military could provide, and shortly thereafter he named National Security Council member Robert Komer his special assistant for pacification. Komer was an advocate of military control, whose master plan was to unite all agencies involved in pacification under his personal management and direct them against the VCI.

Meanwhile, the Saigon Embassy commissioned a study on the problem of interagency coordination. Begun in July 1966 under mission coordinator George "Jake" Jacobson, the Roles and Missions Study made eighty-one recommendations, sixty-six of which were accepted by everyone. Consensus had been achieved, and a major reorganization commenced. Notably, the policy for anti-VCI operations as stated by the Roles and Missions Study was "that the Police Special Branch assume primary responsibility for the destruction of the Viet Cong Infrastructure."[1]

"We did claim in Roles and Missions," according to Brickham, the CIA representative on that committee, "that the police should have a major civilian role and be the spearhead of the effort because it was the police over the long haul, and in terms of ultimate victory, that would have to settle the problem . . . and that therefore we should not let the military run eveything till the end of the war, then let everything fall into chaos when the military was brought out."[2]

But in pursuit of total victory, the size and pace of military operations were steadily escalating in 1966, more and more to the exclusion of the concerns of the civilian agencies involved in pacification. For example, the military was more concerned with gathering intelligence on the size and location of enemy combat units than on its political infrastructure. Military agent nets and interrogators zeroed in on this type of information, reflecting what Brickham termed the military mentality, the object of which is "to set up a battle." The police mentality, according to Brickham, is "to arrest, convict, and send to jail," while the intelligence mentality "is to capture, interrogate, and turn in place."

Expanding on this theme, Brickham said, "If the military were going into a province, the sector adviser and the sector S-two [sector intelligence adviser] would be brought in, do their thing, and come out without ever being aware of the enormous intelligence capability residing in the Special Police. When—in provinces manned by bright military officers—they did bring in the Special Police, it was done on an ad hoc basis. Conversely, anytime the military took over a civilian operation or activity, nine times out of ten it would be a perversion of the civilian capability into a military support arm. And when that happened, we would almost invariably find that the so-called civilian intelligence operation was quickly perverted to provide tactical combat intelligence for U.S. or ARVN forces. This was a tendency which had to be constantly opposed."

However, Brickham qualified his opposition to the emphasis on tactical military concerns by noting: "The CIA could not claim exclusive jurisdiction for an attack on the VCI. We would not have wanted to. Special Branch wasn't strong enough. It suffered from incompetent leadership and from poor training, even though Special Branch personnel and leadership were a cut above the regular staffing of the National Police."

What was needed was cooperation. But while turf battles between the CIA and the military were obstructing the war effort, the problem was exacerbated when the Vietnamese were factored into the equation. "Talk about bureaucratic infighting." Brickham laughed. "Well, it was far worse on the Vietnamese side. There was unquestionably contempt held by the ARVN for the National Police. The Vietnamese military had no use for them. And to the extent that the U.S. military may have reflected the ARVN point of view, if there was a joint ARVN-American operation, well, the Special Police would have been systematically cut out of the thing."

Into this bureaucratic minefield in August 1966 stepped Robert Komer, packing a mandate from President Johnson and intent upon effecting the military takeover of pacification. Predictably the civilian agencies recoiled in horror. The State Department cited the political nature of pacification, and neither the Agency for International Development nor the CIA thought the military capable of doing the job. So, under pressure from Ambassador Lodge (who bestowed upon Komer the nickname Blowtorch), President Johnson gave the civilians one last shot. The result was the Office of Civil Operations (OCO).

Formed in October 1966, OCO combined the field operations units of AID, USIS, and CIA and on this basis was organized into branches for psychological operations, political action, defectors, public safety, refugees, and economic development. Under the director, Wade Lathram, and his military deputy, General Paul Smith, OCO region directors were assigned to each corps; John Vann from AID in II Corps; State Department officer

Art Koren in I Corps; CIA officer Vince Heyman in IV Corps; and Robert Mattson in II Corps. Ed Lansdale was slated for Mattson's job but turned it down.

Given four months to show results, the Office of Civil Operations was doomed from the start, but it did prove valuable by forcing the civilian agencies to work together. Faced with the prospect of military control, agency chains of command—extending from Washington to Saigon to the provinces—were wrenched apart and realigned. And even though nothing was achieved in terms of improving pacification, the formation of the Office of Civil Operations spared MACV commander Westmoreland from having to reorganize the civilian agencies himself. In March 1967 President Johnson was to incorporate OCO within MACV under the Revolutionary Development Support Directorate, managed by General William Knowlton. Announced in May 1967, the Military Assistance Command for Civil Operations and Revolutionary Development (CORDS) was to be the bureaucratic vessel from which Phoenix would be born.

"During the big reorganization at the end of 1966," Brickham recalled, "they were trying to clean up the RD programs and streamline the war effort. So all the field operations, both covert and police Special Branch, were more or less divorced from the station and put under OCO, which was later called CORDS, in the Revolutionary Development Cadre Division. Lou Lapham came out from Washington to become the new deputy chief of station and chief of the RDC. I moved over from Rocky Stone's jurisdiction to Lapham's jurisdiction and answered to him. Lou was a very quiet, laid-back ex-professor with thick-rimmed glasses. He did not have a paramilitary background; his bag was propaganda and psychological warfare.

"RDC took over the CIA's covert action programs under its operations branch, RDC/O," Brickham explained, "while a second branch, RDC/P [Plans], took over police field operations. That was my shop. I no longer had the title of chief of field operations. But it was the same job with basically the same duties, except we were theoretically working toward a coordinated system. I became chief of RDC/P, and we and RDC/O moved from the embassy annex to another building called USAID Two. Donohue went home, and a new guy, Renz Hoeksema, came out from Washington and took over that shop. Renz and I had done two tours together in Teheran. He was a hard-driven officer, very smart . . . one of those Midwest Dutchmen of whom we have several in the agency." Brickham described Hoeksema as "ruthless" and "an expert on self-promotion."

"During the reorganization," Brickham continued, "the station adopted the Special Branch field operations organizational structure as a model for coordinating liaison and covert operations, only instead of using six regions, they used the four corp zones. My Tho and Ban Me Thuot were no longer regional offices." After that all CIA activities in a region were brought under one officer called the region officer in charge (ROIC). Likewise, province officers in charge followed automatically. "The POIC was in charge of all CIA operations, covert and liaison, in a province," Brickham explained. "He could have been drawn from liaison or covert operations, depending on who the ROIC thought was the best guy in the province. Incidentally, we did not actually assign POICs right away, because the rivalry and lack of trust between FI and PM people wouldn't allow it. When I talk about coordination problems in Vietnam, the fact is that we could not even coordinate the station programs in province.

"After the ROICs were named, we set up bases. The engineers went out and built vaults in each of these places and set up the complete multichannel automatic teleprinter encryptographic system radio communications. From this point on the line command went from the chief of station to the deputy chief of station for RDC, to the ROICs, then to the POICs. Renz Hoeksema and I were no longer supervisors in the chain of command to the field operations; we were now running branches as staff assistants to the chief of RDC, outside the station. It made little difference, except the ROICs would occasionally thumb their noses at us. But I didn't object. You couldn't run it any other way.

"So the major result of the fall 1966 decision was to separate the station and the counterinsurgency effort. That was a result of Stone's attitude toward this. And he was right. It's mixing oil and water."

One other significant event occurred at this juncture. "The Provincial Reconnaissance Units were offered to me in the fall of 1966," Brickham recalled. "It was one of the options discussed at the time of the reorganization. This offer was made to me in terms of John Hart's dissatisfaction with the reputation the CTs had acquired. He wanted to turn the CTs into an intelligence arm for capturing prisoners and documents, and not a paramilitary service. But I didn't want them," Brickham said, "mainly because I didn't think we could manage them properly. My Foreign Intelligence guys were in no way, in terms of experience, able to control or direct PRU teams." Consequently, as of November 1966 the recycled counterterrorists were called Provincial Reconnaissance Units and were thereafter managed by CIA officer William Redel in Renz Hoeksema's operations shop in CORDS's Revolutionary Development Cadre Division.

It is commonly agreed that the U.S. military went to Vietnam to fight a conventional war. However, by late 1966 it was clear that gains on the battlefield were transitory and that the war would not be won by seizing pieces of territory. Grudgingly the military was forced to admit that VCI political power could offset U.S. firepower. "Bear in mind," Brickham told me, "that the military was only over there from mid-1965, so it took a period of time for this realization to sink in. The exploitation of province National Police resources by the U.S. military was sporadic at best up until the fall of 1966, when we made a systematic procedure out of it."

Indeed, the process of systematizing the attack against the VCI began in the fall of 1966, when Rocky Stone arranged for Nelson Brickham to brief General Westmoreland on the subject. The impetus for the briefing came from the Roles and Missions Study and the conclusion reached at the 1966 Combined Campaign Plan that "increased emphasis will be given to identifying and eliminating the VC Infrastructure and to small unit operations designed specifically to destroy guerrilla forces."[3]

"These things were all evolving and coming together because of the Office of Civil Operations," Brickham noted. "People wanted to know what you meant when you said 'attack against the VCI.'" So, while preparing for his hourlong briefing of Westmoreland, Brickham wrote a paper aptly titled "Attack Against the Viet Cong Infrastructure." His purpose was to summarize everything that was known about intelligence sources and reaction forces involved in the antisubversive facet of the war. "I don't think Westy had ever heard of the Special Branch before our briefing," Brickham quipped, "or the fact that we had provincial interrogation centers or political order of battle files on VC in the villages and districts."

In any event, "Attack" was circulated among the MACV and CIA staffs and was accepted as the definitive statement on the VCI. Written on November 22, 1966, "Attack" is significant for three reasons. First was its definition of the VCI "as the VC organizational hierarchy, the management structure, as opposed to guerrillas, troops, and even in many cases VC terrorists. Many if not most of these categories—guerrillas, troops and even terrorists—are young people who have been either impressed or seduced into the VC and cannot in any way be considered 'hard core' Communists."[4]

Specifically cited in "Attack" as VCI were "all Party members and front organization officers, as opposed to the rank and file of these front organizations. Thus all members of a village chapter, all District Committee and all Province Committee cadre are included, as of course are the higher echelons, Region and COSVN. We would also include members of the so-called sapper units—these people are hardened Communist troops, organized in military formations to carry out sabotage and terrorism of the larger and more dramatic nature—hotel bombings in Saigon, Long Binh Ammunition dump, General Walt's residence. These latter are not casual acts of terrorism, but carefully planned and fully organized military operations—Commando type operations."[5]

About the word "infrastructure," Brickham said during our interview, "it may be peculiarly applicable to insurgency, due to the animistic conceptual view held by rural people in want of literacy and hygiene, let alone technology." Brickham held the revisionist view that in an insurgency among such people, only 5 percent of the population is politically active, with 2½ percent for the insurgents, and 2½ percent against them. The rural population is not the driving force. Their attitude, he said, is "a pox upon both your houses.

"Without an infrastructure," Brickham said, "there is only a headless body. Destroy the infrastructure, you destroy the insurgency. However, this is not such an easy thing to do, despite any disaffection on the part of the majority of the people. Nor is it exclusively a matter of winning hearts and minds. That only makes it easier to destroy the infrastructure." Brickham viewed the VCI as a criminal conspiracy, a Mafia operating under the pretense of political ideology, coercing people through the selective use of terror. The insurgency, in his opinion, attracted people oriented toward violence and, through political fronts, "naive" individuals. The presence of such marginal characters, he contends, made the attack on the VCI a difficult task.

Secondly, "Attack" is significant in that it defines "the attack against the VCI" in terms of Special Branch field operations—informants, interrogations, and penetrations—of which interrogations are "by far the most important source." Informant operations produced information mostly on hamlet and village cadres and guerrillas, while penetrations could produce "substantial bodies of infrastructure information—identification of cadre, movements and activities—and at times advance information of meetings and conferences." As of September 30, 1966, as stated in "Attack," there were 137 penetrations of district committees, 93 belonging to Special Branch, 44 to the CIO. Special Branch was then developing 92 more penetrations, and the CIO 61.

The "action tools" in the attack on the VCI were primarily "ambushes by the police, PRU or Regional Forces and Special Forces elements" and "military search and destroy, hamlet search, or 'Country Fair' type operations. For these operations," Brickham explains in "Attack," "the police prepare search lists from their files . . . and collect VC defectors and other sources to use as 'identifiers' of VC caught in these cordon and sweep operations." Even though William Colby later testified to Congress that Phoenix was a South Vietnamese police program, Brickham in "Attack" states: "A final and not insignificant tool are direct military operations. . . . For example, 175m artillery fire was directed on the reported site of a combined conference [of] COSVN representatives." On the basis of afteraction reports, Brickham writes, "we are confident that the damage to the infrastructure, in terms of key personnel killed, is significant."[6]

"Attack" also mentions "A special Task Force . . . organized to launch a combined intelligence/police/military assault against the MR-4 (Saigon/

Cholon/Gia Dinh Special Zone Committee) headquarters and base area."[7] This is the third significant point raised by "Attack." Called Cong Tac IV by its Vietnamese creators, it is the operational model for Phoenix and as such deserves a detailed explanation.

General McChristian writes that Cong Tac IV evolved, concurrently with the joint U.S.-Vietnamese Combined Intelligence Staff, from an intensive intelligence program (Project Corral) which he initiated in the spring and early summer of 1966 and directed against MR-4. The purpose was to produce "intelligence on the identification and location of Viet Cong operating in MR-4" and "the dissemination of this intelligence to user agencies for apprehension and exploitation of enemy personnel."[8]

In September 1966 McChristian met with General Loan to discuss his plans for a combined intelligence staff. The idea was approved in November by Prime Minister Ky, the Vietnamese Joint General Staff, and the U.S. Mission Council. As a result—and as a substitute for Hop Tac—Operation Fairfax was begun in December, using three American and three ARVN battalions for the purpose of "searching out and destroying VC main force units, guerrillas, and infrastructure in the MR-4 area." Operation Fairfax and the Combined Intelligence Staff (CIS) were the primary elements of Cong Tac IV.[9]

"The initial actions of the Combined Intelligence Staff," McChristian writes, "were to compile a blacklist of MR-4 infrastructure personalities in support of the combined US and Vietnamese military actions in this area." In the process, the Combined Intelligence Staff compiled, by hand, more than three thousand names, which were stored in a central registry and made available to U.S. and Vietnamese units. Later "the systematic identification and location of VC and the rapid retrieval of these data in usable form was [*sic*] made possible by the use of the automated data processing system located at the Combined Intelligence Center, Vietnam."[10]

In fact, the foundation for the Combined Intelligence Staff was laid, on the American side, in 1964, when CIA security chief Robert Gambino created the Combined Security Committee inside Saigon's First Precinct headquarters. Through a secure radio network linking each of Saigon's nine precincts, the Combined Security Committee coordinated CIA and State Department security officers at the American Embassy with MACV and Vietnamese Military Security Service officers at Tan Son Nhut and with the Special Branch at National Police headquarters and alerted them of pending VC attacks. The Combined Security Committee was directed by Colonel Nguyen Ngoc Xinh, chief of staff of the Saigon police and the deputy to the Saigon police chief, Lieutenant Colonel Nguyen Van Luan. By mid-1967 the Combined Security Committee's "Blue Network" covered all of CT IV.

* * *

For deeper insights into Cong Tac IV we turn to Tulius Acampora, a U.S. Army counterintelligence officer and Korean War veteran who was detached to the CIA in June 1966 as General Loan's adviser. As an officer on General James Van Fleet's staff in Korea, Acampora had had prior dealings with John Hart, who as station chief in Korea had masqueraded as an Army colonel and had interfered in military operations to the extent that General Van Fleet called him "an arrogant SOB."[11] The old grudges were carried forward in Saigon to the detriment of Phoenix.

"I *assisted* Hart." Acampora sighed when we first met in 1986 at Ft. Myers. "He called me in and said, 'We're dealing with an enigma. A cobra. General Loan.' Now Loan had a mandarin Dai Viet background, and his father had rescued Diem. Consequently, under Ky, Loan was very powerful; and Hart resented Loan's concentration of power. Although he was not a political animal, Loan was substantial. So Hart took away first his supervision of the Military Security Service and eventually his oversight of Central Intelligence Organization. But for a while Loan ran them both, along with the National Police.

"When I arrived in Saigon," Acampora continued, "at the national level, the U.S. Embassy, with the agency and MACV, had decided to take over everything in order to change the *political climate* of Vietnam. Through the CIO, the agency was running all sorts of counteroperations to VC infiltration into political parties, trying to find *compatible elements* to create a counterforce to take over control from Ky, who was a peacock. This was done by intercepting VC political cadre: surveilling them, then arresting them or moving toward them, then buying them over to your side in order to destroy the integrity of the VC." Acampora qualified this statement by noting: "The VC would always say yes, but they were usually doubles.

"It was a dual-level scheme," Acampora went on. "We were faced with the threat of terrorism from sappers, but we also had to stop them at the political level. We stopped them at sapper level with PRU under the Special Operations Group and at the political level through the CIO—the centerpiece of which was the National Interrogation Center under [Special Branch chief Nguyen] Tien. The CIO operated over and above CT Four. It could take whatever it wanted—people or information or whatever—from any of its elements. Its job was to turn around captured VCI and preempt Loan. When it came to CT Four, however, Loan wanted control. Loan said to Hart, 'You join us; we won't join you.' In effect, Loan told Hart to go screw himself, and so Hart wanted *me* to assuage Loan—to bring him in tow."

But this was not to be, for General Loan, a dyed-in-the-wool nationalist, had his own agenda. In fact, the basis for CT IV derived, on the Vietnamese side, from a countersubversion program he commissioned in the summer of 1966. The thrust of the program was to prevent VC agents from infiltrating pro-GVN political parties and to prevent sappers from entering Saigon. Called the Phung Hoang program, it was, according to Acampora, "wholly inspired and conducted by the Vietnamese."

The man who conceived Phung Hoang at the request of General Loan was the Special Branch deputy director, Colonel Dang Van Minh, a Claude Rains type of character who, according to Acampora, was "a stoic who took the path of least resistance." Born on Con Son Island, where his father was a nurse, Minh at age eighteen joined the accounting department of the French Sûreté. During the Ngo regime he received CIA training overseas and was then appointed chief of the Judicial Police—the only National Police branch with the power to arrest. After the coup Minh became deputy director of the Special Branch.

Insulated behind his desk at Special Branch headquarters on Vo Thanh Street, Minh weathered each successive regime by serving his bosses as "a professional intelligence officer." Indeed, when I met Minh at his office in 1986, he attributed the fall of Saigon to "the many changes of command in Saigon, while North Vietnam had only one leader and one chain of command."[12] That, plus the fact that the Vietcong had infiltrated every facet of the GVN—a fact Loan also acknowledged when he confessed to Acampora, "We're twenty percent infiltrated, *at least*."

Minh's attack against the VCI was measured, sophisticated and diametrically opposed to American policy. In contrast with Brickham, Minh viewed the VCI as village-level cadres "to be monitored, not killed." As Minh conceived the attack on the VCI, all Vietnamese agencies receiving information on the VCI would forward their reports to the Special Branch for inclusion in its political order of battle file. The goal was the "combination of intelligence," as Minh termed it, *phoi hop* in Vietnamese. Seeking an appropriate acronym, Minh borrowed the *Ph* from *phoi* and the *Ho* from *hop* and christened the program Phung Hoang, after the mythological Vietnamese bird of conjugal love that appears only in times of peace. In Vietnamese myth, the Phung Hoang bird holds a flute and represents virtue, grace, peace, and concord. Its song includes the five notes of the Vietnamese musical scale, and its feathers include the five basic colors.

Before long, however, Phung Hoang was transformed into Phoenix, the mythological bird that perpetually rises from its own ashes. As the Americans drew it, the bird held a blacklist in its claw. In this manifestation, Phoenix is an omnipotent, predatory bird that selectively snatches its prey—a symbol of discord rather than harmony.

Nowhere is the gap between American and Vietnamese sensibilities more apparent than in their interpretations of Phoenix and Phung Hoang, which also represent the struggle between General Loan and John Hart for control over the attack on the VCI. In this contest, Loan scored first when, for legal reasons, Cong Tac IV was placed under his control. Loan assigned as many as fifty officers to the program from the participating Vietnamese agencies, with Major Nguyen Mau in charge of operations, assisted by Dang Van Minh. The United States provided twenty MACV counterintelligence officers, each of whom served as a desk officer in a Saigon precinct or outlying district capital. CIA officer Tom Becker supervised the headquarters staff; the Australians assigned their embassy security officer, Mike Leslie; and the Koreans provided a representative. Members of CT IV were not part of any separate unit but remained identified with their parent agencies and did not have to back-channel to bring resources to bear.

Cong Tac IV came into existence on November 1, 1966, the day Lou Lapham arrived in Saigon to take over the "second" station, as the Revolutionary Development Cadre program was sometimes called. Curiously, it was the same day that VC mortars first fell on Saigon. U.S. generals, dozing in reviewing stands only a few blocks away, were oblivious of the fact that the VC were using a nearby church spire as a triangulation point for their fire.

From November 1 onward, Tully Acampora managed CT IV with Major Mau. The program kicked in when Tom Becker, assisted by MACV officers Larry Tracy and John Ford adopted the standard American police ID kit (replete with Occidental facial features). With their ID kits in hand, CT IV desk officers ventured into the precincts and districts, accompanied by Special Branch and Military Security Service officers. They screened suspects who had been corralled by military units conducting cordon and search operations, took photographs, put together composites of suspected VCI members, then compiled the results and sent their reports to CT IV headquarters in the National Police Interrogation Center in Saigon, where it was collated, analyzed, and used to compile blacklists of the VCI.

"They called it police work," Acampora said, "because the police had the constitutional responsibility for countersubversion. But it was paramilitary. In any event, Loan was going to bring it all together, and he did, until Komer came out in February 1967 and was briefed by Mau and Tracy."

In a 1986 interview with the author, Tracy agreed that the demise of CT IV came from "politicking" on the part of the Americans. "It was short-lived," he told me, "because Komer saw it as a prototype and wanted to make it nationwide before working out the methodology. Komer wanted to use CT Four as a showcase, as part of the Combined Intelligence Staff, but General Loan was reluctant to participate and had to be strong-armed by Komer in February 1967."[13]

By April 1967 the Combined Intelligence Staff would have entered more than sixty-five hundred names in its Cong Tac IV data base and would be adding twelve hundred per month. As the methodology was developed, a search unit consisting of three forty-nine-man Field Police platoons began accompanying the U.S. and Vietnamese military units conducting cordon and search operations in MR-4. With the military providing a shield, the Field Police checked IDs against blacklists, arrested VCI suspects, and released innocent bystanders. According to General McChristian, "From the inception of the Combined Intelligence Staff until 1 December 1967, approximately 500 VC action agents were apprehended in Saigon and environs. The significance of these arrests—and the success of the staff—cannot be fully measured, but unquestionably contributed to the Communist failures in Saigon during the 1968 Tet offensive."[14]

Whether or not Tet was a failure for the VC will be discussed later. But once the CIA had committed itself to the attack on the VCI, it needed to find a way of coordinating its efforts with the other civilian agencies, American and Vietnamese, working independently of each other in the provinces. Considering the number of agencies involved, and their antipathy, this was no easy thing to do. To wit, at Nelson Brickham's request, the liaison officer in Gia Dinh Province, John Terjelian, did a study on the problem of coordination. "The count he made," Brickham recalled, "was something like twenty-two separate intelligence agencies and operations in his province alone. It was a Chinese fire drill, and it didn't work because we had so many violently conflicting interests involved in this thing."

But while the bureaucratic titans clashed in Saigon, a few military and CIA officers—in remote provinces where battles raged and people died—were trying to cooperate. In the northernmost region, I Corps, the Marines and the CIA had especially good relations, with the Marines supplementing many of the agency's personnel needs and the CIA in turn sharing its intelligence. Because of this reciprocal relationship, a solution to the problem of interagency coordination was developed there, with much of the credit going to Bob Wall, a CIA paramilitary officer in Quang Ngai Province. In December 1966 Wall was made deputy to I Corps region officer in charge, Jack Horgan. Wall recalled, when we met in 1987: "In the winter of 1966 to '67, General Lou Walt was the First Marine Amphibious commander and we [the CIA region staff] would cross the river to attend his briefings each morning. Casualties were minimal, and he was the picture of a marine, taking his briefings quickly, sitting erect at his desk. Within the next two months, however, casualties rose from two or three a day to ninety a day—and yet the VC body count was minimal." Said Wall: "Walt went to the picture of abject frustration, slumped at his desk, his head in his hands. He needed help.[15]

"My experience had been as cadre officer in Quang Ngai, where I ran the PATs, the PRU, and Census Grievance," added Wall. "Forbes was the Special Branch adviser but there was no coordination between us and the military or AID. There were about fifteen separate programs in Quang Ngai, and it took me awhile to realize this was the problem. Then I got transferred to Da Nang, where as a result of Walt's inability to make contact with the enemy, I personally proposed Phoenix, by name, to establish intelligence close to the people. Based on a British model in Malaya, we called it a DIOCC, a District Intelligence and Operations Coordination Center."

Having learned through the Quang Ngai Province Interrogation Center the structure of the VCI in the province, Wall was aware that the VCI operated from the hamlet up and that to destroy it the CIA would have to create in the districts what the PICs were doing in the provinces. Hence the DIOCC.

"Walt grabbed it," Wall recalled. "He assigned a crackerjack sergeant to make the necessary equipment available, and this sergeant set it up in Dien Ban, just south of Da Nang in Quang Nam Province. Then we did two more"—in Hieu Nhon and Phuong Dien districts in Thua Thien Province.

The Dien Ban DIOCC went into effect in January 1967 and was the model on which Phoenix facilities were later built throughout Vietnam. A prefab building ten by forty feet large, it was built by marines and located in their district compound. On duty inside were Sergeant Fisher and Lieutenant Morse, along with two people from Census Grievance, one from RD Cadre, and one from Special Branch. There were two interpreter-translators and three clerk-typists. Census Grievance supplied desks, typewriters, and a file cabinet. The Marines supplied the wall map and an electric fan. Office supplies came from the CIA's paramilitary officer in Quang Nam Province. A radio was used for high-priority traffic, with normal communications going by landline to other districts and Third Marine HQ. It was not a sophisticated affair.

The purpose of the DIOCC was that of an intelligence clearinghouse: to review, collate, and disseminate critical information provided by the various intelligence agencies in the area. But what made it innovative was that dissemination was immediate at the reaction level, whereas the member agencies had previously reported through their own channels to their province headquarters, where the information was lateraled to other interested agencies, which then passed it down to the districts. Also, a summary was made at the end of each day. In the Dien Ban DIOCC, the Americans handled the record keeping, with Lieutenant Morse managing the order of battle reporting and Sergeant Fisher taking care of the VCI files and source control cards. In order to protect agents, each agency identified its own sources by number.

Local Marine and ARVN commanders made units available as reaction forces for the DIOCC. More than one hundred policemen in Dien Ban were also made available, along with the Provincial Reconnaissance Unit from the province capital in Hoi An. The DIOCC provided guides from Census Grievance, and the police supplied ID kits, to the operating units. The Marines screened civilian detainees (CDs) arrested in operations, using informants or Special Branch officers to check names against the DIOCC's blacklist. When a positive identification was made, they delivered the suspect to the PIC in Hoi An. A marine detached to the PIC, Warrant Officer Richardson, made a daily run from the PIC to the DIOCC, bringing interrogation reports and other province-generated information. Most CDs were turned over to district police, at which point, the Americans complained, they paid bribes and returned home, there to be arrested again and again.

"Phoenix," insisted Wall, "represented the strategy that could have won the war. The problem was that Phoenix fell outside Foreign Intelligence, and paramilitary programs are historically trouble for intelligence. So Phoenix never got primary attention. MACV did not have the mentality to work with the police, the police were not trained to win hearts and minds, and [Minister of Interior] Khiem, fearing a coup, mistrusted the police and would not assign quality personnel. Phoenix did not work in Vietnam because it was dominated," Wall told me, "by the military mentality. They couldn't believe they would lose."

CHAPTER 9

ICEX

In May 1967 CIA officer Robert Komer arrived in Saigon as deputy for Civil Operations and Revolutionary Development. Thereafter he was called the DEPCORDS, a job that afforded him full ambassadorial rank and privileges and had him answering only, in theory, to MACV Commander William Westmoreland and Ambassador Ellsworth Bunker.

"I'd known Komer from 1952, when he was with the Office of National Estimates," Nelson Brickham told me,[1] "which from the beginning was a high-level organization. Komer would go on to move from one high-level job to another, and in 1967, of course, he was working for the national security adviser, Walt Rostow, in the White House. Komer and I always chatted when he came around and talked to the branches, as he had been doing since February 1967. But in May he was even more acerbic than before. Komer was intensely ambitious, intensely energetic, intensely results-oriented.

"In May," Brickham continued, "in connection with Komer coming out to run CORDS, Hart called me into his office one day and said, 'I want you to forget your other duties—you're going home in June anyway—and I want you to draw me up a plan for a *general staff for pacification.*' I was still chief of field operations," Brickham noted, "so my replacement, Dave West, was sent out early to free me up while I was working on this special paper. Then I asked for another officer in the station [John Hansen] to work with me on this paper. He was counterespionage. But he was also into computers, and he could say the right things about computers and be persuasive in ways that I could not. So Hansen was assigned to me, and we set about writing it up. Hansen focused on the computer end of this thing, and I focused on the organizational end.

"In complying with John Hart's request for a general staff for pacification, there were three things I had to review: strategy, structure, and management. Now the important thing to remember is that *we were never at war in Vietnam*. The ambassador was commander in chief. The MACV commander was under him. So all the annual military operations and everything else were focused under the Country Plan rather than a strictly military plan. And I was the principal agency representative each year for the development of next year's Country Plan.

"Regarding strategy, basically this was it: We had an army to provide a shield from North Vietnamese field units and to engage in military sweeps to go after Vietcong units. . . . And the Vietnamese Army did basically the same thing. That's in-country military. Pacification efforts . . . were to operate behind the military shield to stabilize and to secure the situation. That's the civilian side. Then you had out-of-country military, which was aircraft reconnaissance, naval blockades, bombing operations in the DMZ and along the Ho Chi Minh Trail, and operations in North Vietnam, Laos, and Cambodia.

"My point," Brickham emphasized, "was not to change anything, just do it better. We didn't need more intelligence; we needed better intelligence, properly analyzed and collated. That's the strategy.

"Next, the structure, which, of course, was interagency in nature and encompassed MACV, CIA, CORDS, Revolutionary Development, and the embassy. Now when you start fooling around with other agencies, you're in trouble. Each one has its own legislative mandate, meaning its job prescribed by Congress or as defined in the Constitution. Then there is legislative funding, funds allocations, accounting procedures, and the question of who is going to pay for something. Those legislative givens have to be respected. I as a CIA officer cannot set up an organizational arrangement where I'm going to spend Pentagon money unless the Pentagon gives it. And even if they give it to me, it still has to be within the framework of the congressional appropriation. Then there are the bureaucratic empires, in both Saigon and Washington, all deeply committed to these things. You have overlap, contradictory programs, ill-conceived ventures which receive hearings; time is wasted, and you get corruption, embezzlement, and low morale. And yet somehow you have to pull all these different agencies together."

In looking for a solution, Brickham seized on the personality and presidential mandate of Robert Komer. "Komer had already acquired the nickname Blowtorch," Brickham said, "and his position was a bureaucratic anomaly. He was a deputy ambassador on a par with General [Creighton] Abrams . . . but actually he was reporting to Lyndon Johnson, and everyone knew that. So my idea was to set up a board of directors in which each agency head or his deputy was a member, then establish a reporting system that would allow a guy like Komer to hold their feet to the fire—to make each agency responsive, to give it goals and targets, and to criticize its failures in performance, whether deliberately or inadvertently through sloppiness.

"Remember, the strategy was to sharpen up intelligence collection and analysis and to speed up the reaction time in responding to intelligence, whether on a military or a police level. So the idea was to set up a structure in which agencies *had* to participate and *had* to bring their own resources and funds to bear, without interfering with their legislative mandate or financial procedures."

In determining how to do this, Brickham borrowed an organizational model from the Ford Motor Company, which, he said, had "set up a command post to run their operations, with the policy of the corporation coming from the chief executive officer and a board of directors. Call it the operating committee at the top, supported by a statistical reporting unit that put everything together for the chief executive and the board of directors, giving management the bottom line for them to consider and make decisions. . . . This became the basic structure for the general staff, which Hart was calling ICEX—intelligence coordination and exploitation. I wrote it so the different agencies would provide their own money, personnel, and direction, but as part of a machinery by which they would be directed to a specific purpose."

Having formulated a strategy and structure, Brickham turned to management, which for him boiled down to two things: the bottom line, telling management only what it needed to know; and using reporting as a tool to shape behavior, as articulated by Rensis Likert in *New Patterns of Management*.

"Basically," Brickham explained, "a reporting format fosters self-improvement, *if* the people reporting know what they are expected to do, and are provided with objective measurements of performance in terms of those expectations. . . . So we designed the reporting structure to provide critical types of information to the ICEX board of directors, primarily Komer. But also, by focusing attention in the regions and the provinces on the things we felt were important, we tried to guarantee that those things worked properly."

In particular, Brickham hoped to correct "the grave problem of distortion and cover-up which a reporting system must address." In explaining this problem to Komer, Brickham quoted a CIA officer who had criticized "the current system of reporting statistics that prove . . . that successive generations of American officials in Vietnam are more successful than their predecessors." The officer observed that "Americans in the field, the majority of whom serve a one-year tour . . . go through a honeymoon phase in which they try to see everything good about their counterpart and about the situation and report it thus. Then they go through a period of disillusionment in which they realize that nothing has been accomplished, but by this time they have become the victims of their own past reports and they have to maintain the fiction. Ultimately they go out of there very discouraged and probably very unhappy with their own performance because about the same time they become knowledgeable enough to really do something they are on their way home and have no desire to hurt their own professional career."

Explained Brickham: "The key to ICEX was decentralization"—in other words, forcing field officers to do their jobs by putting responsibility on the scene, while at the same time trying to deliver to these officers the kinds and amounts of information they needed, fast. "This means feedback," Brickham stressed, "which reflects and recognizes the province officer's own activities, tells him what other people are doing, identifies to him the important and reportable activities, and induces a competitive and emulative spirit."

Keyed to Special Branch reporting cycles, the initial ICEX reporting format was submitted monthly and contained narrative and statistical data responding to requirements from Washington, Saigon, and the regions. It reflected the activities, understanding, and writing abilities of field officers, enabling managers like Komer to judge performance. It also revealed program progress and functioning of related systems. Meanwhile, John Hansen was developing a comprehensive input sheet capable of listing every piece of biographical information on VCI individuals, operations, and organization in general. He was also designing collated printouts on the VCI, which were to be sent to region, province, and district ICEX officers plugged into the ICEX computer system.

"Anyway," said Brickham, "those were the ideas that involved this statistical reporting unit for the ICEX staff, which was to pull everything together and analyze it. The statistical reporting unit was the guts, with a plans and programs unit and a special investigations unit tacked onto it."

On May 22, 1967, Nelson Brickham and John Hansen delivered to Komer a three-page memo titled "A Concept for Organization for Attack on VC Infrastructure." Hurriedly prepared, it recommended four things. First was the creation of a board of directors chaired by the DEPCORDS and including the senior intelligence and operations officers from MACV, CIA, and CORDS—a general staff for pacification under Robert Komer. Next, it recommended the creation of a command post in Saigon and ICEX committees in the regions and provinces. Thirdly, it recommended that the Americans "coordinate and focus" the attack on the VCI and that they "stimulate" their Vietnamese counterparts. Lastly, it recommended that province officers create DIOCCs, which Brickham called "the essential ingredient in the Phoenix [as ICEX would eventually be renamed] stew."

The concept paper was approved by the CIA station, then sent to Komer, who turned it down. As Brickham recalled, "Komer said, 'A concept paper is not what I want. I want a *missions and functions* paper—something in military style that the military can understand.'"

"At this point," Brickham said, "I was seconded over to Komer's office. He was buying everything that we proposed to him, but he wanted to develop 'action papers.' He kept repeating, over and over again, that he wanted a 'rifle shot' approach—a sniper's attack, not a shotgun approach—against the VCI. And Komer is a stickler. He was constantly throwing papers back at me to rewrite over and over again until they satisfied him in those terms."

In response to Komer's demands, Brickham and Hansen incorporated the major themes of the concept paper into a detailed missions and functions paper titled "A Proposal for the Coordination and Management of Intelligence Programs and Attack on the VC Infrastructure and Local Irregular Forces." What resulted, according to Brickham, "was not a general staff planning body, but an executive action organization that was focused on getting the job done, not thinking about it, by taking advantage of Komer's dynamic personality."

Eleven pages long (plus annexes on interrogation, data processing, and sceening and detention of VCI), "A Proposal" was accepted by Komer in early June 1967. Its stated purpose was: "to undertake the integration of efforts of all US and GVN organizations, both in intelligence collection and processing and in operations directed against the elimination of the VC Infrastructure and irregular forces" and "to insure that basic programs conducted by different organizations and components, as they relate to the elimination of the VCI, are made mutually compatible, continuous, and fully effective."[2]

ICEX as the embodiment of executive action had emerged as the solution to the problem posed by the VCI. It was a "machine" composed of joint committees at national, corps, province, and district levels. At the top sat Robert Komer as chairman of the board, setting policy with the approval of the ambassador and MACV commander. Serving as Komer's command post was the ICEX Directorate in Saigon, to be headed by "the senior U.S. coordinator for organizing the overall attack on the VCI."[3]

The ICEX Directorate was to be subdivided into three units. The intelligence unit was to be composed of two senior liaison officers—one from MACV and one from the CIA—who were to prepare briefings, conduct special investigations, and evaluate the effectiveness of the attack on the VCI.

The operations (aka the plans and programs) unit was to be composed of three program managers who planned activities, set requirements, managed funds, and were responsible for three specific problem areas: (1) intelligence collection programs and their coordination and reaction operations; (2) screening, detention, and judicial processing of VC civil defendants; and (3) the interrogation exploitation of VC captives and defectors. How ICEX handled these problem areas will be discussed at length in Chapter 10.

The reports management unit was to refine the attack on the VCI through the science fiction of statistical analysis. Reports officers were to help program managers "in developing reports to be required from Region and Province" and to analyze those reports. The reports dealt with province staffing; prisoner and defector accession and disposition; RD team locations, actions, and casualties; quantitative and qualitative descriptions of intelligence reports and PRU operations; and province inspection reports, among other things. The reporting unit included an inspections team because, as Brickham observed, "Everybody lies. . . . These guys are supposed to be on the road most of the time, dropping in unexpectedly to look at your files and to verify what was being reported to us in writing was true."

ICEX field operations were to be grafted onto the CIA's liaison and covert action programs, with the region and province officers in charge continuing to manage those programs and in most cases assuming the added job of ICEX coordinator. The ICEX Province Committee was to be "the center of gravity of intelligence operations against the VCI." The ICEX province coordinator in turn was to establish and supervise DIOCCs (usually seven or eight per province), "where the bulk of the attack on the low level infrastructure and local guerrilla forces must be generated and carried out." ICEX committees at each level were to be composed of the senior intelligence, operations, and pacification officers. And the ICEX coordinator was to "recommend and generate operations for the attack on infrastructure" and "stimulate Vietnamese interagency cooperation and coordination."[4]

"I'm a great advocate of committee meetings," Brickham told me, "provided they're properly run. That's why Phoenix wound up as a committee structure at nation, region, province, and district levels. A joint staff at every level down to district is the essence of Phoenix. We hoped the committee structure would be a nonoperative kind of thing, but we had to have some machinery for bringing together everybody involved in these programs."

Added Brickham: "Some Phoenix coordinators were from the Agency for International Development or the military. They didn't have to be CIA. Same with the province officer in charge; the POIC would be a member of the Phoenix committee, whether or not he was the coordinator." However, insofar as the PICs and the PRU were the foundation stones of Phoenix, if someone other than the CIA province officer in charge was the ICEX Province Committee chairman or its coordinator, that person was totally dependent on the POIC for access to information on, and reaction forces for use against, the VCI. In addition, the committee structure allowed the CIA to deny plausibly that it had anyone operating in the DIOCCs.

"I was opposed to the DIOCCs at the beginning," Brickham admitted, "but after I visited three places up north and wrote the early June paper, I had converted into believing in them as important. . . . And then Komer said we could have as many men as we asked for, and at that point we tried to get district officers." In any event, according to Brickham, "ICEX institutionalizes the thing."

"Okay," said Brickham. "Komer approved this, and we sent a cable to Washington headquarters outlining the situation and requesting approval. And we got a cable back from Colby which basically said, 'Well, we don't know what you're going to do.' And as I recall, they suggested that we sort of pull in our horns."

"Well, we said, 'This is the only way to do it, so we'll just go ahead and do it.' We came up with the ambassador's approval out there in the field, so back in Washington they were left with a fait accompli. And the irony is, Colby had *nothing* to do with ICEX or Phoenix. He *had* to go along with it. It was approved by Komer and the ambassador and the White House, so we implemented it." At that point Nelson Brickham returned to Washington for a job on the Vietnamese desk, and a new personality appeared on the scene, willing and ready to pick up where Brickham had left off.

Having chatted with Roger Trinquier in Vung Tau in 1952, Evan Parker, Jr., was no stranger to Vietnam. As the son of an American pilot who had served in King George's Royal Flying Corps in the First World War, Parker was also well connected. Upon graduating from Cornell University in 1943, Parker, who was fluent in French, was invited to join the fashionable OSS. Trained with the jaunty Jedburghs,* he was slated to parachute into France but instead was sent to Burma, where he served in Detachment 101, as an interrogation and logistics officer fighting with Kachin hill tribes behind the Japanese lines. Parker later served as Detachment 101's liaison officer to Merrill's Marauders and the British Thirty-sixth Division. His service with the OSS (followed by a brief stint as a traveling salesman) led to a career in the CIA's clandestine services and to personal relationships with many of the major Vietnamese, French, and American players in Vietnam.

Parker began his CIA career as a courier in the Far East, then was graduated to case officer, operating mostly in Hong Kong and China. Over

*Elite OSS officers trained at Camp David. Colby, Ward, Parker, and Buhto all were Jedburghs.

the ensuing years, he told me when we met in 1986, he made "four or five" trips to Vietnam and, when he arrived again in Saigon in June 1967, was slated to become the station's executive director, its third-highest-ranking position. However, Robert Komer and John Hart thought that Parker could better serve "the cause" as ICEX's first director.

Parker was chosen to manage ICEX, first and foremost, because Komer needed a senior CIA officer in that position. The CIA alone had the expertise in covert paramilitary and intelligence operations, the CIA alone was in liaison with the Special Branch and the CIO, and the CIA alone could supply money and resources on a moment's notice, without the red tape that strapped the military and the State Department. As a GS-16 with the equivalent rank of a brigadier general, Evan Parker, Jr., had the status and the security clearances that would allow him access to all these things.

Parker's persona and professional record also made him the perfect candidate for the job. Having just completed a tour as the CIA officer assigned to the Pentagon's Pacific Command, Parker had helped draw up the military's strategic plan for Vietnam and was well aware of how Vietnam fitted into the "big picture." Possessing the persuasive skills and political connections of a seasoned diplomat, Parker also enjoyed the status and the style necessary to soothe the monumental egos of obstinate military officers and bureaucrats. And "as *the* expert on unconventional warfare," which was how Tully Acampora facetiously referred to him, Evan Parker had the tradecraft qualifications required to launch a top secret, highly sensitive, coordinated attack on the VCI.

Upon arriving in Saigon, Parker prepared himself by reading Brickham's papers and reviewing "the fifty to sixty" programs we already had in place to deal with the "infrastructure," a word Parker described to me as "hideous."[5]* At an informal conference in Da Nang called to discuss the attack on the VCI, Parker learned that Brickham "and his partners in crime" wanted to concentrate their efforts initially on the Americans, then on the Vietnamese, but that Komer first had to ram ICEX through the impervious Saigon bureaucracy.

This was not hard to do, considering that President Johnson had given Komer a mandate that encompassed not only the formulation of an integrated attack on the VCI but also the reorganization of the Republic of Vietnam's armed forces, management of the October 1967 Vietnamese presidential elections, and revitalizing South Vietnam's economy. When faced with the irresistible force called Robert "Blowtorch" Komer, the immovable Saigon

*According to Parker, Komer liked the phrase "attack on the infrastructure" because "he thought it sounded sexy."

bureaucracy gave way quickly, if not altogether voluntarily.

Flanked by John Hart and General George Forsythe, MACV's chief of Revolutionary Development, Komer on June 14, 1967, presented MACV's chiefs of staff with Brickham's "Proposal." Komer made a forceful presentation, writes Ralph Johnson, but Generals Phillip B. Davidson Jr., Walter Kerwin, and William Pearson balked, "because MACV personnel requirements were not included."[6]

But it did not matter that the majority of DIOCC advisers were slated to be military men. Komer, backed by Hart, simply took his case to MACV commander Westmoreland, who, having been informed of President Johnson's wishes in the matter by Ambassador Bunker, overruled his staff on June 16. A few days later the White House Coordinating Committee (Director of Central Intelligence Richard Helms, Secretary of State Dean Rusk, Chairman of the Joint Chiefs of Staff Earle Wheeler, and Chairman William Sullivan) nodded their final approval. And so it was that ICEX—soon to be Phoenix—was born. And not without resentment. General McChristian recalled, "On my last day in Vietnam, I became aware that a new plan for attacking the VCI was to be implemented. It was to be called ICEX. To put it mildly, I was amazed and dismayed."[7] McChristian was amazed that he had not been told earlier, and was dismayed because ICEX was going to replace Cong Tac IV.

On the morning of June 20,* Evan Parker met with General Davidson (McChristian's replacement as MACV intelligence chief) and General Pearson, the MACV chief of operations. At this meeting, Parker recalled, the generals agreed "to staff this thing out." But, he added, "I think from the point of view of the military, well, they may have felt this was being shoved down their throats by the chief of station.

"Anyway," said Parker, "[Komer and Hart] said, 'Do it,' and they identified me as the man they proposed to head up this staff, and the agency said they would supply assistance. Okay, but immediately you have a problem because there are already advisers to the Special Branch . . . and if all of a sudden I come in and am put in charge, that means I'm getting into somebody else's business. So if I want to get to the Special Police, I have to sound out the American adviser to see if he wants to cooperate with this. Maybe he wants to, and maybe he doesn't. Maybe he feels he's already doing this.

"Well, he may not like it"—Parker smiled—"but he has to do it, because the chief of station tells him to. So he does it. But that doesn't make the pill

*That afternoon Parker had "a brief conversation with General Loan," during which Loan rejected the ICEX proposal, claiming it infringed on Vietnamese sovereignty.

any easier to swallow. In effect he's getting another layer of command or, I should say, coordination, over him."

Ed Brady, an Army officer on contract to the CIA and assigned to the ICEX Directorate, elaborated when we met in his office in 1987. "There certainly was a conflict going on," Brady said.[8] "Dave West [Nelson Brickham's replacement] didn't want to share his prerogatives with another powerful CIA guy. . . . Why should there be two organizations working with the Special Branch? It wasn't proposed that [ICEX] be under his control. It was proposed that it interact with the Special Branch on a separate basis and that separate Special Branch officers would be assigned over there to do that. And West wouldn't have any control or influence over it.

"The Special Branch," Brady explained, "was supposed to be carrying out internal surveillance and operations against subversives. That's its job. The problem . . . was that the vast majority of Special Branch energy went into surveilling, reporting on, and thwarting opposition political parties. Non-Communists. Every now and then they did something about a VC—if he was in Saigon. But they didn't have any systematic program against the Communists. Their main activity was to keep the existing regime in power, and the political threat to the existing regime was not the Communist party, 'cause the Communist party was outlawed! What the Special Branch was doing was keeping track of the so-called loyal opposition—keeping track of what Tran Van Don or what Co Minh Tang or what the Vietnam Quoc Dan Dang was doing.

"Phoenix," Brady explained, "at an absolute minimum caused a focus to be brought to bear on anti-Communist activities."

Having pulled rank to get MACV and the liaison branch in line, John Hart then assigned four CIA officers to Evan Parker on a temporary basis, as well as the services of "key CIA personnel stationed outside of Saigon" and "integrated and CIA-funded programs such as Census Grievance Teams, PRU, RD Cadre, and Special Police."[9] Parker was then told to select a military deputy, and he asked for an old friend from OSS Detachment 101, Colonel Junichi Buhto, then the MACV chief of counterintelligence.

"Junichi agreed to assist," Parker said when we met at his home, "even though he had plenty to do in his own job. It was agreed he would keep his regular job and be my assistant on a part-time basis as another duty. And with his assistance we found a bunch of Army officers, all of whom were near the end of their tours but who could be spared from whatever they were doing. And so it went. That's the ICEX staff.

"Then the police were brought into it," Parker added, referring to the National Police. "Leaving aside the agency people, the key people are John Manopoli and myself because he was head of the National Police."

A retired New York State Police lieutenant, Manopoli had served as a police adviser in Vietnam from 1956 through 1959 and had returned to Saigon as chief of Public Safety in 1966. Although he had no authority over Special Branch, as senior adviser to the National Police, Manopoli was responsible for meeting its, as well as ICEX's, logistical and administrative needs.

"Manopoli," Parker pointed out, "was actually the senior police adviser in-country. I didn't have that kind of responsibility. Mine was a staff responsibility. We in Phoenix were not put over the police or military; we simply gave a directive in the name of MACV or Komer or Colby. The idea was to come up with an organization that would pool intelligence on the infrastructure and try to get these people to use that intelligence to go out and arrest them. This is so easily said and so difficult to do because all these agencies have their own jobs and they existed long before Phoenix."

Manopoli also got the job of kicking Tully Acampora out of his office and moving Parker's staff in. "They found some space for us in USAID Two," Parker said. "We were squeezed in." He was given some part-time secretarial help, and with the officers lent from Hart, "what we did first was come out with a MACV staff paper which described what this program was, what we were going to do, and what this coordinated program—this ICEX—was going to be."

This staff paper, titled "Intelligence, Intelligence Coordination, and Exploitation for Attack on VC Infrastructure (C)," short title: ICEX (U), commonly known as MACV 381-41, was promulgated on July 9, 1967, and marked the birth of ICEX as a formal entity. It also signaled the end to the escalation of the Vietnam War. Five days later the Defense Department imposed a 523,000-man troop limit on the Joint Chiefs of Staff.

One of the authors of MACV 381-41 was CIA officer Jim Ward, who was then preparing to replace Kinloch Bull as region officer in charge of IV Corps. "The first meeting back in those days," Ward recalled, "was between Evan, me, and Junichi Buhto. That's early July 1967. I had known Juni from Germany and OSS Detachment One-oh-one. Just by chance all three of us had been in Detachment One-oh-one of OSS in World War Two. In fact, Evan and I were together at Camp David, where the Jedburghs were trained."[10]

A paramilitary expert who had commanded a unit of Kachin guerrillas operating behind Japanese lines, Ward—whose CIA career began in 1948 in Malaya, where he was schooled by Claude Fenner—was well aware of the prominence of the Special Branch in counterinsurgency warfare. According to Ward, "The key to the Vietnam War . . . was the political control of people. And the Communists were doing a better job of this than we were, and the best way to stop this was to get at the infrastructure. Not the people who were sympathizers or supporters in any way of the VC. They didn't count. The people who counted were the key members of the People's Revolutionary party. These were the people behind the NLF.

"Anyway, Evan set up this meeting. He wanted input from someone with field operations experience and know-how, and what we talked about was concepts: what we had to do to bring everybody together who was collecting intelligence and that everybody should be channeling intelligence into the DIOCC. There intelligence would be collated, analyzed, interpreted, and then reaction operations could be undertaken almost immediately. And new intelligence directives would be drafted. Whoever was in charge was supposed to be doing that all the time—that is, letting people know that a particular piece of information [needed to mount an operation against a particular VCI] was missing, or asking, 'What's the pattern of this guy's movements every day?' Then you decide who should get these directives—the police if you're talking about an infrastructure guy or the military if you're talking about a battalion of VC. Anyway, the guy who runs the DIOCC—be it Special Branch or MSS or S-two or whoever—usually does the laying of requirements.

"First we talked about the coordination of intelligence. For instance, in the Delta there were approximately ten thousand intelligence reports a month coming in from different levels . . . a few hundred were coming up through police channels, some through ARVN and American battalions, and others through the Green Berets and their [Vietnamese] counterparts. All of them were sending information through their own chains of command, rather than using it laterally and exploiting it locally. And we wanted them, at the reaction level [the DIOCC], to collate the information and exploit it. That's the first objective.

"The second objective—assuming the military intelligence gets exploited by the military units—is making sure the infrastructure intelligence gets exploited by whoever appears to be the most appropriate unit to coordinate it. If it's the kind of thing that can be handled only by a large military organization, fine. Even the largest of the American outfits get involved in this, like the First Air Cavalry and the Hundred First Airborne, which was especially good at cordon and search operations. They would take PRU or Field Police units along with them and Special Branch units to do the interrogating. But generally the outfit that's best equipped to get a single guy in a remote place is the PRU."

These concepts of intelligence collection and exploitation, as outlined by Ward, were incorporated in MACV 381-41 along with Brickham's organizational concepts. Timetables were set for the region officers in charge to draft missions and functions statements, to determine in which districts the first DIOCCs were to be built, and to prepare guidelines for DIOCC operations. All this was to be done by the end of July. MACV 381-41 also charged the CIA's region officers in charge with briefing their Vietnamese counterparts as soon as possible.

With MACV 381-41 in hand, Evan Parker and John Hart visited each ROIC. "We told them what we had in mind," Parker recalled, "what the objective was and what their function was. Briefly stated, they were to be the nucleus to get it going. This was all done orally. . . . They were simply told, 'You've now heard what Ev's in charge of—you'll get it done here; you'll pass the word to your people.' Then we briefed the senior military people in the four regions."

Parker attributed his success in co-opting the ROICs to the fact that "in addition to being the Phoenix fellow, I was also a senior CIA officer wearing my other hat." In that capacity he attended CIA station meetings three times each week. In July 1967 the ROICS, who may be thought of as Phoenix's first field generals, were Jack Horgan in I Corps, Dean Almy in II Corps, Kinloch Bull in IV Corps, and Bob Wall in III Corps.

Each region was unique, geographically and politically, and Phoenix in flight conformed to those contours. As Parker explains, "Four Corps was different because there weren't as many Americans there." The Delta was also the breadbasket and population center of Vietnam, thus the locus of the counterinsurgency and Phoenix. I Corps was distinct by virtue of its proximity to North Vietnam and the extent to which Phoenix was directed against Thieu's domestic political opponents. Headquartered in Nha Trang under the shadow of Fifth Special Forces, II Corps was an admixture of SOG and Phoenix operations. And as the region encompassing Saigon and the Central Office of South Vietnam, III Corps was perhaps the most critical region—although one in which, according to Nelson Brickham, there was little success against the VCI.

In June 1967 Robert Komer sent a cable to Richard Helms commending Nelson Brickham for "an outstanding job in helping design new attack on infrastructure" and asking that Brickham be made available for occasional temporary duty in Vietnam "if critical problems arise." Three weeks after arriving back in Langley, with yet another feather in his cap, Brickham was transferred from the Vietnamese desk to the office of the special assistant for Vietnamese affairs (SAVA).

"SAVA was up at the DCI level," Brickham noted, "as a coordination point for all agency and interagency activities relating to Vietnam. The reason I was brought up there was that [SAVA Director George] Carver was obliged to brief [the secretary of defense] and other people on ICEX/Phoenix, and he didn't have a clue. He couldn't understand. Nobody in Washington could understand what we had done out there in the station. So Carver called me in and asked me to write a memorandum."

Brickham described Yale graduate Carver as the person who "provided the theoretical basis for U.S. intervention in Vietnam in an article he wrote for *Foreign Affairs* magazine ["The Faceless Viet Cong"] on the nature of the Vietnam insurgency and American interests there.

"I stayed in SAVA for two months," Brickham continued. "Then I went back out to Vietnam TDY to work with Ev Parker . . . to assist him in the reporting formats, the requirements, and this and that and to implement the philosophy I explained earlier. And it was at this point that we ran into problems with Bob Wall.

"Bob Wall was a paramilitary type." Brickham sighed. "He was first assigned as a province officer, then as deputy in I Corps, and in that capacity he was instrumental in creating the first DIOCCs. He invited some Brits from Kuala Lumpur to explain what they had done there, and he was always hustling papers around the station. He was not a regional officer before the reorganization, but he ended up as our ROIC in Third Corps, in Bien Hoa. Now that was shortly before I left country, and I had very little to concern myself with that situation. It was when I came back TDY to help Evan Parker in the fall of 1967 that it became evident that Bob Wall was one of our less satisfactory region officers.

"One of our problems in Vietnam," Brickham philosophized, "is that that part of the world seems to generate the warlord. It's the damnation of the Far East and a disease that infects the white man when he goes there. . . . And the upshot in Vietnam, before someone came out with the sledgehammer to knock heads together, was that you had forty-four different wars in forty-four different provinces and forty-four different warlords . . . and American region advisers often would fall victim to this same virus. Bob Wall is a prime example. So I recommended disciplinary action and relief from duty.

"Ev Parker, of course, was in charge of it, and he didn't do that. I'd never known Ev Parker before that, but just a finer gentleman you'll never know; he's what the Russians would call a cultured individual. Now Ev Parker is less abrasive than I am; he would see a problem and seek a diplomatic solution. Whereas I would rock a boat and sometimes sink it, Ev Parker would steer it in a different course, so it wouldn't take the waves. Ev Parker has a Chinese mind, and he chose a different way to soften Wall's position."

That position, according to Brickham, was that "Bob Wall was permitting the military people in Third Corps to turn the entire intelligence operation into a military support adjunct, ignoring the infrastructure. Even though he was pushing the DIOCCs like crazy, he and his military counterpart in Region Three were using the PRU as blocking forces for military operations. He was not following policy. He was pursuing his own war out there in the region. This became the issue between Bob Wall and myself in Third Corps."

Bob Wall, a balding, roly-poly man, emphatically denied Brickham's charges. "No way!" he said, adding that it was perfectly proper to use the Provincial Reconnaissance Units in village sweeps, because "the PRU could actually deal with the people. They spoke their language and knew what to look for, whereas U.S. forces were only interested in killing people."

Wall did solicit the help of his corps's deputy intelligence chief, Lieutenant Colonel John Kizirian, who anted up fifteen second lieutenants as DIOCC advisers in III Corps. But that in itself did not make him a warlord. For a CIA region officer could push Phoenix only to the extent that his military counterpart provided qualified personnel to run the DIOCCs. And the military always wanted something in return. And then, of course, there was the overriding question of Vietnamese participation.

On this issue Brickham said, "We put [Phoenix] together and presented it to the Vietnamese. General Loan by this time was chief of the National Police. Everybody knows what he looks like—they've seen pictures of him shooting the VC on TV—but I'm convinced that Loan was an absolutely honest, dedicated patriot. Anyway, this ICEX proposal was presented to Loan, and it didn't take him long to turn it down, mainly because they looked upon it as an infringement on their sovereignty. When I say Loan was a patriot, he was! He was looking out for the Vietnamese. He recognized the fact that Vietnamese and American interests were not always identical. So they turned it down flat.

"We said, 'Well, that's okay 'cause we're gonna do it anyway.' . . . Regardless of what the Vietnamese were going to do, we were going to go ahead with it anyway, if nothing else, to try to serve as an example. And there was really no need for the Vietnamese to string along with us, although up in Da Nang they did. Which, as you know, is where the name Phoenix came from.

"Jack Horgan was our ROIC up there," Brickham went on. "He was in good liaison with both the Vietnamese military and police, and when he presented this to the Vietnamese up there, one of them said, 'Well, we should really call this Phoenix, because it's to rise from the ashes and seek victory.' So Jack Horgan came down with a cable and said, 'By the way, so-and-so has coined the name Phoenix for this activity,' and it took immediately. It became known as Operation Phoenix, and everybody was happy with that. By then it was beginning to go."

CHAPTER 10

Action Programs

Before he bade adieu to Vietnam in November 1967, Nelson Brickham helped put together what was entitled "Action Program for Attack on VC Infrastructure 1967–1968." Signed by the CORDS assistant chief of staff, Wade Lathram, "Action Program" represented Robert Komer's administrative and operational directives for the ICEX program. It is the most significant Phoenix document, charting the program's dimensions and course over its first eighteen months. It set in place Brickham's reporting requirements, established tables of organization, identified major problems, and formed groups to find solutions.

"Action Program" consisted of twelve separate tabs, each addressing a separate mission or function to be accomplished by a specific deadline. First on the list, Tab 1, called for promulgating the ICEX mission directive, MACV 381-41. Tab 2 called for briefing all corps senior advisers, and Tab 3 directed the CIA region officers to designate corps and province ICEX coordinators, all by July 31, 1967. By year's end ICEX committees were operating in thirty-nine provinces, thirty-four of which were chaired by CIA officers. Most were meeting monthly and had initiated anti-VCI operations. Also by year's end twenty-nine Province Intelligence Operations Coordination Centers (the province equivalents of a DIOCC) were functioning and sending reports to the ICEX Directorate. In certain provinces, such as Vinh Long in the Delta, the PIOCC doubled as a Phoenix committee.

Tab 4 called for continuation and expansion of DIOCC development. At the time "Action Program" was issued, 10 DIOCCs were in operation; by year's end there were 103, although most were gathering tactical military intelligence, not infiltrating and attacking the VCI. In November 1967 more than half a million dollars were authorized for DIOCC construction, salaries of Vietnamese employees, office equipment and supplies, and transportation. "These were not operational funds in the sense of supporting anti-infrastructure activities."[1] Money for anti-VCI operations came from the parent agency.

To his credit, Evan Parker did not approve of the rapid pace at which Phoenix was expanding. "I didn't think we needed an elaborate structure everywhere in the country," he told me. "Some of the provinces didn't have enough people or activity in them to warrant it. I would have preferred to concentrate on the more populated active areas where you knew that you had people to work with and something to work against."[2]

There were too many variables, Parker contended, to have "a uniform program." The methodology had not been perfected, and too much depended "on the personal likes and dislikes of the senior Vietnamese people in the field . . . and their adviser. . . . For instance, in I Corps there was a lot of activity, not so much concerned with the VCI as with the machinations of rival political parties—the Buddhists or whatever. . . . These are things that were hung over from the French days. . . . This was always the problem with Thieu. . . . [it] was sort of open season on the enemy—of settling scores."

Tab 5 of "Action Program" prescribed ICEX staff organization along the committee lines proposed by Brickham. In Saigon the ICEX board of directors consisted of the DEPCORDS as chairman, the CIA station chief, the MACV intelligence (J2) and operations (J3) chiefs, and the CIA chief of Revolutionary Development. In fact, the board met only once, and Robert Komer quickly assumed control of Phoenix, setting policy as he saw fit, with the directorate serving as his personal staff. "Komer or Colby [who replaced Komer as DEPCORDS in November 1968] said, 'You'll do it.' My job," explained Parker, "was to say, 'Okay, Colby says you'll do this, and this is how you're gonna go about doing it.' What I did was help people carry out what they were ordered to do. And I firmly believe in the soft sell."

In practice, Parker's CIA kinship with Komer and especially Colby enabled him to manage the Phoenix Directorate without having to consult agency heads. He had merely to state his wishes to the DEPCORDS in order to bypass the various chains of command.

"Colby was my division chief in the field, and in Washington also," Parker explained. "I served with him in World War Two when I was in England. I met him when we were both in a program known as the Jedburghs. He went into the field in Europe, and I went into the field in the Far East.

"Colby is a fine gentleman, I'll tell you. He was tremendously helpful to me. So was Komer. But their personalities were very different. Komer was essentially a rasping, grating sort of voice . . . but he was consistently staunch in his support of the program. . . . He may have given orders, he may have been sarcastic—all those things—but at the same time he was not one to stand on ceremony, not one to do things because that's the way it's always been done. He didn't give a damn about that. He'd say, 'I want Parker's organization to get four trucks! I don't give a good goddamn where they come from, just give him four trucks!'

"Colby was quieter, more soft-spoken, but just as firm in terms of getting things done. . . . He would suddenly say, 'Let's go visit so-and-so,' in a province or region. That meant you would call up and get a helicopter or a plane, with no notice, and he would just go there and see them. That made it a whole lot more secure because we traveled without bodyguards."

Case in point: While serving as Phoenix coordinator in Quang Tri Province, Warren Milberg was visited by Colby, who was on an inspection tour. As Milberg recalled it, Colby decided to spend the night, so Milberg assigned a Nung guard to watch over him. That night there was a mortar attack. The Nung guard grabbed Colby by the scruff of the neck, dragged him backward down the stairs (Milberg arrived in time to see Colby's heels bouncing on the steps) into the basement of the building, threw him on a cot, and threw himself on top of the future director of Central Intelligence. Somewhat dismayed at the treatment the Nung had afforded the DEPCORDS, Milberg half expected the ax to fall when Colby and his entourage assembled for breakfast the following morning. But Colby merely thanked the earnest Nung for the gesture of concern.

The consummate insider, Colby would win many friends with his "just folks" management style, while using his considerable influence to refine and redirect the broad policies put in place by Komer—the outside agitator who rode roughshod over everyone. Together, Komer and Colby were the perfect one-two combination required to jump-start Phoenix and keep it running for five years.

As of August 15, 1967, Parker's part-time staff had been replaced by three permanent CIA officers: Joe Sartiano as executive director; William Law as chief of operations; and James Brogdon as administrative officer; Colonel William J. Greenwalt had replaced Junichi Buhto as deputy director, and six MACV officers were assigned as full-time employees, along with a smattering of AID and State Department people.

"We set up a working organization built around agency people," Parker said, "with other individuals made available from the different agencies, but still paid for by the agencies they belonged to." By then there were American women serving as secretaries, MACV and CIA officers advising the Vietnamese, and others in the office keeping records. "There were probably three or four people I counted on more than anyone else," Parker remarked, but "in order to make this work, I would say that the core people were the agency people in charge of the special police—the senior agency advisers."

Tab 6 provided for military augmentation of ICEX field units. As Parker put it, "Then you realize you're going to have a nationwide organization as well as a headquarters staff, and that you're going to need a lot more people than you envisioned. So the Army becomes the principal.

"In due course a table of organization was set up which assigned people to region, then to province, and most of them were Army. You'd have a captain at province and a major or [lieutenant colonel] at region with assistants—corporals and sergeants and so forth. MACV took the bodies at first as they came in-country and assigned them regardless of the fact that they may have been intended for something else. For example, my deputy was going to a military unit but found himself in ICEX instead. Another fellow who was going to be assigned to MACV counterintelligence instead was assigned to an intelligence function in ICEX. That's where the first people came from."

The first MACV allotment to Phoenix was for 126 military officers and noncommissioned officers (NCOs), all counterintelligence specialists. One officer, one NCO, and one clerk-typist had been sent to each corps by September 15, and one officer and/or NCO to each province. By the end of 1967 one NCO had been assigned to each of the 103 DIOCCs then in existence. All military officers and enlisted men assigned to the Phoenix program in 1967 took orders from the CIA.

Tab 7 provided for briefing and coordination with senior GVN officials. While the groundwork was being laid on the American side of the program, Parker said, "we were working with the Vietnamese to sell them the idea. Although they were militarily assisting, the Vietnamese police had the major role because after all, you're dealing primarily with civilians. So the person who worked most closely with us was the director general of the National Police."

But General Nguyen Ngoc Loan was wary of the CIA, which was supporting Nguyen Van Thieu—not Nguyen Cao Ky—in the campaign leading up to the October 1967 presidential elections. And even though Ky was persuaded to run as Thieu's vice-president (they joined forces against "peace" candidate Tran Van Dzu), the two were bitter enemies. As Ky's enforcer General Loan opposed Phoenix not only because it infringed on Vietnamese sovereignty but because he believed it was being used to promote Thieu. Their opposition to Phoenix was to spell trouble for General Loan and his patron, Ky.

General Loan's opposition to Phoenix, however, did not mean that he refused to work with Americans on an equal basis. His support for CT IV disproves that. And Cong Tac IV "was a program that was doing well, too," said Tully Acampora, "until February 1967. Then Robert Komer arrived, grabbed the political implications, and, after returning to Washington and conferring with his boss, Walt Rostow, purloined it from the Vietnamese."[3]

CT IV differed, fundamentally, from Phoenix in that the U.S. military units it employed were not empowered to arrest Vietnamese civilians. Phoenix, on the other hand, relied primarily on the PRU, which operated under the exclusive jurisdiction of the CIA and thus were beyond General Loan's control. General Loan naturally preferred to work with General McChristian's Combined Intelligence Staff. But when McChristian left Vietnam in July 1967, Komer immediately exploited the situation. At Komer's direction, MACV officers assigned to CT IV were gradually withdrawn by McChristian's replacement, General Phillip Davidson, whom Tully Acampora described as "beholden" to Komer for his job.

"Komer was disastrous," Acampora stressed. "He more than anyone politicized MACV. He was forcing for a treaty, promoting Phoenix and promising Westmoreland the job of Army chief of staff, if he went along. In mid-1967 it was a completely political situation."

Indeed, by deducting more than a hundred thousand Self-Defense Forces and "political cadre" from the enemy order of battle, Westmoreland, Komer, and Hart were able to show success and in the process convince President Johnson that "the light" really was at the end of the tunnel. Meanwhile, having backed themselves into a corner, they decided to do the job themselves. So what if General Loan was resistant? As Nelson Brickham had said, "That's okay 'cause we're gonna do it anyway!"

Symbolizing this "get tough" policy was Phoenix, rising from the devastation of two years of a stalemated war. Phoenix in this hawkish manifestation represented the final solution to the problem of distinguishing between a covert Communist enemy and an inscrutable ally. Uninhibited by family ties, Americans in charge of irregular forces, or by themselves, began hunting the VCI in its villages, doing what the Vietnamese were reluctant to do—even though they were never quite sure of whom they were stalking.

This desperate policy was not without its American detractors. Tempestuous Tully Acampora called it "detrimental and contradictory." Ed Brady, the Army captain assigned to the Phoenix Directorate as a cover for his CIA activities, concurs. "It's very hard to carry out secret covert operations and repressive kinds of things in order to separate guerrillas from people—and then make a speech to them about how their individual rights are so important," Brady said in an interview with Al Santoli.[4]

But while Acampora and Brady believed the United States had no business preempting the Vietnamese when it came to the attack against the VCI, other Americans thought that the time for patience and cooperation had come and gone. From Evan Parker's perspective, the problem was competition between the Special Branch and the ARVN. "It involved one Vietnamese agency saying, 'Well, we can't give [information] to them, because they're penetrated by the VC.' That sort of thing. And in some cases undoubted it was true."

Parker raised a legitimate point. In order for an intelligence coordination and exploitation program like Phoenix to work, institutional mistrust between the police and the military had to be overcome. But, Parker explained, "Having the Special Branch have such an active role made it difficult in many provinces and many of the more rural areas, because the special policeman was probably the equivalent of a sergeant. So . . . he doesn't have much clout. . . . And the [outgunned, outmanned] police are pretty subordinate to the military, so you have all this business of army versus police. It's a wonder it worked at all."

Moreover, frustration with Vietnamese security leaks gave Americans yet another reason *not* to wait for the Vietnamese to throw their support behind Phoenix. As Evan Parker said, "One of the great problems with the Vietnamese in getting this started was that the classification of the directive was so high—in order to prevent it from falling into enemy hands—that it was very difficult to handle these documents in the field . . . and tell people what they were supposed to do."

Typically, Tully Acampora refuted Parker's explanation and interpreted the emphasis on secrecy in political terms. According to Acampora, for whom the switch from CT IV to Phoenix meant a loss in status, Parker "always envisioned Phoenix as a wholly U.S.-promoted, -managed, and -supported program." Moreover, "Hart's one mission was to undermine Loan's influence, to reduce his power base, and to superimpose Phoenix on CT Four. They bought off the head of Special Branch, Major Nguyen Tien. Then Parker started suborning guys on the MACV intelligence staff. He seduced Colonel Junichi Buhto [MACV's chief of counterintelligence] by promising to make him a GS-nineteen if he went along with the CIA. . . . Davidson's mission was to destroy CT Four, and in August, Davidson and the CIA began withdrawing Americans from the Combined Intelligence Staff. This involves the election of 1967."

There is no doubt that Phoenix, in its fledgling stage, was conceived and implemented by the CIA. Furthermore, Ralph Johnson writes, "The results obtained by ICEX by the end of 1967 were primarily, if not totally, stimulated and supported by the Americans."[5] There was early acceptance of Phoenix by the Vietnamese in I Corps, but as Parker himself noted, much of that activity was directed against Thieu's non-Communist political opponents. Otherwise, the majority of Vietnamese hesitated to embrace a program as politically explosive as Phoenix. As Johnson observes, "most province chiefs were waiting for instructions from the Central Government."[6]

The first step in that direction was taken in late December 1967, two months after Thieu had been elected president and Ky had begun to lose influence. On December 20, 1967, Prime Minister Nguyen Van Loc signed Directive 89-Th.T/VP/M, legalizing Phung Hoang, the Vietnamese clone of Phoenix. However, the directive was not signed by President Thieu and thus carried little weight with cautious province chiefs hedging their bets while Thieu established himself more solidly.

It is also important to note that Prime Minister Loc's reasons for authorizing Phung Hoang were directly related to Robert Komer's attempt to undermine General Loan and Nguyen Cao Ky by ending support for CT IV. After December 1, 1967, when Komer managed to terminate Operation Fairfax, Loc had no choice but to support Phoenix. And, according to Tully Acampora, by withdrawing the U.S. units that shielded CT IV's Field Police, "Komer opened up all the avenues which led to Tet." Making matters worse, in an attempt to stimulate the South Vietnamese economy and, in the process, allow Thieu to reap the political rewards, Komer went so far as to remove police roadblocks and checkpoints around Saigon.

Meanwhile, Tully Acampora was pleading with as many American generals as he could find, asking them not to withdraw American forces from CT IV. "Loan was saying that there was a massive influx of VC into Saigon," Acampora recalled, "but Komer was calling it light, and Hart backed him. They wouldn't listen to Loan, who was trying to convince them for sixty days prior to Tet."

Nelson Brickham, for one, admitted to having been fooled. "The VC had pulled their good people out and sent them up North in 1966. We knew that. Then, in the summer and fall of 1967, they came back. But I misinterpreted it. In October 1967 I told Colby that we were in a position that no NVA or VC unit could move without us knowing it. We saw Loan's warnings as crying wolf."[7]

"We were picking up massive numbers of infiltrators," Acampora told me, "so Loan countermanded the Joint General Staff's orders to withdraw; he refused to pull out all of his people. He kept a paratroop unit and a marine unit in Saigon and canceled all police leaves. Those units, with the police, met the first assault in Tet. Then, of course, Loan was resurrected."

But by then it was too late. In Acampora's judgment, Komer's machinations brought about Tet. "The fact is," he said, "that Parker contributed to that disaster, too. Parker said Phoenix was the only impediment, that it turned defeat into victory. But the embassy was attacked! How could that happen? The fact is, Phoenix was a failure, and it was only because of Loan that the VC suffered a setback."

"In any event, the prime minister said, 'Do it.' He gave the order," Evan Parker said, "and he wrote the letters to empower them to do it, and Phung Hoang came into being on the Vietnamese side. . . . A Phung Hoang staff was set up by the Vietnamese consisting primarily of people from Special Branch. Then they set up quarters for them" at the National Police Interrogation Center. "The two organizations had separate quarters," Parker added, "because we wanted the Vietnamese to feel that Phoenix was a Vietnamese program and that the Americans were simply advisers."

"So anyway"—Parker sighed—"we went through this organizational phase. The Vietnamese went through the same thing, pulling together the police and whatever, trying to set up staffs, finding places for them to sit, providing them with pencils and paper, and trying to get them to actually conduct some sort of operations. And here you come to the nitty-gritty."

Tab 8 of "Action Program" called for review of VCI intelligence collection requirements and programs, especially Project Corral, a unilateral American operation started in October 1966 solely to collect information on the VCI at province level. After completing their review, CIA officers on the Phoenix staff began to prepare a standard briefing on the VCI for incoming officers and interested officials. They also began compiling handbooks, interrogation guides, and "related materials" like most wanted lists.

Especially effective against the VCI, most wanted lists had been used for years by Special Forces when, in April 1967, Renz Hoeksema's deputy, Robert Brewer, initiated a Most Wanted program in Saigon and expanded it nationwide. "Every province was directed to examine its files for a list of ten,"[8] Brewer explained noting that the object of the exercise was to show that the enemy was not "faceless." Soon most wanted "posters," replete with composite drawings (prepared by Special Branch officers using New York City Police Department makeup kits) of VCI suspects were being nailed to trees, DIOCC walls, and market stalls throughout Vietnam. The posters offered cash rewards and had a picture of the phoenix to catch people's attention. (See enclosure.)

In the spring of 1967 Komer appointed Brewer as senior adviser in Quang Tri Province. "When I got there, I got all the intelligence-gathering outfits together," Brewer recalled, "and we wrote up a list of the twenty-one most wanted VCI. One guy on my list, Bui Tu, had killed a district adviser's sergeant, and I wanted to get him. So I went to the high school and found his picture in the yearbook. That really paid off. On a sleepy afternoon in July the word came in from Special Branch that Bui Tu was in the area. The

DIOCC notified district, district notified village, and the Marine combined action patrol went after him.

"Bui Tu had been spotted in a shelter on a rice paddy. Three guys jumped up and ran, and the Popular Force team and the Marines mowed them down. Bui Tu was number one. The top. He had captain's bars and a briefcase full of notes, with a quarter inch of papers on me! They knew where I slept in the compound and they were planning to kill me." Thanks to Bui Tu's documents and information provided by the defector, Brewer said, "We blew the VCI apart."

What Brewer described is a typical Phoenix operation: A most wanted poster led to a high-ranking VCI suspect's being spotted and killed, while his captured documents revealed the whereabouts and identities of many of his VCI comrades. Most wanted posters also served to inhibit the VCI. As Jim Ward explained to me, "All of a sudden this guy who used to travel from place to place begins to wonder who is going to turn him in! It begins to prey on him. We found out later that this really had a significant psychological impact on these guys, making them hide and becoming less effective." Said Ward: "It *suppresses* them."[9]

By the end of 1967 thirty-five provinces were compiling blacklists of VCI members, and twenty-two more had most wanted lists.[10]

Tab 9 of "Action Program" called for review and recommendations for action programs to exploit infrastructure intelligence. In theory this meant the training, direction, and coordination, by U.S. personnel, of Field Police and PRU in anti-VCI operations. Between the two, the PRU were more effective, accounting for 98 percent of all anti-VCI operations in I Corps alone. In November 1967, Ralph Johnson writes, "II Corps and III Corps reported that 236 significant VCI were eliminated by the PRU, which continued as the main action arm of the 'rifle shot' approach."[11]

"Basically the PRU were effective," Parker stated. "In some cases the police were effective. And in many areas more got done in capturing VCI in military operations. But I was interested in getting key people. You can arrest the little ones, but the operation goes on and on, and you haven't really hurt them. But it's very hard to get a really important man.

"I personally wasn't involved in any operations," Parker stressed. "Operational control was exercised at whatever level it was happening at, by the so-called action agencies. The idea was to use resources wherever they were. . . . If there needed to be cooperation, the Vietnamese would consult . . . if they trusted the head of the other agency. Unfortunately the Americans would conduct operations without telling the Vietnamese. And vice versa."

By the end of 1967 the Field Police were conducting anti-VCI operations in twenty-six provinces; thirty-nine provinces were using systems taught by Phoenix staffers on how properly to "debrief" defectors, who were used as spotters, PRU, and interrogators. Included in the Phoenix arsenal were joint military-police search and destroy and cordon and search operations, population and resources control, and riverine and maritime operations.

Tab 10 charged the Phoenix program with improving the civilian detention system. About this subject Nelson Brickham remarked, "The one major element left out of all this was the civilian detainee problem. It starts with the Province Interrogation Centers, but the larger problem is, How do you screen detainees, and then what do you do with identified VCI?

"When you'd go through these village sweeps, you'd have whole *corrals* filled full with Vietnamese just sitting there looking at you all day long. In rural provinces you'd wind up with barbed-wire cages with tin roofs packed with people. It was a major problem basically because we were running a revolving-door operation. We'd capture VC; then a week later we'd capture them again . . . assuming they were VC. The Vietcong always knew about these sweeps several days beforehand and always pulled out before we hit. In a lot of sweeps all you would get were the old men and women and kids. There were VC in there, too . . . but nobody knows *really* who they are.

"There were legal questions. Do we reindoctrinate them? Do we shoot them? Do we put them back on the farm? It was just out of control. So one of John Hart's tasks on the original ICEX charge was, What to do with these civilian detainees? Do they have prisoner of war status? Remember, there's no war going on! But in Geneva Americans were saying, 'We're treating these people like POWs.' The Swiss were saying, 'Okay. We want a look into the prison system.' So Hart became concerned with the problem, and the reason it shows up in the ICEX proposal is at John Hart's insistence.

"It went 'round and 'round, and the long and short of it was, nobody wanted to get the name of the Jailer of Vietnam attached to them. USAID didn't want to touch the problem with a ten-foot pole. . . . Same with the military. Their attitude was 'He's a POW. Forget him. When the war's over, we'll ship him back to the farm.' And so one of our tasks was to investigate the problem and recommend a solution to it. But we never did. What we did was to beg the question. We tasked the problem over to the new plans and programs element of the ICEX staff. What they did, I don't know."

What the ICEX staff did was state the problem. As listed in Tab 10, the major issues were: (1) overcrowding, substandard living conditions, and indiscriminate crowding of POWs, common criminals, VC suspects, and innocent bystanders in ramshackle detention facilities; (2) lack of an adequate screening mechanism to determine who should be interrogated, jailed, or released; and (3) a judicial system (lacking due process, habeas corpus, arrest warrants, and lawyers) that might delay someone's trial for two years while he languished in a detention camp or else might release him if he could afford the bribe.

In seeking solutions to these problems, Tab 10 proposed: (1) the construction of permanent detention facilities; (2) a registration system, coordinated with refugee and Chieu Hoi programs, to eliminate the revolving-door syndrome; and (3) judicial reform aimed at the rapid disposal of pending cases, as devised by Robert Harper, a lawyer on contract to the CIA. In addition, a study team from the CORDS Research and Analysis Division (where Phoenix operational results were sent along with a weekly summary of significant activities) conducted "a comprehensive and definitive study of all aspects of the problems of judicial handling and detention of civilian infrastructure."[12] This three-man study team (John Lybrand, Craig Johnstone, and Do Minh Nhat) reported on apprehension and interrogation methods; the condition and number of jails, prisons, and stockades; and graft and corruption.

Regarding overcrowding, by early 1966 there was no more space available in the GVN's prison system for "Communist offenders." And as more and more people were captured and placed in PICs, jails, and detention camps, a large percentage was necessarily squeezed out. Hence the revolving door.

In the fall of 1967 the forty-two province jails where most VCI suspects were imprisoned had a total capacity of 14,000. Of the four national jails, Con Son Prison held about 3,550 VCI members; Chi Hoa Prison in Saigon held just over 4,000; Tan Hiep Prison outside Bien Hoa held nearly 1,000; and Thu Duc held about 675 VCI, all women. Approximately 35,000 POWs were held in six MACV camps scattered around South Vietnam. VC and NVA prisoners fell under U.S. military supervision while ARVN camps handled ARVN deserters and war criminals.[13]

As attorney Harper wrestled with the problem of judicial reform, a mild-mannered, medium-built, retired Marine Corps colonel, Randolph Berkeley, tackled the detention camp problem. Before retiring in 1965, Berkeley had been the corps's assistant chief of staff for intelligence. In 1966 he was hired by the Human Sciences Research Corporation to do a study in Vietnam on civil affairs in military operations, and in early 1967 he briefed Komer in the White House on the subject. Komer liked what he heard and hired Berkeley (who had no corrections experience) as his senior adviser on corrections and detentions, in which capacity Berkeley returned to Saigon in July 1967 as a member of the ICEX staff.

Upon arriving in Saigon in July 1967, Berkeley was assigned by Evan Parker to manage the SIDE (screening, interrogation, and detention of the enemy) program. Berkeley and five assistants—all experienced corrections officers—were listed on paper as employees of Public Safety's Department of Corrections.

"Shortly after my arrival," Berkeley recalled in a letter to the author, "I was called to report to General Westmoreland. I found him with staff members and Ambassador Komer, and it was explained to me that I needed to draft a plan, within a few weeks, which would make the prisons secure from attacks, as valuable lives were being lost in capturing VC who would then be sprung quickly to fight again. . . . The Westmoreland meeting turned me into an operator so busy with his requirements," Berkeley explained, "that my focus was more on prisons than detentions.[14]

"The CIA provided me space in one of their offices at MACV headquarters, and for several weeks I flew about in an Air America plane, scouting locations for attackproof detention facilities and prisons, taking aerial photographs myself, and developing the plan." While doing this, Berkeley learned: "There were over forty prisons nationwide, detention facilities [usually 'just a barracks surrounded by barbed wire'] in every province, and the GVN had neglected all of them in nearly every aspect, including protection from attack by the enemy.

"When my plan was presented on schedule, General Westmoreland approved it and directed that I execute it. In the next few months the prisons were provided defensive weapons and guards trained to use them, and . . . attacks on prisons quickly lost their popularity. One other device we used was to fly VC prisoners to Con Son Island, which was secure from *any* enemy attack."

Having satisfied Westmoreland's requirement for prison security, Berkeley turned to the issue of detention facilities. "I visited Singapore and Malaya to look at prefab construction for possible use in detention camp construction but decided it was cheaper to do the job with local resources available in Vietnam. Meaning the detention problem was dropped like a hot potato, this time into the hands of the GVN." ICEX Memo No. 5, dated November 2, 1967, handed responsibility for the operation and security of detention camps to the province chiefs, with advice and some resources provided by MACV through Berkeley and the Department of Corrections.

On December 27, 1967, MACV issued Directive 381-46, creating Combined Tactical Screening Centers and stating: "The sole responsibility for determining the status of persons detained by U.S. forces rests with the representatives of the U.S. Armed Forces." Case closed. In every Combined Tactical Screening Center, the detaining unit did the screening, interrogating, and classifying of POWs and civilian detainees, sending enemy soldiers to POW camps or to Saigon if they had strategic intelligence, to provincial jails if they were common criminals, or to PICs if they were deemed to be VCI.

"There were, in effect," Evan Parker explained, "two prison systems: "the civil one under USAID and the military one for POWs. PICs were separate and staffed as an agency program . . . but there had to be a lot of understanding between us in order not to waste money." For example, the CIA would provide PICs with vans but not gas or oil or mechanics. The

Phoenix coordinator would then have to persuade the Public Safety adviser to persuade the Vietnamese police chief to provide these materials and services to the Special Branch, which, considering the ongoing rivalries, got done grudgingly, if at all.

"The problem Phoenix dealt with," Evan Parker added, "was making sure that when a knowledgeable person got picked up, the right person got to talk to him and he just didn't disappear in the system." This weeding-out process happened in the PICs "because there you had the Vietnamese whose salaries were paid by the agency. They weren't beholden to the military or AID."

Ultimately Phoenix did nothing to alleviate the problems of civilian detainees. Rather, as Phoenix threw its dragnet across South Vietnam, tens of thousands of new prisoners poured into the already overcrowded system, and the revolving door syndrome was simply converted by province chiefs into a moneymaking proposition. Meanwhile, ICEX lawyers tried to paper over the problem by compiling a handbook on national security laws and procedures, which legalized the attack against the VCI by permitting the administrative detention of VCI suspects for up to two years without trial. No steps were taken to establish due process for civilian detainees.

Tab 11 called for the Phoenix Directorate "to conduct an on the ground review of interrogation facilities, practices and procedures, including coordination, exploitation, and follow through, with a view to optimum support to the attack on the infrastructure." The object was to focus interrogations on intelligence concerning the VCI at province and district levels and to improve coordination with other agencies. No report was required from the CIA compartment within the Phoenix Directorate on this sensitive subject.

Regarding the "practices" of the PIC program, what is known of official policy comes from Nelson Brickham. "I had an absolute prohibition in field operations activities toward conducting or sanctioning or witnessing any acts of torture," he said. "I said the same thing to my province officers from the third day I was in-country. . . . My statement [which he never put in writing] simply was 'Any of you guys get caught in this stuff, I'll have you going home within twenty-four hours.' And there never was such a case that came into existence, although it's possible that there was and the reports never got to me."

Brickham also directed his province officers "to run the PICs from a distance. It's a Special Branch operation; Americans are not to be identified with the program. These guys were not to go near the PICs on a day-to-day basis. They were not to participate in interrogations there or anything like that."

Brickham's directive was ignored. Warren Milberg, for example, spent

"15 percent" of his time in the Quang Tri PIC, supervising interrogations and advising on questions and topics to pursue. His experience is typical; an earnest Phoenix officer *had* to be at the interrogation center to obtain intelligence quickly. Indeed, in the final analysis, interrogation practices were judged on the quality of the reports they produced, not on their humanity. "Phoenix advisers who took an interest in PIC operations," Milberg writes, "normally attempted to improve the quality of interrogation techniques by carefully going over reports and pointing out leads that were missed and other items which should have been explored in greater detail."[15]

As for torture, "While the brutalization of prisoners did occur, interested Phoenix personnel could curtail support for the PIC unless such unauthorized activities ceased." However, Milberg adds, "Since most advisers were neither intelligence nor interrogation experts, the tendency existed to provide passive support and not to try and improve PIC operations."[16]

According to Robert Slater, director of the Province Interrogation Center program from July 1967 until April 1969, "The first thing the Vietnamese wanted to do was tie the guy up to a Double E-eight." As advisers, however, there was little he and his training team could do to prevent this use of an electric generator, other than to try to raise the professional standards of PIC personnel. Slater and his team (augmented and eventually replaced by a Vietnamese team) taught Special Branch employees how to track VCI suspects on maps, how to keep files and statistics on suspects, and how to take and process photos properly. They did not teach agent handling; that was done in Saigon by CIA experts imported from Washington. "The whole concept of the PIC," according to Slater, "was to get them in and turn them around. Make them our agents. It didn't work for us, though, because we didn't reward them well enough."[17]

The major "procedural" problem in the Phoenix interrogation program concerned the disposition of high-ranking VCI suspects. According to Parker, "High-level prisoners and Hoi Chanhs were invariably taken to higher headquarters and never heard from again." Milberg agrees: "People [at region or in Saigon] grabbed our best detainees on a regular basis, so you tended not to report that you had one. You'd keep him for two or three days," to get whatever intelligence he had on other VCI agents in the province, *then* report that you had him in custody." Milberg writes that when "prisoners of high position in the VCI were removed from local PICs for exploitation at other levels, morale of PIC personnel decreased. Often the result was that the PICs became auxiliary jails and were used to house common criminals."[18]

For Robert Slater, the transfer of important VCI prisoners to higher headquarters was merely standard operating procedure. "We trained Special

Branch people how to properly keep statistics and files, how to use a board in the office to track cases, but most important, to send hot prospects from province to region to the National Police Interrogation Center [NPIC]." In other words, Phoenix interrogation procedures at the province (tactical) level were superseded by interrogation procedures at the national level—the political-level Phoenix seeking strategic intelligence.

Having been the CIA's senior adviser at the National Police Interrogation Center, Slater had valuable insights into the interrogation system at its summit. His story began at Camp Pendleton in early 1967, when he was asked to join a presidentially directed counterinsurgency program that trained and sent fifty Vietnam veterans from the various military services back to Vietnam to serve as province officers and Phoenix coordinators. "But I was a separate entity," he noted in a conversation with the author, ". . . although we went over at the same time." A Vietnamese linguist with three years of interrogation experience in-country, Slater was assigned to the NPIC "on the basis of a decision made in Saigon. Dave West said he won me in the lottery, when the station people sat around and reviewed the résumés of the people coming over."

Slater's cover desk was in USAID II, where he sat beside his boss, a tall, muscular, blond CIA officer named Ron Radda, who served as an adviser to Dang Van Minh. Slater attended briefings given by Minh every morning at the NPIC on Vo Thanh Street, where he had his covert office. "When a prisoner came in from, say, Da Nang," Slater explained, "the reports would come over to my section. I'd put them on an eight-foot-long blackboard and report anything hot to Ron." At that point Radda and Minh's interrogators went to work.

Headquarters for both the Special Branch and the National Police, the NPIC was "a monstrous French compound with a separate, restricted wing for the Special Branch. We cleaned it up," Slater said. "Actually whitewashed it." After Tet, the CIA also built the Special Branch social club, the Co Lac Bo, on the gravesite of the VC killed during Tet. The NPIC held between three and four hundred prisoners, most of whom, Slater says, "were packed forty or fifty in little black holes of Calcutta."

The fact is that prison conditions and interrogation practices in Vietnam were brutal—especially those taken out of sight. Case in point: "At a quarter after twelve on June 16, 1967, I was driving home from work to have lunch with my wife," writes Tran Van Truong in *A Vietcong Memoir*. Suddenly a car cut him off. Two men jumped out, pushed their way into his car, and told him that General Loan had "invited him to come in for a talk." Instead of going to the NPIC, however, Truong's captors took him to the old Binh Xuyen headquarters in Cholon. As he was led into the reception room, he found himself "face to face with a burly, uniformed man whose slit eyes and brutal expression were fixed on me in concentrated hatred . . . a professional torturer who had personally done in many people." The interrogator said to Truong, "I have the right to beat you to death. You and all the other Vietcong they bring in here. There aren't any laws here to protect you. In this place you are mine."[19]

Truong describes this secret interrogation center. "Sprawled out on the floor the whole length of the corridor were people chained together by the ankles. Many of their faces were bloody and swollen; here and there, limbs jutted out at unnatural angles. Some writhed in agony, others just lay and stared dully. From the tangle of bodies came groans and the sound of weeping, and the air was filled with a low, continuous wail. My heart began to race. On one side of the hallway were the doors that apparently led to the interrogation rooms. From behind these came curses and spasmodic screams of pain."[20]

Later Truong was invited inside one of these rooms; it "looked like a medieval torture chamber," he writes. "Iron hooks and ropes hung from the ceiling, as did chains with ankle and wrist rings. These latter devices were well known among the activists and Front prisoners, who called them the Airplane. In one corner was a dynamo. Several tables and benches stood in the middle of the floor or were pushed up against the walls." What happened next, you can imagine.

The last tab of "Action Program," Tab 12, directed Evan Parker and his staff to establish "requisite" reporting systems, "for purposes of program management and evaluation, and for support to field collection and collation activities and operations against infrastructure."[21] At first, each agency used its existing system. Province officers gathered information on the VCI from the collation sections of PICs. They then sent this information to region officers, who used liaison branch reporting formats to relay the information to RDC headquarters in Saigon. There it was analyzed and plugged into a data base "against which future developments and progress may be measured." MACV sector personnel sent their reports on the VCI through military channels to the MACV Joint Operations Office in Saigon, which then coordinated with ICEX.

As MACV and CIA Phoenix personnel were gradually incorporated within CORDS province advisory teams and assigned to PIOCCs and DIOCCs, monthly narrative reports were sent directly to the Phoenix staff in Saigon; meanwhile, the Vietnamese used their own parallel, uncoordinated reporting systems.

Standardized reporting was fully authorized on November 25, 1967, and focused on three things: (1) the number of significant VCI agents eliminated;

(2) the names of those eliminated; and (3) significant acquisition, utilization, and other remarks. Until mid-1968 reports about the DIOCCs would occupy as much time as reports generated *by* the 103 DIOCCs in business at the time. Ultimately information gathered on individual VCI suspects in the DIOCCs became the grist of the Phoenix paper mill.

CHAPTER 11

PRU

In early 1967 Frank Scotton left his post in Taiwan and returned to Saigon to help set up CORDS. Upon arriving in-country, Scotton found Colonel Nguyen Be, who was investigating corruption within RD units, "in Qui Nhon being set up for assassination. While the hit team [dispatched by General Lu Lam, the II Corps commander] was hunting him down," Scotton told me, "I flew him to safety in Pleiku."[1] In the meantime, Ed Lansdale arranged with the RD minister, General Nguyen Duc Thang, for Be to assume control of Vung Tau from Tran Ngoc Chau. Chau went on to campaign for a seat in the National Assembly, itself recently instituted under South Vietnam's new constitution.

Soon after this changing of the guard, Tom Donohue (then George Carver's deputy at SAVA), paid a visit to Vung Tau. Robert Eschbach had replaced Ace Ellis as director of the National Training Center; Jean Sauvageot had taken over the Revolutionary Development Cadre training program; and Tucker Gougleman managed the PRU. On the Vietnamese side, Donohue told me, "Be was in charge. But he wasn't in the same league as Mai," who "was in the Saigon office cutting paper dolls."[2]

Under the tutelage of Nguyen Be, according to Jim Ward, "the RD teams no longer had a security mission."[3] In order to foster a democratic society, Be had transformed RD from the "intelligence and displacement" program Frank Scotton had started three years earlier in Quang Ngai Province into one that emphasized "nation building." But with little success. Of South Vietnam's fifteen thousand-odd villages, only a few hundred were secure enough to hold elections in 1967. And where elections were held, they were typically a sham. The RD teams had nominated all the "elected" village chiefs after the chiefs had been recruited by the CIA and trained at Vung Tau. Nevertheless, the village chiefs really didn't know what they were supposed to do or represent, and, as a matter of practicality, their top priority often was accomodating the local VC. And so with the Revolutionary Development teams on the defensive, the attack against the VCI fell to Phoenix or was contracted out. For example, in order to ferret out the VCI in critical Tay Ninh Province, President Johnson hired, at the cost of thirty-nine million dollars, the services of a Filipino Civic Action team.[4]

Meanwhile, in Saigon fantastic amounts of money were being spent (seventy-five million dollars in 1967) in support of RD. But corruption was rife, and much of the money was diverted into people's pockets. For example, while inspecting Quang Ngai Province in mid-1967, RDC/O chief Renz Hoeksema found eight hundred "ghost" employees out of a total of thirteen hundred cadres on the province RD Cadre payroll. Hoeksema set up a fingerprinting system to prevent further abuses, which, considering that each cadre was paid the equivalent of ten dollars a month, continued unabated.

Despite the problems of corruption and accommodation, the RD program continued to have "intelligence potential," mainly through its static and mobile Census Grievance elements. According to Robert Peartt, who in late 1967 replaced Renz Hoeksema, the RD program's primary mission was still to "put eyes and ears in districts where there were none before."[5] To this end, Peartt managed 284 paramilitary officers in the provinces, each of whom fed information on the VCI into DIOCCs and PIOCCs, while passing information gotten from unilateral sources to the CIA station in Saigon through secure agency channels. On the Vietnamese side, information on the VCI was fed to the province chiefs, who, according to Jim Ward, "may or may not turn this over to Phoenix."

In any event, the political war was not going well in late 1967, and with the shift in emphasis to "nation building," Phoenix emerged from the RD matrix as the CIA's main weapon against the VCI. Its two major action arms, as stated in MACV Directive 381 and Action Program Tab 9, were the PRU and Field Police. Of the two, the PRU were "by far the most effective and suffered the lowest casualties," according to the 1966 Combined Campaign Plan, which also noted that "the type of target attacked by the PRU was strategically most significant."[6]

This chapter focuses on the PRU, which more than any other program is associated with Phoenix. But first a quick review of the Field Police, which at the behest of Robert Komer was to be "redirected" against the infrastructure, "as its main function."

Naturally Colonel William "Pappy" Grieves did not respond favorably to this "redirection" of the Field Police, calling it "a misreading of its mission" and calling Phoenix "a phase that set us back."[7] As an example of the proper use of Field Police, Grieves, in a briefing for General Abrams, cited Operation Dragnet in Binh Dinh Province, "in which three companies of Field Police at a time, for two four-month cycles, worked with the 1st Cavalry Division in Cordon and Search operations." As another example of the proper use of Field Police, Grieves cited CT IV and Operation Fairfax, in which Field Police "search" teams operated under the protection of security squads provided by the 199th Light Infantry Brigade. Working in six-man teams, the Field Police searched hooches for hidden documents and weapons and set up screening centers for suspects, where they checked names against blacklists and faces against photos obtained from the Family Census program. Field policemen also checked ID, voter registration, and draft cards. Such were the functions Grieves believed were appropriate for a law enforcement organization dedicated to providing police services to the public. He complained to Abrams:

> Then Phoenix was upon us. At the direction and insistence of Ambassador Komer, the Field Police SOP was drastically reoriented and reworded, with new emphasis on the anti-subversive mission, which was the only mission which was spelled out, and which was emphasized as the first priority mission.
>
> This mission statement resulted in the tremendous underutilization of the Field Police. Proper Field Police missions, other than anti-subversive, were ignored. Police commanders, local officials, and US advisors considered the job done when a Field Police platoon was given carte blanche to a DIOCC, completely ignoring the fact that Phoenix agencies were not producing enough real targets to keep any of the multiplicity of reaction forces available to them fully occupied on this single mission.

Perfectly appropriate and suitable missions assigned to Field Police units not fully in use by Phoenix were constantly reported by US advisers and observers, including Komer, as misuse of Field Police.

In other words, in the rush to destroy the VCI, a successful police program was derailed. Likewise, with the redirection of the Field Police against the VCI, much to Grieves's dismay, Public Safety advisers like Doug McCollum found themselves working more closely than ever with the Special

Branch and its CIA advisers. In accordance with procedures instituted by Robert Komer, McCollum began receiving Aid-in-Kind funds through the province senior adviser. "I was given twenty thousand dollars a month," he recalled, "which I *had* to spend, to develop agent networks in Darlac Province."[8]

McCollum developed three nets, comprised 90 percent of Montagnards, and presented the intelligence these nets produced at weekly meetings among himself, the CIA's province officer, and the MACV sector intelligence officer. These meetings compared notes on enemy troop movements, VCI suspects, double agents, and double dippers—agents who were working for more than one U.S. agency. The CIA's province officer, according to McCollum, got his intelligence from the PRU and the Truong Son Montagnard RD program. When VCI members were identified, individual or joint operations were mounted. When called upon to contribute, McCollum dispatched his Field Police company under former Special Forces Sergeant Babe Ruth Anderson. The PRU adviser, Roger, was a mercenary hired by and reporting only to the province officer.

"It was two halves of the apple," McCollum recalled. "Collection and operations. We would get blacklists from the province officer with names of people in villages or hamlets. The Field Police went out with ARVN units or elements of the U.S. Fourth Division, usually on cordon and search operations. We'd select a target. The day before we were going to hit it, we'd get picked up in the morning by white Air America choppers. I'd take twenty-five or thirty Field Police, and we'd land about ten miles away and set up a base camp with elements of the Fourth Division.

"We'd get up at three A.M., surround the village, and at daybreak send in a squad to check for booby traps. Then we'd go in, search the place, segregate women and children from men, check people against the blacklist, and take them into custody. We'd get money, boots, and medicine and sometimes NVA. If the VCI were classified A or B, hard core, they were sent to the PIC. At that point it was out of my hands. We'd take the other prisoners back to Ban Me Thuot in police custody; we did not give them to the military. Coming back to camp, the U.S. Fourth Division would use the Field Police as point men."

As McCollum described them, the Field Police were used (as Grieves intended) as roving patrols outside Ban Me Thuot more often than they were used against the VCI. However, because they did on occasion go after the VCI, by 1967 the Field Police were being compared with the PRU. In an October 1967 article in *Ramparts,* David Welch quotes the Khanh Hoa Province psychological warfare officer as saying that the Field Police "work just like the PRU boys. Their main job is to zap the in-betweeners—you know, the people who aren't all the way with the government and aren't all the way with the Viet Cong either. They figure if you zap enough in-betweeners, people will begin to get the idea."[9]

"Just like the PRU boys"? Unlikely. On February 18, 1967, Chalmers Roberts, reporting for the Washington *Post* on the subject of counterterror, wrote that "one form of psychological pressure on the guerrillas which the Americans do not advertise is the PRU. The PRU work on the theory of giving back what the Viet Cong deals out—assassination and butchery. Accordingly, a Viet Cong unit on occasion will find the disemboweled remains of its fellows along a well trod canal bank path, an effective message to guerrillas and to non-committed Vietnamese that two can play the same bloody game."

Komer may have wished that the Field Police would operate like the PRU, and in some cases it did, but the PRU had counterterror and intelligence collection missions which the Field Police never had, even under Phoenix. Moreover, the PRU were not a law enforcement organization; in fact, as CIA assets they operated outside the law and had no legal powers of arrest. The PRU were the personification of the Special Forces' behind-the-lines mentality, which in a counterinsurgency meant getting the VCI in its own villages.

Jim Ward put it this way: "To get a guy in enemy territory, you've got to get an armed intelligence collection unit where the guy's got the balls to go into an area to perform the mission. You're not going to get police officers who are walking a beat in town or the Special Branch guy who deals with agents. Generally, the PRU is the outfit that's best equipped."

The problem with the PRU, writes Warren Milberg, was that "the idea of going out after one particular individual was generally not very appealing, since even if the individual was captured, the headlines would not be very great in terms of body counts, weapons captured, or some other measure of success." As Milberg observes, "careers were at stake . . . and impressive results were expected."[10]

In view of these conflicting pressures—the official call for small-unit operations against the VCI and the dirth of "impressive results" the job afforded—by 1967 a new breed of officer was being introduced to the Vietnam War. While conventional warriors continued to search for big battles, highly trained and motivated unconventional warfare officers, with an abiding appreciation for public relations, were called upon to manage the counterinsurgency.

One of the new breed was Navy Lieutenant John Wilbur, a tall, husky, sensitive Yale graduate. In April 1967 Wilbur journeyed to Vietnam as deputy commander of SEAL Team 2, a twelve-man detachment, with no combat veterans in its ranks, which was assigned to a naval riverine warfare group and quartered in a Quonset hut at the My Tho River dock facility in the middle of the Mekong Delta.

"Frankly," Wilbur (now an attorney in Palm Beach) told me, "the Navy didn't know what to do with us. They didn't know how to target us or how to operationally control us. So basically they said, 'You guys are to go out and interdict supply lines and conduct harassing ambushes and create destruction upon the enemy however you can.' Mostly, we were to be reactive to, and protective of, the Navy's PBRs [river patrol boats]. That was probably our most understandable and direct mission. The PBR squadron leaders would bring us intelligence from the PBR patrols. They would report where they saw enemy troops or if there was an ambush of a PBR. Then we'd go out and get the guys who did it."[11]

Knowing what to do and doing it, however, were two vastly different things. Despite their being highly trained and disciplined, Wilbur confessed, "That first month we started out with the typical disastrous screw-up operations. In our first operation . . . we went out at low tide and ended up getting stuck in mud flats in broad daylight for six hours before we could be extracted. . . . We didn't have any Vietnamese with us, and we didn't understand very basic things. . . . We didn't know whether it was a VC cadre or a guy trying to pick up a piece of ass late at night. The only things we had were curfews and free fire zones. And what a curfew was, and what a free fire zone was, became sort of an administrative-political decision. For all we knew, everybody there was terrible.

"We got lost. We got hurt. People were shooting back at us, and other times we never got to a place where we could find people to shoot at. . . . There was a lot of frustration," Wilbur said, "of having no assurance that the information you got was at all reliable and timely."

As an example, Wilbur cited the time "we raided an island across from where the U.S. Ninth Infantry Division was based. We surrounded the settlement that morning and came in with our guns blazing. . . . I remember crawling into a hut—which in Vietnam was a sort of shed encompassing a mud pillbox where people would hide from attacks—looking for a VC field hospital. There I was with a hand grenade with the pin pulled, my hand on my automatic, guys running around, adrenaline going crazy, people screaming—and I didn't know who the hell was shooting at who. I can remember that I just wanted to throw the goddamned grenade in the hut, and screw whoever was in it. And all of a sudden discovering there was nothing but women and children in there. It was a very poignant experience.

"This was during that first two-month period," Wilbur said, shaking his head. "Then one day a SEAL Team One enlisted man who was assigned to the CIA came down to My Tho. His name was Dave, and he was one of two advisers to the PRU, whom we vaguely knew to be independent. Dave presented us with a whole new perspective. He was dressed in blue jeans and a khaki shirt, he had his own jeep, and he went where he wanted and did what he wanted to do. He had a sense of place. He gave me a fairly broad brief, which attracted the hell out of me. Then he said, 'I've got some people, and I'd like to run some operations with you.'"

In exchange, the SEAL team provided the PRU with increased firepower. Explained Wilbur: "We had all the toys: M-seventy-nines, CAR fifteens, Swedish Ks, grease guns, and grenades. Not only that, we had tremendous support capabilities through the Navy chopper squadron [the Sea Wolves] and the PBRs. And we got immediate reaction through the Navy chain of command. So it was advisable for the PRU to work with us. The Vietnamese wanted helicopter rides and that reaction requirement. In exchange, they had the skills, the intelligence, and the experience to know where the bad guys were—who to shoot at and who not to shoot at. It had the potential for a very beneficial relationship."

One of the attributes of the PRU was that they were required to be from the province in which they operated. "So they had relatives and friends in the area," Wilbur explained, and "they had their own intelligence network set up. They'd go back to their hometown for a couple of days, sit around and drink tea and say, 'What's happening?' And a friend would say, 'Tran's a buddy of mine; I'll tell him about the VC district chief meeting.'" Tran would then tell the PRU adviser and, Wilbur said, "Dave, would come down and say, 'My guy says there's a VC district chief meeting. We need some helicopter gunship support. We want to be able to air-evac. You give us the Sea Wolves, we'll give you the operation, and together we'll score a victory.'"

At first Dave assigned one of the PRU to Wilbur as a scout, so the SEALs could adjust to working with a Vietnamese. The teenage scout "could more or less indicate where the VC were set up, when they might come by, and where we might ambush them," Wilbur told me. "He was the kind of person to say, 'We aren't going to go on a PBR into this town. We'll take a little water taxi, and we'll hide on the river till night, then go in at three A.M. and . . . go there.'

"He helped us chart a course for the war," Wilbur added respectfully. "He gave me a sense of confidence and made us feel that we weren't spinning our self-destructive wheels. I was very aware of how minimally trained most Americans were. I remember being in the Sea Wolf helicopters, and people shooting at peasants on water buffaloes, or at fishermen in dugouts because they happened to be in free fire zones, or rocketing huts and burning things down. But with the PRU, I had the ability to control things better than the William Calleys did. I was a professional officer in an elite organization that had a lot of pride, and we were not going to mess up.

"I remember one evening on an LST, right after an operation, sensing there was nothing but anarchy bordering on idiocy in how we were conducting the war." Wilbur sighed. "I remember writing a letter in my mind to [Yale University President] Kingman Brewster, telling him how important it was for people who had some moral training and education to be on the ground to prevent the negligent cruelties that occurred. I saw myself as that person. I saw an opportunity for SEAL team assets and training to multiply exponentially by working with the PRU. I didn't have any master plan, but I felt, when I am with this kid, I think I know where he's going, and when he puts his hand on my arm and whispers, 'Don't shoot,' I know that I shouldn't shoot. And those were significant things. You felt he was guiding you to do something you ought to do and preventing you from doing what you ought not to do.

"This guy proved himself to me," Wilbur stated emphatically. "He was able to command in the field. He was at home, and I wanted to be like that. He was a very good influence. Plus which the Vietnamese are very sweet, affectionate people. You'd go to places and they'd be walking around holding hands with American sergeants. Or they'd come up behind you, put their arms around you, hug you, and offer you some cigarettes. The kid was like that. He was friendly. He reacted. He hung around and became our mascot, which he liked."

Wilbur was also intrigued by the CIA mystique. "Dave had this freedom and economy. He was working with intelligent people, whom I got to know, and so I indicated to him that I'd like to get into the PRU program. By coincidence, this happened just when the agency wanted to expand the PRU and develop its mission—as they envisioned it, a PRU unit in every province with a Special Forces adviser doing the daily operational control. Special Forces, including SEALs, Force Recon Marines, Green Berets, and SAS [British Special Air Service].

"So, lo and behold, just as I became anxious to get into this area, word came down that the Navy was to suggest an officer to go up to a two-week briefing in Saigon, to develop a SEAL adviser system in this program. This was July 1967. I was sent to Navy headquarters in Saigon and told to go to a huge house with servant quarters around the walls outside. There we were organized by Bill Redel. This was his baby," Wilbur said. "There were no Vietnamese visible, unlike the RD program. The PRU program was American-controlled, which is absolutely essential. It was the breakdown of that control that eventually led to the destruction of the PRU concept."

It is also important to recall that before July 1967 PRU teams were organized and directed by CIA advisers at the province level through the province chief's special assistant for pacification. It was only with the formation of ICEX that the PRU became a national program under CIA officer William R. Redel, a veteran of Greece and Korea who wore a Marine Corps colonel's uniform. "He and I were old and close friends," said Evan Parker, a lieutenant colonel in the U.S. Army Reserve, "and there again we cooperated with him and helped."[12] Collocated in USAID II, Redel and Parker worked as equal partners.

"His program was also for going after the VCI," according to Parker. "These were paramilitary people, mostly former Vietcong. In many instances the province chief preferred to use them as his action arm against the infrastructure, rather than regular army forces, which were not as responsive. That's the key; the PRU were directly responsive because you were dealing with the convinced."

John Wilbur recalled: "Bill Redel was a good-looking guy: Nordic, blue eyes, tanned—a model type of guy. He was a good salesman, too, smooth bureaucratically and very political. He greased palms well.

"Bill organized it like a tour," Wilbur said of the briefing in Saigon. "There were fifteen or twenty of us; SEALs . . . Special Forces . . . Force Recon Marines, and straight-leg Army infantry types. Maybe four or five of each. The way it was set up, the Force Recon people were to be advisers in Eye Corps; by and large the Special Forces in Two Corps; the Army in Three Corps, and the SEALs in Four Corps. Most of us were officers or senior enlisted men.

"During the first week we all stayed at the same hotel . . . and we were indoctrinated in what Civil Operations and Revolutionary Development Support (CORDS) was all about—Census Grievance, Revolutionary Development, et cetera. We were given a presentation indicating that we were all volunteers, then were told what the PRU mission was: to target the political infrastructure of the Vietcong, to gather and compile accurate information about it, and to react upon that information to try to destroy the political and economic infrastructure of COSVN. A lot of our briefing concerned COSVN's political, economic, and military arms. We were told what the VCI was, how it operated, and why we were targeted against it. It was almost like learning about CORDS. It was exciting and heady, too. Coming from the military envelope, I was awakened into this whole new world. It was 'Hey! This is a secret' and 'We're the tough guys!' I was pretty impressed with myself.

"Then we spent two days down at the Vung Tau training camp. It was actually a short helicopter ride north, off in the dunes on the South China Sea. The training facility was a corrugated iron compound with classrooms and barracks, a chow hall, and lecture rooms. Two or three hundred people. Then there were rifle ranges and the operational course. There were American instructors, but not many, and the chief administrator was an American—one of the colorful names—baldheaded, barrel-chested, tough, marinish. It was also at Vung Tau that I met Kinloch Bull. Then we all returned to our tactical areas of responsibility. I went to Can Tho to talk further with Kinloch Bull."

Described by Nelson Brickham as "a strange person, devious and sly,"[13] Bull was one of the few Foreign Intelligence officers to serve as a CIA region officer in charge. A confirmed bachelor, Bull worked undercover as the director of a Catholic boarding school, where he would "preside at the head of the table like a headmaster." Tall and thin and fastidious, Bull was a gourmet cook and protégé of William Colby's. He was also an intellectual who confided to Wilbur that his ambition was to sit at a typewriter on the southern tip of the Ca Mau Peninsula and, like Camus, write existential novels.

"We lived in Binh Se Moi," recalled Wilbur, "the motor vehicle hub of Can Tho. Actually it was about five kilometers up the river, halfway between the city and the airport. We were down an alley surrounded by whorehouses and massage parlors where all the enlisted troops would go. There were five or six of us in the place, and I was by far the junior. The others were all in their second careers. There was Bill Dodds, a retired Army colonel with unconventional warfare experience in Korea and Africa. He was the RDC/O in charge of the paramilitary program of which the PRU was a part. Another guy living there was Wayne Johnson, the Phong Dinh province officer. The Special Branch person, the RDC/P, lived with Kinloch. They were all very paternal, very loyal, very fine people.

"So I started working for Kinloch Bull," Wilbur said, "but the Navy wanted me still to work for them. They wanted to make the PRU program theirs, so they could brag about it. But the CIA told me not to provide the Navy with operational reports, so the Navy tried to have me relieved. At which point Kinloch said, 'Well, we'll kick the Navy out of the Delta program then.' It progressed into a tremendous bureaucratic tug-of-war. Everybody wanted to have the PRU because they inflated their statistics."

In describing how the PRU program was structured, Wilbur recalled, "When I got to Can Tho in July, eleven of the sixteen provinces had PRU units. By September they all did. The number of PRU varied from province to province. We had a very large detachment in Can Tho, maybe a hundred. The smallest was twenty in Kien Giang.

"I tried to make sure my advisers were all senior enlisted men," Wilbur continued, "from either SEAL Team One or Two. I had about half and half. We wanted them for a long period of time, but the SEAL teams wanted to rotate as many people as possible in the program, to keep it theirs. I recommended one-year billets, but it turned out to be six months.

"The advisers were assigned to CORDS province teams and came under the direct command of the CIA's province officer," Wilbur explained. "They were not under my direct operational control, and much to my horror, I found myself in an administrative position. And the senior enlisted people were very political in terms of how they tried to maximize their independence. They loved wearing civilian clothes and saying they worked for the CIA, having cover names and their own private armies, and no bloody officers or bullshit with barracks. So a lot of my job was . . . maintaining good relations between the PRU advisers and the province officers, many of whom were retired Special Forces sergeant majors with distinguished military careers. Often there were sparks between the PRU adviser and province officer because it was a little too close to their old professions."

Province officers with military backgrounds often exerted more control over the PRU teams than young, college graduate-type officers who had difficulty controlling their hard-bitten PRU advisers, many of whom were veterans of OPLAN 34A and the counterterror program before it was sanitized. "So where I had the most problems," Wilbur explained, "it was usually when the province officer had more expertise in what the PRU were doing and would run it more hands-on and, in many instances, better than the PRU adviser. And in those instances I had to relieve the PRU adviser . . . Also, to be honest, a lot of PRU advisers were being manipulated by their PRU people. You can't have people go out on combat operations three times a week indefinitely. It's like having teams in the National Football League play two games a week. It takes time to recover, and the PRU had a natural and understandable desire to bag it. So the PRU would figure out excuses to get their advisers to resist the operation. Then the PRU adviser would become the man in the middle. Sometimes he'd say, 'Well, we can't go out; we don't have enough people.'

"In other cases the PRU advisers tried to win popularity contests with their cadre," according to Wilbur, "and then the province officer would get mad at the PRU adviser for being less responsive to him than the PRU cadre themselves. Then that would create a problem between me and the PRU adviser and in many instances between me and the province officer. Bill Redel had the same problem. He was the national PRU adviser, but he had no authority over the region officers. He would tell me to do things, and I would do exactly what my enlisted men would do. If I didn't want to do it, I'd go to Jim Ward and say, 'Do I have to do this?' And he'd say, 'No. I'm going to tell Bill Redel to go shove it.' In the same way, my PRU advisers would hide behind their province people, so as not to do what I wanted them to do."

As for the quality of his PRU advisers, Wilbur said, "The original SEALs were tough guys who did a lot of training but hadn't fought in any wars. Then they went over to Vietnam. By that time they had kids and they weren't that aggressive. The senior guys wanted to send the PRU people out on operations and stay by the radio. Which was a problem.

"We had one situation where we got the operational report that they went out and killed two people and captured two weapons. But they didn't kill anyone the second time . . . and it was the same weapon. My PRU adviser would drop the PRU team off in his jeep, and he'd pick them up, and he'd transport them back and forth. So he never discovered that they were going out and planting weapons.

"Other guys really rose to the occasion," Wilbur noted, adding that because the older men played it safe, the people who started dominating the SEAL ranks "were the young tiger enlisted men. They'd go out and waste people."

One of those "young tiger enlisted men" was Navy SEAL Mike Beamon, who worked "on the Phoenix program in the Ben Tre and My Tho areas" from mid-1968 through February 1969. Beamon's recollections of the PRU resemble Elton Manzione's more than John Wilbur's. He described the PRU as "made up by and large of guys who were doing jail time for murder, rape, theft, assault in Vietnam. The CIA would bail them out of jail under the condition that they would work in these mercenary units."[14]

Beamon spoke of the PRU using ears as evidence to prove they had assassinated a particular VCI and of PRU stealing weapons from South Vietnamese armories and selling them to the CIA. "I can remember ambushing a lot of tax collectors," he added. "After they made all the collections, you'd hit them in the morning and rob them of the money and, of course, kill them. And then report that all the money was destroyed in the fire fight. They'd carry a thousand dollars at a time. So we'd have quite a party."[15]

From Beamon's perspective, Phoenix was a "carefully designed program to disrupt the infrastructure of the Viet Cong village systems. And apparently on some occasions the plan was to come in and assassinate a village chief and make it look like the Viet Cong did it." The idea, he explained, was to "break down the entire Viet Cong system in that area. . . ."—a plan which did not work because "the Viet Cong didn't organize in hierarchies.[16]

"If you organize in a big hierarchy," Beamon explained, "and have one king at the top and you wipe out the king, that is going to disrupt the leadership. On the other hand, if you organize in small guerrilla units, you'll have to wipe out every single leader. Plus if you organize in small units, you have communication across units and everybody can assume leadership. . . . It is my feeling," he said, "that later on we were hitting people that the Viet Cong wanted us to hit, because they would feed information through us and other intelligence sources to the CIA and set up a target that maybe wasn't a Viet Cong, but some person they wanted wiped out. It might even have been a South Vietnamese leader. I didn't understand Vietnamese. The guy could've said he was President for all I knew. He wasn't talking with me. I had a knife on him. It was just absolute chaos out there. Here we are, their top unit. It was absolutely insane."[17]

"From that you can perceive what my job was," Wilbur told me, referring to the dichotomy between the theoretical goals of administrative officers and the operational realities endured by enlisted men trying to achieve those goals. "It was quality control," he said. "I spent a lot of time traveling between the provinces, doing inspections and field checks on the efficiency of these groups. My objective was to go out on operations with all the units so I could report from firsthand knowledge on what their capabilities and problems were. I was constantly on the road, except when Dodds would make me sit in the office and handle the reports which were sent to me from the PRU advisers in the field. The biggest problem was the thousands of reports. Everybody became deskbound just trying to supply the paper that fed Saigon and Washington."

They were not only deskbound but oblivious as well. "Intelligence people operate in a closet a great deal," according to Wilbur. "It got so the guy literally didn't know what was happening on the street corner where he was, fifteen feet away from him, when he could find the answer by asking someone over coffee."

"Operationally our biggest grapple was the demand to go out and capture VC cadre," Wilbur continued. "Word would come down from Saigon: 'We want a province-level cadre,'" Wilbur said. "Well, very rarely did we even *hear* of one of those. Then Colby would say, 'We're out here to get the infrastructure! Who have you got in the infrastructure?' 'Well, we don't have anyone in the infrastructure. We got a village guy and a hamlet chief.' So Colby would say, 'I want some district people, goddammit! Get district people!' But operationally there's nothing more difficult to do than to capture somebody who's got a gun and doesn't want to be captured. It's a nightmare out there, and you don't just say, 'Put up your hands, you're under arrest!'

"First of all," Wilbur explained, "the targets in many cases were illusionary and elusive. Illusionary in that we never really knew who the VC district chief was. In some cases there wasn't any district there. And even if there was someone there, to find out where he was going to be tomorrow and get the machinery there before him—that's the elusive part. Operationally, in order to do that, you have to work very comprehensively on a target to the exclusion of all other demands. To get a district chief, you may have to isolate an agent out there and set in motion an operation that may not culminate for six months. It was much easier to go out and shoot people—to set up an ambush.

"So what happened, the American demand for immediate results to justify this new program, ICEX, started to swamp our operational capabilities. Also at this particular juncture, the province chiefs started seeing the

PRU as their only effective combat reaction force, and they ultimately were not guys you could say no to all the time. So the province adviser had to spend a tremendous amount of time trying to keep the province chief from using the PRU as his personal bodyguards, to guard his house or bridges or to go fight VC battalions. We literally had times when the province chiefs ordered the PRU to go engage a battalion, and therein was the daily tension of trying to keep the PRU on track, to respond to the demand for high-level cadre-type targets."

The value of pursuing such an illusionary and elusive policy was, of course, debated within the CIA itself, with Jim Ward and Kinloch Bull personifying the CIA's schizophrenia on the subject. "Kinloch was a plans-oriented person," Wilbur stated. "He saw the problems of the inability to control a PRU-type operation. It was the battle of the bulge. Less staff people . . . more contract people . . . and less quality among the contract people. More and more programs. More involvement in overt paramilitary activities. Paying for Revolutionary Development and things other than classic intelligence functions."

But whereas Bull tried to stem the tide, his replacement, Jim Ward, hastened the inevitable. "PRU was Jim Ward's baby," Wilbur remarked. "That was his love."

"PRU in the Delta," said Ward, "were the finest fighting force in the country."

How does Ward know? "I went out with the PRU," he answered, "but just to see how they were operating." And Ward expected his province officers to do likewise. "We encouraged the province officers to go on enough of these operations to make sure they're properly connected. But the SEAL guy had to go on more," he added. "Doc Sells down in Bac Lieu Province used to go on three-man operations. He went out at night dressed in black pajamas, his face darkened with root juices. . . . They'd go deep into enemy territory. They'd grab some figure and they'd bring him back."

On the subject of terror, Ward said, "The PRU started off as a counterterror program, but that wasn't too well received in certain areas. That wasn't the basic mission anyway. They were to get at the guys who were ordering the assassinations of schoolteachers and the village headmen. They were trying to 'counter' terror. Their basic mission was as an armed intelligence collection unit—to capture prisoners and bring back documents."

RDC chief Lou Lapham agreed, when I spoke with him in 1986, saying that he directed that the PRU capture VCI members and take them to PICs for interrogation. "But none of us were so naive," he added, "as to think that we could stop every PRU team from carrying out the assassination mission they had as CTs. . . . We lived in the real world. You just cannot control the people fighting the war"—[18] as Phoenix attempted to do.

"Jim Ward wanted ICEX to work," Wilbur said apologetically. "ICEX was something that Jim came in and proselytized. Committees were set up. But since ICEX was a broad term that assumed coordination of multiagencies, I perceived it as something that was going to make the intelligence-gathering capabilities more efficient and that we in the PRU program were simply going to continue doing what we were doing. The idea of ICEX was to give us better and more timely information on the VCI, and we were to be the reaction arm of ICEX. The Field Police were the reaction arm of the plans people. We're on call; ICEX comes in with a hot number, and we go out with the ambulance. ICEX was a name and appeared to create a process, but the process was informally in place anyway."

As for the viability of the Phoenix-PRU program, Wilbur commented, "People didn't recognize the practical difficulties of achieving what its academic objective was to be, which somehow was to be an ambulance squad that went out and anesthetized the district people and brought them in [to the DIOCC or PIOCC or the PIC], where they were mentally dissected and all this information would come in. It was a rhetorical approach that just didn't work out there."

In any event, Wilbur said, "Tet put all that in abatement. Tet happens and it's 'Don't give me all this ICEX crap. Go out and get the guys with the guns.' Tet propelled the PRU into conventional-type small-unit infantry tactics, which, really, they felt more comfortable with than this sophisticated mission, which was elusive and illusionary. 'There's a VC squad in the woods! Let's go get 'em!' It was a more tangible and interesting thing to do. It's easier to go on an ambush."

This dissolution of the PRU, according to Wilbur, marked the beginning of the end of the program. "People began perceiving them as a strike force, a shock troop sort of thing," he said, adding, "With Tet, the PRU got visible. They produced staggering statistics, which became attractive for manipulation and distraction. The objectives started becoming slogans."

CHAPTER 12

Tet

In September 1967 John Hart developed detached retinas ("From playing too much tennis," Nelson Brickham quipped)[1] and was medevaced to the States for treatment. At William Colby's request, RDC chief Lou Lapham stepped in as acting station chief, juggling both jobs until late November, when Hart returned to Saigon, at which point, according to Tully Acampora, "Hart fell out of bed"[2] and detached his retinas again. Three weeks later, fearing for his sight, would-be soldier of fortune John Hart left Vietnam forever. In January 1968 Lewis Lapham was officially appointed Saigon chief of station.

Unlike his "dynamic" predecessor, scholarly Lou Lapham favored classic intelligence rather than paramilitary operations. His priorities, as he articulated them to the author, were: the political stability of the GVN, understanding the GVN's plans and intentions, unilateral penetrations of the VCI and COSVN, and RD programs, including Phoenix.

Lapham assured GVN stability, his number one priority, by lending to President Thieu whatever support was necessary to keep him in power, while steering him toward U.S. objectives through the use of "compatible left" parties managed by CIA assets like Senator Tran Van Don. As for priority two, Lapham's senior aides secretly recruited Vietnamese civilians and military officers "with something to tell us about GVN plans and strategies."[3]

Vietnamese nationals working for the CIA did so without the knowledge of their bosses. Their motive, for the most part, was money.

Unilateral penetrations of the VCI, Lapham's third priority, were managed by Rocky Stone's special unit. According to Lapham, "This was the toughest thing, getting an agent out in Tay Ninh into COSVN, to learn about VC and NVA plans and strategies. But we thought we did. The operation was a valid one when I left [in December 1968]."[4]

Lapham described his first three priorities as "strategic" intelligence. Phoenix, the other RD programs, and SOG were "tactical." "Phoenix was designed to identify and harass VCI," Lapham said, while "the station kept its strategic penetrations and operations secret." And even though tactical intelligence was not as desirable as the strategic sort, Lapham was careful to point out that it was not always easy to delineate between them. "What you get at a low level often reflects a high-level directive. That's why the station has analysts reading captured documents, intelligence reports from region officers, and briefings from interrogators. They put it all together for us, with bits and pieces adding up to reflect guidelines from Hanoi. That's how you do it, unless you can read Ho's reports."

When put in the proper context, Phoenix-generated intelligence on occasion had strategic implications. So CIA officers on the Phoenix staff also briefed station officers in liaison with the CIO, and Evan Parker himself attended station meetings thrice weekly. In these ways the station kept abreast of strategic intelligence Phoenix stumbled on while coordinating its sapper-level programs.

Despite its strategic potential, Phoenix was designed primarily to sharpen the attack against the sapper-level VCI. Renz Hoeksema explained how: "With the PRU you didn't have controlled sources, and so the information wasn't reliable. . . . That's why I didn't mind Phoenix. It was a way to corroborate low-level intelligence. For instance, if Special Branch has an informer, say, a ricksha driver, who falls into something and passes the information back, then we've got to check on it. But otherwise, everybody was too busy with their own operations to check. Phoenix steps in to do coordinating."[5]

"That's why," Lapham said, "the relationship between Special Branch and the PRU is so important. The PRU was the only *station* means to respond in an operational way to the VCI. When we got hot information through a DIOCC or PIOCC, we could mount an attack."

Clearly, in its fledgling stage, when the majority of Phoenix coordinators were CIA officers operating under cover of CORDS, the program was designed primarily to improve coordination between the station's liaison and covert action branches. It also provided Phoenix coordinators with American and Vietnamese military augmentation and intended to redirect them, by example, against the VCI. However, as John Wilbur explained, "Tet put all that in abatement."[6]

And Tet was a result of Robert Komer's desire to show success, which prompted him to withdraw U.S. forces from Cong Tac IV—even though General Loan was predicting a major assault against Saigon—and to realign South Vietnam's political forces behind Thieu. This is the strategic "political" aspect of Phoenix—alluded to earlier by Vietnam's Diogenes, Tulius Acampora—as conducted by the CIO. The CIO, according to Lou Lapham, "didn't trust the police and wouldn't leave high-level penetrations to the Special Branch." And because "Thieu and Ky were just as concerned with suppressing dissidents as Diem," Lapham explained, "There was an element in the police under the CIO for this purpose."

Liaison with the CIO, an organization Lapham described as "basically military intelligence," was handled by the special unit created by Rocky Stone, which met with the CIA's region and province officers and absconded with their best penetrations.

"The CIA is strategic intelligence," Howard "Rocky" Stone asserted when we spoke in 1987. "We were more interested in talking than in killing. . . . So in 1967 I set up an intelligence division at the National Interrogation Center with the Military Security Service and with McChristian." Within this division, Stone revealed, "I set up a separate unit to select targets—to recruit people with something to tell us. This is the precursor to Phoenix. But when I described Phoenix to [Director of Central Intelligence Richard] Helms, he said, 'Give it to the military.' And the military broadened it into something else."[7]

Short, moonfaced, and a member of the CIA's Vince Lombardi clique, Stone said solemnly, "This has never been told, but we thought that by contacting North Vietnamese and South Vietnamese Communists and giving them secure communications, we could initiate a dialogue toward a settlement. We began negotiating with powerful people. It was only after [Senator Eugene] McCarthy entered the [U.S. presidential] race [on November 30, 1967] that problems developed."

What those problems were, Stone would not divulge, but he did refer obliquely to "lines of communication being compromised." He would also like to have the record show that "we were close in terms of timing and political considerations. There were potential avenues for political negotiations in late 1967, but when those collapsed, the Vietnamese thought we were delaying. Negotiations became impossible in 1968, and that resulted in Tet."

Stone's revelation flies in the face of contemporary wisdom. Stanley Karnow, for one, writes that a settlement was impossible in late 1967 because the Communists "had been planning a major offensive since the summer . . . that would throw the Americans and the Saigon regime into utmost confusion."[8]

Regardless of why it happened, Tet surely did throw the GVN into utmost chaos. On January 31, 1968, thousands of VC simultaneously attacked hundreds of South Vietnam's cities and towns and in the process destroyed the credibility of the American war managers who had pointed to "the light at the end of the tunnel." Not only did Tet pour gasoline on the smoldering antiwar movement, hastening the American withdrawal, but it also prompted the war managers to ponder how the VCI could mount such a massive campaign without being detected.

CIA analyst Sam Adams suggests that by lulling people into a false sense of security, imprecise estimates of VCI strength precipitated Tet. That opinion is backed by Tom McCoy, the CIA's chief of East Asian political and psychological operations, who quit the agency in November 1967 to join McCarthy's campaign. Said McCoy: "LBJ was the victim of a military snow job. Three members of the CIA were back-channeling information, contravening the advice of McNamara, the State Department, and the Joint Chiefs of Staff." But "the directive from the field was to report positively," and "the CIA was outdistanced by regular channels of communication."[9]

In any event, Tet proved to the world that the VCI shadow government not only existed but was capable of mobilizing masses of people. From the moment it erupted, Tet revealed, for all the world to see, the intrinsically political nature of the Vietnam War. Even if the U.S. and South Vietnamese governments found it impossible to admit that the outlawed VCI was a legitimate political entity, they could not deny that it had, during Tet, dictated the course of events in South Vietnam. And that fact pushed Phoenix into the limelight. For while operations against the VCI were overshadowed by the military crisis during Tet, in many areas the DIOCCs were the only places where intelligence on VC military units could be found.

At 3:00 A.M. on January 31, 1968, John Wilbur dragged himself out of bed, grabbed his weapons, strapped on his gear, straddled his Lambretta, and put-putted from Bien Se Moi to Can Tho airport. The trip was uneventful, the road empty of traffic, and Wilbur's thoughts were on the dawn raid the PRU were planning to conduct that morning in Kien Tuong Province. But when he stepped into the operations center in the CIA's command post, "It was like walking into pandemonium. People were going crazy. Everybody was on radios, and all the big Special Forces sergeants who had finally graduated to the C Team were walking around with flak jackets and guns. I asked, 'What's going on?'

"One of the sergeants said, 'Eye Corps, Two Corps, Three Corps, and twelve province capitals in the Delta are under simultaneous attack.' All the calls coming in were from province officers saying, 'We're under attack. We're under attack!'

"So," Wilbur recalled, "I ran out to the helicopter pad, and here come these helicopters. I think, 'This must be my operation.' So I literally ran out to this helicopter, and the closer I got to it, the closer it got to me! And the helicopter starts landing right on top of me! I was yelling—and you can imagine the noise—'Is this the PRU operation to Kien Tuong?'

"And the guy said, 'PRU operation? Bullshit! We've just evacuated from Vinh Long! The airport at Vinh Long is under VC control!' And that," said Wilbur with a shake of his head, "was the commencement of Tet."

It was the same all over South Vietnam, but particularly bad in Quang Tri, where the province capital was under siege for five days and everybody had been reported killed. "The first twenty-four hours were pretty much run on adrenaline," Warren Milberg remarked when we met in 1986. "Then the fighting tailed off, and I began to realize that we had very little chance of surviving any kind of massed assault. This is when I began to burn files and make preparations for my death."[10]

But Milberg decided to stick it out, even though the province chief climbed on a helicopter and left. "I knew if I left the province, which I had the option to do, I could never come back and be effective," he said. "So I stayed for five days. And somehow I survived.

"When the Tet offensive was over," Milberg went on, "the month of February was one of cleaning up and trying to resurrect whatever kinds of agent networks you had—of finding out who survived." For Milberg, this meant traveling to Hue to look for Bob Hubbard, one of several CIA province officers killed during the first hours of Tet, when the VC aimed their attacks at the CIA's interrogation centers and embassy houses.* Milberg described Hue as "a scene of what Germany must have been like during the Allied bombings. I'd never seen anything like it. Fighting was still going on. You heard shots here and there. Some armor units were still in a pitched battle against the NVA in the citadel.

"What happened in Hue was pretty traumatic for me," Milberg confided. "At one point, in looking through the rubble for Hubbard, I stumbled on a Marine colonel alive and well and looting bodies. . . . I nearly killed him, I was so angry. But I wound up drawing my pistol instead, taking him into custody and driving him, screaming and shouting, to the nearest Military Police unit. I won't give you his name, but he was court-martialed.

*CIA compounds in the provinces were called embassy houses, because they were extensions of the State Department's consulates.

"Next," said Milberg, "I confronted what the North Vietnamese had done in the city of Hue and probably elsewhere. They had lists of all the people who had collaborated with the Americans and apparently had lined a lot of these people up and summarily shot them. But the most grotesque thing was to find some of the graves where hundreds of people had been pushed in alive and were buried." After a long period of silence Milberg added softly, "It's the kind of thing I still think about."

When asked if he thought the lists used by the NVA and VC in Hue were any different from Phoenix blacklists, Milberg said, "I see a lot of qualitative differences." He would not say what those qualitative differences were.

Quantitative discrepancies need explaining, too. The number of persons buried in Hue, as estimated by Police Chief Doan Cong Lap and reported by Stewart Harris in the March 27, 1968, *Times* of London, was two hundred. The mayor of Hue, according to Harris, found the bodies of three hundred local officials and prominent citizens in the mass grave. Stanley Karnow agrees with these figures but questions how many of the dead in the mass graves were civilians killed in the retaliatory U.S. bombardment "that also inflicted a heavy toll on the civilian population."[11]

Journalists allowed to view the graves while they were being opened reported seeing tire tracks and scour marks around the edges. Considering that the NVA did not have bulldozers, this suggested that civilians killed in the retaliatory bombing were bulldozed into the graves. Just as disturbing is a February 1972 article in the *Washington Monthly*, by Oriana Fallaci, titled "Working Up to Killing." Fallaci writes that more than a thousand people were killed *after* the liberation of Hue "by Saigon forces," including VC cadres, who surfaced during Tet and were identified and killed by the secret police.

One person who knows what happened in Hue in February 1968 is PVT, the I Corps PRU and Phoenix inspector. The background of this unilaterally controlled CIA asset bears examination. Because his father was a police officer in Hue, PVT was accepted into the Sûreté Fédérale in 1954. When the Americans took over in 1955, he moved over to the Vietnamese Bureau of Investigation, rising through the ranks to become chief of Region 1 in Hue. Unfortunately for his career, his job included investigating the Buddhist immolations, and after the Diem coup PVT was jailed on suspicion of being Can Lao. Released a few months later, he and many of his tainted Catholic colleagues went to work for the CIA "because they didn't like the government" of General Nguyen Khanh.

Intelligent and tough, PVT served the CIA well as a Special Branch administrator in Nha Trang, Phan Thiet, and My Tho. In 1965, when Nguyen Cao Ky sold the CIA the right to organize Counterterror, Census Grievance, and Political Action franchises in the provinces, PVT went to work for CIA officer Rudy Enders in Bien Hoa, as his special assistant for pacification. A fast friendship formed between the two men, and when Enders was reassigned to I Corps as the CIA's senior paramilitary adviser, PVT tagged along and helped his patron manage the region's PRU, RD Cadre, Census Grievance, Special Branch, and Phoenix programs.

The CIA officer in charge of Hue in February 1968 was William Melton, "an older man," according to PVT, "hard and mean," who was angered over the death of his PRU adviser. While the battle for Hue was raging, Enders came down from Da Nang to lend Melton a hand. After a quick look around Enders decided to go after "the VCI who had surfaced at Tet. We had troop density," Enders explained to me, "and we had all these [ICEX] files, so now we grab hold."[12]

Also arriving on the scene at that moment were Evan Parker, Tully Acampora, and General Loan, who a few days earlier, on February 2, 1968, had achieved notoriety when, in retaliation for the murder of several of his secret policemen, he had summarily shot a VC sapper in the head in front of a TV camera crew. Bringing the same avenging spirit to Hue, Loan officially sanctioned Vietnamese participation in Phoenix operations in I Corps when he tacked the ICEX chart to the wall of the Hue City police station.

But in order actually to "grab hold" of the VCI operating in Hue, Rudy Enders required the services of PVT, whom he brought down from Da Nang to interrogate VCI prisoners. As PVT told it, he and "a small team of five or six people" crossed the Perfume River into Hue and went directly to the interrogation center, where "Rudy left me in charge." PVT and his team then interrogated the captured Communists and "took photos and fingerprints and made blacklists."

Reports Karnow: "Clandestine South Vietnamese teams slipped into Hue after the Communist occupation to assassinate suspected enemy collaborators; they threw many of the bodies into common graves with the Vietcong's victims."[13]

On February 24, 1968, the most bitter battle of the Vietnam War ended, and out of the mass graves of Hue rose Phoenix, its success prompting Defense Secretary Clark Clifford to recommend on March 4, 1968, that "Operation Phoenix . . . be pursued more vigorously" and that "Vietnamese armed forces . . . be devoted to anti-infrastructure activities on a priority basis."[14]

One day later, on March 5, 1968, with the Pentagon, hence the Armed Forces of Vietnam, now embracing the CIA's controversial Phoenix program, Prime Minister Nguyen Van Loc ordered the activation of Phung Hoang committees at all echelons, and he appointed Dang Van Minh chief of a special Phung Hoang Task Management Bureau. Doubling as the Special Branch representative on the Phung Hoang Central Committee, Minh immediately assigned Special Branch teams to the most important DIOCCs and PIOCCS on a twenty-four-hour basis and charged them with coordinating intelligence, the theory being that if Phoenix worked in Hue, it could work anywhere.

On March 16, 1968, the same day as the My Lai massacre, General Creighton Abrams replaced William Westmoreland as MACV commander. And by the end of the month Lyndon Johnson had pulled himself out of the upcoming presidential campaign. Warren Milberg, who was on leave in the States, recalled the mood of the country: "I remember coming back and listening to LBJ tell everybody that he wasn't going to seek reelection. That kind of reinforced in my mind the futility of the whole endeavor. It really made a big impact on me. I mean, LBJ was a casualty of the Tet offensive—among other things."

Many dedicated American soldiers and civilians, after Tet, felt the same way. On the other hand, while demoralizing many Americans, the trauma of Tet spurred others on to greater acts of violence. For them, Phoenix would become an instrument to exact vengeance on a crippled, exposed enemy. "Up until the 1968 offensives," Robert Slater writes, "the VCI cadre were almost untouchable. Any losses suffered prior to then were insignificant. Confident of almost certain victory during the Tet Offensives, however, they surfaced their key cadre. The results are well known; the attacks cost the Viet Cong thousands of their most valuable cadre, including irreplaceable veterans with ten to twenty years of revolutionary activity."[15]

Professor Huy concurred, writing that "many agents whom the VC had planted in the towns and cities were discovered because of their activities during the attack, and were eliminated by the Saigon government."[16]

It is a fact that Tet was a psychological victory for the VCI. But it was a Pyrrhic victory, too, for in proving itself a viable political entity, the VCI backed the GVN into a corner. Fear, and a chance to exact revenge, finally brought Phoenix to the forefront of the GVN's attention. All that remained was for Lieutenant Colonel Robert Inman to bring everyone together at the middle management level.

Having served in Vietnam with the Army Security Agency from 1963 till 1965, Robert Inman had already had, like many Phoenix officers, a tour of duty under his belt. Also like many Phoenix veterans who contributed to this book, Inman is compassionate, intelligent, and more than a little irreverent. "At the time I arrived in Saigon in early 1968," he told me, "there was a U.S. staff but no corresponding Vietnamese staff. On the U.S. side there were about twenty people, mostly military, although the key management-level positions at the directorate were CIA. . . . We had two read files: one for everybody and one for the CIA only. The distinction was maintained throughout my tour, but"—he chuckled—"I got to read the CIA stuff."[17]

The reason for the compartmentation, according to Inman, was that "CIA coordination with Special Branch continued at a higher level than Phoenix." Likewise, the parallel chains of command extended into the field, with CIA province officers receiving operational direction from ROICs while at the same time, in their capacity as Phoenix coordinators and members of the CORDS province advisory team, reporting administratively to the CORDS province senior adviser. U.S. military personnel serving as Phoenix coordinators fell administratively within CORDS but received operational direction from MACV. The CIA-MACV schism was to be narrowed in some provinces, but the gap was never universally bridged.

At the time Inman arrived at the Phoenix Directorate, there were three State Department officers on staff: Lionel Rosenblatt, Bernard Picard, and their boss, John E. MacDonald. According to Inman, MacDonald's job "was never revealed." Picard, now a prominent Washington lawyer, would not explain to me what he did. Rosenblatt merely said, "As a [twenty-two-year-old] junior officer . . . I was assigned to CORDS-Phoenix in December 1967 and served there till June 1969. During this time my principal duties were: (one) orientation and visits to DIOCCs, December 1967 until March 1968; (two) Cam Ranh City Phung Hoang coordinator, March 1968 through September 1968; and (three) Phung Hoang liaison officer in Saigon."[18]

Executive Director Joe Sartiano, Inman recalled, "spent a lot of time with agency officers in the provinces, trying to coordinate the RDC/P people who ran the PICs with the RDC/O people who ran the PRU under the province officer system."

Inman himself was assigned to the operations section of the Phoenix staff, of which, he said, "There was a unilateral agency effort and a binational effort. And they were separate, too." The Phoenix Reports Branch, under Lieutenant Colonel Lemire, was headquartered not in USAID II but in the old embassy building on the river. "Nothing was computerized," Inman stated. "It was all pens and pencils and paper." There were, in addition, a plans and training section under Lieutenant Colonel Ashley Ivey and an administrative section under CIA officer James Brogdon.

As for the mood of the Phoenix staff, according to Inman, "The problem on the U.S. side was that cynicism was developing. Gooks, slopes, dinks: You didn't hear those words in the Saigon office, but the attitude was there." This racist attitude generally belonged to proponents of unilateral operations, as opposed to people, like Inman, who wanted to hand the job to the Vietnamese. "There were definitely two sides." He sighed, adding, "A lot of people after three months said, 'Why should I waste my time with the Vietnamese at the national level? I can get into the Special Branch files, and I can run the PRU, so what the hell?' " When asked if this was due to legitimate security concerns, Inman responded, "Lack of security was often just an excuse for incompetency."

Inman did not blame Even Parker for the bigotry evident at the Phoenix Directorate. "Parker was not paternal," he said. "But he had reached a point in his career where he was functioning more on a diplomatic than an operational level. And Ev had frustrations with his own people inside the CIA who viewed the RDC/P and RDC/O systems as competitive. Each side would say, 'Yeah, talk to them, but don't tell them too much.' No one wanted to divulge his sources."

There were other problems with Phoenix. "For example," Inman commented, "one province in Three Corps was relatively pacified, and the province senior adviser there thought Phoenix would only stir things up. He thought his ninety-five percent HES [Hamlet Evaluation System] rating would drop if they started looking for trouble." The problem, Inman explained, was that "The U.S. had tremendous resources, enough to fund twenty-five programs, all first priority. Bigger pigs, and better rice, and Phoenix. Now, some province senior advisors simply said, 'There's no way to do it all,' and picked one or two to focus on—and not always Phoenix."

The other major problem, Inman said, was that "Phoenix was used for personal vendettas."

When Inman arrived at the Phoenix Directorate, Evan Parker's military deputy was Colonel William Greenwalt, "an administrator trapped in an office." Inman and his best friend on the Phoenix staff, Lieutenant Colonel William Singleton, concluded that "the CIA had Greenwalt there to take the rap if anything went wrong." What went wrong was Greenwalt's career. Greenwalt was slated to become a brigadier general, but by virtue of his association with the CIA, via Phoenix, his career jumped track, and he retired as a colonel when his Phoenix tour ended.

"Operations was run by a civilian," Inman recalled, "a retired full colonel on contract to the CIA. His name was William Law. He'd been the military attaché in Laos. Singleton and I were assigned to Law, and Law told us to review everything in the files because he didn't know what the next step was going to be. After a month it got to be a drag, so I complained to Greenwalt. I said, 'I want another job. I'm wasting my time.' "

Greenwalt relented. "He gave me and Singleton three or four actions, which we resolved in about an hour," Inman recalled, and shortly thereafter "Law was sent down to the Delta to be the CIA's contact with the Hoa

Hao." Law was replaced by George French, "a very personable, very experienced CIA officer who had done some very dramatic things in his career, from the OSS to Cuba."

George French's first job was as a demolitions expert in an Arizona lead mine, in the years before World War II. For that reason he was recruited into the OSS's Underwater Demolitions Unit in 1943 and assigned to Detachment 404 in Ceylon. Over the course of his CIA career, French did tours in Korea, Turkey, Pakistan, and Saipan and, as a member of the CIA's Special Operations Division, in Laos, Cambodia, and elsewhere. In the summer of 1967 French was assigned to III Corps as Bob Wall's deputy in charge of PRU, even though he actually outranked Wall. Nor did he appreciate that Wall acted "like a dictator." So he asked for a transfer and was assigned to the Phoenix Directorate, replacing William Law as operations chief. French described the job as mostly traveling to the provinces to see what was going on and asking, "How's your body count?" The rest of the job, he told me, "was just paper shuffling: compiling information and passing it on up to MACV."[19]

In March 1968 the Phoenix-Phung Hoang program began to gel. Passing up the opportunity to manage the Soviet/Russia Division (with Rocky Stone as his deputy), William Colby instead had returned to Vietnam, at the request of Richard Helms, to serve as acting chief of staff of CORDS. Because he was too overbearing to communicate effectively with the Vietnamese, Robert Komer needed Colby to work with Interior Minister Tran Thien Khiem in formulating counterinsurgency policy and procedure at the national level. Colby understood Vietnamese sensibilities and knew enough about the country to select and assign CORDS advisers where they were needed most. He also understood the dynamics of the attack on the VCI: that Phoenix advisers were needed specifically to help local authorities develop card files and dossiers modeled on the Diem-era ABC system. In the process Colby was to achieve infamy as the man most closely associated with Phoenix and as its principal apologist.

"At the time I arrived," Inman recalled, "Parker was meeting with Colby and Khiem, developing proposed action programs, writing documents, and sending them down. Khiem was saying yes to everything, but nothing was happening on the Vietnamese side. So I went to Greenwalt and asked permission to contact some lieutenant colonels and majors in the Vietnamese Ministry of the Interior. Greenwalt said okay, and I approached Phan Huu Nhon, my counterpart during my first tour and the J-seven special intelligence officer to the Joint General Staff. Nhon sent me to see Lieutenant Colonel Loi Nguyen Tan, the action officer for Phoenix at the Interior Ministry, where he had a desk, but nothing coming in."

Here it is worthwhile to pause and realize that one reason the Vietnamese were slow in creating their own version of the Phoenix Directorate was their difficulty in finding a suitable translation for the word "infrastructure." To solve the problem, President Thieu appointed a commission consisting of senior American and Vietnamese intelligence officials. Attending as an interpreter-translator was Robert Slater.

"After five lengthy and rather hot (both in temperature and temperament) sessions," Slater writes, "a decision was reached that the term that was presently in use would be retained. The Vietnamese term was *ha tang co so* . . . meaning 'the lower layer of an installation' or 'the underlying foundation.'" According to Slater, this misinterpretation was the "crux of the problem in the Allied attack against the VCI. If the South Vietnamese government cannot get across to the South Vietnamese people the danger of the VCI through an adequately descriptive word, then how can they hope to combat them?"[20]

The "crux" of the problem, of course, was not a lack of understanding on the part of the Vietnamese but the fact that the Americans insisted on defining the VCI in terms that conformed to their ideological preconceptions. Ed Brady put the problem in perspective when he explained that for the Vietnamese, "Committees at lower levels are the infrastructure of any higher-level committee." In other words, village committees are the infrastructure of district committees, district committees of province committees, and so on ad nauseam. According to Brady, "The word 'infrastructure' drew no distinctions at all, and whatever level the VCI existed at depended solely on each individual's own semantic interpretation."[21]

"They were writing documents," Inman said, "and sending them down for translations, but no one understood what the word 'infrastructure' meant, and no one dared go back to Khiem and say, 'I don't understand.' Tan said to me, 'What is this infrastructure?' They were looking it up in the dictionary and coming up with highways and electrical systems and such. . . . I said, 'It's their leaders.'

"And Tan said, 'Oh. *Can bo*. "Cadre." That's what we call them.'"

What Thieu's national commission could not resolve in five days, two lieutenant colonels resolved in five minutes. Next, Inman said, "Tan introduced me to a major who was Thieu's personal chief of staff. Tan, this major, and I sat down and wrote up Thieu's Presidential Directive.* Then this major

*Decree Law 280 defined the VCI as all party members from COSVN to hamlet level and as cadre that "direct and control other parties and organizations such as . . . the Alliance of National Democratic and Peace Forces, or other similar organizations in the future." The only people named as not being VCI were "VC military units" and "citizens forced to perform as laborers." Law 280 charged the Ministry of the Interior, not the Defense Ministry, with footing the Phung Hoang bill.

got the papers to Thieu. The papers were issued in July, and Tan moved into the National Police Interrogation Center, with about ten senior people from Special Branch, as Khiem's man in charge of Phung Hoang. Duong Tan Huu [a former precinct chief in Saigon and, before that, Nha Trang police chief] was assigned as the senior National Police officer. Major Pham Van Cao became the day-to-day manager of the Phung Hoang Office, and I spent the next eight months there as liaison to the Vietnamese national-level staff."

A self-proclaimed "true believer" in the right of the Vietnamese to settle their own affairs, Inman had little to do with the U.S. side of Phoenix. "I was mostly at NPIC headquarters," he stated. "My role was as salesman. I'd check in with George French for thirty minutes in the morning, sometimes only once or twice a week. I'd get input through him from a lot of people; he'd say, 'Sell this to the Vietnamese.' I'd channel policies and directives and manuals from French—all in English—over to the Phung Hoang Office, and they translated them. Then I'd spend time getting everybody to read and understand and sign off on them. I'd run them past Census Grievance and RD, Field Police and Special Branch, the Interior Ministry and ARVN, and everybody would sign off." And that is how the Vietnamese Phung Hoang Office got its marching orders from Colby and the Phoenix Directorate.

The other reason why the Vietnamese were slow in creating the Phung Hoang Office concerned the struggle between President Thieu and Vice President Ky, a struggle that in 1968 reflected changes in the relationship between America and South Vietnam brought about by Tet. The first signs of realignment appeared when President Johnson withdrew from the presidential campaign, at which point his influence in Saigon began to wane. Johnson, however, remained committed to a negotiated settlement because success at the bargaining table was the Democratic party's only chance of getting Hubert Humphrey elected.

But Republican candidate Richard Nixon seized the issue and used it to subvert the Democrats. The darling of the Kuomintang-financed China Lobby, Nixon, through intermediaries in Saigon, persuaded Thieu to postpone negotiations until after the elections, assuring himself the presidency of the United States, at the expense of prolonging the Vietnam War.

Reflecting those developments in Washington, a similar political realignment began in Saigon in May 1968, when the VC initiated a second wave of attacks on Saigon, and Thieu, writes Professor Huy, "as usual had no quick response." But Ky did react decisively. "He tried to mobilize young people for the defense of Saigon and received a favorable response."[22]

"With Tet," said Tully Acampora, "Loan made a comeback. Thieu was in another camp, watching and waiting. Through February the attacks increased, and by May, with the second offensive, Loan thinks he can walk on water. Then he gets shot outside of MSS headquarters, and that's the beginning of the end. It's all downhill after that."

On May 5, 1968* General Nguyen Ngoc Loan was seriously wounded and quickly replaced as director general of the National Police by Interior Minister Khiem, who appointed his own man, Colonel Tran Van Pham. Next, writes Professor Huy, Thieu "began his plan to weaken Ky."[23] His first move was to dismiss Prime Minister Loc and replace him with Tran Van Huong, a former mayor of Saigon and a bitter enemy of Ky's. During the 1967 elections Ky had coerced "peace" candidate Truong Dinh Dzu into pressing blackmail charges against Huong. And so, as soon as he was appointed prime minister, Huong tasted sweet revenge by dismissing most of Ky's backers in the administration.

"Then," writes Huy, "Ky received a new blow when several officers loyal to him and serving in the Saigon police were killed at the beginning of June in Cholon during their campaign against the second attack of the Communists. They were killed by a rocket launched from an American helicopter. Apparently this was a mistake, but many people thought it was due to the American decision to help Thieu against Ky."[24]

The incident occurred on June 2, 1968, when a rocket fired from a U.S. Marine helicopter gunship "malfunctioned" and slammed into a wall in a schoolyard on Kuong To Street. The wall collapsed, killing seven high-ranking officials who had been invited by the Americans to the battlefront in the belief that the VCI leadership was hiding in the home of the Buddhist leader Tri Quang. Killed were Pho Quoc Chu, Loan's brother-in-law and chief of the Port Authority; Lieutenant Colonel Dao Ba Phouc, commander of the Fifth Ranger Battalion; Lieutenant Colonel Nguyen Van Luan, Saigon police chief; Major Le Ngoc Tru, Cholon police chief and Loan's personal aide; Major Nguyen Ngoc Xinh, Combined Security Committee and First Precinct police chief; and Major Nguyen Bao Thuy, chief of staff to Lieutenant Colonel Van Van Cua, Loan's brother-in-law and the mayor of Saigon,

Four days later President Thieu appointed Colonel Tran Van Hai director general of the National Police. On the same day that he took office, Hai dismissed Ky's eight remaining police chiefs in Saigon and replaced Special Branch chief Nguyen Tien with his friend Major Nguyen Mau, who refused to accept Phoenix within the Special Branch and instead incorporated the Combined Intelligence Staff within a new Capital Military District Command (CMDC).

*One day later Colonel Luu Kim Cuong, commander of the First Transport Group and a senior aide to Ky, was killed by border police on the outskirts of Saigon.

A by-product of Tet, the Capital Military District was formed for two reasons: to organize better the resources against the VCI cadres that had aided VC sapper units during Tet and to regulate the half million refugees produced during Tet and pouring into Saigon. It was also with the creation of the Capital Military District that Thieu and Khiem wrenched control away from Ky and Loan once and for all. Encompassing Saigon's nine precincts and Gia Dinh Province, the CMD had as its American counterparts MACV's Capital Military Assistance Command and a Phung Hoang committee in First Precinct Headquarters. Prior to the CMD, Phoenix personnel from Gia Dinh Province had patrolled Saigon's precincts on a circuit rider basis; as of June 1968, Phoenix advisers were placed in DIOCCs in each of the precincts. Phoenix precinct advisers reported to Lieutenant Colonel William Singleton through his deputy, Major Danny L. Pierce, whom Robert Inman describes as "an active Mormon who traveled all over the country on Sundays holding services." In this capacity, Inman informs us, "Singleton and Pierce were involved directly in intelligence and reaction operations in the back alleys of Saigon."

CIA operations in the Capital Military District—aka Region Five—were managed by a series of veteran CIA officers under their cover boss, Hatcher James, the senior USAID adviser to the mayor of Saigon. Headquartered behind City Hall, the Region Five officer in charge monitored all Phoenix operations in the Capital Military District.

A few days after the CMD was created, General Nguyen Khac Binh was appointed director of the CIO and quickly conferred upon station chief Lou Lapham "a charge from Thieu to run intelligence operations anywhere in the country, going after the big ones."

With Ky's people in the grave or the hospital, President Thieu began to shape the government of Vietnam in his own image, appointing ministers, police and province chiefs, and military commanders who would do his bidding. Also, by issuing Law 280, Thieu lifted the monkey off the U.S. Embassy's back, and in return, the Americans looked away when he began persecuting domestic opponents whose "compatible left" political organizations fell under Law 280's definition of VCI "cadre." From July 1968 onward the task of ensuring the GVN's internal security fell to General Tran Thien Khiem, who, according to Dang Van Minh, was "the real boss of administration and intelligence." CIA asset Khiem—serving as interior minister, deputy prime minister for pacification, and chairman of the Phung Hoang Central Committee—thereafter worked hand in hand with William Colby in steering Phoenix into infamy.

With the promulgation of Law 280—which compelled Vietnamese corps commanders and province chiefs to organize Phung Hoang committees—and, one week later, MACV Directive 381-41, which ordered U.S. military and civilian organizations to support Phung Hoang—Phoenix was ready to run on both its American and Vietnamese cylinders.

All that remained was for Lieutenant Colonel Inman to spread the word. "One of my principal functions," he said, "was to take Tan ['polished' and 'above it all'] and Cao ['blunt and offensive'] to visit the PIOCCs and DIOCCs and give a pep talk. I probably visited every district in my last eight months." But, he added, "It was not my job to sell Phoenix to the U.S., so we didn't announce our arrival; the district senior adviser wouldn't even know I was there. My job was to sell Phung Hoang to the Vietnamese, and I stayed on the Vietnamese side."

The people saddled with the chore of selling Phoenix to the Americans were the region Phoenix coordinators—field-grade military officers who began arriving in Vietnam in January 1968. Their role is discussed in Chapter 14. But first some statistics on Phoenix through August 1968.

No aspect of Phoenix is more significant than its impact on civilian detainees, and despite the increase in the number of CDs after the GVN's acceptance of Phoenix in July 1968, the construction of facilities capable of holding them never materialized. Instead, hard-core VCI were transported from mainland camps to Con Son Island, and four "mobile" military field courts were authorized in October 1967 to supplement the four courts authorized in 1962. Confirmed VCI were tried by province security committees, whose proceedings were closed to the public—the defendant had no right to an attorney or to review his dossier. Security committees could release a suspect or send him to prison under the An Tri (administrative detention) Laws or to a special court. Due process for CDs remained on the drawing board.

Nevertheless, in compliance with Law 280, the four Vietnamese corps commanders (General Hoang Xuam Lam in I Corps, General Vinh Loc in II Corps, General Nguyen Duc Thang in IV Corps, and General Nguyen Khanh in III Corps), formed joint Phoenix-Phung Hoang working groups and corps-level Phung Hoang committees, bringing the military and police into varying degrees of cooperation, depending on the commander's personal preferences. For example, Lieutenant Colonel Lemire reported that General Khanh "was reluctant to support police type operations with military resources."[25] Khanh assigned a mere captain as his regional Phung Hoang coordinator.

"In Eye Corps and Two Corps," Lemire noted, "the cordon and search, using Phung Hoang blacklists, appears to get the best results. In Four Corps the PRU is still the main action arm. In Three Corps the joint PRU/Police/RF/PF district operation seems to be most productive."

Everywhere the degree of Vietnamese participation in Phoenix rose steadily. By August 1968 Phung Hoang committees existed in 42 provinces and 111 districts; 190 DIOCCs had been built, at an average cost of fifteen thousand dollars each, and 140 were actually operating, along with 32 PIOCCs. A total of 155 Phoenix advisers were on the job. However, confusion still existed about the proper relationship between PIOCCs and Phung Hoang committees. In some provinces the two were merged, in others they were separate, and sometimes only one existed. Many Phung Hoang committees had no relationship at all with DIOCCs, which were often viewed as an unrelated activity. The change in name from ICEX to Phoenix to Phung Hoang added to the confusion. In Pleiku Province the ICEX Committee became the Phoenix Committee but met separately from the Phung Hoang Committee. Everywhere Americans and Vietnamese continued to conduct unilateral operations, and tension between the Special Branch and the military persisted as the biggest Phoenix-related problem.

The other major problems, cited in a May 1968 report written by CORDS inspectors Craig Johnstone and John Lybrand, were lack of trained DIOCC advisers; lack of agreement on the definition of the word "infrastructure"; inadequacy of reaction forces at district level, the exception being when PRU were sent down from province; improper use of Field Police forces; torture of prisoners*; lack of a standardized filing system; poor source control mechanisms; lack of coordination between Phoenix and other free world forces; and Census Grievance participation in Phoenix.

To facilitate Phoenix operations nationwide, the CIA issued two handbooks in June 1968. The first, a thirty-one-page document titled *The VC Key Organization from Central Level down to Village and Hamlet Levels*, outlined the VCI for Phoenix operators. The other was the Phoenix Directorate's first manual of procedures, outlining the program from Saigon down to the DIOCCs. At this point a detailed picture of the estimated seventy thousand VCI was emerging, targeting was becoming specific and scientific, and results were improving. Lieutenant Colonel Lemire reported that "as the DIOCCs and PIOCCs have refined data bases, gained experience, and mounted more operations against targetted individuals, the neutralization rate has been well over 1000 per month for the last four months." In Gia Dinh Province, Lemire reported, "the combination of an aggressive Province Chief and a dedicated Phoenix Coordinator has more than quadrupled the monthly rate of killed, captured, and rallied VCI."

Much emphasis was placed on neutralization rates, which were deemed the only objective way of measuring Phoenix success. As reports poured into

*Writes Johnstone: "The truncheon and electric shock methods of interrogation were in widespread use, with almost all advisors admitting to have witnessed instances of use of these methods."

the directorate from all over the country, numbers were tabulated and scores posted; by the end of June 1968, more than six thousand VCI had been "neutralized," with exact numbers available from each DIOCC so Phoenix managers could judge performance.

As Evan Parker explained it, "You've got people. You've got some sort of structure set up, some facilities and money and resources. Then you need a record-keeping system. Unfortunately," he added, "people lived on reporting. . . . In order to get brownie points, a guy would say, 'We conducted X many Phoenix operations,' and that looks good on your record. But simply because they were ordered to conduct sweeps, they might pick up some VC, but they could just as easily have been soldiers as civilians. Whatever the results were, it was conducted in the name of Phoenix. A lot of things were done in the name of Phoenix. And this goes into your record-keeping system."

Ralph Johnson writes: "It was this reporting weakness which for a long time attracted much of the foreign press criticism of Phung Hoang."[26]

"Then"—Parker groaned—"Komer took it one step beyond and assigned goals for the number of VCI neutralized. Komer was a great one for setting objectives, then keeping score of your performance against these objectives. And this is how quotas got developed in the summer of 1968."

Borrowing military "kills" to meet Komer's quotas was more than inflationary. John Cook, the Phoenix coordinator in Di An District in Gia Dinh Province, in his book *The Advisor* notes that switching the identity of a VC soldier killed in combat with that of a known member of the infrastructure meant that "If at a latter date the real member was captured or killed, this action could not be reported, for you can only eliminate a man once."[27]

"Komer didn't understand the police nature of the attack against the VCI," Bob Wall said scoffingly. "When LBJ put pressure on him, he invented quotas as a management tool, and this destroyed Phoenix. Quotas gave starving policemen a way to feed families. It let them bring in bodies and say they were VCI."[28]

"I resisted like mad the idea of quotas," insisted Evan Parker, "because I felt this would lead to cheating, or in innocent people being arrested, and this looking good on the quota. Or there might even be names listed on arrest reports that didn't even exist. In one area I was told they were taking names off the gravestones. . . . But"—he sighed—"they had quotas, and they tried to meet quotas, and that's how you get the idea that this was some sort of murder organization."

Indeed, Phoenix was labeled an assassination program, evoking the specter of war crimes and leading many people to minimize the impact of quotas. "I think it was moot," Warren Milberg said. "It was something I just ignored. For the most part it was coming to you from people in Saigon who were going home at night and sitting under the veranda of the Continental Hotel.

You just didn't take that stuff seriously. They couldn't relate to what you were doing, just like you couldn't relate to what they were doing. It was a different war. It was a different part of the world."

Another Phoenix coordinator, a CIA Czechoslovakian desk officer sent to Bien Hoa Province in 1968, saw comparisons between Phoenix and Gestapo tactics in World War II. For him, "The reports I sent in from my province on the number of Communists that were neutralized reminded me of the reports Hitler's concentration camp commanders sent in on how many inmates they had exterminated, each commander lying that he had killed more than the others to please Himmler."

Why one person remained silent and went along with Phoenix while another spoke out against it is the subject of the next chapter.

CHAPTER 13

Parallax Views

"Our PRU in Quang Tri were all victims of Communist terror," said Bob Brewer, who, like many CIA officers in Vietnam, believed he was singled out for assassination. A dedicated anti-Communist who felt personally threatened, Brewer was motivated, and so were his PRU. "They were so red hot you had to control them," he added with delight.[1]

The man with the job of controlling the PRU in Quang Tri Province was Warren Milberg. Elegant and sophisticated, Milberg today is the consummate corporate American male. His employer, the Titan Corporation, designs "Star Wars" lasers. And more than twenty years after the fact—despite a lingering resentment against cynical war managers who send idealistic young soldiers on suicidal rites of passage—Warren Milberg still embraces the cold war ideology and its corresponding Phoenix mythology.

At the core of Milberg's melancholy are two related experiences. Both happened in 1965 during his first tour in Vietnam, when he was deputy chief of security at the Da Nang air base. There Milberg's involvement with agent nets brought him into contact with local CIA operators, who liked his style and invited him to participate in the ongoing SOG operation called Prairie Fire. Milberg joined SOG without the knowledge of his Air Force superiors. He put on black pajamas and worked with a team of Nung mercenaries, leading them on long-range patrols into Laos to monitor and interdict NVA units. Sometimes they sat on the Ho Chi Minh Trail and shot field-grade NVA officers from a thousand yards away, "so they never even heard the report."[2]

"This is where things started to get exciting," recalled Milberg, who along with his other duties, began organizing counterterror teams. "I was doing training of Vietnamese and Americans—Marines and some Army people." As for his indigenous personnel, "The Vietnamese were gansters and thugs—mercenaries who we trained and who were in our pay.... But my perception of the role of the CT teams was to strike terror into the enemy—the NVA and VC—not the population.

"It was during this period of time," Milberg continued, "when I started to think more about the war and my role in it. And I also began to see evidence of how the Vietcong were operating in the hamlets. I saw the messages for the tax collectors and the political officers. And what will always stand out in my mind was the terror and torture they used to strike fear and get compliance from the villagers... an event where a particular village chief's wife, who was pregnant, was disemboweled and their unborn baby's head was smashed with a rifle butt. We stumbled on this incident quite by accident within hours of it happening. I'd never seen anything like it in my life."

Milberg would not talk about the other traumatic incident, other than to say he was asked by the CIA to parachute into North Vietnam. That he did, even though he had never jumped from an airplane before. And something terrible happened, something too painful to describe, something that made him question the motives of war managers who would ask him to do such a reckless thing. He wondered if the mission had any purpose other than testing the men involved—to see how far they could be pushed and to prepare them for equally preposterous missions in the future. He wondered if he was a guinea pig.

"This event resulted in my being afraid, which was a new experience for me. I spent a lot of time between tours thinking about it and wondering how I would react the next time. So it was almost like I needed to test it again." In this way Warren Milberg's self-doubt compelled him to return to Vietnam in August 1967, at the request of the CIA as part of the Presidentially Directed Counter-Insurgency Program that fleshed out ICEX.

On the other hand, remorse drove Elton Manzione out of Vietnam, out of the military, and nearly out of his mind. Consider the cases of Manzione and Milberg: two men equally exposed to a blend of secrecy and terror. Enlisted man Manzione turned on his masters, renounced American imperialism, and spoke out against the misdeeds of the CIA. Officer Milberg submitted to authority and in return became one of the protected few, accepted into the cult of the phoenix, rewarded with the American dream.

Manzione and Milberg are remarkably alike. They have the same kind of build, are the same age, and come from the Greater New York Metropolitan Area. Both have dark complexions and complexes, dark curly hair, and experience in special operations. Both are thoughtful, aggressive, high-strung. Where they part company is where America, too, is divided: over the question of values.

As a SEAL in Quang Tri Province in 1964 Elton Manzione dressed like the enemy, worked with CTs who committed atrocities as standard procedure, and was told to ignore the rules of engagement. "But there was no sense of our role in the war," he said to me forlornly. He will not talk about his comrades who died while on illegal missions into North Vietnam and Laos. But, he noted, "what annoys me is they're not on the Washington monument simply because they ended up getting greased somewhere where they weren't supposed to be."[3]

Manzione's anger went beyond any lack of recognition. He resented the fact that he was trained to kill. "In psychology it's called cognitive dissonance—the notion that once you make a commitment, it's impossible to go back. It's something about the human psyche that makes a person reluctant to admit a mistake. This is what training is all about. You've already killed the gook. So what if it isn't a dummy in the bed this time? So what if it's a living, breathing human being? This is what you're supposed to do. And once the first time comes and goes, it's not as hard the second time. You say to yourself, 'Well, hey, I've killed people before. Why should I have any compunctions about doing it now?'

"Training is brainwashing. They destroy your identity and supply you with a new one—a uniform identity that every soldier has. That's the reason for the uniform, for everyone having the same haircut and going to dinner together and eating the same thing. . . . They destroyed the street kid from Newark and created the sailor. They destroyed the sailor and created the SEAL. But people aren't robots, and despite their training, eventually they react; they turn on their trainers and confront the outside forces that have used them. That's what happened to me.

"I was a guinea pig," Manzione insisted. "There is no doubt in my mind today, and there was very little doubt then, even after five months in Vietnam. All the training and all the 'special' programs—it eventually began to backfire on them. I thought, 'Oh, yeah, great program you got here; you're using me to see how I react. I'm expendable. I'm a pawn.' And that's kind of a heavy realization when you're an eighteen-year-old kid.

"It's a paradox. You know," Manzione continued, "they would send a guy over there to be a replacement for a specific person who was being pulled out. So what consciously came across to you was 'I'm functioning as a part of a machine. And if I fail as a part or break down as a part . . . then another part will come along to replace me.' Then you find yourself thinking, 'The last time I looked at somebody as not a part of the machine, and I thought he was a really great guy, and he's a friend of mine, he stepped on a land mine and came down dust, hair, teeth, and eyeballs.'

"Then you realize, 'I can't afford to do that. Because I feel terrible for a month afterwards.' And you can't function when you feel terrible. The only thing we could deal with at any particular time was survival. 'What do I want to do today? I want to eat, sleep, and stay alive.' And you did it. And you related to those kinds of things. Suddenly you looked around and said, 'Wait a minute! That's what those little guys in black pajamas are doing, too!' You get to a point where you begin to see these people just want to be left alone to grow their rice.

"I'll give you one last example of what I'm talking about. I'm sure you've heard about the laser-guided smart bombs we had. Well, they would drop these laser-guided smart bombs, and what the VC would do was take a bunch of old rags and tires and stuff and start a bonfire with lots of smoke. And the laser beam would hit the smoke particles, and it would scatter, and the bombs would go crazy. They'd go up, down, sideways, all over the place. And people would smile and say, 'There goes another smart bomb!' So smart a gook with a match and an old tire can fuck it up!

"The whole perverse idea of putting this technological, semiantiseptic sort of warfare against these people—who didn't have much more than a stick—was absurd. The sticks won!"

Warren Milberg had a different point of view. He enjoyed being a member of the closed society, in which relating to the enemy in human terms was cause for expulsion. For him, the image of the disemboweled mother and her murdered fetus "formed opinions and justifications for what I was doing. It was the idea that you needed to hate the enemy. It was the beginning of my own personalization of my role in the conflict. It was what resulted in me going back to Vietnam when everybody—my parents, my friends, my wife—told me no one in his right mind would go back to Vietnam. I really believed that I was helping these people defend themselves from the bully. And sometimes that worked well, and sometimes it was horrible. . . . It was horrible if you made some small little village on the periphery of the universe believe they could in fact stand tall and defend themselves against this thing we understood as the enemy, then came back the next day and found them all slaughtered. It happened. And then you had to ask yourself, 'What did I do here? I made these people believe they could do something, and now they're all dead. Maybe it would have been better if I had just done nothing. Just left these people alone.'

"I'm still reconciling it. I still don't think I've worked it all the way through."

Warren Milberg stared into the distance, seeing sights that only combat veterans see. "Things that have happened since then have led me to believe that I don't want to be an instrument of policy anymore," he concluded. "I think the people who devise the policies and cause idealistic young men to go off to war probably need to experience some of the things I've experienced to temper their judgments."

CHAPTER 14

Phoenix in Flight

When his first tour in Vietnam ended in the spring of 1966, Warren Milberg returned to the United States and was assigned to an Air Force base in South Dakota. But his name and accomplishments remained on file at CIA headquarters in Washington, and one year later Milberg was one of fifty officers and enlisted men from the various military services (all Vietnam veterans) whom the Pentagon invited to join a Presidentially Directed Counter-Insurgency Program through a participating agency/service agreement. Those who volunteered were tested and, if accepted by the CIA as junior officer trainees, given extensive training and returned to Vietnam to serve at the discretion of the senior CIA officers in Saigon and the regions. Most were assigned to the provinces as RDC/P or RDC/O advisers, and many became Phoenix coordinators.

Notably, the two other Air Force officers asked to join the program both withdrew, one "as a matter of conscience." Jacques Kline, who is Jewish, was born and reared in France during World War II and withdrew, according to Milberg, because "he felt the means and methods that he thought were going to be used in it were similar to the means and methods used by the Nazis in World War Two."[1]

Milberg, who is also Jewish—but obviously did not agree with Kline—returned to Vietnam in July 1967 and was assigned to CIA region officer in charge Jack Horgan in Da Nang. "I wound up getting a make-work job on the staff there, as liaison to some military units in and around Da Nang, trying to coordinate an intelligence collection and analysis unit for things, like motor units, that the VC used to harass the air base and the city. It was pretty unexciting. I stayed there for maybe a month, bored out of my mind. Then the RDC/P officer in Quang Tri was relieved by Horgan, which left them with a gap. And when I heard about that, I went to him and said, 'I'd like to take the job in Quang Tri.' And he was surprised that I did that—that anybody would want to go to the provinces. . . . But Quang Tri was the end of the line, and it was a way for Horgan to get rid of me.

"So I went up to Quang Tri and was delighted to find that when I got there, somebody actually met me. This was the guy who was leaving. He had three days left in Quang Tri, and in those three days he was going to orient me as to what was going on. After spending virtually the whole day and night talking, we loaded up two jeeps, one full of Nung bodyguards, then drove around to all the districts and met all the people in the Special Branch, the CIO, and anybody else we dealt with that were part of his bilateral operations. And I remember as we crossed the Quang Tri River bridge, heading up Highway One toward Dong Ha, thinking, 'I'm back. Now I'm really back,' and wondering what this was all going to be like.

"I guess we couldn't have been driving for more than half an hour when a bus, one of those Asian buses with pigs and chickens and people hanging off the roof and out the windows, blows up about fifty yards ahead of us. The highway was just a little two-lane road, running along the coastal plain. The bomb was a land mine, constructed out of an unexploded U.S. five-hundred-pound bomb, remotely detonated, and probably meant for us. But either a faulty detonator or vibrations set it off. Whatever, here were a lot of innocent civilians either dead or wounded, and it was like déjà vu: 'Here I am again. What am I doing here? What is this whole thing about?' And I guess I went through a period of depression early on, thinking, 'There's no way to win this thing. This war is going to go on forever. All these programs and activities are just a waste of human and economic resources.'

"All I had left—to justify why I was there—was to do the same thing I had done before, which was to personalize it. What I did while I was there in the midst of all the turmoil and pain and agony—a thing that made absolutely no sense to me—was to apply my own value system to it, which was such that I was going to keep pregnant women from being disemboweled. And it got to be a very personal war for me."

After taking over Quang Tri from his predecessor, Milberg "learned right away that the people you inherited, the counterparts in Special Branch or CIO, had a lot to do with the kind of tour you were going to have. They were either good and competent people or bureaucratic, corrupt functionaries—or variations in between. And I was really fortunate to wind up working with a man named Nguyen Van Khoi, the Special Branch chief in Quang Tri. . . . I was there to advise and assist him, only to find he had been fighting the war his whole life. He was a pro. An incredible man . . . who survived my tour there, often times at great risk to himself." (Khoi was reportedly killed by ARVN deserters in Hue in April 1975.)

In view of Khoi's expertise, there was little for Milberg to do in terms of advising on Special Branch operations. Apart from fighting for his life during Tet, conducting unilateral operations, and monitoring the Province Interrogation Center, Milberg worked largely in financial administration. "I had to go to Da Nang once a month to account for funds I had expended and to bring the region officer and his staff up-to-date on what was going on. And I can remember thinking that I controlled more money as a single individual, that I was sprinkling around the province in one way or another, than what the entire [CORDS] province budget was. I had conversations with the fellow who was the deputy in Da Nang about the fact that we thought that we were providing some measure of economic stability and really weren't interested in the quality of the intelligence we were buying—that by sprinkling this money as we did, to these low-level informant nets, we were creating economic stability as opposed to engaging in intelligence operations. Interesting concept and idea.

"Once a quarter I was called into Saigon," Milberg continued, "and when I went to Saigon, I stayed at the Duc Hotel. And I felt like if the Vietcong ever targeted the hotel or the city, it would be a piece of cake. I was in the business of planning these kinds of things, and I knew that if I had to do it, it would be a simple thing to do. I used to say to myself, 'My God. If this happens, what the hell am I going to do here in Saigon? They have no plans.' People were carrying around little pistols in shoulder holsters because it was fashionable. . . . It was a bureaucratic war in Saigon. All these people supposedly involved in intelligence collection and analysis, planning for the use of intelligence resources and the participation of paramilitary forces—all these people were doing nothing! They lived in their villas in and around town in grand splendor. They'd come to work at eight A.M. and leave at five P.M. It was just like being in an office building, and they had no idea what was going on outside Saigon. None. And I just felt helpless and exposed when I was there. I couldn't wait to get back to the provinces.

"This probably sounds strange," Milberg confessed, "but I felt very much at home in Quang Tri, which was really nothing more than a sleepy province capital consisting of two cross streets and a population between fifteen to twenty thousand people. When I got to Saigon, with its teeming millions, I felt in more danger than I did up-country in my little rural compound in Quang Tri.

"Of course, I wasn't out on operations in the jungle all the time, like I was on my first tour. But whenever we did go out, we were required to send in little spot reports on what we did and why we did it and what the result was. Everybody was manic about body counts—all that kind of crap. In any event, I kept getting warned by the guy [Jack Horgan's replacement, Harry Mustakos] who was in the region office not to go out on operations. That wasn't my job. And this was a guy who was totally paranoid about being in Vietnam. He was living in Da Nang in relative comfort next to the police station, and he could never understand why there was a need to go out on operations when your counterpart was going on those operations, that there was no way you were going to stay home and still maintain credibility with that counterpart. And I remember getting direct orders from him not to do that. Which I ignored.

"I had a compound that was relatively comfortable as things go," Milberg said "and a personal guard force of Nung mercenaries whose only job was to keep me alive. I had virtually unlimited resources to pay for a staff that translated and produced intelligence reports, which I disseminated to anybody in the province, U.S. military or otherwise, that I thought could take action on those reports. And I owned and operated a forty-man PRU force [see photo] which was my personal army. I wound up having a marine working for me who I think was a psychopath. I never saw or participated in what he did, but I was aware of it." (In "The Future Applicability of the Phoenix Program," Milberg called "those abuses that did occur . . . the 'normal' aberrations which result in any form of warfare."[2])

"PRU belonged to the RDC/O side of the province organization until the consolidation," Milberg told me. "I started out as the plans officer, but toward the end of 1967 I was appointed the province officer in charge of both programs. This is where I actually control and direct the PRU myself. Prior to this, if I had need of the PRU, because of some intelligence I had developed, what I did was go and see the RDC/O people—which was a relatively large program, five or six Americans involved—whereas RDC/P was only me. I lived by myself away from them. But I'm not sure if that's the way it was in every province."

In regard to Phoenix, Milberg said, "I'm not sure how you bound Phoenix, but it certainly falls right in the middle. But at this point the agency was beginning to turn the reins of the program over to the U.S. Army, as advisers to the Vietnamese, and going through whatever Orwellian mind-set was necessary to make believe this was a Vietnamese program."

Phoenix operations in Quang Tri Province were different from Phoenix operations in other provinces, Milberg explained, in that "a lot of military activity was going on, as opposed to the Vietcong insurgency. Clearly, both things were going on, but it was a heavily militarily oriented province. So there was a lot of action there."

In "The Future Applicability of the Phoenix Program," Milberg describes a typical Phoenix operation. Capitalizing on their assets in the CIO, PRU, and Special Branch, Milberg and Quang Tri Province Senior Adviser Bob Brewer mounted a Phoenix operation in the village of Thuong Xa, fourteen miles south of the DMZ. As Elton Manzione noted earlier, in this area it was hard to determine anyone's political affiliations, and the tendency was to consider everyone a Vietcong sympathizer. Indeed, Thuong Xa had served as a staging area for the Vietminh in the First Indochina War, and in 1968 its inhabitants were supporting the Vietcong in the same manner against the Americans. Milberg writes this was because "the people were afraid to offer information since they feared VC reprisals."[3]

A decision to conduct a Phoenix operation of "massive proportions" against Thuong Xa was made by Quang Tri's Province Security Council at Brewer's urging. Once permission had been granted, "Only the barest essential information was given to the various Vietnamese agencies in Quang Tri," Milberg writes. In this way, it was thought, those Vietnamese officials who had been coerced by the VC could not interfere with the "planning process." To ensure security, "The actual name of the targeted village was not released to the Vietnamese until the day before the operation."[4]

In preparing the Thuong Xa operation, information from Special Branch informers and PIC reports was fed into DIOCCs in and around Thuong Xa—a phenomenon rarely observed in provinces where the Phoenix coordinator was an MACV officer, not a CIA employee. As a blacklist of suspected VCI was compiled in Quang Tri's Province Intelligence and Operations Coordination Center, it was cross-checked with neighboring Quang Tin's PIOCC and "against master Phoenix lists" in Saigon (to ensure that penetration agents were crossed off the list), then fed to Quang Tri's DIOCCs.

Next, PRU teams were sent to locate and surveil targeted VCI. Escape routes were studied for ambush sites, and "the [province senior adviser] personally arranged" for local U.S. Army and Marine units to act as a "blocking force" to seal off the entire town.[5] At dawn on the day of the operation MACV psywar planes dropped leaflets on Thuong Xa urging identified VCI to surrender and offering rewards and Chieu Hoi status to informers.

No one took advantage of the deal. Instead, the residents of Thuong Xa braced for the shock. In the early-morning hours twenty-five-man PRU teams—accompanied by Special Branch interrogators and CIA advisers—began searching hooches for booby traps, weapons, documents, food caches, and VCI suspects. They "compared the names and descriptions on the blacklists with every man, woman, and child in Thuong Xa."[6] Suspects were sent to screening zones, where innocent bystanders were fed and "entertained" by RD teams. The hard-core VCI, meanwhile, were systematically driven into the northeast corner of town, where they were cornered, then killed or captured as they tried to escape through Brewer's "ring of steel."

The result was two VCI captured. One was the district party chief; the other was the chief of the local NLF farmers' association. Both were sent to the interrogation center in Da Nang. Eight other targeted VCI were killed or escaped. Two fifty-nine-member Revolutionary Development teams stayed behind to assert the GVN's presence, but within a month they were driven out of town and Thuong Xa reverted to Vietcong control. As Milberg observes, "Even with this unusual amount of coordination, the fact that the village reverted to communist control and known members of the VCI escaped strongly suggests that the operation failed as a future model for counterinsurgency operations."[7]

Perhaps the inhabitants of Thuong Xa resisted the intrusion into their village because they feared Vietcong reprisals. Or maybe they really did support the Vietcong. In either case, the point is the same. Even under ideal conditions Phoenix operations failed where the Vietnamese were determined to resist. Where ideal conditions did not exist—where Vietnamese officials were included in the planning of operations and where U.S. military officers replaced CIA officers as Phoenix coordinators—the program failed to an even greater degree.

In early 1968 each of the CIA's region officers in charge was assigned a military intelligence officer, either a major or a lieutenant colonel, to serve as his Phoenix coordinator. In IV Corps the job was given to Lieutenant Colonel Doug Dillard, an easygoing Georgian who, at sixteen, lied about his age, enlisted in the Eighty-second Airborne Brigade, and fought in World War II. After the war Dillard became a commissioned officer, and in Korea he served in the Combined Command for Reconnaissance Activity, which, under CIA auspices, coordinated special operations behind enemy lines. Dillard gained further espionage experience in the late 1950's as a case officer in Germany running agent operations in conjunction with the Army's attaché office and the CIA. After a stint teaching airborne and amphibious "offensive" counterintelligence operations at Fort Holabird, Dillard was made deputy chief of intelligence at the Continental Army Command, where he trained and deployed "practically every army intelligence unit that went to Vietnam."[8]

Speaking in a drawl, Dillard told me, "I went over to Vietnam in February 1968 as the Phoenix coordinator for Four Corps, reporting to the CIA's region officer in charge. Branch called me and said, 'We have what we consider a critical requirement. We can't discuss it over the phone—it's classified—but you'll find out what it is when you get there.'

"So," Dillard continued, "when I arrived in Saigon, I immediately contacted several of my friends. One, Colonel Russ Conger, the senior adviser in Phong Dinh Province, gave me some tips on getting different agencies to cooperate and on overcoming the terrorist psychology in the villages and hamlets. He also informed me that there were many people around who felt Phoenix was a threat to them—to their power base." In other words, military officers commanding units in the field "considered Phoenix, on occasion, as getting in their way and inhibiting resources they could otherwise use for their own operations."

Right away Dillard understood that his job would be to bridge the gap, so that conventional military forces could be made available for unconventional Phoenix operations planned by the CIA. But he also sensed another problem festering beneath the surface. "It's kind of in conflict to our culture and experience over the years," he explained, "to take a U.S. Army element—whatever it may be—and direct it not only toward the military and paramilitary enemy forces but also toward the civilians that cooperate with them."

General Bruce Palmer, commander of the U.S. Ninth Infantry Division in 1968, put it more bluntly. "My objection to the program," he wrote in a letter to the author, "was the involuntary assignment of U.S. Army officers to the program. I don't believe that people in uniform, who are pledged to abide by the Geneva Conventions, should be put in the position of having to break those laws of warfare."[9]

Most military officers, however, resented Phoenix on other than legal grounds. The notion of attacking an elusive and illusionary civilian infrastructure was anathema to conventional warriors looking for spectacular main force battles. For an ambitious officer assigned to Phoenix, "the headlines would not be very impressive in terms of body counts, weapons captured, or some other measure of success," as Warren Milberg notes. In addition, Phoenix coordinators were merely advisers to their counterparts, not commanders in the field.

After being informally briefed by his friends, Dillard reported to the Phoenix Directorate, which "represented the program at the national level, ensuring that we got the kind of personnel and logistical support we felt we needed." However, because of the staff's "very narrow administrative type of intelligence background," it did not "understand how the program was going to develop. As the ICEX program," Dillard explained, "it was run directly at the province level, principally by the agency. But Parker's staff didn't grasp that when MACV took over and fleshed out Phoenix with hundreds of military officers and money, it really was a joint operation—that CIA was a supporter and partial sponsor, but really MACV had to account for it. This is how it evolved."

While the Saigon staff was content to view Phoenix as a CIA subsidiary, Dillard set about asserting MACV's presence in Phoenix operations in the Delta—a task made easier by the relative absence of regular military units and by Dillard's engaging personality and wide experience in command, staff, and operational positions. Ultimately, though, Dillard's leverage was logistics.

"As a matter of protocol between itself and the CIA," Dillard explained, "MACV assumed half of the agency's operational expenses in support of Phoenix. For example, every time the agency's aircraft were used to support a Phoenix activity, technically it should have been charged against the fund allocation MACV had given to the Phoenix program. So when I found out about that, I contacted the Air America operations people in Four Corps and said, 'Just to keep everybody honest, I want a record of what you're charging for aircraft support against the Phoenix program.' And thereafter I tried to get air support from U.S. Army region headquarters at Can Tho, so I didn't have to squander MACV operational funds reimbursing the agency for use of its aircraft."

By protecting MACV's financial interests, Dillard won the support of IV Corps commander, General George Eckhardt. "Most of my work with the MACV staff was either with General Eckhardt directly, or with the intelligence chief, Colonel Ted Greyman," Dillard recalled. "Ted and I worked hand in hand coordinating the activity, and it paid off. . . . General Eckhardt and Colonel Greyman set aside for me a light gun platoon and six helicopter gunships to run Phoenix operations throughout the region." This contingent became "a regional reaction force to haul troops and provide fire support." With it, Dillard was able to provide the PRU with air mobility and thus get access to CIA intelligence in exchange.

Jim Ward spoke highly of Doug Dillard, saying, "He was assigned to me because they wanted the best man they could get down in the Delta."[10] The admiration was mutual. About Ward and his deputy, Andy Rogers, Dillard said, "They were great guys to work with. There was an immediate acceptance of my credentials." That was not always the case. But Dillard and Ward agreed on what constituted a legitimate Phoenix operation—be it an ambush dreamed up at a DIOCC or a multiprovince operation concocted by the CIA—and together they would push Phoenix beyond the narrow rifle shot parameters advocated by Robert Komer.

Dillard's liberal interpretation of Phoenix is partially the result of his perception of the "terrorist psychology" in Vietnam. "I arrived in Can Tho on a Friday afternoon," he recalled. "The two army sergeants that had come in to be my administrative assistants met me at the airport and took me over to the compound and settled me in the CIA's regional house, which was also being used by the local Phong Dinh Province CIA personnel. There was a vacant room, so I took it, and the next morning I reported in to Andy Rogers. I was given a little office with the two enlisted men [who] handled reports and requests from the field. I was also assigned a deputy, Major Keith Ogden.

"Anyway, I found out there was a helicopter going up to Chau Doc Province on the Cambodian border on Sunday morning, so I went up there. It was my first introduction to the real war. . . . It was right after Tet, and there was still a lot of activity. The young sergeant there, Drew Dix, had been in a little village early that morning. . . . The VC had come in and got a couple out that were accused of collaborating with the government, and they'd shot them in the ears. Their bodies were lying out on a cart. We drove out there, and I looked at that . . . and I had my first awareness of what those natives were up against. Because during the night, the damn VC team would come in, gather all those villagers together, warn them about cooperating, and present an example of what happened to collaborators. They shot them in the ears on the spot.

"So I knew what my job was. I realized there was a tremendous psychological problem to overcome in getting that specific group of villagers to cooperate in the program. Because to me the Phoenix program was one requiring adequate, timely, and detailed information so we could intercept, make to defect, kill, maim, or capture the Vietcong guerrilla forces operating in our area. Or put a strike on them. If either through intercepting messages or capturing VCI, you could get information on some of the main force guerrilla battalion activity, you could put a B-fifty-two strike on them, which we did in Four Corps."

For Jim Ward, "intelligence was the most important part of Phoenix." Handling that task for Ward was "a regular staffer with the agency who worked full time on intelligence—the real sensitive, important operations"—meaning unilateral penetrations into the VCI and GVN. The staffer "had military people assigned to him," working as liaison officers in the provinces, as well as CIA, State Department, and USIS officers and policemen from the United States. His job was "making sure they were properly supervised." Of course, the station's special unit could abscond with any penetrations that had national significance.

At the other end of the spectrum, "the first and most important purpose of the DIOCC," according to Ward, "the one that got General Thanh behind Phoenix," was getting tactical military intelligence. When managed by a military officer, as they usually were, DIOCCs focused on this area, while the PIOCCs, where the CIA exerted greater influence, focused on the VCI.

According to Ward, when information generally obtained from interrogation centers or hamlet informants indicated that a person was a VCI, the CIA's liaison officer started a three-by-five card file on that person at the Province Intelligence and Operations Coordination Center, which was often located in the embassy house. When a second piece of information came in—from the provincial reconnaissance units or the Regional and Popular Forces—a folder was opened. After a third source had incriminated the suspect, he or she was targeted for penetration, defection, or capture and interrogation at the PIC, then turned over to the Province Security Committee with evidence for sentencing.

This was the rifle shot approach. But where large concentrations of people or security teams surrounded the targeted VCI, Jim Ward favored a variation on the cordon and search method employed by Brewer and Milberg in Quang Tri, "where you move in at three A.M., surround the entire area, and block everybody off." However, because Ward lacked the "troop density" enjoyed in I Corps, in his Phoenix operations he used light observation helicopters "to buzz the paddy fields to keep people from running off. You don't have enough men to cordon off an entire village when you have only a hundred PRU and two Americans," he said, the two Americans being the PRU adviser and the Phoenix coordinator.

Using this approach, which relied on surprise, Ward would conduct five operations in a day. "They would go in on one side of the village. The first outfit would jump off a helicopter with one adviser and set up a block. Then another helicopter would land a hundred yards further down. Then a third and a fourth, with the other U.S. adviser. These guys would branch out in a skirmish line and start moving into town. They would catch everybody with rifles stacked, unprepared. When a helicopter is coming in low," Ward explained, "you don't even hear it coming in your direction. All of a sudden there's a tremendous roar, and they see people landing in different places.

"The PRU knew exactly what to do," Ward continued. "They'd get all these people [VCI suspects] out in a larger helicopter and take them back to where the province chief could put them in a special stockade. Then they'd get Special Branch people going through identifying each one. Meanwhile, the PRU would reequip with more ammo and go to the next drop."

Ward's method closely resembled the hunter-killer technique developed in 1962 and detailed by Elton Manzione. Omitted from Ward's sanitized account, however, was what happened before the arrival of the killer team, when the hunter team "snatches and/or snuffs" the cadre. Ward also neglected to describe the conduct of the PRU.

"Sometimes we'd go out with a whole pack of mercenaries," recalled Mike Beamon. "They were very good going in, but once we got there and made our target, they would completely pillage the place. . . . It was a complete carnival. . . ."[11]

In balancing MACV's and the CIA's interests in Phoenix, Colonel Doug Dillard was destined to rain on somebody's parade. In IV Corps the man who got soaked was the regional Public Safety adviser, Del Spiers.

Dillard as the regional Phoenix coordinator had the job of bringing police resources to bear against the VCI. The idea was to prevent region officers in charge like Jim Ward and Bob Wall from using PRU as blocking forces during Phoenix operations, so the PRU would be available to conduct rifle shot operations. "Our concept," Dillard said, "was to put the Field Police in a location as a blocking force and let the PRUs do the dirty work."

In 1968, however, most province chiefs were still feeling the aftershocks of Tet and preferred to use the Field Police as bodyguards in the province capital. "Unless you had an effective Regional and Popular Forces organization at the district level," Dillard explained, "the only thing you had . . . was the Field Police, and hell, he was guarding the province chief's house, not out trying to run operations in support of your activity."

Compounding the problem were the Public Safety advisers themselves, whom Dillard described as "principally responsible for getting new jeeps and radios and supplies and funds for the National Police. And that was about it. Their proclivity was to support the Field Police, as opposed to trying to see that force engaged in operations.

"As I began to get out in the provinces," Dillard continued, "it seemed the Public Safety adviser was never there. He was either en route to Saigon or coming back from Saigon. When I talked to the U.S. people in the province, they would say, 'Well, this guy is either drunk or shacked up with his girl friend.' . . . Many of them were former policemen or policemen on leave," Dillard grumbled, "or they came from some law enforcement activity and were plunged into that environment . . . [and] based on my experience, there was almost a total incompetence."

Nor was the problem alleviated when "after Tet, they brought in a group of enlisted men out of the Military Police. They were going to be advisers to the Field Police, but many of them were inept, too. I know from talking to them that they had never been in combat, and their experience was analogous to Shore Patrol," Dillard said. "They were principally experienced as physical security guards, and many of them had drinking problems.

"Anyway, we just wrote the Field Police off. When it came to trying to get their resources on the ground, to put them in helicopters and move them around, we began to find that the province chief had one problem after another: Either the Field Police weren't available, or the Public Safety advisers weren't aware of the nature of Phoenix operations, or [the operations weren't] cleared with the province chief. And the Public Safety adviser would be running against the grain if he took the province chief's resources or even tried to influence him to free up the Field Police to run our operations.

"So the senior CORDS advisor, 'Coal Bin' Willie Wilson, came down to Four Corps, and he called me over and asked, 'What can we do to improve the Phoenix program?' And I complained about the lack of use of Field Police. I said I wanted to use it as a light infantry strike force, which would give us, if you added in the PRU, about a four-thousand-man strike force in the Delta. 'We know the PRU are damn good,' I said, 'but we can't get them all killed trying to do everybody's job.'

"What I proposed is that there be some kind of central control set up that would give us the capability to use police in the Delta to support Phoenix operations. I added that with the kind of people there were out advising in the provinces, 'that ain't ever gonna get done.'"

When confronted by Coal Bin Willie, Doug Dillard recalled, Del Spiers said, "I can't fire the province senior adviser. I have to put up with the people he assigns to me. It's not like the military," where an officer can transfer an unsatisfactory subordinate.

Said Dillard: "Well, I am a military man, and I have a job to get done." And from that day on the Field Police and their Public Safety advisers were the Phoenix program's scapegoats in the Delta. At their expense Dillard achieved peace between the CIA and MACV in the Delta. He convinced the CIA that by sharing its information, military resources could be used against the VCI. In exchange for supporting the CIA's attack on the VCI, the military benefited from CIA intelligence on the location of main force enemy units. That translated into higher body counts and brighter careers.

"I could do what I wanted within the guidelines of the Phoenix program," Doug Dillard said with satisfaction, "which to me was the overall coordination of the units that existed in the Delta to destroy the infrastructure." With his regional reaction force ready and raring to go, Dillard mounted regional Phoenix operations on the Ward mini-cordon and search technique.

"At the province level we had almost daily involvement with the CIA's province adviser and SEAL team PRU adviser," Dillard explained. "This was either trying to help them get resources or going over the potential for operations. A good example is the time we got good intelligence on the VC staff on sampans in the U Minh Forest. The idea was to work in coordination with the U.S. Ninth Infantry Division in Chuong Thien Province. It was good timing because they had troops and could expand their artillery fire into An Xuyen, where the U Minh Forest was. We decided to use the PRU team from Kien Giang, with their SEAL adviser, and Major Leroy Suddath [the Phong Dinh paramilitary adviser, who as a major general in 1986 commanded the First Special Operations Command at Fort Bragg]."

As in the Milberg-Brewer operation in Quang Tri, the Vietnamese were cut out of the planning. "We decided we should lift out without a lot of notice," Dillard said. "So the SEAL adviser put his PRU on alert. But we didn't want to spook them, so they were told they were going on an operation in their province. . . . We took the PRU team out of Kien Giang with Leroy in the lead, and with the Ninth Division helicopters and artillery support to cover our infiltration and exfiltration. This way we could put the PRU on the canal, capture those people, and get in and out during daylight.

"We went over to Chuong Thien and loaded out of there. I flew out of there in the command and control helicopter. We went up to Kien Giang, and Leroy had the PRU team ready. . . . We loaded up early that morning, flew down, and inserted the team on the canal. Then the chopper went back to Chuong Thien; I stayed over there with the radio and talked to Leroy to get a progress report. Leroy went in with the PRU-SEAL team. There were two Americans, and the rest were Vietnamese. They scarfed up twelve people almost immediately but couldn't find the sampan they were looking for. We think the damn operation got leaked, and they got spooked."

As in the Thuong Xa operation, despite elaborate planning and security precautions, a large-scale Phoenix operation failed to accomplish its mission. However, by showing that military assets could be used in support of Province Reconnaissance Units and that CIA intelligence could generate a sizable operation, the U Minh Forest operation did prove to MACV that Phoenix was a viable coordinating mechanism.

"In working with Ted Greyman in the Can Tho Advisory Group," Dillard said, "we were trying to piece together patterns of the main force guerrilla battalions, which constituted the single greatest danger to a district or even a province. Ted very closely coordinated with us in our Phoenix activities, plotting information where VC attacks had occurred, in what force, when, and so forth. When these facts came together, he would coordinate a B-fifty-two strike in that area."

In particular, Dillard was concerned with the movements of the Muoi Tu Battalion, which periodically emerged from its sanctuary in Cambodia and conducted operations in Chau Doc, Kien Phong, and Kien Tuong provinces. "Annually they'd come down and cut a wide swath through these three provinces, then go back into Cambodia," Dillard explained. "That's where Ted Greyman and I began to work very closely to try to plot every piece of information that we could get on the Muoi Tu Battalion."

The job of finding the Muoi Tu in Cambodia belonged to the Special Operations Group and its Vietnamese assets, which ran agent nets and reconnaissance missions into Cambodia. But, explained Dillard, "Quite often there was a lot of clumsy, heavy-handed type of activity, and I don't think [Special Forces] were appreciative of the nuances of being supercautious in collecting and evaluating intelligence before running operations. I think it was in Kien Phong on the border; the sun rose one morning, and they went into position there, and every man on the line had been shot through the back of the head. This was the Vietnamese Special Forces. They were infiltrated constantly by the VC."

Dispersed along South Vietnam's borders since 1962, the Fifth Special

Forces A teams, augmented by the 403d Special Operations Detachment and an unnumbered intelligence group, routinely fed intelligence to MACV and the CIA. "The sophistication of the intelligence apparatus," General McChristian writes, "allowed for operations against the infrastructure."[12]

However, by September 1967 it was clear, as Doug Dillard noted, that the Vietnamese Special Forces were too heavily infiltrated to be trusted. So concurrent with the creation of ICEX and the reorganization of SOG, the CIA commissioned Project Gamma. Also known as Detachment B-57, Gamma was charged with the mission of organizing cross-border counterintelligence operations to find out who within the Cambodian government was helping the NVA and VC infiltrate and attack Special Forces A camps, recon teams, and agent nets. While posing as medical and agricultural specialists in a "dummy" civil affairs unit, Gamma personnel coordinated intelligence from A teams, identifying the key VCI cadres that were mounting penetration operations against them. Detachment B-57 coordinated its activities with SOG and the various Special Forces projects, including Delta, Sigma, Omega, and Blackjack out of Tay Ninh. In defense of its A camps, Special Forces mounted its own attack on the VCI through a combination of agent nets, "specialized patrolling," mobile strike forces, and a "kill on sight" rewards program. In this way, SOG and Phoenix were united.

As for the "heavy-handedness" cited by Dillard, on November 27, 1967, Fifth Special Forces Captain John McCarthy was sitting beside his principal agent, Inchin Hai Lam (a Cambodian working for B-57 out of Quang Loi), in the front seat of a car parked on a street in Tay Ninh. A suspected double agent, Lam was a member of the Khmer Serai, a dissident Cambodian political party created by the CIA to overthrow Cambodia's Prince Sihanouk. Without warning, McCarthy turned and put a bullet between Lam's eyes.

McCarthy was tried for Lam's murder, and the ensuing scandal raised questions about the legality of "terminating with extreme prejudice" suspected double agents. The issue would surface again in regard to Phoenix.

Regardless of where the VCI were—in South Vietnam, Cambodia, Laos, or North Vietnam—"the idea," said Dillard, "was that if we knew their pattern and if we could put the fear of God in them, then we could influence their movements so they could never assemble as a battalion. Our forces could resist any company-sized attacks, and that pretty much cut back their capabilities by preventing them from operating at a battalion-level force."

MACV "could do a fifty-two strike pretty easily," Dillard explained. And once MACV began using B-52 strikes as a way of harassing VC guerrilla units, "Thereafter we had pretty good evidence that the VC were doing just what we wanted them to do. They were not assembling in large battalion-sized forces, and we could route them around. We continued to try to do that from the summer of 1968 on, and we started getting in some pretty good defectors because of that pressure. The overall coordination was working."

Indeed, when B-52 strikes were mounted, coordination was essential. For example, the CIA could not run a PRU operation in enemy territory without first consulting MACV, because, as Dillard put it, "it's conceivable that the operations people have scheduled a strike in that area." Yet everyone mounted unilateral operations anyway. "An element of the five-twenty-fifth"—Dillard sighed—"their collection and special security unit, was trying to get the VCI to defect—this was in the summer of 1968. They had a lead to a VCI cadre meeting, and they ran the operation, and there was nothing there. We were all called into General Eckhardt's office to find out who the hell had approved this special operation without Ted Greyman knowing it.

"There's always that problem," Dillard contended, "when some outfit perceives that they're going to pull off a coup. Then it backfires. The damn thing was a total embarrassment. Just like the sale of arms to Iran."

As long as unilateral operations persisted, Phoenix could never fly. "It was kind of hard at times to determine just who was operating in that environment," Dillard remarked. "Quite often the main mission of the Special Branch guy may have been to keep tabs on the ARVN people. In the case of the Military Security Service, if I was able to get to the guy through [his counterpart, MSS Colonel] Phuoc or through the Army security unit in the Delta . . . I would try to push an operation or try to find out what they knew that we were not being informed of. But in the whole time I was there, I was convinced that there was a lot of unilateral reporting that did not get into the U.S. system, whether it was Phoenix or something else. It had to do with the different axes people had to grind."

CHAPTER 15

Modus Vivendi

The inclusion of the Vietnamese in Phoenix in the summer of 1968 was not welcomed by meticulous CIA security officers. These professional paranoids, Doug Dillard said with a sigh, "did not realize you cannot become so secretive that you can't even run an operation. We were always aware of the need for secrecy, and where we suspected there was a leak we tried to hold everything as close as possible. But sometimes you just couldn't do it. You had to plan and coordinate with the Vietnamese to run operations."[1]

On the other hand, from the Presidential Palace to the most decrepit DIOCC, VC agents were everywhere. It was a fact that was factored into every equation, it was the reason why Phoenix began as a unilateral operation, and it was why the program failed, for Phoenix was not a counterintelligence program meant to uncover enemy agents but a positive intelligence program designed to neutralize the people managing the insurgency.

The job of counterintelligence was shared by the Special Branch and the Military Security Service, with the Special Branch protecting the government and the MSS protecting the South Vietnamese armed forces, at times at cross purposes. For example, like many of his MSS colleagues, Colonel Nguyen Van Phuoc was placed under house arrest and accused of being implicated when Diem and Nhu were assassinated. Afterward Phuoc was "tainted" but was resuscitated by the CIA, which valued him for his contacts, according to Dillard, in "the Catholic intelligence network that extended into Cambodia. As a matter of fact, he offered to bring them into the fold because of the sanctuary that main force guerrilla battalions enjoyed in Cambodia."

With CIA sponsorship, Phuoc was to enjoy a number of prominent positions, not least as deputy IV Corps commander and counterpart to Doug Dillard and Andy Rogers. But Phuoc lived on the edge and, like Generals Do Cao Tri and Tran Thanh Phong, eventually perished in a mysterious plane accident.

"Colonel Phuoc's problems on the Vietnamese side were greater than ours because the province chiefs were appointed by the president," Dillard explained. "There were all kinds of rumors about 'some bought their jobs,' and there were other kinds of arrangements, too. There were businesses that flourished and were never bothered by the VC in the provinces, so it was obvious that someone was being paid off."

In fairness to the Vietnamese, a point should be made about cultural values. For what Americans define as corruption, the Vietnamese consider perfectly proper behavior. Accepting gifts and returning favors—taking bribes and making payoffs—were how, after generations of colonial oppression, Vietnamese officials supplemented measly salaries and supported extended families. The system was a form of prebend, the same right ministers have to a portion of the Sunday offering as a stipend. And rather than fight the system, the CIA compensated for it by paying its Phung Hoang, secret police, and PRU assets exorbitant salaries. Conversely, for the average Vietnamese citizen caught in a war-torn economy, dealing with the Vietcong was a matter of survival. And while this modus vivendi provided American intelligence officers with a line of communication to the enemy, it also gave them migraine headaches.

"For example," Dillard said, "in Bac Lieu there was a great suspicion that the province chief was on the take from the VC tax collector. The PRU team leader in Bac Lieu, Doc Sells, had firsthand evidence of that. But the VC tax collector, who lived in Ba Xuyen Province, was a wealthy businessman, and the way he stayed wealthy was by paying extortion and ransom. . . . Now Doc knew, based on the way the province chief had acted in the past, that never in the world would they [the PRU] be allowed to coordinate an operation in Ba Xuyen without compromising it. So the Bac Lieu PRU ran an operation over into Ba Xuyen and kidnapped this guy. It caused all kinds of grief between the two provinces, and when it surfaced at our level, they had to release him. Then there were threats that 'Well, next time he won't survive.' They put a price on Doc's head. I remember a kid came into the restaurant where Doc was eating and put a cigarette lighter on the table. It was a booby trap that exploded but luckily didn't hurt him."

All this means that if the VCI was a criminal conspiracy, then its partners in crime were government officials—particularly province chiefs, police, and security officials. Robert Slater writes: "During the period 1964–1967, it was fairly common to read of a hand grenade being thrown into a bar. This was normally attributed by the press to terrorism, but police investigations usually showed that the owner had refused to pay taxes to the VC. It is uncommon to read or even hear of this now [in 1970]; undoubtedly the bar owners have agreed to pay their taxes." Likewise, "From 1965 to 1969," Slater knew "of no American oil company trucks being ambushed. On one occasion a VC road block let an American oil company truck pass by, then fifteen minutes later stopped a South Vietnamese bus, disembarked all the passengers, collected 'tax' money, and then shot two ARVN soldiers who were in uniform."[2]

This modus vivendi between the VCI and GVN officials frustrated many Phoenix coordinators who were trying to distinguish one from the other. Some simply threw up their hands, held their breaths, and marked time. Others were spurred to indiscriminate acts of violence. Those who took the hard line, like III Corps DEPCORDS John Vann, believed that it was not enough for the Vietnamese simply to be pro-Phoenix. According to Vann's deputy for plans and programs, who shall hereafter be known as Jack, Vann insisted that in order for Phoenix to succeed, the Vietnamese had to fight actively against the VCI. But that was impossible, Jack explained, because "the Vietnamese were protected in the day by the GVN, but were left to the VC at night. So the little guy in the village survived day to day knowing when to say yes and when to say no. The wrong answer could cost him his life."[3]

Unfortunately for the Vietnamese who preferred to remain neutral, it was the most highly motivated Americans—those who were most avidly anti-Communist—who were listened to in Washington and who ipso facto determined policy.

As hard as it was to involve province chiefs in the attack on the VCI, the rural population was even harder to incite. Earnest Phoenix coordinators like Doug Dillard tried "to get the people in the villages to tell you when the VC were coming, so you could put the PRU on them or a B-fifty-two strike." However, why the Vietnamese would not cooperate is understandable, especially in the case of B-52 strikes, "one of which," Dillard recalled, "occurred right between Kien Hoa and Dinh Tuong. There was pretty good evidence that a VC battalion had assembled in that area," Dillard said, "and Ted put a strike on it. They went in later to assess the damage, and said it looked like a butcher shop."

For that reason, damage assessment was not a popular job in Vietnam and was a task often assigned to PRU units or unpopular American soldiers like Air Force Captain Brian Willson who, with the 823d Combat Security

Police Squadron, commanded a mobile security unit at Binh Thuy Air Base four miles west of Can Tho. As punishment for fraternizing with enlisted men, Willson was given the job of damage assessment in areas bombed by B-52's.

"In the Delta," Willson told me, "the villages were very small, like a mound in a swamp. There were no names for some of them. The people in these villages had been told to go to relocation camps, because this was all a free fire zone, and technically anyone there could be killed. But they wouldn't leave their animals or burial grounds. At the same time, the U.S. Air Force had spotters looking for muzzle flashes, and if that flash came from that dot, they'd wipe out the village. It was that simple.[4]

"It was the epitome of immorality," Willson suggested. "One of the times I counted bodies after an air strike—which always ended with two napalm bombs which would just fry everything that was left—I counted sixty-two bodies. In my report I described them as so many women between fifteen and twenty-five and so many children—usually in their mothers' arms or very close to them—and so many old people. When I went to Tan Son Nhut a few days later, I happened to see an afteraction report from this village. A guy I knew showed me where to look. The report said one hundred-thirty VC dead.

"Another time I was driving up near Sa Dec. It was a coincidence. I didn't even know it was happening. There was an air strike, and I was very near this village where it was happening. I'd never seen a localized air strike on a village before. I was stunned. The ground shook like an earthquake, and that was scary. But there I was, watching as the last sweep came in and dropped some napalm, sending up balls of fire that finally wiped everything out. And I was standing in my jeep, kind of in shock, and this old man came running out of the village. I was about one hundred fifty feet from him, and our eyes met for like two seconds. Then he turned and ran away.

"I remember driving down this little lane . . . thinking I'd wake up and not be there. I drove for three or four miles like that. Then I saw this old Vietnamese woman with a yoke on her back, holding a couple of pails of water. Then I saw this water buffalo just kind of meandering through a rice paddy. I remember stopping and thinking, 'Man, I am here. I'm still in Vietnam.' I'd been there three months. After that I wanted to desert."

Why would the inhabitants of a Vietnamese village voluntarily announce to U.S. or GVN authorities the presence of VC guerrillas or political cadres, if doing so meant a bath in five-hundred-pound bombs or a pack of plundering PRU? This question reaches to the heart of Phoenix and the "collateral damage" it caused.

One explanation was offered in a series of articles written in late 1970 and early 1971 for the liberal Catholic newspaper *Tin Sang* (*Morning News*). Published in Saigon by Ngo Cong Duc, a nationalist in the Vietnamese legislature, half of all its issues were confiscated by the police on orders from the minister of information, Truong Buu Diem, a long-standing CIA asset. Nearly all issues, however, are preserved in the Yen Ching Library at Harvard University. Translated by a Vietnamese woman at the University of Massachusetts, this series of articles, titled "The Truth About Phoenix," provides rare insights into the Vietnamese perspective on Phoenix.

The author of "The Truth About Phoenix" used the alias Dinh Tuong An, but his true identity is known to CIA officer Clyde Bauer, who claims An was a Communist sympathizer. Red-baiting, of course, requires no substantiation. But it is a fact, as corroborated by Phoenix adviser Richard Ide, that An was a translator for Major Oscar L. Jenkins, the CIA's Special Branch adviser in the Trung Giang inner-Mekong area, running Phoenix operations in Sa Dec, Vinh Long, and Vinh Binh provinces in 1968 and 1969.

"Phoenix," writes An, "is a series of big continuous operations which, because of the bombing, destroy the countryside and put innocent people to death. . . . In the sky are armed helicopters, but on the ground are the black uniforms, doing what they want where the helicopters and B-52's do not reach. . . . Americans in black uniforms," according to An, "are the most terrible."[5]

Also according to An, the CIA always sent PRU teams in the day before cordon and search operations, to capture people targeted for interrogation. The next day, An notes, the PRU would return in U.S. Navy helicopters with ARVN troops. "When they go back to their base at Dong Tam [the sprawling PRU facility near My Tho], they bring people's bleeding ears. But," asks An rhetorically, "are these the ears of the VC?"[6]

The purpose of Phoenix, An contends, was "to avenge what the VC did during Tet. Which is why Thieu did not hesitate to sign Phoenix into law. But," he adds, "local officials knew nothing about the program except the decree. The central government didn't explain anything. Furthermore, the CIA and their assistants had a hard time trying to explain to province chiefs about operations to pacify the countryside and destroy the VCI."[7]

Indeed, the Vietnamese were confused by contradictory American programs. For example, B-52 strikes and Agent Orange dustings served only to impoverish rural villagers, prompting them to deduce that these operations were directed against *them,* not the VCI. Making matters worse, province chiefs reported the damage, ostensibly to get compensation for those hurt by the attacks, but kept the money for themselves. Then Revolutionary Development Cadre appeared, promising to offset the damage with economic development. Meanwhile, the U.S. Army was pursuing a scorched-earth policy and the Agency for International Development was withdrawing support for RD reconstruction projects—a reversal in policy, An contends, that stemmed from the CIA's belief that reconstruction projects only helped the wives and families of VC who returned from their jungle hideouts when the projects were done.[8] All that led most Vietnamese to agree with An that "Revolutionary Development only teaches the American line."

The end result of the contradictory programs and double-talk was a lack of trust in the GVN, not in the VCI, which rarely failed to make good on promises. Likewise, the Vietnamese interpreted Phoenix, the program designed to provide security to the rural population, as an attempt by the Americans to prolong the war. Like B-52 strikes and Agent Orange, Phoenix only made people's lives more difficult. People wondered, An informs us, how Phoenix could turn things around.[9]

In responding to these concerns, An writes, the CIA argued that Phoenix was needed because B-52 strikes and defoliation operations did not destroy "the VC lower structure." But in attacking the VCI, the CIA never considered the human concerns of the Vietnamese, declares An. For example, many rice fields were owned by Vietcong, and as more and more fields were destroyed by Agent Orange, people had no choice but to buy rice from these VC. This included wealthy merchants who were subsequently accused by security forces of collaborating with the enemy and were forced to pay bribes to keep from being arrested. In this way GVN officials extorted from people caught in between them and the Vietcong.

Nor, An adds, did the CIA care that many Vietnamese during Tet—including policemen and soldiers—visited their families in areas controlled by the Vietcong, thus becoming VCI suspects themselves. Or that Vietnamese civil servants, especially schoolteachers with families living in VC areas, became informants simply as a way of getting advance notice of Phoenix operations, so they could warn their relatives of pending attacks. In return for protecting their families, these Vietnamese were surveilled and extorted by government security forces.

Nor did the CIA take steps to protect people from false accusations. An cites the case of five teachers working for a Catholic priest in Vinh Long Province. These women refused to attend a VC indoctrination session. When the VC were later captured by PRU, they named these teachers as VC cadres. The teachers were arrested and jailed without trial or evidence. "That's why people feared Phoenix," An explains. "The biggest fear is being falsely accused—from which there is no protection. That's why Phoenix doesn't bring peace or security. That's why it destroys trust in the GVN, not the VCI."[10]

Adding to this mistrust was the fact that the CIA rewarded security officials who extorted the people. "The CIA," An writes, "spends money like water." As a result, MSS and Special Branch operators preferred to sell information to the CIA rather than "give" it to their Vietnamese employers.

And even though the CIA had no way of corroborating the information, it was used to build cases against VCI suspects. The CIA also passed quantities of cash to the various religious sects. "Many priests in the inner-Mekong," An reports, "have relations with the CIA, so people in the provinces refuse to have contact with them.[11]

"Many agents from the different police in IV Corps receive money from the CIA," An reports, "in the form of merit pay." Money was spent beautifying Special Branch offices—buying telephones, generators, air conditioners, Lambrettas, and Xerox machines for dutiful policemen and pretty secretaries. Big bucks were lavished on local officials, particularly those sitting on Phoenix committees. "Conveniences" given to committee members, writes An, made it easier for them "to explore information from agents," leading to the arrest of suspected VCI.[12]

Recall what Warren Milberg said: "I had virtually unlimited resources to develop agent operations, to pay for a staff that translated and produced intelligence reports . . . more money . . . than what the province budget was."[13] But while Milberg saw this as "creating economic stability," the incentive to sell information had the side effect of tearing apart Vietnamese society.

Perhaps the most disturbing charge made by An is that CIA operators encouraged the illegal activities of Phoenix personnel. He cites as an example the time Military Security Service agents in Sa Dec observed Special Branch agents taking payoffs from the local VC tax collector. Naturally, the MSS agents sold this information to the CIA, which took no action—because payoffs were a vehicle for penetration operations. Writes An: "The CIA works to keep some Communist areas intact so they can get information."[14] This, of course, was in direct opposition to the Phoenix mission.

As an example of the intelligence potential of the modus vivendi, An notes that unilateral CIA penetration agents into the VCI often posed as pharmacists and were supplied with desperately needed antibiotics, which they would smuggle into Vietcong jungle hideouts in Cambodia in exchange for information. "Phoenix," explains An, "was watching and talking to the VC while at the same time working to prevent the NLF from reorganizing the VCI."[15]

All this leads An to conclude that America was never interested in ending the war. Instead, he thinks the goal was to show success, "even if many lives must be lost." For An, Phoenix was not a mechanism to end the war quickly, but a means to extend it indefinitely, with a minimum of American casualties. The nature of Phoenix, he suggests, was to pit the Vietnamese against each other, to undermine their efforts at rapprochement while fueling the conflict with money and lies and psychological operations designed to destabilize the culture.[16]

In conclusion, An contends that the Vietnamese neutralists wanted only for the United States to grant South Vietnam the same status it granted Taiwan and Israel. But this was not to be, for in South Vietnam advocating peace with the Communists was punishable by death or imprisonment without trial for two years under the An Tri (administrative detention) Laws. And like Phoenix, An Tri was a boondoggle for corrupt GVN officials. Persons arrested as VCI suspects or sympathizers could be held indefinitely and were released only when their families scraped together enough money to bribe the local Security Committee chairman. That is why, An suggests, the roundup was the worst of all the hardships Phoenix imposed on the Vietnamese people.

The practice of extorting ransoms from VCI suspects served CIA interests however, by elevating security personnel into a privileged class that was utterly dependent on the CIA, in the process, thoroughly destabilizing the society. Through the ICEX screening, interrogation, and detention program, the CIA expanded this psywar tactic into the districts, enabling every minor official to get a piece of the action.

As Colonel Dillard remarked, "I became a major construction tycoon in the Delta as a sideline to my Phoenix business." As well as giving fifteen thousand dollars to every district chief to build a DIOCC, he worked with the CIA in building "those little jails, as I call them, which really were interrogation centers." Dillard recalled: "The agency sent down an elderly gentleman from Maryland who was a contractor. His job in the Delta, one of many, was to get these interrogation centers constructed. . . . Pacific Architects and Engineers did the work, but this guy was an agency employee.[17]

"What you needed in a lot of these little derelict-type districts in the Delta where they really didn't have any facilities," said Dillard, "was a place to secure and interrogate prisoners. . . . They were for anyone. . . . I remember going into one we'd built in Chau Duc that had several monks inside. They had a steel chain chained to their legs so they wouldn't run off.

"We pretty much constructed them throughout the Delta. Those that went up quickest were in the districts that were most accessible. But as fast as they went up, the VC knocked them down with satchel charges." That did not disturb the district chiefs, for whom each new construction project meant another lucrative rake-off. Indeed, the Phoenix program offered a wide range of financial opportunities.

"Phoenix in Sa Dec," An writes, "was an occasion for many nationalists to get rich illegally. Many innocent people were chased away from their homes to the district hall where they were extorted or confined in the interrogation center behind the town hall. Even water buffalo guardians were taken to the district hall, and their parents had to pay for their release or else they would be sent to Vinh Long Prison."[18]

Writes An: "One visiting U.S. congressman said our province was lucky because we had no prison. But actually this is unfortunate, because innocent people—and the Police Special Branch know who is innocent—are confined in the town hall. There is no room to lie down there. The people suffocate. They are put in an empty pool without water."[19]

As a result of Phoenix placing interrogation centers in the districts, the GVN soon gained the reputation as a prison regime. The catchphrase of its jailers was *khong, danh cho co* (if they're innocent, beat them until they're guilty), bringing to mind the Salem witch trials. But whereas in Salem the motive for torture was an ingrown libido, the motive for torture in Vietnam was an ingrown ideology. Tran Van Truong, mentioned in Chapter 10, explains: "It was part of the regime's ideology that anyone who opposed them must be a Communist. They could not accept the fact that there might be people who hated them for the travesty they had made of the country's life, for their intolerance and corruption and cold indifference to the lot of their countrymen."[20]

Truong writes from experience. By bribing "a high National Police official for the information," Truong's wife discovered that her husband was being held in a secret prison. Fearing her husband would be killed there, "and nobody would ever know," she persuaded Truong to sign a full confession. "About ten days later," Truong writes "I was bundled into a car and driven to National Police headquarters. My wife had indeed found someone else to bribe. I found out later it was the butcher himself. His price had been $6,000."[21]

Truong's wife paid two bribes—one to locate him, and one to have him transferred from the secret jail to the NPIC.

Truong adds ruefully, "Had she known about conditions at the [NPIC], it isn't likely that my wife would have paid anything to anyone." He describes six months of solitary confinement and "sensory deprivation" in a pitch-dark cement cell with a steel door and no windows. "I was like an animal in a cave. . . . I thought of my cell as my coffin."[22]

The CIA treated its prisoners at the National Interrogation Center no better. In *Decent Interval,* former CIA officer Frank Snepp cites the case of Nguyen Van Tai, the Cuc Nghien Cuu agent who organized the attack on the U.S. Embassy during Tet. Tai was captured in 1970 and, "With American help the South Vietnamese built him his own prison cell and interrogation room, both totally white, totally bare except for a table, chair, an open hole for a toilet—and ubiquitous hidden television cameras and microphones to record his every waking and sleeping moment. His jailers soon discovered one essential psychic-physical flaw in him. Like many Vietnamese, he believed his blood vessels contracted when he was exposed to frigid air. His quarters and interrogation room were thus outfitted with heavy-duty air conditioners and kept thoroughly chilled."[23]

In April 1975, Snepp notes, "Tai was loaded onto an airplane and thrown out at ten thousand feet over the South China Sea. At that point he had spent over four years in solitary confinement, in a snow-white cell, without ever having fully admitted who he was."[24] As perverse as anything done in Salem, Tai was disposed of like a bag of garbage simply because he would not confess.

But unlike Truong and Tai, most Vietnamese jailed under Phoenix were anonymous pawns whose only value was the small bribe their families offered for their release. Anyone confined in a PIC or province or district prison was in the belly of the beast. The range and extent of torture are beyond the comprehension of the average middle-class American but are well documented, as is the fact that American advisers rarely intervened to reduce the level of abuse.

So the question then becomes, Who were these American advisers?

CHAPTER 16

Advisers

By 1968, half a million American soldiers were in South Vietnam, supported by sailors on aircraft carriers in the South China Sea, airmen maintaining B-52's on Guam, and free world forces from Korea, Australia, the Philippines, and Thailand. Many thousand more civilians were advising the GVN on every conceivable facet of its operations, from police and public administration to engineering and agriculture. All were joined with the government and the Armed Forces of South Vietnam in a war against a well-organized, well-disciplined insurgency supported by North Vietnam and other nonaligned third world, socialist, and Communist nations.

With nearly one thousand NVA and VC soldiers dying each week, and no one keeping count of civilian deaths, the undeclared war in Vietnam had reached epic proportions, but its meaning was shrouded in ambiguities and contradictions. The insurgency was said to be managed along a single chain of command emanating from Hanoi, but the insurgent leadership was elusive, its numbers impossible to gauge. And while the enemy was unified but illusory, the allied effort was clearly defined but hopelessly discombobulated. Something had to be done, and that something fell to several hundred Phoenix advisers, each serving a one-year tour.

"This was moving so fast in early 1968," Doug Dillard recalled, "that young lieutenants and captains coming through the MACV advisory assignment system began arriving in-country, receiving orders, and going right out to the district or province. People didn't even know they were getting a Phoenix assignment at this stage of the game. But the program had one of the highest priorities in MACV for personnel, and as fast as they arrived in-country, they were assigned out directly to the province and district. In Four Corps we tried to intercept them, if I could find out about it in time and coordinate earlier with Saigon. Others we had to pull back from the field. We'd arrange to have them stay in Can Tho from two to three days so we could give them an orientation and tell them what we expected of them as Phoenix coordinators."[1]

At this orientation, according to Dillard, "We outlined their mission, which was to be aware of the entities operating in their area of responsibility, to establish contact with the personalities, to develop a rapport . . . and to try to convince them that the only thing we were trying to do in Phoenix was to focus all our resources on the VCI. And to report directly to me any obstacles they were encountering, to see if there was anything we could do about it. I made an effort to establish direct one-to-one relationships with them so they knew . . . that I was their friend and truly meant what I said in trying to help them. And time and time again it paid off. They would come in demoralized, and I'd find out about it and work it out with the district adviser to let the guy come in to Can Tho. We'd put him up in our own facility and take him over to the club so he could have a decent meal."

Nor did Doug Dillard sit in Can Tho and wait for problems to come to him. "Phuoc and I tried very hard to breathe some life into the coordination process," he said. "We tried to hit one or two districts every day. I would get the U.S. people together and really give them the hard sell on making Phoenix work. 'What are the problems? Do they have resources? How can I help?' And while I was doing that, Phuoc would get the Vietnamese district people together out in the district compound and give them a patriotic lecture. We did that day after day.

"I remember going to Phong Hiep District." Dillard cited as an example. "That was a bad district for VC activity, and Colonel Phuoc and I went down there, and we were walking from the helicopter pad toward the district compound when this kid came out shouting, 'He's just no good!' and 'I almost killed him myself!'

"I said, 'Calm down, Captain. Let's go have a drink and you tell me what happened.'

"Well, they'd been out on an operation that morning to zap some VCI, and as I recall, one of the VCI was the leader of the communications cadre, and they ran into him on the canal and had a fire fight and captured this guy. They were trying to subdue him, but he kept on resisting, violently, so the Vietnamese S-two pulled out his pistol and shot him. My captain almost went out of his mind. He said, 'For Christ's sake, you just killed the best source of information for VC activity in the district. Why'd you do that?' And the S-two said, 'Well, he obviously wanted to die, the way he was resisting.'

"So, you see"—Dillard sighed—"you had a mentality problem."

But there was another side of the "mentality problem." "Down in Bac Lieu," Dillard said, "one of the district chiefs had a group, and they went out and ran an ambush. The district chief stepped on a land mine and had a leg blown off and bled to death before the medevac chopper got there. So I got a report on this and told Jim Ward, and we got it into the system so the corps commander could address the problem, the problem being if these guys see they're not going to be medevaced when they're seriously wounded, they're not going to go out."

To show success to his evaluators in the Saigon Directorate, a Phoenix adviser needed a competent Vietnamese counterpart. But it is wrong to blame the failure of the program solely on the Vietnamese "mentality." To do so is to assume that Phoenix advisers understood the purpose of the program and the intelligence process and that all were mature enough to work with interpreters in a foreign culture. Many were not. As Jim Ward noted, "Very few had the proper training or experience for their work. . . ."[2]

Ward did not blame any one individual. "The effectiveness of a Province or District Intelligence and Operations Coordination Center," he said, "generally depended on three people: the American adviser and the senior South Vietnamese army and police official assigned to the center. When all three were good and had a harmonious working relationship, the DIOCC functioned effectively." But harmony was the exception, and as in most groups, the strongest personality dominated the others. If it was the Vietnamese army intelligence officer, then DIOCC operations focused on gathering tactical military intelligence. If the Vietnamese policeman was dominant, then the DIOCC concentrated on the VCI. But because the ARVN S2 generally prevailed, the overall impact of Phoenix in the Delta, according to Ward, "was spotty. Really effective in some districts, partially successful in half, and ineffective in the rest."

Contributing to the misdirection of Phoenix operations away from the VCI toward military targets was the widening gap between Province and District Intelligence and Operations Coordination Centers. Explained Ward: "Because most Phoenix-Phung Hoang planning took place at province [where the CIA Special Branch adviser was based], and because the DIOCC was run by the ARVN S2 advised by U.S. Army officers as part of the MACV district advisory team, the CIA Special Branch adviser was not going to share his intelligence or dossiers with these people." This lack of cooperation reinforced the tendency on the part of military intelligence officers to do what they could: to gather information on impending guerrilla attacks, not the VCI.

For this reason, said Colonel George Dexter, who organized Special Forces A teams in Vietnam in the early 1960's and served as the CORDS assistant chief of staff in IV Corps in 1972, "It would seem that Army Intelligence Corps officers were not a good choice for this role since they were basically oriented toward combat intelligence rather than police intelligence. However, U.S. civilians [meaning CIA officers] were almost never assigned at district level because the risk of combat was too high."[3]

Warren Milberg suggests that "the biggest deficiency in the advisory program was the lack of an 'institutional memory.' Phoenix advisers did not know the history of their provinces [or] how the insurgents operated there." Moreover, "Nothing was done to improve the situation. . . . Not being able to speak the language of their counterparts, and knowing they were only going to stay in Vietnam for a relatively short period of time, most advisers tended to neglect the political and social aspects of the situation in which they found themselves. Unable to cope with, or accept, the people of the RVN, many advisers became ineffective, and the overall result was the degradation of the Phoenix-Phung Hoang program."[4]

Colonel Dexter was more forgiving: "The lieutenant spent his whole tour in Vietnam as a member of a five- or six-man district advisory team in a small town in the middle of nowhere, 'advising' a Vietnamese counterpart (who was probably several years older and surely many more years experienced in the war) and holding down any number of additional duties within the advisory team." Said Dexter: "His success depended primarily on the competence of his counterpart and, to a lesser degree, on his own energy and imagination. His major handicap was the inability to speak Vietnamese with any degree of fluency."

A difficult language and an inscrutable culture; lack of training and experience; institutional rivalries and personal vendettas; isolation and alienation: all were obstacles the typical Phoenix district adviser had to face. All in all, it was not an enviable job.

Colonel Dillard's fatherly concern for his young district advisers, "fresh out of college and through the basic course at Fort Holabird," was as exceptional as the harmony he had achieved with the CIA in the Delta. More often than not, Phoenix advisers received little guidance or support from cynical region and province officers. Nor were the first Phoenix advisers even minimally prepared for the intrigues they encountered. The first batch of junior officers sent to Vietnam in February 1968—specifically as Phoenix advisers—consisted of forty second lieutenants trained in the art of air defense artillery—of which there was no need in South Vietnam insofar as the Vietcong had no aircraft. In addition, most were Reserve Officer Training Corps graduates who had been called upon to meet the unanticipated personnel requirements imposed on the Army Intelligence Corps after the deeply resented troop limit had been imposed on the Joint Chiefs of Staff.

Such was the case with Henry McWade. A 1965 graduate of East Tennessee State, McWade was commissioned a second lieutenant in 1966 and called to active duty in 1967. In December 1967 he attended Fort Holabird, where, in his words, "we were trained in European methods for the cold war."[5] In May 1968 McWade and twenty-one other second lieutenants, a group he referred to as "the last idealists," were sent to South Vietnam as Phoenix district advisers. Now a realist, McWade told me wearily, "They needed seven-year captains."

Following a week's orientation at the Combined Intelligence Center, McWade was assigned to Go Vap District in Gia Dinh Province as part of CORDS Advisory Team 44. He resided in a prefab facility with other members of the district team, while the province Phoenix coordinator, Major James K. Damron, lived in opulent splendor in the CIA's lavish embassy house, "a cathedral" complete with a helicopter landing pad on the roof and a contingent of PRU bodyguards—a "goon squad" whom "the Vietnamese feared and considered criminals."

"He gave us no direction at all," McWade said of Damron. "The people at the PIOCC . . . located five miles away in the old Special Branch headquarters . . . kept us at arm's length. The few times we drove up there, they gave us no guidance or advice at all. Only money." For McWade, this was a big disappointment. "As a green second lieutenant I needed that operational guidance. But I didn't get it. . . . And the Company man, the Special Branch adviser, just didn't deal with us at all. They had their own advisory system compartmented away from Phoenix.

"The program had been more autonomous, flexible, and experimental under the agency," McWade continued. "But as Army advisers—whom CIA officers consider amateurs—filtered in at every level, the program shifted under the CORDS province senior advisers or their deputies. And if the CIA can't control it," McWade explained, "they get rid of it."

From his DIOCC in Go Vap, McWade observed that Major Damron was "an empire builder. The life-styles were incredible. Damron contracted with an American construction company to build safe houses, where he entertained and kept women. He had civilian identification that allowed him to go anywhere. He carried a CAR-15 until the Uzi became fashionable. Then he carried that. And Damron was shrewd. When the province senior adviser or his deputy was around, he talked intelligence jargon. He had files and computers. But when they were gone"—McWade winked—"the conversation was all construction. Damron was the best at building buildings. He built great DIOCCs and safe houses. But he couldn't catch any VCI."

The Phoenix program had begun in 1967 under the management of CIA province officers, but as junior grade army officers like Henry McWade mounted the Phoenix ramparts in 1968, the CIA instructed its officers to retreat to the safety and seclusion of the embassy houses. "And once they found out I was against physical torture," McWade added, "they preferred that I stay away from the province interrogation center altogether." Thereafter, whenever the Go Vap DIOCC produced a VCI suspect, "they removed the prisoner from our sight. They solved the problem by taking it out of sight."

Complicating matters, McWade said, was the fact that "the Special Branch was playing us against the CIA." In other words, in order to meet Phoenix quotas, the Vietnamese Special Branch would arrest common criminals and present them as VCI, while behind the scenes they were extorting money from genuine VCI in exchange for not arresting them. "And the CIA," McWade sighed, "was stretched too thin to know."

As for oversight from the Phoenix Directorate, McWade said it was negligible. "They'd send down a computer printout [containing biographical information on known VCI]. We got them sporadically. Fifty names per page, six inches thick. But we couldn't use them because they lacked the diacritical marks which were necessary for proper identification." And that pretty much left McWade on his own to manage Phoenix operations in Go Vap.

Vietnamese assigned to the Go Vap DIOCC included PRU, a Regional and Popular Forces company, Census Grievance cadre, National Police, and Field Policemen. McWade's counterpart was the ARVN S2, "a weak person I put too many demands on. The only time he moved was the time a ranger brigade came to Go Vap to conduct cordon and search operations with the police. When Saigon units, which were there to prevent coups, came out to our area, things happened. Then it was a genuine Phoenix operation."

Otherwise, said McWade, "We ran every conceivable type of operation, from night ambushes in the rural areas north of Go Vap, to Rambo-style counterintelligence operations in the city—the kind where you personally had to react." McWade went on village sweeps with the local Regional and Popular Forces company, checking hundreds of IDs with the police. Based on tips gotten from informers, he would also surveil and target houses in Go Vap where VCI suspects lived, contact points where VCI met, and places where commo-liaison cadres crossed the river. He took photographs, submitted reports, and "fed the computer in Saigon.

"We were going out every other day, sometimes every day," he recalled. "I worked eighteen hours a day, six or seven days a week." And yet, he was never really in control. "I had no operational control over any units, and I had to rely one hundred percent on my counterpart," he said. "So every operation had to be simple," primarily because of language. "I was at the mercy of an interpretor with a five-hundred-word vocabulary," McWade sighed. "It was like being deaf and dumb. And I just assumed every operation was compromised, at a minimum because my interpretor was an undercover Military Security Service agent." And even though he monitored agent nets, "No one reported directly to me; it would have been impossible to try, if you can't speak the language. There was no such thing as a secure agent, and we didn't have walk-ins because the people couldn't trust the police." Making matters worse, there were at least a dozen intelligence agencies operating in the area, each with what it assumed were its own unilateral agents in the field. But because the various intelligence agencies refused to share their files with one another, they never realized that each agent, as McWade put it, "was selling information to everybody."

The picture is one of total chaos. Indeed, most of McWade's initial operations were conducted—without his realizing it—by his police counterparts against common criminals or dissidents. He recalled his first day on the job, which coincided with the beginning of the second Tet offensive. "The first one in February came through Cholon," McWade said. "This one came through Go Vap. We were out with the Regional and Popular Forces company, picking up anyone who looked like an ARVN draft dodger. Meanwhile the Vietnamese police were shaking them down, although I didn't learn about it till much later."

There were other surprises. In an area outside Go Vap, for example, over thirty thousand refugees lived in a sprawling ghetto. McWade told me, "They were mostly prostitutes working for organized crime—meaning the police. I thought we were investigating the VCI, but actually I was used by my police counterpart to raid the madams who hadn't paid him off." When he figured out what was really going on, McWade said, "I developed what I called 'McWade's Rule'; fifteen percent for graft, eighty-five percent for the program. And this was a complete reversal of what was happening when I arrived!"

But Henry McWade did not become bitter, nor was he unable to cope with Vietnamese culture. Unlike many of his colleagues, he did not interpret Vietnamese customs as insidious schemes designed to deceive him. "The Vietnamese had a different vocabulary and different goals. They were *not* interested in acquiring bodies," he said. "They were interested in acquiring money and items on the black market." In other words, their motives were practical, geared toward surviving in the present, while it was generally only their American advisers who were obsessed with eliminating Communists from the face of the earth.

* * *

As a means of bringing Vietnamese and American procedures into closer sync, the Phoenix Directorate in July 1968 issued its first standard operating procedures (SOP 1) manual. SOP 1 stressed the leadership role of the police and the need for paramilitary forces to support the police in the attack on the VCI. It subdivided Intelligence and Operations Coordination Centers (IOCCs) into three areas. The Plans and Operations Center devised plans and organized available forces in operations against guerrilla units and individual VCI. The Situation Center maintained files, handled agent security and operations, produced reports, and set requirements. It had a military order of battle section under the Vietnamese army intelligence officer, the S2, gathering intelligence on and targeting guerrilla units, and a political order of battle section under the Special Branch, targeting VCI. The Message Section communicated with the district or province chief, who exercised overall responsibility for any particular IOCC.

In practice, SOP 1 had little effect. "It didn't do any harm," Henry McWade observed; but it was issued only to Americans, and the Vietnamese continued to organize the IOCCs according to their own "separate goals and missions. The double standard persisted, even after a translation (minus diacritical marks) was circulated."

Ralph Johnson acknowledges this, noting that the GVN's instructions to its own people—by making no reference to the role of U.S. Phoenix advisers in the IOCCs—widened the gap between Americans and Vietnamese. At first only the CIA, which "controlled the salaries, training and support of critical elements in Phung Hoang," was able to exert influence, by parceling out resources and funds. Otherwise, when Phoenix advisers received adequate funds through CORDS, they, too, "were able and willing to use monetary leverage to drive home needed advice and guidance. And a CORDS agreement with President Thieu gave CORDS the right to call attention to officials who should be replaced."[6]

In any event, Phoenix advisers found themselves caught in the middle of intrigues beyond their comprehension. Woefully unprepared, they stood between their Vietnamese army and police counterparts; their CIA and U.S. Army superiors; and the GVN and the sect or opposition political party in their area of operation. Everything was expected of them, but in reality, very little was possible.

Shedding light on the problems of Phoenix advisers is Ed Brady, a slender Army officer who served his first tour in Vietnam in 1965 as an adviser to the Twenty-second Ranger Battalion in Pleiku. After that, Brady volunteered for another tour and was assigned as a Regional and Popular Forces adviser in Da Lat, where he learned about the connection between politics and the black market in Vietnam. "Both the VC and the ARVN tried to avoid military operations in Da Lat," Brady told me, adding that as part of the modus vivendi, it was "a neutral city where you could have meetings and where financial transactions could take place, legal and illegal. It was a place where the VC could raise and wash and change money. It was sort of what Geneva was like in World War Two. There were many businesses in the province, like woodcutting, rubber and tea plantations, and the *ngoc mam* [fish sauce] industry. All were sources of money for the VC and the GVN."[7]

In Da Lat Brady worked with CIA Province Officer Peter Scove, who introduced him to Ted Serong, who at the time was handing over control of the Field Police to Pappy Grieves. "I was learning a lot," Brady said. "I learned Vietnamese from the officer I was working with . . . the words that dealt with money and corruption. Then Serong asked me if I would be willing to go on loan to his team. They had a new kind of platoon . . . that they wanted to train in small-unit tactics. More like guerrilla warfare than what the police did. And would I be willing to train this platoon because he didn't think that the Australian warrant officers he had there were the right people?"

Brady agreed and spent the next few months at the Field Police center, training what turned out to be "the first experimental PRU team in Tuyen Duc Province . . . recruited by the CIA to be the action arm of the province officer." The platoon had four squads, two composed of Nungs and two of Montagnards. "They couldn't speak to each other." There were also squad leaders and a platoon commander, all of whom were South Vietnamese Special Forces officers, none of whom could speak Montagnard or Nung or English either.

"It was really the strangest thing you ever saw," Brady said. "And I taught them small-unit tactics."

As was generally the case, Brady's association with the CIA spelled trouble for his military career. "I had a lot of problems with my sector boss over these activities," he told me. "He thought I should eat in the sector house with the rest of the team, not with the Aussies and CIA people. I also spent most of my off time with Vietnamese officers in their homes, in bars, doing the things they did. I rented a house on my own, lived off the economy, learned how you buy your jobs, and met a lot of general officers' mistresses who liked to come to Da Lat for the weather. The American colonel I worked for thought this was atrocious, and I got a zero on my performance report."

Having been suborned by the CIA, enticed by the Vietnamese, and excommunicated by the Army, Brady—whose family was connected to a powerful U.S. senator and the III Corps commander—was reassigned to the Vietnamese Joint General Staff (JGS), "in their command center. We were a division of the MACV Combat Operations Center. The main purpose of this group was to collect data on Vietnamese operations and feed it to the MACV so it could be reported to Washington.

"General Cao Van Vien was commander of the Joint Staff," Brady continued, "and these guys were his operations staff. They traveled to every major Vietnamese battle to find out what happened—they placed no reliance on any official message—and I went on every one of those trips. I met all the key commanders. Plus which I was moving in Vietnamese social circles."

Brady became friends with General Vien's executive officer and with the JGS operations chief, Major General Tran Tran Phong. "And for some reason," he added, "a number of the ranger officers and people I knew in Da Lat had moved into key positions in Thieu's administration. They had sort of been in exile when I met them—you didn't get assigned to a ranger outfit because you were in good graces with the administration . . . —but later they showed up in Saigon. And I had a great bond with them. I'd been in combat and brothels with them. But they were now full colonels. And I met many of their bosses, who were generals in powerful positions."

When Brady's tour at the JGS ended, the CIA station asked him to capitalize on his well-placed connections and report on what he learned about GVN plans and strategies. Brady agreed, and was assigned to the Phoenix Directorate as a cover for his espionage activities. "Somebody called me up one day and said, 'We're starting a new organization, and we'd like you to consider joining it.' This was ICEX. So I went over there . . . and spent a couple hours talking to Evan Parker. He said, 'We're interested in targeted operations against the civilian part of the Communist party. . . . The main force war doesn't address the real problem . . . the shadow government.' And I was ready for that—psychologically and emotionally. Everything I knew said, 'That's exactly right.'

"ICEX was to work with the Special Branch," Brady continued, "which set up a separate building in the National Police compound to be the Phung Hoang Central Office. They detailed mostly Special Branch policemen to work there, but there were a few military officers and a few National Police officers to round out the staff. Their office was only two months old when I arrived. There were a couple of CIA advisers down there to be the people who worked with them. Joe Sartiano was the senior CIA guy down in the Phung Hoang Central Office. And me and Bob Inman were down there from the Phoenix operations section."

The Phoenix assignment put Brady in close contact with Dang Van Minh, Duong Than Huu, and Lieutenant Colonel Loi Nguyen Tan. About his relationship with Tan, Brady said, "Since Colonel Tan was a military officer, we knew people in common, so there was an immediate rapport. Tan was very friendly, very easy to talk to. But he was not, from an American point of view, demanding. We would go out on inspection teams together, to operations centers, and he'd have a discussion with the chief. Meanwhile, his Vietnamese subordinate and I pored through the dossiers, looked at their procedures and what operations they had run recently. And a lot of it was a sham—a facade that they were meeting the letter of the law. So they had a hundred dossiers. Big deal! Seventy-five had nothing in them. Fifteen of the other twenty-five had a couple of newspaper clippings from the local newspaper about the VC district chief. But they had no real intelligence, no real targeted operations that they were setting up or running. And Tan would never crack down on them or lean on them in some way that was acceptable to us from the West.

"Now in Vietnamese he would make a few remarks to them: 'You really ought to try to do better.' And when he got back, he'd file a report that this place was not in very good shape. But he didn't say, 'Damn it, I'm going to be back here in three weeks and you'd better have something going by then!' That's why it's difficult to say if he was effective."

Brady, who has deep affection for the Vietnamese, explained why their approach to Phoenix was at odds with the one pressed by Evan Parker: "If you really want to get down to cases, no Vietnamese of any significance in the military or in the police didn't know who the truly high-level people were—the district chiefs and the province chiefs. Let me give you an example. Colonel Tan and Mr. Huu and I were eating in a market stall up near the border in Three Corps. The place was a hotbed of VCI support for NVA units. There was lots of money flowing there, donated by French rubber plantation owners without much coercion. They didn't like the GVN. Anyway, this woman comes in. She's got three or four kids, the youngest is maybe two, the oldest about seven. And Tan says to me, 'You see this woman?' We're there eating soup and drinking Vietnamese coffee. She's there feeding her kids at a nearby table in the market stall.

"I say, 'Yeah.'

"He says, 'You know who she is? She's the province chief's wife.'

"I looked around and said, 'I don't see the province chief. You're telling me there's an honest province chief, and his wife doesn't own a jeep and go around collecting money all day?'

"No, no," he says. "The *VC* province chief."

"So, being young and naive, I say, 'Well, look at how many young kids she has. She either goes to see him, or he comes to see her. Or she's got a lover.'

"He says, 'Right.' But they are his kids. They even look like him.

"So I say, 'Well, he must come in to see her, then, or she goes to see him.' I'm really excited. I say, 'This is something we can really work with.'

"He says, 'You don't understand. You don't live the way we live. You don't have any family here. You're going to go home when this operation is over with. You don't think like you're going to live here forever. But I have a home and a family and kids that go to school. I have a wife that has to go to market. . . . And you want me to go kill his wife? You want me to set a trap for him and kill him when he comes in to see his wife? If we do that, what are they going to do to our wives?'

"How many wives were ever killed?" Brady asked rhetorically. "Zero—unless they happened to drive over a land mine, and then it was a random death. The VC didn't run targeted operations against them either. There were set rules that you played by. If you went out and conducted a military operation and you chased them down fair and square in the jungle and you had a fight, that was okay. If they ambushed you on the way back from a military operation, that was fair. But to conduct these clandestine police operations and really get at the heart of things, that was kind of immoral to them. That was not cricket. And the Vietnamese were very, very leery of upsetting that."

Likewise, as Tran Van Truong notes in *A Vietcong Memoir:* "Thieu's chief of psywar hid in his own house a sister-in-law who was the Vietcong cadre in charge of the Hue People's Uprising Committee. Neither had any particular love for their enemies, but family loyalty they considered sacrosanct."[8]

"Atrocities happened," Brady said. "Those things happened by individual province officers or people who worked for them and the PRUs. . . . It happened in the U.S. units. My Lai happened. No matter what anybody says about 'it didn't happen,' it did happen. I've watched people torch Montagnard villages for no real reason except they were frustrated by not being able to catch the VC. And the Montagnards must have known about the VC, which I believe they did. But we didn't have to burn their houses."

When asked if Phoenix encouraged atrocities, Brady answered that it depended on whether or not the PRU and the PICs were defined as part of Phoenix. "If you want to say that all the intelligence activities that were *supposed* to be coordinated by Phoenix *are* a part of Phoenix, then yes," Brady said. "But if you want to say, 'Did Phoenix go do these things?,' then my answer is no. Because Phoenix was too inactive, too incompetent, and too passive. Now, Phoenix should have been doing many more things directly, and if it had, then my belief is that Phoenix would have perpetrated some atrocities, because they would have been in the position these other people were in, where they were frustrated, they were angry, and they would have done some things.

"Furthermore," Brady added, "you can make the case that Phoenix was helping to repress the loyal opposition political parties and prevented a neutral Vietnam from occurring. The Vietnamese said that, because the Special Branch guy who planned the operation to nullify their political operations was also running Phoenix operations. . . . So it depends on how you want to interpret the data and how you want to say things were connected together. . . . I'd say either of those interpretations are valid.

"I think the director of Phoenix never planned such things," Brady concluded in defense of Evan Parker and American policy in general. But he also said, "Yes, people assigned to Phoenix did such things."

CIA officer Ralph Johnson, in safari jacket and baseball cap, standing beside his donkey in Muong Sai, Laos, circa 1959 (Johnson family collection)

Phoenix officials, spring 1969; *left to right:* National Police officer Duong Tan Huu; Lt. Col. Loi Nguyen Tan; Phoenix Director Evan J. Parker, Jr.; Parker's replacement, John H. Mason; Lt. Col. Robert Inman; two unidentified Vietnamese (Parker family collection)

American pacification officials in Binh Dinh Province, circa 1963; *left to right:* Major Harry "Buzz" Johnson; State Department officer Val Vahovich; USIS officer Frank W. Scotton; Special Forces Sergeant Joe Vaccaro (Johnson family collection)

Nelson H. Brickham, Jr., in Dalat, circa 1966 (Brickham family collection)

William Colby, circa 1969 (Colby family collection)

Tulius Acampora with General Nguyen Ngoc Loan, circa 1966 (Acampora family collection)

Acampora with Major Nguyen Mau (Acampora family collection)

Colonel William "Pappy" Grieves walking behind National Police Field Forces chief Colonel Nguyen Van Dai, February 1970 (Grieves family collection)

Khanh Hoa Province Interrogation Center, Nha Trang, circa 1966 (Brickham family collection)

Province Interrogation Center, unidentified province, circa 1966 (Brickham family collection)

Colonel Douglas Dillard with the director of the Military Security Service, General Vu Duc Nhuan, circa 1969 (Dillard family collection)

Province Interrogation Center program director Robert Slater in Dalat, December 1968, holding Bridget Bardot Rose, with Vietnamese Special Branch officers in background (Slater family collection)

Slater flanked by PIC program advisers Frank Cerrincione, *left,* and Orrin DeForest in Bao Loc, Lam Dong Province, December 1968 (Slater family collection)

Phoenix officer Warren Milberg standing beside I Corps National Police Chief Vu Luong, in Danang, spring 1968 (Milberg family collection)

Quang Tri Province Provincial Reconnaissance Unit (PRU), circa 1967 (Milberg family collection)

Delta PRU adviser John Wilbur with the Kien Hoa Province PRU team, circa 1967 (Wilbur family collection)

PRU cadre, Vung Tau training center, circa 1967 (Wilbur family collection)

II Corps PRU advisers, circa 1969; *left to right:* Aussie Ostera; Blue Carter; Captain John McGeehan; Sergeant John Fanning; Major Paul Ogg; Captain Charles Aycock; Captain John Vaughn; Sergeant Buzz Brewer; Sergeant Al Young; Sergeant Larry Jones (Ogg family collection)

II Corps PRU adviser Paul Ogg with Colonel Ruel P. Scoggins, circa 1970 (Ogg family collection)

Phoenix training officer Lt. Col. Walter V. Kolon, *right,* with John E. MacDonald, senior State Department representative to the Phoenix staff, circa 1969 (Kolon family collection)

From left: Phoenix Director John H. Mason, Phoenix Operations Chief Lt. Col. Thomas P. McGrevey, and Deputy Phoenix Director Colonel James W. Newman, circa 1970 (Newman family collection)

From left: Phung Hoang chief Colonel Ly Trong Song, John Mason, James Newman, and senior Phung Hoang officer Lt. Col. Pham Van Cao, circa 1970 (Newman family collection)

Sergeants Ed Murphy, *left*, and Blane Baisley outside Dragon Mountain Combined Interrogation Center, 4th Military Intelligence Detachment, Pleiku Province, circa 1968 (Murphy family collection)

Public Safety Adviser Douglas McCollum at National Police Field Force outpost in Darlac Province, circa 1968 (McCollum family collection)

Member of the Bien Hoa special Phoenix team, displaying Phoenix tattoo

Ancient and Oriental Order of Phoenicians certificate, provided by Phoenix district adviser Major Claude Alley

VIET-NAM CONG-HOA

THE

ANCIENT AND ORIENTAL ORDER OF PHOENICIANS

Be it Known By All Those Here Present That:

Lieutenant Claude R. Alley

Is Initiated Into This Venerable Society With The Title Of

NUMBER ONE BIRDWATCHER FIRST CLASS

With All Rights, Priviledges And Responsibilities Appurtenant Thereto

WHEREAS:

By virtue of having served in the PHOENIX Program during the period 11 March, 1969 to 11 March 1970 Said recipient has endured the flapping of the PHOENIX Bird's wings, honed its talons, unsnarled its ribbons, smoothed its tailfeathers, nestled in its breast, been pecked upon ad infinitum and cleaned its cage, to the extent that he has been infinitely, totally, and incurably neutralized. He may therefore upon his return to the world pursue such birdwatching as his title health and pocketbook permit.

Signed, sealed, & attested this [illegible] day of [illegible] 1970 A. D.

IMPERIAL BIRDWATCHER

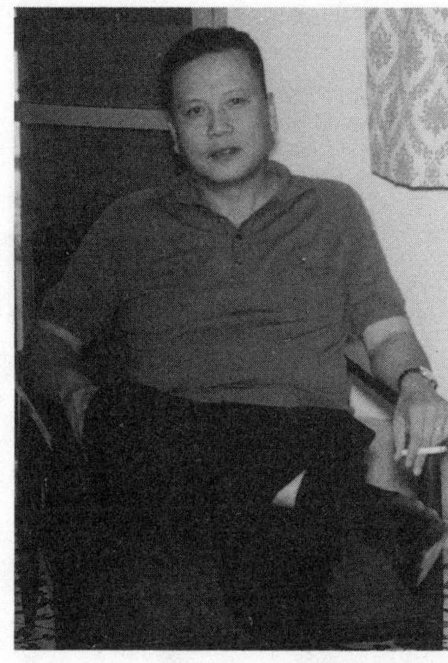

Special Police Saigon chief, Major Pham Quant Tan (Roberts family collection)

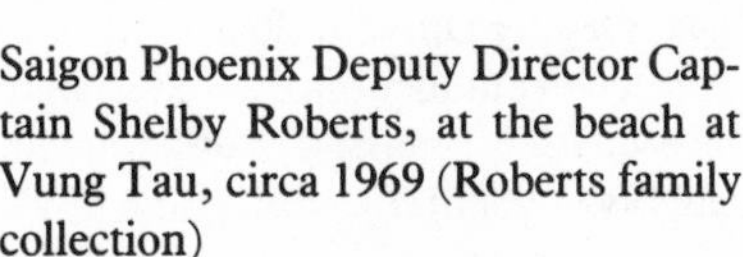

Saigon Phoenix Deputy Director Captain Shelby Roberts, at the beach at Vung Tau, circa 1969 (Roberts family collection)

Phoenix Directorate staff, circa 1972; *left to right:* Operations Chief Lt. Col. George Hudman; Phoenix Director John S. Tilton; Deputy Director Colonel Herb Allen; Major Carl Moeller (*seated*); unidentified secretary; unidentified officer; unidentified secretary; Major Doug Collins; unidentified secretary; Sergeant Jim Marcus; unidentified officer, unidentified civilian; unidentified secretary (Hudman family collection)

Phoenix Directorate function, circa 1971; *left to right:* Deputy Director Colonel Chester B. McCoid; Director John S. Tilton; Lt. Col. Russ Cooley; unidentified Public Safety officer; Colonel Ly Trong Song; National Police adviser Frank Walton; Captain Albright; Special Branch Deputy Director Dang Van Minh; Lt. Col. John Ford (McCoid family collection)

Criminal Investigation Division Sergeant William J. Taylor (Taylor family collection)

CIA officer and senior SOG adviser George French flanked by Special Operations Group chief Colonel J. F. Sadler, *left,* and unidentified SOG officer, circa 1971 (French family collection)

Lt. Col. Walter Kolon and Lt. Col. Al Weidhas at a Tai Kwon Do exhibition in Saigon in 1969, sponsored by the Vietnamese American Association (Baillargeon family collection)

Phoenix officers at a farewell ceremony for State Department officer Seton Shanley; *left to right:* Captain Paul Baillargeon; National Police Chief Colonel Tran Van Hai; John Mason; Colonel Robert E. Jones; Captain Richard Bradish; Seton Shanley; Charles Phillips; unidentified Vietnamese officer (Baillargeon family collection)

CIA officers Bruce Lawlor and Patry Loomis in Quang Nam Province, circa 1972 (Lawlor family collection)

CHAPTER 17

Accelerated Pacification

The election of Richard Nixon in November 1968 signaled a shift in U.S. policy in Vietnam. Reflecting the desire of most Americans, in the wake of Tet, for an honorable withdrawal, the policy balanced negotiations with the bombing of North Vietnam. Called the Nixon Doctrine, the policy had as its premise that the United States has a moral obligation to support foreign governments fighting Communist insurgents, on the condition that those governments supply their own cannon fodder.

Shortly after taking office, Nixon instructed his national security adviser, Henry Kissinger, to start negotiating with the North Vietnamese in Paris. On the assumptions that Tet had dealt the VCI a deathblow and that the Thieu regime was firmly in control of the country, Nixon began planning for troop reductions. Following in the footsteps of the French, U.S. forces began a gradual retreat to coastal enclaves. And MACV, under General William Westmoreland's replacement, General Creighton Abrams, prepared to fight a sanctuary war based on CIA estimates that forty thousand NVA soldiers hunkered down in Cambodia constituted the major outside threat to the Thieu regime. The bombing of these potential invaders began in February 1969, with the consent of Cambodia's Prince Norodom Sihanouk, whose agents provided the Special Operations Group (SOG) with information on the location of enemy forces, many of which were located in densely populated areas. Conducted in secret, the illegal raids into Cambodia were revealed in May 1969 and resulted in increased opposition to U.S. government conduct in Southeast Asia.

The Nixon Doctrine as applied in Vietnam was called Vietnamization, and the man upon whom the mantle of Vietnamization fell was William Colby, godfather of the Covert Action program that had set the stage for American intervention ten years earlier. In November 1968 Colby was appointed DEPCORDS, replacing Democratic party loyalist Robert Komer, whom President Johnson had named U.S. ambassador to Turkey. Colby reported to Henry Kissinger, who supported Colby's ambitious pacification program, geared to facilitate Vietnamization.

Colby subdivided his pacification plan into three main categories, beginning with military security, which he called "the first step in the pacification and development process"—in other words, borrowed from Nelson Brickham, "shielding the population from the Communist main forces," a job which "is the task of the Vietnamese regular forces."[1]

Often generated by Phoenix intelligence, the resulting air raids, artillery barrages, and search and destroy operations were an integral part of pacification, insofar as they created defectors, prevented guerrillas from assembling in large concentrations, and, by creating refugees, separated the fish from the water.

Part II of Colby's strategy was territorial security, the 1969 manifestation of Revolutionary Development, in which the Regional and Popular Forces—thereafter called Territorial Security Forces—were advised by U.S. Army mobile advisory teams (MATs) under the auspices of CORDS. In combating VC guerrilla units and the VCI, Territorial Security Forces were assisted by the People's Self-Defense Forces.

In a Defense Department report titled *A Systems Analysis of the Vietnam War 1965–1972,* Thomas Thayer says that as of 1968, "The Revolutionary Development program had significant problems in recruiting and retaining high quality personnel." The RD Cadre desertion rate was over 20 percent, "higher than for any GVN military force, perhaps because they have a 30% better chance of being killed than the military forces." Thayer notes that in response, the RD ministry had directed its cadre "to concentrate on building hamlet security and to defer, at least temporarily, the hamlet development projects which formerly constituted six of the teams' eleven RD tasks."[2]

Under these revised guidelines, providing intelligence to Phoenix replaced "nation building" as the RD program's top priority. Reflecting this change, the RD Cadre program was incorporated within the CORDS Pacification Security Coordination Division in November 1968, at which point MACV officers and USAID employees moved in to manage the program, bringing about, according to Robert Peartt and Jim Ward, a decline in performance and morale. In line with Lou Lapham's redirection of the station away from paramilitary operations back toward classic intelligence functions, the CIA's role in RD diminished, although it continued to skim off whatever strategic intelligence was produced. As Peartt noted, the station was "interested in going after region people, and would get involved at that point in RDC/O operations."[3] To a lesser degree, the CIA's PRU program was also affected.

"The agency made a decision," John Wilbur said, "to get their ass out of Vietnam as fast as they could, for all the reasons Kinloch Bull foretold. It was losing control . . . diluting its cadre . . . being misdirected. It had become the sponsoring agency for a hodgepodge thing, and Phoenix was going to be the mechanism by which it was going to withdraw its control and sponsorship . . . and transition it over to the military. And that . . . meant that the PRU were no longer going to be the CIA's exclusive boys, which foretold a real human crisis in the units."[4] Their "élan and morale had been carefully nurtured," Wilbur explained. "We protected them from the dilution of control . . . from the province chiefs and battalion commanders. We insulated them from being used for whatever multiple good and bad reasons other people wanted to use them for. We would pay them a little better, we would take care of their dependents, and we would provide them with the best military support there was." That, according to Wilbur, motivated them to "go out and do the things they did."

But, he added, "they had incurred a lot of resentment by the Vietnamese to whom they had previously been untouchable. . . . The leadership levels were marked men among many Vietnamese political forces." And as soon as the Vietnamese got control in the summer of 1968, "everybody started messing with them." The PRU began to be used as bagmen.

"I was hurt in the last attack on Can Tho," Wilbur continued, "and when I got back [from the hospital], my replacement had already arrived . . . and I spent most of the next six weeks introducing Chuck [Lieutenant Commander Charles Lemoyne] to the provinces, to all the hundreds of people he would have to deal with." At that point Wilbur went home, where he remained until May 1968, when the CIA asked him to return to Vietnam to help Bill Redel "develop a national PRU unit which was targeted to recover American POWs in South Vietnam. It was the only thing that seemed worth fighting for," Wilbur said, so he accepted the job. He was transferred to a naval security group, assigned to MACV, given an office (formerly occupied by Joe Vacarro) on the second floor of USAID II, and went to work for Redel.

"We were going to set up a unit that would go around the provinces and try to collate whatever extant information there was, and in the event there was something that indicated [a POW camp] was there, we would try to put an in-place person, or try to develop . . . somebody to deal with an agent in place, and then gather the intelligence sufficiently to mount some sort of rescue operation."

But the rescue program was scuttled, and Wilbur instead got the job of transferring management of the PRU to the Vietnamese. He was introduced to Special Forces Mayor Nguyen Van Lang,* the first PRU national commander, and they began traveling around the country together. "And it became very apparent when I showed up with a Vietnamese colonel . . . what was going to happen. It meant the military, and that meant that the leadership elements of the PRU were in jeopardy of maintaining allegiance—they weren't colonels and majors and captains."

Wilbur sighed and said forlornly, "The fact that there was no national overlay allowed the CIA to maintain autonomy over the PRU program longer than they would have otherwise." But by the summer of 1968 "The official word had to go out that the PRU was becoming part of the Phoenix program: 'We're going to lose control. Get ready for the transition.'

"It was the dissolution of American protection of the units that was mandated in our withdrawal," Wilbur explained, "that corrupted the quality of control, which in turn allowed the PRU to be turned into a department store. And I became an agent of that. I was going to try to convince people to give up control of the PRU, after I had spent all this time arguing for its insulation and control and independence."

To effect territorial security, Colby intended "to get weapons into the hands of the Vietnamese villagers, so they could participate in their own defense" and to provide "funds to the elected village leaders to carry out local development programs."[5] The mechanism for this was Ralph Johnson's village chief program at Vung Tau, about which Professor Huy writes: "[A]fter 1968, when Thieu succeeded to restore security in the countryside, several province and district chiefs used fraud and threats to put their men in the village and hamlet councils. These men were often the children of rich people living in cities. They needed the title of 'elected representatives of the population' to enjoy a temporary exemption from military service, and their parents were ready to pay a high price for their selection as village councilors. Thus, even the fiercely anti-Communist groups became bitter and resentful against Thieu."[6]

That brings us to Part III of Colby's plan, internal security, otherwise known as Phoenix, the two-track CIA program to destroy the VCI and ensure

*Lang's sister had married Tucker Gougleman when Gougleman was managing SOG operations in Da Nang in 1964.

the political stability of the Thieu regime by insulating him from the backlash of his repressive policies. As it was in the beginning, the pacification purpose of Phoenix was to weaken the link between the "people" and the VCI, while the political-level Phoenix was designed to exploit that link.

To implement his plan, Colby forged ahead with a three-month start-up program dubbed the accelerated pacification campaign (APC). Begun in November 1968, APC was designed to bolster Kissinger's negotiating position in Paris by boosting the GVN presence in the hamlets, and was expected to show its effect by Tet [of 1969]. The goal was to add twelve hundred hamlets to the five thousand already classified under the Hamlet Evaluation System (HES) as "relatively secure." Afterward APC was to be followed by an annual "full year pacification and development program." To facilitate this process, Colby created the Central Pacification and Development Council as his personal staff and private conduit to Tran Thien Khiem, who replaced Tran Van Huong as prime minister in August 1969.

Said Evan Parker about his patron William Colby: "The interesting thing was his relationship with Khiem . . . they would travel around the countryside in the same plane, each sitting there with his briefcase and a stack of working papers, writing like mad, answering memoranda, writing memoranda, passing memorandum back and forth. . . . There's your coordination on this stuff—one of them or both would use his authority to support what I was asking the Vietnamese to do."

To assist him on the council, Colby hired Clayton McManaway as program manager; Tony Allito for HES reports; Harry "Buzz" Johnson for territorial security; and Ev Bumgartner and Frank Scotton for political liaison. With his personal staff in tow, Colby spent two days each week canvassing the provinces, bringing pressure to bear on people in the field, and promoting the accelerated pacification campaign.

Phoenix adviser John Cook describes the accelerated pacification campaign as "an all out nationwide effort to put as many hamlets under government control as soon as possible. The Viet Cong violently opposed this action, since its primary purpose was to eliminate them and their control. It involved large military operations coupled with psychological operations, resulting in increased emphasis on the pacification program." Insofar as the attack on the VCI strengthened Henry Kissinger's bargaining position, Cook writes, "Pressure was placed on the Intelligence and Operations Coordinating Centers to provide more valid information about the enemy's location. This required more of an effort from all of us, which meant an increase in the number of raids, ambushes and operations."[7]

The hour of Phoenix was at hand. With American troops withdrawing and emphasis being shifted from military to political operations, the pressure began to mount on Phoenix advisers, who were expected to eliminate any vestiges of revolutionary activity in South Vietnam. Reasons why they failed to accomplish this goal are offered by Jeffrey Race in his book *War Comes to Long An*.

Blaming "overcentralization," Race observes that the district, where the DIOCCs were located, "was the lowest operational level" of Phoenix, "one having no significance in terms of social or living patterns, and staffed by outsiders whose interests bore no necessary connection to the districts. By contrast, the revolutionary organization was the essence of simplicity . . . and intimately familiar with the local population and terrain." Race traces the lack of "security" at the village level to the GVN's disdain for the common people and its "failure to develop a highly motivated and trained local apparatus."[8]

Operational as well as organizational errors also factored into the equation. Forces under the Phoenix program, Race explains, "operated in the manner of a conventional war combat organization—independently of their environment—and so they did not have the enormous advantage enjoyed by the party apparatus of operating continuously in their home area through a personally responsive network of friends and relatives. This in turn severely handicapped their ability to locate intended targets and to recognize fortuitous ones. The program was also handicapped in developing a sympathetic environment by the use by the Saigon authorities of foreign troops and by the program's intended purpose of maintaining a distributive system perceived as unfavorable to their interests by much of the rural population."[9]

Responding to the grievances of the rural population and taking steps to correct social injustices might have enabled the GVN to collect intelligence and contest the VCI in the villages. But acknowledging the nature of the conflict would have undermined the reason for fighting the war in the first place. And rather than do that, Race says, "attention was turned to the use of such new devices as starlight scopes, ground surveillance radar, and remote listening devices, as well as the previously employed infrared and radio transmission detection devices."[10]

In August 1968, concurrent with Robert Komer imposing, as "a management tool," a nationwide quota of eighteen hundred VCI neutralizations per month, the science fiction aspect of Phoenix was enhanced with the advent of the Viet Cong Infrastructure Information System. VCIIS climaxed a process begun in February 1966, when Secretary of Defense Robert McNamara established the Defense Department's Southeast Asia Programs Division. The process was carried forward in Saigon in January 1967, when the Combined Intelligence Staff fed the names of three thousand VCI (assembled by hand at area coverage desks) into the IBM 1401 computer at the Combined

Intelligence Center's political order of battle section. At that point the era of the computerized blacklist began.

As the attack against the VCI exploded across South Vietnam in 1968, reports on the results poured into the Phoenix Directorate, inundating its analysts with reams of unreliable information on individual VCI and anti-VCI operations. In DIOCCs the data could be processed manually, but in Saigon it required machines. Hence, with input from the Defense Intelligence Agency, the FBI and the CIA—all of which had an interest in analyzing the finished product—VCIIS became the first of a series of computer programs designed to absolve the war effort of human error and war managers of individual responsibility.

The cerebellum of Phoenix, VCIIS compiled information gathered from all U.S. and free world field units on VCI boundaries, locations, structures, strengths, personalities, and activities. The end product, a monthly summary report, was a statistical summary of Phoenix operational results by province, region, and the country as a whole and showed the levels and methods of neutralizations at each echelon within the VC infrastructure. A monthly activity listing listed each "neutralized" VCI by name. In July 1970 the Vietnamese were invited to contribute to the program and started key punching at the National Police Interrogation Center. Until then the computerized blacklist was a unilateral American operation.

In January 1969 VCIIS was renamed the Phung Hoang Management Information System. The PHMIS file included summary data on each recorded VCI in the following categories: name and aliases; whether or not he or she was "at large"; sex, birth date, and place of birth; area of operations; party position; source of information; arrest date; how neutralized; term of sentence; where detained; release date; and other biographical and statistical information, including photographs and fingerprints, if available. All confirmed and suspected VCI members were recorded in this manner, enabling Phoenix analysts instantly to access and cross-reference data, then decide who was to be erased. All of this added up to hard times for NLF sympathizers, Thieu opponents, and those unfortunate enough to be creditors or rivals of Phoenix agents.

As a management tool PHMIS was used by Komer and Colby to measure and compare the performance of Phoenix officers—unless one believes those like Tom McCoy, who claims that Komer was a fraud who went to Vietnam "not *to do* pacification but *to prove* that it was being done."[11] In that case the numbers game was computerized prestidigitation—an Orwellian manipulation of statistics to shape public opinion.

According to McCoy's scenario, PHMIS was part of a larger hoax begun in January 1967, when Robert Komer introduced the Hamlet Evaluation

System (HES)—eighteen factors subject to computer analysis for each of South Vietnam's fifteen thousand hamlets. These factors included data on VC military activity, GVN security capabilities, the strength of the VCI, Revolutionary Development activities, etc. The data were assembled by MACV district advisers, with the computer then putting the hamlets into one of three classes: A, secure; B, contested; or C, controlled by the VC.

On the verge of Tet in December 1967, nearly half of South Vietnam's hamlets were rated A. One year later more than half were rated A. As Public Safety chief Frank Walton told me, "We would get reports of provinces being eighty-five percent pacified and ninety percent pacified, and then, when it got to the point that they were near a hundred percent, figures had to be revised downward. It was done with computers, and that's where I first heard the term 'GIGO' for 'garbage in; garbage out.' "[12]

The Hamlet Evaluation System also included input on "the known strengths of the 319 currently identified, upper-level VCI organizations at COSVN, region, province and district levels." The HES guesstimate of VCI strength in January 1969 was 75,500.

Statistics on the VCI; definitions of the VCI; attitudes toward the VCI—all were subjective. Yet despite his own admission that "we knew there was a VCI, but we could not be said to know very much about it," William Colby set about attacking it. Armed with technology that rendered due process obsolete, he "set up standards and procedures by which to weed out the false from the correct information." To ensure that Phoenix operations were mounted on factual information, "The general rule was established that three separate sources must have reported a suspect before he could be put on the rolls." Thus, the VCI was put into three classes of offenders: A, for leaders and party members; B, for holders of other responsible jobs; and C, for rank-and-file members and followers. "And the decision was taken that those in the 'C' category should be ignored, since Phoenix was directed against the VCI command and control structure and not the occasional adherent or supporter."[13]

To complement these safety procedures, Phoenix advisers and their Vietnamese counterparts were issued, in July 1968, the Yellow Book, published by the CIA under cover of the RAND Corporation. Officially titled *The Modus Operandi of Selected Political Cadre,* the Yellow Book described the operational patterns and procedures of VCI cadre and suggested "possible actions" to exploit them.

In November 1968 came SOP 2, telling how to manage a DIOCC, and in December 1968 appeared the Green Book, *Current Breakdown of Executive and Significant VCI Cadre.* The bible of Phoenix advisers, the Green Book listed all VCI job titles, assigned each an A, B, or C rating, and prescribed the duration of detention suitable for each functionary. It told how the VCI routed messages, how they constructed and hid in tunnels, who was likely to know whom in the party organization, and other tips that would allow earnest Phoenix advisers to prioritize their targets, so they could go after the big fish recorded in the Black Book kept in the situation section of each DIOCC and PIOCC.

Other publications made available to Phoenix advisers included a biweekly newsletter that enabled advisers to share their favorite interrogation, operational, and briefing techniques; MACV's monthly "Summary of VCI Activities"; Combined Document Exploitation Center and Combined Intelligence Center readouts; the PHMIS monthly report; and an eagerly awaited Phoenix End of Year Report.

Perhaps the most far-reaching innovation of 1968 was the Phoenix Coordinators Orientation Course (PCOC), which held its first classes at Vung Tau's Seminary Camp in November 1968. The PCOC represented a final recognition that, as Doug Dillard remarked, "MACV *really* had to account for it."[14] To state it simply, military careers were now hitched to the Phoenix star.

The advent of the PCOC dovetailed neatly with the folderol of the accelerated pacification campaign and the infusion into the Phoenix Directorate of a new generation of staff officers, who brought with them new ideas and were confronted with new concerns, most concerning public relations. On the CIA side, Robert E. Haynes replaced Joe Sartiano as executive director, and Sartiano and two State Department officers began writing a plan to put Phung Hoang under the control of the National Police. On the military side, Colonel Robert E. Jones replaced William Greenwalt as deputy director.

In September, Army Security Agency officer Lieutenant Colonel Richard Bradish stepped in as the military liaison to Special Branch. Bradish "provided direct assistance" to the Phung Hoang staff in Special Branch headquarters at the NPIC. He and the sergeant assisting him were the only military personnel who had desks there. "We were very busy," Bradish told me, "primarily advising the Special Branch in anti-infrastructure operations."[15] Bradish also advised Vietnamese inspectors visiting Phung Hoang committees on "how to bolster morale and improve record keeping on VCI neutralizations."

Bradish noted that Parker's military deputy, Colonel Jones did not provide "close supervision," a condition that was "characteristic of the whole thing. . . . I was compartmented," Bradish said about himself and the other military personnel on the staff. "We were outsiders. When I was there, Special Branch was Phung Hoang"—meaning that the CIA still controlled Phoenix, with the military there as window dressing. Likewise, Bradish observed, the

Vietnamese at the Phung Hoang Office "were putting on a show. They were not acting like they were at war, but like it was a normal job." In his judgment, "The North Vietnamese were more committed."

The Central Phung Hoang Permanent Committee as of November 1968 looked like this:

Chairman: General Tran Thien Khiem
Assistant Chairman: Colonel Ly Trong Song
Phung Hoang Plan: Lieutenant Colonel Loi Nguyen Tan
Planning Bureau: Mr. Duong Than Huu
Intelligence Operations: Mr. Ha Van Tien
Action Programs: Mr. Mai Viet Dich
Inspections Bureau: Mr. Nguyen Van Hong
Chieu Hoi Representative: Mr. Le Doan Hung
Statistics Bureau: Military Security Service Captain Dinh Xuan Mai

Also arriving at the Phoenix directorate in September 1968, concurrent with its reorganization into separate branches for plans and training, was Lieutenant Colonel Walter Kolon. Put in charge of training, Kolon's job was "to prepare incoming personnel at Seminary Camp at Vung Tau,"[16] which in 1969 was still the private property of the CIA; only Air America was authorized to fly in and out. Having worked with the agency at various stages in his career, including his first tour in Vietnam in 1965 with the Special Military Intelligence Advisory Team (SMIAT), Phoenix was a program that Walter Kolon was well suited for. Assembled by CIA officer William Tidwell within MACV's Technical Intelligence Branch, SMIAT was a deep cover for sophisticated "black" operations against the VCI before Phoenix. "The premise and charter of SMIAT," said Kolon, "laid the groundwork conceptually for Phoenix."

When Kolon arrived on the scene, CIA contract officers like Bob Slater and veteran Phoenix coordinators like Doug Dillard and Henry McWade were teaching classes at Vung Tau. Recalled Dillard: "There was a compound and classrooms and different kinds of training facilities out on the grounds. Colonel Be was there with his RD Cadre training school, although they kept them separate. And of course, I was involved only with American personnel. They had agency people who had been with ICEX as instructors. The U.S. cadre down there were all agency people; later they began to get some Army personnel in."

Phoenix personnel assigned to Seminary Camp shared their mess hall with PRU advisers. "We had two elements," Walter Kolon recalled. "One was the Phoenix school; the other was PRU. Those were the only two there. The RDC training area was separate. But the people being assigned were neither fish nor fowl; counterintelligence and intelligence people had no understanding of police or judicial procedures, and former policemen were not the solution either," he added, noting that they and people from other agencies sometimes had no intelligence training at all. "What was needed was a new breed of cat, a person who understood collection, analysis, and response units like the National Police Field Force, and how all that jibed with gathering evidence and building a case."

So, Kolon continued, "We made recommendations to Colby to get a new program under way in the States. Then I went back to brief the people at SACSA, CIA, Fort Holabird, and the Continental Army Command at Fort Lee as to what our needs were, not just immediately, but into the foreseeable future as well—always remembering that Phoenix was a coordinative function. As a result, the military intelligence branch of the Army, on instructions from the acting chief of staff for intelligence, actively began identifying in the United States people to volunteer as Phoenix advisers, on the understanding that they would be able to choose their next assignment after Vietnam. This would eventually develop into what was called the Phoenix Career Program."

Phoenix curriculum was soon introduced to the Foreign Service Institute; the Defense Intelligence School; the Army Intelligence School; the Institute for Military Assistance at Fort Bragg; the Civil Affairs School at Fort Gordon (home of the Military Police); the Army Intelligence School in Okinawa; and Joint U.S. Military Advisory Group in Thailand. Walter Kolon then returned to Vung Tau, where he supervised the creation of the ten-day bimonthly Phoenix Coordinators' Orientation Course. The staff was "originally about a dozen people. Some were former DIOCC advisers, and the CIA also supplied a number of guest lecturers."

About his experience as a Phoenix facilitator, Henry McWade said, "I gave two classes. The first class was how the DIOCC should be, as set forth in SOP One and SOP Two. In the second class I said, 'Forget the first class; this is how it really is.' Then I explained how they had to adjust to the Vietnamese, how they would get money for expenditures but no money for bodies, and how sometimes they would get money for agents."

Kolon and his deputy, Major Kelly Stewart, also provided advice and support to Special Branch training courses begun in Bien Hoa in December 1968, then expanded to the other corps. In this capacity Kolon traveled with Ed Brady and Loi Nguyen Tan. By the end of 1969 corps centers had trained eighteen hundred students, primarily in how to be case officers. Beginning in February 1969, American advisers to ARVN ranger battalions, along with police advisers and Free World Military Assistance Forces, were also given Phoenix instruction.

In addition to classes at Vung Tau, the CIA gave instruction to Phoenix advisers at the Vietnamese Central Intelligence School. John Cook attended one of the sessions. He writes:

> There were forty of us in the class, half American, half Vietnamese. The first day at the school was devoted to lectures by American experts in the insurgency business. Using a smooth, slick delivery, they reviewed all the popular theories concerning communist-oriented revolutions. . . . Like so many machines programmed to perform at a higher level than necessary, they dealt with platitudes and theories far above our dirty little war. They spoke in impersonal tones about what had to be done and how we should do it, as if we were in the business of selling life insurance, with a bonus going to the man who sold the most policies. Those districts that were performing well with the quota system were praised; the poor performers were admonished. And it all fitted together nicely with all the charts and figures they offered as support of their ideas.[17]

Like many of his colleagues, Cook resented "the pretentious men in high position" who gave him unattainable goals, then complained when he did not reach them. In particular, as a result of mounting criticism in the American press, Phoenix advisers were called to task for their failure to capture rather than kill VCI. The problem stemmed from the press's equating Phoenix with the PRU teams it employed. For example, in December 1967 the Minneapolis *Tribune* described the PRU as "specially trained Vietnamese assassins" who "slip silently by night into sleeping hamlets to carry out their deadly function." The *Tribune* noted: "This aspect of ICEX has a tradition that goes back far beyond the Vietnam conflict, and its methods are those of hired killers everywhere."

The "hired killer" label was to stick to Phoenix, with hapless DIOCC advisers taking the heat for PRU advisers conducting their business with impunity. Writing for the *Wall Street Journal* on September 5, 1968, reporter Peter Kann described the VCI as "the invisible foe," adding that "the target is assassinated, sometimes brutally as an object lesson to others."

In this way Phoenix developed a reputation as an assassination program. That is why it became imperative that the CIA disassociate itself from the program through public statements building a case for plausible denial. Such was the tack William Colby took at a press conference held for thirty news correspondents on December 28, 1968, in response to mounting public queries about Phoenix. In his opening statement Colby called Phoenix "a Vietnamese program" in which Americans were involved "only as part of military operations." The MACV information officer assisting Colby added that no American units were allocated to Phoenix. Colby stressed that the goal was to capture, not to kill, VCI. Nothing was said about wanted dead or alive posters, the PRU, or the Army's combined reconnaissance and intelligence platoons (CRIPS), which Jeffrey Race calls "Far more effective than even the PRU at eliminating members of the VCI."[18]

When asked how advisers prevented people from using Phoenix as a cover for political assassination, Colby cited systematic record keeping as the fail-safe mechanism, producing charts and graphs to show statistics backing his claims. He did not mention the massacre of Ky's people on June 2, 1968, or Tran Van Don's claim that Phoenix helped Truong Dinh Dzu in the 1967 election, or the station's special unit, whose victims' names never appeared on Phoenix rolls.

Colby made no reference to the CIA's having built the province interrogation centers and said that advisers were "seldom" present at interrogations. He then outlined American-conceived legal procedures for detaining suspects.

The *essence* of Colby's dissembling was his definition of Phoenix as an organization rather than a concept. As stated in the previous chapter, when Ed Brady was asked if Phoenix generated atrocities, his answer was that it depended on whether or not the PRU and the PICs were defined as part of Phoenix. The *reason* for Colby's ignoring these two foundation stones of Phoenix was to conceal CIA involvement in the program, as well as to protect unilateral CIA penetrations, what Nelson Brickham called "the most important program in terms of gathering intelligence on the enemy." What Jim Ward called "the real sensitive, important operations."[19] And, according to Colby, it worked: "We were getting more and more accurate reports from inside VCI provincial committees and regional Party headquarters from brave Vietnamese holding high ranks in such groups."[20]

"CORDS provided an umbrella," said John Vann's deputy, Jack. "But people, especially the CIA, were always back-channeling through their own agencies to undermine it. . . . Komer insisted that CIA people would run Phoenix through regular channels. But on highly sensitive matters, like tracking high penetrations, it wasn't reported in CORDS."

In a conversation with the author, Jack noted that the informal lines of command are more important than formal lines, that, as he put it, "*real* power gravitates off the organizational charts. The way it gets organized isn't critical; it had to be done some way, and it can adapt. For example, in Hau Nghia it was military, while in Gia Dinh it was Special Branch. It has to be flexible to account for HES A and B hamlets as opposed to C and D hamlets. Military or police, depending on the environment. In any event the CIA advised Special Branch had cognizance over Phoenix."[21] And Phoenix was a concept, not an organization.

CHAPTER 18

Transitions

Saigon has been called a wicked city. It is said that the pungent smell of opium permeated its back alleys, that its casinos never closed, that its brothels occupied entire city blocks, and that a man could sell his soul for a hundred dollars, then use the money to hire an assassin to kill his lover, his boss, his enemy.

Anything was possible in Saigon. And given the massive infusion of American soldiers, dollars, and matériel that began in 1965, criminally minded individuals had the chance to make fortunes. This could be done in all the usual ways: by selling military supplies and equipment on the black market, by taking kickbacks for arranging service and construction contracts, and through extortion, gambling, prostitution, narcotics, and money changing. The dimensions of the black market were limitless and included corrupt officials, spies seeking untraceable funds and contact with the enemy, and mafiosi in league with military officers and businessmen out to make a fast buck. By late 1968, with the psychological defeat brought about by Tet, the crime wave was cresting, and the transition from a quest for military victory to making a profit had begun in earnest.

As one CIA officer recalled, "When the so-called Vietnamization of the war began, everyone knew that even though the Company would still be running CORDS, it was the beginning of the end. The contract employees began getting laid off, especially those running operations in Laos. The others, mostly ex-Army types, knew their turn was coming, so they began trying to make as much money as they could. Air America pilots doubled the amount of opium they carried.* The Americans in CORDS, with the help of the PRU, began shaking down the Vietnamese, arresting them if they didn't pay protection money, even taking bribes to free suspects they'd already arrested. Everyone went crazy for a buck."

"Here you have a very corrupt environment, a culture that tolerates corruption," Ed Brady observed, "and now you're going to run covert operations."[1]

Considering that the Special Branch—which had cognizance over Phoenix—was responsible for investigating corruption, it was inevitable that some Phoenix coordinators would abuse the system. Much of that abuse occurred in Saigon under the nose of John O'Keefe, the CIA officer in charge of the Capital Military District. Described by Nelson Brickham as a "very capable officer"[2] and a "raconteur" who spoke excellent Parisian French, O'Keefe was a veteran case officer with years of experience in Europe. In Vietnam he had served as the officer in charge of Chau Doc Province and Hue before being transferred to Saigon in September 1968.

Headquartered on the second floor of the three-story building behind City Hall on Nguyen Hue Boulevard, O'Keefe on paper reported to Hatcher James, the senior USAID adviser to Saigon Mayor Do Kin Nhieu, whose deputy "really ran things" (foremost among those things being the loan and default payments the GVN owed the "five communes," the principal Chinese families in Cholon who served as South Vietnam's major moneylenders). Tall, with sandy hair and a fondness for drinking scotch with the CIA's notorious finance officer, alias General Monopoly, at the Cosmos, O'Keefe supervised Special Branch and Phoenix operations in Saigon beginning in September 1968.

Also arriving in Saigon in September 1968 was Captain Shelby Roberts. In 1965 Roberts had been a warrant officer flying photoreconnaissance missions for MACV's Target Research and Analysis Division, locating targets for B-52 strikes. Another creation of Bill Tidwell's, TRAC was used by General McChristian as the nucleus for the Combined Intelligence Center. In 1966 Roberts was commissioned an officer and, after completing the military adviser training program at Fort Bragg, returned to Vietnam and was assigned as Phoenix coordinator to Saigon's high-rent neighborhood, Precinct

*Drugs were also smuggled on CIA/SOG black flights, which were exempt from customs checks. Likewise, SOG personnel carried military assistance adviser "Get out of Jail Free" cards, exempting them from search and seizure by their adversaries in the Military Police and Criminal Investigation Division.

1. Snuggled on the east side of Saigon, far from the squalor of Cholon and Tan Son Nhut's sprawling shantytowns, Precinct 1 had been the private domain of the French colonialists. By 1969 many of those rambling villas were occupied by Americans, including John O'Keefe, Hatcher James, and William Colby, who lived on treelined Hong Tap Thu Street.

Abutting Precinct 1 on the east was Gia Dinh Province, fiefdom of Major James K. Damron, whom Roberts described in an interview with the author as "the agency's man in Gia Dinh" and "a warlord who went overboard and built a tremendous building. But he played from a position of power," Roberts said. "He demanded total loyalty from his people, and the Vietnamese respected that and were terribly loyal to him." Majors James Damron and Danny Pierce—who served as deputy coordinator of the Capital Phung Hoang Committee—were "business partners."[3]

Roberts described Danny Pierce as "an operator" who "abused the system." An officer in the Mormon Church, Pierce was linked to the black-market supply and service industry through a secret "ring-knock" identification system. Pierce was allegedly fired for possession of a stolen jeep traced to the SOG motor pool located at 10 Hoang Hoa Tam Street, where the Army Counterintelligence Corps had originally set up shop in Vietnam in 1962.

In early 1969 Captain Roberts replaced Major Danny Pierce as the Capital Phung Hoang Committee deputy coordinator. Thereafter once a month Roberts visited the Gia Dinh Province embassy house to exchange information with warlord Damron, until Damron himself was reassigned by William Colby in early 1969 to an administrative post in the IV Corps Phoenix program.

Unlike his freewheeling predecessor, who had fallen under the influence of the CIA, Shelby Roberts was not a member of the Phoenix Directorate. In an effort to achieve greater control over the program, MACV had Roberts report to John O'Keefe on operational matters, while reporting administratively to the chief of MACV's Saigon Capital Advisory Group (SCAG). As a result, Roberts was not as closely involved in CIA operations in Saigon as Pierce had been. But he was collocated with O'Keefe, and he did have insights into the CIA side of Phoenix operations in Saigon.

"My office was behind City Hall, on the floor below O'Keefe's office," Roberts recalled. "We had about twenty Vietnamese employees, eight in the translation section, the rest doing clerical work." The officer representing the Phoenix Directorate in Saigon was Lieutenant Colonel William Singleton, whom Roberts described as "working on the operations side, in covert activities. He had safe houses and a plantation house with a small staff." A tall man from Tennessee, Singleton was "particularly interested in Cholon." The Special Branch officer running Phoenix operations in Saigon was Captain

Pham Quat Tan, a former ARVN intelligence and psywar officer featured in a January 12, 1968, *Life* magazine article.

According to Roberts, Phoenix in the Capital Military District was entirely a CIA operation run out of Special Branch headquarters. "We fed nothing to the Phoenix Directorate," Roberts said. "The reports all went back to the Combined Intelligence Center, or I would give a briefing to O'Keefe, and he'd go to the embassy, to the sixth floor"—where analysts in the station's special unit sifted through names and chose candidates for penetration.

Anti-infrastructure operations in Saigon were difficult at best. The city had ten precincts, with those outside downtown Saigon resembling the suburbs in Go Vap District, as described by Henry McWade. Security in outlying precincts was maintained not by the Metropolitan Police but by the paramilitary Order Police patrolling in armored cars, American infantry brigades, and ranger battalions. There was a strict curfew, and in the aftermath of Tet new interrogation centers were built in all of Saigon's precincts. In Precinct 1 a large interrogation center was built by Pacific Architects and Engineers directly behind the U.S. Embassy. In other precincts interrogation centers were constructed "under existing roofs." In either case Roberts tended to avoid them. "I was reluctant to get involved because the Special Branch tried to use me during interrogations. They'd say, 'If you think we're bad, he'll cook you and eat you!' So I didn't care to participate."

Each precinct had wards called *phung,* which were further subdivided into *khung,* a group of families, usually ten, which the Special Branch monitored through "family books" maintained by the Metropolitan Police. The finished product of the Family Census program, family books contained biographical information and a photograph of every family member. One of the *khung* families was responsible for keeping track of visitors to the other families, and on the basis of these family books, the Special Branch compiled blacklists of suspected VCI members.

In discussing the tactics of the Special Branch, Shelby Roberts said, "They ran all their operations at night. They'd turn the floodlights on, tear down entire neighborhoods . . . and arrest entire families. They were mainly interested in shakedowns. The 'Send your daughter to my office'-type harassment. And making money on the side. Everyone," Roberts added, "was in the black market."

There were other intrigues. "We chased commo-liaison people," Roberts explained, "and if we caught them, the police would get reward money and money for their captured weapons. This led to the same weapons being turned in over and over again. Over half a million were paid for, but there were less than a quarter million at the armory." Meanwhile, "The Special Branch hid information from us so it wouldn't go up to O'Keefe and the CIA. It was common knowledge that if you gave good information to Phoenix, you wouldn't get the reward money." And that, according to Roberts, "was the death of the program."

Despite its heavy-handed methods, "The Special Branch was considered a white-collar job," Roberts explained, "whereas the Saigon Metropolitan Police . . . were looked down upon." So out of spite the Metropolitan Police turned from law enforcement to graft. Precinct chiefs sold licenses for every conceivable enterprise, from market stalls to restaurants and hotels, and managed prostitution, gambling, and narcotics rackets. The police were paid off by the crooks and the Vietcong alike. As a result, according to Roberts, "They got no respect. They were so corrupt they tried to corrupt the Phoenix coordinators."

Making matters worse, Roberts said, was the fact that when information on suspected VCI members was forthcoming, Phoenix coordinators—reflecting the CIA's desire to have total control over sources that might generate strategic intelligence—were told to ignore it. This prohibition and the frustration it caused, plus the fact that the police tried to bribe the precinct coordinators, resulted in more than twenty Phoenix advisers passing through Saigon's ten precincts in 1969. Most lasted only a few weeks, although those who were suborned by the CIA held their jobs for years. For example, Captain Keith Lange, who replaced Roberts in Precinct 1, was "pulling off national-level operations" for two and a half years. On the other hand, Roberts put Captain Daniel Moynihan in Precinct 2, "so I could watch him, because he had trouble with finance."

Indeed, money was the answer to, and cause of, all problems in Saigon. Insofar as AID withdrew its Public Safety advisers from Saigon after Tet, Roberts said, "We, the Phoenix coordinators, were the only Americans in the precincts. Some guys were so busy they slept in their offices." And because the CIA was no longer disbursing funds through AID, Phoenix coordinators by default became the conduit of monetary aid to the National Police and the Special Branch. "So the police chiefs really liked us a lot," Roberts added.

Phoenix coordinators also became the conduit for AID funds ostensibly destined for community development, refugee, and health programs. In reality, the money bought information and influence. Roberts recalled one housing project in an area of Cholon that had been leveled during Tet. The cost was $150,000. Roberts got the money from CIA finance officer General Monopoly at the embassy annex. "Short, potbellied, and in his sixties," General Monopoly "sat in the same seat every night at the Cosmos. He was there at three o'clock every day drinking scotches with Damron, Singleton, and O'Keefe."

As the pursuit of money began to rival the pursuit of intelligence, a new twist was added to The Game, as the competition for intelligence sources was called. "Especially in Precinct Five [which encompassed Cholon]," Roberts said, "we'd get U.S. deserters working with the VCI through the black market. They were dealing arms and supplies from the PX. We knew of five deserters in Cholon. Each one was operating with several IDs. The MPs and CID ran a number of operations to get one guy in particular. He would sneak past guards, masquerading as an enlisted man. And he was actually detained several times. But because he had phony ID, he was always released."

There may be another reason why this traitor was never caught. It has to do with the CIA's practice of nurturing deviant communities as a source of assassins. John Berry quotes one such "contractor" in his book *Those Gallant Men on Trial in Vietnam*: "Well, I walk behind this screen and I don't see this guy's face, but he give me 5,000 piasters and a picture and an address, and I go kill the dude and then go get my other 5,000."[4]

With Vietnamization, Phoenix came under closer scrutiny. The repercussions were evident everywhere. Toward the end of 1968, Henry McWade recalled, "Major Damron got into a power play for intelligence resources"[5] and Damron's bosses reached the conclusion that he was all smoke and mirrors.

"Damron was losing control," McWade explained. "So he put the blame on us, the DIOCC advisers, to gain time and space for himself. We were sacrificed." A few days later McWade and a group of scapegoats (not including John Cook) were transferred out of Gia Dinh to other provinces. McWade landed in Hau Nghia in III Corps as deputy to the province Phoenix coordinator, Captain Daniel L. Smith.

Back in Gia Dinh, Damron and his loyalists were hunkering down. But Colby was intent on cleaning house, and Damron was transferred out of Gia Dinh. Doug Dillard recalled the scandal precipitated by Damron's infamous excesses: "I'll never forget Colby's admonition to us on one of his visits down in the Delta. Up in Three Corps there was an agency guy who had built a magnificent building with a helicopter landing pad on the roof. And Colby said, 'There ain't gonna be any more monuments built in Vietnam. I'm glad to see you guys have a conservative program for just getting the job done.'"[6]

Ironically, the new Gia Dinh province officer in charge proved more troublesome for Colby than Damron. For whereas Damron was guilty of mere greed, the new province officer was prey to a far more dangerous master: his conscience. A veteran CIA paramilitary officer, Ralph McGehee had already spent fifteen years fighting the Holy War in a number of Asian countries when he arrived in Vietnam in October 1968. His biggest success had been in Thailand, where he had developed survey teams for rooting out the Communist infrastructure. McGehee's survey teams consisted of police, military, and security officials who entered Thai border towns to "interrogate anyone over ten years old"[7] about Communist efforts to organize secret political cells. However, in a cruel twist of fate which engendered his crisis of faith and his fall from grace, McGehee naively relayed information uncovered by his survey teams indicating that the Communist insurgency had overwhelming popular support. Although accurate in their assessment of the situation, his reports defied policy and were summarily dismissed by his bosses in Washington. Feeling rejected, McGehee arrived in Saigon teetering on the brink of heresy. What he saw of Phoenix pushed him over the edge.

As the CIA's Gia Dinh province officer in charge, McGehee reported to the CIA's III Corps ROIC; as the Gia Dinh Province Phoenix coordinator, he reported to the CORDS province senior adviser. In his book *Deadly Deceits,* he writes that "the primary CORDS program was the Phoenix operation" and that "CIA money was the catalyst."[8] But McGehee's problem with Phoenix had nothing to do with the attack on the infrastructure; in an interview for this book, he said the PRU program "was admirable." McGehee's gripe was that "the agency was not allowed to report the truth."

Writes McGehee: "The assignment to Gia Dinh gave me the opportunity to see how the agency's intelligence program worked, or more accurately how it did not work at that level. One or two sentence intelligence reports poured in, were translated, and were filed or thrown away. A typical report, one of hundreds like it received each week, said: 'Two armed VC were seen moving south of the village of . . . this morning.' A massive agency/CORDS/Phoenix file system processed this daily flow of nonsense. Collation and analysis never applied. I wondered how this intelligence effort could possibly give our leaders and generals anything even approaching an accurate picture of what was going on.[9]

"Our policy," McGehee deduced, "was based on 'intelligence' reports of the numbers of communists in Vietnam that had nothing to do with reality. Either they were the result of unbelievable incompetence or they were deliberate lies created to dupe the American people."[10]

McGehee settled on the second explanation, a belief he shares with Sam Adams, the controversial CIA analyst who quit the agency in 1973 in protest over what he claimed was "the sloppy and often dishonest way U.S. intelligence conducted research on the struggle in Indochina."[11] A member of George Carver's SAVA staff, Adams wrote the CIA's handbook on the VCI and for five years taught a class on the VCI to CIA case officers bound for Vietnam. After quitting the agency, Adams claimed that the CIA had falsified statistics, and in 1982 in a CBS documentary called *The Uncounted Enemy: A Vietnam Deception,* he accused General William Westmoreland of a deliberate cover-up. Humiliated, Westmoreland filed his famous $120 million libel suit against CBS.

The origins of the "Vietnam deception" date back to January 11, 1967, when SAVA director Carver wrote a memo, introduced as evidence at the Westmoreland trial, indicating that the number of confirmed Vietcong, put at over a quarter of a million by MACV, was "far too low and should be raised, perhaps doubled." Despite indications presented by General McChristian substantiating the CIA estimate, MACV rejected it and instead, by excluding Vietcong Self-Defense Forces from its order of battle, contrived a lower number. CIA analysts persisted in arguing for an estimate approaching half a million, and a stalemate ensued until August 30, 1967, when Director of Central Intelligence Richard Helms, describing the issue as "charged with political and public relations overtones,"[12] arranged for Carver to lead a delegation of senior intelligence officers to Saigon to negotiate an agreement on the exact size of NVA and VC forces.

Two days after arriving in Saigon and meeting with McChristian's replacement, General Davidson, Carver notified Helms that MACV was "stonewalling" and that "circumstantial indicators . . . point to inescapable conclusion that Westmoreland . . . has given instructions tantamount to direct order that strength total will not exceed 300,000 ceiling. Rationale seems to be that higher figure would not be sufficiently optimistic and would generate unacceptable level of criticism from the press."[13]

Although the CIA knew that the estimated 120,000 VC Self-Defense Forces (which Westmoreland described as "old men, old women and children") were the integral element of the insurgency, Carver, after being shown "evidence that I hadn't heard before," cut a deal on September 13. He sent a cable to Helms saying: "Circle now squared. . . . We have agreed set of figures Westmoreland endorsed."[14] In November National Security Adviser Walt Rostow showed President Johnson a chart indicating that enemy strength had dropped from 285,000 in late 1966 to 242,000 in late 1967. President Johnson got the success he wanted to show, and Vietnam got Tet.

Sam Adams's claim that the agency had "misinformed policymakers of the strength of the enemy" was backed at the CBS libel trial by Carver's deputy, George W. Allen, who claimed that Westmoreland "was ultimately responsible" for "this prostitution" and that the CIA, "by going along with it," had "sacrificed its integrity on the altar of public relations and political expediency." Allen added that the end result of the deception was that Washington was left "essentially with an inadequate understanding of what we were up against" in Vietnam. According to Allen, the Self-Defense Forces were not old women and children but hardened guerrillas who were responsible for 40 percent of all U.S. combat casualties in Vietnam.

As a result of Adams's claims, a congressional inquiry was conducted in 1975. The investigating committee, chaired by Otis Pike, concluded that juggling of numbers "created false perceptions of the enemy U.S. forces faced, and prevented measurement of changes over time. Second, pressure from policymaking officials to produce positive intelligence indicators reinforced erroneous assessments of allied progress and enemy capabilities."[15]

Sam Adams has said that "the reason [Phoenix] did not work was that its needs, although recognized in theory, were never fulfilled in practice. The divorce between hope and reality became so wide that the program degenerated into a game of statistics, in which numbers were paramount, and the object of the exercise—the crippling of the Communist Party—was never even approached."[16]

Likewise, Ralph McGehee found the CIA squaring statistical facts with ideological preconceptions in Vietnam, just as it had in Thailand. "The station's intelligence briefings on the situation in South Vietnam confirmed all my fears," he writes. The briefers "talked only about the numbers of armed Viet Cong, the slowly increasing North Vietnamese regular army, and the occasional member of the Communist infrastructure. They made no mention of the mass-based Farmer's Liberation Association, or the Communist youth organization, all of which in some areas certainly included entire populations."[17]

The reason for this deception, McGehee contends, was that "U.S. policymakers had to sell the idea that the war in the South was being fought by a small minority of Communists opposed to the majority-supported democratic government of Nguyen Van Thieu. The situation, however, was the opposite. . . . The U.S. was supporting Thieu's tiny oligarchy against a population largely organized, committed, and dedicated to a communist victory."[18]

McGehee blames the American defeat in Vietnam on "policy being decided from the top in advance, then intelligence being selected or created to support it afterwards." In particular, he singles out William Colby as the principal apostle of the Big Lie. A veteran of the Far East Division, McGehee at one point served as Colby's acolyte at Langley headquarters and bases his accusations on firsthand observations of Colby in action—of watching Colby deliver briefings which were "a complete hoax contrived to deceive Congress."[19] Writes McGehee of Colby: "I have watched him when I knew he was lying, and not the least flicker of emotion ever crosses his face." But what made Colby even more dangerous, in McGehee's opinion, was his manipulation of language. "Colby emphasized the importance of selecting just the right words and charts to convey the desired impression to Congress. He regarded word usage as an art form, and he was a master at it."[20]

Years later they met again in Gia Dinh Province, at which point McGehee describes Colby as "a harried, self-important, distracted bureaucrat" who "began calling for statistics. 'How many VC killed this month? How many captured? How many firefights?' Each unit chief answered. Colby checked the replies against the figures in his books, and questioned each chief about discrepancies or outstanding figures." All this was a waste of time, McGehee contends. "Here the U.S. was trying to fight an enemy it only slightly acknowledged. Why? What had happened to all the idealism, all the rules of getting and reporting intelligence? Why did the agency blind itself while pretending to look for intelligence? Why did we insist on killing people instead of talking to them? How long would this insanity go on?"[21]

In his defense Colby said to me, "We were getting all the statistics, and if you could get them on the computer, you could play them back and forth a little better, and see things you couldn't see otherwise. It was really quite interesting. I never really believed the numbers as absolute, but they helped you think about the problems. We would use it for control of how local people were doing," he explained, "how if one province reported they had captured a lot of category Cs, but no As, and another province said it captured 15 category As, first you'd check if there were any truth to the second story, and if it is true, you know the second province is doing better then the first one. You don't believe the numbers off-hand, you use them as a basis for questions."[22]

Numbers as a basis for questions were a management tool, but they were also a way of manipulating facts. And William Colby is a scion of the gray area in between. In his autobiography, *Honorable Men,* Colby explains how his father converted to Catholicism, and how Colby himself, when he entered Princeton, was excluded from the in crowd as a result. An articulate man trained as a lawyer and spy, but with only one foot in the door, Colby embraced "the art of the possible" and cultivated his "grey man" mentality to achieve success in the CIA bureaucracy, as well as to dissolve the lines between right and wrong, enabling him to give Phoenix a clean bill of health. "I have no qualms about accepting responsibility for it," he writes.[23]

So it was in Vietnam, that just as criticism of Phoenix was building within the program, the press began turning its attention toward the subject. The calamity called Tet had subsided, the elections were over, and the Paris Peace Talks were about to start. The Communist shadow government was emerging into the light of day, and U.S. efforts to deal with it became the pressing concern.

Glimpses of Phoenix began appearing in print. On June 29, 1968, in his "Letter from Saigon" column in *The New Yorker,* Robert Shaplen identified the program by its Vietnamese name, Phung Hoang, calling it the "all-seeing bird." Shaplen rehashes the thrust of the program, citing statistics and quoting Robert Komer as saying "some 5,000 arrests have been made of alleged members of the [VC] command structure." According to Shaplen, the program's major weakness was "a tendency on the part of the Vietnamese to build up a massive dossier on a suspect until he gets wind of what is happening and disappears." Shaplen notes that "district and village chiefs are sometimes loath to furnish or act on intelligence on the grounds that the war may soon be over."

Indeed, the possibility of a negotiated settlement raised the specter of those in the VCI—the people Phoenix was arresting *and killing*—gaining legal status. And that scenario sent chills running up and down every war manager's spine. But the transition from supporter to critic of American conduct of the war did not come easily to reporters used to acting as cheerleaders. Reasons for withdrawing support had yet to be uncovered. However, sensing momentum in that direction, the information managers began to search for scapegoats. And who better to blame than the Vietnamese themselves? GVN shortcomings, which were previously swept under the carpet, were suddenly being aired. Suddenly the Vietnamese were corrupt and incompetent, and that, not any fault on the part of the Americans, explained why the insurgency was growing.

Moreover, war crimes in 1968 still went unreported. The VC were "faceless," an abstract statistic whose scope was negotiated by the CIA and MACV. *Wall Street Journal* reporter Peter Kann, in a September 1968 article on Phoenix, called the VCI "the invisible foe." For Kann, they were an insidious "underground" enemy who could only be eliminated "at night" in their homes.

Kann employed similar imagery in March 1969 in an article titled "The Hidden War: Elite Phoenix Forces Hunt Vietcong Chiefs in Isolated Villages." Here Phoenix is characterized as a "systematic, sophisticated application of force." The PRU and their U.S. advisers are "elite," while far from having any popular support, the VCI members are outcasts in "isolated villages," far removed from cities and civilization.

On January 6, 1969, *The New York Times* reporter Drummond Ayres gave Phoenix a favorable review, saying that "more than 15,000 of the 80,000 VC political agents thought to be in South Vietnam are said to have been captured or killed." He also expresses the belief that "the general course of the war . . . now appears to favor the Government" and predicts that Phoenix would "achieve much greater success as the center's files grow."

Despite the good reviews, the surfacing of Phoenix in the press sent the publicity-shy CIA running for cover. Under National Security Council Directive 10/2, the CIA is authorized to undertake *secret* political and paramilitary operations. As Ralph Johnson writes, "CIA was empowered to develop and test programs through its *covert* assets. If these programs were successful, and if approved, and if they supported U.S. policy objectives, then they would be turned over to appropriate *overt* U.S. agencies." And so, in December 1968, the newly arrived CIA station chief informed DEPCORDS

William Colby "that the Agency had fulfilled its function. [Phoenix] was now functional and CIA proposed to withdraw all its management and overall responsibility."[24]

Making this pivotal decision was Ted Shackley. A veteran CIA officer with experience in Germany and in Miami running operations against Cuba, Shackley had just completed a two-year tour as station chief in Vientiane, Laos, where he had acquired a detailed understanding of the situation in South Vietnam, primarily through meetings in third countries with John Hart and Lou Lapham, at which regional issues were discussed, strategy was coordinated, and briefings of deep-cover agents were held. "The big item," according to Lapham, "was the NVA coming down the Ho Chi Minh Trail."[25]

Tall, thin, and pale, Shackley, in an interview conducted in his Arlington office, concurred. "It was the same war in the Laotian panhandle," he said, "although Laos, in addition, had the basic political problem of coalition."[26]

No stranger to the types of programs the CIA was running in South Vietnam, Shackley reviewed them all upon arriving in Saigon in November. "It became clear to me then," he told me, "that the pacification programs had come of age . . . that the agency contribution was no longer required. So my original proposal was to see about getting others to manage these . . . programs, to free up CIA resources to improve the quality of the intelligence product, to penetrate the Vietcong, and the NVA supporting them, and to concentrate more against the North and the VC and the NVA in Cambodia.

"So negotiations were undertaken," Shackley continued, "and an agreement was reached to phase out the CIA. Pacification programs were to go to the GVN, and CORDS was to provide the transition. We took a mission approach. Each program was approached specifically, including Phoenix, and a certain level of top management was provided for coordination. Static Census Grievance was taken apart; some functions went to Revolutionary Development, some to the Hamlet Evaluation System, and some were dropped. By 1969, static Census Grievance was out of business. RD and Territorial Security were merged and Phil Potter and Rod Landreth saw that the GVN took over the PRU program." And Phoenix, too, was discarded.

On December 14, 1968, MACV notified DEPCORDS William Colby of its intention to assume "responsibility for intelligence matters as they pertain to the VC infrastructure."[27] By June 1969 the transfer of Phoenix from CIA to MACV-J2 was complete.

In early December, Evan Parker recalled, "I became the author of memos back and forth from Colby to Shackley putting myself out of business." Parker, however, was not pleased with the reorganization, his main objection being that "the military staff officers were not ready to take over."[28]

"This was a difficult assignment for the military," Shackley concurred, because there "had to be liaison with the Special Branch. You had to have a manager to coordinate intelligence problems. For instance, leads came out of the PICs and had to be coordinated with the highest levels of CIA."

To facilitate the process, Colby incorporated the Phoenix program as a division within CORDS, but with a senior CIA staff officer as director, functioning as the American counterpart to the secretary general of the Central Phung Hoang Permanent Office. In this way the CIA could, when necessary, direct Phoenix advisers and exercise jurisdiction over prisoners and penetration agents spun out of the program. Chairmanship of Phoenix committees at region and province became the responsibility, respectively, of the corps DEPCORDS and the province senior adviser. CIA region and province officers became deputy chairmen and ostensibly supported their new military managers with CIA intelligence.[29]

"The idea," according to Shackley, "was that Evan Parker, and three or four others, would slowly peel back people as the military marched in." Thereafter the role of the Phoenix director was to meet "once or twice a week with the [Vietnamese] to iron out problems. Was there a province chief not willing to cooperate with the PIC? Was he funneling people to the Military Security Service, rather than to the Special Branch? Maybe there was overcrowding in a PIC that province or region couldn't resolve. What to do? Well, the Phoenix director would go to the secretary-general and cite specific cases. There might be a knowledgeable source in a PIC who needed to be brought to Saigon. Were the line managers looking at the dossiers? Yes or no?"

Despite the fact that the Phoenix director, a senior CIA staff officer, had cognizance over the PIC program, "Phoenix," insisted Shackley, "had nothing to do with intelligence operations. It was completely separate from Special Branch trying to penetrate the Vietcong. Any guy who could be used as a penetration agent was spun out of Phoenix." That was the job in 1969 of special unit analysts under the management of CIA officer George Weisz. In this way, Phoenix evolved into a massive screening operation, with its parent organization, the Special Branch, having, in the words of Ralph Johnson, the "intelligence coordination mission" of "keying important VCI political leaders and activists so as not to clog up the system with volumes of low level VCI cadre or front members."[30]

And so, in June 1969, the CIA receded into the dark corners of CORDS. Evan Parker, having brought the Phoenix program to fruition, was appointed deputy chief of the CIA's Special Operations Division and was replaced as Phoenix director by veteran CIA officer John Mason. Described by Shackley as "a highly decorated World War Two Army colonel who served with the agency mostly in Europe (and with George French in Turkey)," Mason was a personal friend of General Creighton Abrams. "He followed Abrams's tanks through Europe with an infantry battalion," said Jim Ward, who, as the

CIA's Vietnam desk officer in 1969, asked Mason to take the job. At first he refused, but eventually Mason succumbed to Ward's supplications—to his eternal regret.

"Mason caught all the Phoenix flak." Ward sighed. "The last time I spoke with him, the only thing he said to me was 'You bastard.'"

CHAPTER 19

Psyops

The fabric of South Vietnamese society, always loosely knit, began to unravel in 1969. As prospects for a clear-cut military victory for either side slipped away, psychological operations became the weapon of choice in what was an increasingly political war. Both sides played the psywar game. Its only rule: Post your own score.

The insurgents scored the first points in June 1969, when they formed the Provisional Revolutionary Government (PRG) to represent them in South Vietnam and at the negotiating table in Paris. The PRG was immediately recognized by thirteen Communist bloc and ten nonaligned nations—mostly Arab. Support was expressed as well by Scandinavian, African, and Latin American countries. One month later COSVN issued Resolution 9 directing its officers "to prepare political cadre to insure a capability to govern in anticipation of a coalition government in South Vietnam."[1] Liberation Committees were made subordinate to the PRG and were renamed Revolutionary Committees. At the village and hamlet level the insurgency was reinvigorated.

Back at CIA headquarters in Washington, it was recognized that: "There were sufficient communist forces to keep the war going, and progress depended on the morale and determination of the communists."[2] Morale, however, is intangible, so CIA propagandists cited irrefutable statistical evidence as proof that the VCI was losing, not gaining—as was the reality[3]—support in the villages. In April 1969 HES reports indicated that more than three quarters of all Vietnamese were living in "secure" villages.

The purported success was attributed to VCI manpower shortages caused by aerial and artillery bombardment, defoliation campaigns, forced relocations, and mass arrests. The VCI was said to be collecting less tax money as a result of Phoenix and, out of desperation, to be using as cadre children who were too young to be issued IDs. But "the bulk of manpower shortages," the Phoenix 1969 End of Year Report claimed, "were caused by deserters who rallied to the GVN." In Vinh Long and Sa Dec provinces, it said, "manpower shortages at district, village and hamlet levels ranged from 45 to 100 percent during 1969. Unable to cope with the GVN accelerated pacification campaign, VCI members by late November 1969 had fled to areas of sparse population and even Cambodia where they could exert little influence over the population."[4]

From the language of the Phoenix report, one could easily think that the few VCI members who had not defected were hiding in Cambodia. But the author of "The Truth About Phoenix," whose area of operations included Sa Dec and Vinh Long provinces, claims that most Chieu Hois simply regurgitated the American line in order to win amnesty, make a quick visit to their families, enjoy a few home-cooked meals, then return to the fray, fat and rested. Legitimate Chieu Hois, An writes, were pariahs who were not accepted back in their villages, while other Chieu Hois were trained by the VC to infiltrate the program and become spies.[5]

In any event, from 1967 onwards, all "rallied" VCI members were included in Phoenix neutralization statistics, and by 1969 more than a hundred thousand defectors had been processed through fifty-one Chieu Hoi centers. The Chieu Hoi program was managed from 1966 until March 1969 by Ogden Williams, then turned over to Eugene P. Bable, a career CIA officer who had served with Ralph Johnson in the Flying Tigers.

Evan Parker stated that Chieu Hoi offered more satisfaction than Phoenix, and "Chieu Hoi," said Jim Ward, "was a great program. Well done." Ward explained that most Chieu Hoi advisers were from the U.S. Information Service, although some were State Department or military officers. "But they wouldn't have more than one American adviser in a province and," Ward added, "it was usually the Vietnamese operating at district level."[6]

Upon arriving at the Chieu Hoi center, the defector was "interviewed" and, if he had information on the VCI, was sent to the PIC; if he had tactical information, he was sent to military interrogators. Next came political indoctrination, lasting from forty to sixty days, depending on the individual. "They had a formal course," said Ward. "They were shown movies and given lectures on democracy." Upon graduation each was given an ID card, a meal, some money, and a chance to repent. Political indoctrination was handled by defectors who said they had been well treated by the Americans and had decided it was better to live for a *free* Vietnam than to die for the totalitarian North Vietnamese. "Chieu Hoi had lots of guys who had been with the enemy before," Ward continued, "who knew how to talk to these people and would persuade them to join the Territorial Forces or the PRU." Others joined armed propaganda teams, which went back into VC territory to contact Vietcong families and recruit more Vietcong defectors.

"The great thing about the Chieu Hoi program," Ward noted, "is that we didn't have to put people in jails or process them through the judicial system, which was already overcrowded. You could talk to the Chieu Hois when you brought them in—talk to them about what the government was doing for the people.

"They'd say, 'But it's a crooked government.'

"You'd say, 'Wait a minute. The government's providing seeds for rice. This enables us to grow three to four times as much rice in the Delta as in the past. Now that's good.'

"The guy'd say, 'I didn't know that.' All they'd hear from the Communists were the contradictions they'd devise, if they didn't already exist. But now he was getting the picture from our side. And a lot of them would flip-flop because of it. Now some guys would come in, Chieu Hoi, spend time with their families, then go back out in the field again. That happened, but not to the extent that you might think. I'd say less than ten percent."

Despite his praise for the Chieu Hoi program, Jim Ward said that "Americans should have been targeted only against the North Vietnamese and left the South Vietnamese forces to handle the insurgency," even though such a strategy would have precluded Phoenix. However, having made the mistake of military intervention, Americans looked for psychological ploys, other than an appeal to nationalism, to win people over to the GVN. High on the list were bounty programs. The Phoenix 1969 End of Year Report cites as an example Kien Phong Province, where the Phung Hoang Committee printed and had distributed a wanted poster featuring photographs of eight members of the Cao Lanh City sapper unit. "While a RD Cadreman was tacking up a poster he saw one of the members passing by," the report says. "He called the police who arrested the suspect. Two other members were later arrested. Three were induced to rally claiming they were rendered ineffective having their names and faces known."[7]

In Phong Dinh Province the Vietnam Information Service (VIS) broadcast the names of VCI through loudspeakers mounted on sampans while traveling through the canals of Phung Hiep District. "While the team was conducting the operation, a village level VCI cadre walked into the Phung Thuan DIOCC," saying he had to rally, "because *Phung Hoang* must know about him if the members of the District Revolutionary Committee were known to Phung Hoang, as broadcast by VIS."[8]

No one wanted to find his name on a Phoenix blacklist; it meant the PRU would creep into his hooch some night, or black helicopters would swoop down on his village. And because fear of Phoenix was an effective means of creating informers and defectors, an intensive publicity campaign called the Popular Information Program began in October 1969. Under the banner of "Protecting the People from Terrorism," U.S. and GVN psywar teams crisscrossed the countryside, using Phoenix-supplied radios, leaflets, posters, TV shows, movies, banners, and loudspeakers mounted on trucks and sampans to spread the word. Using the eye of God technique, taped broadcasts were pitched at specific VCI members. A typical broadcast would say, "We know you, Nguyen Van Nguyen; we know where you live! We know you are a communist traitor, a lackey of Hanoi, who illegally collects taxes in Vinh Thanh Hamlet. Soon the soldiers and police are coming for you. Rally now, Nguyen Van Nguyen; rally now while there is still time!"[9]

So important were psyops that the Phoenix Directorate produced a thirty-minute movie explaining how Phoenix "Helps Protect the People from Terrorism." A copy of the film was sent to each province for use on local TV stations and in movie theaters. Writes Phoenix Coordinator John Cook: "[T]he concept was simple; in practice it was suicidal."[10] Suicidal, he explains, because the VC found the lightly armed psyops teams easy targets. Cook therefore used the psyops team as bait to flush out the VC, whom he then ambushed with his Phoenix task force. In this way psyops were transposed into combat operations, turning psychological defeat into military victory, with a body count to boot.

In addition to the Phoenix movie, hundreds of thousands of copies of "an illustrated booklet describing the Phung Hoang Program in cartoon* format" were also distributed throughout Vietnam (in Montagnard and Cambodian dialects as well), "with the goal of placing ten to fifteen in each hamlet. Culture-drama teams used the booklet as a scenario for skits."[11]

On January 22, 1970, thirty-eight thousand of these leaflets were dropped over three villages in Go Vap District. Addressed to specific VCI members, they read: "Since you have joined the NLF, what have you done for your family or your village and hamlet? Or have you just broken up the happiness of many families and destroyed houses and land? Some people among you have been awakened recently, they have deserted the Communist ranks and were received by the GVN and the people with open arms and family affection. You should be ready for the end if you remain in the Communist ranks. You will be dealing with difficulties bigger from day to day and will suffer serious failure when the ARVN expand strongly. You had better return to

*See Addendum 1 in Appendix.

your family where you will be guaranteed safety and helped to establish a new life."[12]

Psyops leaflets stressed traditional Confucian values of obedience to authority and family and portrayed the Communists as a socially disruptive force that could be stopped only by Phoenix. But the fact that the GVN could reach the "people" only through "media" like leaflets and loudspeakers indicates how far removed it was from the reality of life in rural villages. As An notes in "Truth About Phoenix" while the GVN relied upon cartoon books to sell itself to a largely illiterate people, "The VC goes from person to person talking to ears," proving that technology was no substitute for human contact.[13]

Consequently, in 1969, the Phoenix Directorate directed Phung Hoang Province committees to expand the Hamlet Informant program (HIP) drastically. District chiefs were instructed to conduct classes "on GVN programs, progress, potential and ideology for residents who had VC/VCI relatives or leanings." There was a one-week course "with extensions for problem individuals." Day care and lunch were made available in "vacated" homes. Chieu Hoi was emphasized, "counseling" was provided, and insofar as the goal was the neutralization of VCI, "the populace was encouraged to report the activities of the VCI by dropping a note addressed to the police in local mailboxes." This method "was credited with approximately 40% of the information used in Phung Hoang operations" in Dinh Tuong Province.[14]

Psyops in support of Phoenix became such a potent weapon in the attack on the VCI that in August 1970 SACSA described Phoenix as "the number one MACV PSYOPS priority."[15] Four months later John Mason reported: "There have been more than twelve million leaflets, posters, banners and booklets printed and distributed throughout Vietnam in support of the program."[16]

Despite the emphasis on psyops, combat operations were still preferred by the military officers managing the Phoenix program in the field. Such operations most often began at the hamlet level when paid informers reported to Vung Tau-trained village chiefs, who then mobilized Territorial Forces under their command, and advised by American military officers, against VCI suspects. Likewise, unilateral American Phoenix operations usually began with informants' feeding names to a DIOCC, whose adviser then informed the counterintelligence section of the nearest American outfit. An operation was then mounted. In the wee hours of the morning a unit of infantrymen would be deployed around the village to provide security, and a team of commandos would snatch the VCI suspect and bring him or her to the military intelligence interrogation center. Such was the standard procedure which involved the average American soldier in Phoenix operations.

CIA paramilitary officers also continued to mount unilateral Phoenix operations via their PRU advisers. As reported in the December 1986 issue of *Soldier of Fortune* magazine, Long An PRU adviser Captain Frank Thornton circumvented orders not to accompany his PRU into the field by putting his name on the SEAL Detachment Alpha roster "for administrative purposes," and "Saigon never knew the difference." A combat enthusiast, Thornton obtained intelligence on the location of VCI members from a PRU agent net comprised of "old women, kids and former ARVN soldiers who'd lost arms and legs fighting the VC. To ensure security, he rarely passed along his intel products other than to SEALs."

On October 11, 1969, Thornton's agents reported a district-level VCI meeting in Can Giuoc district. Putting two SEALs and four PRU in a Cobra "killer" helicopter for backup, Thornton climbed into a light observation "hunter" chopper, flew to a point near the target area, got out, and alone (just as Elton Manzione had done five years earlier) slipped into the VCI's hooch, grabbed him, and radioed for extraction. The man he snatched, Pham Van Kinh, was the commanding officer of four VC battalions. The mission garnered Thornton a Vietnamese Cross of Gallantry, awarded by Rung Sat Special Zone PRU commander Major Nguyen Hiop.

Thornton's heroic deed was the exception, however, not the rule. In "The Phoenix Murders" Joseph Treaster quotes an Army captain who spent three years advising PRU teams: "Unless somebody made a mistake, you're not going to find a guy alone. And if you go in and try to tangle with a whole village, you're in deep. . . . If the guy is important, it's very hard to extract him."[17]

This captain recalled only one case when the PRU targeted a specific individual, a VC district official in a province on the Cambodia border. It was the man's wedding day—he was marrying the daughter of a GVN village official—and the PRU burst into the room, yelling for everyone to freeze. "But," the captain told Treaster, "some VC in the wedding party goes for his gun and our guy opens up. The next two or three guys through the door open up, too, and the first thing you know, there's a lot of blood on the sand. So that didn't work too well. We didn't lose anybody, but there were 22 people in the wedding party and 20 were killed."

A typical district-level Phoenix operation, cited in the 1969 year-end report, began when Deputy Party Secretary Dang was caught in a tunnel. During interrogation, Dang informed on his comrades, who were captured along with incriminating documents. One of them revealed during his interrogation that the district party chairman, Nguyen Van Kia, was a horse cart driver. PRU teams were stationed at the main traffic intersection in Kia's area of operations. He was caught the same day without a fight. Four other cadre members were snatched in their homes. "The next target was Nguyen Thi Bah, the message section chief; a description of her route of travel was furnished by the DIOCC. The PRU posed as VC and set up an ambush along her usual route. On the second evening of the trail watch, Bah was captured."[18]

Province-level Phoenix operations, like the following one in Long Khanh, tended to be more elaborate. In this case the operation developed when the province chief assigned the job of resources control to the Phoenix coordinator and his Phoenix task force. In response, the Phoenix coordinator mounted three concurrent long-term operations lasting two months.[19]

Part I was the establishment of "mobile resource control checkpoints." Three six-man teams—two national and two field policemen and two PRU—were assigned to checkpoints. The National Police provided trucks; blacklists came from the Special Branch. Roadblocks were set up, and while the National Police checked IDs and the Field Police stood guard, the PRU searched and detained suspects, who were carted off to the PIC for interrogation.

Part II occurred in three phases. First, a special airmobile resource control (SARC) team was formed to interdict VCI commerce. Next, under the command of the Phoenix coordinator and his interpreter, a search element consisting of two PRU, three Special Branch and one national policeman, was formed. A security element was formed of two squads from the U.S. First Cavalry. Thirdly, the cavalry provided a command and control chopper, a light observation helicopter (LOCH), and a Cobra gunship—the traditional hunter-killer team with an added "eye in the sky." SARC operations were mounted on the basis of intelligence reports providing "targets of opportunity." When a target of opportunity presented itself, the SARC force would galvanize into action, swoop down from the sky, cordon off areas, send in search teams, stop vehicles, and capture and kill VCI members.

Part III, Operation Cutoff, was designed to capture suspects who could produce leads to the VCI. To this end, DIOCCs sent lists to the PIOCC, where priority targets were selected. After two months of preparation, thirty-eight hamlets were targeted. Special Branch provided lists of relatives of the suspects. Territorial Forces and the U.S. 199th Infantry Brigade provided security forces to cordon off each hamlet. Operations began at 4:00 A.M. with National and Field Police and PRU searching hooches while a psywar team broadcast names and instructions over loudspeakers. People were gathered together at a Special Branch "processing station," where IDs were checked against blacklists. RD Cadre drama teams entertained the innocent while various agencies interrogated suspects, who were then sent to the Province Interrogation Center.

By the end of the Long Khanh Phoenix campaign, 168 VCI "sympathizers" had been caught and confined. Although suppliers and supporters were category C, not genuine VCI, they did inform on their authentic A- and B-grade comrades. Over the next three months VCI neutralizations in Long Khanh soared to their highest levels ever. There was a corresponding rise in Hoi Chanhs.[20]

A typical Saigon operation began in March 1969, when a People's Intelligence Organization agent submitted a report on Nguyen Nuoi to the First Precinct Special Police. Suspecting Nuoi of being VCI, the Phoenix coordinator assigned a six-man surveillance team to watch him. The six special policemen worked in two-man teams, one on foot, one on a bike. In this way they learned where Nuoi lived and worked and where his "contact points" were. The Special Branch set up agents in business in a soup shop one block away from Nuoi's house and established a bicycle repair shop near his favorite café. Two agents continued to follow him. Three houses Nuoi frequented were also placed under surveillance.

Three weeks later Nuoi was arrested along with several comrades in the safe houses who had leaflets produced by the Saigon Women's Revolutionary Association. During interrogation Nuoi informed on his bosses in the party. His testimony led to more arrests, including several cadres in the district party committee. One member was "enticed to work for the police" and went back to the party committee as a penetration agent. He stayed there three months in his former position, secretly channeling information to the Special Branch which led to more arrests.

As the 1969 Phoenix End of Year Report notes, "Before allowing their penetration agent to be freed, Special Police personnel took photos of the agent enjoying himself in the company of other Special Police agents and required him to sign a sworn statement that he was in fact working for the GVN. These documents would find their way back to the VC if the agent did not cooperate with the police in the future. A surveillance team was assigned to watch the agent's activities as an added precautionary measure."[21]

So successful was Phoenix in 1969 that the directorate boasted in its End of Year Report that "the first generation" of COSVN military proselytizers has been reduced to seven personnel." In supporting its claims of success at every level, the report quotes a high-ranking VCI who described COSVN Resolution 9 as "a desperate VC plan, written in an attempt to save an otherwise hopeless political and military situation. He said that the Phung Hoang (Phoenix) program has been given top priority for destruction by the VC."[22]

One could deduce from this that the GVN stood on the verge of a great victory. But the view from the field was not so rosy. As Phoenix adviser Wayne Cooper said to Joseph Treaster,

> A typical DIOCC would have an impossible clutter, with wheat and chaff filed together. The alphabetical files we insisted they keep would not be cross-referenced by alias, family location, or any other useful designation. The dossiers so vital to province security committee prosecution would contain poor sketchy information; perhaps enough for an operation but not enough for prosecution. Other files—Most Wanted lists, potential guide files, mug shots, and so on—were maintained so poorly as to be useless, or never kept at all. There would be no intelligence collection plan, and agents received little direction.[23]

Ralph Johnson agrees with Cooper's dismal assessment of Special Branch capabilities. "DIOCC files on VCI personalities did not reflect much progress toward Phung Hoang intelligence objectives," he writes. He also contradicts Colby's statement that "We were getting more and more accurate reports from inside VCI provincial committees and Regional Party headquarters from brave Vietnamese holding high ranks in such groups."[24] Says Johnson: "The Special Branch rarely if ever managed to recruit agents who had access to high-level VCI planning." He adds that "the GVN arrested suspected agents and attempted to destroy VCI organizations instead of surveilling or recruiting agents in place for long term exploitation." The result was that "most VCI captured were low-level in the province or below," and "most intelligence was generated and exploited from counter-guerrilla operations, casual walk-in informants, captured VCI, VCI caught in Resource Control operations, captured documents, cordon and search operations, and especially Chieu Hoi defectors from VCI."[25]

With the transition of Phoenix to CORDS, a new and improved means of judging, evaluating, and proving success was needed. Hence, Big Mack, "An instructive type document that directs the territorial intelligence system to quantitatively and qualitatively evaluate the VCI and lower level military units."[26] Big Mack reported on the number of identified and unidentified VCI members, their influence in the area, and their identity by position for inclusion in the Green Book. Compiled monthly by U.S. military advisers without Vietnamese input, Big Mack reflected the military's emphasis on operations against enemy military units, the type that resulted in big body counts.

"It was a reporting requirement that could choke a mule," recalled Colonel Doug Dillard, "to the point of designing data entry sheets to feed the computer in Saigon. . . . I met with Ted Greyman, and we coordinated with other staff members, and we came to the conclusion that if we implemented Big Mack, we would stop pursuing the war and start reporting on it." But the Saigon bureaucracy prevailed, and—Dillard sighed—"we began implementing portions of Big Mack."[27] By the end of 1969 Big Mack reports were pouring into Saigon from South Vietnam's 250 districts. A comparison with the statistics from 1968 shows the number of captured VCI decreased, while the number of VCI killed more than doubled.[28]

	1968	1969
Captured	11,288	8,515
Killed	2,229	4,832
Rallied	2,259	6,187
Total	15,776	19,534

Within this total, 4,007 VCI security agents were cited as having been neutralized: 3 COSVN level VCI; 64 regional VCI; 226 from provinces, 881 from districts, 235 from cities, 2,081 from villages, and 511 from hamlets. An estimated 74,000 VCI were still "at large"; but overall, neutralizations were up, and the directorate boasted that 60 percent were A and B priority targets. Meanwhile, the VCI in 1969 had "murdered" 6,000 GVN officials and "ordinary citizens," had "kidnapped" 6,000 people, and had wounded 15,000 more.[29]

Statistical evidence of success so pleased the Washington brain trust that additional computer systems were quickly introduced. In March 1969 the National Police Evaluation System went on-line, recording "police assignment data" for analysis and "counter-measures." In 1970 Big Mack's bilingual replacement, the Big Mack Special Collection Program, shifted the burden of reporting and accountability to the RVN Territorial Intelligence System. In January 1970 the VCI Neutralization Information System was inaugurated to record all anti-VCI operations. The National Police Criminal Information System (NPCIS) was implemented in April 1970 to track VCI who were held beyond "statutory limitations." Designed to "interface" with a Chieu Hoi "tracking system," which aided province security committees in the "post-apprehension monitoring of released VCI," NPCIS was also compatible with the VCI Neutralization and Identification Information System, which stored in its classified files "a history of the VCI member from the time of his identification to his neutralization."[30]

Complementing these "tracking systems" was the National ID Registration Program System. Within twenty-four hours of arrest, detainees were booked. A report was then sent to the proper Province Intelligence and Operations Coordination Center, and a fingerprint card sent to the National

Identity Records Center in Saigon, where a data sheet was plugged into the computer. In the field, nearly two thousand policemen worked in two shifts, seven days a week, sending twenty thousand documents from the provinces to Saigon every day. By November 1970 more than seven million laminated fingerprint cards had been classified, searched, and placed in the fingerprint bank for instant access.

Climaxing the computer process in January 1971 was the National Police Infrastructure Analysis Sub-System-II (NPIASS-II), which was used to plan "countermeasures" against the 73,731 confirmed and suspected VCI still "at large" (and called "logical records" in its files). NPIASS-II functioned until March 1973, when, with the assistance of technicians from the Computer Science Corporation, it was transferred to the Vietnamese along with PHMIS and the National Police Identification Follow-up Sub-System (NPIFUSS). Yet another "tracking system," NPIFUSS "provided a means of determining the action taken on wanted person notices and statistics on the disposition of wanted person cases." There was even a National Police Directory Table Sub-System on National Police units and correction centers. However, the reliance on computer systems was a poor substitute for a judicial system based on due process. As Public Safety officer L. M. Rosen wrote on November 27, 1970, "The NPCIS will not of itself improve the administration of justice or the processing of detainees."[31] Further reforms remained to be made.

CHAPTER 20

Reforms

Caught between its stated goal of building democratic institutions and its operational goal of ensuring internal security, the South Vietnamese government, in order to improve its public image vis-à-vis the Provisional Revolutionary Government, began instituting in 1969 a series of cosmetic "reforms" designed to square its security needs with the civil rights of its citizens. In essence it was an attempt to resolve the problem posed by Nelson Brickham back in 1967, when he asked, "What do you do with identified VCI?"

The "reform" process got off to a feeble start on March 24, 1969, with Ministry of Interior Circular 757, "Classification and Rehabilitation Guidelines for Proper Processing of VCI." Signed by Interior Minister Tran Thien Khiem, it was created by William Colby specifically to enable province security committees to ensure faster prosecution and sentencing of VCI suspects. However, as Ralph Johnson notes, "there was a general recognition that the circular was neither understood nor properly applied throughout the country."[1]

Circular 757 reiterated who was a class A, B, or C Communist offender, how long each could be detained, and who decided. It directed the coordination of "All local National Police Services . . . with the Phung Hoang Committee and the Correction Center involved." As for the status of VCI held in detention centers, 757 reasoned circularly that "The method of classification and the detention period for these Communist Offenders shall be carried out like that for those who are captured under the Phung Hoang Plan."[2]

In addition, Circular 757 directed the National Police to establish "PsyWar Groups" to "carry out the rehabilitation of offenders." PsyWar Groups were to teach Communist offenders how to recognize and abide by constitutional government. Circular 757 also ordered GVN's Directorate of Corrections to form five Mobile Corrections Groups and to include in them "Corrections Cadre qualified in culture and propaganda indoctrination." Cadres came from the ministries of Information and Chieu Hoi and the CIA-advised Directorate of Political Warfare, which had cognizance over the Military Security Service. One mobile group was assigned to each corps, and the fifth handled Con Son, Chi Hoa, Thu Duc, and Tan Hiep prisons. Mobile Correction Groups supported PsyWar Groups in the "rehabilitation" of Communist offenders and provided cover for CIA "talent scouts" who recruited convicts into the PRU and armed propaganda teams, and as prison informers.

To oversee psywar and intelligence operations inside correctional facilities, in September 1969 the CIA created the GVN's Central Security Committee, chaired by General Khiem and including Director of Corrections Colonel Nguyen Psu Sanh (advised by Donald Bordenkircher), the director general of the National Police, and the prison wardens. More important, the Central Security Committee reviewed cases of Communist offenders considered for conditional or early release from the five national correction centers, recommending further detention if the offender was deemed dangerous, as was universally the case. The Vietnamese National Assembly tried unsuccessfully to abolish the Central Security Committee in December 1970.

Province Security Committees were reorganized to include a province prosecutor as legal adviser, although the deputy chief for security—the CIA asset on the province chief's staff—secretly managed the affairs of the Committee. Pressure for more meaningful reforms was brought, however, when the lower house of the National Assembly interpellated the ministers of justice, defense, and the interior on June 20, 1969, concerning alleged abuses by officials in the Vinh Binh Province Phoenix program. This action came after a delegation composed of the Interior, RD, and Anticorruption committee chairmen returned from Vinh Binh Province with reports of illegal arrests, torture, corruption, and abuses of authority. The interpellation resulted from a petition signed by eighty-six deputies asking for an explanation of the no longer secret Phoenix program.

Justice Minister Le Van Thu outlined the stated goals of the program, noting that the Province Security Committees had the power to sentence VCI members for up to two years without accusing or convicting them of any specific crime. His explanation that the practical difficulties of amassing solid evidence made it necessary to arrest everyone suspected of complicity for further interrogation and investigation was not well received. A cross section of legislators bitterly cited examples of abuses in their own provinces.

Tin Sang publisher and Anticorruption Committee Chairman Ngo Cong Duc charged the Vinh Binh police chief with "knowingly" arresting innocent people for the purpose of extortion. A Buddhist legislator from Thua Thien Province alleged that suspects were often detained for six to eight months (instead of the one-month maximum cited by Justice Minister Thu) before their cases were heard and that suspects were frequently tortured to extract confessions. She said the people "hated" the government for starting the Phoenix program. Other deputies were incensed that American troops forcefully and illegally detained suspects during military operations. Deputy Ho Ngoc Nhuan, a Saigon Catholic, charged that village chiefs were not consulted before VCI suspects were arrested during military operations, contrary to what Thu and Khiem claimed.

Khiem responded by promising further reforms. He said the Joint General Staff had already moved to prevent further detentions by American forces, with the exception of the VCI caught flagrante delicto. His conciliatory tone assuaged the deputies, and an improved circular was issued.

As a remedy for what Ralph Johnson calls "various deficiencies" in the judicial system, Colby and Khiem, in August 1969, issued Circular 2212, "Improvements of the Methods of Resolving the Status of Offenders."[3] As a result of Circular 2212, a Political Security Office was formed to provide policy guidance for the three GVN agencies—the Central Phung Hoang Committee, the National Police, and the Directorate of Corrections—that were involved in processing Communist offenders. Plans were made to send more prosecutors to the provinces to assist "in the proper legal handling of such cases" and "to ensure the proper functioning of Province Security Committees."[4] However, in a nation with fewer lawyers than warlords, establishing due process was like tilting at windmills.

As a way of reducing prison overcrowding and ending the revolving-door syndrome, Circular 2212 provided for the "mandatory" sentencing and transfer of class A and B VCI from the mainland to Con Son Prison. Province Security Committees were given thirty days to open an offender dossier on each VCI detainee, scrutinize the evidence therein, and pass judgment. To speed the process, a short-form offender dossier (on which the detainee signed a confession) highlighted the incriminating evidence which the Security Committee needed for a quick conviction. To reduce backlog, Circular 2212 required security committees to meet at least once a month and to submit transcripts to the Political Security Office for review before passing judgment. Such was the judicial system in South Vietnam.

* * *

In response to the charges leveled by the lower house deputies in June, Annex II of Colby's 1970 pacification and development plan, "Protection of the People from Terrorism," called for "notification to village chiefs of planned Phoenix operations in their villages." However, notifying village chiefs was tantamount to notifying the VCI, and again, the operational goal of security was at odds with the stated goal of notification, which in practice rarely occurred. So a few more Phoenix reforms were crafted, including an improved quota system stipulating that VCI be identified before they were neutralized, rather than "revealed" after being captured or killed. Under this proposal, suspected VCI were to be counted as "captured" only after being convicted and sentenced, rather than upon apprehension.

The other significant and related "reform" of 1969 was Decree 044, dated March 12, 1969, placing the PRU under the jurisdiction of the director general of the National Police. Canceling out this decree was a long-standing law, never rescinded, that prohibited PRU from serving in the Vietnamese Army or government in any capacity. Operational control in each province remained with the province chief in conjunction with a PRU province commander, and even though, as of September 1969, Americans were prohibited from venturing out on PRU operations, they did (see Frank Thornton in the previous chapter). Americans continued to advise and assist in the planning of operations.

Prior to June 1968, when President Thieu embraced Phoenix, the PRU operated only at province level under the direction of the CIA. After June 1968 the national PRU commander, Major Nguyen Van Lang occupied himself primarily by selling "PRU-ships" to the highest bidders at the province and region levels.

The CIA staff officers who managed the PRU program at the national level along with Lang's brother-in-law Tucker Gougleman were Phil Potter and Rod Landreth. Harvard graduate Phil "Potts" Potter was an old Vietnam hand who in the early 1950's had been case officer to Emperor Bao Dai and had hired some of the CIA's first assets in the Sûreté. During the battle for Saigon Potter had served as acting chief of station, as liaison to Ngo Dinh Nhu and Dr. Tran Kim Tuyen, and as control of the station's ten or twelve intelligence officers running agents in the field. During his stint as acting chief of station, while Saigon was in turmoil and the piaster was nearly worthless, Potter had purchased property—safe houses and such—for the CIA at 10 to 15 percent of its real value. His efforts in this respect laid the groundwork for a generation of spooks to come.

Potter also served as station chief in Tanzania and Greece and as consul general in Norway and Hong Kong. But his heart was in Vietnam, where he formed close friendships with Ralph Johnson and Tucker Gougleman. During his years in Saigon Potter developed personal and professional relationships with the most influential Vietnamese, including the CIO chief, General Nguyen Khac Binh, and President Thieu. First and foremost, though, Potter was an intelligence officer actively engaged in recruiting and running agents in the field.[5]

The other PRU manager, Rodney Landreth, described by a colleague, Harry "Buzz" Johnson, as "the kind of guy you'd like to have as an uncle," arrived in Saigon in 1967 and served as a deputy to Ted Shackley. Station Chief Shackley, described by Buzz Johnson as "a cold pale fish,"[6] relied on likable Rod Landreth to represent him at diplomatic functions and on the interagency committees formed to investigate GVN corruption and drug dealing. While Potter was case officer to CIO Chief Binh, Landreth was case officer to General Dang Van Quang, Thieu's national security chief. Potter and Gougleman are credited with having organized the Special Branch, while Ralph Johnson and Landreth worked more closely with the CIO. All four were intimately involved in formulating CIA policy regarding Phoenix, the Special Police, and the PRU.

Opinions vary on the impact Potter, Johnson, Gougleman, and Landreth had on the course of events in South Vietnam. To some people they were the consummate insiders; to others they were tired old men who were totally out of touch with the war in the villages and who, like clones of the colonialists they had displaced, gathered every evening at the Circle Sportif to drink by the pool and bask in the adoration of beautiful Vietnamese women.

Likewise, the inner circle of Landreth, Johnson, Gougleman, and Potter had little patience with the ambitious technocrats Langley sent out to Saigon to play at being station chief, or with their corrupt GVN lackeys. In private they ridiculed Ted Shackley, calling him Tran Van Shackley for his reliance on Senator Tran Van Don. Tom Polgar, who replaced Shackley in 1972, fared even worse and was described as "rigid" and "a bureaucrat" who "was not well versed in intelligence field work."[7]

For his part, Tom Polgar called Landreth and Potter "fine officers" who were "past their prime."[8] Ed Brady concurred: "These people had their jobs. . . . But they weren't trying to achieve anything. They had no objectives."[9]

Brady gave an example of how the Washington bureaucrats shamed "old Vietnam hand" Potter into submission. "Potter lived with a Vietnamese woman whom he wanted to marry," Brady recalled. "He was near retirement, but the agency, citing operational security, said, 'No. If you marry her, you're through. But it's okay if you live with her.' It was the height of hypocrisy."

Perhaps the "old Vietnam hands" do symbolize the proprietary, but essentially moribund, American policy in Vietnam after 1969; those who had understanding were subordinated to the ideologues and functionaries. Living in splendid sand castles, they alternately cursed and ignored the rising tide of corruption and deception that was engulfing South Vietnam. For example, Landreth's main job was chairing the interagency committee charged with investigating the black market, an inquiry he deflected away from the CIA. Likewise, the interagency narcotics committee chaired by Landreth focused entirely on the North Vietnamese, studiously avoiding General Dang Van Quang, who Stanley Karnow notes was "accorded the rice and opium franchise in his region" while commander in the Delta. Writes Karnow: "Among those allegedly involved in the trade were Prime Minister Nguyen Cao Ky and his successor, General Tran Thien Khiem, said to have funneled the proceeds from the business into their political machines."[10]

Although Rod Landreth was the agency's liaison to General Quang, who on behalf of President Thieu set PRU policy, the day-to-day business of the PRU was handled by CIA officers Ben Mandich and William Buckley, both of whom are deceased, as are Potter, Landreth, Gougleman, and Johnson. Of those who were involved in PRU matters, only Ralph Johnson has left behind statements for the record. "The impact of the GVN on the PRU was negative," Johnson writes, because of "the failure of PRU commanders to work closely with the PIOCCs. The PRU commanders, supported by the Province chiefs, excused this failure by citing poor security in the PIOCCs, as a result of which the PRU were failing to report intelligence to the Coordinating Centers." Furthermore, says Johnson, "when the ARVN and the RF/PF absorbed the tactics of the PRU during 1968–1969, then the PRU probably should have been disbanded and their members integrated into one of the nation-building programs which constituted the major portion of the Pacification Program. Or, the PRU should have been returned to their native villages as part of the Refugee Program, to bolster the People's Self-Defense Forces."[11]

Veteran CIA paramilitary officer Rudy Enders disagreed when we met and insisted that the PRU operated effectively at least until the cease-fire, when they were put under control of the Special Branch.[12] In any case, the March 1969 decree putting the PRU under the National Police facilitated plausible denial. It enabled William Colby to swear on a stack of Bibles that the CIA was not operationally involved. The GVN became accountable as the CIA maneuvered to scapegoat its oblivious client. But the GVN could not afford (even with CIA-sanctioned corruption and drug trafficking) to support the PRU on its own, nor was the CIA willing to abandon the rifle shot approach at the moment it said it had the VCI on the ropes. But resources channeled through the Phoenix program could not compensate for the reduction in CIA support and supervision, so the PRU turned to shakedowns of lucrative targets in the private sector to keep their organization intact. Phoenix and the PRU became captive to criminal enterprises and the subject of increasing controversy.

Always inextricably linked, the Phoenix and PRU programs were simultaneously brought under military review in 1969. On October 20, 1969, in a secret memo to Defense Secretary Melvin Laird, Army Secretary Stanley Resor referred to "the social and moral costs and the desirability of a selective attack" and expressed "concern over these programs."[13] Later that day Laird conveyed his concern over "lack of progress in the Phoenix/Phung Hoang Program" to General Earle Weaver, chairman of the Joint Chiefs of Staff.[14] One month later Laird, referring to the My Lai massacre and the Green Beret murder case, informed Wheeler of his "growing anxiety over the PRU [sic] program in view of recent events concerning U.S. military conduct in South Vietnam."[15]

In response to Defense Secretary Laird's concerns about the Phoenix program, MACV Commander Abrams assured Washington that "Statistically [sic] the program has made significant progress in recent months." Abrams recounted the "reforms" cited on the preceding pages but then offered a candid and somewhat ominous appraisal, saying, "[I]t is clear to me and to the commanders in the field that the program does not yet have the degree of sophistication and depth necessary to combat the highly developed and long experienced VC infrastructure (VCI) in South Vietnam." Abrams noted that Ambassador Bunker had agreed to talk to President Thieu about Phoenix, "especially with respect to improving GVN local official attitudes." Abrams closed by promising "a separate report . . . on the PRU."[16]

At this point the Pentagon had three elements interested in Phoenix: The Joint Chiefs were involved through SACSA, the Defense Department was involved through its office of International Security Assistance (ISA), and MACV was involved through CORDS.

For its part, SACSA was not in any chain of command but served the Joint Chiefs by bringing together representatives from the State Department, CIA, U.S. Information Agency, Agency for International Development, and the Department of Defense. Broad policies came down to SACSA from the White House through the National Security Council, while specific ideas regarding psywar and counterinsurgency came up from MACV or the individual services. SACSA assigned staff members to present recommendations for consideration by the Joint Chiefs. When the chiefs reached a decision on how a policy was to be implemented, the service responsible for implementing that policy was directed to provide manpower, matériel, and money. The Army Intelligence Corps had responsibility for over Phoenix.

SACSA itself was divided into three parts: for special operations in South Vietnam; for special operations elsewhere; and for Revolutionary Development programs in Vietnam, including Phoenix. MACV reported data on Phoenix to SACSA only when solicited. SACSA's Revolutionary Development component did studies and drafted papers on Phoenix for the Joint Chiefs' signature.

From the inception of Phoenix until January 1969, Major General William DuPuy served as SACSA. A former CIA deputy division chief, DuPuy met regularly with State Department officer Phil Habib and CIA Far East Division chief William Colby to coordinate unconventional warfare policy in South Vietnam. DuPuy was replaced by Major General John Freund, commander of the 199th Infantry Brigade while it supported Cong Tac IV. Freund had little clout with the Joint Chiefs and was fired after six months. Replacing him was the former SOG commander Brigadier General Donald Blackburn, under whose management SACSA had little involvement in Phoenix.

The Defense Department's office of International Security Affairs (ISA) was, by comparison, more deeply involved with setting Phoenix policy. According to its charter, ISA "provides supervision in areas of security assistance, Military Assistance Advisory Groups and Missions, and the negotiating and monitoring of agreements with foreign governments." Insofar as Phoenix was a security assistance program funded by the military through CORDS—which ISA authorized in May 1967—ISA had overall supervision of the program.

Called the Pentagon's State Department by Robert Komer, ISA coordinated State and Defense department policy on Vietnam. ISA representatives sat on the State Department's Ad Hoc Psyops Committee, and ISA representatives, along with CIA officers Jack Horgan and Tom Donohue, sat on the State Department's Vietnamization Task Force, which, through the National Security Council, determined how to turn the war, including Phoenix, over to the Vietnamese.

Within ISA, policy regarding Vietnamization was coordinated by the Vietnam Task Force (VNTF). Created in mid-1969, the VNTF was headed by Major General George Blanchard until October 1970, by Major General Fred Karhohs till May 1972, and by Brigadier General David Ott till the cease-fire. Each VNTF chief in turn reported to ISA chief Warren Nutter's deputy for East Asian and Pacific affairs, Dennis Doolin, and Doolin's assistant, Tom Constant. It was at the VNTF that Phoenix policies were coordinated between Saigon and the concerned parties in Washington.

So it came to pass that in November 1969 the VNTF was saddled with the task of bringing into line with "USAID budgets and the law," as one VNTF coordinator put it, a program that had been conceived by the CIA without any regard for legalities, and to do it without treading on the CIA's ability to conduct covert operations. It was a ticklish job that required squaring the hard reality of political warfare in Vietnam with the fluctuating political situation in Washington. The major effects were to bring the military into an adulterous relationship with the Special Branch and to set the State

Department on a collision course with international law.

The Vietnam Task Force's assistant for concepts and strategies became the staff officer responsible for Phoenix. A Marine lieutenant colonel standing over six feet tall and weighing over two hundred pounds, he was a tough Korean War veteran with a résumé that included employment with the CIA and the State Department as well as with the military. From 1964 to 1967 he prepared military officers for civil operations service in Vietnam, and from late 1967 to early 1969 he was a member of CORDS, serving as John Vann's deputy for plans and programs in III Corps. Jack, as he has been dubbed, preferred to remain anonymous when we met at his home in 1987.

Jack was at the center of the Phoenix drama as it was acted out in Saigon and Washington, and according to him, the VNTF was "Laird's baby; it was his locus."[17] Jack often briefed the defense secretary and prepared "hundreds" of memos for his signature; he wrote papers for and briefed the ISA director Warren Nutter; he coordinated on a daily basis with members of the National Security Council, the Vietnam Working Group, the Special Studies Group, the Vietnamization Task Group (over which the VNTF "had cognizance"), and Tom Donohue at SAVA. On matters affecting the Joint Chiefs, Jack coordinated with its representative, Colonel Paul Kelly—later commandant of the Marine Corps. Jack's contact at SACSA was Colonel Ray Singer, and he worked with members of Congress investigating various facets of the Vietnam War. All in all, Jack was the man in the middle. He is an experienced military theorist, and his recollections and assessment of the Phoenix program are especially incisive and well worth noting.

Jack adhered to Robert Thompson's theory that in order to succeed, a counterinsurgency requires a coordinated military-police-intelligence attack against the insurgent's political leadership. But, Jack contended, although the theory is valid, Thompson's extrapolation from Malaya to Vietnam was doomed to fail, for whereas the ethnic Chinese leading the insurgency in Malaya were visibly different from the Malayan people, those in the VCI were indistinguishable from other Vietnamese and impossible to track by foreigner advisers. What's more, said Jack, "the Brits were shrewd enough to offer large rewards . . . to informers. But no Vietnamese was going to turn in Uncle Ho for fifty bucks."*

Jack cited this misuse of resources as a major flaw in America's counterinsurgency policy in Vietnam. "Komer was trying to solve problems through Aid-in-Kind," he explained. "Komer would evaluate people on how

*Jack suggested that a point system—ten points for a COSVN cadre down to one point for a messenger boy—with a monetary equivalent would have resulted in a truly qualitative attack.

many piasters they gave away. He did what corporate managers do; he set goals . . . which were higher than people could achieve. But these were managerial-type solutions, a repeat of World War Two, and this was a political war. And the way to win hearts and minds was through security."

In order to establish security, Jack said, "You don't need to get each individual VCI; you just need to *neutralize* their organization. For example, the presence of a terrorist unit confers influence, so the idea is to prevent any accommodation. As John Vann explained, it's not enough to agree *not* to fight. That means you can still sell guns and medicine to enemy, like the Filipino group did in Tay Ninh. That is an active accommodation. The people had to have a dual commitment. They had to reject the VC *and* support the GVN. Many would support GVN, but not betray VC, and that was the problem."

Even if the Vietnamese had not identified with the VCI, and even if American resources had been properly used, Thompson's three-pronged attack on the VCI was doomed to fail, explained Jack, because the CIA did not report to CORDS on highly sensitive matters, like tracking high-level penetrations. Phoenix could have been effective only if the CIA had brought its CIO, PRU, and Special Branch assets to bear. But when the CIA relinquished control of the program in 1969, it took those assets—which were the only effective tools against the VCI—with it. In order to protect its political intelligence operations, the CIA never shared its sources with the military officers or Public Safety advisers assigned to Phoenix—unless, of course, those people had been suborned.* In this way the CIA kicked out from under Phoenix one of the three legs it stood upon. After June 1969 the agency conducted its own unilateral operations against the VCI, apart from Phoenix, through the PRU in rural areas and through the Special Branch in the cities. MACV and the Office of Public Safety in Saigon complained to their headquarters in Washington, making reform of the Special Branch and the PRU the central Phoenix-related issues, but these were areas over which the Defense and State departments had no influence.

After mid-1969 MACV tried desperately to obtain access to Special Branch intelligence in the DIOCCs. But, as Jack explained, Special Branch worked at the province level and above, primarily in urban areas, and avoided the rural areas where most DIOCCs were located. Nor did the Special Branch

*According to Michael McCann, Saigon Public Safety director from July 1969 until April 1972, his biggest Phoenix problem was that the CIA used the Public Safety program as a cover for its case officers, bringing all Public Safety advisers under suspicions.[18] Likewise, said Fred Dick, chief of the Bureau of Narcotics and Dangerous Drugs in Vietnam, "Everyone had his rock to hide under, but CIA kept using our rocks, listing its officers as narcotics advisors to the embassy."[19]

desire to share sources with its rival, the MSS, forcing the CIA into greater dependency on the PRU for its rural operations. Having been excluded by the CIA, military advisers to Phoenix relied totally on their ARVN counterparts, with a corresponding emphasis on tactical military rather than political operations.

There were rare instances when a CIA province officer would send the PRU down to a DIOCC to assist the Phoenix adviser. Other times the PRU fed "washed-out" bodies into the PICs. On the other side of the coin, the Special Branch was usually chasing dissidents, not the VCI. A study by Robert Thompson on behalf of the National Security Council revealed the Special Branch to be undertrained, understaffed, suffering from bad morale, and racked by corruption. Jack put it this way: "Whereas the average cop on the street would take fifty piasters as a bribe, when the Special Branch got involved, the price went up." He added, "There was good reason to believe that the VC had penetrated the inner circle of the Special Branch. This is why Colby requested that two FBI agents be sent to Saigon to set up a counterintelligence operation."

Knowing that the PRU and Special Branch were fractured beyond repair but that problems within them would remain hidden under layers of CIA security and that CIA officers would continue to mount their own operations apart from Phoenix, the State and Defense departments were compelled to seek other solutions. The question became whether—in the absence of intelligence officers—soldiers or policemen were better suited to mount anti-infrastructure operations.

"What you needed," Jack suggested, "was to be flexible in order to conform to Hamlet Evaluation System ratings; you needed police forces in secure areas, and the military in areas controlled by the enemy. But generally, in guerrilla warfare it's more military than police, and so that's where the emphasis should fall." Nevertheless, Jack explained, this flexible approach, applied to Phoenix after 1969, was slow to develop and basically ineffective. "In the beginning of the Phoenix program," he said, "the Army and Marines had a surplus of armor and artillery officers, who were assigned to the program but had no knowledge of running intelligence operations. We were sending out the third team against the first team. Then, when they began staffing the DIOCCs and PIOCCs with military intelligence officers, it became clear that their training was inadequate for the job. Six weeks is not enough time to train a Special Branch officer.

"So it became clear that what they needed was experienced police officers, and in 1970 the police through USAID began playing a larger role. But there were defects on this side, too. They should have had seasoned civilians coming into AID, but instead they got all the losers in that one. The civilians coming to AID were running away from bad marriages and bad careers. Many were alcoholics; they'd get a Vietnamese girl and enjoy the cheap living. These people had a good war." But they had little success against the infrastructure.

Jack said he believed that military policemen were the answer, and on his advice, on a trial basis, Colonel Albert Escola was appointed the Phoenix region coordinator in IV Corps. Now corporate secretary of Bechtel, Escola had received a degree in police administration from Michigan State in 1957 and was known as a protégé of General Abrams's. For "improving procedures against the VCI," Escola was awarded the Legion of Merit in 1970 and a few years later was promoted to major general—rewards never bestowed upon Doug Dillard.

In any event, Phoenix as an organization proved far less than the sum of its parts. Moreover, by 1969 concerns about its concept had moved from the boardroom into the courtroom, where Phoenix was coming under attack as an assassination program. Suddenly its problems were legal and moral, not organizational and procedural.

Jack said, "Colby pushed Khiem to get Phoenix legitimized so it would have a constitutional basis in Vietnamese law, similar to the FBI or the CIA. Colby tried to make Phoenix legitimate internal security—that to be a member of the Communist party is illegal. This is the nail upon which Phoenix is hung: If you're a Communist, you're breaking the law. Then Phoenix goes out and gets these guys."

Of course, Phoenix had been going out and getting those guys for fifteen years by the time 1970 rolled around. The effect of those fifteen years of illicit covert action, on both Vietnamese and Americans, is the next subject.

CHAPTER 21

Decay

After August 1969, writes Professor Huy, "Power in Saigon belonged to three generals: Nguyen Van Thieu as President; Tran Thien Khiem as Prime Minister; and Cao Van Vien as Chief of the Joint Staff. They kept their positions until the eve of South Vietnam's collapse."[1]

As was customary in Vietnam, according to Huy, power was administered by each man's wife. "Mrs. Thieu dealt with the businessmen, especially those of Chinese origin, and had her shares in profits obtained from import, export and international trade." Mrs. Khiem "fixed a price for new appointments for the posts of chief of province, chief of district, and chief of police services at the provincial and district levels. Mrs. Vien's domain was the army: contractors working with the army could pass through her intermediary, and she had her tariff for a quick promotion in the army."[2]

With the consolidation of power by these three men came a resurgence of what CIA Summary 0387/69, dated September 12, 1969, called "influence by the widely hated Can Lao group of the Diem era." The CIA memo named as members of the neo-Can Lao cabal "Foreign Minister Lam, as well as the ministers of information, economy, finance and legislative liaison." The memo noted that Duong Van "Big" Minh had predicted "that renewed Can Lao influence could lead to a tragic clash between Catholics and Buddhists." And, the memo noted, "apprehension is likely to increase over reports that the new information minister [Thieu's cousin, Hoang Duc Nha] has appointed some 20 cadre from the Nhan Xa Party—a neo-Can Lao group—to key subordinate positions."

Indeed, political developments in 1969 mirrored those of 1955, when Ed Lansdale was told that Diem "needed to have his own political party."[3] Likewise, to strengthen Thieu's position, the CIA in 1969 financed the creation of the National Social Democratic Front, described by former CIA officer Frank Snepp as "a pro-government coalition of political parties." And, just as in Diem's day, Snepp writes, "the CIA lavished large sums of money on the Thieu government to be used in cowing and 'neutralizing' its opposition,"[4] the opposition being those nationalist parties, like the Dai Viets, that had relations with the Buddhists. With the Americans chasing the VCI, these domestic groups became primary targets of the Special Branch and its stepchild, Phung Hoang.

In particular, Thieu felt threatened by Tran Ngoc Chau, the popular nationalist whose persecution was said to symbolize the "fratricidal" nature of the Vietnam War. But in fact, Chau's persecution had less to do with regional differences than with rampant corruption, itself fueled by the CIA's bottomless black bag and irrational obsession with internal security at any cost.

Chau's problems began in 1969, when he launched an anti-corruption campaign against Thieu, his old classmate from Fort Bragg. The gist of Chau's claim was that Nguyen Cao Thang—a wealthy pharmacist and former Can Lao from Hue—was using CIA funds to undermine the National Assembly. Chau's crusade was seen as a threat to GVN stability, and as a result, the CIA sent two case officers to offer him enough money to start his own political party in exchange for backing off. When Chau declined, Rod Landreth informed General Dang Van Quang that Chau was secretly in contact with his brother, Tran Ngoc Hien, a senior Cuc Nghien Cuu officer in North Vietnam. Quang issued an arrest warrant for Chau, charging him with the capital crime of espionage.

Hien was arrested, Chau went into hiding, and on orders from Washington, Ambassador Bunker ordered Chau's case officer, John Vann, to break off contact. At that point Vann, in June 1969, summoned Frank Scotton from Taiwan and arranged for him and Chau to meet in a safe house in Gia Dinh. The conversation, according to Scotton, went like this: "I said to Chau, 'Sergeant Johnson is standing by near the Cambodian border with some of his Special Forces friends. They're dependable, and they'll help you get out. But it's now or never.'"[5]

"Chau was very emotional that night in Gia Dinh," Scotton continued. "He said, 'To run now would be the same as admitting I'm a Communist.

And I'm not. So I will not run.'" And so Chau remained in hiding until captured in late 1969.

Ironically, while Thieu was using Phoenix to repress his domestic opponents, his own cabinet was crawling with Communist agents. But in order to perpetuate the myth of GVN stability, the CIA was reluctant to publicize this fact. Consequently, says renegade CIA officer Sam Adams, in May 1969 station chief Ted Shackley "indicated on a visit to Washington his belief that the Vietcong had only 200 agents in the South Vietnamese Government. He spoke from ignorance. An in-depth research study going on at that time suggested the real number of such agents was more like 30,000."[6]

Although thirty thousand sounds improbably high, the extent to which the GVN was infiltrated was revealed in a counterintelligence operation mounted by CIA officer Ralph McGehee in 1969. Begun in 1962, Operation Projectile relied on a penetration agent inside what the 1969 Phoenix End of Year Report called "a COSVN level intelligence net directed against the office of the President of South Vietnam and other ministries of the GVN." The leader of the spy ring was Vu Nhoc Nha, President Thieu's friend and chief adviser on Catholic affairs. Nha, a Catholic, had resettled in South Vietnam during the 1954 Lansdale-inspired exodus from North Vietnam. The spy ring's highest-ranking member was Huynh Van Trong, Thieu's special assistant for political affairs and director of the Central Intelligence School, a position that placed him at the top of the CIO.

McGehee inherited Projectile in 1969, when, after six weeks as Gia Dinh province officer in charge, he became the CIA's liaison to the Special Branch in Region V. "In this capacity," he explained, "I supervised [six] other agency case officers working with specific elements of the Special Police in and around Saigon."[7]

The principal Vietnamese player in the drive against the Cuc Nghien Cuu's strategic intelligence networks was Special Branch chief Nguyen Mau. Born in Ninh Thuan Province (where Thieu was born and reared), Mau was graduated from the Da Lat Military Academy in 1954. In 1963 Diem appointed him sector commander and province chief of Thua Thien Province and mayor of Hue, in which capacity he put down the Buddhist crisis leading up to the coup. In the reorganization after the coup, Mau was made a Montagnard task force commander with the ARVN Twenty-second Division, a job he held until 1967, when he was put in charge of Cong Tac IV. The following year he was promoted to lieutenant colonel and made director of the Special Branch of the National Police.

Soft-spoken and smart, Mau wanted nothing to do with Phoenix. In a letter to the author, he says his "great concern in taking command of the

Special Branch was the unjustified arrest, false accusation and arbitrary detention. Those bad manipulations couldn't be stopped since the province chiefs, police chiefs and other officials would do anything to make Phoenix score, which assured them job security and higher regard. They knew that Phoenix was under the supervision of an American Ambassador, and that President Nguyen Van Thieu always listened to this powerful personage. They kept the Special Branch in the provinces too busy with arrest in village, confession worksheet and charge procedure at the Provincial Security Committee, while I wanted to direct the Special Branch into professional activities: organizational penetration gathering information relating to policies and campaign plans, spotting the key leaders for neutralization. But I did not argue with them. I felt so alone I kept my mouth shut."

Mouth shut, Mau concentrated on smashing the Cuc Nghien Cuu's strategic intelligence networks within the GVN. When McGehee gathered enough evidence to convince Shackley to let him roll up Nha's net, Mau galvanized his forces, and the Special Branch sprang into action. Mau's "small *secret police cadre* prepared individual files on each person to be arrested," McGehee writes. "Late one afternoon he called a task force in to his office, then cut them off from outside contact: He briefed each three-man arrest team separately then passed them copies of the file on their target individual. At midnight the police fanned out through Saigon and pulled in the net."[8]

The operation was a smashing success. House searches turned up "microfilm of secret documents, document copying cameras, one-time radiop encoding and decoding pads, radios, secret ink"[9] and other tools of the trade. The Special Branch also had the good fortune of arresting a visitor of one of the targets, who "turned out to be the head of a military intelligence net"[10] in the MSS. All in all, fifty people were arrested and forty-one spies were tried and convicted. The group included businessmen, military officers, teachers, students, and two top-ranking Chieu Hoi officials.

However, showing that the GVN was "so riddled by enemy spies that they were able to operate under the nose of the President," McGehee laments, was "not the kind of success that the CIA's top officials wanted to see." That reinforced his suspicion that the CIA was unwilling to admit either the strength of the enemy or the weakness of its ally. To McGehee "it was obvious that we were bolstering a hopelessly corrupt government that had neither the support nor respect of the Vietnamese people."[11]

Meanwhile, other CIA officers were reaching the same conclusion. When Frank Snepp arrived in Saigon in 1969, he was assigned the task of putting together background profiles on targets for assassination by "plowing through documents" and conducting interrogations at the National Interrogation Center. "I would put together a list and I would turn it over to Mr. Colby's people," Snepp says in *The Ten Thousand Day War*. "He would feed this list out to the strike teams, and they would go to work. . . . And that is how you become a collaborator in the worst of the terrorist programs, in the most atrocious excesses of the US government."[12]

Others became involved in other ways. Consider the case of Bart Osborn, a Phoenix critic who enlisted in the Army in October 1966, was trained at Fort Bragg and Fort Holabird, and was classified an intelligence area specialist. "My training was designed to prepare me as an agent handler and consisted of classes designed to teach recruitment and training of agents and management of agent networks," Osborn testified before Congress in 1973. He added that his training included a session concerning the termination of agents through various methods, including assassination.[13]

A corporal with no knowledge of Vietnamese language, history, or culture, Osborn arrived in Da Nang in September 1967 and was assigned to the 525th Military Intelligence Group. His area of operations was south of Da Nang, outside a Marine air base in Quang Nam Province. Having been assigned to the unilateral branch of the military intelligence team, whose activities were "extra-legal," Osborn used an alias and, for plausible denial, was provided with false identification indicating he was a civilian employee with the CORDS refugee program. Osborn slipped into his military uniform when it was necessary for him to see military maps or documents.

Osborn's team leader put him in touch with a principal agent who was running six subagents in a single cell. The subagents were political specialists, gathering positive intelligence on VC cadres. Eager to expand his network, Osborn hired as additional agents people whose names he got from the employment files of a local American construction company. He sent his intelligence reports to the 1st Marine Division, the 3d Marine Amphibious Force, the 525th MIG, the American Division, and, unknown to him, the Da Nang Phoenix coordinator.

Osborn's association with Phoenix was cemented when, to his surprise, he was told that the 525th's Intelligence Contingency Fund was empty and that he would henceforth be unable to pay his agents. At this point Osborn had two principal agents, forty subagents in five cells, and operating expenses averaging half a million piasters per month—lack of which prompted him to check his list of users for new sources of revenue. Recalled Osborn: "I was able to ascertain that the Phoenix program was receiving and utilizing my information. . . . I visited the Phoenix Coordinator, a US Army major, and talked to him about the information that was laterally disseminated to him. He . . . told me that any information I gathered would be used in the context of the Phoenix program. In return I was guaranteed financial remuneration for my agents, use of various 'safe houses' for clandestine meetings, and access to Air America transportation."[14]

Osborn also obtained drugs, draft deferments for his agents through phony enrollment in the Civilian Irregular Defense Group program, and fifteen thousand dollars quarterly for bribing the local police. The Phoenix coordinator also offered a bonus of a hundred thousand piasters for high-ranking VCI members. In this way, regular military personnel across South Vietnam became involved in Phoenix abuses.

When asked to explain *why* Phoenix abuses occurred, Snepp says the program was "jerry-built" because of "the CIA's concern that the VC had penetrated the Special Branch and Military Security Service. The more fragmentation, the better the security. They didn't want it central so it could be exploited."[15]

Unfortunately, writes Snepp, "For lack of finite guidance the Phoenix strike teams opted for a scattershot approach, picking up anyone who might be a suspect, and eventually, when the jails were packed to overflowing, they began simply taking the law, such as it was, into their own hands."[16]

Explanations for why Phoenix was open to abuse depend on a person's politics. Snepp, who harbors a grudge against the CIA, says his former employer "jerry-rigged" Phoenix for its own security. Others say Phoenix was handed to the military as a cover for CIA negotiations with the VCI in Tay Ninh and Saigon. From Phoenix director John Mason's perspective, accommodation was the root cause of all Phoenix woes. In an August 19, 1969, *New York Times* article, Terrence Smith quotes Mason as saying, "Favoritism is a part of it. Sometimes family relationships are involved. We know very well that if one of our units picks up the district chief's brother-in-law, he's going to be released."

For Nguyen Mau, Phoenix was subject to "bad manipulations" by officials seeking job security and high regard. Likewise, South Vietnamese nationalists pointed to corrupt officials as the evil inherent in Phoenix, as was made clear in June 1969, when legislators complained that the police used Phoenix to extort money from wealthy citizens and that VCI agents supplied names of loyal citizens to the police, getting around the Colby fail-safe cross-check system by reporting through several different agencies. In this way, innocent people found their names on the dreaded Phoenix blacklist.

Mismanagement by design, ineptitude, accommodation, corruption, and double agents were reasons why Phoenix abuses occurred. However, the actual reporting of abuses fell to Third Force Vietnamese and noncareer American military personnel. It is to this aspect of the Phoenix story that we now turn.

One of the first people to criticize Phoenix publicly was Ed Murphy, a native of Staten Island, New York, who spent nine months in a Catholic seminary before enlisting in the U.S. Army. Following his tour in Vietnam, Murphy, from June 1969 through January 1970, was stationed in Washington, D.C., doing background investigations and security checks for the 116th Military Intelligence Group. At the time he was one of a growing number of Vietnam veterans, almost exclusively enlisted men, who were publicly demonstrating against the war. In October 1969 Ed Murphy was also one of the few Americans acquainted with Phoenix.

Murphy's determination to make Phoenix a political issue in the United States began on October 15, while he was participating in the March Against Death outside the Pentagon. There he encountered colleagues from the 116th MIG. "I was being surveilled," he told me. "I know, because the people doing it told me so. 'I've been reading about you,' one of the officers said."[17]

Having fought for his country in defense of its liberties, Murphy was angry to find that military intelligence was being used against American citizens who were exercising their constitutional rights. To him, this represented "the Phoenix mentality in the United States." Just how serious Murphy considered this threat is made clear by his definition of the program. "Phoenix," he said, "was a bounty-hunting program—an attempt to eliminate the opposition. By which I mean the opposition to us, the Americans, getting what we wanted. Which was to control the Vietnamese through our clients—the Diems, the Kys, the Thieus." For Murphy, all other definitions of Phoenix are merely "intellectual jargon."

Murphy is a man of conscience, a former novitiate at a seminary in Baltimore whose deep-seated patriotism prompted him to enlist, despite his compunctions about the morality of the Vietnam War. After basic training, Murphy was sent to Fort Holabird, where he was trained as a counterintelligence specialist, then to the Defense Language Institute in Texas for Vietnamese-language training. From there he was assigned to Fort Lewis. "On the plane from Fort Lewis to Cam Ranh Bay," he recalled, "I was given an article to read. It was a study by the American Medical Association on . . . interrogation methods used in the Soviet Union. It showed how to do things without laying a hand on a person—how you could torture a person just by having them stand there." That manual was his introduction to the doctrine of Contre Coup.

Upon his arrival in Vietnam on May 12, 1968, Murphy was assigned to Fourth Division headquarters outside Pleiku City, where his understanding of counterinsurgency warfare rapidly evolved from theory to reality. There were five enlisted men in his counterintelligence team, each with a sector, each sector having ten agents. Murphy's job was to conduct sabotage investigations and to run undercover agents, furnished by the MSS, who acted as day workers on the military base. Murphy also inherited agents eleven miles away in Pleiku City and acted as the Fourth Division's liaison to the local Phoenix coordinator, a CIA contract officer named Ron who was posing as a Public Safety adviser conducting currency investigations.

Once a week Murphy went to the local CIA compound, along with various civilian and military intelligence people in the vicinity, to submit to the Phoenix Committee the names of VCI suspects their agents had fingered. Surrounded by a concrete wall, its gate manned by a Montagnard Provincial Reconnaissance Unit, the embassy house was located in a remote corner of Pleiku. Inside the compound was a barbed-wire "cow cage" for prisoners. The cage, according to Murphy, was too small for prisoners to stand up in. Murphy was not permitted in the PIC, which "sat on a hill and looked like a U-shaped school."

As for the identity of the people his agents surveilled and targeted, Murphy said, "I would never see a North Vietnamese or Vietcong soldier. This is post-Tet, and those people are all dead. What we're talking about are civilian infrastructure people supporting the NVA and VC. It could be anybody. It could be somebody who works in a movie theater . . . somebody sweeping up."

When asked what kind of information he needed before he could have a suspect arrested, Murphy answered, "None. Whatever you wanted." When asked what sort of criteria he used to classify VCI suspects, Murphy replied, "Nothing. One of my agents says somebody's a spy. If I had reason to believe . . . that he was telling the truth, and if I wanted to bring somebody in for interrogation, I could do it. It was that easy. I had an agreement with the team leader that I could do anything I wanted. I even wore civilian clothes. My cover identity was as a construction worker with Pacific Architects and Engineers."

Murphy called his agents "hustlers—entrepreneurs making money off intelligence." After noting the difficulty of verifying information submitted by agents at Phoenix Committee meetings, "the lack of files and things like that," Murphy told how one suspect was raped and tortured simply because she refused to sleep with an agent.

"Phoenix," said Ed Murphy, "was far worse than the things attributed to it. It was heinous, but no worse than the bombing. And I don't apologize. But it was a watershed for me. It focused things. I realized it wasn't just a war, but that based on the assumption that nothing is worse than communism, the government of Vietnam, backed by the U.S., felt justified in suppressing all opposition while extending its control throughout the country." That control, Murphy explained, served an economic, not an idealistic, purpose. "Phil Lapitosa [an employee at Pacific Architects and Engineers] told me about two million dollars in matériel and cash being unaccounted for at PA and E . . . that goods being sold on the black market didn't come from the Vietnamese, but from the Americans.

"In order to get into military intelligence school," Murphy continued, "I and the other candidates had to write an essay on the debate about the

Vietnam War. And the thrust of my paper was 'What we do in Vietnam will come back to us.' It was a one world thesis. Well, I go to Vietnam and I see the bullshit going down. Then I come back to the United States and see the exact same thing going on here. I'm at the Hundred Sixteenth MI unit, and as you leave the room, they have nine slots for pictures, eight of them filled: Rennie Davis, Abbie Hoffman, Ben Spock, Jerry Rubin. And I'm being sent out to spot and identify these people. This is Phoenix. This is Phoenix," he repeated, then added for emphasis, *"This is Phoenix!"*

"In Nam I had composite descriptions," Murphy acknowledged. "But then I wasn't in a place where we had technology. It doesn't make any difference. The point is that it was used in Vietnam, it was used in the U.S., and it *still* is used in the United States."

Thus, Murphy felt justified in taking tactics the military had taught him and using them against his former masters. "To me," he explained, "Phoenix was a lever to use to stop the war. You use what you got. I got Phoenix. I'm a former intelligence agent, fluent in Vietnamese, involved in Phoenix in the Central Highlands. That means I'm credible. I'm using it."

Intent on making Phoenix a domestic political issue to be used to stop the war, Murphy joined two other Vietnam veterans—Bob Stemme and Mike Uhl—in an effort to inform the public. At news conferences held simultaneously in New York, San Francisco, and Rome on April 14, 1970, the three veterans issued a joint press release—without naming names—laying out the facts about Phoenix. And even though the release was not widely reported, it did perpetuate the controversy that had begun in February, when Phoenix was first examined by the Senate Foreign Relations Committee. By then Phoenix was nearly three years old.

How the Senate hearings came to address Phoenix is unusual. It concerns Francis Reitemeyer, a Seton Hall Divinity School dropout who was drafted and attended officer candidate school in late 1968. Along with forty other air defense artillery officers, Reitemeyer was trained at Fort Holabird for duty as a Phoenix coordinator in Vietnam. He was appalled by the instruction he received from veteran Phoenix advisers. Loath to participate in what he considered a program that targeted civilians for assassination, Reitemeyer approached American Civil Liberties Union lawyer William Zinman in November 1968. On behalf of Reitemeyer, Zinman filed a petition for conscientious objector status in U.S. District Court on February 14, 1969, while the rest of Reitemeyer's class was departing for Vietnam.

In the petition Reitemeyer said that he was told that he would supervise and fund eighteen mercenaries "who would be explicitly directed by him" to "find, capture and/or kill" as many VCI as possible within a given area. The VCI were defined as "any male or female of any age in a position of authority or influence in the village who were politically loyal or simply in agreement with the VC or their objectives." Reitemeyer was told that he would be required to maintain a "kill quota" of fifty bodies per month and that for him to locate VCI, "resort to the most extreme forms of torture was necessary." As an example of what was expected of him, Reitemeyer was told of one VCI suspect being killed by "said mercenaries and thereafter decapitated and dismembered so that the eyes, head, ears and other parts of the decedent's body were displayed on his front lawn as a warning and an inducement to other VC sympathizers, to disclose their identity and turn themselves in to the Advisor and the mercenaries."

Reitemeyer was told that Phoenix "sought to accomplish through capture, intimidation, elimination and assassination what the U.S., up to this time, was unable to accomplish through the . . . use of military power." The Vietnamese were characterized in racist terms, so that the cruelties perpetrated upon them might be more easily rationalized. Reitemeyer was told that if captured, he could be tried for war crimes under "precedents established by the Nuremberg Trials as well as . . . the Geneva Convention."

On the basis of this account of his Phoenix instruction, Reitemeyer was granted conscientious objector status on July 14, 1969. The Army filed an appeal but, for public relations purposes, withdrew it in October, just as the March Against Death was getting under way. Meanwhile, the ramifications of the case set in motion the series of events that brought Phoenix under congressional scrutiny. Reitemeyer was satisfied with having escaped service in Phoenix and faded into obscurity. Zinman, however, like Murphy, saw Phoenix as a lever to be used to stop the war. He pressed a copy of the petition into the palm of a senator on the Foreign Relations Committee. While the committee prepared to hold hearings on CORDS in February 1970, a staff aide to Senator William Fulbright leaked a copy of the petition to reporters Judy Coburn and Geoffrey Cowan. Their investigation resulted in an article titled "Training for Terror: A Deliberate Policy?" Printed in the *Village Voice* in December 1969, the article brought the subject of Phoenix into open debate.

The military responded to Coburn and Cowan's article and Reitemeyer's "wild allegations" on the day they appeared in print. Colonel Marshall Fallwell, commandant of Fort Holabird, suggested that some instructors might have told "war stories," but he insisted that torture and assassination were not part of the school's curriculum. He did acknowledge that Fort Howard contained a mock Vietnamese village where Phoenix advisers "Plan[ned] and mount[ed] an operation for seizure of the village," then rehearsed interrogating VCI suspects whom they identified from blacklists. Because the object of such "proactive" operations was uncovering the enemy's secret agents, this was called an offensive counterintelligence operation.

Fallwell's answers fell short of allaying congressional concerns, however, and one week later gasoline was poured on the smoldering controversy when George Gregory—an attorney representing one of seven soldiers charged with murdering a Vietnamese agent—discussed his investigation at the Atlanta Press Club. According to Gregory, Phoenix advisers were flocking to military lawyers in Saigon in the wake of the famous Green Beret murder case, in which seven American Army officers in the B-57 detachment were nearly put on trial for murdering one of their agents. Apparently, the Phoenix advisers were concerned that they were susceptible to similar charges.

Here it is important to note that the killing of enemy spies was a counterintelligence function, while the attack against the VCI was a "positive" intelligence function aimed at bureaucrats managing the insurgency's terror campaign. However, the termination with extreme prejudice of agents and the assassination of civilian members of the enemy's underground organization did overlap in cases in which penetration agents inside the VCI were found to be doubles, playing both sides of the fence. Dealing with such people was the prerogative of the CIA and its special unit.

In any event, the results of the Green Beret murder case were the termination of B-57 and a blow to the morale of Phoenix advisers in the field—although their anxieties were relieved in September 1969, when, at the request of President Richard Nixon and DCI Richard Helms, charges against the soldiers were dropped by Army Secretary Resor. The agent's wife, who worked for the CIA, was awarded death benefits, and the case was closed. A Gallup poll showed 58 percent of all Americans disapproved of the war.

On January 12, 1970, *Newsweek* ran a story called "The Rise of Phoenix," in which the program was described as "a highly secret and unconventional operation that counters VC terror with terror of its own."

In response, ISA's director of East Asian and Pacific affairs, Dennis Doolin, professed that a counterterror program of the kind Phoenix was alleged to be "would subvert and be counter-productive to the basic purpose of pacification in reorienting the allegiance of all the South Vietnamese people toward support of the government of Vietnam."[18] And rather than acknowledge Contre Coup as official policy—as legitimate conflict management—the war managers mounted a congressional "information" campaign. Leading the charge up Capitol Hill was Henry Kissinger, "who," writes Erwin Knoll, "is known to believe the program can play a crucial role in destroying the Vietcong opposition during the period of American military withdrawal from South Vietnam. Emissaries from Kissinger's White House National Security staff," Knoll says, "have carried encouraging reports on Phoenix to Capital Hill."[19]

As the Senate hearings approached, the battle lines were drawn. On one side were senators who on faith accepted Kissinger's explanation that Phoenix was part of an overall strategy to protect the retreating American army—hardly something a patriot could fault.* These senators used the hearings to praise Phoenix as it was defined by William Colby and his entourage, which included John Vann, then IV Corps DEPCORDS; Clayton McManaway; Hawthorne Mills, the Tuyen Duc Province senior adviser; a district senior adviser; a mobile advisory team adviser; and a member of the Quang Nam Marine combined action platoon.

No Phoenix advisers were invited to testify, so presenting the other side of the argument were several senators armed with newspaper and magazine articles written by established reporters sent to Vietnam specifically to investigate Phoenix. Among the journalists were Robert Kaiser of the Washington *Post* and Peter Kann from the *Wall Street Journal*. Portions of their articles portrayed Phoenix as a program employing "assassination" and "counterterror."

One article in particular, "The CIA's Hired Killers," by Georgie Anne Geyer, raised congressional eyebrows. Calling the PRU "the best killers in Vietnam," she compared them to terrorists, with the qualification that "our terror" was different from "their terror" in that "there was no real political organization—no political ideology—behind our terror. Their boys did it for faith; our boys did it for money."[20]

Apart from Geyer's failure to recognize the worship of Mammon as religion, her allegation that the CIA hired killers to commit terror cast a dark cloud over the hearings, one that William Colby, despite his initial opposition to the program, was called on to dispel. Colby's testimony earned him the reputation as Phoenix's staunchest defender.

*Kissinger meanwhile was plotting the Cambodian invasion for the same purpose.

CHAPTER 22

Hearings

On February 17, 1970, the same day the Senate Foreign Relations Committee began hearing testimony on U.S. government pacification policy in South Vietnam, Robert Kaiser reported that some people were calling Phoenix "an instrument of mass political murder . . . sort of Vietnamese Murder Inc."[1] Coming on top of the Green Beret murder case and reports about the My Lai massacre, sensational reports like Kaiser's formed a disturbing pattern, one suggesting that terror and political repression were official policies of the U.S. government. The senators wanted to know if that was true. William Colby was willing to put their minds at ease.

Colby's strategy was outlined in State Department Telegram 024391, dated February 17, 1970, which says in part: "We believe the line of questioning attempting to establish the Phoenix program as an assassination program [can be] successfully blunted by repeated assertions regarding US/GVN policies, coupled with admissions of incidents of abuses." Using this approach, Colby alternately confounded and assuaged his congressional challengers. By saying, "I will not pretend to say that no one has been wrongfully killed there,"[2] Colby came across as a decent, honest, fallible human being. He did not admit premeditated murder, but the master of the "art of the possible" did lay a credible foundation for the plausible fictions that followed.

Making his job easier were the absence of witnesses who might contradict his claims, the fact that lurid reports of Phoenix abuses were often derived from secondhand sources and were replete with melodramatic language which detracted from their reliability, and the lack of background information available to the senators—a blank slate Colby used to his advantage early in the proceedings by introducing a carefully prepared "Statement for the Record on the Phung Hoang Program," which defined Phoenix not as a broad symbol of Contre Coup, but in the context of the CORDS bureaucracy. Phoenix in this manifestation was merely a block in an organizational chart, a box on a shelf with a warning label listing all its dangerous ingredients, not a concept of counterterror.

Colby defined Phoenix as an internal security program designed to protect "the people" from "Communist terrorism." And by defining "the people" apart from the VCI, as the object of VCI terror and as voluntarily participating in the program, he established a moral imperative for Phoenix.

Next, he established a legal basis for the program. Phoenix, Colby said, was designed "to single out key personnel for primary attention." The "key people" were guilty of "crimes against national security" and were subject to judicial proceedings in military courts and to "administrative detention under emergency powers" similar to those used in Malaya, Kenya, and the Philippines. He cited the preamble to Ministry of Interior Circular 757, which said, "Government policy is to completely eliminate the VCI by capturing as many as possible, while the lenient rehabilitation policy aims at releasing as many as possible." He did not mention that the circular was not understood or properly applied. Nor did he mention the existence of Province Interrogation Centers, or that the CIA asset—the deputy chief for security—managed the affairs of the Province Security Committee, or that "mandatory sentencing" was an official policy that meant two years in Tan Hiep, Chi Hoa, Thu Duc, or Con Son Prison. The laws were on the books; did it matter that they were not enforced?

Colby then proceeded to abstract fact from form. Citing Directive 044 of March 1969, he described the PRU as part of the National Police. However, in order to protect an ongoing covert action, he neglected to mention, as Colonel Pappy Grieves explained, that "The PRU were supposed to voluntarily enter the police, province by province, man by man. But none of them ever did."[3]

Meanwhile, in early 1970, National Police Chief Tran Van Hai gave Field Police Chief Nguyen Van Dai oversight of the PRU. "To be a 'Force,'" writes Colonel Dai, "I must accept PRU in the Support Division, which originally consisted of the Field and Marine police forces." But, Dai adds, he only monitored the PRU, while Major Lang actually commanded them under the supervision of Tucker Gougleman. "I did not have any major problems between NPFF and PRU," Dai continues. "Only myself and the

American PRU advisers had a misunderstanding, and the PRU advisers accused me of having 'anti-American' spirit."[4]

According to Pappy Grieves, the trouble between Dai and Gougleman developed when Dai inspected a company of PRU in I Corps, "and found they were short 400 tons of plastique. . . . They couldn't account for a number of M-sixteens and pistols either," Grieves revealed. "I said, 'Dai, where did they go?' He said, 'Colonel, there's only one place they could go.'

"This again is the problem of the Company." Grieves sighed. "No accountability out of Saigon."

Or in Washington. As reported at the hearings, the CIA funded the PRU in 1969 at a cost of more than five million dollars, and, Colby said, "plans are in progress for the transition of the PRU to full GVN funding and support." In 1970 the CIA funded the PRU at an increased cost of more than six million dollars.

Having defined Phoenix as moral, "popular," and legal, Colby took questions from the senators, some of whom used the opportunity to promote themselves. Others tried to get at the truth. For example, Tennessee Senator Albert Gore asked Colby to explain "the difference between the Vietcong terror efforts against the political infrastructure of the Saigon government, on the one hand, and the counter-terror program of the [GVN] against the political infrastructure of their opposition, the NLF."[5]

Dodging the question, Colby said, "There is no longer a counter-terror effort." One had existed a few years earlier, for about "six months to a year," but, he said, he had stopped it because they did "some unfortunate things."

After some verbal jousting, Gore asked Colby, "What were the goals of the Phoenix program when it was, by your terms, a counter-terror program?"[6]

COLBY: ". . . to capture, rally or kill members of the enemy apparatus."[7]

GORE: "As I understand your answer, the goals are the same. You used identically the same words—capture, rally or kill. I do not quite get either a distinction or a difference. . . ."[8]

COLBY: "The difference . . . was that at the time there were these special groups which were not included in the normal government structure. . . . Since that time, this has been more and more integrated into the normal government structure, and correspondingly conducted under the government's rules of behavior."[9]

Was it really? In her article "The CIA's Hired Killers," Georgie Anne Geyer tells how "[i]n the absence of an American or South Vietnamese ideology, it was said in the early days, why not borrow the most workable tenets of the enemy's. After all," she quotes Frank Scotton as saying, "they stole the atomic bomb secrets and all from us." And so, Geyer writes, "Scotton and a few other Americans . . . started a counter-guerrilla movement in northern Quang Ngai Province. . . . Terror and assassination were included in their bag of tricks. At one point, USIS printed 50,000 leaflets showing sinister black eyes. These were left on bodies after assassination or even—'our terrorists' are playful—nailed to doors to make people think they were marked for future efforts.

"But," Geyer goes on, "whereas Scotton's original counter-guerrillas were both assassins in the night and goodwill organizers of the people, the PRUs are almost exclusively assassins in the night." Their emphasis "of late," she writes, "has been . . . to murder, kidnap, terrorize or otherwise forceably eliminate the civilian leadership of the other side." In one village "a VC tax collector will be assassinated in his bed in the night. In another, wanted posters will be put up for a VC leader, offering a reward to try to persuade his friends to turn him in. The PRU may also drop down from helicopters and terrorize whole villages, in the hope that they will be frightened to deal with the VC in the future." Furthermore, "the PRUs are excellent torturers. . . . Torture has now come to be so indiscriminately used that the VC warn their men to beware of any released prisoner if he has not been tortured."

"Sometimes we have to kill one suspect to get another to talk," Geyer quotes a PRU adviser as saying. Another PRU adviser told her that "he ate supper with his PRUs on the hearts and livers of their slain enemies." Another one said, "I've been doing this for 22 years all over the world." He cited Egypt when Nasser was coming to power and the Congo "when we were trying to get rid of Tshombe." Writes Geyer about the PRU adviser: "His job, like that of many Americans in South Vietnam, was terror." And she calls American PRU advisers "really the leaders,"[10] a view that contrasted with Colby's claim that Americans were limited to "advice and assistance."

As for the instructors who taught Francis Reitemeyer how to manage PRU, Colby said, "[W]e have some rather direct instructions to our people as to their behavior in Vietnam."[11] Colby was referring to an October 15, 1969, memo sent to the Phoenix staff "and forwarded for inclusion in the training of Phung Hoang advisers in Vietnam and at Fort Holabird." The memo stated that "U.S. personnel are under the same legal and moral constraints with respect to operations under the Phung Hoang program as with respect to military operations against enemy units in the field."

The final word on Phoenix policy was contained in MACV Directive 525-36, issued on May 18, 1970. Noting the "unlawful status of members of the VCI," MACV Directive 525-36 cites "the desirability of obtaining these targetted individuals alive and of using intelligent and lawful methods of interrogation to obtain the truth." It says that Phoenix advisers were "specifically unauthorized to engage in assassination" and that if they were to "come in contact with activities conducted by Vietnamese (never Americans) which do not meet the standards of land warfare," they were "[n]ot to participate further" but were "expected to make their objections of this kind of behavior known to the Vietnamese conducting them" and "expected to report the circumstances to the next higher U.S. authority." The directive closes by saying that "if an individual finds the police type activities of the Phoenix program repugnant to him, on his application, he can be reassigned from the program without prejudice."

In response to the article by Geyer, which focused attention on the PRU and the issue of terror, and in defense of William Colby, his patron, John Vann* said, "[T]here is always a tendency to report extremes. . . . But when those exceptions . . . are used by people who are in basic disagreement with the policy in Vietnam as a means of criticizing the effort, they are taken out of context. They in no way reflect anything that is normal."[13]

Kentucky Senator Sherman Cooper asked Vann, "Is the Phoenix organization a counter-terror organization?"[14]

Vann replied, "The counter-terrorist organization bore and bears no resemblance at all to . . . Phoenix."[15]

COOPER: "Is the U.S. involved in any way in carrying out what can be called a "terrorist" activity?"[16]

VANN: "Well, the answer very shortly, sir, is no, we do not."[17]

Compare Vann's statement with that made by Charlie Yothers, the CIA's chief of operations in I Corps in 1970: "Sure we got involved in assassinations. That's what PRU were set up for—assassination. I'm sure the word never appeared in any outlines or policy directives, but what else do you call a targeted kill?"[18]

According to Tully Acampora, Phoenix was a two-tiered program, with the PRU working against terrorists on the tactical level and the CIO operating above that on strategic affairs. This aspect of Phoenix was addressed by New Jersey Senator Clifford Case when he asked William Colby if Phoenix might be used "by ambitious politicians against their political opponents, not the Viet Cong at all."[19]

COLBY: ". . . it is our impression that this is not being used substantially for internal political purposes. . . . I have heard the President and Prime Minister on many occasions give strong directions that the focus is on the

*"I made the biggest impact of the war when I pulled John out of III Corps and sent him to IV Corps because," Colby said to me, "that was going to be the major area of the pacification battle. He did a spectacular job." A compulsive liar and adulterer, Vann committed statutory rape in 1959. However, his wife lied on his behalf, and after rehearsing for days and going forty-eight hours without sleep, Vann passed a lie detector test and was exonerated. Like many senior American officers in Vietnam, Vann had several mistresses in Vietnam.[12]

Vietcong . . . and that it is not to be used for other purposes."[20]

Picking up on this line of questioning, Committee Chairman William Fulbright asked Colby: ". . . where is Mr. Dzu, the man who ran second in the last election?"

When Colby said, "Mr. Dzu is in Chi Hoa jail in Saigon," Fulbright asked him to "reconcile that with your statement of the very objective view of the Prime Minister." Colby replied that Truong Dinh Dzu "was not arrested under the Phoenix program." Dzu was arrested under Article 4, which made it a crime to propose the formation of a coalition government with the Communists.[21]

FULBRIGHT: "But you say they are giving instructions to be so careful not to use the program for political purposes, when Thieu himself has put a man in prison for no other crime that we know of than that he ran second to him in the elections."[22]

At that point Senator Case came to Colby's rescue, saying, "I think that just, perhaps, suggests this is a privilege reserved for higher officials."[23]

But the point had been made: If Phoenix were to be judged by the behavior, not the stated policies, of Thieu's administration, then it *was* an instrument of political repression. Moreover, as indicated in a letter from Tran Ngoc Chau to Senator Fulbright, political repression in South Vietnam was carried out with the tacit approval of the U.S. government. In his letter to Fulbright (which was inserted into the record of the hearings), Chau claimed that his contacts with his brother had been authorized by, among others, William Colby, Ev Bumgartner, Tom Donohue, Stu Methven, John O'Reilly, Gordon Jorgenson, and John Vann, who instructed Chau not to inform Thieu of his contacts with Hien.

Chau wrote, "Present political persecution of me is consequence of combined action taken by U.S. officials and CIA and Vietnamese officials in an attempt to sabotage Vietnamese and Communist direct talks for Peace Settlement."[24]

In February 1970 Chau was sentenced to twenty years in jail. In May 1970, writes Professor Huy, "the Supreme Court rendered a judgment stating that Chau's arrest and condemnation were unconstitutional. Despite this judgment, Thieu refused to free Chau."[25]

What happened to Chau and Dzu proved that stated policy in South Vietnam was ignored in reality. Likewise, attempts to portray Phoenix as legal and moral were transparent public relations gimmicks meant to buy time while Thieu consolidated power before the cease-fire. To ensure Thieu's internal security, CIA officers were willing to betray their assets, and this capacity for treachery and deceit is what really defined American policy in regard to Phoenix, the PRU, and the war in general. What the Senate concluded, however, was only that diametrically opposed views on Phoenix existed. The official line advanced by William Colby portrayed Phoenix as imperfectly executed—but legal, moral, and popular. The other view, articulated by Senator Fulbright, was that Phoenix was "a program for the assassination of civilian leaders." But that was not proven.

"The Senate Foreign Relations Committee may have been confused by last week's testimony on Operation Phoenix," observed Tom Buckley. "The problem," he explained, "is one of definition."[26]

Unable to decide which definition was correct, the press tended to characterize Phoenix as an absurdity. In a February 18, 1970, article in *The New York Times,* James Sterba said that "the program appears more notorious for inefficiency, corruption and bungling than for terror. . . . If someone decided to make a movie about Phoenix . . . the lead would be more a Gomer Pyle than a John Wayne."

Playing on the notion that the Vietnamese, too, were too corrupt and too stupid to be evil, Tom Buckley wrote that the PRU "were quicker to take the money, get drunk, and go off on their own extortion and robbery operations than they were to sweep out into the dangerous boondocks"—hardly a description of what Jim Ward called "the finest fighting force in Vietnam." But for Buckley and Sterba there was no motive behind the madness. Phoenix was a comedy of errors, dopey disguises, and mistaken identities. There was nothing tragic in their depictions; even the people directing the show were caricatures subject to ridicule.

So it was that Phoenix began sinking in a morass of contradictions which seemed to reflect the intensely human, moral ambiguity of the Vietnam War itself. Even the dead-end debate between Colby and Fulbright mocked America's babbling, hilarious schizophrenia. Whom to believe?

Twenty years later the facts speak for themselves. When Fulbright asked Colby if cash incentives were offered to Vietnamese for neutralizations, Colby said no. Six months later the deputy director of the Joint Chiefs of Staff, General Frank Clay, sent a memo (JCSM-394-70) to Defense Secretary Melvin Laird, noting that General Abrams had recommended "an incentive program to foster greater neutralization achievement."

One of the more significant Phoenix documents, Clay's memo enumerated the Defense Department's major concerns regarding Phoenix: the national identity and registration program, information support of Phoenix, inadequacy of prison space, surveillance of released VCI, Phung Hoang leadership, and exchange of intelligence. These six concerns, notably, derived from a survey conducted by Robert Komer in June 1970.

Upon arriving in Turkey as U.S. ambassador, Komer had been dogged by demonstrators charging him with war crimes. Consequently, he resigned his post even before his nomination was confirmed by the Senate. Seeking vindication, he hired on with RAND, returned to Saigon, and wrote a scathing report called "The Phung Hoang Fiasco." In it Komer says, "[A]s the military war winds down and the conflict assumes a more politico-subversive character, a much more sophisticated and intensive effort to destroy the VCI becomes well nigh indispensable to a satisfactory outcome."

The former champion of quotas rails against "fakery," charging that "half the kills are falsely listed as VCI just to meet Phung Hoang goals." He cites instances where "we may have as many as 10 or 12 dossiers on the same man," and he complains that "each agency still keeps its own files." Special Branch is "grossly overstaffed with poor quality results," the Field Police are "a flop as the action arm of Phung Hoang," and as for the PRU, Komer writes that "everywhere their effectiveness is apparently declining greatly."

Komer is especially critical of the Vietnamese. In III Corps "fully half the province chiefs don't really support Phung Hoang," he writes, and in II Corps Lu Lan "gives only lip service." Komer names Lieutenant Colonel Thiep (who replaced Loi Nguyen Tan, who took command of Chi Hoa Prison) as "the senior full-time Phung Hoang officer," then adds contemptuously that Thiep's "incompetent boss Colonel Song is apparently being kicked upstairs. As I put it bluntly to Thieu and Khiem," Komer says, "there are 65 generals in RVNAF: how come only a LTC to run Phung Hoang?"

Basically, Komer's anger stemmed from Thieu's decision to transfer the Central Phung Hoang Permanent Office from the prime minister's office to the National Police Directorate as a separate bloc. Noting that "the Phung Hoang bloc is completely separate from the key Special Branch bloc," Komer argues that the Central Phuong Hoang Permanent Committee had been "downgraded." He calls the transfer "a case where one of the most crucial of all current GVN priority missions is given to one of the weakest and least effective GVN agencies, the National Police."

In a May 3, 1970, telegram to the secretary of state, Ambassador Ellsworth Bunker explained that Phung Hoang was being transferred from Prime Minister Khiem's office to the National Police to "move it toward Vietnamization" and improve its overall operations. Noting that the "US advisory position on this question had been established through coordination between MACV/CORDS, OSA and Embassy," Bunker concludes by stating his belief that the "most important contribution National Police can make to future Vietnam lies in vigorous and proper execution of Phung Hoang Program against Viet Cong Infrastructure." Case closed.

As compensation for the transfer, Komer proposed getting "the best young, hard driving major general to be found—Phong or Minh of CMD—and make him Minister or Vice-Minister of Interior to give him status." Other reforms Komer suggests: to "increase reward money," to "go after the five best dossiers," and to concentrate efforts "in eight provinces [where] well over half the estimated VCI are concentrated." The provinces were Quang Nam, Quang Tin, and Quang Ngai in I Corps; Binh Dinh in II Corps; and Kien Hoa, Vinh Long, Vinh Binh, and Dinh Tuong (where Komer found the "only . . . Phung Hoang program worthy of the name") in IV Corps.

Summarizing, Komer writes, "For better or worse, CIA produced . . . the only experienced hands who were really good at the game. . . . If I couldn't think of a better solution, I'd transfer operational control over the whole business to OSA [office of special assistant, cover designation for the CIA]."

But Bunker, in his May 3, 1970 telegram, had already nixed that idea. "Integration into Special Police would complicate important public information aspects of program," he said, "and produce *complications* to US advisory element. When VCI reduced to manageable level," he said, turning Phoenix over to the Special Branch "could be reviewed." In any event, the "VC turn to protracted war reemphasizes necessity of Phung Hoang effort against infrastructure during coming year . . . and is of higher priority in Vietnam today than civil law enforcement as contribution to Vietnamization."

Three years into the program the Phoenix brain trust was back on square one, wondering, as Evan Parker had recommended, if it should focus its efforts not on legions of low-level VCI, but on the big fish and, as Parker had also observed, if CIA Special Branch advisers were not already doing the job. Having come full circle, Komer finally realized that the "Special Branch and its U.S. advisers seem to run an almost completely separate operation . . . usually when I asked why no fingerprints in dossiers, I was told they were over in the Special Branch office in the PIC."

Komer was right. Phoenix was a fiasco, but not just because the CIA had decided to hide behind it for "public information" purposes. The notion that reporting formats and quotas as "management tools" could supplant a thousand years of culture and forty years of Communist political development at the village level was simply a false premise. Yes, Phoenix was a fiasco—it had become unmanageable, and it encouraged the most outrageous abuses—but because it had become "of higher priority . . . than civil law enforcement," it was a fiasco with tragic, not comic, consequences.

By 1970 an armistice was inevitable, and Phoenix had become the vehicle by which America was going to transfer responsibility for internal security to the Vietnamese. As a result, General Abrams asked, "That it be made clear to all US and RVN agencies contributing to the Phung Hoang/Phoenix program that the objective of neutralizing the infrastructure is equal in priority to the objectives of tactical operations." As a way of going after strategic VCI targets—the big fish running COSVN—and as a way of protecting Phoenix from penetration by enemy agents, Abrams also asked that "consultation be initiated with the Attorney General . . . to secure a team of two or three FBI counter-espionage experts to be sent to the RVN for the specific purpose of providing recommendations for the neutralization of important national level members of the [VCI]."[27]

Meanwhile, in Washington General Clay advocated increased attention on the DIOCCs, "the cutting edge of Phoenix," because "the district and village level infrastructure remains the key element in the enemy plan to subvert the Government . . . and continues to produce the major threat against GVN efforts to consolidate pacification gains made in the past 18 months." Clay also noted that "Phung Hoang leadership is being improved by recognizing and expanding the prominence of the role of the Special Police in the functioning of the DIOCC."[28]

But in order to mount an attack against the VCI, the U.S. Army needed to gain access to Special Branch files in the DIOCCs. So in February 1970 a third Standard Operating Procedure manual was issued with instructions on how to use the ultimate Phoenix "management tool," the VCI "target folder." As stated in the Phung Hoang Adviser Handbook, "preparation of target folders is the foundation from which successful operations can be run and sentencing be assured by Province Security Committees."[29]

Target folders also served a public information function, by allowing William Colby to say that "our first step was to make sure that the intelligence we gathered on the VCI was accurate, and for this we set up standards and procedures by which to weed out the false from the correct information."[30]

Target folders were specifically designed to help Phoenix advisers focus on high-level VCI. Divided in two, a target folder contained a biographical data on the left side and operational information on the right, in which the suspect's habits, contacts, schedule, and modus operandi were recorded, along with captured documents and other evidence. The folder was the responsibility of the Special Branch case handler in the DIOCC, although a source on the suspect might be handled by another agency. Each Special Branch case handler was required to maintain ten People's Intelligence Organization (PIO) cells—each consisting of three agents—in each hamlet in his area of operations. As stated in the third Standard Operating Procedure manual, the tracking of a VCI suspect began when an informant reported someone making "suspicious utterances" or "spreading false rumors." As more and more sources informed on a suspect, he or she graduated from blacklist D to C to B, then finally to blacklist A—most wanted—at which point the VCI suspect was targeted for neutralization and an operation mounted. The folder was sent to the PIC while the suspect was being interrogated and to the Province Security Committee to assure proper sentencing.

In order to help Special Branch case handlers gather the precise evidence a security committee needed for quick convictions, training programs were started in each corps, where the case handlers were taught how to maintain target folders, a hundred thousand copies of which the Phoenix Directorate prepared and distributed in August 1970. To assure proper target folder maintenance, the Army also assigned a counterintelligence-trained enlisted man to each DIOCC. In 1970, 185 of these counterintelligence specialists graduated from the Phoenix Coordinators Orientation Course. They acted as liaison among the PIC, DIOCC, and PIOCC. In addition, a third officer was added to each PIOCC staff to coordinate with Chieu Hoi and Field Police, and in an effort to upgrade the status of Phoenix coordinators vis-à-vis the CIA's Special Branch advisers, region slots were filled by full colonels, with majors in PIOCCs and captains in DIOCCs. However, cooperation between province Phoenix coordinators and CIA province officers rarely occurred.

A survey of each corps in November 1970 produced these results: I Corps reported "that certain member agencies in the DIOCCs have a wealth of knowledge and information which had hithertofore never been tapped." II Corps reported that "professional jealousies and even distrust among agencies continue to impair progress." III Corps reported that "support comes from only one or two of the agencies represented, while others tend to ignore results." IV Corps reported that "each GVN intelligence agency closely guards its information, thus making dossier construction difficult."[31]

The problem, not explicitly stated, was that CIA officers, extracted from Phoenix by Ted Shackley and hidden away in embassy houses, saw only liabilities in sharing their sources with "amateurish" Phoenix coordinators.

Said Ed Brady: "They had their relationship with the PIC. Many of them either participated in or observed or were close at hand during the interrogations. So they had firsthand output from it. Very few of them, however, ever went and put that in the PIOCC or in the DIOCC . . . which they were *required* to do by the procedures. . . . What they really did," he complained, "was go out and get their own organization, the PRU, and run their own separate operations. It wasn't a Special Branch operation. It belonged to the province officer. So if he thought he had some intelligence that could be acted upon, the U.S. tendency was to act on it unilaterally. They might invite a few Special Branch people to go along, but the Special Branch might not accept the invitation. Then if they caught somebody, they brought him back and turned him over to the Special Branch. They were so caught up in the mythology themselves, they'd say, 'Hey! I'm running a Phoenix operation.' "[32]

Here Ed Brady chose to define Phoenix in its narrow organizational sense, as a division of CORDS with its own SOP, offices, and employees. But insofar as Phoenix is a symbol for the attack against the VCI and insofar as the PICs and PRU were the foundation stones upon which Nelson Brickham built ICEX, the province officers were in fact running Phoenix operations.

What is important to remember is that in order to achieve internal security in South Vietnam, America's war managers had to create and prolong an "emergency" which justified rule by secret decree and the imposition of a military dictatorship. And in order to gain the support of the American public in this venture, it was necessary for America's information managers to disguise the military dictatorship—which supported itself through corruption and political repression—as a bastion of Christian and democratic values besieged by demonic Communists.

In this context, Phoenix is the mask for the terror of the PICs and the PRU, and for the CIA's attempts at the political level "to eliminate the opposition to us and to control the Vietnamese through our clients."[33] Phoenix in the conceptual sense is all the programs it coordinated, as well as the "public information aspects" that concealed its purpose. All other definitions are merely "intellectual jargon."

"The point," Ed Murphy reminded us, "is that it was used in Vietnam, it was used in the United States, and it *still* is used in the United States."

CHAPTER 23

Dissension

Soon after the Senate hearings concluded in mid-March 1970, the Phoenix controversy was again obscured by a larger event. On April 30, 1970, ten days after he had proposed withdrawing 150,000 American troops by the end of the year, Richard Nixon announced that U.S. and South Vietnamese forces had invaded Cambodia.

A deviation from the Nixon Doctrine, the Cambodian invasion was the culmination of twelve years of covert actions against the government of Prince Norodom Sihanouk. The final phase began on March 12, 1970, while Sihanouk was abroad and his prime minister, Lon Nol, under instructions from the CIA, ordered all North Vietnamese out of Cambodia within seventy-two hours. That same day Deputy Prime Minister Sirik Matak canceled a trade treaty between Cambodia and the Provisional Revolutionary Government. Four days later the U.S. merchant ship *Columbia Eagle,* which was ostensibly carrying munitions for U.S. Air Force units in Thailand, was commandeered by two CIA officers, who steered it into the port of Sihanoukville. Armed with guns and ammunition from the *Columbia Eagle,* and backed by the Khmer Kampuchea Krom (Cambodian exiles trained by the CIA in South Vietnam) and the Khmer Serai (Cambodians under Son Ngoc Thanh, trained by the CIA in Thailand), Lon Nol's forces seized control of the government and moved against the Khmer Rouge (Cambodian Communists) and the Vietnamese who supported Prince Sihanouk.

The CIA had been planning the operation since August 1969, when the murder of Thai Khac Chuyen had brought about an end to Detachment B-57. The CIA plan called for the Khmer Serai to attack Khmer Rouge positions from their base in Thailand, while Lon Nol seized Phnom Penh, using deserters from Sihanouk's palace guard, backed by Khmer Kampuchea Krom (KKK) forces from South Vietnam. But the plan quickly got off track. Stanley Karnow notes: "Cambodia was convulsed by anarchy in late March 1970. Rival Cambodian gangs were hacking each other to pieces, in some instances celebrating their prowess by eating the hearts and livers of their victims. Cambodian vigilantes organized by the police and other officials were murdering local Vietnamese, including women and infants."[1]

What Karnow describes is Phoenix feasting on Phnom Penh. Aided by the CIA, the Cambodian secret police fed blacklists of targeted Vietnamese to the Khmer Serai and Khmer Kampuchea Krom. The Vietnamese woman who translated the "Truth About Phoenix" article recalled what happened. "These were not VC being killed," she said. "I remember that. These were mass killings of Vietnamese merchants and Vietnamese people in Cambodia. Oh, yeah. Oh, yeah! I remember because a friend of mine told me. He was one hundred percent Vietnamese, but he didn't succeed in Vietnam, so when he was young, he became a Cambodian citizen and served in the Cambodian government. There were many many Vietnamese people who went to Cambodia to settle. They were leaders of the economy and the government. But the Vietnamese were not loved by the Cambodians—like the Chinese in Vietnam—and there was a mass execution of all those Vietnamese. They cut off their heads and threw them in the river."[2]

On April 4 the Communists counterattacked, and by late April the forces of Lon Nol were faltering. As planned, Nol asked Washington for help, and soon South Vietnamese planes were flying supplies to Phnom Penh. Hastening to support his besieged client, Nixon "encouraged General Abrams to propose intervention by American combat units as well. Abrams broadened the targets to include sanctuaries in the Fish Hook border region further north, where he also claimed to have located the legendary Communist headquarters, COSVN."[3]

The ultimate mission of Phoenix, of course, had always been to neutralize what John Vann at the Senate hearings called the "brains" of the insurgency; and insofar as COSVN was the locus of the VCI, the Cambodian invasion was a massive attack against the VCI. Indeed, the Phoenix Directorate contributed directly to this last desperate attempt to win the war, primarily as a result of the personal relationship John Mason shared with his comrade from World War II General Creighton Abrams. The bond of trust these two men enjoyed enabled them to bridge the bureaucratic abyss that often separates the CIA and the military.

As important as the relationship between Mason and Abrams, however, was the relationship between Mason and Lieutenant Colonel Thomas P. McGrevey, who in July 1969 became the directorate's operations chief, replacing Lieutenant Colonel Al Weidhas. An engaging and immensely likable man, McGrevey was a graduate of West Point (where he roomed with Richard Secord) who in 1964 was sent to the Joint U.S. Military Advisory Group (JUSMAG) in Bangkok as an adviser to Thai intelligence. In Bangkok McGrevey met weekly with the MAG commander, General Richard Stilwell, with the CIA station chief, Red Jantzen, and with John Mason, who was stationed in Hawaii but made frequent trips to Bangkok. In effect, McGrevey was working as the military's liaison to the CIA in Southeast Asia, establishing coordinated intelligence operations in Cambodia, Laos, and South Vietnam, in which capacity he visited South Vietnam at one-month intervals, was introduced to the senior Special Branch, MSS, and PRU officials, and became intimately aware of their operations.

In 1966 McGrevey returned to the United States to become chief of the 108th Military Intelligence Group in Boston, where he supervised operations throughout New England. Then, in 1967, at the request of the acting chief of staff for intelligence, General Chester Johnson, McGrevey returned to Bangkok to facilitate a trilateral agreement among the United States, Thailand, and South Vietnam. As a result of this agreement, Thai intelligence began running joint operations in Cambodia and Laos (where Secord was managing the air war for the Vientiane station chief, Ted Shackley) with the Vietnamese CIO and the CIA.

In July 1969, McGrevey was assigned to be the MACV intelligence chief in II Corps. When John Mason learned that McGrevey had arrived in Saigon, Mason immediately arranged for him to be reassigned to the Phoenix Directorate. In turn, McGrevey had a number of his former aides in Thailand transferred to the directorate, and after a period of orientation in respect to Phoenix operations in the provinces, he and his team began utilizing their contacts in Thailand in preparation for the Cambodian invasion. McGrevey obtained information on COSVN through his sources in Thai intelligence and through the handful of penetrations the directorate had inside COSVN. These penetrations existed at several levels, but the most significant penetration was COSVN's deputy finance director, who alerted McGrevey when the finance director was going on vacation, enabling McGrevey to mount a black propaganda campaign in which he said the finance director was running off with embezzled funds.

In February 1970 Lieutenant Colonel Cao Minh Thiep was transferred from his job as chief of the Combined Intelligence Center to become McGrevey's counterpart in the Phung Hoang Office. At this point General Abrams asked John Mason to intensify Phoenix operations in the border provinces in preparation for the invasion. This was done primarily through PRU teams that searched for infiltration routes and supply caches. Meanwhile, McGrevey was reading reports from the Special Operations Group, which, under Colonel Steve Cavanaugh in liaison with CIA officer Joe Moran, was mounting its own operations against COSVN. McGrevey also read reports submitted from Special Forces A camps and from the Army Security Agency (ASA), which was attempting to locate COSVN through its radio transmissions. But the best intelligence on COSVN came from Thai units in Cambodia. To obtain this information, McGrevey and Cao Minh Thiep, in the company of a team of Vietnamese CIO officers, were flown by the CIA to Bangkok, to the military side of the airport, where they met in the security center with Colonel Sophon and Colonel Panay from Thai intelligence.

Said McGrevey: "In April we provided [to General Abrams] a picture of what COSVN looked like and where the key people were."[4]

On May 11, 1970, *Newsweek* reported that "near the town of Mimot, COSVN's reinforced concrete bunkers are believed to spread 15 to 20 feet beneath the jungle's surface and to house some 5,000 men." Upon arriving in Mimot, however, "American troops found only a scattering of empty huts, their occupants having fled weeks before in anticipation of the assault."

As Karnow quips, "The drive against COSVN . . . turned out to be quixotic."[5]

"Quixotic," yes, but only in the sense that the VCI was not headquartered in a particular set of underground bunkers in Mimot. The invasion deflected attention from the CIA-engineered coup and bloodbath in Phnom Penh, it enabled Lon Nol to install a pro-American government in Cambodia, and it allowed Union Oil of California to secure concessions for all onshore and much offshore Cambodian oil.

The Phoenix Directorate's participation in the Cambodian invasion—if the program is viewed as a bell curve—was certainly its climax. It was not, however, the extent of the directorate's role in operations against the VCI. Operations chief Tom McGrevey managed, from his office in Saigon, several actions against high-level VCI in South Vietnam. He cites as an example the time the Pleiku Province Phoenix officer got information of an impending VCI regional meeting near a tea plantation in II Corps. McGrevey asked the Army Security Agency to pinpoint the location of the meeting, and it obliged him by intercepting and tracking VCI radio communications. McGrevey then sent in a SEAL team that captured several high-ranking VCI.

In conjunction with the CIA station, the Phoenix Directorate also mounted penetrations of, and ran operations against, high-level VCI through special teams that never appeared on any of its rosters. American soldiers assigned to this highly compartmentalized aspect of Phoenix were enlisted men trained in the United States by the CIA, then sent to Vietnam, where they were briefed by CIA, SOG, and MACV intelligence officers at the Ho Ngoc Tau Special Forces camp on such matters as liaison procedures with the Vietnamese, the role of hunter-killer teams, how to screen detainees, district and province chief responsibilities, where input would come from, and where resources were available. Members of these special teams were given a sterile unit cover, usually as part of an Army Security Agency radio research unit, and were assigned only at corps and division level. While they were out on anti-VCI operations, their daily activity reports were falsified to show that they had been present at high-level briefings. Said McGrevey: "The teams were in place when I got there."

The team in Bien Hoa, for example, was assigned for administrative purposes to the 175th Radio Research Unit, which was headquartered on the Bien Hoa military base. The team itself, however, was located in a safe house next to an old train station in Bien Hoa City. The team was composed of ten enlisted men divided into five two-man teams under the region Phoenix coordinator. The team's top priority was collecting tactical military intelligence in support of the Bien Hoa military base, but it also conducted currency investigations and an attack against the VCI.

Regarding this latter function, the special team in Bien Hoa reported to the CIA's special unit (which included women analysts) at the embassy annex. These CIA analysts read Phoenix reports on a daily basis, assessed them for potential intelligence recruitment leads (PIRLs), then decided how a particular VCI could be approached in order to be developed as a penetration agent.* Generally, VCI were told they could work for the CIA, or they could appear to have been killed by their own people. The program was basically a system of identification and control within the VCI, so GVN officials could assume positions of power after the impending cease-fire.

Special teams like the one in Bien Hoa operated above the Phoenix province organization, so there were occasional accidents. For example, in one case a VCI was removed from the blacklist and approached as a PIRL. However, the Phoenix team in the district got to him first and killed him. The Phoenix adviser was just doing his job, and doing it well, but it ruined the recruitment, which had taken three months to develop.

Another case in which the Bien Hoa special team was involved concerned a village chief who was supposedly loyal to the GVN. He was a former Vietminh, a southern Vietnamese who had not gone north. A strong nationalist, he hated Americans; but he also saw the North Vietnamese trying to

*PIRLs were provided with incentives from the black market, including narcotics that CIA contractors brought in from Thailand, Laos, and Cambodia.

control the South, and he hated the North too, and that was his motivation to work with the CIA. But it was a shaky motive, and when a team of NVA agents came and made him feel comfortable with their presence, he became a double agent.

The chief was also the Vietcong tax collector, in which capacity he went around with the VC political officer, who gave him access to unit cadre. At that point he was also working for the CIA, and when it gave him a polygraph test, he failed. Then a GVN team got ambushed en route to meet him, so he was terminated with extreme prejudice, which meant along with his entire family, in such a way that it was made to appear that he was taken out by the Vietcong. The job was done by the Vietnamese ranger team assigned to Bien Hoa special team. Other times the Americans did the terminations themselves, making sure to kill everyone so there would be no witnesses and using brass catchers so there would be no incriminating evidence. Other times the special team sent in SEALs.

Make no mistake about it: Americans who were involved in Phoenix suffered wounds that were not just physical. Many returned to the United States emotionally wrecked, fearful of being prosecuted for war crimes. Many began to doubt the reasons they were given for fighting the war.

Back home in the United States in 1970, many people were reaching the same conclusion, although belatedly because facts about the covert operations that fueled the war were slow to emerge. For example, not until he was released from prison after the war did Tran Ngoc Chau reveal that "a systematic campaign of vilification by use of forged documents was carried out during the mid-1950s to justify Diem's refusal to negotiate with Hanoi in preparation for the unheld unifying elections of 1956." According to Chau, the forging was done by U.S. and British intelligence agencies, which helped gather "authentic" documents that permitted plausible foundations to be laid for the forgeries. These were distributed to various political groups as well as to writers and artists who used the false documents to carry out the propaganda campaign.[6]

Forged documents used to justify and conceal illegal activities often appear in the form of captured documents similar to the type described by Chau. As two aides to the Senate Foreign Relations Committee reported about the Cambodian invasion, "There seems to be captured documents to prove any point or to support, retrospectively, almost any conclusion."[7]

When used against an individual, forged documents are called a compromise and discreditation operation. Along with recruitment in place, defection, capture, and killing, the compromise and discreditation operation was a standard procedure employed by Phoenix personnel. Its purpose was to create dissension among the VCI, to make them suspect that one of their own had betrayed them. Compromise and discreditation were accomplished by conducting whisper campaigns and by planting forged documents or incriminating evidence, usually to reflect dishonesty, immorality, or greed.

Forged letters are a CIA specialty. Writes former CIA officer Philip Agee:

> I would say our most successful operation in Ecuador was the framing of Antonio Flores Benitez, a key member of the Communist revolutionary movement. By bugging Flores' phone, we found out a lot of what he was doing. His wife was a blabbermouth. He made a secret trip to Havana and we decided to do a job on him when he landed back in Ecuador. With another officer, I worked all one weekend to compose a "report" from Flores to the Cubans. It was a masterpiece. The report implied that Flores' group had already received funds from Cuba and was now asking for more money in order to launch guerrilla operations in Ecuador. My Quito station chief, Warren Dean, approved the report—in fact, he loved it so much he just had to get into the act. So he dropped the report on the floor and walked on it awhile to make it look pocket-worn. Then he folded it and stuffed it into a toothpaste tube—from which he had spent three hours carefully squeezing out all the toothpaste. He was like a kid with a new toy. So then I took the tube out to the minister of the treasury, who gave it to his customs inspector. When Flores came through customs, the inspector pretended to go rummaging through one of his suitcases. What he really did, of course, was slip the toothpaste tube into the bag and then pretend to find it there. When he opened the tube, he of course "discovered" the report. Flores was arrested and there was a tremendous scandal. This was one of a series of sensational events that we had a hand in during the first six months of 1963. By late July of that year, the climate of anti-Communist fear was so great that the military seized a pretext and took over the government, jailed all the Communists it could find and outlawed the Communist Party.[8]

Likewise, according to Donald Freed in *Death in Washington,* the catalyst for the 1973 coup in Chile was a forged document—detailing a leftist plot to start a reign of terror—which was "discovered" by the enemies of President Salvador Allende Gossens. The result was a violent military coup, which the CIA officers (who had set it in motion through disinformation in the press) sat back and watched from a safe distance.

Compromise and discreditation operations are a tried-and-true method used in America, too. For example, CIA officer Howard Hunt forged State Department documents showing that President John Kennedy ordered the assassination of Ngo Dinh Diem. And the FBI discredited, through the use of forged documents, Martin Luther King, Daniel Ellsberg, and Jean Seberg. Among others.

When genuine, however, captured documents provide valuable insights into the enemy's plans and strategies. Indeed, said Jack from the Vietnam Task Force, "Colby proved Phoenix effectiveness through captured documents."

For example, in its 1970 End of Year Report, the Phoenix Directorate quoted captured documents signed by the deputy secretary of COSVN as saying that Phoenix and the accelerated pacification campaign "were the most dangerous and effective measures used by the GVN against the insurgency." Another captured document, quoted in the report, stated that "personnel of the Phung Hoang intelligence organization are the most dangerous enemies of the Revolution in suburban and rural areas. Judging by information from captured documents, interrogations of captured personnel and Hoi Chanh debriefings," the directorate concluded that "Phung Hoang is an effective program."[9]

Captured documents, when genuine, also serve as something of a double-edged sword, revealing U.S. plans and strategies, including those pertaining to Phoenix, that might otherwise remain secret. Consider, for example, a circular titled "On the Establishment of the Enemy Phung Hoang Intelligence Organization in Villages." Issued by the Vietcong Security Service in Region 6 on March 29, 1970, captured on May 15, 1970, and cited as Document 05-3344-70 by the Combined Document Exploitation Center (CDEC), it describes how the VCI viewed and planned to combat Phoenix.

As stated in the circular, "the most wicked maneuvers" of Phoenix "have been to seek out every means by which to terrorize revolutionary families and force the people to disclose the location of our agents and join the People's Self-Defense Force. They also spread false rumors . . . and make love with our cadres wives and daughters. Their main purpose is to jeopardize the prestige of the revolutionary families, create *dissension* between them and the people, and destroy the people's confidence in the revolution. In addition, they also try to bribe poor and miserable revolutionary families into working for them."

Phoenix agents are described as "village or hamlet administrative personnel, policemen and landowners," who set up the People's Intelligence Organization and work with "pacification personnel and intelligence agents" to organize "family cadre, issue ID cards, and classify the people." Phoenix agents were said to have made a list of the cadre to be eliminated when the cease-fire took place. "Their prescribed criteria are to kill five cadre in each village in order to change the balance between enemy and friendly forces in the village."

According to the circular, the primary task of GVN village chiefs is to "assign Phoenix intelligence organization and security assistants to develop and take charge of the PSDF [and] select a number of tyrants in this force to activate 'invisible' armed teams which are composed of three to six well trained members each. These teams are to assassinate our key cadre, as in Vinh Long Province."

What the circular is describing is the culmination of Ralph Johnson's Contre Coup process, in which counterterrorists were extracted from People's Self-Defense Forces by Vung Tau-trained village chiefs under the aegis of the Phung Hoang program.

By 1970 political warfare was also being managed through Phoenix. The 1970 End of Year Report cites an experimental program in which "Armed Propaganda Teams of seven men were placed under the operational control of the DIOCCs. On a day to day basis, the DIOCC provided targeting information on specific VCI or VCI families to the APT [which] would then contact them in an effort to induce them to rally." Ralliers were interrogated immediately, "thereby achieving a snow-ball effect . . . in the targeting subsequent neutralization process." Defectors were dubbed "Phoenix Returnees."[10]

By 1970 Phoenix was also sponsoring indoctrination courses. In May Phung Hoang agents in Dien Ban district organized the "People's Training Course to Denounce Communist Crimes." This training course—its name evoking memories of Diem's denunciation campaign—was attended by 280 local residents.

The problem was that Contre Coup had no corresponding ideology. Ralph Johnson could turn the enemy's tactics against him, but not his beliefs. On this point the captured circular reads, "[A]s a result of the victories of the Revolution, the enemy has been forced to accept serious failures and to de-escalate the war. In the face of the situation, the U.S. imperialists have been forced into withdrawing their troops. This fact has caused great confusion and *dissension* within the enemy ranks. The people have developed great hatred for the enemy . . . In addition, there is *dissension* among the Phoenix intelligence members, pacification personnel, policemen, and espionage agents due to internal conflict."

Fanning this dissension was the ability of the VCI to penetrate IOCCs. A captured Vietcong document, dated July 1, 1970, and issued by the Dien Ban District Security Service (An Ninh), instructs its agents to penetrate all Phung Hoang Hanh Quan (intelligence operations coordination centers), to establish blacklists of personnel (especially Special Branch and PSDF), and to report on their activities for elimination.

Da Nang City and Quang Nam Province were particularly well penetrated. A Combined Document Exploitation Center (CDEC) report dated November 23, 1970, cites three messages "pertaining to Phoenix and the PSDF committee in Danang City, and the location and activities of the GVN intelligence service in Danang City"; a blank release slip from the Dien Ban DIOCC "copied by an unidentified individual"; and an undated note regarding a Phung Hoang meeting at the Quang Nam PIOCC at Hoi An.

According to another captured document provided by the Combined Document Exploitation Center on October 21, 1970, a member of the Da Nang military interrogation center escaped after the MSS had discovered he was a double agent. Still another captured document notes that "an agent of the Phung Hoang organization in the 2nd Precinct, Da Nang City," who was the son of the secretary of the VNQDD (Vietnamese Kuomintang) in Vinh Phuoc Village, "provided detailed information on a Phung Hoang training course he attended on 15 June 1970 and the assignment of the trainees upon completion of the course"—meaning the VCI in Da Nang knew every move Phoenix was making.

Nelson Brickham viewed Vietnam as a war that would be "won or lost on the basis of intelligence," and he created Phoenix as the vanguard in that battle. Unfortunately the Phoenix front line unraveled faster than the VCI's; dissension between the Americans and Vietnamese, and the CIA and the military, doomed the program to failure. And while the insurgents held tight, mistrust of U.S. government policy in Southeast Asia, born during Tet 1968 and brought to a boil by the Cambodian invasion, began to unravel American society.

Immediately following the Cambodian invasion, massive antiwar demonstrations erupted across the country. In Ohio Governor James Rhodes reacted violently, vowing to "eradicate" the protesters. On May 4, 1970, the Ohio National Guard responded to his exhortations, firing into a crowd of demonstrators at Kent State College, killing four people.

The spectacle of American soldiers killing American citizens had a chilling effect on many people, many of whom suddenly realized that dissent was as dangerous in the United States as it was in South Vietnam. To many Americans, the underlying tragedy of the Vietnam War, symbolized by Phoenix, was finally felt at home. Nixon himself articulated those murderous impulses when he told his staff, "Don't worry about decisiveness. Having drawn the sword, stick it in hard. Hit 'em in the gut. No defensiveness."[11]

Nixon backed his words with actions. He ordered one of his aides, a former Army intelligence specialist and president of the Young Americans for Freedom, Tom Huston, to devise a plan to surveil, compromise, and discredit his domestic critics. The Huston Plan was called evidence of a "Gestapo mentality" by Senator Sam Ervin of North Carolina.[12]

What Ervin meant by the "Gestapo mentality" was Phoenix in its conceptual sense—the use of terror to stifle dissent. Reflecting Nixon's "Gestapo mentality," offensive counterintelligence operations were directed against dissenters in America: blacks, leftists, pacifists, the Vietnam Veterans Against the War (VVAW), and American Indians. The most famous example may have been mounted by the CIA's domestic operations branch against the Black Liberation Movement; as in Chile, it provoked a violent reaction by security forces and served to justify repression.

Colston Westbrook, according to Mae Brussell in a July 1974 article in *The Realist,* was a CIA psywar expert. An adviser to the Korean CIA and Lon Nol in Cambodia, Westbrook from 1966 until 1969 reportedly worked (undercover as an employee of Pacific Architects and Engineers) as an adviser to the Vietnamese Police Special Branch. In 1970 Westbrook allegedly returned to the United States and was gotten a job at the University of California at Berkeley. According to Brussell, Westbrook's control officer was William Herrmann, who was connected to the Stanford Research Institute, RAND Corporation, and Hoover Center on Violence. In his capacity as an adviser to Governor Ronald Reagan, Herrmann put together a pacification plan for California at the UCLA Center for Study and Prevention of Violence. As part of this pacification plan Westbrook, a black man, was assigned the task of forming a black cultural association at the Vacaville Medical Facility. Although ostensibly fostering black pride, Westbrook was in truth conducting an experimental behavior modification program. Westbrook's job, claims Brussell, was to program unstable persons, drawn from California prisons, to assassinate black community leaders. His most successful client was Donald DeFreeze, chief of the Symbionese Liberation Army (SLA). It was Westbrook who designed the SLA's logo (a seven-headed cobra), who gave DeFreeze his African name (Cinque), and who set Cinque and his gang on their Phoenix flight to cremation, care of the Los Angeles SWAT Team, the FBI, and U.S. Treasury agents.

In 1971 Nixon was to direct his domestic affairs officer, John Erhlichman, to form a special White House internal security unit called the Plumbers. Chosen to head the Plumbers were certified psychopath Gordon Liddy and "false document preparation" expert Howard Hunt. In charge of "controls" was Egil Krogh, who once said, "Anyone who opposes us, we'll destroy. As a matter of fact, anyone who doesn't support us, we'll destroy."[13]

Just as Thieu's domestic political opponents were targets on Phoenix blacklists in Vietnam, so the Plumbers' "enemies list" included critics of

Nixon—people like Gregory Peck, Joe Namath, and Stanley Karnow. And just as illegal methods were used to discredit and compromise "neutralists" in Vietnam, so, too, the Plumbers turned to crime in their attack against "anyone who doesn't support us." Along with Hunt and several other government officials, Krogh (a devout Mormon) was to be convicted of breaking into the home of Daniel Ellsberg's psychiatrist.

Offensive counterintelligence operations directed against the antiwar movement were mounted by the Plumbers; the CIA through its Operation Chaos; the FBI through its COINTELPROS under William C. Sullivan, whose favorite trick was issuing Kafkaesque "secret" subpoenas; the National Security Agency, which used satellites to spy on dissenters; and the Defense Intelligence Agency, servicing the Joint Chiefs and working with the Army chief of staff for intelligence, General William Yarborough, through Operation Shamrock, headquartered at Fort Holabird. Shamrock's main targets were former military intelligence personnel like Ed Murphy and special operations veterans like Elton Manzione, both of whom, by then, were members of the Vietnam Veterans Against the War. Allegedly as part of Shamrock, the 111th Military Intelligence Group (MIG) in Memphis kept Martin Luther King, Jr., under twenty-four-hour-a-day surveillance and reportedly watched and took photos while King's assassin moved into position, took aim, fired, and walked away. As a result, some VVAW members contend that the murders of King, and other less notable victims, were the work of a domestic-variety Phoenix hit team. Some say it still exists.

Be that as it may, it is a fact that during the Vietnam War the government sought to neutralize its domestic opponents, using illegal means, in the name of national security. The fear of surveillance being as effective as surveillance itself, the result was that many Americans refrained from writing letters to their representatives or otherwise participating in the democratic process, knowing that to do so was to risk wiretaps on their phones, FBI agents' reading their mail, being blackmailed for past indiscretions, made victims of vicious rumor campaigns, losing their jobs, or worse.

Moreover, the suppression of dissent in America was championed by the same people who advocated war in Vietnam. And when it became apparent that America had been defeated in Vietnam, these reactionaries—like the Germans after World War I—vented their bitterness and anger on the disparate groups that formed the antiwar movement. Using Phoenix "offensive counterintelligence" tactics, the security forces in America splintered the antiwar movement into single-issue groups, which were isolated and suppressed during the backlash of the Reagan era. Today the threat of terrorism alone remains, pounded into the national consciousness, at the bequest of big business, by abiding media.

Indeed, without the complicity of the media, the government could not have implemented Phoenix, in either Vietnam or America. A full disclosure of the Province Interrogation Centers and the Provincial Reconnaissance Units would have resulted in its demise. But the relationship between the media and the government is symbiotic, not adversarial. The extent to which this practice existed was revealed in 1975, when William Colby informed a congressional committee that more than five hundred CIA officers were operating under cover as corporate executives and that forty CIA officers were posing as journalists. Case in point: reactionary columnist and TV talk-show host William Buckley, Jr., the millionaire creator of the Young Americans for Freedom and cohort of Howard Hunt's in Mexico in the 1950's.

When it comes to the CIA and the press, one hand washes the other. In order to have access to informed officials, reporters frequently suppress or distort stories. In return, officials leak stories to reporters to whom they owe favors. At its most incestuous, reporters and government officials are actually related—for example, Delta PRU commander Charles Lemoyne and his *New York Times* reporter brother, James. Likewise, if Ed Lansdale had not had Joseph Alsop to print his black propaganda in the United States, there probably would have been no Vietnam War.

In a democratic society the media ought to investigate and report objectively on the government, which is under no obligation to inform the public of its activities and which, when it does, puts a positive "spin" on the news. As part of the deal, when those activities are conducted in secret, illegally, reporters tend to look away rather than jeopardize profitable relationships. The price of success is compromise of principles. This is invariably the case; the public is always the last to know, and what it does learn are at best half-truths, squeezed into five-hundred-word columns or thirty-second TV bites, themselves easily ignored or forgotten.

So it was with Phoenix.

CHAPTER 24

Transgressions

In the introduction to this book, Elton Manzione described the counterterror campaign he joined in 1964. He told how as a U.S. Navy SEAL working in a hunter-killer team, he broke down from the strain of having to kill not just enemy soldiers but their families, supporters, and innocent bystanders as well. In September 1964 Manzione's crisis of faith compelled him to go AWOL in France. His military records show he was never even in South Vietnam.

The tragedy of the Vietnam War is that with the arrival of regular American units in 1965, the attack on the elusive and illusory VCI became everyone's job, not just that of elite units. And once the license to kill was granted carte blanche to all American soldiers, a corresponding moral turpitude spread like an infectious disease through their ranks. The effects were evident in fragmentation grenades thrown into officers' tents, crippled Vietnamese orphans selling vials of heroin to addicted GIs, Confederate flags unfurled in honor of Martin Luther King's assassination, companies refusing to go out on patrol, and thousands of deserters fleeing to Canada, France, and Sweden.

The problem was one of using means which were antithetical to the desired end, of denying due process in order to create a democracy, of using terror and repression to foster freedom. When put into practice by soldiers taught to think in conventional military and moral terms, Contre Coup engendered transgressions on a massive scale. However, for those pressing the attack on the VCI, the bloodbath was constructive, for indiscriminate air raids and artillery barrages obscured the shadow war being fought in urban back alleys and anonymous rural hamlets. The military shield allowed a CIA officer to sit behind a steel door in a room in the U.S. Embassy, insulated from human concern, skimming the Phoenix blacklist, selecting targets for assassination, distilling power from tragedy. As the plaque on Ted Shackley's desk says, "Little minds are tamed and subdued by misfortune—but great minds rise above it."

Others, meanwhile, sought to prevent the "negligent cruelties" they witnessed. William Grieves, for one, is proud of the fact that his Field Police were able to protect civilians from marauding Vietnamese Ranger units. And as Doug McCollum recounted, on one occasion they even held their own against a U.S. Army unit.

The military and the police, McCollum explained, divided Vietnam into areas of responsibility. In white areas, considered safe, and gray areas, considered up for grabs, the police had jurisdiction, but in red areas, considered war zones, the military could do whatever it wanted. It was in red areas that "the military shenanigans I reported" took place, McCollum recalled.[1]

McCollum told how, in 1968, in a joint operation with elements of the U.S. Fourth Division, he and his Field Police platoon entered a "red" Montagnard village in search of VC. But "there were only women and children and old men. That was generally the case," he said. What happened next was no aberration either. A military intelligence captain called in armed personnel carriers and loaded the women and children in them. Everyone was taken out to a field, several miles from the village. The armed personnel carriers formed a semicircle with their backs toward the people. Soldiers manned the machine guns, and the people, knowing what was about to happen, started crying. The frantic Field Police platoon leader asked McCollum, "What are they doing?"

McCollum in turn asked the captain, "Who's doing this?"

"Higher headquarters," he was told.

"Well then, you'll have to kill my Field Police and me," McCollum said, deploying his forces in a line in front of Montagnards. "So the military drove away," he told me, shaking his head. "They just left everyone there. And the next morning, when I told the police chief what happened, the only thing he said was, 'Well, now you've got to transport everyone back to the village.' That was what he was upset about."

About the massacring of civilians by U.S. infantry troops, Doug McCollum stated, "There wasn't too much of that. It was mostly raising skirts and chopping off fingers." However, as more and more soldiers succumbed to anger and frustration, more and more incidents occurred.

* * *

The My Lai massacre was first reported in March 1969, one full year after the event. In April 1969, because of congressional queries, the case was given to the Army inspector general, and in August Army Chief of Staff William Westmoreland turned the case over to the Army's Criminal Investigation Division (CID). In November 1969 Seymour Hersh broke the story, telling how 504 Vietnamese civilians were massacred by members of a U.S. infantry company attached to a special battalion called Task Force Barker.

Ten days after Hersh broke the story, Westmoreland ordered General William Peers to conduct an official inquiry. Evan Parker contended to me that Peers got the job because he was not a West Point graduate.[2] However, Peers's close ties to the CIA may also have been a factor. In World War II, Peers had commanded OSS Detachment 101, in which capacity he had been Evan Parker's boss. In the early 1950's he had been the CIA's chief of training and its station chief in Taiwan, and as SACSA in 1966 Peers had worked with the CIA in formulating pacification policy. Having had several commands in Vietnam, he was well aware of how the war was being conducted. But the most conclusive evidence linking Peers to the CIA is the report he submitted in March 1970, which was not made available to the public until 1974 and which carefully avoided implicating the CIA.

The perfunctory trials that followed the Peers inquiry amounted to slaps on the wrist for the defendants and fueled rumors of a cover-up. Of the thirty people named in the report, charges were brought against sixteen, four were tried, and one was convicted. William Calley's sentence was quickly reduced, and in conservative quarters he was venerated as a hero and scapegoat. Likewise, the men in Calley's platoon were excused as victims of VC terror and good soldiers acting under orders. Of nearly two thousand Americans surveyed by *Time* magazine, 65 percent denied being upset.

Yet, if most Americans were willing to accept the massacre as necessary to ensure their security, why the cover-up? Why was the massacre portrayed as an isolated incident?

On August 25, 1970, an article appeared in *The New York Times* hinting that the CIA, through Phoenix, was responsible for My Lai. The story line was advanced on October 14, when defense attorneys for David Mitchell—a sergeant accused and later cleared of machine-gunning scores of Vietnamese in a drainage ditch in My Lai—citing Phoenix as the CIA's "systematic program of assassination," named Evan Parker as the CIA officer who "signed documents, certain blacklists," of Vietnamese to be assassinated in My Lai.[3] When we spoke, Parker denied the charge.

A defense request to subpoena Parker was denied, as was a request to view the My Lai blacklist. Outside the courtroom CIA lawyer John Greaney insisted that the agency was "absolutely not" involved in My Lai. When asked if the CIA had *ever* operated in My Lai, Greaney replied, "I don't know."

But as has been established in this book, the CIA had one of its largest contingents in Quang Ngai Province. Especially active were its Census Grievance cadre, directed by the Son Tinh District RD Cadre intelligence chief, Ho Ngoc Hui, whose VNQDD cadres were in My Lai on the day prior to the massacre. A Catholic from North Vietnam, Hui reportedly called the massacre "a small matter."[4]

To understand why the massacre occurred, it helps to know that in March 1968 cordon and search operations of the type Task Force Barker conducted in My Lai were how RD Cadre intelligence officers contacted their secret agents. The Peers report does not mention that, or that in March 1968 the forty-one RD teams operating in Quang Ngai were channeling information on VCI through Hui to the CIA's paramilitary adviser, who shared it with the province Phoenix coordinator.

The Phoenix coordinator in Quang Ngai Province at the time of the My Lai massacre was Robert B. Ramsdell, a seventeen-year veteran of the Army CID who subsequently worked for ten years as a private investigator in Florida. Ramsdell was hired by the CIA in 1967. He was trained in the United States and sent to Vietnam on February 4, 1968, as the Special Branch adviser in Quang Ngai Province. Ramsdell, who appeared incognito before the Peers panel, told newsmen that he worked for the Agency for International Development.

In *Cover-up,* Seymour Hersh tells how in February 1968 Ramsdell began "rounding up residents of Quang Ngai City whose names appeared on Phoenix blacklists."[5] Explained Ramsdell: "After Tet we knew who many of these people were, but we let them continue to function because we were controlling them. They led us to the VC security officer for the district. We wiped them out after Tet and then went ahead and picked up the small fish."[6] The people who were "wiped out," Hersh explains, were "put to death by the Phoenix Special Police."[7]

Ramsdell "simply eliminated everyone who was on those lists," said Gerald Stout, an Army intelligence officer who fed Ramsdell names. "It was recrimination."*[8] Recrimination for Tet, at a minimum.

Unfortunately, according to Randolph Lane—the Quang Ngai Province MACV intelligence adviser—Ramsdell's victims "were not Vietcong."[9] This fact is corroborated by Jeffrey Stein, a corporal working undercover for the

*In August 1966 the CIA's paramilitary adviser in Quang Ngai, Reed Harrison, unwittingly sent USAID employee Dwight Owen into an ambush outside Tu Nghia. The guerrillas who killed young Owen were from the Forty-eighth VC Battalion.

525th MIG, running agent nets in Quang Nam and southern Thua Thien provinces. According to Stein, the VNQDD was a Vietnamese militarist party that had a "world fascist allegiance and wanted to overthrow the Vietnamese government from the right! The people they were naming as Communists were left-wing Buddhists, and that information was going to the Phoenix program. We were being used to assassinate their political rivals."[10]

Through the Son Tinh DIOCC, Phoenix Coordinator Ramsdell passed Census Grievance-generated intelligence to Task Force Barker, estimating "the 48th Battalion at a strength of 450 men." The Peers report, however, said that 40 VC at most were in My Lai on the day prior to March 16 and that they had left before Task Force Barker arrived on the scene.[11]

Ramsdell told the Peers panel, "Very frankly, anyone that was in that area was considered a VCS [Vietcong suspect], because they couldn't survive in that area unless they were sympathizers."[12]

On the basis of Ramsdell's information, Task Force Barker's intelligence officer, Captain Kotouc, told Lieutenant Colonel Frank Barker that "only VC and active VC sympathizers were living [in My Lai and My Khe]." But, Kotouc said, because leaflets were to be dropped, "civilians would be out of the hamlets . . . by 0700 hours."[13]

Phoenix Coordinator Ramsdell then provided Kotouc with a blacklist of VCI suspects in My Lai, along with the ludicrous notion that all "sympathizers" would be gone from the hamlet by early morning, leaving 450 hard-core VC guerrillas behind. Yet "the link between Ramsdell and the poor intelligence for the 16 March operation was never explored by the Peers Panel."[14]

As in any large-scale Phoenix operation, two of Task Force Barker's companies cordoned off the hamlet while a third one—Calley's—moved in, clearing the way for Kotouc and Special Branch officers who were "brought to the field to identify VC from among the detained inhabitants."[15]

As Hersh notes parenthetically, "Shortly after the My Lai 4 operation, the number of VCI on the Phoenix blacklist was sharply reduced."[16]

In an unsigned, undated memo on Phoenix supplied by Jack, the genesis of the blacklist is described as follows:

> There had been a reluctance to exploit available sources of information in the hamlet, village and district. It was, therefore, suggested that effective Cordon and Search operations must rely on all locally available intelligence in order to deprive the Viet Cong of a sanctuary among the population. It was in this context that carefully prepared blacklists were made available. The blacklists were furnished to assist the Allied operational units in searching for specifically identified people and in screening captives or local personnel

> held for questioning. The information for the blacklists was prepared by the Police Special Branch* in conjunction with intelligence collected from the Province Interrogation Centers.

Kotouc was charged by the Peers panel with concealing evidence and falsifying reports, with having "authorized the killing of at least one VC suspect by members of the National Police," and with having "committed the offense of maiming by cutting off the finger of a VC suspect."[17]

The CIA, via Phoenix, not only perpetrated the My Lai massacre but also concealed the crime. The Peers panel noted that "a Census Grievance Cadreman of Son My Village submitted a written report to the Census Grievance chief, Quang Ngai, on 18 March 1968," indicating that "a fierce battle with VC and local guerrillas" had resulted in 427 civilian and guerrilla deaths, 27 in My Lai and 400 in the nearby hamlets of Thuan Yen and Binh Dong!"[18] The appearance of this report coincided with the release by Robert Thompson of a "captured" document, which had been "mislaid" for nineteen months, indicating that the Cuc Nghien Cuu had assassinated 2,748 civilians in Hue during Tet.

The only person named as having received the Census Grievance report is Lieutenant Colonel William Guinn, who testified in May 1969 that he "could not recall who specifically had given it to him." In December 1969 Guinn, when shown a copy of the Census Grievance report, "refused further to testify and accordingly, it was not possible to ascertain whether the 18 March Census Grievance report was in fact the one which he recalled having received."[19] With that the matter of the Census Grievance report was dropped.

The My Lai cover-up was assisted by the Son Tinh District adviser, Major David Gavin, who lost a report written on April 11 by Tran Ngoc Tan, the Son Tinh district chief. Tan's report named the 504 people killed at My Lai, and Tan said that "he discussed [the report] with Gavin" but that "Gavin denies this." Shortly thereafter Major Gavin became Lieutenant Colonel Gavin.[20]

The Eleventh Brigade commander dismissed Tan's charges as "baseless propaganda."[21] Barker's afteraction report listed no civilian deaths. Civilian deaths in South Vietnam from 1965 until 1973 are estimated at 1.5 million; none is reported in U.S. military afteraction reports.

The Peers panel cited "evidence that at least at the Quang Ngai Province and Son Tinh District levels, and possibly at 2nd ARVN Division, the Senior

*In June 1988 Quang Ngai Special Branch chief Kieu participated in a Vatican ceremony which elevated Catholics killed in Vietnam to the status of martyrs.

U.S. military advisors aided in suppressing information concerning the massacre."[22]

Task Force Barker commander Lieutenant Colonel Barker was killed in a helicopter crash on June 13, 1968, while traveling back to My Lai as part of an investigation ordered by the Quang Ngai Province chief, Colonel Khien. Khien is described "as a big time crook" and a VNQDD politico who "had a family in Hue" and was afraid the VC "were going to make another Hue out of Quang Ngai." Province Chief Khien and the deputy province senior adviser, Lieutenant Colonel Guinn, both "believed that the only way to win the war was to kill all Viet Cong and Viet Cong sympathizers."[23]

The last piece in the My Lai puzzle concerned Robert Haeberle and Jay Roberts, Army reporters assigned to Task Force Barker. After the massacre Roberts "prepared an article for the brigade newspapers which omitted all mention of war crimes he had observed and gave a false and misleading account of the Task Force Barker operation." Roberts was charged by the Peers panel with having made no attempt to stop war crimes he witnessed and for failing to report the killings of noncombatants. Haeberle was cited by the panel for withholding photographic evidence of war crimes and for failing to report war crimes he had witnessed at My Lai.

As Jeff Stein said, "The first thing you learn in the Army is not competence, you learn corruption. And you learn 'to get along, go along.' "[24]

Unfortunately not everyone learns to get along. On September 3, 1988, Robert T'Souvas was apparently shot in the head by his girl friend, after an argument over a bottle of vodka. The two were homeless, living out of a van they had parked under a bridge in Pittsburgh. T'Souvas was a Vietnam veteran and a participant in the My Lai massacre.

T'Souvas's attorney, George Davis, traveled to Da Nang in 1970 to investigate the massacre and while there was assigned as an aide a Vietnamese colonel who said that the massacre was a Phoenix operation and that the purpose of Phoenix was "to terrorize the civilian population into submission."

Davis told me: "When I told the people in the War Department what I knew and that I would attempt to obtain all records on the program in order to defend my client, they agreed to drop the charges."[25]

Indeed, the My Lai massacre was a result of Phoenix, the "jerry-built" counterterror program that provided an outlet for the repressed fears and anger of the psyched-up men of Task Force Barker. Under the ageis of neutralizing the infrastructure, old men, women, and children became the enemy. Phoenix made it as easy to shoot a Vietnamese child as it was to shoot a sparrow in a tree. The ammunition was faulty intelligence provided by secret agents harboring grudges—in violation of the agreement that Census

Grievance intelligence would not be provided to the police. The trigger was the blacklist.

As Ed Murphy said, "Phoenix was far worse than the things attributed to it." Indeed, the range of transgressions generated by Phoenix was all-encompassing but was most evident in its post-apprehension aspect. According to Jeff Stein, the CIA "would direct the PRU teams to go out and take care of a particular target . . . either capture or assassination, or kidnapping. Kidnapping was a common thing that they liked to do. They really liked the whole John Wayne bit—to go in and capture someone at night. . . . They'd put him in one of these bins—these garbage collection type bins—and the helicopter would pick up the bin and fly him off to a regional interrogation center.

"I think it's common knowledge what goes on at the interrogation center," Stein writes. "It was common knowledge that when someone was picked up their lives were about at an end because the Americans most likely felt that, if they were to turn someone like that back into the countryside it would just be multiplying NLF followers."[26]

Bart Osborn (whose agent net Stein inherited) is more specific. "I never knew in the course of all those operations any detainee to live through his interrogation," Osborn testified before Congress in 1971. "They all died. There was never any reasonable establishment of the fact that any one of those individuals was, in fact, cooperating with the VC, but they all died and the majority were either tortured to death or things like thrown out of helicopters."[27]

One of John Hart's original ICEX charges was to develop a means of containing within the GVN's judicial system the explosion of civilian detainees. But as Nelson Brickham explained, no one wanted to get the name of the Jailer of Vietnam, and no agency ever accepted responsibility. So another outcome of Phoenix was a prison system filled to overflowing.

It was not until April 1970, when ten Vietnamese students put themselves on display in a room in the Saigon College of Agriculture, that treatment of political prisoners gained the attention of the press. The students had been tried and convicted by a military field court. Some were in shock and being fed intravenously. Some had had bamboo splinters shoved under their fingernails. One was deaf from having had soapy water poured in his ears and his ears pounded. The women students had been raped as well as tortured. The culprits, claims Don Luce in his book *Hostages of War,* were Saigon's First District police, who used false documents and signatures to prove guilt, and used torture and drugs to extract confessions.

The case of the students prompted two congressmen to investigate conditions at Con Son Prison in July 1970. Initially, Rod Landreth advised station chief Shackley not to allow the congressmen to visit, but Shackley saw denial as a tacit admission of CIA responsibility. So Landreth passed the buck to Buzz Johnson at the Central Pacification and Development Council. Thinking there was nothing to hide, Johnson got the green light from General Khiem. He then arranged for Congressmen Augustus Hawkins and William Anderson and their aide Tom Harkins to fly to Con Son accompanied by Public Safety adviser Frank Walton. Acting as interpreter for the delegation was Don Luce, a former director of the International Volunteer Service who had been living in Vietnam since 1959. Prison reform advocate Luce had gained the trust of many Vietnamese nationalists, one of whom told him where the notorious tiger cages (tiny cells reserved for hard-core VCI under the supervision of Nguyen Minh Chau, "the Reformer") were located at Con Son Prison.

Upon arriving at Con Son, Luce and his entourage were greeted by the prison warden, Colonel Nguyen Van Ve. Harkins presented Ve with a list of six prisoners the congressmen wished to visit in Camp Four. While inside this section of the prison, Luce located the door to the tiger cages hidden behind a woodpile at the edge of a vegetable garden. Ve and Walton protested this departure from the guided tour, their exclamations prompting a guard inside the tiger cage section to open the door, revealing its contents. The congressmen entered and saw stone compartments five feet wide, nine feet long, and six feet high. Access to the tiger cages was gained by climbing steps to a catwalk, then looking down between iron grates. From three to five men were shackled to the floor in each cage. All were beaten, some mutilated. Their legs were withered, and they scuttled like crabs across the floor, begging for food, water, and mercy. Some cried. Others told of having lime buckets, which sat ready above each cage, emptied upon them.

Ve denied everything. The lime was for whitewashing the walls, he explained, and the prisoners were evil people who deserved punishment because they would not salute the flag. Despite the fact that Congress funded the GVN's Directorate of Corrections, Walton accused the congressmen of interfering in Vietnamese affairs. Congressman Hawkins expressed the hope that American POWs were being better treated in Hanoi.

The extent of the tiger cage flap was a brief article in *The New York Times* that was repudiated by U.S. authorities. In Saigon the secret police cornered Luce's landlady and the U.S. Embassy accused Luce of being a Vietcong agent. Rod Landreth approached Buzz Johnson with the idea of circulating evidence of Luce's alleged homosexuality, but Johnson nixed the idea. When Luce began writing articles for *Tin Sang,* all issues were promptly confiscated and his press card was revoked. Finally, Luce was expelled from Vietnam in May 1971, after his apartment had been ransacked by secret policemen searching for his records. Fortunately Luce had mailed his notes and documents to the United States, and he later compiled them in *Hostages of War*.

Michael Drosnin, in the May 30, 1975, issue of *New Times*, quotes Phoenix legal adviser Robert Gould as saying, "I don't know for sure, but I guess Colby was covering up for Con Son too. Nothing really was changed after all that publicity . . . the inmates who were taken out of the Tiger Cages were simply transferred to something called 'cow cages,' which were even worse. Those were barbed wire cells in another part of the camp. The inmates were shackled inside them for months and left paralyzed. I saw loads of spidery little guys—they couldn't stand and they couldn't walk, but had to move around on little wooden pallets."[28] According to Gould, "It was a well known smirking secret in certain official circles that with all the publicity about the Tiger Cages, no one ever found out about the cow cages."[29]

Added Gould: "The responsibility for all this is on the Americans who pushed the program. We finally made some paper reforms, but it didn't make any difference. The Province Security Committees did whatever the hell they wanted and the pressure our 'neutralization' quotas put on them meant they had to sentence so many people a month regardless. And God, if you ever saw those prisons."[30]

In *Hostages of War* Don Luce refers to the GVN as a "Prison Regime" and calls Phoenix a "microcosm" of the omnipotent and perverse U.S. influence on Vietnamese society. He blames the program for the deterioration of values that permitted torture, political repression, and assassination. "While few Americans are directly involved in the program," Luce writes, "Phoenix was created, organized, and funded by the CIA. The district and provincial interrogation centers were constructed with American funds, and provided with American advisers. Quotas were set by Americans. The national system of identifying suspects was devised by Americans and underwritten by the U.S. Informers are paid with US funds. American tax dollars have covered the expansion of the police and paramilitary units who arrest suspects."[31]

Thus, Luce writes, "the U.S. must share responsibility for the nature of the Saigon government itself. It is a government of limited scope whose very essence is dictated by American policy, not Vietnamese reality."[32] But the CIA absolved itself of responsibility, saying that abuses occurred in the absence of U.S. advisers and that oversight was impossible. However, if the CIA had accepted responsibility, it would have nullified the plausible denial it had so carefully cultivated. Like Phoenix, the prison system was intentionally "jerry-built," enabling sadists to fall through the gaping holes in the safety net.

Writes Luce: "Abuses of justice are not accidental but an integral part of the Phoenix program." For example, "The widespread use of torture during interrogation can be explained by the admissibility of confession as evidence in court . . . and by the fact that local officials are under pressure from Saigon to sentence a specific number of high level VCI officials each month." He adds that "Phoenix was named after the all seeing mythical bird which selectively snatches its prey—but the techniques of this operation are anything but selective. For many Vietnamese, the Phung Hoang program is a constant menace to their lives."[33]

CHAPTER 25

Da Nang

Jerry Bishop served in the Da Nang City Phoenix program from July 1968 until March 1970. An ROTC and Fort Holabird graduate, he arrived in Vietnam with thirty other lieutenants in August 1967 and was assigned to the Huong Thuy DIOCC near Hue. Shortly thereafter, in July 1968, he was transferred to Da Nang, where he became Major Roger Mackin's deputy in the Da Nang City Intelligence and Operations Coordination Center.

Like many young men who wound up working for the CIA, Bishop felt constrained by the military and preferred the company of freewheeling agency officers like Rudy Enders, who had married PVT's* sister and had formed the Da Nang City PRU as a means of providing his in-laws with draft deferments and steady employment. Working undercover in the CIA motor pool, the Da Nang City PRU specialized in deep-penetration operations into the jungle area in the districts outside Da Nang where the ARVN feared to go. Said Bishop: "We relied on the PRU and the U.S. Special Forces Mobile Reaction (Mike) Forces,† because the Regional and Popular Forces could

*The CIA's unilateral Vietnamese asset PVT was in charge of PRU and Phoenix operations in Da Nang.

†The PRU and Special Forces Mike Forces were trusted because they were under CIA control, with no official Vietnamese involvement.

not be trusted. Also, it was hard to convince the Vietnamese to run operations, which is why having the PRU was so important."

The Da Nang City PRU were the subject of much controversy. They were the only PRU team assigned to a city in all Vietnam and did not have the approbation of Captain Pham Van Liem, the Quang Nam PRU chief, or of Major Nguyen Van Lang, the national PRU commander, who made his living selling "PRU-ships" and resented the fact that PVT had gotten his job for free. In fact, when Bishop arrived in Da Nang in July, his boss, Roger Mackin, was embroiled in a dispute with Police Chief Nguyen Minh Tan over the mere presence of the PRU in Da Nang. And while Enders was home on leave, Liem transferred PVT to Quang Ngai Province. When Enders returned to Da Nang, he brought PVT back and assigned him and his PRU to the newly created IOCC as the action arm of Phoenix in Da Nang. Tan was transferred to the newly created Central Phung Hoang Permanent Office in Saigon, and the controversy over the Da Nang City PRU simmered.

Meanwhile, Bishop stepped in as deputy Phoenix coordinator in Da Nang City, in which capacity he coordinated the various Vietnamese intelligence agencies in Da Nang. The city, incidentally, was strictly off limits to U.S. troops living in nearby military bases. Apart from Phoenix personnel, only a few military policemen, CID investigators, SOG spooks, and CORDS advisers were permitted within the city proper.

Bishop's top priority was collecting data on VCI infiltrators living in the shantytowns on the outskirts of the city. He did this by reading translated Special Branch reports provided by Dick Ledford, the senior CIA Special Branch adviser headquartered at the Da Nang Interrogation Center with his Vietnamese counterpart, Lieutenant Colonel Tien, and the PIC chief, Major Mao. Ledford used Bishop to interrogate high-level VCI prisoners, whom Bishop would isolate and humiliate in order to make them lose face with the other prisoners, on the theory that breaking a man's spirit was the quickest way to get him to talk. In hard cases Bishop administered drugs to disorient his prisoners, then offered a return to sanity in exchange for information. Business was brisk. The Da Nang PIC held five hundred prisoners, most supplied by the PRU, which did their interrogations there. The PIC,* in Bishop's words, was the "cornerstone" of anti-VCI operations in Da Nang, while Phoenix was "just coordination."

Phoenix operations in Da Nang, like those described by Shelby Roberts

*Bishop noted that the American sergeant in charge of PIC administration sold food and clothing on the black market and had to be relieved. The Da Nang City IOCC and the three district IOCCs had their own interrogation and detention facilities.

in Saigon, consisted mainly of the National Police cordoning off neighborhoods where VCI activity was suspected, then searching homes and checking IDs. The city was ringed by police checkpoints which Bishop, carrying photographs of VCI suspects, regularly visited in the company of Special Branch personnel. Bishop also worked closely with the Public Safety adviser to the Da Nang Field Police, which Bishop described as "mobile riot cops riding around in trucks with truncheons and shields," enforcing the 10:00 P.M. curfew, arresting suspects, putting them in CONEX garbage containers and hauling them off to prison. Bishop called Phoenix operations in Da Nang "an example of big brother police state tactics."

As Phoenix coordinator Bishop also worked with the MSS, an outfit he likened to the Gestapo and said included "the kind of people who torture people to death." While the police had Da Nang City as their beat, the MSS operated primarily in the districts outside town. Each of Da Nang's three districts had its own IOCC and Phoenix coordinator. The Third District IOCC—located across the bay in a rural area—was advised by an Army lieutenant, but neither he nor the other two DIOCC advisers, one of whom hailed from the Food and Drug Administration, were intelligence officers. They averaged twenty-two or twenty-three years old and were unable to speak Vietnamese.

Another part of Bishop's job was working with the Military Police recovering property—mostly jeeps and trucks—stolen from the U.S. Army, and he often met with Army and Marine commanders to obtain helicopters for joint operations. At times these operations had nothing to do with the VCI. "We had problems with deserters, mostly blacks near the Marine air base, hiding out in the shantytown across the bay," Bishop explained. "They were trying to make noodles and stay underground, but they were heavily armed and, at times, worked with the VC. So we had cordon and search operations to round them up. After the MPs started taking casualties, though, we used American military units, airborne rangers provided by General Lam, and the Nung Mike Force from Special Forces."

Bishop also ran operations against the local Koreans, who "had their own safe houses and their own black-market dealings." The Koreans "were selling weapons to the NVA through intermediaries and were shipping home U.S. Army trucks, which is what finally brought the MPs and Police Chief Duong Thiep together. But the Koreans were too tough—they all had black belts in karate—for the police to handle by themselves." So Bishop used the Da Nang City PRU to raid the safe house where the deals were being done. "We confiscated their vehicles, which they did not take lying down. They were so pissed off," Bishop recalled, "that they later tossed a grenade in my jeep."

Despite his trouble with the Koreans, Bishop and the other Americans in Da Nang frequented the Korean social club, which was located next door to the CIA's embassy house on Gia Long Street. It was a favorite spot for Americans because the Vietnamese had outlawed dance halls. On the other hand, the Vietnamese maintained a number of opium dens in Da Nang. "The Vietnamese didn't give a damn about drugs," Bishop explained, "so we left them alone. That was Public Safety's problem."

In late 1968 Roger Mackin left Vietnam, and Jerry Bishop assumed command of the Da Nang City IOCC, and in early 1969 Dick Ledford bequeathed the I Corps Phoenix program to Colonel Rosnor, the Phoenix region coordinator. As part of the MACV takeover, Rosnor was forced to move Phoenix region headquarters out of the CIA compound into the mayor's office. And shortly thereafter Rosnor was himself replaced by Colonel Daniel Renneisen, a Chinese linguist brought in from Taiwan to assuage the Vietnamese. With Renneisen's approval, Bishop built a new IOCC "off the harbor road three blocks from the water." Promoted to captain in early 1969, Bishop became Renneisen's deputy and liaison to Lieutenant Colonel Thiep.

The CIA's pullout from Phoenix had a big impact on Bishop. "Previously," he explained, "I would see Ledford for coordination; I would go to the PIC, get the hot information, and bring it into the Da Nang City IOCC, which was important, because the Special Branch wouldn't share its information with the Vietnamese police or the military. But once Ledford was gone, we had no more access. The new people coming in were lost." Phoenix, said Bishop, "became a mechanism to coordinate the Vietnamese, while the CIA began running its own parallel operation. . . . The problem," Bishop explained, "is that the CIA sees itself as first. You're supposed to give your agents and your information to them, and then they take over operational control. So everyone tried to keep something for themselves." Bishop, for example, ran his own secret agent, whom he had recruited from the local Chieu Hoi center.

Not only had Bishop lost access to Special Branch information, but he had also lost his major source of funding, and he had to find a way to involve the Vietnamese more directly in the program. His response was to give PVT money from the Intelligence Contingency Fund, which PVT used to throw a party for the top-ranking Vietnamese officials every two or three weeks. PVT would hire a band and invite high-ranking officers from the mayor's office, the MSS, the National Police, and Special Branch, and everyone would make small talk and share information. It was an informal way of doing things which, Bishop pointed out, reflected Vietnamese sensibilities.

"The people in the villages," Bishop pointed out, "had no concept of communism. They couldn't understand why we were after the VCI, and they didn't take sides. They'd help the guerrillas at night and the GVN during day." In Bishop's opinion, "We were helping the wrong side. The GVN had no real sense of nationality, no real connection to people. They were trained by the French to administer for the Saigon regime. Those who worked with Chieu Hoi and RD understood communism somewhat, but the GVN had no ideology. Just negative values."

Over time the parties organized by PVT evolved into formal Phung Hoang meetings held in the mayor's office. PVT acted as translator (Americans wore headsets) and facilitator, setting the agenda and making sure everyone showed up. The Phung Hoang Committee in Da Nang consisted of the mayor and his staff and reps from the MSS, Special Branch, National Police, Census Grievance, RD Cadre, and Chieu Hoi—nine to ten people in all. They had never gotten together in one spot before, but from then on the Phung Hoang Committee was the center of power in Da Nang, even though it was split into opposing camps, one led by Thiep, the other by Mayor Nguyen Duc Khoi, Thiep's business rival.

Bishop was aligned with Thiep, and in order to strengthen Thiep's hand, he persuaded Colonel Renneisen to persuade General Cushman, the American military commander in I Corps, to ante up a helicopter, which Bishop and Thiep then used to visit each of I Corps's five PIOCCs on a circuit-rider basis.

The Special Branch representative on the Phung Hoang Committee reported (but always on dated information) to Mayor Khoi—a former MSS officer who had at one time been Diem's security chief. As the agency with the closest ties to the civilian population, the Special Branch had the best political intelligence and thus was a threat to the I Corps commander, General Lam. For that reason, when General Khiem had become prime minister in early 1969, he appointed his confidential agent, Lieutenant Colonel Thiep (an MSS officer from Saigon) police chief in Da Nang, with cognizance over the Special Branch. Thiep reported to General Lam and was able to post an MSS officer in the region PIC. However, PIC chief Mao—in fact, a Communist double agent—isolated the MSS officer, leaving Phung Hoang Committee meetings as the only means by which Thiep could keep tabs on the Special Branch.

The CIA's region officer in charge in 1969, Roger McCarthy, and his deputy, Walter Snowden, retreated from sight, leaving Renneisen and Bishop to fend for themselves. But MACV was not providing sufficient funds to maintain either the Da Nang PRU or existing agent nets, and so Bishop began issuing special passes to the Special Forces team in Da Nang in exchange for captured weapons, which he traded to the Air Force for office supplies, which he gave to Thiep for his Phung Hoang headquarters. When Bishop learned, through PVT, that the Navy Civic Action center was in possession of stolen jeeps, he confiscated the jeeps, painted them green and white at the PRU motor pool, forged legal papers, and gave them to Thiep.

One of Bishop's confrontations with the local MPs occurred when Marine investigators tried to recover the stolen vehicles but found they now belonged to Thiep and the National Police. Tension between the Da Nang Phoenix contingent and Marine investigators mounted because, according to Bishop, "People got corrupted by Phoenix."

With the loss of CIA funding, the Phoenix program in Da Nang suffered other setbacks. The Da Nang City PRU were suddenly on their own. PVT, the indispensable link between the Americans and Vietnamese, began to worry, so Bishop was forced to take action. "We heard through PVT what really went on," Bishop said. But in order to keep PVT as an asset and carry out the attack against the VCI, it was necessary to maintain the PRU in Da Nang. "Our PRU were English-speaking and could translate documents and act as interpreters for us," Bishop explained. "We couldn't get along without them." Knowing that the Da Nang Phoenix program was on the verge of collapse, Bishop wrote a letter to Prime Minister Khiem, asking that the PRU be retained as draft-exempt employees of the Da Nang City Phung Hoang program, working as auto mechanics in the motor pool, paid through the MACV Intelligence Contingency Fund.

The letter was not well received by PRU commander Lang in Saigon. Nor was the 525th MIG thrilled at the prospect of shelling out money for a program that was coming under increasing criticism. "The PRU were hated by everyone," Bishop explained. "They were considered worse than the MSS Gestapo."

Colonel Renneisen did not want to get involved either, "But we needed interpreters," Bishop said, "and the letter was signed by Thiep, and Thiep arranged for PVT to meet with Colonel Pham Van Cao at the Phung Hoang Office in Saigon. Cao wrote a letter to the director general of the National Police, who approved it, as did General Lam after prodding from Renneisen. And so on the condition that they be directed only against the VCI, the PRU were allowed to stay in Da Nang."

The establishment of the Da Nang PRU as an official arm of the city's Phung Hoang program coincided with the transfer of PRU national headquarters to the National Police Interrogation Center in Saigon, and the transfer of PRU logistical support was transferred to Colonel Dai and the National Police. While the PRU had been paid directly by the CIA before, as of 1969, funds were channeled through intermediaries—usually Phoenix—while uniforms and equipment came through the Field Police.

Having profaned the sacred chain of command with his letter to Khiem, Bishop soon found himself in hot water. "A red-haired guy from Saigon, a young kid, came up to Da Nang and replaced me at the Da Nang City IOCC with a major from the Third Marine Amphibious Force," Bishop recalled. "I was kicked upstairs and became Renneisen's full-time deputy, and the major—responding to General Cushman, who was upset because vehicles kept disappearing—decided to get rid of all renegade vehicles in the PRU motor pool. The last I heard, the steering wheel fell off his jeep while he was driving around the city."

Jerry Bishop left Vietnam in March 1970 and returned to college, badly disillusioned. Colonel Renneisen was transferred to Saigon as operations chief at the Phoenix Directorate. A new I Corps Phoenix coordinator settled into the job. In Quang Nam Province, the Phoenix adviser was Lieutenant Bill Cowey; Captain Yoonchul Mo was the Korean liaison; and the PRU, under Major Liem, were advised by Special Forces Sergeant Patry Loomis. The Da Nang City PRU continued to be advised by PVT. Major Thompson ran the Da Nang City IOCC, and the Da Nang PIC was advised by Vance Vincent.

The question this book has tried to answer is, Was Phoenix a legal, moral, and popular program that occasionally engendered abuses or was it an instrument of unspeakable evil—a manifestation of everything wicked and cruel? Consider the case of William J. Taylor. A former Marine Corps investigator and veteran of three tours in Vietnam, Taylor now owns his own detective agency, one of the foremost in the country. He served as chief investigator and consultant in the Karen Silkwood, Three Mile Island, and Greensboro murder cases. He was also involved in the investigations into the My Lai massacre, the Atlanta missing and murdered children case, and the Orlando Letelier assassination. A man who has been shot and stabbed in the course of his work, Taylor is tough as nails, but when we met in the fall of 1986, it was in an attorney's office, in the presence of a witness; for what he had to say lent credence to all the horror stories ever told about Phoenix.

Bill Taylor enlisted in the Marines in 1963. He did his first tour in Vietnam in 1966 as a member of a unit guarding a mountaintop radio relay station that monitored enemy and allied radio traffic in the valley below. When the post was attacked and overrun by an NVA unit, Taylor was nominated for a Silver Star for his gallantry in action.

Taylor returned to Vietnam in 1968 as an investigator with the Marine Corps Criminal Investigation Division (CID). His duties involved investigating robberies, arsons, murders, rapes, fraggings, race riots, and other serious crimes committed by American military personnel. Taylor transported dangerous prisoners, acted as a courier for classified messages, and maintained a network of informers in Da Nang. In 1969 Taylor returned to Da Nang as a CID investigator with the Third Marine Amphibious Force. He resided at the Paris Hotel and worked, half a mile away, with a team of Marines in the Army's CID headquarters. Taylor's supervisor was Master Sergeant Peter Koslowski.

"Pete liked me." Taylor laughed. "He was always mad at me, but he liked me."

It was through Koslowski that Taylor first heard about Phoenix. "Koslowski said Phoenix was a great organization and that it would right a lot of wrongs over there," Taylor recalled. "He said it was necessary, sometimes, to cut throats and that it was also important, for psychological reasons, that some times it be made to look like the Communists had done it. That included terrorist activities in Da Nang and Saigon, which were Phoenix projects."

Expressing his own disgust with such a policy, Taylor said, "I was young and didn't understand political realities. That's what Koslowski said. Well, now that I'm mature, I understand them less."

Taylor's account of Phoenix is set in Da Nang in July 1970. The incident occurred on a Sunday morning. As was his habit, Taylor was rummaging through the garbage cans in the alley behind the White Elephant restaurant near the Da Nang Hotel, loading the back of his jeep with discarded fruit, vegetables, and bread, which he gave to Vietnamese members of his informer network who were having a hard time making ends meet. Some of these people worked at Camp Horn; others, for the mayor of Da Nang. Most he had known since 1968.

While poking around in the trash, Taylor saw a U.S. Army intelligence officer, accompanied by a Korean intelligence officer, pass by in a jeep. Taylor had been investigating the American for several months, so he quickly dropped what he was doing and followed them. Taylor had opened the case when a number of his Vietnamese sources began complaining to him that an American military officer, in cahoots with the Koreans, was murdering Vietnamese civilians for the CIA. The American officer was regularly seen at the Da Nang Interrogation Center, assaulting women prisoners and forcing them to perform perverse acts. He had a reputation as a sadist who enjoyed torturing and killing prisoners. A psychopath with no compunctions about killing people or causing them pain, he was the ideal contract killer.

That the CIA should recruit such a man was not unusual. Taylor himself had investigated a racial incident in which four blacks threw grenades into the Da Nang enlisted men's club while a movie was being shown. One of the blacks told Taylor that a CIA "talent scout" had offered to get him and his comrades off the hook if they would agree to perform hits for the CIA on a contract basis, not just in Vietnam but in other countries as well.

Taylor's principal source was a Vietnamese woman who knew where the American assassin lived. Together they watched the house, and when the man emerged, Taylor recognized him immediately. The man was the Da Nang Phoenix adviser, in which capacity he periodically appeared at the CID compound dressed in the uniform of a U.S. Army intelligence officer.

"The guy was crazy," Taylor explained. "He was my height, slightly taller. He had dark hair and a runner's build. He had three or four names and eyes you'd never forget—like he was acting at throwing a tantrum. Like Jim in *Taxi*. He was angry all the time," Taylor continued. "When he walked through a crowd of Vietnamese, he just pushed people aside. The first time I saw him, as a matter of fact, was outside Koslowski's office. A Vietnamese sentry blocked his way, so he slammed the guy up against the guardhouse. Right then and there I knew that someday we were going to fight.

"He didn't look or act like a military officer," Taylor added. "That's why I started watching him."

Over the next few months Taylor compiled a comprehensive dossier on the man, with more than a hundred pages of notes and twenty rolls of film, including pictures of the Koreans and American civilians with whom he met. When Koslowski discovered what Taylor was doing, he tried to dissuade him. But Taylor persisted. He continued to surveil the Phoenix agent, noting that much of his contact with other Americans occurred at the Naval Claims Investigation building, a "gorgeous mansion" that served as a "CIA front." Known to Jerry Bishop as the Civic Action center, it was the place where Vietnamese went to collect indemnities when their relatives were accidentally killed in U.S. military operations or by U.S. military vehicles. Although there were only six claims adjusters, the building had dozens of spacious rooms and doubled as a beer hall on Saturday nights. Taylor and his colleagues would party there with the intelligence crowd, local American construction workers, and reporters from the Da Nang Press Club. At these parties Taylor watched while the Phoenix agent met and took instructions from civilians working undercover with the Da Nang Press Club.

Sensing he was on to something unusual, Taylor wrote to L. Mendel Rivers, a congressman in South Carolina. "A few weeks later," he noted, "Koslowski hinted that maybe I shouldn't be writing to politicians."

Taylor began to feel uncomfortable. Thinking there was an informer in Rivers's office, he began mailing copies of his reports and photographs to a friend in Florida, who concealed the evidence in his house. What the evidence suggested was that Phoenix murders in Da Nang were directed not at the VCI but at private businessmen on the wrong side of contractual disputes. In one case documented by Taylor, Pepsi was trying to move in on Coke, so the Coke distributor used his influence to have his rival's name put on the Phoenix hit list.

Taylor's investigation climaxed that Sunday morning outside the White Elephant restaurant. He followed the Phoenix adviser and his Korean accomplice as they drove in smaller and smaller circles around the northwest section of Da Nang. Satisfied they weren't being tailed, the two parked their jeep, then proceeded on foot down a series of back alleys until they reached an open-air café packed with upper-middle-class Vietnamese, including women and children. Taylor arrived on the scene as the two assassins pulled hand grenades from a briefcase, hiked up the bamboo skirting around the café, rolled the grenades inside, turned, and briskly walked away.

Taylor watched in horror as the café exploded. "I saw nothing but body parts come blasting out. I drove around the burning building and the bodies, hoping to cut them off before they reached their jeep. But they got to it before I did, and they started to drive away. They passed directly in front of me," Taylor recalled, "so I rammed my jeep into theirs, knocking it off the road.

"After the initial shock," he continued, "they reached for their weapons, but I got to them first. I wanted to blow them away, but instead I used my airweight Smith and Wesson to disable them. Then I took their weapons and handcuffed them to the roll bar in the back of my jeep. I drove them back to the CID building and proceeded to drag them into Koslowski's office. I got them down on the floor and told Ski they'd killed several people. I said that I'd watched the whole thing and that there were witnesses. In fact, the crowd would have torn them apart if I hadn't brought them back fast.

"Meanwhile, the American was screaming, so I stepped on him. I'd taken the cuffs off the Korean, who was trying to karate-chop everything in sight, so I cuffed him again. Then Ski told me to go back to my office to write up my report. Ski said he'd handle it. He was mad at me."

It was soon apparent why Koslowski was upset.

"While I was in my office across the courtyard, in another wing of the CID building," Taylor said, "one of the other CID agents came in and asked me if I had a death wish. 'No,' I replied, 'I have a sense of duty.'

" 'Well,' " he said, " 'nothing's gonna get done.' " By this time reports describing the incident as an act of Vietcong terrorism were streaming into the office. Fourteen people had been killed; about thirty had been injured.

"Then," Taylor said, "a second CID agent came in and said, 'Ski's letting them go!' I charged back to the main building and saw the American Phoenix agent walking down the hall, so I started bouncing him off the walls. At this point Koslowski started screaming at me to let him go. A Vietnamese guard came running inside, frantic, because there was a lynch mob of Koreans from the Phoenix task force forming outside. One of the CID guys grabbed me, and the Phoenix agent screamed that I was a dead man. Then he took his bloody head and left.

"I really didn't care." Taylor sighed. "Sanctioning of enemy spies is one thing, but mass murder . . . I told Ski, 'If it's the last thing I do, I'm going to get those guys.' "

Shortly thereafter Koslowski received a phone call and informed Taylor that "for his own safety" he was being restricted to his room in the Paris Hotel. Two marines were posted outside his door and stood guard over him through the night. The following morning Taylor was taken under custody to the Third MP Battalion and put in a room in the prisoner of war camp. Now a captive himself, he sat there for two days in utter isolation. When the Koreans learned of his whereabouts, and word got out that they were planning an attack, he was choppered to a Marine base on Hill 37 near Dai Loc on Route 14. Taylor stayed there for two more days, while arrangements were made for his transfer back to the States. Eventually he was flown back to Da Nang and from there to Cam Ranh, Yokohama, Anchorage, and Seattle. In Seattle he was relieved of his gun and escorted by civilians posing as personal security—one was disguised as a Navy chaplain—to Orlando, Florida.

"When I got to Orlando, where my family was waiting," Taylor recalled, "there was still mud on my boots. I had five days' growth of beard, and I was filthy. I cleaned up, contacted Marine headquarters, and was told to stand down. Nothing happened for about forty-five days, at which time I was ordered to Camp Lejeune, where I was debriefed by a bunch of military intelligence officers. I was told not to tell anyone about what had happened. They said I could go to jail if I did."

And so Bill Taylor's account of Phoenix came to an end. Almost. Within a month of his return to the States, his friend's house was broken into and the incriminating evidence stolen. In a predictable postscript Taylor's service records were altered; included in the portion concerning his medical history were unflattering psychological profiles derived from sessions he never attended. He never got the Silver Star either. Yet despite his losing battle with the system, Bill Taylor still believes in right and wrong. He is proud of having brought the Phoenix assassins in for justice (never dispensed), for having torn the masks off their faces, and for putting them out of business temporarily in Da Nang.

Nor has the Phoenix controversy ended for Taylor. He has seen the fingerprints of the "old Phoenix boys" at the scene of a number of murders he has investigated, including those of American journalist Linda Frazier and Orlando Letelier. The "old Phoenix boys" Taylor referred to are a handful of Cuban contract agents the CIA hired after the Bay of Pigs fiasco to assassinate Fidel Castro. Some served in Vietnam in Phoenix, and a few operate as hired killers and drug dealers in Miami and Central America today. Taylor included the CIA case officers who manage these assassins in his definition of the "old Phoenix boys."

CHAPTER 26

Revisions

By 1971, as the war subsided and the emphasis shifted to police operations, it was finally understood, as General Clay had said in August 1969, "that the objective of neutralizations of the infrastructure is equal in priority to the objective of tactical operations."[1]

Brighter than ever, the spotlight shone on the Phoenix Directorate, which boasted in its 1970 End of Year Report: "The degree of success of the RVN counter-insurgency effort is directly related to the success in accomplishing this neutralization objective." Noting that "This *concept* [author's emphasis] will receive even more emphasis in 1971" and that "The Phung Hoang program has been given the highest priority in the GVN's pacification effort," the report says: "Full participation of all agencies will be maintained until VCI strength is greatly reduced; then it will be feasible to transfer complete responsibility for VCI neutralizations to the Special Police."[2]

Despite the optimism, there were problems. The pending cease-fire, aka the stab in the back, meant that just as the coup de grace was about to be delivered to the VCI, Washington politicians were preparing to grant it legal status, a development which would enable its agents, the directorate warned, "to increase their activity in controlled and contested areas and, with their anonymity, be free to proselytize, terrorize and propagandize in the GVN controlled rural and urban areas." Citing captured documents that revealed plans for Communist subversion after the truce, the directorate said, "It is imperative that the Phung Hoang or a similar anti-VCI effort be continued, particularly during an in-place ceasefire." Moreover, because the politicians were hastening to withdraw American troops, the directorate suggested "[c]areful and studied consideration . . . to ensure that the Phung Hoang Program is not adversely affected by the premature withdrawal of advisory personnel."[3]

Apart from the cease-fire and the drawdown, what the directorate feared most was the inability of the Vietnamese to manage the attack on the VCI. The pressure began to mount on December 3, 1970, when *The New York Times* quoted Robert Thompson as saying that captured documents indicated that hundreds of South Vietnamese policemen were Vietcong agents, that there were as many as thirty thousand Communist agents in the GVN, and that Phoenix was *not* doing the job and was itself infiltrated by Communists. Thompson's charge was substantiated when, in 1970, a CIA counterintelligence investigation revealed that Da Nang's PIC chief was a Communist double agent who had killed his captured comrades during the Tet offensive in order to maintain his cover.

As a result of these problems, it was suggested that further revisions in the Phoenix program be made. One of the first steps was to hire two private companies—Southeast Asia Computer Associates (managed by CIA officer Jim Smith) and the Computer Science Corporation (under CIA officer Joe Langbien)—to advise the two hundred-odd Vietnamese technicians who were scheduled to take over the MACV and CORDS computers. The Vietnamese were folded into Big Mack, and the Phung Hoang Management Information System (PHMIS) was joined with the National Police Criminal Information System, which tracked the VCI members from their identification through their capture, legal processing, detention, and (when it happened), release.

Personnel changes designed to strengthen National Police Command support of Phoenix began at the top with the promotion of Colonel Hai to brigadier general in September 1970.* Five months later twenty-five thousand ARVN officers and enlisted men and ten thousand RD Cadre were transferred to the National Police. Three policemen were sent to each village having at least five hundred residents, and in urban areas two cops were assigned for each thousand people. Field Police platoons were sent to the districts, and twenty-six hundred additional special policemen were hired into the force.[4]

As a way of addressing what General Clay called "the critical shortage

*In December 1970 Hai was reassigned as commander of the XXXXIV Corps Tactical Zone, and as Komer suggested, Major General Tran Thanh Phong became National Police chief.

of qualified Special Police case officers," the directorate focused greater attention on the case officer training courses and seminars at the regional Phung Hoang schools, emphasizing the use of target folders.

Regarding American personnel, Phoenix inspection teams were given the authority to remove unsatisfactory Vietnamese, and more than two hundred senior enlisted men scheduled to return to the United States as part of the drawdown were transferred instead to Phoenix as deputy DIOCC advisers, mostly in the Delta. Because these men could speak Vietnamese and were counterintelligence experts, Jack called this a windfall. These counterintelligence specialists maintained target folders, reviewed agent reports, PIC reports, and Chieu Hoi debriefings, and liaisoned among PICs, PIOCCs, and Chieu Hoi centers.

September 1970 also marked the creation of the Phoenix Career Program and the Military Assistance Security Advisory (MASA) course at Fort Bragg, climaxing a process begun in 1950, when the U.S. Army had established its Psywar Division at Fort Riley. Requirements for MASA training included an "outstanding" record and Vietnamese-language "ability and aptitude." Prior service in Vietnam was "desirable," and military intelligence officers were given top priority. Field-grade officers were promised entry into the Command and General Staff College. Other ranks were promised, among other things, preference of next assignment; civil schooling upon completion of the tour; an invitation to join the Army's Foreign Area Specialist program; and, while in Vietnam, five vacations and a special thirty-day leave, including a round-trip ticket anywhere in the free world.

"The only bad side to that," said Doug Dillard, "is that it didn't work. When I came from the War College to take over as chief of Military Intelligence Branch, we were getting a lot of complaints from the youngsters saying, 'You're not living up to your promise. I wanted to go to Fort Bragg and you're sending me to Fort Lewis.' It was part of the turmoil of the drawdown, that all these jobs were not going to exist when these kids started coming out of Vietnam. I immediately did everything I could to change that program and not make any commitment to those youngsters."[5]

In July 1970 the Phoenix Coordinators' Orientation Course was renamed the Phung Hoang Advisory School and moved from Seminary Camp to the Driftwood Service Club on the Vung Tau Air Base. Classes began in August and were taught by CIA instructors and a team of intelligence officers assigned to Lieutenant Colonel C. J. Fulford. As the National Police assumed greater responsibility for Phoenix, more Public Safety advisers began to receive Phung Hoang training and were folded into the program as PIC and Phoenix task force advisers.

Another development in 1970 was the proliferation of Phoenix task forces. For example, in September 1970 in Quang Tin Province, a Phoenix task force composed of 180 field policemen, 60 PRU, and 30 armed propagandists was organized and used as a private army by the Phoenix coordinator in Tam Ky. Called Hiep Dong, the force was broken down into platoons that operated independently and in combined operations with U.S. or ARVN forces. The Quang Tin province chief wrote Hiep Dong's operational orders, which were cosigned by the local U.S. and ARVN commanders. In one Hiep Dong operation, 24 Regional Force companies, 99 Popular Force platoons, and the entire 196th and 5th ARVN regiments were committed. Of the operation's 132 objectives, 116 were VCI targets, 99 of which were neutralized.

In addition, the Territorial Forces and People's Self-Defense Forces provided "intelligence and reconnaissance units" to the force. "In my hamlet," said a resident of Quang Tin Province quoted in *Hostages of War*, "the Phoenix men come at night and rap on our doors. They are dressed in the black pajamas of the Liberation soldiers and tell people they are with the Liberation army. But they are really the secret police. If the people welcome them with joy, these policemen kill them or take them away as Viet Cong. But if they are VC soldiers and we say anything good about the Saigon government, we are taken off as rice bearers or soldiers for the Front."[6]

All in all, 8,191 VCI were killed in 1970—more than any year before or after; 7,745 VCI rallied and 6,405 were jailed, for a total of 22,341 VCI neutralized, all class A and B. Approximately 40 percent of all VCI kills were credited to Territorial Forces. The Field Police were still "underemployed," according to the 1970 End of Year Report, and "Coordination of the PRU with the DIOCCs was somewhat less than ideal in some areas. The PRU, in some cases justifiably critical of the security in the DIOCCs and PIOCCs, generally did not contribute intelligence regularly to the DIOCC but instead reacted to intelligence they had gathered on their own." PRU matters, however, were not within the directorate's bailiwick but were "addressed by the advisory elements at the Saigon level."[7]

In *A Systems Analysis View of the Vietnam War*, Thomas Thayer reports that the PRU in 1970 were "per man . . . at least ten times as effective as any other anti-VCI action force."[8] He also writes: "The PRU are being incorporated into the Special Branch" and that "Hopefully [*sic*] they will serve as a nucleus around which an improved police force may be built."[9] However, in March 1972 William Grieves told General Abrams, "To date . . . not a single application has been received from a member of the PRU for enrollment in the National Police."[10]

Thayer is far more critical of Phoenix than the revisionist directorate. According to Thayer, "Results through April 1971 indicate that Phoenix is still a fragmented effort, lacking central direction, control and priority. Most neutralizations still involve low level, relatively unimportant workers gained as a side benefit from military operations. . . . Only 2% of all VCI neutralized were specifically targeted and killed by Phoenix forces, and there have been very few reports of such assassinations from the field." He faults the judicial system for being unable to "process the 2500 or so suspected VCI captured each month," and citing a "constant backlog" of detainees, he observes: "Significant numbers of alleged VCI wait 6 months before going to trial."[11]

Meanwhile, the issues of incentives and internal security were dominating Phoenix planning. Regarding internal security, General Frank Clay, the deputy director of the Joint Chiefs of Staff, blamed the CIA for the "critical shortage of qualified Special Police case officers."[12] Colby, meanwhile, in a December 12, 1970, presentation to Defense Secretary Melvin Laird (titled "Internal Security in South Vietnam—Phoenix"), complained about the "continuing predominance of military leadership in the program." Colby then made twenty-seven recommendations for "improving GVN internal security in general and Phung Hoang in particular." Chief among his recommendations were that an FBI officer be sent to Saigon and that an incentive program be implemented.

The request for FBI assistance was initially made by General Abrams in the summer of 1970 "for the specific purpose of providing recommendations for the neutralization of important national level members of the [VCI]."[13] It fell to Colby to get the ball rolling. He assigned Jack, the assistant for concepts and strategy on the Vietnam Task Force, as action officer on the matter. "People in Washington, D.C., wanted Colby's scalp," Jack explained. "Things weren't moving, Phoenix being one. What there was was tension between the CIA and the Pentagon. And so the FBI was called in."

On February 4, 1970, through General Fritz Kramer, Jack met with FBI Internal Security Division chief William C. Sullivan, who told him "that any request for FBI assistance would have to come from the White House as a directive signed by Kissinger." Sullivan said he would call Kissinger "on a quiet" basis and apprise him of the request. The problem, said Jack, was that "Senior people were very sensitive about the FBI screwing around in the embassy" and that AID Assistant Director Robert Nooter thought that the task being assigned to the FBI was a police function rightly belonging to AID.

To clear the way for the FBI, Colby back-channeled instructions to his friend and CIA colleague Byron Engel, the chief of Public Safety. Engel passed those instructions along to his Vietnam desk officer, John Manopoli. When Jack met with Manopoli on February 8, the latter said that AID had changed its mind and had no objections to the FBI visit. That day Jack drafted a "talking paper" for General Karhohs, which the Vietnam Task Force chief used to brief Defense Secretary Laird the next day. Jack called Sullivan "to clear the action," and on February 12 Warren Nutter signed the necessary letter of transmittal, which Laird sent to the White House for approval. On February 23, FBI Director J. Edgar Hoover received the directive, signed by National Security Adviser Henry Kissinger.

On March 30 Jack received a copy of a White House memo directing the FBI to send two people TDY to Vietnam. Hoover approved it and sent Harold Child, the FBI's legal adviser at the Tokyo Embassy, to Saigon for four or five days on a "diagnostic" basis, to see if an investigation was warranted. "It was a perfunctory execution of a White House directive." Jack chuckled. "There was not enough time to do a thorough review."

Harold Child writes:

> Early one morning I received a telephone call from FBI Director J. Edgar Hoover. [He] wanted me to go immediately to Saigon to talk with all the people concerned to help him reach a conclusion as to whether there was anything that the FBI could constructively do in South Vietnam. . . . John Mason turned out to be the individual in Saigon who was designated to assist me in my contacts and provide information and background that I required.
>
> Until I landed in Saigon, I had no idea whatever as to what the Phoenix program was. In fact, even after the first two or three days, what they were doing and what they had accomplished were very confusing to me. Upon return to Tokyo, I furnished a detailed report to Mr. Hoover . . . [and] my recommendations were in summary: 1) No information had been presented to me to demonstrate that operations of the Phoenix Program had any direct relation to FBI internal security responsibilities; 2) There was much confusion and inconsistency inherent in the program, which had developed over a considerable period of time, making it impractical for the FBI to come in at this late stage; and 3) I recommended against the FBI becoming involved in insurgency problems or other local problems in Vietnam.[14]

John Mason's military deputy, Colonel Chester McCoid, has a different recollection. According to McCoid, in an interview with the author, Child was there to obtain information on Vietnamese supporters of American antiwar groups; the FBI wanted current intelligence, but the CIA would not share what it had. Mason presented "the CIA's perspective, not the CORDS perspective," McCoid claimed.[15] Citing the separate charters of the CIA and FBI, "Mason lectured Child on cognizance, arguing that overseas intelligence is the CIA's job.

"Phoenix was a creature of the embassy," McCoid said. "The footwork was done by uniforms, but the tone was set by the CIA—by Ted Shackley and John Mason."*

Colby denied any shenanigans. "I just wanted FBI ideas on how to improve Phoenix," he said to me.[18] Yet while seeming to advance the process, Colby actually blunted it. On April 30, 1971, Hoover reported to Colby that FBI services were not required in Saigon. Jack terminated the action on May 24. "Colby sent a letter killing it," he said. Instead of the FBI's advising the directorate, the Internal Security Bureau of the National Police was expanded from forty to six hundred personnel.

For a view of Phoenix in the field, we turn to a December 1970 report by the III Corps DEPCORDS, Richard Funkhouser. At the time, according to Funkhouser, the VCI were lying low, concentrating on recruiting new cadres, penetrating the GVN, and bumping off the occasional GVN official. The III Corps commander, General Do Cao Tri, had approved "a combined U.S.-GVN Phung Hoang Task Force" to inspect IOCCs and "get the horses galloping in the same direction." General Tri (who was killed when his helicopter was shot down on February 23, 1971) had approved the task force as part of a "crash VCI program" that "Thieu kicked off . . . himself at a special secret meeting at Vung Tau on 31 October."[19]

Funkhouser reported that PIOCCs were being integrated into police operation centers, that the VCI was stronger in urban than rural areas, and that "the leadership of the police traces itself back to the Ministry of Interior which reportedly makes assignments after the proper payoff is made." He deemed quotas "redundant, difficult to attain and in fact not susceptible to accurate measurement," the problem being that neutralization figures were inflated to meet goals. He said that most Vietnamese police officers were too busy to devote time to Phoenix but that targeting of the VCI had improved with the assignment of senior noncommissioned officers as deputy DIOCC advisers in thirty-five of III Corps's fifty-three districts. "Coordination with PICs ranges from good to fair," he reported, "but advisors often conducted supplementary interrogations." To be successful, Funkhouser noted, anti-VCI operations required "the sensitive and instant use of informers and total secrecy."

"We stayed on our own side of the fence," said the III Corps senior Public Safety adviser Walt Burmester. "And the Vietnamese felt the same

*Few members of the directorate held Mason in high esteem. Walter Kolon described him as "duplistic in all of his dealings. He would be honey smooth to a man's face, then vitriolic as soon as he left the room."[16] James Hunt said, "I was never quite sure if he was being clever or straightforward."[17] Everyone agrees that his loyalty was to Ted Shackley and the CIA station.

way. . . . People didn't come to the police for help, because the only places attacked by the VC were government installations." Burmester added that the National Police merely supplied Phoenix with equipment and that Phoenix itself acted more as a resource center than an action agency.[20]

In fact, the attack against the VCI in the early 1970's was carried out primarily by the CIA through the PRU. As reported by Funkhouser, "The increase in PRU effectiveness throughout the region has been spectacular, and is due primarily to the strong leadership of the Region PRU commander and his U.S. adviser." That PRU adviser was Rudy Enders.

In 1965, with only nine cadres (one of whom was PVT), Rudy Enders had formed III Corps's original counterterror team in Tan Uyen. In 1970 he returned to Bien Hoa, at Ted Shackley's request, to manage the region's paramilitary forces. "Our main job was to keep rockets from raining on Saigon," Enders said to me, although he also managed the attack on the VCI.[21] However, he added, "There were simply too many party committee structures. To unscramble this, we centralized in Bien Hoa. We got access to high-level guys in the Chieu Hoi center, the PIC, or the hospital—anyone we could get our hands on. We'd take him around, watch him for two weeks, and try to win him over.

"Sam Adams was making a case that the commander of VC military subsection twenty-two, Tu Thanh, had recruited four hundred fifty penetrations in Hau Nghia," Enders said, then told how he proved Adams wrong. The process began when "Our Long An officer and a defector from COSVN were going past the market one day." Quite by accident, the defector spotted Tu Thanh's secretary. She was grabbed and taken to the embassy house, where, during interrogation, it was learned that she was in love with Tu Thanh's son and that Tu Thanh's family had established legal residence under aliases in Hau Nghia after the Cambodian invasion. However, because Tu Thanh had forbidden his son to see his secretary, the woman decided to defect. Blessed with a photographic memory and eager to exact revenge, she supplied the CIA with Tu Thanh's identification number, along with the real names and addresses of another two hundred VCI in Tu Thanh's network.

Having managed the Vietnam desk in 1962 and 1963, III Corps CIA region officer in charge Donald Gregg understood the importance of the secretary's information. He immediately focused everyone in the region on Tu Thanh's network, which was diagrammed on a wall map to show where his deputies and family members lived. Enders and Gregg then dispatched Special Branch surveillance teams to take pictures of the suspects; meanwhile, they tried to place a penetration agent inside the apparatus.

"We tried to recruit a district cadre from Hau Nghia," Enders recalled. "Tu Thanh's secretary knew he had a girl friend, so we got her to narrate on a tape cassette a plea for him to work with us. The girl friend brought the tape to the cemetery where her mother was buried, and they exchanged it there. Next we sent a three-man PRU team from Hau Nghia to make a pitch, to get the guy to defect. But they came back empty-handed. Then we got wind that the next night the VC had come in for the tape recorder, so we ran a counterintelligence operation on the PRU and found out that the PRU commander was a VC penetration agent. So we changed commanders; Mr. Nha became the PRU commander."

It was as a result of this failure that Gregg gave up on penetrations. "Shackley was interested in penetrations," he recalled, "and the vehicle for doing that was the Special Branch working closely with PIC advisers." Gregg added emphatically, "This is not Phoenix." As for the nature of Phoenix operations in III Corps, he said, "The PIOCCs and DIOCCs had a guy asleep at the desk."[22]

As Gregg explained it, "Because Three Corps had hard-core VC units in heavily mined areas, I decided I couldn't penetrate. So I wound up trying to take apart the remaining elements of the VCI by putting together a chart of it from ralliers, prisoners, et cetera. I told ARVN I'd take all the POWs they couldn't handle. We'd get battered people and treat them well. In return we'd get information on caches, supply dumps, river crossings, et cetera. We'd get them to point out the location on the map. Then Felix Rodriguez would take them up in a light observation helicopter to point out the hiding places on the ground. A PRU team would follow with the First Air Cav and [Phoenix Region Coordinator] Johnny Johnson. Felix would locate the bunker by drawing fire; then he'd mark it with smoke. The First Air Cav would provide two or three Hueys for fire support and two more with the PRU. Then they'd go in." When bigger operations were mounted, the First Air Cavalry provided troops.

"So we went after Tu Thanh during Tet of 1971," Rudy Enders went on. "We missed him by a step but found his hiding place and brought twenty-three people hiding there to the PIC. The PIC chief in Region Three, Colonel Sinh, did the interrogations. We brought guys in from Con Son to flesh out the reports, and we had guys analyzing reports, marking photographs, putting the pictures together on the wall, and then photographing that. As a result, we learned the names of ninety-six people in the organization, only two of whom had access to ARVN or the police. One was the province chief's valet; the other was in the Hau Nghia police. But instead of four hundred fifty, like Adams said, it was only two.

"In the process of going after this organization," Enders continued, "we got all of [III Corps Commander] General Hollingsworth's assets, and together we took photos of the houses where they lived . . . then took the photos back to the helicopter where we had the twenty-three people plus the woman from Long An. The twenty-three people were hooded, and they circled the faces of the VCI. Felix Rodriguez was the guy doing this. Felix also got the choppers from Hollingsworth."

Like Gregg, Enders claimed this was not a Phoenix operation. "Phoenix was just a record-keeping thing," Enders said. "No organization is going to share intelligence because you didn't know who was a double." In other words, by 1971 the CIA was carrying the attack against the VCI, while Phoenix was merely keeping score.

Phoenix as defined in official reporting also differed from Phoenix in fact. While the directorate was promoting Phung Hoang as a Vietnamese program, the commander in chief, Pacific, was saying, "The GVN has not been able to secure the cooperation of officials at hamlet, village and district level that is required for a successful Phung Hoang-Phoenix program."[23] Likewise, Pacification Attitude Analysis System results revealed that Phoenix was penetrated by the VCI and that most Vietnamese considered Phoenix a U.S. program, preferred a modus vivendi, and had "a grudging admiration for the VCI struggle."[24]

"I reported to this guy in the station, who I only knew by the name George," Ed Brady said to me. "I told him, 'Your flow of information is through guys like Joe Sartiano and Dave West. But what does Minh Van Dang tell Dave West?' I said, 'They know he's there for you; they tell him what you want to hear. How would you like something in context? Something that wasn't told to an American official?' And I had a good record of doing that, so I was reassigned to become special assistant to the director, John Mason."

Unfortunately, Brady's reports did not show success and were roundly ignored. As he explained it, "I had a view that was different from the official reports. But this put the CIA in the position of having to decide, Is he right or not? Sometimes they'd go with me, but more often not. They frequently didn't want to use material I generated—they didn't want to report it to Washington—because it made them look bad."

For another inside view of Phoenix in 1971, we turn to Colonel Chester McCoid, who in February 1971 replaced Colonel James Newman as deputy to John Mason. A veteran of four years and ten separate assignments in Vietnam, McCoid chronicled the program's major developments in letters to his wife, Dorothy. On February 18 he writes:

> Yesterday afternoon . . . with two other Americans . . . from the Saigon City Advisory Group, I drove first to 6th Police Precinct Office and then on to the 7th. Our purpose was to inspect the work in progress to eliminate the enemy agents and shadow government apparatus in these critical areas.

> The net result was an acute sense of distress! This was due directly to the inadequate job the American advisers were doing in both precincts. Here, in a situation where the enemy are hardcore old timers, we are employing callow young lieutenants to give advice to Vietnamese National Policemen who have been on the job for as many as 17 years. Naturally our people are far over their heads and find that they are rarely listened to by those whom, in theory, they are to give operational assistance. One of the officers, a captain, knows what should be done. He is familiar with his duties and does know a great deal about the precinct—population, size, state of the economy, ethnic breakdown, enemy strength, recent VC activity, who their supporters are, the true identity of the VC leaders, etc. His only difficulty is that he hasn't won the confidence of the National Police chief yet.
>
> In the 7th Precinct the situation is so unsatisfactory that it is sickening. There a lazy young punk is absolutely without any influence and, unless there is a dramatic improvment in his efforts, there is little hope there ever will be. This member of the "Pepsi Generation" knows almost nothing of the area for which he is supposedly accountable. In response to questions relating to the enemy . . . he had no answers. He complained that the Chief of the Special Police would spend no time with him, and that he, our lieutenant, was never approached for advice. Small wonder.
>
> What are our advisory personnel like? Well, they range from being as useless as the clod in the 7th Precinct to some who have spent years in the Counter-Intelligence Corps. Most of these are majors or chief warrant officers; they know their trade and they manage to establish effective relationships with the National Police and Province S2s early on. Our best people aren't in Saigon because the need is greater out in the remote border areas where the Vietnamese dump their duds. They naturally concentrate their most competent searchers for the VCI here in the nation's capital; after all, they don't want to have the Prime Minister or the President unhappy with the program.

In an April 2 letter, McCoid discusses the Thu Duc training center, where two thousand ARVN officers were to be sent for Phoenix training in preparation for assignment as village police chiefs:

> The frustrations of working with some of these little bastards are formidable. They absolutely cannot do anything requiring any in-

> itiative—or perhaps the term should be "will not." The school is for their case officers, yet they rely almost exclusively on the efforts of one of our personnel to draw up the program of instruction, the lesson plans, and the schedules. The course is to commence on the 19th and they've invited the Prime Minister to attend the opening ceremony; yet the building needs repairs and there is little or nothing available in the way of furnishings. There are only four of the required 10 instructors and few of the other personnel on hand—and no steps are being taken to correct the situation. By this time, if they were Westerners, they would be in a state of emotional collapse; but the Vietnamese face the situation with perfect equanimity—in fact, Monday the 5th is a holiday and they all are taking the day off. What are they waiting for? Well, American funding for one thing. They know that we will eventually come through with about seven million piasters ($25,000) and they see no reason to get excited until our money starts to flow.

In an April 14 letter McCoid announces the transfer of power on April 25 from John Mason to the third and final Phoenix director, John Tilton.* A graduate of George Washington University, Tilton had served most of his career in Central and South America, where he served as operations officer in two countries. He also served as chief of station in two other Latin American countries, including Bolivia, where he mounted the successful manhunt and capture of Che Guevara. Colonel Paul Coughlin, chief of operations at the Phoenix Directorate throughout 1971, claimed that a photo taken of Che's spread-eagled corpse—which was leaked to the press and depicted the revolutionary as a crucified Christ figure—was the reason why Tilton was exiled from his area of expertise to Southeast Asia.[25] Tall and thin, gaunt and gangly, Tilton, according to McCoid, was like Mason insofar as they both held Ted Shackley "in awe."†

Tilton served as Phoenix director from May 1971 till August 1973. From August 1972 till August 1973, he also served as deputy chief of station and senior adviser to the Special Branch in Vietnam. Under Tilton, Phoenix was reunited with its foster parent, the Special Branch.

*When I interviewed Tilton in 1986, he was forthcoming and helpful. After I presented him with a magazine article that was critical of Phoenix (and which had been mailed to me by Nelson Brickham), Tilton asked not to be quoted.

†In 1971 George French replaced Bob Dunwoodie as CIA liaison to SOG, Bob Wall was back as senior adviser to the Special Branch, and Tully Acampora had returned as adviser to Tran Si Tan, chief of the metropolitan police and, according to Acampora, "to Thieu what Loan had been to Ky."[26]

Tilton considered himself a hands-on manager who worked closely with his region and province officers on operational matters. He inspected DIOCCs, evaluated the military officers posted to the directorate, attended Central Phung Hoang Committee meetings, and occasionally visited the Phung Hoang Office. In return, the Phung Hoang chief, Colonel Ly Trong Song, was frequently in Tilton's office and house. Song, Tilton noted, was replaced by Colonel Nguyen Van Giau.

Tilton defined Phoenix as basically committees and cited this as one of the program's faults—because committees are okay in setting broad policy, but a single agency in charge of the program would have been more effective. His other gripes were that Americans were trying to organize a country that wasn't a country, that Phoenix advisers were too dependent on their interpreters, and that most informants were working for both sides. Tilton described Phoenix as a Special Forces program run out of Fort Bragg, and he tried hard to conceal the role of his parent agency. Prior to an interview with reporter Michael Parks, Tilton told McCoid not to reveal that Tilton was with the CIA. "He was very cherry about that," McCoid noted.

On May 30, 1971, on orders from President Thieu, Colonel Ly Trong Song assumed command of the Phung Hoang bloc, and the program began going downhill. Always late, often not appearing at work at all, Song busied himself picking up order blanks for Sears or Montgomery Ward, snatching pens and pencils from people's desks, and asking Colonel McCoid to buy him booze at the PX. A political appointee, Song had the job of preventing Phung Hoang personnel from disrupting Thieu's influence in the provinces.

Morale problems began to affect the directorate. In a June 2 letter McCoid writes that more and more Phoenix advisers were requesting early releases, which were being granted as a means of scaling down U.S. involvement. Otherwise, CORDS was not filling vacancies. McCoid mentions how one captain assigned to the directorate asked for release after five weeks and how most of the others were badly disaffected. McCoid notes that more and more enlisted men were turning to drugs and that more and more NCOs were finding solace in the bottle. "Our strength here in the Directorate is scheduled to fall steadily while our work load sky-rockets," he says, adding that he spent one third of his time responding to flag notes from William Colby, whom he called "a monumental figure."

In a July 3 letter, McCoid notes that Colby had gone home to testify once again before Congress about Phoenix. Colby was to remain in Washington as executive director-comptroller of the CIA until his appointment as director in August 1973. Colby's job at CORDS was taken over by George Jacobson, and CORDS, too, began its descent into oblivion. "Our supply and funding officer," McCoid once wrote, "theorizes that only the Americans feel strongly about the necessity of rounding up the political cadre of the VC." Indeed, with the ineluctable withdrawal of American "advisers," Vietnamese determination steadily deteriorated, and the war effort staggered to its dishonorable conclusion.

CHAPTER 27

Legalities

In his aptly titled master's thesis for American University, Ralph Johnson poses the question: "The Phoenix Program: Planned Assassination or Legitimate Conflict Management?"[1]

The answer is that Phoenix was both. Insofar as the rifle shot concept was the essence of the attack against the VCI, Phoenix was "planned assassination." At the same time, in the sense that the key to the Vietnam War was the political control of people, Phoenix was also conflict management. The question is if, under the aegis of conflict management, everything from ambush and assassination to extortion, massacre, tiger cages, terror, and torture was legitimate and justifiable? Indeed, by 1971 the legality of Phoenix was being questioned not just by antiwar activists but by the House Subcommittee on Foreign Operations and Government Information, cochaired by William Moorehead and Ogden Reid.

As usual, it was a whistle-blower who provided Congress with its ammunition. In late 1970 Bart Osborn approached an aide on Congressman Moorehead's staff with a copy of the training manual he had been issued at Fort Holabird. Said the aide, William Phillips: "It showed that Phoenix policy was not something manufactured out in field but was sanctioned by the U.S. government. This was the issue: that it is policy. So we requested, through the Army's congressional liaison officer, a copy of the Holabird training manual, and they sent us a sanitized copy. They had renumbered the pages."[2]

This stab at disguising policy prompted Congressman Pete McCloskey to visit the Phoenix Directorate in April 1971, in preparation for hearings on Phoenix to be held that summer. His visit was recalled by Phoenix training chief James Hunt: "Colby was out of town, Jake [George Jacobson] was in charge, and Mason was there. And just as I was getting up to go to the platform to give my briefing, Mason whispered into my ear, 'We gotta talk to them, but the less we say, the better.' Well, the first question McCloskey asked was if anyone in the program worked for the CIA. And Mason denied it. He denied any CIA involvement. Jake, too."

Hunt recalled that McCloskey, Mason, and Jacobson immediately went into executive session. He did not know what happened there. But it bothered him that Mason "blatantly lied." Hunt added parenthetically, "Phoenix had been under the CIA; then MACV supposedly took it over. But we didn't really understand it, and that bothered us. There was always a suspicion. My impression was that John Mason worked for Colby through Jake, but he also had a close relationship with the chief of station—a professional relationship, back-channeling messages."

Also bothered by the lies, McCloskey returned to Washington and charged that planned assassinations under Phoenix denied due process and that Phoenix "violated several treaties and laws."[3] The legal basis for McCloskey's charge was Article 3 of the Geneva Conventions, which prohibits "the passing of sentences and the carrying out of executions without previous judgment pronounced by a regularly constituted court, affording all the judicial guarantees which are recognized as indispensable by civilized peoples." It also prohibits mutilation, cruel treatment, and torture.

Having agreed to the conventions, the United States government was well aware of the substance of Article 3. The problem was a letter written on December 7, 1970, by Imer Rimestead, the American ambassador to the International Committee of the Red Cross (ICRC). In his letter Rimestead says, "With respect to South Vietnamese civilians captured by U.S. forces and transferred by them to the authorities of the RVN, the U.S. Government recognizes that it has a *residual responsibility* to work with the GVN to see that all such civilians are treated in accordance with the requirements of Article 3 of the Conventions."

To the consternation of the war managers, Rimestead's letter meant that the U.S. government could no longer dismiss the problem of civilian detainees—corralled in droves by the Phoenix dragnet—as an internal matter of the GVN. Rimestead reasoned that the U.S. government, by funding Phoenix and the GVN Directorate of Corrections, automatically assumed "residual responsibility." And the truth of the matter was, without U.S. aid there never would have been a Phung Hoang bloc or Directorate of Corrections.

In response to Rimestead's letter, which implied that U.S. war managers were war criminals, the Vietnam Task Force began coordinating with State Department and Pentagon lawyers in an attempt to prove that Phoenix did not violate Article 3. At the same time, the CORDS Research and Analysis staff and the U.S. Embassy in Saigon began a review of Phoenix procedures, and William Colby marched off to face his critics in Washington. However, as was so often the case, when Colby and the Phoenix controversy landed in America, a larger event grabbed the headlines. On June 13, 1971, *The New York Times* began printing lengthy excerpts from the *Pentagon Papers*—a painstakingly edited stack of documents that, even by name, deflected attention away from the CIA and Phoenix. Consequently, little public attention was paid when the *Times*, on July 15, 1971, reported: "Previously classified information read into the record of a House Government Operations subcommittee today disclosed that 26,843 non-military Vietcong insurgents and sympathizers were neutralized in 14 months through Operation Phoenix."

So it was again, four days later, when, in regard to those 26,843 non-military insurgents, Congressman Reid asked William Colby, "Are you certain that we know a member of the VCI from a loyal member of the South Vietnamese citizenry?"[4] Colby replied no but assured Congress and the American public that Phoenix did abide by the Geneva Conventions.

Read into the hearing transcript on July 19 was a memo titled "The Geneva Convention and the Phoenix Program." Prepared by the Vietnam Task Force, it argued that the Geneva Conventions afforded no protection to civilian detainees because "nationals of a co-belligerent state are not protected persons while the state of which they are nationals has diplomatic representation in the state in whose hands they are." It asserted that Article 3 "applies only to sentencing for crimes and does not prohibit a state from interning civilians or subjecting them to emergency detention when such measures are necessary for the security or safety of the state." Skirting the issue of executions carried out "without previous judgment pronounced by a regularly constituted court," it asserted that because An Tri [administrative detention] procedures involved "no criminal sentence," they were "not violative of Article 3."

In other words, the United States had the right to intern Vietnamese civilians because they, unlike soldiers, were not "protected persons" under the Geneva Conventions. Likewise, the GVN could place citizens in emergency detention to ensure its internal security, without violating the Geneva Conventions, as long as those citizens were not sentenced but merely detained.

Regarding due process, Congressman Reid asked Colby if civilian detainees had a right to counsel. Colby replied no.

Noting that there were often cases of mistaken identity, Reid asked, "How can you possibly put that together with a quota for sentencing?"

Responded Colby: "There is additional pressure in the assignment of public prosecutors to the Province Security Committee."[5]

But, Congressman Pete McCloskey asked Colby, "The administrative detention applies to those against whom there is insufficient evidence to convict, isn't that right?"

Colby agreed.

So McCloskey inquired, "If Article 3 . . . requires a trial by court, how are we working with the GVN to see that these civilians are receiving the proper attention under the Geneva Convention?"

Referring to the various reforms and revisions, Colby answered, "We are trying to put in the standards of due process . . . and we have achieved a number of them."[6]

But, McCloskey blurted, "the defendant informed against, or identified, has no right to appear in his own defense, no right to counsel, no right to confront his accusers, no right to see his dossier; is that correct?"[7]

"That is correct," Colby said, producing statistics to show that only hard-core Communist offenders generally had their sentences extended indefinitely by the Central Security Committee, while many category Cs were released.[8]

"That brings me to the real problem with the Phoenix program that I saw while I was there," McCloskey countered. "If the evidence is insufficient to convict a man, and also insufficient to show a reasonable probability that he may be a threat to security, then he may still be sent to the PIC."[9]

Regarding verification, Ogden Reid asked Colby: "Do you state categorically that Phoenix has never perpetrated the premeditated killing of a civilian in a noncombat situation?"

Colby, differentiating between concept and organization, replied: "Phoenix as a program has never done that. Individual members of it . . . may have done it. But as a program it is not designed to do that."[10]

Regarding Americans involved in Phoenix, Reid asked Colby, "Do they perform any actual arrests or killings, or do they merely select the individuals who are to be placed on the list who are subject to killing or capturing and subsequent sentencing?"

Colby replied, "They certainly do not arrest, because they have no right to arrest." But, he added, "American units may capture people in the course of a raid on a district VC headquarters base," and "Occasionally a police advisor may go out with a police unit to capture somebody [but] he would not be the man who reached out and grabbed the fellow."[11]

Reid said, "I have here a list [signed by the CIA's Special Branch adviser in Binh Dinh Province] . . . of VC cadre rounded up . . . after that area was secured by Operation Pershing in February 1967. It is of some interest that on this list, 33 of the 61 names were women and some persons were as young as 11 and 12."[12]

Colby: I think that is an example of exactly the situation that this program is designed to eliminate."[13] He then submitted written responses to questions on every aspect of Phoenix, from PICs to PRU and refugees, explaining why conflict management in wartime required the suspension of habeas corpus and due process.

On August 3, 1971, Congressman Reid, referring specifically to Phoenix, offered an amendment to the Foreign Assistance Act which would have barred assistance to any nation or program that employed assassination or torture. In offering the amendment, Reid expressed his feeling that some activities of Phoenix were "violative at the time they took place of the Geneva Conventions." Said Reid: "At least as shocking as the assassinations, torture, and drumhead incarcerations of civilians under the Phoenix program is the fact that in many cases the intelligence is so bad that innocent people are made victims." In making his case, Reid observed that Colby had replied no when asked, "Are you certain we know a member of the VCI from a loyal member of the South Vietnamese citizenry?" Reid asked rhetorically, "Who knows how many innocent people have been assassinated or tortured in the name of the Phoenix program?"[14]

In any event, congressional hearings are not trials, and William Colby was not charged with wrongdoing. But neither was he believed, for whereas the Senate hearings of 1970 had allowed him to define Phoenix in terms that supported his ideological preconceptions, the House allowed people to refute Colby by citing for the record specific instances of abuse.

For example, despite Colby's claim that standards of due process were being put in place, CORDS official Ted Jacqueney testified that "arrest without warrant or reason" was a major complaint of the people of Da Nang. "I have personally witnessed poor urban people literally quaking with fear when I questioned them about the activity of the secret police in the past election campaign. One poor fisherman in Danang, animated and talkative in complaining about economic conditions, clammed up in near terror when queried about the police, responding that 'he must think about his family.' After many personal interviews in Vietnam on this subject, I came to the conclusion that no single entity, including the feared and hated Vietcong, is more feared and hated than the South Vietnamese secret police."[15]

Jacqueney said, "In every province in Vietnam there is a Province Interrogation Center—a PIC—with a reputation for using torture to interrogate people accused of Vietcong affiliations. These PICs have a CIA counterpart relationship with the AID police advisor. Not in all cases however. Last year the senior AID police advisor of Danang City Advisory Group told me he refused, after one visit, to ever set foot in a PIC again, because 'war crimes are going on in there.' . . . Another friend, himself a Phoenix advisor, was ultimately removed from his position when he refused to compile information on individuals who would, he felt, inevitably be 'targeted' however weak the evidence might be."[16]

Referring to Colby's testimony about Americans' not being the ones "who reached out and grabbed the fellow," Jacqueney said, "I know of Americans that have actually battered down the door—so help me—in going after people."[17]

Also contradicting Colby was Michael Uhl, who served in Vietnam in 1968 with the Eleventh Brigade's First Military Intelligence Team (MIT). As a first lieutenant Uhl administered the team and supervised its counterintelligence section. He said, "Ambassador Colby gave the impression that Phoenix targetted specific high level VCI whose identity had been established by at least three unrelated intelligence sources. . . . Colby thus would have us believe that the vast majority of these people were targetted according to the rules that he outlined." But, Uhl added, "It was my experience that the majority of people classified as VC were 'captured' as a result of sweeping tactical operations. In effect, a huge dragnet was cast out in our area of operations and whatever looked good in the catch, regardless of evidence, was classified as VCI."[18]

Uhl testified that he was told by a superior officer "that the only justification for MI people to be on a patrol was for the hunting down of VCI. From that point on, any 'body count' resulting from an MI patrol were automatically listed as VCI. To my knowledge," said Uhl, "all those killed by the 1st MIT on such patrols, were classified as VCI only after their deaths. There was never any evidence to justify such a classification. . . . Not only was there no due process . . . but fully all the detainees were brutalized and many were literally tortured." He added that "All CDs [civilian detainees] . . . were listed as VCI" and that even though Colby denied that Americans actually exercised power of arrest over Vietnamese civilians, "In Duc Pho, where the 11th Brigade base camp was located, we could arrest and detain at will any Vietnamese civilian we desired, without so much as a whisper of coordination with ARVN or GVN authorities."[19]

As for the accuracy of information from "paid sources who could easily have been either provocateurs or opportunists with a score to settle," Uhl said, "The unverified and in fact unverifiable information, nevertheless was used regularly as input to artillery strikes, harassment and interdiction fire, B-52s and other air strikes, often on populated areas."[20]

Bart Osborn agreed: "I had no way . . . of establishing the basis of which my agents reported to me suspected VCI. . . . There was no cross-check; there was no investigation; there was no second opinion. There was no verification and there was no discrimination." Osborn added, "I never knew of an individual to be detained as a VC suspect who ever lived through an interrogation in a year and a half, and that included quite a number of individuals."[21]

"They all died?" Congressman Reid asked increduously.

"They all died," Osborn replied. "There was never any reasonable establishment of the fact that any one of those individuals was, in fact, cooperating with the VC, but they all died and the majority were either tortured to death or things like thrown out of helicopters."

At the end of the hearings Representatives McCloskey, John Conyers, Ben Rosenthal, and Bella Abzug stated their belief that "The people of these United States . . . have deliberately imposed on the Vietnamese people a system of justice which admittedly denies due process of law. . . . In so doing, we appear to have violated the 1949 Geneva Convention for the protection of civilian peoples at the same time we are exerting every effort available to us to solicit the North Vietnamese to provide Geneva Convention protections to our own prisoners of war.

"Some of us who have visited Vietnam," they added, "share a real fear that the Phoenix program is an instrument of terror; that torture is a regularly accepted part of interrogation . . . and that the top U.S. officials responsible for the program at best have a lack of understanding of its abuses." They concluded "that U.S. civilian and military personnel have participated for over three years in the deliberate denial of due process of law to thousands of people held in secret interrogation centers built with U.S. dollars," and they suggested that "Congress owes a duty to act swiftly and decisively to see that the practices involved are terminated forthwith."[22]

Was William Colby really unaware? When Congressman Reid asked if any Phoenix advisers had "resigned on the grounds that they could not morally be satisfied that they were identifying the right individuals," Colby said he could not recall any who had resigned "for that reason."[23] Yet, considering his close contact with George Jacobson, John Tilton, John Vann, and Wilbur Wilson, is it likely that Colby was unaware of the case of Sid Towle, who on August 1, 1971 (while the hearings were in progress) requested release from Phoenix for exactly that reason?

A graduate of Yale University, Lieutenant Sid Towle in June 1969 was assigned to the 116th MIG in Washington, D.C. As chief of a counterintelligence team Towle assigned and reviewed cases (including an investigation into Ed Murphy's antiwar activities) and conducted offensive counterintelligence operations in the nation's capital. One task was disrupting antiwar demonstrations by building bonfires and inciting people to riot, so the capital police could be called in to bash heads. During this period Towle was rated by his commander as "one of the most dedicated, professionally competent and outstanding junior officers I have had the privilege to serve with anywhere."[24]

But Sid Towle did not want to go to Vietnam, and upon receiving orders to head overseas in January 1971, he requested release from active duty, citing in his application his "complete abhorrence for the Vietnam War and the continued U.S. presence there." Towle filed for release under Army Regulation 635-100; but his request was denied, and his counterintelligence credentials were withdrawn. Towle was sent to Vietnam in March 1971 as the Phung Hoang coordinator in Vung Liem district in Vinh Long Province.

During his stint as a Phoenix adviser, Towle spent most of his time "sifting through the DIOCC's target folders looking for aliases."[25] A sergeant assigned to the DIOCC managed funds obtained from the CIA for informers and PRU and acted as liaison with the Vinh Long PIC and PIOCC. Towle lived in a villa with five or six other people in the CORDS district team. Behind the villa were the PRU quarters. Said Towle: "We turned up the radio when we heard the screams of the people being interrogated. . . . I didn't know what the PRU were doing ninety percent of the time," he explained. "They were directed by province."

To clear operations against the VCI, Towle had to get permission from the province officer in charge, Tom Ahearne. Regarding operations, Towle said, "I went after an average of eight to ten VCI per week. The Special Branch people next door . . . would come up with the names, which I would check. Then the PRU went out. They went out every night and always killed one or two people. But verifying whether or not they were VCI was impossible. They would tell you who they had killed, and it was always a name on the list, but how could I know? We had charts on the wall, and we'd cross off the name, and that was it."

In effect, Towle was keeping score—until the day the district chief took him for a ride in a helicopter. As they were flying over a village, they spotted an old man and a girl walking hand in hand down the main street. The district chief said to the door gunner, "Kill them."

The gunner asked Towle, "Should I?"

Towle said no.

"That was the beginning of the end," he reported. "Ahearne called me on the carpet. He told me the province chief was angry because I had caused the district chief to lose face."

There were other reasons why Towle did not enjoy working in Phoenix. According to Towle, Ahearne (who was taken hostage while serving as CIA station chief in Teheran in 1979) and the province senior adviser, Colonel

D. Duncan Joy, initiated a bounty program in the province, in which cash prizes were offered to the Vietnamese as an incentive. Ahearne and Joy even arranged a contest between the Phoenix advisers to see who could rack up the biggest body count. Disgusted, the advisers got together and decided not to participate.

That was in June 1971. A few days later John Vann arrived in his private helicopter. "He flew right into the DIOCC," Towle recalled. "He was very critical. He asked where the bodies and weapons were, then sent me into a funeral in progress. He had me open the casket to identify the body. I hated Vann," Towle said. "He was really into body counts."

On another occasion, while Towle was eating his dinner in the CORDS villa, the district chief stormed into the room with the PRU team and dumped a dirty bag on the table. Eleven bloody ears spilled out. The district chief told Towle to give the ears to Joy as proof of six VCI neutralized. "It made me sick," Towle said. "I couldn't go on with the meal.

"After the ear thing," Towle explained, "I went to Vinh Long and joined up with the air rescue team on one of its missions. I was promoted to captain while I was there and received a message from the district senior adviser saying, 'Don't come back.' So I went to see a friend in the judge advocate general's office in Can Tho, and he reported the incident to General Cushman. The general went down in a chopper and handed Joy a letter of reprimand. After that I knew I could never go back, so I had one of my friends in Vung Liem bring my bags up to Can Tho."

Captain Sid Towle was officially removed as the Vung Liem Phoenix coordinator on July 20, 1971. While awaiting reassignment, he worked at the Combined Document Exploitation Center, reading reports on NVA infiltration along the Ho Chi Minh Trail and giving briefings to senior MACV officers. Then, on August 1, he received orders reassigning him to Kien Phong Province. "It was the proverbial one-way ticket to Cambodia." He sighed. "The last two guys sent out there as Phoenix coordinators were killed by their own PRU. So I went back to see the major running Phoenix administration in Can Tho [James Damron], and he said he would not reassign me. So from there I went to the JAG [judge advocate general] office, where my friend and I drafted a letter to the Phoenix Directorate in Saigon."

In his letter to Tilton, Towle said that "War crimes as designated by the Geneva Conventions were not uncommon" in Phoenix and that he "had expressed my negative feelings on the program to the province Phung Hoang Coordinator and had given much thought to applying for release under MACV 525-36." He then requested "immediate release" from Phoenix.

The next day Major Damron, with the approval of the IV Corps Phoenix adviser, Lieutenant Colonel Efram E. Waller, reassigned Towle to the Tuyen Binh DIOCC—the same DIOCC where the previous two "triple sixers" had been killed in action. Damron noted that General Cushman was aware of the move, as was the JAG. Meanwhile, Towle's request for release was in the pipeline. So, taking two weeks' vacation, he hid at a friend's house in Can Tho until August 10, when the new CORDS chief of staff, General Frank Smith, approved his release. (Postscript: Referring to "the case that appalled us all," Wilbur Wilson wrote to George Jacobson, at the request of John Tilton, suggesting: "A records check in Saigon before an officer or enlisted man is assigned to a Phung Hoang position in Vietnam could reduce chances of assignment of unsuitable personnel.")

While William Colby was assuring Congress that no Phoenix adviser had resigned on moral grounds, or through MACV 525-36, and that incentive programs were not policy, John Tilton was organizing, with the National Police Command, a High Value Rewards Program (HVRP). In explaining the program to his wife, Colonel McCoid writes, "A very substantial reward is placed on highly placed VC political leaders, as much as $8,000 at the rate on the blackmarket or twice that amount on the official rate of exchange. Our idea is to induce the lower-grade VCI to turn their bosses in for the bounty money." Sadly, says McCoid, "our original proposal . . . was watered down by the bleeding hearts, who think placing a price on your enemy's head is excessively cruel! This despite Colby's support."

A conference of police and CORDS personnel, including Tilton, was scheduled for July 23, to select a list of VCI whose names were to be passed down to Phoenix officers in four pilot provinces (Binh Dinh, Quang Nam, Bien Hoa, and Vinh Binh) crucial to Thieu's election in October. Selected VCI were to be district rank or higher, dangerous, and confirmed with enough evidence to convict. Province chiefs, in their role as Phoenix committee chairmen, were to select dossiers and coordinate with the PIOCC. The list was to be approved by the region's military commander, and as stated in Interior Ministry Directive 1223, the "Phung Hoang Bloc of the National Police Command, acting for the Central Phung Hoang Committee, will review and make final selection of the VCI to be placed on the rewards list and will be submitted to the Major General Commander of the National Police, Vice Chairman concurrently Secretary General of the Central Phung Hoang Committee for final approval."

The HVRP, which was to be expanded into all provinces and administered by Phoenix advisers, was tentatively approved on July 31 by Josiah Bennett, director of the Vietnam Working Group; Henry Sizer at the Saigon Embassy's Internal Unit; the State Department's Vietnam desk officer, Lars Hydle; MACV; and the Joint U.S. Public Affairs Office (JUSPAO). However, the conference to select HVRP targets was indefinitely postponed as a result of Decree 1042. Promulgated in secret by General Khiem on August 2, 1971, its provisions known only to the Central Security Committee, the decree granted VCI suspects the right to an attorney and the right to appear in person at their trials. As a result, "public action" on the HVRP was deferred until after the election.

On October 3, 1971, Thieu was reelected with nearly 90 percent of the vote. The next day *The New York Times* reported that more than twenty thousand innocent civilians had been killed under the Phoenix program and that a congressional subcommittee had criticized the Pentagon for not investigating war crimes. A few days later the High Values Reward Program was scrapped by Ambassador Bunker, and plans to phase out American involvement in Phoenix were begun in earnest.

The process had begun on August 11, 1971, when Gage McAfee, a legal adviser to William Colby, submitted his end of tour report. Citing reports that the VCI was actually growing in number, McAfee writes, "There is doubt that the Phung Hoang Program is achieving its desired goal of eliminating the infrastructure. It can be argued that its resources and energy are actually being diverted to other undesirable activities that are . . . counterproductive in the context of supporting a viable and responsive government which will provide an effective alternative to the insurgent government." He adds that "some if not the majority of the war results from the social grievances of the part of the population, separate and distinct from the military aggression of the North," and that "No really responsive government should ever need such a program at all."

McAfee notes that An Tri "lacks a legislative base, there being no specific statute enacted by the National Assembly which empowers the Executive in time of war or emergency to administratively detain." He cites the legislature's opposition to Province Security Committees, which, he adds, "were generally acknowledged to be extra-constitutional if not unconstitutional." He rejects as "irrelevant" the argument that no residual responsibility for civilian detainees exists, citing *Nuremberg and Vietnam,* in which Telford Taylor says that if the GVN did not abide by the Geneva Conventions, "then the original captor power [the United States] must take effective steps to correct the situation, or shall request the return of the prisoners."[26]

McAfee emphasizes that Province Security Committees were not "regularly constituted courts" and that support for them was "a departure from the standards" of Article 3. "From a strictly legal standpoint," he concludes, the Rimestead letter required that the United States either demand the elimination of security committees or take steps to insure that no prisoners captured by U.S. forces were sentenced by them. "Not only are we now in the difficult position of having supported these committees in the past," he writes, "but many Vietnamese now think that Security Committees are as American as apple pie and baseball. The Phung Hoang program itself has always been associated with the Americans and of course the CIA. If the U.S. decides

. . . to recommend the elimination of these Committees, it might be useful for the Vietnamese . . . to blame it all on the U.S. So with the Phung Hoang program in general. If it fades into and is totally absorbed by the Special Police, it might help the Vietnamese to eliminate the bad aftertaste by blaming the entire program on their misguided benefactors." The only alternative, McAfee suggests, was "to force the GVN to make necessary improvements."

But the U.S. government would not go along with McAfee's recommendations that the Stalinist security committees "should die," that trials be made public, or that "The kill quota be eliminated as the ultimate misuse of the body count." Instead, it stalled until the problem could be sloughed off on the GVN. The Defense Department denied any "residual responsibility" whatsoever, and the Saigon Embassy minimized the problem, saying that only "between 1500 and 2500 individuals out of a VCI correction population of about 17,000 are the subject of that responsibility."[27]

The final word on U.S. policy regarding civilian detainees was stated on November 12, 1971, in State Department telegram 220774, which directed the Saigon Embassy to work with the Directorate of Political Security to guarantee "humanitarian treatment of detainees" and to ensure that An Tri was implemented "in terms of fundamental concepts of due process and to improve conditions of internment." This, despite State Department attorney Robert Starr's admission that "We cannot justify secrecy of procedural reforms in Circular 1042," which failed to provide for judicial review, "meaningful" appeal, "free choice" of an attorney, or the right to cross-examine witnesses. Noting that confessions alone were enough to convict a suspected VCI, Starr urged that "there should be a requirement of corroborating evidence." He cautioned Bunker that An Tri "is subject to attack on grounds it does not simply provide for emergency detention, but involves actual findings of guilt or innocence and sentencing of persons," and he suggested that Bunker work to implement "new legislation establishing a clear and detailed basis for program."

What Starr envisioned was legislation transferring security committee responsibilities to regularly constituted courts. But that never happened. Until the fall of Saigon, only the CIA-advised Directorate of Political Security could reverse Province Security Committee recommendations to extend detention. In November the GVN did withdraw from security committees the power to recommend An Tri detention against Communist offenders whose sentences had expired, VCI suspects who were released before trial for lack of evidence, and VCI suspects who were referred and had been acquitted. Unless "new factors" were specified. In December Prime Minister Khiem announced a parole and conditional release program "to release selected prisoners and also provide a system for post-release surveillance."

On December 13, 1971, Robert Starr reported to William H. Sullivan:

"These reforms are another welcome step in the right direction but fall short of effectively dealing with the underlying problems."[28] The next day the Washington *Post* printed an article by Peter Osnos headlined US PLAN FAILS TO WIPE OUT VC CADRE. The year 1971 closed without a resolution of An Tri or Phoenix.

CHAPTER 28

Technicalities

In early October 1971 Lieutenant Colonel Connie O'Shea arrived at the Phoenix Directorate and was assigned by John Tilton as liaison officer to Colonel Song at the Phung Hoang bloc office in the National Police Interrogation Center. His job, he told me, "was to tell Tilton what Song was thinking."[1]

A veteran intelligence officer who had served in Vietnam in 1966 and 1967, O'Shea described the directorate in late 1971 as "Sleepy Hollow. . . . There were ongoing discussions between U.S. and Vietnamese police officials," he recalled, "as to how to get the program transferred. Tilton and [operations chief Paul] Coughlin were doing their PHREEX [Phung Hoang reexamination] report, and coming down from Washington was a proposed list of things we should back away from. They were going to turn the dossiers over to the Vietnamese, and the Special Branch was apprehensive; they didn't want to turn their files over to anybody. . . . The other big thing was PHMIS [Phung Hoang Management Information System], but it was not ready to be used yet by the Vietnamese."

Coauthored by the CORDS Research and Analysis Division, PHREEX, according to Phoenix operations chief Paul Coughlin, "came from John Tilton," who initially wanted to call it Phung Hoang Reprise.[2] "It involved four months of depth research and included slides and graphs," explained Coughlin, "and basically outlined how to transfer Phoenix to the Vietnamese and how to deal with lessening assets [in 1972 the directorate had at most fifteen staffers]. But it also addressed what activities U.S. forces should be involved in, and to what degree; the whole idea of Revolutionary Development support and CORDS, which was the program's Achilles' heel, because everyone was answering to a different master. . . . Detention was not a PHREEX issue," Coughlin added, "but military justice and the moral aspects of the program were, as were our concerns over Vietnamese loyalty. After all of these things were considered together, we decided not to let the program die on the vine, but just to let the dead areas go." Otherwise, Coughlin noted, "Our concern in the directorate was that people in the field got what they needed—jeeps, communications equipment, et cetera—which we learned about through reports."

He added that "reports on operations ran up through another channel—through Special Branch." As for the relationship between the Special Branch and Phoenix, Coughlin observed that the directorate was "very compartmented," that a reserve officer on staff might have worked for the CIA, and that Chester McCoid's replacement as deputy director, Colonel Herb Allen, "was not in the know" and "was selected for that reason." Coughlin asserted that the Green Beret murder trial "changed the whole thing" and that employees of the Defense Investigative Service started arriving, running agents, and doing background investigations for Phoenix in 1972.

A different perspective on PHREEX was provided by Coughlin's deputy, Lieutenant Colonel George Hudman, a veteran intelligence officer who was also a friend of John Tilton's. "Coughlin was not an intelligence officer," Hudman explained, "and, as a result, was not trusted by Tilton. So I briefed PHREEX to Jake [George Jacobson] and General Forrester. . . . Basically, it explained why Phoenix didn't work. People in the agency were looking for a way to back out, and PHREEX was it. We took all the data compiled from all Phoenix centers, put it all together, and showed that the program was failing because it was too big and because the military had no understanding of it. They had no understanding of intelligence. They would round up VCI suspects, and they resorted to body counts. But intelligence isn't predicated on body counts."[3]

Despite blaming the military for the failure of Phoenix, Hudman explained that "Shackley, then Polgar to Tilton was the real chain of command" and that "Bob Wall [then senior adviser to the Special Branch] oversaw Phoenix."

Indeed, as the U.S. military prepared to leave Vietnam, the CIA needed to find a new way of managing the attack against the VCI without appearing to do so. In other words, the concept of an attack against the VCI was still considered vital; what was sought was a new organization. The process began when General Abrams suggested in October that "responsibility for the full anti-VCI mission should be assigned to the National Police Command on a time-phased basis commencing 1972"[4] and that Phung Hoang committees and centers be deactivated as a way of "increasing the emphasis on the anti-VCI responsibilities of district and province chiefs."

These recommendations were studied in Washington by a working group composed of Josiah Bennett (State), John Arthur (AID), George Carver (CIA), John Manopoli (Public Safety), General Karhohs (ISA), the Joint Chiefs of Staff, and SACSA. After each agency had considered the proposals, Bennett shot a telegram (196060) back to Saigon indicating tentative approval, although, in deference to the CIA, "with the Special Branch collating intelligence and maintaining dossiers on the VCI, and with positive action responsibilities assigned to the PRU, NPFF and other elements as required." A few weeks later Ambassador Bunker sent a telegram (17357) to Secretary of State William Rogers saying that Robert Thompson and the GVN had also approved of the plan. The working group then prepared to send a team, headed by the Vietnam Task Force's action officer Jack, to Saigon to determine which "key people" could be reassigned to Phoenix. When the team arrived in Saigon in mid-November, according to Jack, "Tilton got the okay from Carver to give me the Phoenix information."

Despite its tentative approval of the plan to phase out Phoenix and turn the management of the attack against the VCI over to the National Police Command (NPC), the CIA had no such intentions. In fact, in October 1971 orders went out to all province Special Branch advisers to begin forming Special Intelligence Force Units (SIFU). Eight-man teams composed of four volunteers each from the Special Police and Field Police, the SIFU were targeted specifically at high-level VCI, as substitutes for the PRU. They were also a sign that the CIA planned to manage the attack on the VCI through the Special Branch, while keeping Phoenix intact as a way of deflecting attention and accountability.

For Phu Yen Province PIC adviser Rob Simmons—who worked under cover of the CORDS Pacification Security Coordination Division but who never even met the CORDS province senior adviser—Phoenix in 1972 was merely a library of files to cross-check information, not the CIA's partner in the attack on the VCI. "We would go to Phoenix," Simmons told me, "and they'd show us a file, and we'd use the file to build a case. And every report we generated, we sent to the PIOCC. But Special Branch had its own files. And if at the PIC we got someone who cooperated, we would withhold his file—if he was going to be doubled—because we knew the PIOCC was penetrated."[5] Furthermore, according to Simmons, the Phu Yen Province officer in charge concentrated on unilateral operations and political reporting, because he considered (as had Rocky Stone) Special Branch liaison too exposed to be secure.

As William Colby explained it, "CORDS people were kept out of the station. And even though Special Branch coordinated through the province senior adviser, the station had a clear chain of command in intelligence matters."[6]

Indeed, Phoenix was a valuable resource, and it allowed the CIA to say that it had no officers in the districts. But the CIA was not about to turn over its Special Branch files to the National Police Command (NPC) or submit its agents to NPC authority. And when those proposals returned to Carver's desk for final approval, there they died. In December 1971 Carver wrote a working paper entitled "Future U.S. Role in the Phung Hoang Program." Its stated purpose was "to ensure that the GVN Phung Hoang Program continues to receive effective U.S. advisory support during up-coming 18–24 month period with an option for continuance if required."

Using familiar terms, Carver defines Phoenix as: a) "the intelligence effort against the higher levels of the VCI who possess information . . . on enemy plans and intentions; b) the intelligence effort directed against the lowest level of the VCI [who] perform an essentially political function of relating the Communist party mechanism to the population; and c) an action effort to neutralize the targets in (a) and (b)." He also notes that, on November 27, 1971, General Khiem changed his mind and said that "Phung Hoang Centers and Committees will be retained," that the Central Phung Hoang Committee would be upgraded and chaired by Khiem himself, that the Phoenix program "will be continued indefinitely," and that "included . . . will be a rewards program funded by the GVN." One month after Bunker had killed the High Value Rewards Program, it was born anew as a GVN program, as part of Phung Hoang.

The main reason for not scrapping Phoenix, Carver writes, was the "crucial" need to destroy the VCI. However, he suggests that the titles Phoenix and Phung Hoang adviser be dropped, and he warns against withdrawing advisers in provinces where the VCI presence was heavy. "The minimum staffing level appears to be about thirty positions which would provide coverage of the program at national, regional and a few key provincial echelons," Carver writes, adding, "Plans should be drawn up to have the normal U.S. advisory structure absorb anti-VCI advisory duties beyond the transitional period of the drawdown." He envisioned the complete withdrawal of Phoenix advisers by the end of 1972, but only in a way that would provide the United States with "a capability to monitor not only the GVN program but also to develop some semblance of an independent estimative capability." That job would fall, after 1973, to the 500th Military Intelligence Group as well as the CIA.

As ever, the CIA got its way. On December 28, 1971, State Department officer Lars Hydle, in response to Carver's paper, wrote "that Phung Hoang should be handled by the Special Branch within the National Police Command . . . that Phung Hoang Committees should continue in existence," and that province and district chiefs should assume responsibility "beginning with the most secure areas where there are few RVNAF main forces. Perhaps U.S. military advisors will continue to be needed as long as RVNAF retains action responsibilities for Phung Hoang, but *as action is transferred to the Special Branch, the advisory role should be taken over by the Special Branch advisor, the CIA man*" (author's emphasis).

This is the "reprise" John Tilton imagined: the return of the Special Branch to prominence in anti-VCI operations. By 1972 it was policy, as articulated by Bob Wall: "I was really pushing Special Branch to support Phoenix during the Easter offensive, while the VC were overrunning Hue. [The National Police commander Major General] Phong had the chief of police in Hue on the phone. I told him what to do, and he relayed the message. . . . Where the Special Branch contributed," Wall said, "was in Hue in April 1972; there was success."[7]

As soon as the North Vietnamese Army (NVA) attacked, the VCI in Hue were to begin sabotage and terror attacks within the city, direct NVA artillery fire, and guide assault columns. However, reports Robert Condon, the Phoenix coordinator on the scene, "Before the enemy agents could be activated, about 1000 of them who had been long identified by the PIOCC were arrested. Our intelligence indicated that the NVA commanders were blind in Hue, due to this timely Phung Hoang operation."[8]

"Phoenix," Bob Wall insisted, "represented the strategy that could have won the war." But, he lamented, "Ted Shackley stuck to the traditional route of only collecting intelligence and gave Phoenix away." Removing the Special Branch in 1969, Wall contended, "kicked the teeth out of the program.

"The Special Branch was up to the job," Wall added. "Mau had instituted a training program in 1970, but Khiem prevented them from getting good-quality people because Mau had demonstrated the operational capabilities necessary to pull off a coup. Not that he was close to trying it, but when Thieu listed the possibilities, Mau was at the top: He was smart, charismatic, courageous, cold-blooded, politically minded, and he had access to the agency and troops who could pull it off."

A Catholic and central Vietnamese with Can Lao connections, Mau was good at his job. But he was a consultant to PA&E, and he had given the CIA access to the accounting records of the Special Branch, and he had organized his own political party, the Nationalist Students, all of which combined to make him a liability. So after Thieu had won reelection in October 1971, Mau was replaced as chief of the Special Branch by Brigadier General Huynh Thoi Tay; Colonel Song was replaced as the chief of Phoenix by Nguyen

Van Giau; and General Phong* was replaced as the director general of the National Police by CIO chief Nguyen Khac Binh, even though, according to Tom Polgar, it was a mistake to have one man in both positions. Polgar added that Rod Landreth and Phil Potter negotiated the transfer of Phoenix and the PRU to the GVN with Generals Binh and Dang Van Quang.[9]

Meanwhile, the CIA was distancing itself from the PRU. III Corps adviser Rudy Enders noted that PRU national commander Major Nguyen Van Lang was fired for selling positions and shaking down his region commanders and that "by the time 1972 rolls around, Ho Chau Tuan [former commander of the Eighth Airborne Battalion at Tan Son Nhut] had taken over in Saigon."[10]

Michael Drosnin quotes Ho Chau Tuan as saying, "The main mission of PRU was assassination. I received orders from the Phoenix office, the Vietnamese and Americans there, to assassinate high-level VCI. We worked closely with Saigon with the CIA from the Embassy, and in the provinces with the CIA at the consulates, to decide who to kill." Writes Drosnin: "Tuan offered to name names of high-level Americans who directly ordered assassination strikes, but then he backed off. 'I have enough experience in this profession to be afraid,' he explained. 'I know the CIA. I might be killed' " (*New Times*, 1975).[11]†

In 1972 the PRU were advised in I Corps by Patry Loomis, in II Corps by Jack Harrell and Bob Gilardo, in III Corps by Rudy Enders and Felix Rodriguez, and in IV Corps by John Morrison and Gary Maddox.

Phoenix operations in the field in 1972 varied from region to region. Rudy Enders told me he had the VCI on the run in III Corps. And in IV Corps, where the PRU were most active, success was reported against the VCI. But in I Corps and II Corps, where the NVA concentrated its attacks in 1972, the situation was much harder to handle. Quang Tri fell in April, and in early May the NVA captured Quang Ngai City, which it held until September. In Binh Dinh Province, forty thousand Koreans refused to fight, several thousand unpaid ARVN soldiers threw down their rifles and ran away, and the NVA seized three district capitals. With the ARVN and Territorial Forces in retreat, Thieu turned to Phoenix.

In May 1972, writes Michael Klare, "Thieu declared martial law and

*Phong was killed with five bodyguards and advisers William Bailey and Luther McLendon in a plane that exploded on the ground on December 1, 1972, in Tuy Hoa, the capital of Phu Yen Province.

†*New Times* is an English-language version of *Nove Vremya,* which is published in Moscow and distributed in various countries.

launched a savage attack on the remaining pockets of neutralism in the big cities. Government forces reportedly cordoned off entire districts in Hue, Danang and Saigon and arrested everyone on the police blacklists. The reputable *Far Eastern Economic Review* reported on July 8, 1972, that 50,000 people had been arrested throughout Vietnam during the first two months of the offensive, and *Time* magazine reported on 10 July that arrests were continuing at a rate of 14,000 per month."[12]

For an eyewitness account of Phoenix operations in II Corps in 1972, we turn first to Lieutenant Colonel Connie O'Shea, who in January 1972 was transferred from Saigon to Phoenix headquarters in Nha Trang, as deputy to II Corps Phoenix Coordinator Colonel Lew Millett.

"The problem with the program," according to O'Shea, "was that people were being rotated out, but replacements were not being made. And as the intelligence officers went home, the Phoenix guy took over that job, but not the reverse. It was a one-way street, and Phoenix fell to the wayside.

"Millett was trying to keep Phoenix people doing their Phoenix job," O'Shea continued, "and he spent a lot of time going around to the province chiefs, trying to keep them focused on the VCI. But it was hard during the spring offensive. So Millett and [Region II Phung Hoang chief] Dam went around trying to keep the organization in place, telling the Phoenix coordinators that if they had to do S-two work, not to forget their anti-VCI job. That was number one. Our other job was making ourselves visible with Colonel Dam, so the Vietnamese would not get the sense that we were pulling out. We kept a high profile. We were missing a couple of province guys, and an awful lot of DIOCCs were missing advisers. The district senior advisers were not taking over but were trying to get the Vietnamese to take over. So we spent a lot of time touring and helping the Phung Hoang Committees and DIOCCs collect intelligence and prepare operational plans.

"Thirdly," O'Shea said, "Millett was an operator, trying to conduct as many missions as possible himself." Millett's biggest success was "turning" the Montagnard battalion that had led the attack on Hue during Tet of 1968.

Fifty-two years old in 1972, Medal of Honor winner Lew Millett—who in 1961 had helped create the Vietnamese rangers and later did likewise in Laos—was known as a wild man who participated in ambushes and raids against VCI camps with Connie O'Shea and some of the more aggressive Phoenix coordinators.

According to Millett, "Phoenix was coordinated at corps level by the CIA, and I had to back-channel to get around them."[13]

According to O'Shea, "The Phoenix program had gotten to the point where the region office was a manager's office. Millett was trying to coordinate provinces and districts, and where we did run operations, it was in a province where the PIOCC was not doing much. We as senior officers did not theoretically coordinate with the CIA's province officer in charge; that was the job of the major at the PIOCC."

One such major at a PIOCC in 1972 was Stan Fulcher, the Phoenix coordinator in Binh Dinh Province. "Stan had taken over all the programs," O'Shea noted. "He was running the whole show. He kept taking on everything, including the PRU, which was true in many cases."

The son of an Air Force officer, Stan Fulcher was brought up in various military posts around the world, but he brands as "hypocritical" the closed society into which he was born. "The military sees itself as the conqueror of the world"—Fulcher sighed, "but the military is socialism in its purest form. People in the military lead a life of privilege in which the state meets each and every one of their needs."[14]

Having served in the special security unit at Can Tho Air Base in 1968—where he led a unit of forty riflemen against the VCI—Fulcher fully understood the realities of Vietnam. He told me of the Military Security Service killing a Jesuit priest who advocated land reform, of GVN officials trading with the National Liberation Front while trying to destroy religious sects, and of the tremendous U.S. cartels—RMK-BRJ, Sealand, Holiday Inns, Pan Am, Bechtel, and Vinnell—that prospered from the war.

"The military has the political power and the means of production," Fulcher explained, "and so it enjoys all the benefits of society. . . . Well, it was the same thing in Vietnam, where the U.S. military and a small number of politicians supported the Vietnamese Catholic establishment against the masses. . . . Greedy Americans," Fulcher contended, "were the cause of the war. The supply side economists—these are the emergent groups during Vietnam."

During a tour in London from 1968 to 1971, in which he saw British businessmen trading with the North Vietnamese, Fulcher learned there are "no permanent allies." During his tour in Phoenix, he became totally disenchanted. "When I arrived in Saigon," he recalled, "an Air America plane was waiting and took me to Nha Trang. That night I talked with Millett. The next day I got in a chopper and went to Qui Nhon, the capital city of Binh Dinh Province, where I met the S-two, Gary Hacker, who took me to my quarters in a hotel by the ocean." Hacker then took Fulcher to meet the province senior adviser, "a young political appointee who lived in a beautiful house on the ocean. When I walked into the room, he was standing there with his arms around two Vietnamese girls. The tops of their ao dais were down, and he was cupping their breasts."

Next, Fulcher met Larry Jackson, the CIA province officer in Binh Dinh. Jackson had "about twenty contract workers, USIS types who thought they were Special Forces. They all had Vietnamese girl friends and important dads. They were all somewhat deranged and did nothing but play volleyball all day." Fulcher described the CORDS advisory team as "a sieve."

As the Binh Dinh Province Phoenix coordinator, Stan Fulcher supervised nearly a thousand U.S. technicians and Vietnamese nationals, including a Special Forces sergeant who ran Binh Dinh's PRU. The PRU adviser reported both to the CIA and to Fulcher. "His Vietnamese wife had been cut open," Fulcher said. "He was a dangerous man who went out by himself and killed VC left and right." Fulcher mistrusted the PRU because they did not take orders and because they played him against the CIA.

Fulcher's Vietnamese counterpart was MSS Major Nguyen Van Vinh. "The Vietnamese with the MSS," Fulcher contended, "were the worst. They kept track of what the Americans were doing, they had friends in the VCI, and they would deal with Phoenix before the police." The National Police had its own adviser, "a former cop from Virginia who ran the Field Police." The PIC "was terribly disgusting," and there was an interrogation center behind the Province Operations Center, Fulcher said, "right behind the province senior adviser's house. Our barracks were next door."

Mr. Vinh was paid by Fulcher, who also had an interpreter and seven other Vietnamese on his Phoenix staff. "I could influence each one," he stated, noting that with no replacements coming in, the advisory vacuum was easily filled by an aggressive person such as he. "As more and more Americans left," Fulcher explained, "more Vietnamese came under my control. They needed consolidation. The structure was so corrupt, with everyone power grabbing, that independent units couldn't do a job. And that meant added jobs for me."

For example, Fulcher inherited Binh Dinh's Civic Action program—including the fifty-nine-man RD teams—which had been getting one million dollars annually in U.S. aid. "Then the well dried up, and funds were cut off," Fulcher explained, "which caused much bitterness. Like the contras or, before them, the Cubans. Everyone was turning against the government." As the province psywar officer, Fulcher also controlled the Qui Nhon TV station, where he spent one day a week working with the actors and staff, organizing parades, producing broadcasts and puppet shows, printing leaflets, and distributing radios tuned in to the GVN station. According to Fulcher, the embittered Vietnamese psywar officer absconded with the TV money and sold the radios on the black market.

Fulcher also managed the Chieu Hoi program. During the spring offensive, he recalled, "We gave them rifles and sent them up to the front lines. . . . I sat on top of a knoll and watched while they threw down their guns and ran away."

Territorial security was a job that involved "checking villages every two weeks for a day or so. The Territorial Forces," he pointed out, "were a motley crew, mostly old men and women and little kids." Fulcher also liaisoned with the Korean White Horse Division, "which would steal anything it could get its hands on." According to Fulcher Americans were involved with the Koreans in drug dealing, and he said that the Koreans were "sadistic and corrupt."

In explaining the meaning of Phoenix, Stan Fulcher said, "You can't understand it by creating a web. There were several lines of communication, which skipped echelons, and I could go to whatever side—military or Phoenix—that I wanted to. . . . Phoenix was more of a political program, like what the Germans had on the eastern front—Gestapo/SS, but half assed." For that reason, Fulcher explained, "The regular military didn't like Phoenix, and the province senior advisers [PSAs] hated it, too.

"Twice a week I'd brief the PSA at the TOC [tactical operations center]. Each member of the province team would brief through his deputy. The operations officer was the main guy, then the G-two, then Phoenix, PRU and the CIA rep. The Province Phung Hoang Committee met twice a month, at which point the MSS would exercise whatever influence it had with the province chief, who'd say, 'We need fifty VCI this week.' Then the Special Branch would go out and get old ladies and little kids and take them to the PIC. They'd send us on special operations missions into the hamlets, and the village chiefs would take the old and maimed and give them to us as VCI. 'If you don't give me rice, you're VCI.' It was perverted.

"The ARVN supplied us with cards on everyone they didn't like," Fulcher went on, "but we could never find them. On night operations during curfew hours, we'd seal off the exits and go after a specific guy. We'd be running through houses, one guy lifting up a lamp, another guy holding pictures of the suspect and taking fingerprints. But everyone had the same name, so we'd search for weapons, maps, documents. It was just impossible"—Fulcher sighed—"so after two months I started to find ways to let people go—to get their names off the list. You see, Binh Dinh had something like thirty-seven political parties, and *no one* could say who was VC. By 1972 most district chiefs were NLF, and even though they were appointed by Saigon, most were from the North and were kept off hit lists due to friendships."

What finally convinced Fulcher to work against Phoenix was the "disappearing" of thirty thousand civilians in the aftermath of the spring offensive. Rocking back and forth in his chair, his head buried in his hands, sobbing, Fulcher described what happened: "Two NVA regiments hit Binh Dinh in the north, mainly at Hoi An. We went through a pass in the valley to meet them, but a whole ARVN regiment was destroyed. Four hundred were killed and sixteen hundred escaped down Highway Thirty-one. I could see the ARVN soldiers running away and the NVA soldiers running after them, shooting them in the back of their heads with pistols so as not to waste ammunition. . . . I could see our helicopters being shot down. . . . We called in close air support and long-range artillery and stopped them at Phu Mi. There were pitched battles. The NVA attacked on two ridges. Then [II Corps Commander John] Vann was killed up in Kontum, and [Special Forces Colonel Michael] Healy took over. Healy came in with his Shermanesque tactics in August."

The disappearance of the thirty thousand occurred over a two-month period beginning in June, Fulcher said, "mainly through roundups like in the Ukraine. The MSS was putting people in camps around Lane Field outside Qui Nhon, or in the PIC. Everyone was turning against the GVN, and anyone born in Binh Dinh was considered VC. There were My Lais by the score—from aerial bombardments and artillery. . . . Phoenix coordinated it. Me and Jackson and four or five of his contractors. The National Police had lists of people. Out of the thirty thousand, the Special Branch was interested in particular in about a hundred. The MSS put everyone else in camps, and the Vietnamese Air Force loaded them up, flew away, and came back empty. They dumped whole families into the Gulf of Tonkin. This was not happening elsewhere."

How could this happen? "You're a shadow," Fulcher explained, his face contorted with anguish. "You're a bureaucrat. You only *think* things, so you don't investigate."

After the disappearances, Fulcher complained to a State Department officer. As a result, two things happened. First, in addition to his job as province Phoenix coordinator, Fulcher was made senior adviser in the three districts—Hoi An, Hoi Nan, and Binh Khe—that the NVA had seized. Next, an attempt was made on his life.

"Jackson was unhappy with the PRU," Fulcher explained. "He couldn't pay them anymore, so they moved in with Binh Khe district team. I was scheduled to go up there to pay them [from the Intelligence Contingency Fund], but a West Pointer, Major Pelton, the Phoenix guy from Phu Cat, went instead. And the PRU shot him in the helicopter right after it landed. Pelton was killed, and the Phu Cat district senior adviser, Colonel Rose, was wounded. The incident was blamed on the VC, but Mr. Vinh and I went to the landing zone and found Swedish K rounds (which only the PRU used) in the chopper. First I went to [the PSA], then Millett at Nha Trang, then Healy in Pleiku. But nothing ever happened."

In explaining how such tensions might occur, Connie O'Shea (who replaced Lew Millett as II Corps Phoenix coordinator in August 1972) points to the inclusion of key military leaders as well as civilians in the definition of VCI. "Vann put pressure on to get these guys," O'Shea explained, "but Special Branch would not give their names for security reasons. . . . And as a result . . . military advisers started going after the commo-liaison links—those VCI that were more military than political. And when you got very strong personalities like Stan Fulcher in there, that situation became explosive. Stan wanted access, and his solution," O'Shea said, "was to force it back up to Vann or Healy, who would say, 'I can't force them to open up files.' So it was kept at the local level, where it went back and forth between Stan and Jackson. And I had to go down there and try to mediate between them. But we just had to accept that this was not the period of time to be arguing with the CIA that to run an effective PIOCC, we had to have their dossiers. The time to do that was four years prior. But Stan was insisting . . . that he was going to get at them. Well, the CIA would give other stuff—Revolutionary Development or Census Grievance—but not Special Branch."

When asked why he and Millett could not exert influence, O'Shea replied, "This is why Phoenix was not as effective as it should have been."

In March 1972 Ambassador Bunker sent a telegram (040611Z) to the State Department saying, "We question whether the USG should concede failure of an An Tri system to meet test of Article 3." Because he thought that An Tri probably did violate the Geneva Conventions, Bunker asked that a decision be put off until completion of a study written by CORDS legal adviser Ray Meyers. In the study, entitled "An Tri Observations and Recommendations," Meyers suggested, among other things, opening An Tri hearings to the public. On April 11, John Tilton advised against doing that, saying it would "result in the compromise of sources. . . . Under Executive Order 10460," Tilton wrote, "the American public is not allowed to attend U.S. administrative security proceedings nor are transcripts of the proceedings releasable to the public. It is difficult to justify why a nation which is seriously threatened by internal subversion should institute a procedure that is not even allowed in a nation which has no such threat."[15]

Tilton's recommendation on this point was accepted.

Meyers also noted that "the great majority of the Vietnamese people are completely ignorant of the purposes, procedures and results of either Phung Hoang or An Tri." Tilton retorted that that was "a subjective statement . . . and could cause a reader with little background . . . to reach the erroneous conclusion that the programs are pretty much of a failure." Tilton recommended that "many" be substituted for "great majority."[16] That suggestion, too, was implemented.

On April 12, the CORDS Public Safety Directorate added its two cents, calling An Tri "a relaxation of the RVN's right of self-defense and . . . a gratuity." The embassy recommended "that detentions based on a charge of belonging to or supporting the VCI [a crime of status] be eliminated on a province by province basis over a period of years to eliminate gradually the whole An Tri structure instead of institutionalizing it by transferring jurisdiction over VCI from the province security committees to the courts."[17] However, Tilton advised against the province-by-province phaseout, and his position, again, was accepted.

Faced with intractable CIA internal security considerations, the embassy decided to defer reform of An Tri indefinitely. But it did not want to appear to be sanctioning summary executions either, so embassy political officer Steven Winship emphasized that "the mission recognizes this to be a serious problem, particularly when excessive legalism or consideration of public relations are [*sic*] introduced tempting the police to neutralize by killing instead of arrest and prosecution."[18] It was suggested that the computer system at the National Identity and Records Center "be supported and that some provision be made for the review of cases where VCI suspects were released by the Province Security Committees." The ideà was to set up a central control that would prevent abuses at the local level and would allow the GVN to market preventive detention as a "substitute for killing people."

The result was that An Tri was to be reformed into a system not of "sentencing" but of indefinite "detention" with periodic review by the Central Security Committee. It was to apply only to Communists. This system was to be a "temporary" measure, which "offers possibilities for avoiding possible criticism under the terms of the Geneva Convention." Article 19 of Decree Law 004 of 1966 was amended to "preclude charges that the system violates Article 7 (2) of the RVN Constitution," and Bunker put the U.S. seal of approval on An Tri.

While the subject of An Tri was being debated in Saigon, IV Corps Commander Truong in Can Tho authorized, on April 21, 1972, a "special" F6 Phung Hoang campaign designed to neutralize the VCI by moving against suspects with only *one* adverse report on the record. A response to the Easter offensive, the F6 campaign was started in Chau Doc Province on the initiative of the province chief, who was concerned with reports that NVA units were being guided and assisted by the VCI. More than a thousand VCI suspects were quickly rounded up.

Flying as it did in the face of An Tri reforms, F6 was the cause of some concern. "Mission is aware of potential pitfalls in special Phung Hoang campaign and possibilities of adverse publicity if campaign used for mass roundups of suspects," wrote Ambassador Bunker.[19]

A hundred twenty-five Phoenix advisers were left in Vietnam in October 1972, when a tentative agreement was reached calling for the formation of a National Council for Reconciliation and Concord composed of representatives from the GVN, NLF, and Third Force neutralists. On October 24, President Thieu presented sixty-nine amendments to the agreement and, stating that the VCI "must be wiped out quickly and mercilessly," ordered a new wave of arrests. On November 25, 1972, three weeks after Richard Nixon was reelected, Thieu signed Decree Law 020, "Concerning National Security and Public Order." Issued in secret, 020 modified An Tri to the extent, Ambassador Bunker wrote, "that these powers are no longer limited to wartime and may be applied following a ceasefire and the end of an officially declared state of war. The evident purpose of the law is to provide for an extension of An Tri procedures in preparation for a ceasefire confrontation with the Communists."[20]

Broadening An Tri to include people deemed dangerous to "public order," Bunker wrote, "means that virtually any person arrested in South Vietnam can now be held on criminal instead of political charges."

The "public order" provision was included in Decree Law 020 precisely because the cease-fire agreement prohibited the incarceration of political prisoners. According to Decree Law 020, Communist offenders already in jail under the An Tri Laws would also have their sentences automatically extended. Likewise, Province Security Committees were directed to extend automatically the detention of categories A and B VCI until the end of the "present emergency," which did not end with the cease-fire.

As a result of Decree Law 020, thousands of Vietnamese remained incarcerated until April 1975. On December 18, 1972, *Newsweek* estimated that there were forty-five thousand "official" prisoners in Vietnamese prisons and another hundred thousand in detention camps. Amnesty International reported at least two hundred thousand political prisoners, and other observers cited higher estimates. The U.S. Embassy identified on its computer tapes fewer than ten thousand political prisoners and called the criticism unfounded in light of An Tri reforms. In Saigon, three thousand people were arrested in one night. The cost of having an enemy's name placed on a Phoenix hit list, now easier than ever, thanks to Decree 020, was reduced to six dollars.

In December 1972 cease-fire talks collapsed, and Nixon bombed Hanoi. Thieu called for a return to the denunciation of Communists campaign of 1956 and ordered his security officers to target neutralists in the National Council of Reconciliation and Concord. With Decree Law 020 safely in place, Prime Minister Khiem canceled the F6 campaign and ordered a return to the three-source rule. "However," wrote Bunker, "there is some evidence that the National Police do not regard the order as terminating the accelerated Phung Hoang campaign."[21]

By 1973 South Vietnam had come full circle. Only the names had changed. Empowered by secret decrees written by CIA officers, security forces now arrested dissidents for violating the "public order" instead of the "national security." In March 1972 Prime Minister Khiem determined that "it is important not to get hung up on the term Phung Hoang. . . . The problem that the Phung Hoang structure was erected to address will still remain . . . with or without the term."[22] In a report on Phoenix, "Phung Hoang Effectiveness During August and September 1972," John Tilton crossed out the words "Phung Hoang" and inserted in their place the term "Anti-Terrorist," explicitly heralding the modern era of low-intensity warfare.

In Nha Trang in December 1972, Connie O'Shea transferred the records and equipment in the region Phung Hoang office to the Public Safety adviser, "who didn't want them. Then I turned off the lights," he said, "locked the door, walked across the street to the CORDS building, and turned in the key."

CHAPTER 29

Phoenix in Flames

After the cease-fire agreements were signed in Paris on January 27, 1973, the armed forces and government of South Vietnam were expected to stand on their own. To meet the challenge, General Khiem signed Circular 193, creating political struggle committees in every province, city, district, and village. Political struggle committees were described by Ken Quinn, a State Department officer in Chau Doc Province, in a February 24, 1973, memo, as the "principal vehicle for organizing anti-Communist demonstrations" and for combating "the Communist plot for a General Uprising." Each struggle committee's subcommittee for security and intelligence was given jurisdiction over the existing Phung Hoang Committee. But, observed Quinn, "unless more specific instructions are forthcoming, even those village officials who understand *why* they are part of the committee will not understand *what* they are supposed to do."

To ensure that government officials followed the party line, the GVN through its Quyet Tam campaign put an officer in each village as its special political warfare cadre. A member of Thieu's Dan Chu party, the cadre put in place agents who organized networks in the hamlets to spy on local GVN officials as well as Communists and dissidents.

On the American side of the fence, under the terms of the cease-fire agreements, MACV was replaced by a Defense Attaché Office (DAO) in the U.S. Embassy. The DAO consisted of some four hundred civilian Defense

Department employees, fifty military officers, and twenty-five hundred contract workers. Colonel Doug Dillard, who in 1973 commanded the 500th Military Intelligence Group and managed all U.S. military intelligence activities in Southeast Asia, recalled "The Five Hundredth MIG, under Operation Fast Pass, received primary responsibility for intelligence support to the embassy in Saigon during the remainder of the U.S. presence. The other services bowed out, but the Army, via General Alexander Haig, agreed to provide the people."[1]

According to Dillard, "as part of the in-country structure, there was a province observer in each province as liaison with the MSS and Special Branch, in coordination with Phoenix under the U.S. Embassy. But they didn't work at province, really. They worked as liaison with the South Vietnamese Army, Navy, Air Force, and General Staff, because U.S. Navy and Air Force intelligence had phased down and only the Five Hundredth provided support after the drawdown.

"There were several province observers on the Five Hundredth's payroll," Dillard continued, "in a civilian capacity." Many of them had served in Vietnam before, as liaison officers or Phoenix coordinators. But, Dillard added, their function was often so tightly controlled by province State Department representatives, who were "very jealous of their prerogatives . . . and didn't want that billet filled . . . , that they contributed very little and the program never got off the ground."

Other province observers were doing more than merely training and reporting on South Vietnamese units. According to PRU adviser Jack Harrell, his counterpart, Tran Ahn Tho, went to work for Province Observer David Orr (formerly the CIA's paramilitary adviser in Binh Dinh Province) in 1973 as a principal agent organizing stay-behind nets. In "From the Ashes" Jeff Stein writes that "the prime mission of intelligence agencies is to set-up stay behind operations in the event a truce does actually go into effect."[2] Noting that the focus was on political reporting, Stein goes on: "American case officers are meeting frequently with their agents now and developing alternative means of communication so that when the officers are removed to such areas as Bangkok or Phnom Penh or even Tokyo or the United States, they can maintain communication with their agents and direct them toward political personnel, the VCI. So that . . . the operations would be able to continue indefinitely—whether there was one American in Vietnam or not."

As civilians, province observers were often disguised as employees of private companies, like the Computer Science Corporation, on contract to the Pentagon. In a November 1972 article in *The New York Times,* Fox Butterfield wrote that "as many as 10,000 American civilian advisers and technicians, most of them under DOD [Defense Department] contract, will stay on in Vietnam after the ceasefire." Among those staying behind through a loophole in Article 5 of the cease-fire agreements were a number of Public Safety advisers from Japan, Israel, Taiwan, and Australia, as well as from America. In fact, the last two Army officers at the Phoenix Directorate—Colonel Richard Carey and Lieutenant Colonel Keith Ogden—completed their tours as Public Safety advisers.

Other people, like Ed Brady, hired on with the State Department's Reconstruction and Resettlement Directorate or as part of SAFFO (the special assistant for field operations), which replaced CORDS and was managed by George Jacobson.

Several hundred CIA officers also remained in Vietnam beyond the cease-fire. Among them was George French, who as the officer in charge of propaganda broadcasts into North Vietnam managed the Con Te Island complex near Hue until 1974. Frank Snepp continued to interrogate prisoners at the National Interrogation Center. Robert Thompson returned as an adviser to the National Police, and Ted Serong returned as an adviser to the Joint General Staff.

The allied strategy was simple. For the first half of 1973 Henry Kissinger relied on massive B-52 raids into Cambodia as a way of turning Hanoi's attention away from South Vietnam. But then Congress cut off funds for further bombing, and Kissinger and Thieu again turned to Phoenix and a renewed round of political repression.

On May 15, 1973, State Department officer Frank Wisner sent a memo from Can Tho to Washington, subject "Phoenix Goes Underground." "After a two month respite, the Phoenix program is quietly coming back to life," Wisner notes, adding, "Phoenix activities have been generally restrained since the ceasefire, partly because *they violate article 10 of the Paris agreement,* and partly because the working level forces . . . lacked the zeal to pursue their risky business" (author's emphasis).

"For a time [deleted] tried to continue the program under cover of changing the names of the targets from VCI to 'disturbers of domestic tranquility,' " Wisner continues. Noting that that pretext had been dropped, he writes: "Saigon had instructed all province Phung Hoang (Phoenix) Committees to double the number of monthly operations against VCI without the fanfare and publicity that it used to receive. The GVN has assigned it high priority."

Further bolstering the attack against the VCI and the Third Force was Prime Ministerial Decree 090 of May 12, 1973, which authorized detention for up to two years and enforced residence in their homes, confiscation of their property, and/or banishment from prohibited areas of persons deemed dangerous to National Security or Public Order. Province security committees examined cases, which were reviewed by the Central Security Committee in Saigon. The prime minister issued the final decision.

On May 19, 1973, Decree 093 modified Decree 090 to the extent that the director of military justice was given a seat on the Central Security Committee, which then included the minister of the interior; prosecutor general of the Saigon Court of Appeals; director general of the National Police; director of military justice; director of political security and his chief of statistics and records; the chief of the Penitentiary Directorate; and their American counterparts.

In June 1973 State Department officer Dean Brown informed the State Department that the I Corps Special Branch liaison officer had reported that Da Nang Mayor Le Tri Tin had "ordered the cessation of all *overt* Phung Hoang (Phoenix) activities. No more files and correspondence will be maintained," he added, "and most information will be passed by word of mouth. 'Security Suspects' will still be pursued, but quietly. Liaison officer was told that this action was taken because of the possibility of ICCS (International Commission of Control and Supervision) inspection for ceasefire violations."[3]

In July 1973, with the cessation of bombing in Cambodia, Thieu, in violation of the cease-fire agreements, ordered several large search and destroy operations along the border. The North Vietnamese counterattacked, overrunning ARVN outposts in Quang Duc Province on November 6. Declaring that the war had begun anew, Thieu requested American military aid. But the very next day Congress passed the War Powers Act, restricting the President's ability to initiate hostilities against foreign countries. Congress began cutting back aid, and the South Vietnamese economy began to fizzle. More and more the Vietnamese turned to corruption and drug dealing to maintain the standard of living they had known under American patronage. According to CIA officer Bruce Lawlor, the disease was contagious.

A Vietnamese linguist, Bruce Lawlor in early 1972 was assigned to the counterintelligence section of the CIA's Da Nang region office. Lawlor worked at that job through the Easter offensive, during which time he developed a friendship with Patry Loomis. In the summer of 1972, when Loomis was made the region PRU adviser, Lawlor replaced him as the Quang Nam province officer in charge. By then the PRU had been renamed Special Reconnaissance Units and, Lawlor recalled, "had become an adjunct duty of the Special Branch adviser in each province."[4] The CIA funneled PRU salaries in I Corps through the Special Branch to the region PRU commander, Major Vinh, who then doled it out to the province PRU chiefs.

As Rob Simmons had done in Quang Ngai, Lawlor and Loomis created in Quang Nam, with Special Branch Captain Lam Minh Son, a Special Intelligence Force Unit. "Lam recognized that his own people could not run paramilitary operations in rural villages," Lawlor explained. "So we trained a unit of Special Branch guys—taught them infantry formations—so when the PRU came under the operational control of Special Branch in the province after the cease-fire," Lam could utilize them for paramilitary functions immediately.

Prior to the cease-fire, Lawlor's "easy, striped pants" job as Special Branch adviser amounted to coordinating with Captain Lam and getting reports from the Hoi An Province Interrogation Center. He had no dealings with the U.S. military or the province senior adviser and "rarely acted on Phoenix information—just PRU and unilateral sources. There was little Special Branch input, because no one talked to anyone."

According to Lawlor, as the Easter offensive tailed off, the North Vietnamese concentrated on repairing their infiltration routes in preparation for the next offensive. Then came the cease-fire, at which point each village and hamlet identified itself as either GVN- or VC-controlled, and, Lawlor recalled, "all of a sudden there was a lot of business. Because as soon as someone put a VC flag on their roof, they're gone. Not in the sense that they were killed, but we could pick them up and interrogate them. And we basically were flooded."

It was also after the cease-fire, according to Lawlor, that the "country club set" took over. Tom Flores (a protégé of Tom Polgar's) replaced Al Seal as I Corps region officer in charge. Flores brought in his own deputy and chief of operations, and the entire CIA contingent moved into the Da Nang Consulate under State Department cover.

Lawlor described Flores as "a very senior officer on his last tour" whose objective "was to live well, not rock the boat, and take advantage of the amenities that were readily available." That attitude was prevalent. For example, Lawlor says, the Public Safety adviser "was one of the guys who used to set up the [Field Police] shakedowns of merchants. . . . He came out of that war wealthier than you or I will ever be. But you can't prove it." Moreover, when Lawlor brought the matter to the attention of his bosses, he was told, "Don't bother me," or asked, "What do you want me to do?"

Even some province observers were just along for the ride. "The Special Branch liaison in Hue became the Thua Thien province observer," Lawlor recalled. "He had been a retired cop, and he liked the good life. But he had no enthusiasm. He thought it was a joke. He wanted to stay over there when his contract was up, so he became the province observer. He liaised."

Contributing to the decline in morale after the cease-fire was the fact that the Special Intelligence Force Units were disbanded and the PRU were placed under the National Police Command within the Special Branch. "This caused many problems," Lawlor explained. "We started seeing more ghost soldiers, more extortion, more protection money. We couldn't pay them at all, so we lost control." The PRU had the same mission, and they maintained their intelligence agents in field, "but because the CIA adviser was no longer a participant, there were less operations and more excuses for not going."

Instead, Lawlor tried to maintain control by providing "gee whiz" gadgets like UH-1 Night Hawk helicopters with miniguns and spotlights and by being able to get wounded PRU into the hospital in Da Nang.

"Phoenix coordination," according to Lawlor, "was dead. There was nothing left. The Vietnamese gave it lip service, but there was no coördination with the Special Police. When the MSS and Special Branch got together, they tried to take away rather than share information." And once the Special Branch had begun paying PRU teams at province level, "Major Vinh got concerned. Now he has to answer to Saigon. He has to give them a cut. That resulted in Vinh cheating somebody out of his cut, and that fractured what had been a unified unit."

Vinh began putting the squeeze on the Quang Nam PRU chief, Phan Van Liem, who in turn began changing money for the VC. Eventually one of the Quang Nam PRU team, a man named Quyen, came to Lawlor and said, "It's getting out of hand." Ever the idealist, Lawlor investigated. He walked into the Hoi An PIC and saw a woman—who knew about Liem's dirty dealings—stretched over a table. She had been raped and murdered. Said Lawlor: "All of a sudden Mr. Vinh wants me to go on a mission with him, and other PRU guys are telling me, 'Don't go.' "

So it was that the PRU program devolved into a criminal enterprise, like Frankenstein's monster, beyond the control of its creators.

With the cease-fire and the end of American subsidization of Phoenix, PVT and the Da Nang Phoenix Committee had moved into the Da Nang police station. Throughout 1973 PVT divided his time doing Phoenix and drug investigations*—managed by the Air America dispatcher at the Da Nang Air Base—for the CIA. As PVT discovered, the major drug dealers were the Vietnamese police officer in charge of narcotics investigation in Da Nang and his American Public Safety adviser.

The last straw for Bruce Lawlor occurred just before the end of his tour in November 1973. Having worked in Da Nang's counterintelligence office, Lawlor knew that an NVA spy ring still existed in the area and that the

*Phoenix advisers began participating in drug investigations between August and October 1971. Tom Thayer wrote that "reports from field advisers indicate that the joint US/GVN program to dry up South Vietnam's drug traffic may have added to Phung Hoang's chronic problems. Phoenix assets are being used to ferret out drug dealers," he said, adding, "Their attention has in many provinces been turned partially away from anti-VCI efforts. While both problems are essentially police matters, they apparently cannot be handled concurrently. The number of province advisors who mentioned this in their July reports underscores the lack of depth of the Phung Hoang organization."[5]

Special Branch had merely sacrificed a number of low-level cadre in 1971 instead of actually flushing out the most important spies. According to Lawlor, "It was a great deception operation. The high-level people continued to operate." In fact, one of the agents was the girl friend of Tom Flores's operations chief. When Lawlor reported this to Flores, Flores did nothing but accuse Lawlor of having "gone native." Lawlor slipped a copy of his report to the station's security chief in Saigon. The operations officer was sent home, a new operations chief arrived, and Bruce Lawlor ran afoul of the Saigon station. Security teams visited his office, confiscated his furniture, and presented him with a ticket back home.

"After that I became disillusioned," Lawlor confessed. He completed his tour and returned to Langley headquarters, where Ted Shackley—then chief of the Far East Division—offered to accept his resignation.

Lawlor was embittered. "The agency betrayed us," he said. "To go after the VCI, we had to believe it was okay. But we were too young to understand what happens when idealism cracks up against reality. We risked our lives to get information on the VCI, information we were told the President was going to read. Then guys who didn't care gave it to superiors more interested in booze and broads."

(Postscript: In 1984, when he ran for state attorney general in Vermont, Lawlor's opponents uncovered his participation in Phoenix operations and accused him of having committed war crimes. He lost the election. When William Colby heard about the smear campaign, he offered his support. Lawlor was summoned to Langley and interviewed by Rudy Enders, then chief of the Special Operations Division. Despite his willingness to return to the fold and go to work for the CIA in Central America, details of the Da Nang incident surfaced during the interview, and Lawlor was not called back.)

By the end of 1973 the cease-fire, like pacification, was a thing of the past. The Chieu Hoi rate plummeted and, with drastic cuts in U.S. aid, GVN officials who had depended on American aid to maintain their private empires sought their own separate peace with the encroaching Communists. ARVN morale deteriorated as paychecks were diverted into commanders' pockets. Unpaid Territorial Security forces and armed propaganda teams reverted to their pre-Phoenix ways, like the Civil Guard of old, spending most of their time guarding Chieu Hoi centers and the homes and offices of government officials.

At the time Ed Brady was working for the Computer Science Corporation, which had contracted with the Directorate of Political Security to study the "administrative and judicial aspects of the An Tri Laws." Said Brady, who was interviewing Vietcong prisoners at Con Son: "I wrote a lot about how people, if they weren't VC when they were sent to Con Son, were VC when they came out. It was a great training center . . . the people they recruited were made into somebody."[6]

Brady told of one VCI who had been chained to the floor in solitary confinement for refusing to salute the flag. He told Brady, "I'm not South Vietnamese. I'm a VC soldier, and it would be a breach of discipline for me to salute the flag of my enemy. I'll never say yes." Brady pointed out: "He knew what he was and what he believed in, and he was an example to the rest of the camp." Punishing him for sticking to his principles, Brady asserted, "was good for the morale of all the other prisoners. It was a matter of principle to the VC, but it was just a power struggle, like between a parent and a child, for the South Vietnamese. That's what it was all about. None of the propaganda mattered. The VC had principles. The GVN was corrupt."

In 1974, writes Professor Huy, "Corruption, already established as a principle of government by Thieu, Khiem and Vien, now was devouring the social tissue as a growing cancer."[7] Unfortunately, the battle against corruption opened the way for the final Communist offensive.

The push for genuine reform, as the only way to win the political struggle, came from the Catholics and began after Thieu had visited the Vatican and the pope admonished him for packing the jails with political prisoners. Concerned that a Third Force coalition of Buddhists and Communists would exclude them from any position of power in a post-Thieu Vietnam, the Catholics used anticorruption as a pretext to mobilize public opinion against Thieu in July 1974. The movement was led, ironically, by Father Tran Huu Thanh, author of the Vietnamese version of personalism,* which had brought the Ngo regime via the Can Lao party to power in 1954.

At the same time that opposition was building against Thieu, hearings to impeach President Richard Nixon were getting under way in the U.S. Congress. The issues were similar. As a result of the Watergate incident, Congress was concerned that Nixon was using intelligence and security forces to suppress his political opponents. There was also the matter of his having accepted illegal campaign contributions and the bombing of Cambodia and Laos. Likewise, on July 17, 1974, Congressman Otis Pike convened hearings for the purpose of investigating the CIA's role in the Watergate break-in, the disinformation campaign to compromise and discredit Daniel Ellsberg, and other illegal activities the CIA was conducting worldwide.

Back in Saigon, the Catholics, armed with documents showing Thieu's overseas real estate holdings, mounted massive demonstrations in July; by

*See Chapter 1: The Can Lao party—the Can Lao Nham Vi—translates as the "Personal Labor party."

August the capital was in turmoil. On August 18, 1974, the day Nixon announced his plans to resign, David Shipler wrote an article for *The New York Times* headlined SAIGON POLICE FIGHT SUBVERSION BUT ALSO CURB POLITICAL DISSENT. Said Shipler, "[T]hose caught in the web of arrest, torture and imprisonment include not only Communists . . . but non-Communist dissidents . . . apolitical peasants . . . and writers who have simply opposed United States policy and called for peace." Shipler called the wave of political repression "a silent hidden war that runs its course out of the public view."

Phoenix had gone underground, but the bodies it corralled were impossible to hide—despite the efforts of Ambassador Graham Martin, who on July 25, 1974, told the Senate Foreign Relations Committee that "we found no one in prison" who could be regarded as a political prisoner and that charges that there were two hundred thousand political prisoners were part of a Communist propaganda campaign "deliberately designed to force the American Congress to limit economic aid."

Refuting Martin's assertions was David Shipler, who cited one instance after another of perverse torture of women and men—mostly teachers, students, and union workers—in Saigon's First Precinct headquarters. Shipler interviewed Tran Tuan Nham, jailed in 1971 (while running for the National Assembly) by police who cited his anti-American articles as evidence that he was a Communist. Nham wrote about the CIA's involvement in My Lai and the harmful effects of defoliants. Shipler told of another writer "held for three years after he had written newspaper and magazine articles arguing that Vietnamese culture must be preserved against Americanization." And Shipler wrote about a woman arrested in Saigon, taken to the Kien Chuong PIC twenty-two miles away, and viciously, sadistically tortured for absolutely no reason whatsoever, other than for the pleasure of the torturers.

Wrote Shipler: "[D]issidents who are free to speak out say they are mere ornaments, that whenever they begin to accrue political power the police arrest the lesser figures around them, break up their meetings and leave them isolated." The leaders themselves were targeted for assassination.

In his follow-up article on August 20, TO SAIGON, ALL DISSENTERS ARE FOES, ALL FOES ARE REDS, Shipler explained that GVN security forces believed that only Communists opposed Thieu. He quoted Thieu as saying that "the 19.5 million South Vietnamese people should be molded into a monolithic bloc, motivated by a single anti-Communist ideal." Shipler then told how security forces saw Communists—to whom they attributed superhuman powers of deviousness and persuasion—everywhere. And not only were all dissenters Communists, but according to a PRU officer working with the Special Branch, "all dissidents are opportunists."

In reality, soaring inflation—resulting from a lack of U.S. aid—had made mere survival the single ideal uniting the Vietnamese people. Even CIA-supported Special Branch officers were feeling the pinch and in order to make ends meet were packing the jails with "opportunists" who they held for ransom. Shipler described a visit he made to see a group of "opportunists" held for ransom in the Chi Hoa jail. The "movie room" where they were being held was eighteen by twenty-four feet, dimly lit by a single bulb, full of mosquitoes, and the stench of urine and feces on the floor was so bad that the prisoners—all of whom were shackled by one leg to an iron bar running the length of the wall—couldn't breathe. Friends and relatives of prisoners, and "VCI" suspects, were required to report to the Special Branch, then extorted. Indeed, by 1974 there was no middle ground in Vietnam—just the rising blood pressure of a body politic about to suffer a massive coronary thrombosis.

At the same time that the financial supports were being kicked out from under the Thieu regime in Saigon, USAID's Office of Public Safety was put on the chopping block. The process had begun in 1969, when Public Safety adviser Dan Mitrione was captured and killed in Uruguay by guerrillas who claimed he was an undercover CIA officer teaching torture techniques to the secret police. A 1970 movie titled *State of Siege,* which dramatized the Mitrione episode and showed International Police Academy (IPA) graduates torturing political prisoners, brought attention to the practices of the IPA. Consequently, according to Doug McCollum, the State Department "developed animosity toward Public Safety people," and many contracts, including McCollum's, were not renewed.[8]

Charges that the IPA taught torture and political repression gained credence in August 1974, when columnist Jack Anderson printed excerpts from several student papers written at the academy. Wrote one student from South Vietnam: "Based on experience, we are convinced there is just one sure way to save time and suppress stubborn criminal suspects—that is the proper use of threats and force."

On October 2, 1974, Senator James Abourezk inserted into the *Congressional Record* the words of National Policeman Le Van An. Said Le: "Despite the fact that brutal interrogation is strongly criticized by moralists, its importance must not be denied if we want to have order and security in daily life."[9]

In 1972 senior Field Police adviser William Grieves was scheduled for reassignment to Bangkok. "But," he told me, "the ambassador wouldn't let me in because the CIA held a grudge." Instead, Grieves was sent to Washington as deputy to Public Safety chief Byron Engel. Said Grieves: "I lost all respect for Byron Engel. He'd been too long in CIA. He was always asking me to have so-and-so bring things back from Hong Kong, and he was rude to congressmen." But the worst thing, according to Grieves, was Engel's attempt to "rewrite history."[10]

And history was rewritten. The IPA was abolished but, like a Phoenix, was reborn in the guise of a new organization called the Law Enforcement Assistance Administration.

Despite its ability to regenerate and survive, the CIA was taking its lumps in 1974, too. Richard Helms was accused and later convicted on perjury charges after William Colby admitted that the agency had spent eight million dollars to "destabilize" Allende's regime in Chile. Colby himself was under attack, not only for alleged Phoenix-related war crimes but for having censored John Marks's book *The Cult of Intelligence* and for trying to block publication of Philip Agee's *CIA Diary*.

Agee in particular was despised by his CIA colleagues for saying, in an interview with *Playboy* magazine, that there was "a strong possibility that the CIA station in Chile helped supply the assassination lists." Agee asserted that the CIA "trains and equips saboteurs and bomb squads" and that the CIA had "assassinated thousands of people. . . . When the history of the CIA's support of torturers gets written," Agee predicted, "it'll be the all-time horror story.[11]

"Thousands of policemen all over the world," Agee said, "are shadowing people for the CIA without knowing it. They think they're working for their own police departments when, in fact, their chief may be a CIA agent who's sending them out on CIA jobs and turning the information over to his CIA control."

Some of those people were Special Branch officers in Vietnam. For example, in August 1974, Colonel Ben Hamilton prepared a report titled "Results of Communist Infrastructure Neutralization Efforts Made by Phoenix Committees" for Colonel Doug Dillard at 500th MIG headquarters. The report cited the number of neutralizations from February 15 through May 31, 1974. The source of the information was a "friendly Foreign Intelligence agency," meaning the National Phoenix Committee under Colonel Nguyen Van Giau, who signed the report and sent it to the Directorate of Political Security. Noting that the figures were probably "inflated," Hamilton sent the report to the CIA, the Defense Intelligence Agency, and the acting chief of staff for intelligence at the Pentagon. According to the report, I Corps tallied 39 percent of its yearly quota from February till May. In II Corps Binh Thuan Province racked up 54 percent of its yearly goal, with 39 convictions, 47 killed, and 29 rallied. In III Corps Phuoc Long Province tallied 3 VCI killed and 2 rallied, and in IV Corps, 169 VCI were killed in Chuong Thien Province.

In September 1974 William Colby was asked by a panel of citizens why

Watergate burglar and CIA officer James McCord's personnel records had been burned by CIA officer Lee Pennington immediately after the break-in and why the CIA had destroyed tapes of Richard Helms instructing Nixon and John Erhlichman how to respond to congressional inquiries. They asked Colby to defend CIA financing of the National Student Association, and he responded by citing Point 5 of the National Security Act, which allows the CIA to perform "functions and duties related to intelligence affecting the national security as the National Security Council may from time to time direct."

Senator James Abourezk asked Colby, "But you do undertake activities overseas that would be crimes in this country?"

Replied Colby: "Of course. Espionage is a crime in this country."[12]

ABOUREZK: "Other than espionage?"

COLBY: "Of course." Added Colby: "I think . . . the use of an atomic bomb is justified in the interest of national security, and I think going down from there is quite a realm of things you can do in the reasonable defense of the country."

Asked John Marks: "But in peacetime?"

On January 6, 1975, the NVA overran Phuoc Long Province.

A few days later UPI reporter Robert Kaylor reported that the United States was still involved with "the ill-famed Phoenix program," that the program had been renamed the "Special Police Investigative Service (SPIS)" and was being conducted by fourteen thousand special troops whose operations are monitored on a part-time basis by CIA operatives in Saigon and in provincial capitals throughout the country. According to Kaylor, "The U.S. also provides data processing facilities for SPIS through a contractor, Computer Science Services Inc.," which "runs intelligence reports through its machines to classify and collate them and then turns the material over to SPIS."[13]

Writes Kaylor: "According to sources here, about 100 American personnel are now involved in monitoring the program. They said that overall responsibility for watching it rests with a U.S. Air Force officer on detached duty with the American Embassy in Saigon."

When Ambassador Martin read Kaylor's article, he immediately sent a telegram to Washington calling Kaylor's article "journalistic fiction" and assured the State Department that, as regarded Phoenix, "No element of the U.S. Government is involved in any way with any program in Vietnam of any such description."[14] As for the Special Police, "The U.S. Government has no relationships to this organization whatsoever." According to Martin, "There is no U.S. Air Force officer on detached duty," and as for the Computer Science Corporation (CSC), it merely contracted with the National

Police "in logistics and personnel." Said Martin: "At the present time, CSC . . . is uninvolved in any counter-insurgency or other operational matters."

On March 10, 1975, the NVA overran Ban Me Thuot. In desperation, Ted Serong drew up a plan to abandon the Central Highlands and withdraw all ARVN forces to cities along the coast. The South Vietnamese agreed, opening the floodgates to the NVA. Hue fell on March 25. Chu Lai and Quang Ngai City fell on the same day, amid attacks by the South Vietnamese against CIA officers who abandoned their records and agents. Within hours all that remained in I Corps was Da Nang. II Corps was going down just as fast. Kontum and Pleiku had fallen two weeks earlier, and thirteen province capitals were to be gone by April. The Third NVA Division was heading toward Qui Nhon, and a million refugees were fleeing toward Nha Trang.

In Da Nang the scene was one of fire, murder, looting, and rape. ARVN soldiers had seized the airport control tower, and planes meant to evacuate them were frozen on the ground. CIA helicopters were ferrying Americans out of the city, abandoning their Vietnamese assets. Thousands of panicked people moved to the waterfront, piled onto piers and barges, dived into the water, tried to swim to boats. Hundreds of bodies were later washed up on the shore. The CIA contingent joined the exodus, fleeing their quarters while their Nung guards fired shots at their heels. At Marble Mountain airstrip the consul general was beaten into unconsciousness by ARVN soldiers. By March 29 Da Nang was defenseless and being shelled. By the thirtieth Special Branch and Military Security Service officers were being rounded up and shot by NVA security officers.

On March 29 PVT found himself stranded in Da Nang, on the verge of a harrowing experience. "The ranger and airborne generals left, saying they had to go to a meeting," he recalled. "We were told to wait for orders, but they didn't come. After that there was no coordination."[15] Growing impatient, PVT and eight members of his PRU team made their way with Police Chief Nguyen to police headquarters. But "They were all gone." Knowing they had been abandoned, PVT and his comrades decided to stick together and fight their way out. Taking charge, PVT led the group to the waterfront, where, by force of arms, they commandeered a boat and set off down the river into the bay. That night they were picked up by a U.S. Navy vessel crowded with refugees. On April 2 the ship disembarked its human cargo at Cam Ranh Bay. PVT and his crew began walking south down Route 1 but were stopped at gunpoint at an ARVN checkpoint; no one was being allowed to leave the city. Luckily, though, PVT was recognized by an ARVN commander, who put them on a truck going to Nha Trang. Several hours later they arrived there only to find that the American Embassy had been abandoned the day before. Nha Trang would be bypassed by the NVA on its way to Cam Ranh.

With cities in II Corps falling like dominoes, PVT led his group to the home of another friend, Colonel Pham, the Khanh Hoa province chief. After curfew Colonel Pham loaded his own family along with PVT's PRU team in the back of a truck, drove them to the dock, and put them on a ship bound for Vung Tau. PVT could think of nothing else but getting to Saigon and arranging safe passage for his family out of Vietnam. Upon arriving off the coast of Vung Tau, however, PVT and his companions were informed that all traffic to Saigon, both by river and by road, had been cut. In Washington the CIA's Far East Division chief Ted Shackley had ordered the city sealed off from refugees. His heart sinking as fast as Vietnam, PVT sailed off toward Phu Quoc Island.

Still holding hopes for a negotiated settlement, the war managers met one last time in Saigon to plan the city's defense. While evacuation plans were drawn up on a contingency basis, the American brain trust drew a Maginot Line extending from Tay Ninh to Phan Rang and told its Vietnamese clients to defend it to the death. Behind the scenes Air Marshal Ky pressed for a coup d'état, and General Loan—then a special assistant to General Vien—warned station chief Polgar that unless "high-risk" Vietnamese were evacuated as promised, American hostages would be taken. To avert such a catastrophe, an evacuation team under State Department officer Dean Brown was formed in Washington. Among those chosen to select which Vietnamese were to be saved were Lionel Rosenblatt, Frank Wisner, Ev Bumgartner, Craig Johnstone, Ken Quinn, and Frank Scotton. Bill Johnson, the CIA's Saigon base chief, got the job of setting up CIA stay-behind nets.

On April 4, 1975, Congress was debating how much money to give Saigon for its defense, while in Saigon, Valium and scotch were selling at a premium in the besieged U.S. Embassy. Metropolitan Police Chief Tran Si Tan slapped a twenty-four-hour curfew on the city. Panic began to spread. The war reached Saigon four days later when a South Vietnamese Air Force pilot dropped three bombs on the Presidential Palace. Inside, Thieu consulted with fortune-tellers. Tran Van Don and General Khiem, who had resigned as prime minister, nominated General Duong Van "Big" Minh as Thieu's replacement.

On April 12 Henry Kissinger ordered the evacuation of Phnom Penh, Cambodia. As the American contingent boarded helicopters and flew to safety, Sirak Matak cried that he had been betrayed. Five days later, when Khmer Rouge troops rolled into the city, he was arrested and summarily executed. Meanwhile, six NVA regiments were poised north of Can Tho in the Delta, and numerous others were heading south toward Saigon. Knowing the country was doomed, Tucker Gougleman wrote a letter to a friend on April 13, spelling out his plans to rescue his family. Posted from Bangkok, where he managed Associated Consultants Limited, Gougleman's letter told how he planned his "extraction from Phu Quoc Island to Trat near Chantaburi on the southernmost part of the Thai east coast." Gougleman commented on the "totally undependable" ARVN and its "cruel perpetrations on civilian refugees" and noted that "Thieu has killed SVN." He closed the letter with "C'est la fucking vie."

Being stuck on Phu Quoc Island was a frustrating experience for PVT, and as soon as they could, PVT and his PRU comrades boarded a boat heading for Saigon. Immediately four Vietnamese marines armed with M-16's commandeered the boat and stole everyone's money and watches. "But they didn't know we were police or that we were armed," PVT told me with a glint in his eye. "I told my men to wait till dark. When the marines were eating, I organized an assault. We got control." A few hours later PVT arrived in Saigon.

Phan Rang fell on the sixteenth. On Saturday, the nineteenth, the CIA began flying selected Vietnamese out on unauthorized black flights. Ostensibly these were "high-risk" assets from the various security programs who were unable to obtain the necessary exit visas from the Ministry of the Interior. More often they were girl friends of their CIA case officers. On the twentieth the CIA began burning its files. On the twenty-first, Xuan Loc fell, and the evacuation rate was accelerated. Fifteen hundred people were flown out that day.

Having finally set foot in Saigon, PVT reported to Colonel Hai, who only a few weeks before had taken over command of the PRU and who proposed to PVT that he and his PRU team provide security for the CIA. Having been unable to find a single CIA officer to vouch for him in Saigon, PVT refused. Instead, he began making arrangements to save his family. On the twentieth PVT gathered his wife and children together in a house he owned near Tan Son Nhut airport. He visited his brother at the Cholon branch of the Thanh Thien bank and arranged to have his savings transferred to a branch office in Gia Dinh Province. "Communist political cadre were even then moving everyone out of the city," he said. Thieu resigned on the twenty-first and turned the government over to Vice President Huong. That day PVT piled his family into a jeep and drove them to Tan Son Nhut airport, where they were given sanctuary by a police colonel—a close friend of Ky's—whose house was inside the gates.

Inside Tan Son Nhut, PVT contacted his old friend from Da Nang, Police Captain Nguyen Minh Tan. After the flap over the Da Nang City PRU, PVT had used his influence to get Tan a job in the Saigon Phoenix office. When Colonel Nguyen Van Giau assumed command of Phoenix after the cease-fire, he reassigned Tan to the immigration office inside Tan Son Nhut. On the twenty-first Tan told PVT that it was time to go. PVT handed his sister his life's savings—five hundred thousand in piasters—and asked her to change it in Cholon. She returned with two hundred American dollars. On the twenty-second Tan brought PVT into the office of the South Vietnamese Air Force captain in charge of flights to Clark Air Force base in the Philippines. For two hundred American dollars the captain put PVT's name on manifest. At 9:00 P.M. on the twenty-second, while the NVA rolled toward Bien Hoa and Vung Tau, PVT and his family and Nguyen Minh Tan and his family bade adieu to their homeland.

On the same day PVT left Saigon, Lionel Rosenblatt and Craig Johnstone arrived, set up shop in the Regent Hotel, and arranged safe passage out of Vietnam for a number of their friends. By the time the two left on the twenty-fifth (the same day that Thieu and Khiem fled to Taiwan), they had smuggled out anywhere from three to two hundred high-ranking police and PRU officers.

On April 25, while U.S. Marines exchanged rifle fire with South Vietnamese paratroopers, President Huong offered to free the two hundred thousand political prisoners the U.S. Embassy claimed had never existed. The Communists laughed in his face. On the twenty-seventh the road between Tay Ninh and Saigon was cut, rockets began falling in Saigon, and Huong turned the government over to Big Minh. That night CIO chief General Binh bade adieu to Vietnam. By the twenty-eighth there was fighting in the streets of Saigon. U.S. helicopter gunships roamed the smoke-filled skies while Saigon base chief Bill Johnson paid a final visit to his colleagues in the Special Branch and CIO. He suggested that they get out of town fast. According to Frank Snepp, four hundred Special Branch and four hundred CIO officers were left behind, along with "files identifying defectors, collaborators, prisoners, anyone who had helped us or seemed likely to."[16] Snepp says the CIA abandoned "countless counter-terrorist agents—perhaps numbering as high as 30,000—specially trained to operate with the Phoenix program."[17]

On William Colby's orders, U.S. helicopters began flying Americans to ships offshore on the twenty-eighth; the following day the NVA hit Tan Son Nhut. With the army in full retreat and no policemen left to enforce the curfew, rioting and looting broke out in Saigon. Panic spread through the American community while the one man with the most to lose, Tucker Gougleman, decided to go down with the ship. Perhaps he was having a drink on the veranda of the Continental Hotel when Saigon, like the Phoenix in flames, gave up its ghost.

EPILOGUE

In the opinion of Stan Fulcher (who in 1972 was the Binh Dinh Province Phoenix coordinator and whose experiences are recounted in Chapter 28), "Phoenix was a creation of the old-boy network, a group of guys at highest level—Colby and that crowd—who thought they were Lawrence of Arabia."[1]

Indeed, the Phoenix program in South Vietnam was set up by Americans on American assumptions, in support of American policies. Unfortunately America's allies in South Vietnam were people whose prosperity depended on American patronage and who therefore implemented a policy they knew could not be applied to their culture. In the process the definition of the Vietcong infrastructure was misinterpreted to mean any Vietnamese citizen, and Phoenix was broadened from a rifle shot attack against the "organizational hierarchy" into a shotgun method of population control.

It happened, Fulcher said ruefully, because "any policy can find supporting intelligence," meaning "the Phoenix Directorate used computers to skew the statistical evaluation of the VCI. Dead Vietnamese became VCI, and they lucked out the other five percent of the time, getting real VCI in ambushes." As Fulcher explained it, "The Vietnamese lied to us; we lied to the directorate; and the directorate made it into documented fact. . . . It was a war that became distorted through our ability to create fiction. But really, there were only economic reasons for our supporting the fascists in Vietnam, just like we did in Iran."

Professor Huy agrees, asserting that America "betrayed the ideals of freedom and democracy in Vietnam." Furthermore, writes Huy, "American politicians have not yet changed their policy. What happened later in Iran was a repetition of what happened in South Vietnam. Almost the same people applied the same policy with the same principles and the same spirit. It is amazing that some people are still wondering why the same result occurred."[2]

"It's the problem of supporting personalities rather than democratic institutions," Fulcher explained, noting that in Vietnam the issue was not the Vietcong versus the Army of South Vietnam, but land reform and government corruption. "The Vietnamese were victims of our corruption," Fulcher said emphatically. "We smothered them with money. It's the same thing you see in Central America today. You can't take a Salvadoran colonel in a patron army without the corruption he brings along.

"With consolidation we could have had control," Fulcher concluded, "and Phoenix was the culmination of the attempt to solidify control." But the warlords and corrupt politicians we supported in Vietnam refused to sacrifice even a tiny share of their empires for the greater good of Vietnam, and thus were incapable of countering what was a homogeneous, nationalist-inspired insurgency.

In any event, defeat in Vietnam did not repress the impulses that powered America to third world intervention in the first place; it simply drove them elsewhere. Nowhere is this more evident than in El Salvador, where Lieutenant Colonel Stan Fulcher served from 1974 till 1977 as an intelligence adviser with the U.S. Military Group. In El Salvador Fulcher saw the same "old boys" who had run the war in South Vietnam. Only in El Salvador, because of the vast reduction in the CIA's paramilitary forces instigated by the Carter administration, these officials effected their policies through proxies from allied countries. For example, Fulcher watched while Israeli agents taught El Salvador's major landowners how to organize criminals into vigilante death squads, which, using intelligence from Salvador's military and security forces, murdered labor leaders and other opponents of the oligarchy. Likewise, Fulcher watched while Taiwanese military officers taught Kuomintang political warfare techniques at El Salvador's Command and General Staff College: Phoenix-related subjects such as population control through psychological warfare, the development and control of agents provocateurs, the development of political cadres within the officer corps, and the placement of military officers in the civilian security forces. He also saw political prisoners put in insane asylums—facilities he described as being "like Hogarth's paintings."

While other Americans smuggled weapons and funds to the death squads, Fulcher, who was outraged by what he saw, organized at his home a study group of young military officers who supported land reform, nationalization of the banks, and civilian control of the military. In 1979 these same reformist officers staged a successful but short-lived coup, as a result of which the Salvadoran National Security Agency (ANSESAL), which had been formed by the CIA in 1962, was disbanded and reorganized as the National Intelligence Agency (ANI).

This reorganization did not put an end to the death squads. Instead, the landowners and fascist military officers moved to Miami and Guatemala, where they formed a political front called Arena, to which they channeled funds for the purpose of eliminating the reformers. Chosen to head Arena was Major Roberto d'Aubuisson, a former member of ANSESAL who transferred its files to general staff headquarters, where they were used to compile blacklists. Operating out of Guatemala, D'Aubuisson's death squads murdered Archbishop Oscar Romero and El Salvador's attorney general in early 1980. In December of that year six members of El Salvador's executive council were kidnapped, tortured, and killed by a death squad, and the death squads began a rampage which included the murders in January 1981 of José Rodolfo Viera, the head of the land distribution program, along with Viera's American advisers, Michael Hammer and Mark Pearlman.

At this time, according to Salvadoran Army officer Ricardo Castro,[3] death squad supervision passed to Department 5, the civil affairs branch of the Salvadoran general staff. "Department 5 suddenly started coordinating everything," said Castro, a West Point graduate with a master's degree in engineering. Formed in the mid-1970's by the CIA, Department 5, Castro explained, became "the political intelligence apparatus within the general staff." Although it was designed as an investigative, not an operating, agency, Department 5 had "a large paramilitary force of people dressed in civilian clothes," and because it targeted civilians, "They can knock someone off all by themselves, or capture them."

When military as opposed to political targets were involved, Department 2, the intelligence branch of the general staff, would send information gathered from its informant nets to Department 3 (operations), which then dispatched a death squad of its own. Whether the people to be killed were guerrillas or civilians, Castro explained, "the rich people—the leading citizens of the community—traditionally have a great deal of input. Whatever bothers them, if they've got someone who just came into their ranch or their farm and they consider them a bad influence, they just send a messenger to the commander."

In March 1981 Castro himself began leading death squad operations. Using a modus operandi perfected in Vietnam, orders were always verbal and the soldiers in the death squads shucked their uniforms and dressed as left-wing guerrillas. "Basically," said Castro, "you come in after patrolling or whatever . . . and then you're told that at a certain hour you will have to go get up the troops and go do something. . . . They already know what the mission is. They happen just about every night, or they used to.

"Normally," Castro added, "you eliminate everyone. . . . We usually go in with . . . an informant who is part of the patrol and who has turned these people in. When you turn somebody in," Castro noted, "part of your obligation is to show us where they are and identify them. We would go in and knock on people's houses. They'd come out of their houses and we'd always tell them we were the Left and we're here because you don't want to cooperate with us or whatever. And then they were eliminated, always with machetes."

In late 1981, with the government of El Salvador back in the hands of the fascist military, the death squads were moved under the Salvadoran security forces, which generally operated in urban areas and pretended to be and/or used the services of right-wing vigilantes. Castro told of death squads within the treasury police* killing teachers and of death squads within the National Guard killing mayors and nuns—all with the approval of the general staff.

Castro also worked as translator to a series of CIA advisers at general staff headquarters. One course he translated was on interrogation. It was taught by a CIA officer who suggested electric shock and presented architectural plans for a PIClike prison to be built at the cavalry regiment headquarters. "It was going to become a secret jail," recalled Castro, who was enlisted by Department 5 to begin engineering work.

According to Castro, the CIA interrogation instructor also advised the general staff on mounting death squad operations in foreign countries, especially Honduras, and was complicit in these operations insofar as he provided El Salvador's Secret Service with files and photos of Salvadorans in the United States.

As in Vietnam, the proliferation of political assassinations in El Salvador had a ripple effect, which ended in the massacring of innocent civilians. Castro told how in November 1981 a number of civilians were killed following a sweep by the U.S.-trained Atlacatl Battalion. Said Castro: "[T]here were 24 women and children captured, and they were assassinated

*Under Colonel Nicolas Carranza, who, according to the Center for National Security Studies, was recruited by the CIA in the late 1970's at a cost of ninety thousand dollars a year.[4]

right smack in front of me—just one by one, in cold blood." Counterterror-style, the mutilated corpses were left behind as a warning to leftist guerrillas.

In December 1981 Castro met Major Pineda of Department 5, who was operating in Morazán Province. "They had two towns of about three hundred people each," Castro recalled, "and they were interrogating them to see what they knew. Since I had translated in the class and knew something about interrogations, he said they might want me to help. The Major told me that after the interrogation, they were going to kill them all." Said Castro: "I later found out, they did go in and kill them after all."

In August 1982 Castro traveled to Washington on behalf of a group of young Salvadoran officers concerned about corruption and demoralization within the army rank and file. Castro told a CIA officer in Washington about the death squads. The CIA officer said, "We know all that." Nothing was done.

This hands-off policy reflected a maturation in the thinking of the CIA. In the aftermath of Vietnam the CIA set up a special section to study terrorism and third world instability. The "terrorism account" was given to DIOCC creator Bob Wall by ICEX's first director, Evan Parker, who was then deputy director of the CIA's paramilitary Special Operations Division (SOD). In analyzing the problem of terrorism, Wall brought in Foreign Intelligence experts, who determined that the CIA could not reasonably expect to penetrate terrorist groups—like the VCI or the Palestine Liberation Organization—which were "homogeneous." As a result of this determination, the CIA then separated its antiterrorist activities from its counterinsurgency activities, which it renamed "low-intensity warfare."

By 1980 paramilitary expert Rudy Enders was chief of the Special Operations Division, and Enders in turn passed the "terrorism account" to former senior PRU adviser William Buckley, who created a military staffed antiterrorism unit in 1981 under the Pentagon's Joint Special Operations Command.

Meanwhile, El Salvador had emerged as the perfect place to test the CIA's new theory of low-intensity warfare. In March 1983 Vice President George Bush's national security adviser, former III Corps region officer in charge Donald Gregg, wrote to President Ronald Reagan's national security adviser, Robert MacFarlane, saying, "Rudy Enders . . . went to El Salvador in 1981 to do a survey and develop plans for effective anti-guerrilla operations. He came back and endorsed the attached plan."[5] The Pink Plan, written by former PRU adviser Felix Rodriguez, was to launch mobile air strikes with "minimum U.S. participation" at leftist rebels. Rodriguez said the plan would "Be ideal for the pacification effort in El Salvador and Guatemala."[6]

Shortly after proposing the Pink Plan, Gregg introduced Rodriguez to

George Bush* and Oliver North. Rodriguez was sent to El Salvador, where, as an adviser to Department 5, he organized a "high-bird, low-bird" Pink Team, leading the missions himself and using the same techniques he had developed while serving as Gregg's deputy in charge of the PRU in Vietnam. As in Vietnam, civilian security services joined with Department 5 (civil affairs) and Department 2 (intelligence) to provide Department 3 (operations) with information on the location of guerrillas, whose hideouts were bombed by U.S. warplanes, then ravaged in Phoenix-style cordon and search operations in which PRU-type teams hunted enemy cadres in their homes. Rodriguez played the role of coordinator. At the time Colonel Adolfo Blandon commanded Departments 2 and 5.

According to reporter Dennis Volkman, Blandon was advised by a Cuban-American from the consular section of the American Embassy, who met regularly with U.S. military advisers to Departments 2 and 5 in San Salvador.[7]

General Paul Gorman, who commanded U.S. forces in Central America in the mid-1980's, defined this new type of counterinsurgency operation as "a form of warfare repugnant to Americans, a conflict which involves innocents, in which non-combatant casualties may be an explicit object."[8]

Gorman could have been alluding to Operation Phoenix, launched by the Salvadoran Army in January 1986. As reported in the Boston *Globe,* Operation Phoenix began with the military dropping waves of 750-pound bombs over Guazapa volcano, "a defiant symbol of persistence by a few thousand rebels against government forces that outnumber them 10 to one and are backed by the purse and arsenal of the U.S."[9] Next came planes with leaflets and bullhorns offering the rebels rewards for their rifles and safe passage to refugee camps. Meanwhile, thirty-five hundred troops swept the volcano in a tightening circle, burning crops, destroying hideouts, interrogating civilian detainees, and hunting enemy cadres.

The Salvadoran officer in charge of Operation Phoenix said, "We have three goals. Get rid of the idea that Guazapa belongs to the terrorists; to reactivate idle land; and to convince the *masa* (the people) we are different from the reality they've been told." And, he added, "By removing the *masa* from Guazapa, officials hope to disrupt the rebels' vital network of rural support."

In a Public Broadcasting System documentary titled *Enough Crying of Tears,* Operation Phoenix was described as wiping out entire villages.

*In 1983 Bush journeyed to El Salvador and arranged to have the most prominent death squad leaders sent to diplomatic posts abroad. By 1987 nine of eleven were back.

* * *

In the wake of Vietnam, the CIA not only defined antiterrorism apart from counterinsurgency but also separated counterterrorism (defined as "bold and swift action to undo what terrorists have recently done") from antiterrorism, which is the broad spectrum and includes psywar campaigns against countries the United States brands as "terrorist." The best example is Nicaragua, where the CIA mined harbors and inserted insurgents, called contras, who systematically tortured and massacred civilians and assassinated government officials.

When in 1983 tales of contra atrocities began reaching congressional ears, CIA Director William Casey sent CIA officer John Kirkpatrick (an alias) to contra headquarters in Honduras to clean up their act. In October 1983 former Green Beret Kirkpatrick returned to Washington, where he copied a U.S. Special Forces manual issued at Fort Bragg in 1968. He then returned to Tegucigalpa, Honduras, where the manual was printed in Spanish. It was titled *Tayacan: Psychological Operations in Guerrilla Warfare.*

Kirkpatrick was an older man who dressed entirely in black in order "to inspire a cult of death among the fighting men," writes James Dickey in *With the Contras*. "Kirkpatrick thought he knew quite a bit about his end of a paramilitary operation: the psychology of it. . . . He knew about those special circumstances when an assassination might be unavoidable, even appropriate. He knew from studying the methods of the Communists everywhere, and from his own experience in Vietnam and from what he learned from the Phoenix program there, how you could make even an accidental killing work in your favor. But he also knew what My Lai could do, and the way one massacre could destroy your credibility."[10]

Dickey describes *Tayacan* as "a little book with a cover in the blue and white of the Nicaraguan flag. The graphic motif was rows of heads with large holes through them. Targets. It looked as if they were targets for snipers. But the idea was to target their minds."[11]

Indeed, *Tayacan* was based entirely on Frank Scotton's motivational indoctrination principles. The goal was to organize the contras into armed propaganda teams that would persuade the people to stage a general uprising. As stated in *Tayacan,* this was to be done through psychological operations, by reaching beyond the "territorial limits of conventional warfare, to penetrate the political entity itself: the 'political animal' that Aristotle defined." For once his mind has been reached, the "political animal has been defeated, without *necessarily* receiving bullets."

Central to the CIA's doctrine of psychological operations is the "compulsion of people with arms," the notion of "implicit terror," that "the people are internally 'aware' that the weapons can be used against them." There are also times, *Tayacan* adds, when "explicit terror" is required to compel the people to change their minds. Using a modus operandi perfected by the Vietcong, *Tayacan* instructs its armed propaganda teams to gather the villagers together, cut all communication with the outside world, then desecrate symbols of the government while being courteous to the people so as to get the names of government informants and officials, who are then brought before a people's tribunal. Lastly, the team's political cadre gives a prepared speech explaining that force is necessary to give the people power over the government and that the ensuing execution is being done to protect the people and is an act of democracy.

Tayacan specifically calls for "neutralizing" judges, police officials, and state security officials. It also says that "professional criminals should be hired to carry out specific, selective jobs."

What *Tayacan* represents, of course, is Ralph Johnson's doctrine of Contre Coup having come full circle, emerging from the Phoenix *program* in Vietnam as the Phoenix *concept* of "explicit terrorism" disguised as antiterrorism.

It is instructive to hear how people responded to *Tayacan*. Contra defector Edgar Chamorro, who leaked the manual to the American press in 1984, used language lifted from Robert Komer when he said *Tayacan* author John Kirkpatrick "didn't want us to use a shotgun approach; he wanted us to select our targets."[12]

Senator Sam Nunn of Georgia said the word "neutralize" could be interpreted by reasonable people to mean "assassination."[13]

"It does not mean assassination," William Colby said on the October 28, 1984, *David Brinkley Show;* "it means take the person out of action."[14] Ronald Reagan agreed and said that "neutralize" meant "remove from office." When asked how that could be done without violence, Reagan said, "You just say to the fellow that's sitting there in the office, you're not in the office anymore."[15]

Duane Clarridge, the CIA officer in charge of operations against Nicaragua at the time *Tayacan* was printed, acknowledged that "civilians and Sandinista officials in the provinces, as well as heads of cooperatives, nurses, doctors and judges," had been killed by the contras. But, he added, "These events don't constitute assassinations because as far as we are concerned assassinations are only those of heads of state."[16]

Eden Pastora was not a head of state; he was the head of the southern branch of the contras—until May 31, 1984, when an attempt was made on his life at La Penca, Costa Rica, where he was preparing to announce his withdrawal from the contra force. When asked whom he blamed for the attempt on his life, Pastora responded, "We now believe the order came from Oliver North." When asked whom he held ultimately responsible,

Pastora replied, "I could get killed for saying this, but it would have to be Vice-President George Bush."[17]

Is Pastora's accusation totally outrageous? Perhaps not when one considers that in May 1984, in El Salvador, Felix Rodriguez was facilitating the contra resupply effort for Oliver North. Or that the person initially chosen by North to resupply the contras was former SOG commander John Singlaub, who in doing so worked with *Soldier of Fortune* publisher Robert Brown, creator in 1974 of Phoenix Associates. Or that one mercenary group operating in Nicaragua actually called itself the Phoenix Battalion.

There is another disturbing connection in the La Penca bombing. On the night before the bomb went off, Oliver North's liaison to the contras, Rob Owen, was meeting in San José, Costa Rica, with the CIA station chief, Joe Fernandez. Rob Owen is the brother of Dwight Owen, who was killed in an ambush by the same Vietcong outfit that was supplied by the villagers of My Lai.

Consider also that Tom Polgar, former Saigon station chief, was chief investigator for the Senate Select Committee probing the Iran-contra affair. In the February 1986 issue of *Legal Times,* Donald Gregg is quoted as saying that Polgar "wanted to assure me that [the hearings] would not be a repeat of the Pike and Church investigations." When George Bush was director of central intelligence in 1976, Gregg was his representative before the congressional committees that were investigating the CIA's role in criminal activities, including the attempted assassinations of foreign leaders. At the time Gregg presented the committees with an ultimatum: Back off or face martial law. Polgar, it seems, likewise derailed another round of executive-legislative brinkmanship.

In 1985 Tom Polgar was a consultant on George Bush's Task Force on Combatting Terrorism, along with Oliver North and John Poindexter.

What these "old Phoenix boys" all have in common is that they profit from antiterrorism by selling weapons and supplies to repressive governments and insurgent groups like the contras. Their legacy is a trail of ashes across the third world.

And where can Phoenix be found today? Wherever governments of the left or the right use military and security forces to enforce their ideologies under the aegis of antiterrorism. Look for Phoenix wherever police checkpoints ring major cities, wherever paramilitary police units patrol in armored cars, and wherever military forces are conducting counterinsurgent operations. Look for Phoenix wherever emergency decrees are used to suspend due process, wherever dissidents are interned indefinitely in detention camps, and wherever dissidents are rounded up and deported. Look for Phoenix wherever security forces use informants to identify dissidents, wherever security forces keep files and computerized blacklists on dissidents, wherever security forces conduct secret investigations and surveillance on dissidents, wherever security forces, or thugs in their hire, harass and murder dissidents, and wherever such activities go unreported by the press.

But most of all, look for Phoenix in the imaginations of ideologues obsessed with security, who seek to impose their way of thinking on everyone else.

APPENDIX

Addendum 1: Psyops Comic Book: "Phung Hoang Campaign"

The cartoon book titled Gia dinh ong Ba va Chien Dich Phung Hoang **(Mr. Ba's Family and the Phoenix Operation) reads as follows:**

Caption 2. Summary: Mr. Ba and his family are presently living in Phong Thanh village. This village is actually part of the nationalist territory but is still infiltrated by a number of Communist elements; therefore, Phoenix leaders have taken military action against them. They received enthusiastic cooperation from the villagers. As a result of this, and through accurate information provided by local people, many Communist cadres have been arrested. These circumstances help you follow the story of Mr. Ba's family.

Caption 3. The cruel Communists kill innocent people again!

Caption 4. Following is the news: "This morning at nine A.M., a Lambretta was blown up by a Communist mine five kilometers outside Phung Hiep village. Two children were killed, three women wounded. The Communists continue to terrorize people!"

Caption 5. "Hello, sister Tu!"

"Why are you so late?"

"Hello, brother and sister. I am sorry I am late. I left early this morning, but we had to stop at the bridge because it was destroyed by a Communist bomb. We had to wait for the bridge to be repaired by a military engineering unit."

Caption 6. "Mr. Ba, you are asked to pay farm tax to the Liberation Front!"

Caption 7. "This year the crop is poor, but the Communists still collect taxes. It is a miserable situation. I have heard there is much security in Phung Phu village. There taxes are not collected by the Communists any more thanks to the Phoenix operation. I wonder why such an operation has not come to our village?"

"Perhaps because nobody provides them with information! This afternoon the Phoenix operation agents posted a notice at the intersection. I will go and see it tomorrow."

Caption 8. "What is new, my friends?"

"There are two dangerous Communist cadres hiding in our village."

Caption 9. Here are the two Communist cadres sought by the Phoenix Operation. The wanted poster says: "Dear compatriots, If you know the hiding place of the two above-named Communist cadres, please notify the national police or the armed forces. You will be rewarded, and your name will be kept secret."

Caption 10. The radio broadcast says, "Compatriots, please help your government by providing information indicating the hiding place of two Communists, Ba Luong and Hai Gon. You will be rewarded, and your name will be kept secret."

"Did you hear that on the radio?"

"I knew it already. It is exactly the same as it has been posted on the wall at the intersection of the village."

Caption 11. "See, there are so many leaflets!"

Caption 12. "Honey, what do they say in those leaflets?"

"They are the same as those wall posters, as well as the announcements on the radio yesterday. The two Communists Ba Luong and Hai Gon are presently hiding in our village in order to collect taxes. I am determined to report to the Phoenix Operation Committee because I know their hiding place."

Caption 13. "Where are you going so early?"

"I am going to the district headquarters to report about what happened last night."

Caption 14. "Dear Sir, the two Communists you want are hiding in my village. They are hiding in the house number 80/2 by my village boundaries. They only go out at night. If you succeed in arresting them, please keep my name secret!"

"Thank you, Mr. Ba, your name will be kept secret." (The Phoenix Operation provides security and prosperity to the people.)

Caption 15. "Why are so many soldiers entering our village?"

"Perhaps they are conducting a military operation against the Communists in hiding."

Caption 16. "The two Communists are very dangerous. We can only have peace and security when they are captured."

Caption 17. "Ladies, do you know that the two Communists are captured? From now on our village will be secure. There will be no more assassinations or tax collectors. The Phoenix operation is very effective!"

Caption 18. "Mr. Ba, since the two Communists are captured, our village is at peace. Too bad they are in jail! If they returned to our side beforehand, it could have been better for them!"

"They are obstinate indeed. Had they returned like Mr. Thanh from Long Dien village, they certainly would have enjoyed the government's clemency. Mr. Thanh is now reunited with his family."

Caption 19. "Mr. Ba, you have some mail."

"I wonder who sends you this mail?"

"Wait and see!"

Caption 20. "What does the letter say?"

"Dear Mr. Ba, Since you have helped the government by providing information and undermining the local structures of the Communists, you will be rewarded accordingly. You are invited to attend the coming meeting of the Phoenix Operation Committee to receive your award. Sincerely yours."

Caption 21. Poster says: "Mr. Nguyen Van Thanh, former guerrilla at Long Dien village, Gia Rai District, Bac Lieu Province, has returned to the national side. He therefore is allowed to be reunited with his family."

GLOSSARY

AA Air America: subsidiary airline of the Central Intelligence Agency which was active in Asia during the Vietnam War

Agroville (Khu Tru Mat): garrison community into which rural Vietnamese were forcefully relocated in order to isolate them from the Vietcong.

AID Agency for International Development: branch of the U.S. State Department responsible for advising the government of Vietnam, including the National Police

AIK Aid-in-Kind: nonmonetary aid

An Ninh The Vietcong's internal security and propaganda service

APC Accelerated pacification campaign: pacification program begun November 1968 to increase the number of villages rated "secure" under the Hamlet Evaluation System

APT Armed propaganda team: platoon-size unit composed of soldiers with both a combat and psychological warfare mission

ARVN Army of the Republic of Vietnam

ASA Army Security Agency: branch of the National Security Agency working with the U.S. Army to locate the Vietcong through its radio communications

Biet Kich Commando

Cadre Nucleus of trained personnel around which a larger organization can be built

CAP Combined Action Patrol: platoon-size unit composed of U.S. Marines and Vietnamese Territorial Forces

CAS Controlled American source: an employee of the CIA

CD Civilian detainee: Vietnamese civilian detained by U.S. or Vietnamese military forces

CDEC Combined Document Exploitation Center: formed October 1966 to support allied military operations primarily through the translation of captured enemy documents

CG Census Grievance: CIA covert action program designed to obtain information on the VCI through static agents in villages, or mobile agents in armed propaganda teams

CI Counterintelligence: that aspect of intelligence devoted to destroying the effectiveness of enemy intelligence activities

CICV Combined Intelligence Center, Vietnam: created in 1965 to coordinate U.S. and South Vietnamese intelligence operations

CID Criminal Investigation Division: branch of the U.S. Army charged with investigating crimes committed by American soldiers

CIDG Civilian Irregular Defense Group: U.S. Special Forces-trained village and tribal security and reaction forces

CINCPAC Commander in Chief, Pacific: the U.S. military headquarters in Hawaii to which the commander of MACV reported

CIO Central Intelligence Organization: formed in 1961 to

	coordinate South Vietnamese foreign and domestic intelligence operations
CIS	Combined Intelligence Staff: formed in November 1966 to manage the attack against the VCI in Saigon and its environs
CMDC	Capital Military District Command: formed in June 1968 to coordinate military and pacification operations in Saigon and its environs
CMEC	Combined Matériel Exploitation Center: formed in 1965 to coordinate intelligence gained from the analysis of captured enemy matériel
CORDS	Civil Operations and Revolutionary Development Support: organization established in May 1967 under MACV, designed to coordinate U.S. military and civilian operations and advisory programs in South Vietnam
COSVN	Central Office of South Vietnam: mobile headquarters of the South Vietnamese insurgency, created in 1962
CPDC	Central Pacification and Development Council: formed in 1968 by William Colby, who was then chief of CORDS, as a liaison staff to the office of the prime minister of South Vietnam
CPHPO	Central Phung Hoang Permanent Office: formed in July 1968 to manage the South Vietnamese attack against the VCI
CSC	Combined Security Committee: formed in 1964 to protect U.S. government personnel and facilities in Saigon and its environs
CT	Counterterrorist: mercenary soldier employed by the CIA to kill, capture, and/or terrorize the VCI
CT IV	Cong Tac IV (also known as Counterterror IV): joint U.S.-South Vietnamese program begun in December 1966, designed to eliminate the VCI in Saigon and its environs
CTSC	Combined Tactical Screening Center: formed by the U.S. Army in 1967 to distinguish prisoners of war from civilian detainees

Cuc Nghien Cuu Central Research Agency: North Vietnamese intelligence service

DAO Defense Attaché Office: U.S. military headquarters that replaced MACV in 1973 after the cease-fire

DCI Director of Central Intelligence: U.S. official in charge of managing the affairs of the CIA

DEPCORDS Deputy to the MACV commander for Civil Operations and Revolutionary Development Support

DGNP Director General of the National Police: Vietnamese official in charge of the South Vietnamese police

DIOCC District Intelligence and Operations Coordination Center: office of the Phoenix adviser in each of South Vietnam's 250 districts

DMZ Demilitarized zone: stretch of land along the seventeenth parallel, created in 1954 to separate North and South Vietnam

DSA District senior adviser: senior CORDS official in each of South Vietnam's 250 districts

FI Foreign Intelligence: branch of the CIA charged with inserting agents within foreign governments

Free Fire Zone: Area in South Vietnam where U.S. military personnel had the authority to kill anyone they targeted

GAMO Group administrative mobile organization: French-advised and -outfitted combat unit composed of South Vietnamese soldiers

GCMA Composite airborne commando group: French-advised and -outfitted antiguerrilla unit composed mostly of Montagnards

GVN Government of Vietnam

HES Hamlet Evaluation System: computer system developed by the U.S. Defense Department in 1967 to measure trends in pacification

HIP Hamlet Informant program: CIA-funded program managed by CIA officers in liaison with the Special Branch of the South Vietnamese National Police in which secret agents were paid to identify VCI in hamlets

hooch: Dwelling occupied by rural Vietnamese

Hop Tac: Pacification Intensive Capital Area program, begun July 1964 to bring security to Saigon and its environs

HVRP High Values Rewards Program: bounty program proposed by the Phoenix Directorate in July 1971 to induce low-level VCI to turn in high-level VCI

ICEX Intelligence coordination and exploitation: original name of the Phoenix program, formed in June 1967

IOCC Intelligence Operations and Coordination Center

IPA International Police Academy: school in the United States where the Agency for International Development through its Office of Public Safety trained policemen from foreign countries from 1963 to 1974

ISA International Security Affairs: office within the U.S. Defense Department responsible for supervising security asistance programs such as Phoenix in foreign countries, excluding NATO

JAG Judge Advocate General: chief prosecuting general within the U.S. armed forces

JGS Joint General Staff: command organization of the Republic of Vietnam Armed Forces

J1 Personnel branch of the JGS or MACV

J2 Intelligence branch of the JGS or MACV

J3 Operations branch of the JGS or MACV

J4 Logistics branch of the JGS or MACV

JUSPAO Joint U.S. Public Affairs Office: formed in May 1965 under the office of the U.S. Information Agency in South Vietnam, to manage MACV psychological warfare operations and public relations

KKK Khmer Kampuchea Krom: Cambodian exiles trained by the CIA in South Vietnam

KMT Kuomintang: official ruling party of the Republic of China (Taiwan), formed by Dr. Sun Yat-sen in 1911

LLDB Luc Luong Duc Biet: South Vietnamese Special Forces

LRRP Long-range reconnaissance patrol: small team of U.S. soldiers sent to gather behind-the-lines intelligence on enemy troops

LST Landing Ship Transport: naval vessel in which troops are often quartered

MACV Military Assistance Command, Vietnam: arrived in Saigon in February 1962 as a unified command under the Commander in Chief, Pacific, managing the U.S. military effort in South Vietnam

MAAG Military Assistance and Advisory Group: arrived in South Vietnam in November 1955 to provide support and training to the Republic of Vietnam Armed Forces. Its function was absorbed by MACV in 1964.

MASA Military Assistance Security Adviser: U.S. military officer who manages a security assistance program in a foreign country

MAT Mobile advisory team: team of U.S. military personnel assigned to CORDS, charged with training and supporting the Territorial Security Forces of South Vietnam in a province or district

Mike Forces: Mobile strike force commands: corps-level units under the command of the 5th Special Forces

MOI Ministry of the Interior: branch of the GVN with authority over pacification, including Phung Hoang

MSS Military Security Service: counterintelligence branch of the Republic of Vietnam Armed Forces

MSUG Michigan State University Group: employees of Michigan State University contracted in 1954 to provide technical assistance to the GVN

NIC National Interrogation Center: CIA facility built in 1964 inside CIO headquarters in the naval shipyard in Saigon

NLF National Liberation Front: formed in 1960 by the various insurgent groups in South Vietnam

NPC National Police Command: organized in June 1971 to incorporate Phung Hoang within the existing National Police structure

NPCIS National Police Criminal Information System: computer system designed to track identified VCI

NPFF National Police Field Force: paramilitary branch of the National Police

NPIASS National Police Infrastructure Analysis Sub-Section: data bank containing biographical information on the VCI, used to plan countermeasures

NPIC National Police Interrogation Center: located at National Police headquarters on Vo Tanh Street in Saigon

NVA North Vietnamese Army

OCO Office of Civil Operations: formed in Saigon in November 1966 to manage U.S. pacification programs in South Vietnam

OSA Office of the Special Assistant: code name for the CIA station in Saigon

PA&E Pacific Architects and Engineers: private company that did construction work for the GVN

PAAS Pacification Attitude Analysis System: computer system designed to assess the political effects of CORDS pacification programs

PAT People's action team: CIA version of the standard Vietcong armed propaganda team

PCOC Phoenix Coordinators Orientation Course: begun November 1968 at Vung Tau's Seminary Camp to train Phoenix coordinators

PHMIS Phung Hoang Management Information System: computer system containing biographical and organizational data on the VCI, created January 1969

PHREEX Phung Hoang reexamination: study begun in 1971, designed to critique the Phoenix program

Phung Hoang: The mythological Vietnamese bird of conjugal love that appears in times of peace, pictured holding a flute and representing virtue, grace, and harmony. Also the name given to the South Vietnamese version of Phoenix

PIC Province Interrogation Center

PICC	Province Intelligence Coordination Committee: established by decree in November 1964 to serve as the senior intelligence agency in each province, but never put into effect
PIOCC	Province Intelligence and Operations Coordination Center: headquarters of the Phoenix adviser in each of South Vietnam's forty-four provinces
PIRL	Potential intelligence recruitment lead: VCI removed from the Phoenix blacklist and approached to become an agent of the CIA
PM	Paramilitary: branch of the CIA that obtains intelligence through unconventional warfare operations
POIC	Province officer in charge: senior CIA officer in a province, supervising both police liaison and paramilitary operations
PP	Political and Psychological: branch of the CIA that manages black propaganda and political liaison activities
PRG	Provisional Revolutionary Government: formed in June 1969 by the NLF to negotiate the reunification of North and South Vietnam
PRP	People's Revolutionary party: created in January 1962 as the southern branch of the Vietnamese Communist party
PRU	Provincial Reconnaissance Units: mercenary forces under the control of the CIA in South Vietnam
PSA	Province senior adviser: senior CORDS official in each of South Vietnam's forty-four provinces
PSC	Province Security Committee: nonjudicial body charged with the disposition of captured VCI
PSD	Public Safety Division: branch of CORDS responsible for advising the National Police
PSCD	Pacification Security Coordination Division: CIA component of CORDS
PSDF	People's self-defense forces: South Vietnamese civilian militia
psyops	Psychological operations

psywar	Psychological warfare
PTSD	Post traumatic stress disorder: stress that continues after the traumatic event that caused it
RD	Revolutionary Development: CIA program to build support for the GVN in the provinces of South Vietnam
RDC	Revolutionary development cadre: South Vietnamese trained by the CIA at Vung Tau to persuade the citizens of South Vietnam to support the central government
RDC/O	Revolutionary Development Cadre, Operations: CIA officer in charge of paramilitary operations in a province
RDC/P	Revolutionary Development Cadre, Plans: CIA officer in charge of liaison with the Special Branch in a province
RF/PF	Regional Forces and Popular Forces: a National Guard under the control of district and province chiefs
RMK/BRJ	Raymond Morrison Knudson, Brown Root Jorgansen: private company that did construction work for the GVN
ROIC	Region officer in charge: senior CIA officer in each of the four corps and Saigon
RVNAF	Republic of Vietnam Armed Forces
S2	Sector intelligence adviser: senior MACV intelligence adviser to the South Vietnamese forces in a province
SACSA	Special Assistant (to the chairman of the Joint Chiefs of Staff) for Counterinsurgency and Special Activities: office within the Joint Chiefs with responsibility for Phoenix policy
SARC	Special airmobile resource control: method of interdicting VCI attempting to resupply armed Vietcong guerrillas
SAVA	Special Assistant for Vietnamese Affairs: office in the CIA reporting directly to the Director of Central Intelligence on developments in South Vietnam

SCAG Saigon Capital Advisory Group

SEAL Sea-Air-Land: the U.S. Navy's Special Forces

SES Special Exploitation Service: formed in April 1964 as the JGS counterpart to SOG, renamed Strategic Technical Directorate in September 1987

SIDE Screening, interrogation, and detention of the enemy: ICEX program begun in September 1967 to resolve the problem of separating genuine VCI from innocent civilian detainees

SIFU Special Intelligence Force Units: small units formed in 1971 to replace PRU, composed of Special Branch and Field Police

SMIAT Special Military Intelligence Advisory Team: formed in 1965 to mount sophisticated operations against the VCI

SMM Saigon Military Mission: CIA office formed in 1954 to help the South Vietnamese conduct psychological warfare against the Vietminh

Snatch and snuff Kidnap and kill

SOG Special Operations Group: joint CIA-military organization formed in 1964 to conduct operations outside South Vietnam in support of MACV, but under the control of SACSA

SP Special Police: term used in reference to the CIA-advised and -funded Special Branch of South Vietnamese National Police

Trung-doi biet kich Nham dou: people's commando team, formed by Frank Scotton in 1964

USARV United States Army Republic of Vietnam: created July 1965 at Long Binh to control all logistical and administrative units of the U.S. Army in Vietnam

USIS United States Information Service: branch of the U.S. government responsible for conducting psychological operations overseas

TDY Temporary duty

TRAC Target Research and Analysis Section: created in January 1965 to develop targets for Strategic Air Command B-25s in support of MACV

VBI Vietnamese Bureau of Investigation: precursor organization to the Special Branch, also known as the Cong An

VC Vietcong: Vietnamese Communist

VCI Vietcong infrastructue: all Communist party members and NLF officers, plus Vietcong and NVA saboteurs and terrorists

VCS Vietcong suspect: Vietnamese civilian suspected of being VCI

VIS Vietnamese Information Service: branch of the GVN responsible for conducting psychological operations in South Vietnam

VNQDD Vietnam Quoc Dan Dang: Vietnamese branch of the Kuomintang

VNTF Vietnam Task Force: office within ISA responsible for Vietnam

NOTES

CHAPTER 1: Infrastructure

1. "Vietnam Policy and Prospects 1970" (Hearings before the Committee on Foreign Relations, U.S. Senate, February 17–20 and March 3, 14, 17, 19, 1970), p. 723.
2. Stanley Karnow, *Vietnam: A History* (New York: Viking, 1982), p. 60.
3. Karnow, p. 76.
4. Karnow, p. 82.
5. Karnow, p. 87.
6. David Galula, *Counter-Insurgency Warfare: Theory and Practice* (New York: Praeger, 1964) p. 80
7. Robert Slater, "The History, Organization and Modus Operandi of the Viet Cong Infrastructure" (Defense Intelligence School, March 1970), p. 3.
8. Richard Harris Smith, *OSS: The Secret History of America's First Central Intelligence Agency* (Berkeley: University of California Press, 1972), p. 347.
9. Nguyen Ngoc Huy, *Understanding Vietnam* (The DPC Information Service, the Netherlands, 1982), p. 85.
10. Interview with Jack.
11. Edward Lansdale, *In the Midst of Wars* (New York: Harper & Row, 1972), pp. 70–72.
12. Lansdale, p. 72.
13. Kevin Generous, *Vietnam: The Secret War* (New York: Bison Books, 1985), p. 94.
14. Generous, p. 66.
15. Lansdale, p. 211.
16. Huy, p. 85.

17. J. J. Zasloff, "Origins of the Insurgency in South Vietnam 1954–1960" (Rand Memorandum RM-5163), p. 8.
18. Noam Chomsky, *Counter-Revolutionary Violence: Bloodbaths in Fact and Propaganda* (A Warner Modular Publication, 1973, USA), p. 57-18.
19. Huy, p. 85.
20. Lansdale, p. 340.
21. Lansdale, p. 343.
22. Lansdale, p. 344.

CHAPTER 2: Internal Security

1. Graham Greene, *The Quiet American* (New York: Viking, 1956), p. 8.
2. Jeffrey Race, *War Comes to Long An* (Berkeley: University of California Press, 1972), p. 19.
3. Race, p. 67.
4. Race, p. 52.
5. Ralph Johnson, *Phoenix/Phung Hoang: A Study of Wartime Intelligence Management* (Washington D.C.: American University, 1985), pp. 37–38.
6. Lansdale, pp. 82–88.
7. Interview with Clyde Bauer.
8. Don Schrande, "Father Hoa's Little War," *The Saturday Evening Post,* February 17, 1962, p. 76.
9. Schrande, p. 76.
10. Interview with Bernard Yoh.
11. Slater, pp. 38–39.
12. Slater, p. 56.
13. Johnson, *A Study,* p. 64.
14. Johnson, *A Study,* p. 72.
15. "Vietnam Policy and Prospects 1970," p. 724.
16. Karnow, p. 410.
17. Race, p. 196.
18. Interview with William Colby.
19. Karnow, p. 284.

CHAPTER 3: Covert Action

1. Interview with Stu Methven.
2. Ralph Johnson, *Phoenix/Phung Hoang: Planned Assassination or Legitimate Conflict Management?* (Washington D.C.: American University, 1982), p. 5.
3. Methven interview.
4. Ralph Johnson, *Phoenix/Phung Hoang: A Study of Wartime Intelligence Management* (Washington D.C.: American University, 1985), p. 441.
5. Methven interview.
6. Race, pp. 239–240.
7. "Vietnam Policy and Prospects 1970," p. 245.
8. "Alleged Assassination Plots Involving Foreign Leaders" (94th Congress, 1st Session, Senate Report No. 94-465: Church Select Committee, Senate Select Committee on Government Operations with Respect to Intelligence [U.S. G.P.O., 1975], p. 278.

9. "Alleged Assassination Plots," p. 139.
10. "Alleged Assassination Plots," p. 336.
11. "Vietnam Policy and Prospects 1970," p. 722.
12. Interview with Frank Scotton, July 1986.
13. Ngo Vinh Long, "The CIA and the Vietnam Debacle" in *Uncloaking the CIA*, ed. Howard Frazier (New York: The Free Press, 1978), p. 72.
14. Scotton interview.
15. Scotton interview.
16. Karnow, p. 281.
17. Huy, p. 97.
18. Huy, p. 101.
19. Huy, p. 110.
20. Scotton interview.
21. Interview with Walter Mackem.

CHAPTER 4: Revolutionary Development

1. Scotton interview.
2. Peer DeSilva, *Sub Rosa* (New York: New York Times Books, 1978), p. 249.
3. DeSilva, p. 247.
4. DeSilva, p. 245.
5. DeSilva, p. 250.
6. Lansdale, p. 75.
7. Seymour Hersh, *Cover-Up* (New York: Random House, 1972), p. 85.
8. Interview with Tom Donohue.
9. Huy, p. 123.
10. Huy, p. 123.
11. Scotton interview.
12. William A. Nighswonger, *Rural Pacification in Vietnam* (New York: Praeger, 1966), p. 298.

CHAPTER 5: PICs

1. Galula, p. 117.
2. Slater, p. 21.
3. Galula, p. 124.
4. Scotton interview.
5. John Marks, *The Search for the Manchurian Candidate* (New York: New York Times Books, 1979), p. 178.
6. Marks, p. 179.
7. Johnson, *A Study*, p. 400.
8. Major General Joseph McChristian, *The Role of Military Intelligence 1965–1967* (Washington D.C.: Department of the Army, 1974), p. 14.
9. McChristian, p. 71.
10. McChristian, p. 50.
11. McChristian, p. 26.

CHAPTER 6: Field Police

1. Interview with William Grieves.
2. Letter to the author from Nguyen Van Dai.
3. Interview with Douglas McCollum.

CHAPTER 7: Special Branch

1. Interview with Nelson Henry Brickham.
2. Interview with Tom Donohue.
3. Warren Milberg, "The Future Applicability of the Phoenix Program" (Research Study, Report #1835-74, Air Command and Staff College, Air University, Maxwell Air Force Base, May 1974), pp. 33–34.
4. Galula, p. 120.
5. *The Herald Tribune,* October 21, 1965.
6. Anthony Herbert, *Soldier* (New York: Holt Rinehart & Winston, 1973), pp. 105–106.
7. Herbert, p. 106.
8. Milberg, p. 50.
9. Milberg, p. 34.
10. Galula, p. 110.
11. Interview with James Ward.
12. Interview with Sam Drakulich.

CHAPTER 8: Attack on the VCI

1. *The Pentagon Papers* (Washington D.C.: U.S. Department of Defense, 1971), Vol. V, p. 58.
2. Brickham interview.
3. *The Pentagon Papers,* Vol. V, pp. 120–122.
4. Nelson Brickham, "Attack on the VCI" (Saigon: November 1966), p. 1.
5. Brickham, "Attack," p. 1.
6. Brickham, "Attack," p. 4.
7. Brickham, "Attack," p. 4.
8. McChristian, p. 72.
9. McChristian, p. 72.
10. McChristian, p. 74.
11. Interview with Tulius Acampora.
12. Interview with Dang Van Minh.
13. Interview with Lawrence Tracy.
14. McChristian, p. 78.
15. Interview with Robert Wall.

CHAPTER 9: ICEX

1. Brickham interview.
2. Nelson Brickham, "A Proposal for the Coordination and Management of Intelligence Programs and Attack on the VC Infrastructure and Local Irregular Forces (Saigon: June 1967), p. 1.
3. Brickham, "Proposal," p. 3.

4. Brickham, "Proposal," p. 4.
5. Interview with Evan J. Parker, Jr.
6. Johnson, *A Study,* p. 174.
7. McChristian, p. 76.
8. Interview with Edward Brady.
9. Johnson, *A Study,* p. 110.
10. Ward interview.

CHAPTER 10: Action Programs

1. Johnson, *A Study,* p. 196.
2. Parker interview.
3. Acampora interview.
4. Al Santoli, *Everything We Had* (New York: Ballantine Books, 1984), p. 202.
5. Johnson, *A Study,* p. 200.
6. Johnson, *A Study,* p. 200.
7. Brickham interview.
8. Interview with Robert Brewer.
9. Ward interview.
10. Johnson, *A Study,* p. 198.
11. Johnson, *A Study,* p. 197.
12. "Project Take-Off" (Saigon; U.S. Military Assistance Command, Vietnam, November 1967) p. 3.
13. Johnson, *A Study,* p. 391.
14. Letter to the author from Randolph Berkeley.
15. Milberg, p. 60.
16. Milberg, p. 61.
17. Interview with Robert Slater.
18. Milberg, p. 61.
19. Tran Van Truong, *A Vietcong Memoir* (New York: Harcourt Brace Jovanovich, 1985), p. 108.
20. Truong, p. 110.
21. "Project Take-Off," p. 3.

CHAPTER 11: PRU

1. Scotton interview.
2. Donohue interview.
3. Ward interview.
4. Raymond Bonner, *Waltzing with a Dictator* (New York: Random House, 1987) p. 75.
5. Interview with Robert Peartt.
6. *The Pentagon Papers,* Vol. V, p. 120.
7. Grieves interview.
8. McCollum interview.
9. David Welch, "Pacification in Vietnam," *Ramparts,* October 1967, p. 39.
10. Milberg, p. 39.
11. Interview with John Wilbur.
12. Parker interview.
13. Brickham interview.
14. Santoli, pp. 203–204.

15. Santoli, p. 204.
16. Santoli, p. 205.
17. Santoli, pp. 217–218.
18. Interview with Louis Lapham.

CHAPTER 12: Tet

1. Brickham interview.
2. Acampora interview.
3. Lapham interview.
4. Lapham interview.
5. Interview with Renz Hoeksema.
6. Wilbur interview.
7. Interview with Howard Stone.
8. Karnow, p. 514.
9. Interview with Tom McCoy.
10. Interview with Warren Milberg.
11. Karnow, p. 523.
12. Interview with Rudy Enders.
13. Karnow, p. 532.
14. *The Pentagon Papers,* Senator Gravel edition (Boston: Beacon Press, 1971), Vol. IV, p. 578.
15. Slater, p. 48.
16. Huy, p. 129.
17. Interview with Robert Inman.
18. Letter to the author from Lionel Rosenblatt.
19. Interview with George French.
20. Slater, p. ix.
21. Brady interview.
22. Huy, p. 130.
23. Huy, p. 136.
24. Huy, p. 130.
25. "Status of Phoenix/Phung Hoang for Period January–June 1968" (Saigon, MACCORDS, Phoenix Fact Sheet, August 10, 1968, LTC Lemire).
26. Johnson, *A Study,* p. 275.
27. John Cook, *The Advisor* (Philadelphia, Pa.: Dorrance, 1973), p. 195.
28. Wall interview.

CHAPTER 13: Parallax Views

1. Brewer interview.
2. Milberg interview.
3. Manzione interview.

CHAPTER 14: Phoenix in Flight

1. Milberg interview.
2. Milberg, p. 62.
3. Milberg, p. 44.

4. Milberg, p. 50.
5. Milberg, p. 51.
6. Milberg, p. 53.
7. Milberg, p. 57.
8. Interview with Douglas Dillard.
9. Letter to the author from Bruce Palmer.
10. Ward interview.
11. Santoli, p. 204.
12. McChristian, p. 100.

CHAPTER 15: Modus Vivendi

1. Dillard interview.
2. Slater, p. 56.
3. Interview with Jack.
4. Interview with Brian Willson.
5. Dinh Tuong An, "The Truth About Phoenix" (Saigon, Tin Sang, 1970–71).
6. An, "Truth."
7. An, "Truth."
8. An, "Truth."
9. An, "Truth."
10. An, "Truth."
11. An, "Truth."
12. An, "Truth."
13. Milberg interview.
14. An, "Truth."
15. An, "Truth."
16. An, "Truth."
17. Dillard interview.
18. An, "Truth."
19. An, "Truth."
20. Truong, p. 113.
21. Truong, p. 117.
22. Truong, p. 117.
23. Frank Snepp, *Decent Interval* (New York: Random House, 1978), p. 31.
24. Snepp, p. 38.

CHAPTER 16: Advisers

1. Dillard interview.
2. Ward interview.
3. Letter to the author from George Dexter.
4. Milberg, p. 46.
5. Interview with Henry McWade.
6. Johnson, *A Study*, p. 265.
7. Brady interview.
8. Truong, p. 136.

CHAPTER 17: Accelerated Pacification

1. "Vietnam Policy and Prospects 1970," p. 716.
2. Thomas Thayer, *A Systems Analysis of the Vietnam War 1965–1972,* Vol. 10: Pacification and Civil Affairs (Washington D.C.: Office of the Assistant Secretary of Defense, 1975), pp. 40–43.
3. Peartt interview.
4. Wilbur interview.
5. William Colby, *Honorable Men* (New York: Simon & Schuster, 1978), pp. 260–263.
6. Huy, p. 141.
7. Cook, p. 113.
8. Race, p. 239.
9. Race, p. 239.
10. Race, p. 240.
11. McCoy interview.
12. Letter to the author from Frank Walton.
13. Colby, pp. 207–208.
14. Dillard interview.
15. Interview with Richard Bradish.
16. Interview with Walter Kolon.
17. Cook, p. 208.
18. Race, p. 238.
19. Brickham and Ward interviews.
20. Colby, p. 269.
21. Jack interview.

CHAPTER 18: Transitions

1. Brady interview.
2. Brickham interview.
3. Interview with Shelby Roberts.
4. John Berry, *Those Gallant Men on Trial in Vietnam* (Novato, Calif.: Presidio Press, 1984), p. 56.
5. McWade interview.
6. Dillard interview.
7. Interview with Ralph McGehee.
8. Ralph McGehee, *Deadly Deceits* (New York: Sheridan Square Press, 1983) p. 141.
9. McGehee, p. 142.
10. McGehee, p. 142.
11. "Hearing on the Nomination of William Colby" (Committee on Armed Services, U.S. Senate, July 2, 20, 25, 1973), p. 56.
12. *The New York Times,* November 10, 1984.
13. *The Boston Globe,* November 14, 1984, p. 10.
14. *The Boston Globe,* November 14, 1984, p. 10.
15. *The New York Times,* November, 21, 1984, p. B2.
16. "Hearing on the Nomination of William Colby," p. 57.
17. McGehee, pp. 127–128.
18. McGehee, p. 128.
19. McGehee, p. 84.

20. McGehee, pp. 82–83.
21. McGehee, p. 145.
22. Colby interview.
23. Colby, p. 266.
24. Johnson, *A Study*, p. 370.
25. Lapham interview.
26. Interview with Ted Shackley.
27. "Phoenix Reorganization" (Saigon, MACCORDS, February 6, 1969), cited in Johnson, *A Study*, p. 370.
28. Parker interview.
29. Johnson, *A Study*, p. 372.
30. Johnson, *A Study*, p. 304.

CHAPTER 19: Psyops

1. "Phung Hoang/Phoenix 1969 End of Year Report" (Saigon, MACCORDS, February 28, 1970), p. D-3.
2. Scott Breckenridge, *The CIA and the US Intelligence System* (Boulder, Colo.: Westview Press, 1985), p. 170.
3. William Turley, *Far East Asian Economic Review*, May 2, 1985.
4. 1969 End of Year Report, p. B-6.
5. An, "Truth."
6. Ward interview.
7. 1969 End of Year Report, p. B-6-1.
8. 1969 End of Year Report, p. B-3-1.
9. "Phung Hoang Results Due Directly to Psyops" (Saigon, MACCORDS, Phoenix Directorate, December 6, 1970).
10. Cook, p. 182.
11. Johnson, *A Study*, p. 355.
12. 1969 End of Year Report, p. B-10-3.
13. An, "Truth."
14. "Phung Hoang Results Due Directly to Psyops."
15. "Phung Hoang/Phoenix Program" (Washington D.C.: The Joint Chiefs of Staff, Memorandum for the Secretary of Defense, JCSM-394-70, August 15, 1970, from Major General Frank B. Clay, Deputy Director, Joint Staff).
16. "Phung Hoang Results Due Directly to Psyops."
17. Joseph Treaster, "The Phoenix Murders," *Penthouse*, December 1975, p. 147.
18. 1969 End of Year Report, p. B-1-2.
19. 1969 End of Year Report, p. B-2-1-6.
20. 1969 End of Year Report, p. B-2-1-6.
21. 1969 End of Year Report, p. B-1-1 to B-1-3.
22. 1969 End of Year Report, p. D-7.
23. Treaster, p. 147.
24. Colby, p. 269.
25. Johnson, *A Study*, pp. 304–305.
26. "Special Collection Program BIG MACK" (Saigon, MACCORDS, MACJ212-2 Fact Sheet, December 8, 1970).
27. Dillard interview.
28. 1969 End of Year Report, pp. 8 and C.
29. 1969 End of Year Report, pp. 8 and C.

30. "Tracking of Arrested Individuals" (Saigon, CORDS Public Safety Fact Sheet, L. M. Rosen, November 27, 1970).
31. "National Police Redeployment Concept" (Saigon, CORDS Public Safety Fact Sheet, L. M. Rosen, December 8, 1970).

CHAPTER 20: Reforms

1. Johnson, *A Study,* p. 406.
2. Ministry of Interior Circular 757, "Classification and Rehabilitation of Offenders," Saigon, March 21, 1969.
3. Johnson, *A Study,* p. 406.
4. Ministry of Interior Circular 2212, "Improvements of the Methods of Resolving the Status of Offenders," Saigon, August 20, 1969.
5. Interview with Lien Johnson.
6. Interview with Harry Johnson.
7. Interview with Lien Johnson.
8. Interview with Tom Polgar.
9. Brady interview.
10. Karnow, pp. 440–441.
11. Johnson, *A Study,* pp. 374–375.
12. Enders interview.
13. Cited in "The Phoenix/Phung Hoang and Provincial Reconnaissance Units (PRU) Programs," undated Memorandum for the Secretary of Defense, from General Abrams.
14. "The Phoenix/Phung Hoang and Provincial Reconnaissance Units (PRU) Programs."
15. "The Phoenix/Phung Hoang and Provincial Reconnaissance Units (PRU) Programs."
16. "The Phoenix/Phung Hoang and Provincial Reconnaissance Units (PRU) Programs."
17. Interview with Jack.
18. Interview with Michael McCann.
19. Interview with Fred Dick.

CHAPTER 21: Decay

1. Huy, p. 139.
2. Huy, p. 146.
3. Lansdale, p. 343.
4. Snepp, p. 15*n*.
5. Scotton interview.
6. "Hearing on the Nomination of William Colby," p. 58.
7. McGehee interview.
8. McGehee, pp. 153–154.
9. McGehee, p. 154.
10. McGehee, p. 154.
11. McGehee, p. 153.
12. Michael Maclear, *The Ten Thousand Day War* (New York: St. Martin's Press, 1981), p. 261.
13. "U.S. Assistance Programs in Vietnam" (Foreign Operations and Government

Information Subcommittee, Committee on Government Operations, July 15, 16, 19, 21 and August 2, 1971), p. 105.

14. "U.S. Assistance Programs in Vietnam," p. 105.
15. Maclear, p. 263.
16. Snepp, p. 12.
17. Interview with Ed Murphy.
18. Erwin Knoll, "The Mysterious Project Phoenix," *The Progressive*, February 1970.
19. Knoll.
20. Georgie Anne Geyer, "The CIA's Hired Killers," *True*, February 1970.

CHAPTER 22: Hearings

1. *The New York Times*, February 17, 1970.
2. State Department Telegram 024391 from Clayton McManaway to William Sullivan, Subject: "Senate Hearings," February 17, 1970.
3. Grieves interview.
4. Letter to the author from Nguyen Van Dai.
5. "Vietnam Policy and Prospects 1970," p. 200.
6. "Vietnam Policy and Prospects 1970," p. 201.
7. "Vietnam Policy and Prospects 1970," p. 201.
8. "Vietnam Policy and Prospects 1970," p. 201.
9. "Vietnam Policy and Prospects 1970," p. 201.
10. Geyer.
11. Colby interview.
12. Neil Sheehan, "An American Soldier in Vietnam, Part III: An All-Round Man," *The New Yorker*, June 20, 1988, pp. 54–55.
13. "Vietnam Policy and Prospects 1970," p. 212.
14. "Vietnam Policy and Prospects 1970," p. 118.
15. "Vietnam Policy and Prospects 1970," p. 119.
16. "Vietnam Policy and Prospects 1970," p. 120.
17. "Vietnam Policy and Prospects 1970," p. 120.
18. Michael Drosnin, "Phoenix: The CIA's Biggest Assassination Program" (*New Times*, August 22, 1975), p. 19.
19. "Vietnam Policy and Prospects 1970," p. 205.
20. "Vietnam Policy and Prospects 1970," p. 205–206.
21. "Vietnam Policy and Prospects 1970," p. 206.
22. "Vietnam Policy and Prospects 1970," p. 206.
23. "Vietnam Policy and Prospects 1970," p. 207.
24. "Vietnam Policy and Prospects 1970," p. 104.
25. Huy, p. 141.
26. *The New York Times*, February 22, 1970.
27. "Phung Hoang/Phoenix Program" (Washington D.C.: The Joint Chiefs of Staff, August 15, 1970, Memorandum for the Secretary of Defense from Major General Frank B. Clay, Deputy Director, Joint Staff) (hereafter called the Clay memo), p. 2.
28. Clay memo, p. 8.
29. *Phung Hoang Adviser Handbook* (Saigon, MACCORDS, November 20, 1970), p. 10.
30. Colby, p. 268.

31. Johnson, *A Study,* pp. 341–342.
32. Brady interview.
33. Murphy interview.

CHAPTER 23: Dissension

1. Karnow, p, 606.
2. Interview with Lucy Nhiem Hong Nguyen.
3. Karnow, p. 608.
4. Interview with Thomas P. McGrevey.
5. Karnow, p. 610.
6. Chomsky, p. 57-26.
7. Senate Committee on Foreign Relations: Cambodia, May 1970 Staff Report, p. 5.
8. Interview with Philip Agee in *Playboy,* March 1975, p. 60.
9. "Phung Hoang 1970 End of Year Report" (Saigon, MACCORDS, Phung Hoang Directorate, May 11, 1971), p. 43.
10. 1970 End of Year Report, p. 13.
11. Karnow, p. 611.
12. Karnow, p. 612.
13. Karnow, p. 634.

CHAPTER 24: Transgressions

1. McCollum interview.
2. Parker interview.
3. "Calley Defense Asks Disclosure of Top-Secret Data on Song My," *The New York Times,* August 25, 1970.
4. Wall interview.
5. Hersh, p. 87.
6. Hersh, p. 88.
7. Hersh, p. 88.
8. Hersh, p. 88.
9. Hersh, p. 88.
10. Myra MacPherson, *Long Time Passing* (New York: Signet, 1984), p. 625.
11. Joseph Goldstein, *The My Lai Massacre and Its Cover-up* (New York: The Free Press, 1976), p. 256.
12. Hersh, p. 93.
13. Hersh, p. 93.
14. Hersh, p. 95.
15. Goldstein, p. 145.
16. Hersh, p. 95.
17. Goldstein, p. 339.
18. Goldstein, p. 270.
19. Goldstein, p. 277.
20. Goldstein, p. 278.
21. Goldstein, p. 288.
22. Goldstein, p. 313.
23. Hersh, pp. 188–189.
24. MacPherson, p. 625.

25. Interview with George Davis.
26. Jeffrey Stein and Michael T. Klare, "From the Ashes: Phoenix," *Commonweal*, April 20, 1975, p. 159.
27. "U.S. Assistance Programs in Vietnam," p. 53.
28. Drosnin, p. 24.
29. Drosnin, p. 24.
30. Drosnin, p. 23.
31. Don Luce, *Hostages of War* (Indochina Resource Center, 1973) p. 26.
32. Luce, p. 27.
33. Luce, p. 24.

CHAPTER 25: Da Nang

1. Interview with Daniel Jerry Bishop.
2. Interview with Bill Taylor.

CHAPTER 26: Revisions

1. Clay memo, p. 2.
2. 1970 End of Year Report, p. v.
3. 1970 End of Year Report, p. 51.
4. "National Police Redeployment Concept."
5. Dillard interview.
6. Luce, p. 30.
7. 1970 End of Year Report, p. 19.
8. Thayer, p. 82.
9. Thayer, p. 99.
10. Grieves interview.
11. Thayer, p. 95.
12. Clay memo, p. 8.
13. Clay memo, p. 3.
14. Letter to the author from Harold Child.
15. Interview with Chester McCoid.
16. Kolon interview.
17. Interview with James Hunt.
18. Colby interview.
19. "Response to Ambassador Colby's Check List" (to William Sullivan, Deputy Assistant Secretary of State, from Richard Funkhouser, Office of the Deputy for CORDS, II Field Force Vietnam, December 1, 1970).
20. Interview with Walt Burmester.
21. Enders interview.
22. Interview with Donald Gregg.
23. Clay memo, p. 7.
24. "Internal Security in South Vietnam—Phoenix," December 12, 1970.
25. Interview with Paul Coughlin.
26. Acampora interview.

CHAPTER 27: Legalities

1. Johnson, *Planned Assassination.*
2. Interview with William Phillips.
3. *The New York Times,* April 17, 1971, p. 5.
4. "U.S. Assistance Programs in Vietnam," p. 206.
5. "U.S. Assistance Programs in Vietnam," p. 192.
6. "U.S. Assistance Programs in Vietnam," p. 194.
7. "U.S. Assistance Programs in Vietnam," p. 195.
8. "U.S. Assistance Programs in Vietnam," p. 195.
9. "U.S. Assistance Programs in Vietnam," p. 197.
10. "U.S. Assistance Programs in Vietnam," p. 206.
11. "U.S. Assistance Programs in Vietnam," p. 207.
12. "U.S. Assistance Programs in Vietnam," p. 208.
13. "U.S. Assistance Programs in Vietnam," p. 208.
14. "U.S. Assistance Programs in Vietnam," p. 237.
15. "U.S. Assistance Programs in Vietnam," p. 251.
16. "U.S. Assistance Programs in Vietnam," p. 251.
17. "U.S. Assistance Programs in Vietnam," p. 252.
18. "U.S. Assistance Programs in Vietnam," p. 283.
19. "U.S. Assistance Programs in Vietnam," p. 313.
20. "U.S. Assistance Programs in Vietnam," p. 314.
21. "U.S. Assistance Programs in Vietnam," p. 315.
22. "U.S. Assistance Programs in Vietnam," p. 321.
23. "U.S. Assistance Programs in Vietnam," Additional Views of Hon. Paul N. McCloskey, Jr. (Concurred in by Hon. Benjamin S. Rosenthal, Hon. John Conyers, Jr., and Hon. Bella S. Abzug), pp. 105–107.
24. "U.S. Assistance Programs in Vietnam," p. 191.
25. Interview with Sid Towle.
26. Towle interview.
27. W. Gage McAfee, "End of Tour Report" (Saigon, CORDS PP&P, August 11, 1971), p. 5.
28. "End of Tour Report: W. Gage McAfee, Comments of Reviewing Officer" (Saigon, CORDS PP&P, undated, signed by Norman L. Sweet, Director, Plans, Policy and Programs), p. 2.
29. "An Tri Reforms—Saigon 19140" (Cable to William H. Sullivan from U.S. State Department Legal Adviser Robert I. Starr, December 13, 1971).

CHAPTER 28: Technicalities

1. Interview with Cornelius J. O'Shea, Jr.
2. Coughlin interview.
3. Interview with George Hudman.
4. "Recommended Reorganization of the Phung Hoang Program" (State Department Telegram 196060 from Secretary of State William Rogers to Ambassador Ellsworth Bunker in Saigon, in response to COMUSMACV 129816).
5. Interview with Rob Simmons.
6. Colby interview.
7. Wall interview.

8. "The Evolution of American Military Intelligence" (The U.S. Army Intelligence Center and School, Ft. Huachuca, Arizona, May 1973), p. 117.
9. Interview with Tom Polgar.
10. Enders interview.
11. Drosnin, p. 21.
12. Michael T. Klare, "Operation Phoenix and the Failure of Pacification in South Vietnam" (*Liberation*, May 1973), p. 25.
13. Interview with Lew Millett.
14. Interview with Stan Fulcher.
15. "An Tri Observations and Recommendations" (Saigon, MACCORDS, Phoenix Directorate, from John Tilton to the Director, CORDS PP&P, April 11, 1972), p. 1.
16. "An Tri Observations and Recommendations."
17. "An Tri Reform" (Department of State Telegram 02917 from Ambassador Bunker in Saigon to Secretary of State William Rogers in Washington, March 1972), p. 1.
18. "An Tri" (Draft Airgram from Saigon embassy political officer Steven Winship to the Department of State on April 27, 1972), p. 2.
19. "Special Phung Hoang Campaign in the Delta" (State Department Telegram 271149Z, April 1972, Ambassador Ellsworth Bunker).
20. "Presidential Decree Law on Administrative Detention and An Tri Proceedings" (State Department Telegram 050556Z, January 1973, Ambassador Ellsworth Bunker).
21. "Phung Hoang Special Campaign (F6) Ends" (State Department Telegram 051334Z, January 1973, Ambassador Ellsworth Bunker), p. 3.
22. "Phung Hoang Program" (Department of State Telegram 054228 from Secretary of State William Rogers to the Saigon embassy, March 1972), p. 2.

CHAPTER 29: Phoenix in Flames

1. Dillard interview.
2. Stein and Klare, "From the Ashes," p. 159.
3. "Ceasefire and Political Sitrep MR 1, X Plus 137, June 14" (Department of State Telegram 141435Z from Charles Whitehouse, June 1973).
4. Interview with Bruce Lawlor.
5. Thayer, p. 103.
6. Brady interview.
7. Huy, p. 155.
8. McCollum interview.
9. Fred Branfman, "South Vietnam's Police and Prison System" in *Uncloaking the CIA*, ed. Howard Frazier (New York: The Free Press, 1978), p. 103.
10. Grieves interview.
11. Interview with Philip Agee in *Playboy*, March 1975, pp. 48–60.
12. "Master of Deceit" (NACLA's "Latin America and Empire Report," December 10, 1974), pp. 13–15.
13. Robert Kaylor, UPI Bangkok, January 8, 1975.
14. "Phoenix Program—Another False UPI Report" (Department of State Telegram 111317Z from Ambassador Graham Martin to the Secretary of State, January 1973).

15. PVT interview.
16. Snepp, p. 456.
17. Snepp, p. 567.

EPILOGUE

1. Fulcher interview.
2. Huy, pp. 168–170.
3. Allan Nairn, "Confessions of a Death Squad Officer," *The Progressive,* March 1986, pp. 26–30.
4. Jay Peterzell, "The CIA and Political Violence in El Salvador," *First Principles,* Vol. 10, No. 2, November/December 1984, pp. 1–2.
5. "George Bush's Iran-Contra Albatross," *U.S. News & World Report,* January 18, 1988, p. 23.
6. "George Bush's Iran-Contra Albatross."
7. Dennis Volkman, "Salvadoran Death Squads: A CIA Connection?," *The Christian Science Monitor,* May 8, 1984.
8. *The Boston Globe,* July 10, 1984.
9. Pamela Constable, "El Salvador Targets Rebels' Volcano Stronghold," *The Boston Globe,* January 1985.
10. James Dickey, *With the Contras* (New York: Simon & Schuster, 1985), pp. 254–256.
11. Dickey, pp. 254–257.
12. *The New York Times,* November 2, 1984.
13. "Aides: CIA Chiefs Didn't Okay Guide," *The Boston Globe,* October 24, 1984, p. 7.
14. "CIA Manual Said Based on Old Ideas," *The Boston Globe,* October 29, 1984, p. 3.
15. "Reagan Now Says Manual Was Mistranslated," *The New York Times,* November 4, 1984, p. 21.
16. Dickey, p. 257.
17. Beth Hawkins, "Pastora: North Was Behind Bombing," *The Tico Times,* San Jose, Costa Rica, May 15, 1987.

Index

AA (Air America), 48, 81, 153, 267
Abourezk, James, 413, 415
Abrams, Creighton, 129, 161, 181, 253, 278, 297, 302, 321, 323, 328–329, 365–366, 390
Abzug, Bella, 382
Acampora, Tulius, 121–123, 134, 137, 146–149, 174, 176, 180, 186–187, 319, 373*n*
"Action Program for Attack on VC Infrastructure 1967–1968," 142–158, 160
Adams, Sam, 177, 271–274, 305, 369
Advisor, The (Cook), 191
Agee, Philip, 333, 414
Agent Orange, 217–218
Ahearne, Tom, 383, 384
AID (Agency for International Development), 44, 51, 71, 81, 92–93, 96, 99, 125, 132, 217, 301, 366
  Public Safety Division of, *see* Public Safety
AIK (Aid-in-Kind), 81, 162, 299
Akins, Dick, 105
Allen, George W., 273
Allen, Herb, 390
Allende Gossens, Salvador, 333
Allito, Tony, 257
Almy, Dean, 139
Alsop, Joseph, 339
Anderson, Babe Ruth, 162
Anderson, Jack, 413
Anderson, William, 348
An Ninh, 40, 42
ANSESAL (Salvadoran National Security Agency), 422
antiterrorism, counterterrorism contrasted to, 426
APC (accelerated pacification campaign), 257–265, 281, 294
Apple, R. W., 68
APTs (armed propaganda teams), 43–44, 46–47, 54, 56, 65, 106
Aristotle, 426
Arthur, John, 391
ARVN (Army of the Republic of Vietnam):
  intelligence operations of, *see* MSS
  modus vivendi of, 230–231
  Vietcong superior to, 51–52
A teams, 210–211, 226
"Attack Against the Viet Cong Infrastructure" (Brickham), 118–120
Ayres, Drummond, 276

Babineau, Raymond, 32, 35, 41
Bable, Eugene P., 281
Bailey, William, 394*n*

Bao Dai, 23–24, 294
Barker, Frank, 344, 345
Barlow, Jack, 79–80
Bartolomucci, Tony, 78–79
Bauer, Clyde, 34–35, 217
Beamon, Mike, 170–171, 207
Becker, Tom, 123
Ben (intelligence), 80
Benitez, Antonio Flores, 333
Bennett, Josiah, 385, 391
Berkeley, Randolph, 152–153
Berry, John, 271
B-52 strikes, 211–212, 217–218
Biet Kich, 59, 83
Big Mack computer, 288–289
"Big" Minh, *see* Duong Van "Big" Minh
Binh Xuyen, 25, 29, 31, 156
Bishop, Jerry, 351–357, 359
Bissell, Richard, 47
Blackburn, Donald, 76, 298
black propaganda, 48, 49, 50, 339
Blanchard, George, 298
Blandon, Adolfo, 425
Bordenkircher, Donald, 292
Boston Globe, 425
Bradish, Richard, 261–262
Brady, Ed, 136, 146, 185, 230–235, 263, 265, 267, 295, 325, 406, 410–411
Brewer, Robert, 149–150, 193, 202–203, 207, 209
Brewster, Kingman, 166
Brickham, Nelson, 113, 122, 136, 138, 146, 168, 174, 254, 265, 267, 326
  career of, 101–102
  interviews with, 100, 102–112, 114–118, 124, 127–130, 132–133, 139–142, 148
  VCI as studied by, 118–119, 130–132, 142–143, 151, 154, 291
Brogdon, James, 144, 182
Brown, Dean, 407, 417
Brown, Robert, 428
Brussell, Mae, 337
Buckley, Tom, 321
Buckley, William, 296, 424
Buckley, William, Jr., 339
Buddhist crisis, 38, 44, 305
Buddhists, Vietnamese, 46, 52, 61, 95, 143, 303, 304
Buhto, Junichi, 136–137, 144, 147
Bui Tu, 149–150
Bull, Kinloch, 105, 137, 139, 167–168, 172, 255
Bumgartner, Everett, 49–50, 54, 257, 320, 417
Bunker, Ellsworth, 127, 135, 297, 304, 322, 323, 386, 387, 391, 400–402
Burke, Tom, 105
Burmester, Walter, 368–369
Bush, George, 424, 428
Butterfield, Fox, 405
Calley, William, 342, 344
Cambodia, 34, 75, 90, 128, 210–211, 214, 253–254, 281, 314*n*
  invasion of, 327–330
Can Lao Nham Vi, 24, 25, 27, 28, 29, 31, 38, 41, 179, 303, 411
Cao Dai religious sect, 22, 25, 29, 62
Cao Minh Thiep, 329, 330
Cao Van Vien, 232, 303, 411, 417
Carey, Richard, 406
Carranza, Nicholas, 423*n*
Carver, George, 139–140, 159, 272–273, 391, 392
Case, Clifford, 319, 320
Casey, William, 426
Castro, Fidel, 47–48
Castro, Ricardo, 422–424
Cavanaugh, Steve, 330
CDs (civilian detainees), 126, 151–154, 381, 387
Census Grievance program, 63, 124, 179, 277
  as intelligence operation, 70, 72–73, 99, 106–107, 167
  original purpose of, 66–67
Chamorro, Edgar, 427
Chiang Kai-shek, 23, 37
Chieu Hoi (Open Arms) amnesty program, 98, 99, 107
  defectors and, 51, 83, 109
  successes ascribed to, 281–282
Child, Harold, 367
China, People's Republic of, 44, 102
Church Committee report, 48, 428
CIA (Central Intelligence Agency):
  Cambodian invasion engineered by, 327–332
  captured documents used by, 334–335
  compromise and discreditation by, 332–334
  contemporary counterterrorism of, 420–429
  counterinsurgency organized by, 40–42
  development of Phoenix program and, 114–116, 124–126, 128–136
  domestic dissent suppressed by, 338–339
  and end of Vietnam War, 391, 414, 417–419
  interrogation models of, 73–88
  My Lai massacre and, 342–347
  "old-boy network" in, 420, 421, 428
  police models of, 89–112
  political warfare as practiced by, 43–51, 54–56
  psychological warfare models of, 57–72
  security networks established by, 24–37, 52–54
  see also Colby, William; Komer, Robert "Blowtorch"; MACV; Phoenix program

CIA and the Vietnam Debacle, The (Long), 50
CIA Diary (Agee), 414
"CIA's Hired Killers, The" (Geyer), 314
CIDG (Civilian Irregular Defense Group) program, 36–37, 45–46, 55, 64
CIO (Central Intelligence Organization), 41, 42, 74, 77, 78, 79, 84, 103, 121, 175, 176
Circular 757, 291–292, 316
Circular 2212, 293
Civic Action program, 27, 29, 33, 34, 36, 44, 49, 54, 70
Clarridge, Duane, 427
Clay, Frank, 321, 324, 363, 366
Clifford, Clark, 190
CMDC (Capital Military District Command), 187–188, 269
Coburn, Judy, 312
Colby, William, 49, 71, 168, 268, 349, 410, 427
 APTs as described by, 46–47
 background and personality of, 144, 275
 CIA operations directed by, 34–36, 104, 143, 188, 271, 274–275, 277–278, 291, 293, 296, 298, 324, 366, 368, 374, 377, 392, 414–415, 420
 Phoenix program and, 19, 40–41, 119, 184, 301–302, 314–321, 334, 377–382, 385, 420
 Vietnamization and, 254–265, 294
Collier, Bob, 105
colonialism, Vietnam ruled by, 20–22
Combat Police, 95*n*
"combat psywar" model, 25, 44
Combined Intelligence Center, 86–87, 120, 123, 147, 187
Communists, 22, 40, 43, 48, 51, 52, 90, 118
 Diem and, 28–29, 42, 46
 intelligence networks modeled on, 58, 99
 see also VC; VCI
computer systems, 363
 in psychological warfare, 288–290
"Concept for Organization for Attack on VC Infrastructure, A" (Brickham and Hansen), 130–131
Condon, Robert, 393
Conein, Lucien, 13
Cong An, *see* VBI
Conger, Russ, 203
Con Son Prison, 20, 21, 22, 32, 33, 153, 189, 348–349, 411–412
Constant, Tom, 298
contras, 426–428
Contre Coup doctrine, 44, 46, 59, 107, 313, 316, 335, 340–341, 427
 see also counterterrorism, counterterrorists
Conyers, John, 382
Cook, John, 191, 257, 264, 271, 283
Cooper, Sherman, 319
Cooper, Wayne, 288
cordon and search operations, 91, 162, 189, 207, 343, 344
CORDS (Civil Operations and Revolutionary Development), 127, 159, 167, 254, 266–267, 277, 300, 374, 390, 392
 Phoenix program and, 116–117, 157, 175, 182, 230, 272, 278, 288, 316, 325
corruption, 396–397, 407, 411
 South Vietnam blamed for, 276
 Vietnamization and, 266–271
COSVN (Central Office of South Vietnam), 38, 109–110, 167, 174, 175, 280, 287, 305, 328–330
Coughlin, Paul, 373, 389, 390
Counter-Insurgency Warfare: Theory and Practice (Galula), 21
counterterrorism, counterterrorists (CTs), 25, 27, 44–47, 49, 91, 106–107, 117, 172
 interrogation models for, 73–88
 psychological warfare models for, 57–72
 see also specific organizations
covert action:
 characteristics of personnel in, 106
 political and psychological rationales for, 43–73
 see also specific operations and programs
Cover-up (Hersh), 343
Cowan, Geoffrey, 312
Cowey, Bill, 357
CT IV (Cong Tac IV), 120–21, 123, 146–148, 176
CTs, *see* counterterrorism, counterterrorists
Cuc Nghien Cuu (Central Research Agency), 39–40, 305–306, 345
Cult of Intelligence, The (Marks), 414
Cushing, Robert, Jr., 355, 357, 384, 385

Dai Viet party, 22, 38, 52, 53, 64, 304
Dam, Colonel, 395
Damron, James K., 227, 268, 270–271, 384
Da Nang, Phoenix operations exemplified in, 351–361
Dang Van Minh, 122–123, 156, 180–181, 188, 232
Dang Van Quang, 295, 296, 304, 394
Dao Ba Phuoc, 187
d'Aubuisson, Robert, 422
Dave (PRU adviser), 164–166
David Brinkley Show, 427
Davidson, Phillip B., Jr., 135, 146, 273
Davis, George, 346
Davis, Jefferson, 13
Davis, Rennie, 311
Deadly Deceits (McGehee), 272
Dean, Warren, 333
Death in Washington (Freed), 333
death squad operations, in El Salvador, 422–424

Decent Interval (Snepp), 221
Decree Law 280, 185*n*, 188–189
defectors, in political warfare, 48–49, 51, 83, 109, 112, 281–282
Defense, U.S. Department of:
 Phoenix program reviewed by, 297–299
DeFreeze, Donald, 337
Delta Program, 12, 75, 76
 see also Phoenix program
Denunciation of the Communists' campaign, 28–29, 335
DeSilva, Peer, 59–60, 63, 71, 102
Dexter, George, 226
Dick, Fred, 300*n*
Dickey, James, 426
Diem, Ngo Dinh, *see* Ngo Dinh Diem
Dien Bien Phu, 24
Dillard, Douglas, 226, 288, 289, 302, 414
 career of, 203
 interviews with, 205–215, 220, 223–225, 261, 262, 271, 364, 405
 Phoenix program as viewed by, 203–205
Dinh Tuong An, 217–221, 281, 284
Dinh Xuan Mai, 262
DIOCCs (District Intelligence and Operations Coordination Centers), 131, 141, 157–158, 190, 225, 258, 284, 288, 300–301
 purposes of, 125–126, 133, 138, 206, 325
disinformation, in political warfare, 47–48
Dix, Drew, 206
Doan Cong Lap, 178
Do Cao Tri, 214, 368
Dodds, Bill, 168, 171
Do Kin Nhieu, 267
Do Minh Nhat, 152
Donohue, Tom, 65–69, 70–72, 105–106, 116, 159, 298, 299, 320
Dooley, Tom, 26
Doolin, Dennis, 298, 313
Drakulich, Sam, 105, 110–111
Drosnin, Michael, 349, 394
Dulles, Allen, 25, 30
Dulles, John Foster, 25, 30
Dunn, Burke, 111
Dunwoodie, Bob, 373*n*
Duong Tan Huu, 186, 232, 233, 262
Duong Van "Big" Minh, 52–53, 303, 417
Duong Van Khanh, 53–54, 64
DuPuy, William, 298
Durbow, Elbridge, 41

Eckhardt, George, 205, 212
Ehrlichman, John, 337, 415
Ellis, Ace, 159
Ellsberg, Daniel, 334, 411
El Salvador, counterterror operations in, 421–425
Enders, Rudy, 180, 296, 351, 352, 369, 370, 394, 410, 424
Engel, Byron, 35, 92, 366, 413–414
Enough Crying of Tears, 425
Ervin, Sam, 337
Eschbach, Robert, 159
Escola, Albert, 302
eye of God, in psychological warfare, 61–62, 283

Falke, Dick, 84
Fall, Bernard, 89
Fallaci, Oriana, 179
Fallwell, Marshall, 312
Family Census program, 73–74, 269
Far Eastern Economic Review, 395
FBI (Federal Bureau of Investigation), 104, 302, 366–368
Fenner, Claude, 137
Fernandez, Joe, 428
Field Police, 89–99, 124, 150–151, 208, 322, 325, 341
 activities and objectives of, 93–99, 160–162, 173
 need for development of, 89–92
First Indochina War, 23
Fisher, Sergeant, 125
Flores, Tom, 408, 410
Forbes (Special Branch adviser), 124
forced relocation, 50–51
Force Recon Marines, 166
Ford, John, 123
Foreign Affairs, 140
Forsythe, George, 135
Fortin, Dick, 72
France, 20–25
 Diem and, 25
 Vietminh and, 22–24
 Vietnam colonized by, 20–22
Frazier, Linda, 361
Freed, Donald, 333
Freedom Company, 26, 27, 48
French, George, 184, 186, 278, 373*n*, 406
Freund, John, 298
Fulbright, William, 312, 320, 321
Fulcher, Stan, 396–399, 400, 420–422
Fulford, C. J., 364
Funkhouser, Richard, 368, 369
"Future Applicability of the Phoenix Program, The" (Milberg), 107, 201, 202

Gallagher, Phillip, 23
Galula, David, 21, 73, 74, 107–108, 112
Gambino, Robert, 120
Gavin, David, 345
Gene (administrator), 84
Generous, Kevin, 26
Geneva Accords (1954), 24, 27, 28, 34, 40, 42
Geneva Conventions, 13, 204, 312, 380, 382, 384, 386, 400

Article 3 of, 377–379
Gestapo, 192, 337, 353, 398
Geyer, Georgie Anne, 314, 317–318, 319
Gilardo, Bob, 394
Goldwater, Barry, 53
Goodwin, Richard, 48
Gore, Albert, 317
Gorman, Paul, 425
Gougleman, Tucker, 78–80, 102, 103, 109, 159, 256*n*, 294–296, 316–317, 417–418, 419
Gould, Robert, 349
Greaney, John, 342–343
Green Beret murder case, 297, 313, 315, 390
Green Berets, 10, 34, 85, 166
Greene, Graham, 26, 32
Greenwalt, William J., 144, 183, 184, 261
Gregg, Donald, 369–370, 371, 424–425, 428
Gregory, George, 313
Greyman, Ted, 205, 210, 212, 215, 288
Grieves, William "Pappy," 91–99, 161, 162, 231, 316–317, 341, 365, 413–414
Guevara, Che, 373
Guinn, William, 345, 346
Gulf of Tonkin Resolution, 53
GVN (Government of Vietnam), *see* Vietnam, Republic of

Habib, Philip, 298
Hacker, Gary, 396
Haeberle, Robert, 346
Hai, Colonel, 363, 418
Haig, Alexander, 405
Hamilton, Ben, 414
Hammer, Michael, 422
Hansen, John, 127–128, 130–131
Harkins, Tom, 348
Harper, Robert, 152
Harrell, Jack, 394, 405
Harris, Stewart, 179
Harrison, Reed, 343*n*
Hart, John, 79, 106, 117, 121, 122, 136, 139, 146, 148, 174, 277
ICEX developed by, 127–129, 134, 135, 151, 347
personality of, 102–103
Ha Van Tien, 262
Hawkins, Augustus, 348
Haynes, Robert E., 261
Healy, Michael, 399, 400
Helms, Richard, 135, 139, 176, 184, 273, 313, 414, 415
Herbert, Anthony, 107–108
Herrmann, William, 337
Hersh, Seymour, 62, 342, 343, 344
HES (Hamlet Evaluation System), 257, 259–260, 277, 280–281, 301
Heyman, Vince, 116
Hill, Bob, 81
Hilsman, Roger, 73
Himmler, Heinrich, 192
HIP (Hamlet Informant program), 104, 107–108, 284
Hitler, Adolf, 192
Hoa Hao religious sect, 22, 25, 29, 55
Hoang Duc Nha, 304
Hoang Xuam Lam, 189
Ho Chau Tuan, 394
Ho Chi Minh, 22–23, 38, 74, 175
Ho Chi Minh Trail, 34, 61, 128, 277
Hodges, Paul, 78
Hoeksema, Renz, 116–117, 149, 160, 175
Hoffman, Abbie, 311
Hollingsworth, General, 370–371
Honduras, political assassinations in, 423
Ho Ngoc Hui, 343
Ho Ngoc Nhuan, 392
Honorable Men (Colby), 275
Hoover, J. Edgar, 367, 368
Hopper, Sam, 78
Hop Tac (Pacification Intensive Capital Area), 74–75, 120
Horgan, Jack, 124, 139, 141, 198–199, 201, 298
Horus, 62
Hostages of War (Luce), 347, 349
Houle, David, 12
Hubbard, Bob, 178
Hudman, John, 390
Hue, Tet offensive and, 178–180
Hugo, Victor, 62
Humphrey, Hubert, 71, 186
Hunt, Howard, 334, 337–338, 339
Hunt, James, 368*n*, 377
hunter-killer teams, 9–10, 12, 46, 207
Huston, Tom, 337
Huy, Nguyen Ngoc, *see* Nguyen Ngoc Huy
Huynh Thoi Tay, 393
Huynh Van Trong, 305
Hydle, Lars, 385, 392

ICEX (intelligence coordination and exploitation), 127–142, 166, 171, 173, 180, 190, 204, 220, 232, 264, 326, 347
Ide, Richard, 217
Indochina War, First, 23
Inchin Hai Lam, 211
informant operations, 104, 107–108, 112, 119
Inman, Robert, 181–186, 188–189, 232
interrogation, 73–88
development of models for, 73–81
methods and processes in, 81–86, 88
see also PICs; Special Branch
In the Midst of Wars (Lansdale), 25
IOCCs (Intelligence and Operations Coordination Centers), 230, 257
Israel, 220
Ivey, Ashley, 182

Jack (Vann's deputy), 215, 265, 299–302, 332, 344, 363, 366–368, 391
Jackson, Larry, 396–400
Jacobsen, George "Jake," 114, 374, 377, 382, 385, 390, 406
Jacqueney, Ted, 380–381
James, Hatcher, 188, 267, 268
Jantzen, Red, 329
Jenkins, Oscar L., 217
Johnson, Bill, 417, 419
Johnson, Chester, 329
Johnson, Harry "Buzz," 257, 295, 348
Johnson, Johnny, 370
Johnson, Lyndon B., 53, 90, 113–116, 129, 134–135, 146, 160, 177, 181, 186, 191, 254, 273
Johnson, Ralph, 33, 39–40, 51, 58, 84, 135, 147–148, 150, 191, 230, 276, 278, 281, 291, 294, 427
  on counterterrorism, 44, 335, 376
  covert operations of, 44–45, 55, 60, 256
Johnson, Wayne, 168
Johnstone, Craig, 152, 190, 417, 419
Jones, Robert E., 261
Jorgenson, Gordon, 71, 102, 320
Joy, D. Duncan, 384

Kaiser, Robert, 314, 315
Kann, Peter, 264, 276, 314
Karhohs, Fred, 298, 366, 391
Karnow, Stanley, 20, 21, 40, 41, 79*n*, 176–177, 179, 180, 296, 328, 330, 338
Kaylor, Robert, 415
Kelly, Paul, 299
Kelly, Robert, 57, 59, 70
Kennedy, John F., 42, 52–53, 334
Kerwin, Walter, 135
Khiem, Mrs., 303
Khiem, Tran Thien, *see* Tran Thien Khiem
Khien, Colonel, 346
Khrushchev, Nikita, 42
Kieu (Special Branch chief), 345*n*
Kim Chong Pil, 77
King, Martin Luther, Jr., 338
Kirkpatrick, John, 426–427
Kissinger, Henry, 253, 254, 257, 313, 314*n*, 366–367, 406, 417
Kizirian, John, 141
Klare, Michael, 394
Kline, Jacques, 198
Knoll, Erwin, 313
Knowlton, William, 116
Kolon, Walter, 262–263, 368*n*
Komer, Robert "Blowtorch," 123, 130, 133, 137, 142, 149, 152–153, 176, 254, 259, 265, 275, 298
  assessments of, 146, 148, 191
  mandate and methods of, 127, 128–129, 134–135, 143, 161–163, 184, 205, 258, 299–300, 427
  military control favored by, 114, 115
  personality of, 144
  Phoenix program criticized by, 321–323
Korea, South, CIA operations in, 76–77
Koren, Art, 116
Koslowski, Peter, 357–360
Kotouc, Captain, 344–345
Kramer, Fritz, 366
Krogh, Egil, 337, 338
Krulak, Victor, 53
Kuomintang, 23, 186
Ky, Nguyen Cao, *see* Nguyen Cao Ky

Laboon, John, 9–11
Laird, Melvin, 297, 299, 321, 366, 367
Lam Minh Son, 407–408
Landreth, Rod, 277, 294–296, 304, 348, 394
Lane, Randolph, 343
Langbien, Joe, 363
Lange, Keith, 270
Lansdale, Edward, 25–30, 31, 34, 44, 47–48, 62, 71, 113, 116, 159, 304, 339
Lao Dong Central Committee, Reunification Department of, 38, 39
Laos, 12, 34, 37, 44, 60, 81, 90, 128, 195, 277
La Penca, bombing at, 427–428
Lapham, Lewis, 112, 116, 123, 172, 174–176, 188, 255, 277
Lapitosa, Phil, 310
Lathram, Wade, 115, 142
Latin America, CIA operations in, 77
Law, William, 144, 183–184
Lawlor, Bruce, 407–410
Lawton, Gilbert, 36
Leaping Lena program, 12, 61, 75
Ledford, Dick, 352, 354
Le Doan Hung, 262
Le Duan, 38
Legal Times, 428
Lemire, Lieutenant Colonel, 182, 189, 190
Lemoyne, Charles, 255, 339
Lemoyne, James, 339
Le Ngoc Tru, 187
Le Quang Tung, 52
Leslie, Mike, 123
Letelier, Orlando, 357, 361
Le Tri Tin, 407
Le Van An, 413
Le Van Thu, 292–293
Le Xuan Mai, 44, 59, 65, 67, 68, 72, 159
Liddy, Gordon, 337
Likert, Rensis, 129
LLDB (Luc Luong Duc Biet), 26–27, 52
Loan, Nguyen Ngoc, *see* Nguyen Ngoc Loan
"local initiatives," 45, 54–55, 91
Lodge, Henry Cabot, 113, 115
Loi Nguyen Tan, 184–186, 189, 232–234, 262, 263, 322

Lombardi, Vince, 176
Lon Nol, 327–328, 329
Loomis, Patry, 357, 394, 407
Lowe, Bob, 93
Luce, Don, 347–350
Lu Lam, 159, 303, 353, 355
Luu Kim Cuong, 187*n*
Lybrand, John, 152, 190
Ly Trong Song, 262, 374

MAAG (Military Assistance and Advisory Group), U.S., 24, 31, 42, 45–46
McAfee, Gage, 386, 387
McCann, Michael, 300*n*
McCarthy, Emmett, 24
McCarthy, Eugene, 176, 177
McCarthy, John, 211
McCarthy, Roger, 355
McChristian, Joseph, 86–87, 120, 124, 135, 146, 176, 211, 267, 273
McCloskey, Pete, 377, 379, 382
McCoid, Chester, 367, 371–373, 374, 385, 390
McCoid, Dorothy, 371
McCollum, Doug, 97–98, 161–162, 341, 413
McCord, James, 415
McCoy, Tom, 177, 259
MacDonald, John E., 182
MacFarlane, Robert, 424
McGarvey, Pat, 62
McGehee, Ralph, 271–272, 274–275, 305–306
McGrevey, Thomas P., 329–330, 331
Mackem, Walter, 55–56
Mackin, Roger, 351, 352, 354
McLendon, Luther, 394*n*
McManaway, Clayton, 257, 314
McNamara, Robert, 177, 258
MACV (Military Assistance Command, Vietnam), 42, 75, 94–96, 116, 118, 273, 300
  Phoenix program and, 57, 86–88, 115, 126, 131, 135–137, 176, 182, 190, 204–205, 207, 209, 211–212, 224, 276, 318, 355–356
MACV Directive 381-41, 137–139, 188
McWade, Henry, 227–230, 262, 263, 269, 271
Maddox, Gary, 394
Maddox, USS, 53
Magsaysay, Ramón, 25
Mai Huu Xuan, 53
Mai Viet Dich, 262
Malaya, intelligence methods developed in, 73, 79, 92, 125, 299
Mandich, Ben, 296
Mann, Charlie, 93
Manopoli, John, 93, 136–137, 366, 391
Manzione, Elton, 9–13, 53, 60–61, 63, 170, 194–197, 202, 207, 285, 338, 340
Manzione, Lynn, 9
Mao, Major, 352, 355
March Against Death, 309, 312
Marks, John, 77, 414, 415
Martin, Graham, 412, 415–416
Mason, John, 278–279, 284, 308, 328–329, 367–368, 371, 373, 377
Matisse, Mr., 72
Mattson, Robert, 116
Melton, William, 180
Methven, Stu, 44–45, 55, 59, 63–64, 65, 320
Meyers, Ray, 400
Milberg, Warren, 107, 108, 144, 154–155, 163, 202, 203, 207, 219, 226
  ideological convictions of, 193–194, 196–198
  interviews with, 178–179, 181, 192–193, 194, 199–201
  Manzione compared with, 195
Millett, Lew, 395, 396
Mills, Hawthorne, 314
Minh Van Dang, 371
Minneapolis Tribune, 264
Mitchell, David, 342
Mitchum, Robert, 76
Mitrione, Dan, 413
Monk, Harry "The Hat," 70
Monopoly, General, 267, 270
Montagnards, 44, 76, 106, 162
Moorehead, William, 376
Moran, Joe, 330
Morrison, John, 394
Morse, Lieutenant, 125
motivational indoctrination, 58, 75, 426
Mountain Scouts program, 44–46, 51, 60
Mountbatten, Lord Louis, 23
Moynihan, Daniel, 270
MSS (Military Security Service), 87, 99, 121, 123, 176, 212, 213, 301, 306, 308, 353
MSUG (Michigan State University Group), 31–32, 35
Muldoon, John Patrick "Picadoon," 76–86, 91, 104, 109
Murphy, Ed, 308–311, 312, 326, 338, 347
Mustakos, Harry, 201
My Lai massacre, 181, 297, 315, 342–347, 426, 428

Namath, Joe, 338
National Police, 92, 118, 353
  MACV's relationship with, 95–96, 118
  Phoenix program and, 261, 270, 363, 369
  Phung Hoang and, 232, 322
  PICs and, 81–82
  PRU and, 294–296, 316
  see also Field Police; Special Branch
National Revolution Movement, 28
National Security Action Memorandum 273, 53

National Social Democratic Front, 304
Navy, U.S., 164, 168
Nazis, 198
neutralization, neutralization rates, 13, 190–191, 287
Newman, James, 371
New Patterns of Management (Likert), 129
Newsweek, 313, 330
New Yorker, 275
New York Herald Tribune, 107
New York Times, 68, 276, 308, 321, 339, 342, 348, 363, 378, 386, 405, 412
Ngo Cong Duc, 217, 293
Ngo Dinh Can, 24
Ngo Dinh Diem, 47, 51, 62–63, 71, 121, 176, 213, 304, 332, 335
  assassination of, 53, 334
  CIA support for, 24–27
  coups against, 38, 52–54, 179
  internal security as concern of, 27–29, 31–32, 41–42
Ngo Dinh Nhu, 24, 27, 28, 29, 38, 41, 42, 50–53, 54, 213, 294
Ngo Dinh Thuc, 24, 52
Ngo Vinh Long, 50
Nguyen Bao Thuy, 187
Nguyen Be, 58, 70, 159, 262
Nguyen Cao Ky, 42, 54, 69, 71, 120, 121, 145, 148, 176, 179, 186–188, 265, 417
Nguyen Cao Thang, 304
Nguyen Chi Thanh, 90
Nguyen Duc Khoi, 355
Nguyen Duc Thang, 71, 159
Nguyen Hiop, 285
Nguyen Huu Tho, 90
Nguyen Khac Binh, 188, 295, 395, 419
Nguyen Khanh, 179, 189
Nguyen Loc Hoa, 37
Nguyen Mau, 123, 187, 305–306, 308, 393
Nguyen Minh Chau, 348
Nguyen Minh Tan, 352, 418
Nguyen Ngoc Huy, 24, 28, 29, 54, 64, 69, 181, 186, 187, 256, 303, 320, 411, 421
Nguyen Ngoc Le, 27
Nguyen Ngoc Loan, 87, 120, 156, 186–187, 188, 417
  as National Police director, 69, 95, 141
  notoriety of, 180
  Phoenix program opposed by, 121–123, 135*n*, 145–147
  Tet offensive predicted by, 148–149, 176
Nguyen Ngoc Xinh, 120, 187
Nguyen Nuoi, 287
Nguyen Psu Sanh, 292
Nguyen Thi Bah, 286
Nguyen Tien, 121, 187, 352
Nguyen Ton Hoan, 54, 69
Nguyen Tuy, 51
Nguyen Van Dai, 96, 316–317, 356
Nguyen Van Giau, 374, 394, 414, 418
Nguyen Van Hong, 262
Nguyen Van Khoi, 200
Nguyen Van Kia, 285
Nguyen Van Lang, 256, 294, 316, 352, 394
Nguyen Van Loc, 148, 180
Nguyen Van Luan, 120, 187
Nguyen Van Phuoc, 212, 213, 224
Nguyen Van Tai, 221–222
Nguyen Van Thieu, 50, 64, 71, 74, 145, 295, 320, 322, 368, 411
  CIA support for, 174, 176, 274, 385
  Diem and, 41, 52–54
  overthrow of, 417–419
Nguyen Van Thieu, cont.
  political style of, 188–189, 256–257, 304–306
  as president, 69, 148, 185–186, 294, 297, 303, 374, 393
  repressive measures of, 394–395, 401–402, 406–407
Nguyen Van Ve, 348
Nguyen Van Vinh, 397, 399
Nguyen Van Y, 41, 53
Nha, Mr., 370
Nha Trang, 186
Nhu, Madame, 52
Nhu, Ngo Dinh, *see* Ngo Dinh Nhu
NIC (National Interrogation Center), 77, 78, 84, 85, 121, 176, 221
Nicaragua, antiterror operations in, 426–428
Nixon, Richard M., 186, 253, 313, 327, 328, 402, 411–412, 415
  domestic dissent suppressed by, 336–338
Nixon Doctrine, 254, 327
  see also Vietnamization
NLF (National Front for the Liberation of South Vietnam), 38–39, 46, 52, 87, 283
Nooter, Robert, 366
North, Oliver, 425, 427, 428, 429
North Vietnam, *see* Vietnam, Democratic Republic of
NPFF, *see* Field Police
NPIC (National Police Interrogation Center), 79, 103, 123, 149, 156, 186, 221
NSC (National Security Council), 31, 42, 301
Nunn, Sam, 427
Nuremberg War Crimes Trials, 312
Nutter, Warren, 298–299, 366
NVA (North Vietnamese Army):
  casualties in, 223
  and end of Vietnam War, 393, 415–419
  intelligence operations by and against, 48, 55, 88, 175, 273
  in Tet offensive, 178–179

OCO (Office of Civil Operations), 115–116, 118

Ogden, Keith, 205, 406
O'Keefe, John, 267–270
Operation MONGOOSE, 48
Operation Phoenix, 425
OPLANS, 12, 53, 60, 79*n*, 169
O'Reilly, John, 72, 320
"Origins of the Insurgency in South Vietnam 1954–1960" (Zasloff), 28
Orr, David, 405
Orwell, George, 89
Osborn, Bart, 307–308, 347, 376, 382
O'Shea, Connie, 389, 395–396, 399–400, 403
Osiris, 62
Osnos, Peter, 388
Ott, David, 298
Owen, Dwight, 343*n*, 428
Owen, Robert, 428

PA&E (Pacific Architects and Engineers), 81, 310
pacification:
  accelerated, *see* APC
  differing philosophies of, 89–90
  general staff for, *see* ICEX
  see also specific operations
Palmer, Bruce, 204
Panay, Colonel, 330
Paris Peace Talks, 253, 257, 275, 280, 404
Park Chung Hee, 77
Parker, Evan, Jr., 133–140, 148, 152, 157, 175, 180, 183, 184, 232, 233, 235, 278, 323, 342, 424
  background and career of, 133–134
  interviews with, 135–137, 143–145, 147, 149, 150, 153–154, 167, 191, 257, 277, 281
Parks, Michael, 374
Pastora, Eden, 427–428
Pat (paramilitary), 80
PATs (Political Action Teams), 59, 63, 70, 74, 75, 124, 180
PCOC (Phoenix Coordinators Orientation Course), 261
Pearlman, Mark, 422
Pearson, William, 135
Peartt, Robert, 160, 254
Peck, Gregory, 338
Peers, William, 114, 342, 343, 344, 346
Pelton, Major, 399
penetration units, 109–112, 119, 370
Pennington, Lee, 415
People's Self-Defense Forces, 254
Personalist Labor party, *see* Can Lao Nham Vi
Petry, Chuck, 94
Pham, Colonel, 417
Pham Ngoc Thao, 42, 50, 52, 54
Pham Quat Tan, 269
Pham Tuong, 57–58
Pham Van Cao, 186, 189, 356
Pham Van Kinh, 285
Pham Van Liem, 352, 357, 409
Phan Huu Nhon, 184
Philippines, intelligence models developed in, 25, 44, 62
Phillips, Rufus, 29
Phillips, William, 376–377
PHMIS (Phung Hoang Management Information System), 259, 261
"Phoenix Murders, The" (Treaster), 285
Phoenix/Phung Hoang: A Study of Wartime Intelligence Management (Johnson), 33
Phoenix program, 9–18, 57–429
  atrocities aided by, 340–350
  Cambodian invasion and, 328, 330–332
  CIA-MACV conflicts in, 115, 176, 182, 190, 204, 209, 212
  conflicting objectives in evolution of, 94, 98–99, 112, 115
  contemporary implications of, 13–14, 420–429
  cornerstones of, 32, 45, 108–109
  Da Nang operations as example of, 351–361
  differing perspectives on, 101–102, 203–205, 264–265, 316–317, 321, 326, 349, 371, 374, 392, 398
  dissolution and final days of, 389–419
  legality of, 376–388
  objectives of, 13, 38, 39, 60
  orientation materials for, 260–264
  prototypes and models for, 12, 26, 40, 57–72, 111
  reasons for mismanagement of, 308–310, 322–323
  reorganizations of, 266–280, 362–375
  Senate hearings on, 313–322
  as synthesis of intelligence networks, 99, 101, 113–141
Phoenix Program: Planned Assassination or Legimate Conflict Management, The (Johnson), 44, 376
Phong, Major General, 393, 394
Pho Quoc Chu, 187
"Phung Hoang Fiasco, The" (Komer), 322–323, 327
Phung Hoang program, 122, 148, 149, 181, 230, 232, 261–262, 283, 287, 304, 322, 355, 374, 393
  see also Phoenix program
Phuoc Le interrogation center, as PIC model, 80–81
Picard, Bernard, 182
PICCs (Province Intelligence Coordinating Committees), 74, 79, 80, 86
PICs (province interrogation centers), 76–86, 99
  operations and purposes of, 81–86, 109, 126, 151–157, 265, 316, 325–326
  origin and development of, 76–81

PICs *(cont.)*
as Phoenix program foundation, 108–109, 132, 234, 352
Pierce, Danny L., 188, 268
Pike, Otis, 273, 411, 428
Pineda, Major, 424
Pink Plan, 424–425
PIOCCs (Province Intelligence Operations Coordination Centers), 142, 157, 160, 173, 181, 189, 190, 202, 206, 225, 296, 325
plausible denial, in political warfare, 47–48, 49, 60, 72, 133, 296
Playboy, 414
PLO (Palestine Liberation Organization), 424
Polgar, Tom, 295, 390, 394, 408, 417, 428
Poindexter, John, 428
political warfare, 43–51, 54–56, 160, 335–336
defectors in, 48–49, 51, 83, 112, 281–282
forced relocation in, 50–51
"local initiatives" and, 45, 54–55
objectives of, 46–47, 50
plausible denial in, 47–48, 49, 60, 72, 133, 296
propaganda in, 43–44, 47–49, 54
terrorism in, 44–46, 55–56
Popular Force, 36–37, 75, 86, 99, 189
Potter, Phil "Potts," 277, 294–296, 394
Prairie Fire operation, 90, 193
PRG (Provisional Revolutionary Government), 280, 291
prison system, Phoenix program's creation of, 347–350
Project 404, 90
Project Gamma, 211
Project 24, 76
propaganda, 43–44, 47–49, 54
PRP (People's Revolutionary Party), 19, 38–39, 138
PRU (Provincial Reconnaissance Units), 117, 141, 150, 177–178, 201–202, 207, 255–256, 272, 276, 277, 301, 314, 409
CIA management of, 294–296, 347, 369–370
counterterror activities of, 264, 267, 283, 285, 316–319, 351–361, 383
development and objectives of, 162–173
as Phoenix program foundation, 132, 160, 234, 265, 326
psychological warfare, 25–26, 34, 44–45, 57–73, 107–108
anti-VCI operations in, 280–290
Census Grievance program and, 66–67, 72–73
eye of God in, 61–62, 283
terrorism and torture in, 59–60, 61–63, 65, 107–108
Psywar Groups, 292
Public Safety, 35, 36, 74–75, 82, 92, 93, 94, 97, 99, 152, 208, 300
PVT (PRU adviser), 179–180, 351, 352, 354–355, 409, 416–419

Quiet American, The (Greene), 32
Quinn, Ken, 404, 417
Quoc Dan Dang, 136

Race, Jeffrey, 32, 33, 41, 46, 258, 265
Radda, Ron, 156
Ramparts, 162
Ramsdell, Robert B., 343–344
RD (Revolutionary Development), 159–160, 166, 202–203, 218, 254–255, 277
development and purpose of, 57–59, 69–71
RDC (Revolutionary Development Cadre), 64–72, 95, 99, 112, 116–117, 123, 157, 159–60, 217, 262, 342
Reagan, Ronald, 337, 424, 427
Redel, William, 117, 166–167, 169, 255
Regional Forces, 36, 86, 99, 189
Reid, Ogden, 13, 376, 378–380
Reinhardt, George, 29
Reitemeyer, Francis, 311–312, 318
Renneisen, Daniel, 354, 355, 356, 357
Resor, Stanley, 297, 313
Resources Control Bureau, 74–75
Rhee, Syngman, 77
Rhodes, James, 336
Richardson, Warrant Officer, 126
rifle shot approach, in Phoenix operations, 206–207
Rimestead, Imer, 377, 378
Rivers, L. Mendel, 359
Roberts, Chalmers, 163
Roberts, Jay, 346
Roberts, Shelby, 267–271, 352
Rodriguez, Felix, 370–371, 394, 424–425, 428
Rogers, Andy, 205, 214
Rogers, William, 391
Romero, Oscar, 422
Rose, Colonel, 399
Rosen, L. M., 289
Rosenblatt, Lionel, 182, 417, 419
Rosenthal, Ben, 382
Rosnor, Colonel, 354
Rosson, William B., 42
Rostow, Walt, 127, 146, 273
Rothwell, Gordon, 105
Rubin, Jerry, 311
Rural Construction program, *see* RDC
Rusk, Dean, 135
Rygalski, Frank, 84

Saigon:
bureaucracy in, 200
corruption in, 266–271

Saigon Metropolitan Police, 270, 271
Sam, Colonel, 78
Sammers, Ian "Sammy," 78
Sang, Colonel, 322
Sanh, Colonel, 95
Santoli, Al, 146
Sartiano, Joe, 144, 182, 232, 261, 371
SAS (British Special Air Service), 166
Saturday Evening Post, 37
Sauvageot, Jean, 71, 72, 159
Schlacter, Ed, 96
Schrande, Don, 37
Scigliano, Robert, 35
Scotton, Frank, 49–51, 54–55, 57–59, 69–71, 75–76, 159, 257, 304, 317, 318, 417, 426
Scove, Peter, 231
Seal, Al, 408
SEALs (Sea-Air-Land forces), U.S. Navy, 60–61
  objectives and procedures of, 9–11
  PRU assisted by, 164–166, 168, 172
Search for the Manchurian Candidate, The (Marks), 77
Sea Swallows, 37, 50, 55
Seberg, Jean, 334
Secord, Richard, 329
selective terrorism, 21–22, 41, 44
  see also counterterrorism, counterterrorists
Sells, Doc, 172, 214
Senate, U.S., 47–48
  Foreign Relations Committee of, 19, 311, 312, 313–322
Serong, Ted, 92–95, 231, 406, 416
Shackley, Ted, 277–278, 295, 305, 306, 325, 348, 368, 369–370, 373, 390, 393, 410, 417
Shaplen, Robert, 275–276
Sherwood, John, 103
Shipler, David, 412–413
SIDE (screening, interrogation, and detention of the enemy) program, 152
Sihanouk, Norodom, 211, 253, 327
Silkwood, Karen, 357
Simmons, Rob, 391, 407
Singer, Ray, 299
Singlaub, John, 428
Singleton, William, 183, 188, 268, 270
Sinh, Colonel, 370
Sirik Matak, 327, 417
Sizer, Henry, 385
Slater, Robert, 39, 155–156, 181, 185, 215, 262
Smith, Daniel L., 271
Smith, Jim, 363
Smith, Paul, 115
Smith, Terrence, 308
snatch and snuff operations, 46, 56, 207
Snepp, Frank, 221–222, 304, 306–308, 406, 419
Snowden, Walter, 355
SOG (Special Operations Group), 53, 60, 74–76, 107, 121, 175, 211, 253
Soldier (Herbert), 107
Soldier of Fortune, 285, 428
Song, Colonel, 389, 393
SOP (standard operating procedures) manuals, 230, 263
Sophon, Colonel, 330
South Korea, CIA operations in, 76–77
South Vietnam, *see* Vietnam, Republic of
Soviet Union, 69
  CIA surveillance in, 101–102
Special Branch, 74, 78, 81, 99, 118, 228, 232, 296, 298, 355
  development and management of, 104–112, 267, 269, 277–278, 300–301, 373
  functions of, 97, 102–104, 136, 212
  lack of coordination in, 288, 323, 370, 390
Spiers, Del, 207–208
Spock, Benjamin, 311
Sputnik, 101
Starr, Robert, 387–388
State Department, U.S., 115, 177, 206
  Office of Research and Intelligence in, 73
Stein, Jeffrey, 343–344, 346, 347, 405
Stemme, Bob, 311
Stent, Jack "Red," 78, 102–103, 110
Sterba, James, 321
Stewart, Kelly, 263
Stilwell, Richard, 329
Stone, Howard "Rocky," 110–112, 116, 117, 118, 176, 184, 391
Stout, Gerald, 343
strategic hamlet program, 50, 54
Strathern, Cliff, 45, 65
Sub Rosa (DeSilva), 59
Suddath, Leroy, 209–210
Sullivan, William C., 338, 366
Sullivan, William H., 135, 387
supplétifs, 21, 25, 74
suppressive terrorism, 41
Sûreté, 25, 31–32, 104
Swetz, Eddie, 9–11
Systems Analysis of the Vietnam War 1965–1972, A (Thayer), 254, 365
systems approach, in intelligence operations, 101–102

Tacloban Hotel, The (Valentine), 12
Taiwan, 220
Task Force Barker, 342, 343, 344, 346
Tayacan: Psychological Operations in Guerrilla Warfare, 426–427
Taylor, Telford, 386
Taylor, William J., 357–361
10/59 law, 33–34, 36
Ten Thousand Day War, The (Maclean), 306
Terjelian, John, 124

Territorial Security Forces, 254, 277, 282, 284
terrorism:
as psychological weapon, 21–22, 25–26, 44–45, 55–56, 59–60, 61–63, 65
suppressive, 41
see also counterterrorism, counterterrorists
Tet offensive, 124, 148–149, 156, 176–180, 200, 206, 208, 218, 221, 257, 275, 343
significance of, 173, 181, 186, 253, 266
Thai Khac Chuyen, 328
Thayer, Thomas, 254, 365–366, 409*n*
Thich Tri Quang, 52
Thiep, Colonel, 322, 354, 355, 356
Thieu, Mrs., 303
Thieu, Nguyen Van, *see* Nguyen Van Thieu
Thompson, Major, 357
Thompson, Robert, 73, 74, 79, 85, 92, 299–301, 345, 363, 391, 406
Thornton, Frank, 285, 294
Those Gallant Men on Trial in Vietnam (Berry), 271
Thuong Xa, Phoenix operation at, 202–203
Tidwell, William, 262, 267
Tiege, Ian, 57, 59
Tilton, John, 373–374, 382, 385, 389, 390, 391, 393, 400–401, 403
Time, 104, 342, 395
Times (London), 179
Tin Sang, 217, 293, 348
Ton That Dinh, 52, 53
torture, 59, 63, 84–85, 350
Towle, Sid, 382–385
Tracy, Larry, 123
Tran Ahn Tho, 405
Tran Huu Thanh, 411
Tran Kim Tuyen, 29, 41, 52, 54, 294
Tran Ngoc Chau, 49–50, 55, 71–72, 159, 304–305, 320, 332
Tran Ngoc Hien, 304, 320
Tran Ngoc Tan, 345
Tran Quoc Buu, 63–64
Tran Si Tan, 373*n*, 419
Tran Thanh Phong, 214, 363
Tran Thien Khiem, 186, 262, 293, 302, 322, 348, 385, 411, 419
Diem and, 41, 52–54
as interior minister, 126, 184–185, 187–188, 291, 292
as prime minister, 257, 355, 356, 392, 393, 402, 404, 417
Tran Tran Phong, 232
Tran Tuan Nham, 412
Tran Van Don, 52, 53, 136, 174, 265, 295, 417
Tran Van Dzu, 145
Tran Van Hai, 187, 316
Tran Van Huong, 187, 257, 418, 419
Tran Van Pham, 187
Tran Van Thua, 95
Tran Van Truong, 156–157, 221, 222, 234
Treaster, Joseph, 285, 288
Trinquier, Roger, 133
Truong Buu Diem, 217
Truong Dinh Dzu, 187, 265, 320
Truong Son, 55
"Truth About Phoenix, The" (Dinh Tuong An), 217–221, 281, 284, 288
T'Souvas, Robert, 346
Tu Thanh, 369

Uhl, Mike, 311, 381
Uncounted Enemy: A Vietnam Deception, The (Adams), 272
unilateral penetrations, 110–112, 174–175, 190, 212, 265
USIS (U.S. Information Service), 27, 49, 206, 281, 318
U.S.-Vietnamese relations:
duplicity in, 50
ideological problems in, 185–186
value conflicts in, 214, 233–234

Vacarro, Joe, 70–71, 255
Valentine, Ray, 77
Van Fleet, James, 121
Van Lesser, Kenny, 53
Vann, John Paul, 49–50, 51, 54, 89, 115, 215, 265, 299, 300, 304, 314, 319, 320, 382, 384, 399, 400
Van Van Cua, 187
VBI (Vietnamese Bureau of Investigations), 32–33, 35, 38, 41, 48, 56, 74
VC (Vietcong):
ARVN inferior to, 51–52
cruelty and ruthlessness ascribed to, 59, 107–108, 194
modus vivendi of, 196, 213–222, 230–231
VCI (Vietcong infrastructure), 13, 19–404, 424, 427
background and origins of, 19–38
covert action programs of, 43–44, 46–47, 56
and end of Vietnam War, 390–391, 406
infiltration and penetration by, 109–112, 335–336
modus vivendi of, 213–223
organization of, 38–40
PICs and, 73–74, 80, 82, 83, 85, 87–88
psychological warfare and, 280–290
publications of, 334–335
systematizing of operations against, 113–142
VCIIS (Viet Cong Infrastructure Information System), 258–259
Vien, Mrs., 303
Viera, José Rodolfo, 422

Vietcong Memoir, A (Tran Van Truong), 156, 234
Vietminh, 22–29, 58, 74
colonialism opposed by, 22–24
Diem and, 27–29
see also VC; VCI
Vietnam:
colonial rule of, 20–22
political demarcations of, 20, 22, 24
Vietnam: A History (Karnow), 20
Vietnam, Democratic Republic of (North), 53, 90, 128, 194, 195
Vietnam, Republic of (South), 34, 39, 41, 47, 60, 90, 220, 280, 399
ceasefire and last days of, 404–419
Diem's downfall and, 51–56
and end of Vietnam War, 404, 411, 413, 417–419
"infrastructure" as understood by, 185–186
interrogation networks in, 73–88
modus vivendi of, 213–215
"nation building" strategy in, 160
as prison regime, 221, 349
as scapegoats, 276
Soviet Union compared with, 69
U.S. support of, 47, 148–149, 174, 186–188, 256–257, 303–305, 387, 391
Vietnam: The Secret War (Generous), 26
Vietnamese History from 1939–1975 (Huy), 24
Vietnamization, 254–279
corruption and, 266–271
intelligence networks restructured in, 266–279
policies and implementation of, 254–265
reforms in, 291–302
Vietnam War:
end of, 404–419
new breed of officers in, 163
northern bombing as beginning of, 53
suppression of dissent against, 336–339
Village in Vietnam, 105
Village Voice, 312
Vincent, Vance, 357
Vinh, Major, 407, 409
Vinh Loc, 189
VIS (Vietnam Information System), 51, 282
VNQDD (Vietnam Quoc Dan Dang), 22, 64, 67, 344
VNTF (Vietnam Task Force), 298–299
Volkman, Dennis, 425
Vo Nguyen Giap, 22
Vung Tau program, *see* RDC
Vu Nhoc Nha, 305

Wall, Bob, 124–126, 139, 140–141, 184, 191, 208, 373, 390, 393, 424
Waller, Efram E., 384
Wall Street Journal, 264, 276, 314
Walt, Lou, 124–125
Walters, Howard, 51
Walton, Frank, 35, 260, 348
War Comes to Long An (Race), 32, 258
Ward, Jim, 160, 169, 173, 208, 225, 254, 265, 321
interviews with, 109, 137–138, 150, 163, 172, 205–207, 278–279, 281–282
Washington Monthly, 179
Washington Post, 163, 314, 388
Weidhas, Al, 329
Weisz, George, 278
Welch, David, 162–163
West, Dave, 127, 136, 156, 371
Westbrook, Colston, 337
Westmoreland, William, 91, 118, 146, 253
libel suit of, 272–273
as MACV commander, 57, 64, 113, 116, 127, 135, 152–153, 181, 342
on pacification, 89
Wheeler, Earle, 135, 297
Wilbur, John, 163–173, 176, 177–178, 255–256
Williams, Ogden, 57, 281
Willson, Brian, 215–216
Wilson, "Coal Bin" Willie (Wilber), 208–209, 382, 385
Winne, John, 77
Wisner, Frank, 406, 417
With The Contras (Dickey), 426
Woodsman, John, 72, 106
World War I, 22, 62, 100, 338
World War II, 12, 47, 69, 90, 91, 143, 192, 198, 300

Yarborough, William, 91, 338
Yoh, Bernard, 37
Yoonchul Mo, 357
Yothers, Charlie, 319
Young, Stephen, 107

Zasloff, J. J., 28, 33
Zinman, William, 311–312
Zorthian, Barry, 71